BASEBALL UNIFORMS of the 20th CENTURY

THE OFFICIAL MAJOR LEAGUE BASEBALL GUIDE

Researched, Illustrated & Written by
Marc Okkonen

Sterling Publishing Co., Inc. New York

to Kathy & Dave

Library of Congress Cataloging-in-Publication Data

Okkonen, Marc.
Baseball uniforms of the 20th century : the official major league baseball guide / researched, illustrated & written by Marc Okkonen.
p. cm.
ISBN 0-8069-8490-2
1. Baseball—United States—Uniforms—History—20th century.
I. Title.
GV879.7.038 1991
796.357'028—dc20 91–19540
CIP

Photographs courtesy of the National Baseball Library

10 9 8 7 6 5 4 3 2 1

Published by Sterling Publishing Company, Inc.
387 Park Avenue South, New York, N.Y. 10016

Distributed in Canada by Sterling Publishing
℅ Canadian Manda Group, P.O. Box 920, Station U
Toronto, Ontario, Canada M8Z 5P9
Distributed in Great Britain and Europe by Cassell PLC
Villiers House, 41/47 Strand, London WC2N 5JE, England
Distributed in Australia by Capricorn Ltd.
P.O. Box 665, Lane Cove, NSW 2066
Printed and bound in China

Sterling ISBN 0-8069-8490-2

FOREWORD

When the producers of the baseball movie THE NATURAL were determined to recreate the 1939 major league setting with accuracy their research efforts proved to be more frustrating than anticipated. One of the surprising difficulties was authenticating the appearance of the 1939 National League uniforms which were to be portrayed in many scenes. Despite an abundant reservoir of materials available at the National Baseball Library in Cooperstown, positive identification of photographs of the period failed to verify all the correct uniforms of 1939 despite the advantage of a clue which would positively pinpoint a given uniform as 1939 —the square centennial sleeve patch which was displayed only in that season. The uniforms recreated in the movie were fairly representative of the period but lacked the accuracy the producers sought.

I watched the movie and immediately noticed the flaws in the uniforms and wondered why these uniforms could not have been precise duplications as intended. After all, major league baseball is the most thoroughly documented sport in the world — photographs and the most minute data on any player who ever played in the majors are available through all the yearbooks, annual guides, periodicals and encyclopedias containing an endless supply of facts. But one facet of the history of major league baseball has been almost totally neglected in the records —the uniforms. This vast body of useful information has never been fully researched, assembled, and organized into a documentary volume for research purposes. With a fair familiarity with baseball history already lodged in my brain and enough artistic skill to prepare the necessary illustrations, I embarked on my own personal crusade to try to fill the void in this long neglected part of the documentation of major league baseball history.

In order to accomplish a reasonable goal without spending the rest of my days in a bottomless pit of research, I decided to limit my work to the twentieth century. At least, by using 1900 as a starting point, I could fully account for the American League (which began officially in 1901). My initial efforts were simply gathering information —making xerox copies of uniform photos wherever I found them. Gradually, I was able to date the uniforms by years and also make the distinctions between home and road versions. Besides any and all books containing baseball photos, the Reach and Spalding guides were extremely useful in dating the uniforms. Many, many hours were spent meticulously scanning old newspaper microfilms in search of photo verification and rare verbal references to uniforms. Most of this old newspaper search was conducted at the Library of Congress with additional visits to the libraries of several major league cities.

The two most difficult obstacles in the research were: (a) distinguishing between HOME and ROAD uniforms and (b) identifying the COLORS used, especially in the decades up to WWII. All photo information in the early decades of the century were, of course, in black and white —which has created a "mind set" that the whole world was devoid of color up to the late forties. Even the grays on travelling suits were almost impossible to distinguish from home whites in black and white photography. Colors such as blue generally tend to appear in a lighter tone and reds appear darker —a fact that was both helpful and frustrating in color identification. Spring training and pre-season photos provided another pitfall that I learned to be wary of: Even though a photo was clearly from a given year, most clubs conducted their training and pre-season games in the uniforms of the previous season and saved their new spangles for opening day. Occasionally, a team would open the season with one set of uniforms and at one point introduce a new set —I have attempted to record this with overlapping illustrations. I have also used this device to portray optional uniforms worn during a given season.

A standard 2-dimensional "manikin" pose drawing was carefully developed to provide a consistent vehicle to portray each uniform. The feet, the hands, the bat, and the "blank" face are identical in every illustration —as if the "manikin" were dressed and undressed several thousand times. The "faceless" face has already drawn some criticism, but my purpose for this was to keep attention focused on the uniform itself —facial features being irrelevant. Up to about 1947, the flesh tones are exclusively caucasian — darker skin tones are used thereafter in proportionate mix.

I sincerely hope that the critical users of this compilation will be forgiving about a few shortcomings. First, the presentation is purely from the viewpoint of an outside observer —I have no personal experience or working knowledge of the manufacture of uniforms (hence some "makeshift" terminology used throughout) nor do I have any "inside" information about how people involved made their decisions on selecting and designing the uniforms and how they were cared for. Nor have I had the consultation of players, managers, and executives that could have illuminated the research. In attempting to account for over 3000 uniforms over a span of 92 years, some "educated" guesses had to be made on a number of uniforms. Color identification was very often confusing or clearly not available for many years, especially in the early decades. Actual uniform samples from the "black & white" years are painfully scarce and often suspect. Even the color schemes that are correctly presented cannot be expected to be a faithful color match from the original uniforms because of various limiting factors — i.e. a limited range of color shades in the art materials used and the inevitable variations in color photocopying. It is my hope that subsequent updated editions of this document will eventually weed out many of the errors and provide more accurate information for the future.

I wish to express my gratitude to many individuals for their contribution to this body of knowledge. Posthumously, the great baseball photographers of the past —Conlon, Burke, Horner, Chickering, Van Oeyen, Keunzel to mention a few. In the early stages, Mr. Barry Halper was kind enough to permit me to examine his vast collection of actual uniforms. My nephew, Dan Westhoff, willingly participated in some tedious microfilm research and provided valuable input while at Cooperstown. Fellow SABR members Bob Littlejohn, Mike Mumby, Mike Anderson, Art Ahrens, Eddie Gold, Cliff Kachline, Rich Topp, Rich Lindberg, Jim Bready, Lefty Blasco, and Ed Koller offered valuable contributions. Salty Saltwell and Bob Ibach of the Cubs organization provided early encouragement and an initial opportunity to publish a part of my material. To Paul Cimarusti and Tom McMahon a debt of gratitude for their willingness to provide financial assistance at a critical time. A special thanks to Carl Shoen for some difficult newspaper research and to Scott Tackett for some White Sox input. And, last but by no means least, Tom Heitz and staff members at the National Baseball Library and Hall of Fame Museum in Cooperstown. Their initial enthusiasm for the project and their ongoing support and cooperation over the past several years has been crucial to its completion.

To the vast mountain of data that continually nourishes our passion for the national pastime, I add this volume to help fill an unfortunate vacuum. In an effort to "lighten up" the team narratives, I have incorporated historical information and occasional personal comments which I hope will be tolerated. But the primary objective of this work is REFERENCE ("reader-friendly" or not) and at long last movie makers, baseball artists, photo collectors, baseball writers & researchers, etc. will have an invaluable source of information on major league uniforms of the past. To paraphrase Casey Stengel, now "you can look it up!"

TABLE OF CONTENTS

TRENDS & TRIVIA

PRE-1900 UNIFORMS

Since the subject matter of this research deals with the twentieth century, we will defer any discussion of nineteenth century precedents. Certainly, the history of baseball uniforms is evolutionary and the uniforms of 1900 are a continuation of 1899 but the story of earlier uniforms is even more difficult to develop and we will reserve that information for future additional research. An important finding of such research will be establishing the starting point of use of separate uniforms at home and on the road, which was standard for all major league teams by 1900.

FABRICS

Uniform fabrics in 1900 were either 100% wool flannel or a blend of wool and cotton. Summer temperatures and humidity were no different than now and the idea of playing baseball weighted down with these heavy uniforms seems unthinkable today. But play they did, and with as much vigor and dash as the modern, more comfortably clothed players of the 1980's. The weight of these wool and cotton flannels was gradually reduced in half by the 1940's but the problems of durability and shrinkage had not improved much. The advent of synthetic fibers in the post-WWII era (NYLON, DACRON, ORLON) paved the way for improved blends. The most successful of these was the WOOL/ORLON blend in the sixties —seemingly the "ultimate" material for baseball flannels. But the double-knit fabrics introduced in the early seventies provided so many more attractive and practical features over flannel: lighter, cooler, more comfortable, more durable, etc. etc.. Traditionalists insist that the tight-fitting stretchy double knit suits cannot compare with the well-tailored flannel look of the sixties, but the use of the flannel materials for baseball uniforms is "history" — unless some new miracle fabric comes along that more clearly simulates flannel.

FABRIC PATTERNS AND COLORS

Home uniforms for all clubs at the turn of the century were white, while road uniforms were either gray or a darker hue. The material itself was heavy wool flannel which must have been insufferably warm in mid-summer. Pin striping in the fabric first appeared around 1907 —a fine, narrowly spaced line on the road grays that was barely visible from a distance. The Chicago Cubs were probably the first to use this pattern, but the Boston Nationals went a step further with a discernable green pin stripe on their 1907 road suits. The Brooklyn club was yet more daring with a fine blue "cross-hatch" pattern on their '07 road grays. This "checked" effect would be used later by the New York Giants and again by Brooklyn (with wider spacing) on several occasions. The wider spaced, more visible pin striping first appeared on several major league team uniforms in 1912. The finer striping on road uniforms was becoming common and by the mid-teens, half the teams were sporting the more distinct pin-stripes on their home uniforms. The Giants in 1916 provided the ultimate —an almost "plaid" effect with a crossing of multiple fine lines of purple.

A popular alternative to the gray-colored travelling suits in the 1900-1915 era was a solid dark blue or black material with white relief —often a "negative" image of their home whites. Although black and white photography may conceal earlier examples, the color TAN was introduced on the Dodger's 1937 road uniforms (to complement the Kelly Green trim). Charles O. Finley's Kansas City A's in 1963 challenged the entire tradition of home/road colors with a stunning gold and green combination. By the 1970's, light blue was in common use in place of the gray color on road suits.

THE SPALDING TRADE-MARK GUARANTEES QUALITY · ACCEPT NO SUBSTITUTE

Why Spalding Uniforms Are Best

BECAUSE we possess a perfect factory equipment and for over thirty years we have been making Base Ball Clothing, accumulating during that time a superior knowledge of the requirements of the Base Ball Player, which knowledge, together with all the advantages of our superior factory facilities the purchaser receives the benefit of in every Spalding Uniform we make. **All Spalding Uniforms consist of Shirt, Pants, Cap, Belt and Stockings.**

The Spalding Uniform No. 0—Highest Grade Made

Workmanship and material very highest quality throughout. Colors: Red Stripe, Green Stripe, Navy Blue Check, White, Blue Gray, Brown Gray, Dark Gray, Black, Green, Maroon, Navy Blue, Brown and Cardinal.
The Spalding Uniform No. 0. . . Complete, $15.00
Net price to clubs ordering for *entire team*. . Suit, **$12.50**

The University Uniform No. 1

Equal to No. 0 Uniform, but slightly lighter. Colors: Red Stripe, Green Stripe, Navy Blue Check, White, Blue Gray, Brown Gray, Dark Gray, Black, Green, Maroon, Navy Blue, Brown and Cardinal.
The University Uniform No. 1. . . Complete, $12.50
Net price to clubs ordering for *entire team*. . Suit, **$10.00**

The Interscholastic Uniform No. 2

One of our most popular suits, and will give the best of satisfaction. Can usually be worn two seasons. Colors: White, Blue Gray, Brown Gray, Dark Gray, Black, Green, Maroon, Navy Blue, Brown and Cardinal.
The Interscholastic Uniform No. 2. . Complete, $9.00
Net price to clubs ordering for *entire team*. . . Suit, **$7.50**

The Minor League Uniform No. M

A very popular and satisfactory uniform. Well made of very durable material. Colors: Navy Blue, Blue Gray, Dark Gray and White.
The Minor League Uniform No. M. . Complete, $9.00
Net price to clubs ordering for *entire team*. . Suit, **$7.50**

The City League Uniform No. P

Good quality uniform, in neat and attractive checks, plaids and stripes. Finished like our best quality uniforms. Colors: Brown Check, White with Blue Check, Brownish Blue Shadow Plaid, Grayish Brown with Blue Stripe, Bluish Gray, Light Blue Plaid and Brown Stripe.
The City League Uniform No. P. . . Complete, $7.50
Net price to clubs ordering for *entire team*. . . Suit, **$6.00**

Communications addressed to
London England | **A. G. SPALDING & BROS.** | Edinburgh Scotland
in any of the following cities will receive attention
For street numbers see inside front cover of this book

New York Buffalo Syracuse	Boston Pittsburg Cleveland	Philadelphia Washington Baltimore	Chicago Detroit Atlanta	St. Louis Denver Seattle	Cincinnati Kansas City Minneapolis	San Francisco New Orleans Montreal, Can.

Prices in effect January 5, 1909. Subject to change without notice.

Spalding's uniform selections of 1909

CAP STYLES

Several styles of cap design were worn in the first decade by major league clubs. The "pillbox" or Chicago style usually incorporated horizontal striping much like a layer cake and was a survivor of the 1890's. The so-called "Brooklyn" style had a higher, fuller rounded crown than the more common "Boston" style. The Boston style was the forerunner of future cap styles with a rounded close-fitting crown, more abbreviated than current styles and with the top button tilted more toward the front. Variations of the "cake box" crown resurfaced in later years —the A's of 1909-1915, the Giants in 1916 and the Pirates in modern times. The standard modern cap has changed very little in recent decades —slightly fuller crown and larger sun visor than its antecedents.

Spalding's cap varieties in 1922

SHOES

Baseball spikes, up to the TV age, were like Henry Ford's Model T: you could have any color you wanted as long as it was BLACK. The shoe height dropped from just below the ankle bone to a basic low-quarter style by 1910. The KC A's revolutionary white shoes in the sixties opened the door for color matching and hardly an all-black shoe can be found on today's major leaguers.

1904 baseball shoes ad.

JERSEYS AND UNDERSWEATERS

Jerseys at the turn of the century were pretty much flannel pullover "shirts" with a standard fold-down collar and a buttoned or laced front. Even the sleeves were often full length with buttoned cuff and a left-breast pocket was common. It became fashionable with players later in the decade to wear the collar folded up and pinned at the throat. Undersweaters were becoming a part of the color scheme (some even had stripes) and elbow-length sleeves were worn to accent the sleeve colors. An unusual feature that provided a choice in sleeve length was the detachable sleeve —attached at the elbow with buttons.

Hal Chase in his 1911 Yankees home jersey. Note buttonhole for detachable sleeves.

The first radical change in shirt design in the decade was provided by John McGraw's 1906 Giants when they introduced the "collarless" jersey with a lapel contour curiously indentical to that of later decades. The fold-down collar was definitely on its way out but its popular replacement was to be the short, stand-up "cadet" style —first worn by the Cubs in 1909. By 1912, most clubs adopted the cadet collar and some even sported the almost collarless "V" neck style, the next popular trend. Some of the 19th century features persisted into the decade of the teens: the Boston teams had a laced shirt front as late as 1911 and the Detroit Tigers briefly resurrected the fold-down collar during World War I. The shirt pocket had disappeared forever by 1915.

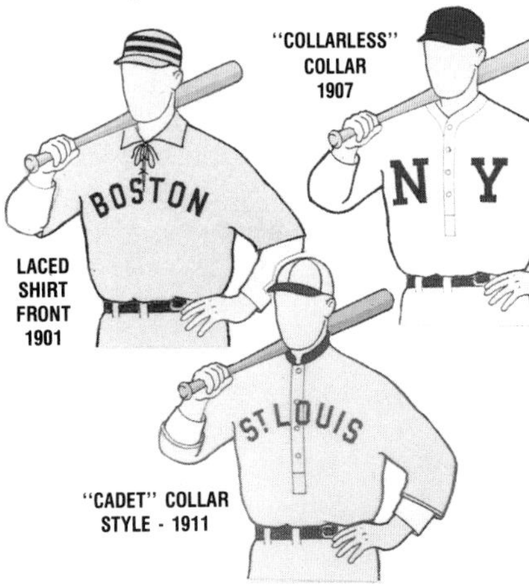

John McGraw in his "V" neck shirt collar

The "V" neck collar style, with a brief tapered extension around the neck, was pretty much the unanimous standard during the twenties. Sleeve lengths varied from 1/2 to 3/4 to full length during the decade. By the mid-thirties, the collar extension disappeared and sleeve lengths were nearly all half (or elbow) length. The first zipper front made its appearance on the all new Cubs uniforms of 1937 and became popular with many clubs for a decade or so. The most innovative jersey of its time —the sleeveless vest —was also introduced by the Chicago Cubs in 1940. The blue undersweater most often used with the vest was also novel —3 red stripes (to match the sox stripes) just below the elbow and sometimes a white crown across the shoulders. The vest survived for 3 seasons and resurfaced in the fifties and sixties with several clubs. The zipper was pretty much history by the sixties, except for an occasional curtain call —most recently by the Phillies.

By the 1970's, the flannel fabrics were lighter and more comfortable with shorter sleeves, but the development of the revolutionary double-knit fabrics doomed the flannels forever. Many of the new-look jerseys were buttonless pullover styles, but the button front has remained popular —indeed current trends indicate a return to the traditional buttons by many clubs.

TROUSERS AND BELTS

Built-in protective padding was a standard part of nineteenth century baseball pants and this "quilting" survived on a few of the post-1900 uniforms. Separate sliding pads on the inside soon became the preferred choice. Belts were considerably wider and were furnished in a variety of colors and materials. Belt tunnels on the sides came into being after 1900 and are a standard feature even on many of today's double-knits. Piping down the sides of the trousers existed in the early 1900's, even before piping became a popular jersey trim feature. Considering the tailoring differences between the old, baggy flannels and the closer fitting double-knits of today, the basic "knickers" concept has really changed very little since 1900.

STOCKINGS

Stockings in 1900 were made of heavy wool and were of one-piece full-length (above the knee) construction. The foot covering part below the ankle bone was white or natural wool and often created the illusion of stirrups. The true stirrup stocking, separate from the "sanitary" foot stocking, first came into being about 1905. The popularity of striped or multi-tone stirrup stockings ebbed and flowed in cycles, becoming widely used around 1910 and less common by the late teens. Except for a few "candy-cane" varieties (particulary by the Giants, Cardinals & Washington), striping was quite minimal during the twenties and, in contrast, enjoyed a revival of sorts in the early thirties. As pant legs became lower and stirrups were stretched higher and higher over the following decades, the stockings became a neglected component in the overall appearance of the uniform. In fact, since the sanitary undersock has gained more and more visibility, its traditional white color, in some cases, has been abandoned for a distinct color to complement the new colored variety of shoes.

STOCKINGS THROUGH THE YEARS

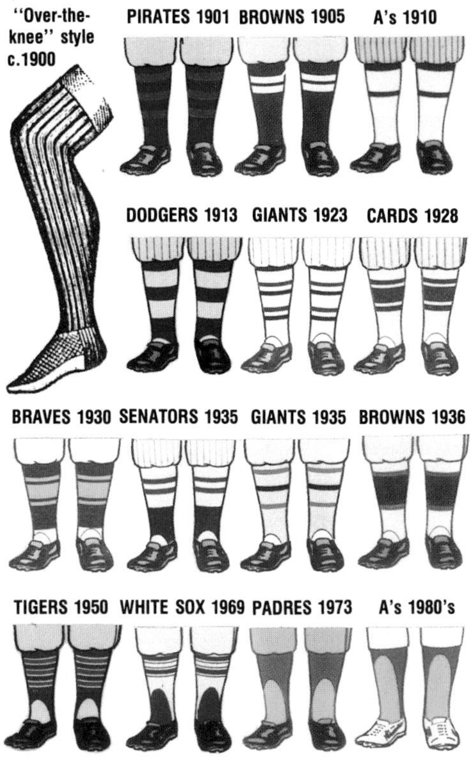

TRIM COLORS AND GRAPHICS

In the 1890's, stocking colors were the principal device in distinguishing one team from another (hence the team names White Stockings, Red Stockings, Browns, etc.) and graphic displays identifying the home city were merely extra window dressing. In fact, some clubs after 1900 elected to wear plain unmarked jerseys and left their unique identification to their stocking colors and caps (i.e. the Chicago Nationals and St. Louis Americans).

STANDARD BLOCK LETTERING

FANCY SINGLE LETTERS

Although trim colors were abundant in uniform schemes, the selection was limited to BLACKS, DARK BLUES, MAROONS or REDS, & BROWNS and seldom in combinations (some exceptions: Pittsburgh's maroon & navy stockings, Detroit's black stockings with a red stripe). Lettering styles for the home city name were usually in plain block capital letters (from the manufacturer's standard stock) and the single letters or monograms were either a similar block style or a heavily ornamental Victorian or Old English type. John McGraw was quite unpredictable and often innovative in dictating the color schemes of his Giants. Once the team's N-Y monogram style was established (c. 1909), he stayed with it but he boldly flaunted color traditions by introducing VIOLET in 1913 as a trim color. The Cubs in 1916 added a second color red to dress up the navy blue trim and a wave of patriotism in the WWI years encouraged a more generous display of red, white and blue on some major league uniforms.

SOME COLORFUL UNIFORMS IN THE TEENS

In the case of many clubs, team nicknames were an unofficial invention of the press and changed constantly. On the other hand, clubs such as the Cardinals, Tigers and Athletics were universally identified by fans and team management alike. However, display of the nickname (or representative symbols of same) on the uniform were rare in the early decades of the century. The first instance of displaying a graphic symbol of the team nickname was the small red tiger on the black cap of the 1901 Detroits. When the Boston Americans decided to adopt the new nickname of RED SOX in 1908, they did so with an unusual graphic display, showing a red sock silhouette (with the word BOSTON inside) on their shirt fronts. The small cub figure inside the Chicago National "C" in 1908 would be the only other such embellishment of this type among NL teams in the 1900-1910 period.

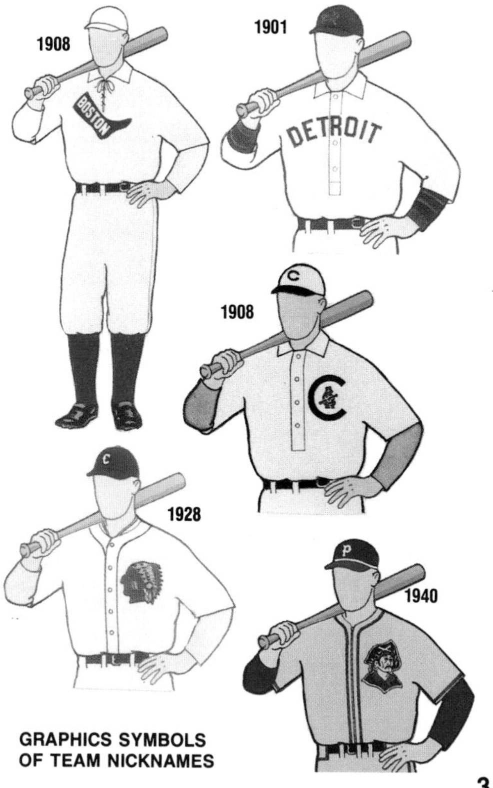

GRAPHICS SYMBOLS OF TEAM NICKNAMES

The first spelling out of the team's nickname on the jersey was on the Washington home shirts of 1905. Determined that they were no longer to be called the "Senators", their now official name "NATIONALS" was displayed in capital letters across the chest. Simpler and more established nicknames [i.e. Cubs, (White) Sox, Reds] soon appeared. By 1910, the new cadet-style collar shirts placed a new emphasis on the front button lapel and it became fashionable to stack up the letters of the team name or city name in a vertical position. By the 1920's, display of the team name had become common (even the conservative Yankees did it for a time on their road uniforms). Oddly, the Philadelphia Athletics had never in their long history displayed so much as a letter P to identify the home city, yet they were the last of the original 16 major league franchises to spell out the full nickname ATHLETICS —in their final year (1954) in the City of Brotherly Love.

FIRST DISPLAY OF TEAM NICKNAMES

EXAMPLES OF SCRIPT LETTERING

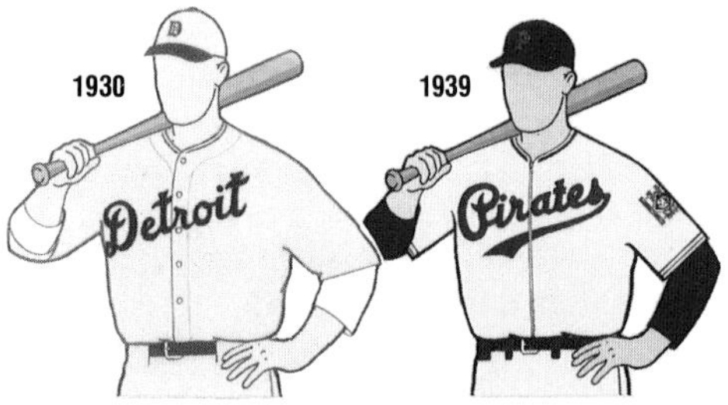

The Detroit Tigers in 1930 established an important precedent by using a script lettering of DETROIT in place of the traditional capital letters. By the end of the decade, the idea of slanted script letters with an underline flourish was widely used. Also, a second trim color became the norm for many other major league teams in the thirties. As for graphic symbols, almost every club by this time had displayed some pictorial version of club identification at one time or another. Even the Athletics exploited their elephant symbol (whose origin is a story in itself) as early as 1905 on their team sweaters and later on the uniform jersey. Many of the team nicknames defy visual identification (Reds? Phillies? Nationals? Dodgers?) and thus escaped usage. Perhaps the St. Louis Cardinals have the most notable and familiar graphic presentation with their 2-birds-on-a-bat design which began in 1922 and, with few interruptions has persisted to this day. In the last years before numbers became standard on the backs of the shirts, the Detroit and Boston NL clubs boldly displayed a colorful tiger's head and Indian head profile respectively, on their backs.

Rogers Hornsby in an early version of the famous Cardinals shirt-front graphics

FULL TEAM NAME DISPLAYED

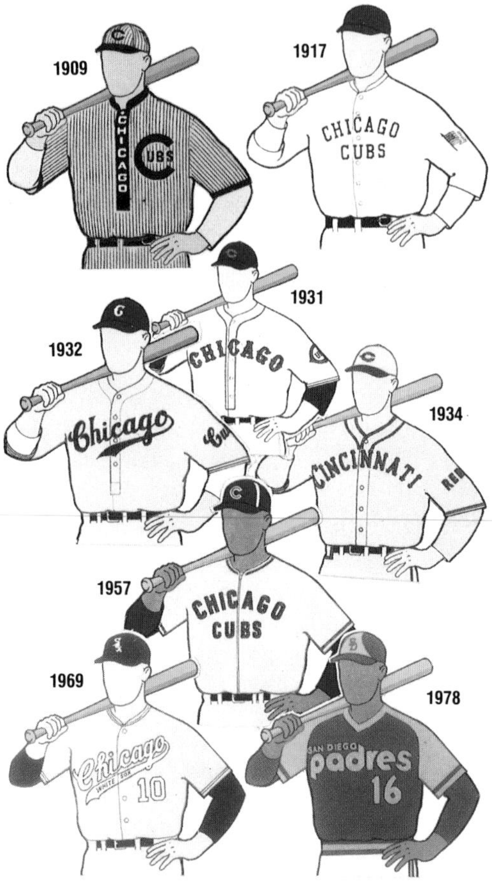

On rare occasions the entire team name (city and nickname) has been spelled out on the uniform. The Cubs in 1909 were the first with CHICAGO in vertical lettering down the button lapel and the CUBS emblem on the left breast. The last major league uniform to show the full team name was by the San Diego Padres in 1978. In recent decades, more imaginative lettering styles appeared —notably, the Indians with an unusual interpretation of American Indian-type calligraphy in the early seventies. Probably the most tasteful and attractive use of a modern type face is exemplified by the current BLUE JAYS uniform set.

The proliferation of color TV coverage of major league baseball probably did more to invite the use of brighter and non-traditional uniform color schemes in the 1960's. The Athletics' gold and green ensembles started a color revolution that culminated in the bizarre "rainbow" jerseys introduced by the ASTROS in 1975. However, in midst of this color orgy, a handful of teams (i.e. the Yankees, Red Sox, Tigers) maintained a fairly consistent conservative image, holding steadfastly to the dictates of a long tradition. Even the trends of the double-knit revolution (pullover jersey, beltless trousers) seem to be reverting to earlier styles (buttoned jerseys and belted trousers). The popular practice of stretching the stirrups far up under the trouser legs also seems to be reversing itself and once again revealing the heretofore unseen striping on the outer socks. Among the expansion teams, the two Canadian entries have maintained stable, consistent uniform designs. The other side of this coin is the the San Diego franchise, which has at times changed its uniform designs almost annually in their nearly 2 decades of existance in the majors.

NUMBERS AND NAMES

The first attempt to identify individual players with numbers affixed to their uniforms occurred with the Cleveland club in 1916. In this early experiment, the numbers were attached to the sleeve, not the back. For reasons unknown, the idea faded away and was not seen again (except briefly by the Cardinals in 1923) until 1929 when the New York Yankees (possibly inspired by earlier trials in the Minor Leagues) boldly took the field with large numbers on their backs, an idea that initially did not escape ridicule. Since teams and batting orders were relatively stable and not likely to change (especially the infamous "murderers row"), the first number sets reflected their position in the batting order — hence, Ruth #3, Gehrig #4, etc. Obviously, if the numbering system were to presevere, this system was eventually incompatible with roster changes in ensuing seasons. In any case, the new system met approval by the fans and this time it was here to stay. By 1932, all major league teams were "numbered". In 1952, the Brooklyn Dodgers repeated the numbers on the FRONT of their home jersey and many other teams soon copied this idea. The sixties saw numbers appearing on the sleeves and by the seventies, even the trousers could not escape number identification by some clubs.

Ruth's famous no. 3 in 1929 —the first year of numbers on the back

White Sox slugger Ted Kluszewski (Kluszewxi?) improperly identified in 1960.

Another feature which was probably inspired by increasing TV coverage, was the display of the player's last name on the back of the uniform. The Chicago White Sox were the pioneers of this idea in 1960. Acceptance was not instantaneous, partly because of the fear of lost revenues from lower scorecard sales, but the fans liked it and almost every team today has adopted the practice. The most notable holdout being the tradition-bound New York Yankees (ironically, the same Yankees who introduced numbers on the back in 1929).

PATCHES

The first recorded use of a shoulder patch on a major league uniform was by the Chicago White Sox of 1907. Still gloating over their humiliation of the cross-town Cubs in the '06 series, this small patch triumphantly certified the new world champions —certainly a more modest statement than McGraw's "WORLD CHAMPIONS" shirts of the previous summer. The patriotic fervor of the WWI period produced an abundance of American flags or red, white & blue shields on the major league uniforms of those years. The year 1925 marked the 50th anniversary of the founding of the National League and the occasion was visually displayed on all NL team uniforms with a large attractive circular blue and gold patch. The city of Boston celebrated its tercentenary year in 1930 with a Pilgrim Hat patch on both Red Sox and Braves uniforms. Similar milestones in other major league cities in subsequent years have been observed with a variety of patches too numerous to list here. The St. Louis Browns commissioned a new official team crest and added it to the sleeves of their 1937-38-39 uniforms. A striking orange and blue patch promoting the upcoming 1939 World's Fair was displayed on the sleeves of all three New York City teams' uniforms in the 1938 season.

The first patch to be worn on all 16 major league uniform sleeves in a given year appeared in 1939 to observe the centennial year of the game's invention (an accepted consensus opinion —the argument continues as to whether baseball was really "invented" or evolved). Indeed, this patch was worn by all of professional baseball, including the minor leagues and it coincided with the grand opening of baseball's Hall of Fame in Cooperstown, New York. The World War II seasons of 1942-45 also produced a universally applied patriotic shield patch— In 1942, the word "HEALTH", then, in subsequent war years, red stripes. The Philadelphia Athletics in 1951 celebrated Connie Mack's incredible 50th year at the helm with a circular gold patch on the left sleeve. In the following season (1951), each league had its own anniversary patch —75 years for the NL, 50 years for the AL. The third patch to be displayed by all teams, was the rectangular Major League Baseball centennial patch in 1969 commemorating 100 years of professional baseball. The nation's bicentennial year of 1976 featured a variety of patches worn by most of the major league teams to celebrate the occasion. Many of the ballpark anniversaries have also inspired special patches and even eulogies to the recently departed have been expressed with patches rather than the traditional black arm bands of earlier decades.

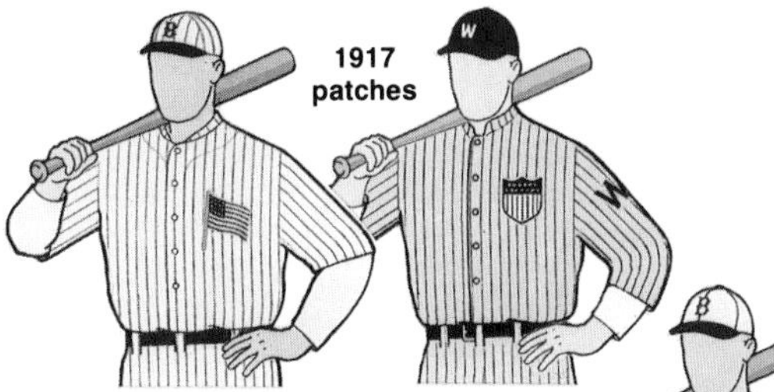

1917 patches

'39 NY World's Fair patch (1938 season)

National League's 50th anniversary patch (1925)

World War II patch (1942)

MAJOR LEAGUE BASEBALL

100th year of professional baseball (1969)

NL 100th anniversary (1976)

American League's 50th anniversary patch (1951)

1939 Baseball centennial patch

National League's 75th anniversary patch (1951)

SPECIAL AND UNUSUAL UNIFORMS

Certain uniforms worn from time to time deserve special mention here because of their unusual outward appearance or the atypical reasons for their existance. The first Baltimore Orioles road uniform in 1901, as personally commissioned by new manager John McGraw, is a classic case of an outlandish color scheme. Apparently inspired by nature's coloring of the oriole, the cap, shirt and trousers were solid black with yellow-orange trim. A large letter "O" on the left breast, a yellow belt and bright yellow-orange stockings with black stripes highlighted the design and invited ridicule by the press in most of the AL towns they visited. The following season, McGraw had heard enough and reverted back to a basic gray road uniform with black trim, similar to the uniforms of the legendary Oriole teams of the 1890's.

1901 ORIOLES

1905 SERIES

When McGraw took over the New York Giants, he resurrected the all-black uniform (this time with white trimmings) especially for the 1905 World Series. Once again, the comments were often derogatory (even by the New York following) but the psychological ploy seemed to work as the shabbily-clad Athletics were defeated. Since McGraw had also been heavily criticized for his refusal to participate in a post-season series in 1904, his smugness was unrestrained and he outfitted his new champions with the words "WORLD CHAMPIONS" across the chests of both the home and road suits for the 1906 season. When the Giants and Athletics met for an encore world championship series in 1911, all-black uniforms were once again specially made for the occasion by McGraw. This time, however, it didn't work as rhe New Yorkers were subdued handily by the awesome talent of Connie Mack's Athletics.

1906 GIANTS

1911 SERIES

The idea of advertising the world championship on the game uniforms of the following season was repeated by the Cleveland Indians in 1921 and once again by the St. Louis Cardinals in 1927. The Cleveland version more or less duplicated McGraw's '06 Giants, while the simple circular inscription of world champions around a solitary perched Cardinal bird in '27 reflected a more modest form of pride in acheivement.

1921 INDIANS

1927 CARDINALS

Occasional world tour and barnstorming teams were often outfitted with special uniform designs. The much heralded world tour by the Giants and Chicago White Sox in 1913 provided specially designed outfits for the Comiskeys, totally unlike their customary apparel in league play. The home (?) version featured pinstriping on a white jersey with the word CHICAGO arched across the chest in fancy capital letters of several hues. The road (?) version was a solid dark blue which also incorporated the name CHICAGO across the chest in plain block capital letters with a white outline. The Giants' uniforms on the tour, were much like their official league suits —trimmed in the current VIOLET color, except that the city name NEW YORK was displayed on the shirt front of one version.

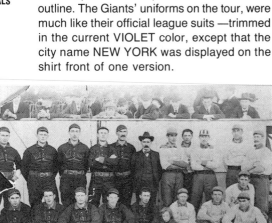

An ancient precursor of the all-star game. American and National League stars played each other on a 1902 barnstorming tour —wearing "American" and "National" uniforms.

Chicago White Sox 1913 world tour uniform

1913 Giants world tour.

A barnstorming tour of National Leaguers in 1915. Dark uniforms with a circled N on the shirts

Britain's King George "inspects" the Chicago White Sox, on a world tour in 1924.

Perhaps the most unusual fabric pattern of any major league uniform was presented by the Giants' edition of 1916. Bands of 5 thin purple stripes were perpendicularly intersected to create a near "plaid" effect. An oversized N-Y emblem (also in violet hue) graced the left breast and the suits were topped off by a ressurrected "Chicago" style pillbox cap reminiscent of earlier decades. The following year, in keeping with the "God Bless America" mentality of the WWI era, the AL champion Chicago White Sox took the field for the 1917 World Series, in an honest-to-goodness, star-spangled, red, white & blue variation of their normal home uniform design. They even broke with an almost sacred team tradition by adding a red and blue stripe to their normally all-white hose. They won the series and immediately retired those garish uniforms —perhaps an appropriate fate for the last world championship team uniform representing the Windy City.

Larry Doyle in the Giants "plaid" uniform of 1916

Eddie Cicotte and Pants Rowland in "battle dress" for the 1917 world series.

When the first all-star game took place at Comiskey Park in 1933, the American League elected to allow their participating players to wear their everyday home uniforms. The visiting National Leaguers, in contrast, decided upon a specially made gray road suit with the words NATIONAL LEAGUE inscribed on the front of the jersey. The solid dark caps displayed an NL similar to the league's umpire caps of a later generation. This uniform was also permanently retired —used for this one historic occasion only —as the National Leaguers also saw fit to wear their regular uniforms for the 1934 game and all future all-star games.

Frankie Frisch in his '33 all-star duds.

The Cincinnati Reds introduced night baseball in 1935 and in the following year they commissioned the Goldsmith Company to produce a special uniform for occasional game use in 1936 and 1937. It is not clear what inspired this so-called "Palm Beach" version (possibly, it was the advent of baseball under the arc lights) but it presented some interesting departures from long standing Reds' uniform tradition. In place of the standard C-REDS logo, the name REDS appeared in the now-fashionable red script lettering on the left breast. And the real shocker was the combination of white jersey and BRIGHT RED pants, which was only one version of the new Palm Beach emsemble.

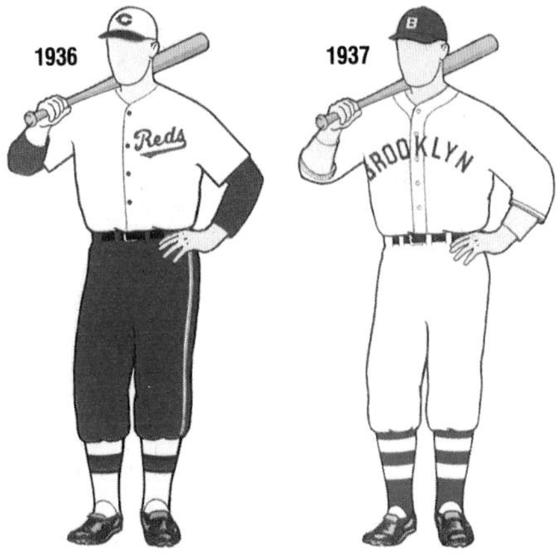

In keeping with the new color craze of the depression years, the Brooklyn Dodgers surprised everyone by changing their more-or-less traditional "Dodger Blue" trim to a striking KELLY GREEN for the 1937 season. All-green caps, stockings and undersweaters — not a trace of blue to be found. Even the normal gray color of the road uniforms was replaced by TAN. It was St. Patrick's Day all season long at Ebbetts Field as even the ushers were outfitted in green jackets. The following season, the Dodgers returned to the real world with all new Royal blue-trimmed uniforms which, incidentally, introduced the now-famous script DODGERS.

The increasing popularity of night baseball also inspired an unusual "night-games only" shiny satin material on the game uniforms. The idea was that this more reflective material would add considerably to the viewing pleasure of baseball under the lights. Several National League clubs participated in this practice during the 1940's —most notably, the Brooklyn Dodgers, whose road version of the night satins was bright powder blue with BROOKLYN displayed across the chest in white script.

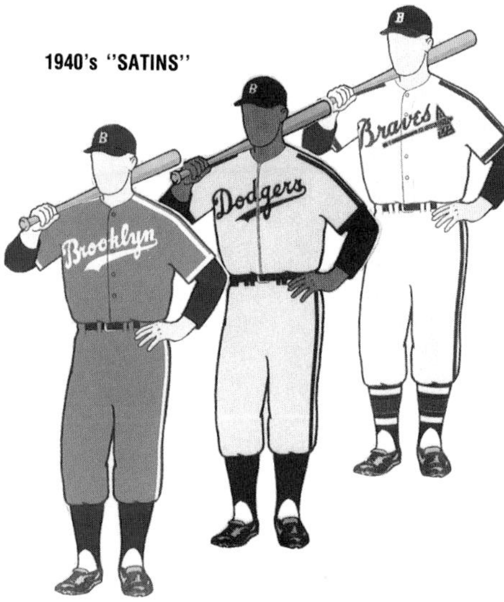

After baseball's "P.T. Barnum", Bill Veeck, re-purchased the Chicago White Sox in the mid-70's, he furnished some innovative uniforms which upheld his reputation as the master merchandiser of the game. With a mix & match combination of whites and navy blues, he concocted a uniform ensemble that was totally new yet suggested features of an earlier age. The jerseys had a straight-cut bottom and were worn "pajama" style—outside the belt. The open collar design incorporated a "pseudo" fold down collar shape (not seen for 60 years) and the lettering style of the name CHICAGO was deliberately reminiscent of earlier Sox road unforms (i.e. 1930, 1902-1915). In another stroke of pure Veeckian "pizazz", he presented a Bermuda shorts version in 1976, which was an instant public relations success and an equally instant failure in terms of player acceptance.

The Cincinnati Reds, in their 1978 Florida spring training exhibition season, pulled off a publicity gimmick with their home uniforms that still has the fans buzzing. On March 17th (St. Patrick's Day of course), they took the field in fully GREEN duplications of their red-trimmed home whites. The effect was mind-boggling —a visual phenomenon for Reds fans at the park. The practical joke was so much fun that similar green abberations of other teams uniforms have made their appearance periodically on this appropriate date in the years following. These Cincinnati GREENS uniforms have, since that time, become treasured collectors items —an irresistable conversation piece among baseball fans everywhere.

In a brief episode in 1979 that most all Philadelphia Phillies fans would prefer to forget, someone in the front office decided that the popular Phillies uniform motif could be modified (for Saturday games only) into an ALL-BURGUNDY version with white trimmings. The reaction was instantaneously negative by everyone —the media, the fans, and the players. The idea was hastily abandoned and entered the realm of nostalgic novelties in major league uniforms.

SWEATERS, COATS AND JACKETS

The outer garments for major league baseball uniforms as with 19th century uniforms is a fascinating, colorful story in itself and deserves more exhaustive coverage in future research efforts. At least a brief overview of trends is worth mention here. At the turn of the century the standard uniform coat seemed more appropriate for a Sousa band than a baseball team. Certainly "spiffy" in its day, it appears to be a garish overstatement from the viewpoint of the 1980's. Double-breasted, fingertip length with large pearl buttons and 2-tone trimmings on the sleeve ends, pocket flaps and collar —a garment which elicits "guffaws" and disbelief from our eyes. These dressy "storm coat" styles faded out by 1910 and the big heavy sweaters became more the standard wear for cooler days and pitcher's arms. But even the color schemes of some of these sweaters evolved into bizarre "Indian blankets" and colorful plaids by the late teens. By the twenties the sweater colors subsided and were soon giving way to shorter "windbreaker" style jackets. In the twenties and thirties, many of these jackets were combinations of high-grade felt, suedes and colored leathers. The windbreaker style with stretch waistband and wrists is still the popular trend, but newer fabrics (i.e. nylon) have displaced the leathers and felts.

Napoleon Lajoie in a turn-of-the-century style dress coat.

Boston manager Lee Fohl in a mid-twenties sweater.

A leather jacket from 1930 modeled by Dave Bancroft of the Giants

Manager Ralph Houk of the Yanks and Cookie Lavagetto of the new Twins wearing typical 1961-style jackets.

BATTING HELMETS & PRACTICE JERSEYS

Since the wearing of protective helmets became mandatory in the seventies, they have become an integral part of the overall uniform motif. Usually they attempt to duplicate the regular home cap in appearance and the same helmets are used on the road even if the soft road cap differs in appearance. And often, for practical reasons, the batting helmets from previous years are retained for use even after a re-design of the soft cap. Colorful practice jerseys are now used by all the teams for exhibition games and pre-game practice. These jerseys have borrowed from the graphic identity of the game uniforms but usually with distinctly re-arranged color schemes. Many of the colorful pullover jerseys adopted as part of the game uniforms of recent years most certainly evolved from practice jerseys.

Len Dykstra in a Mets practice jersey. You won't see this shirt worn in a regular season game.

THE PENDULUM OF UNIFORM DESIGN TRENDS

For the rage of bright colors and multiple color schemes inspired by the color TV and double-knit age, the party appears to be about over for now. The pendulum seems to be swinging toward more conservative and traditional uniforms. Buttoned jerseys, pants with belts, standard whites and grays, and even black shoes are making a comeback. But it has always been cyclical since 1900 —a "tug-of-war" between tradition and innovation. Periods of new ideas are punctuated by years of conservative, stable preferences. With so many more new franchises in recent decades, the cycles are overlapping more and more. But when one examines the evolution of the uniforms of a particular franchise, these cycles are clearly evident. Americans love the game of baseball the way it IS, but they also worship the sport for what it HAS BEEN and they can't always have it both ways. No matter, we accept and idolize the teams of our preference and seldom take issue with the way they are packaged —we adapt with changes in uniforms very quickly.

BOSTON/MILWAUKEE ATLANTA BRAVES

BOSTON BEGINNINGS

At the turn of the century, the Boston Nationals were in their 26th year as a league member, being one of the original franchises from the first year of National League play (1876). Their uniforms by the 1890's were of the laced collar type with either the name BOSTON or an Old English capital B on the shirt fronts. After 1900, both home whites and road grays displayed BOSTON in standard arched block capital letters across the chest. Caps were usually the "Chicago" style, a pillbox shape with horizontal striping of various combinations. The trim color was most often maroon or red through the first five or six years of the decade. The arrival of the Boston Americans in 1901 offered unwanted competition and an eventual identity crisis with respect to uniform identification of the two teams. The upstart Americans, although using blue as a trim color, had pretty much duplicated the uniform look of the Nationals —using the identical lettering style of BOSTON on their shirt fronts and often adopting a similar cap style. Black and white photographs of the period often made the players appear to be from the same team.

When John Dovey assumed control of the Nationals, he had the uniforms radically restyled for the 1907 season. The newspapers had pinned a new nickname on the team, DOVES, and the redesigned suits reinforced the new image. The new home uniforms were WHITE from head to foot with only a maroon Old English B on the shirt front and a yellow leather belt to provide relief. The road uniforms were a gray French flannel material with a fine green striping (one of the first uses of pinstriped fabrics). Road caps were plain gray and the stockings were off-white natural wool. The Old English B was repeated in BLUE on the road jerseys. Buttons replaced the lacing on the shirt fronts in keeping with uniform trends of the new decade. These uniforms received much comment around the league and the Boston Americans assumed that red or maroon was abandoned as a standard trim color by the Doves. Accordingly they seized the opportunity to use RED in their uniform designs for 1908 since no other American League club was so identified.

A group of re-christened "Doves" in 1907

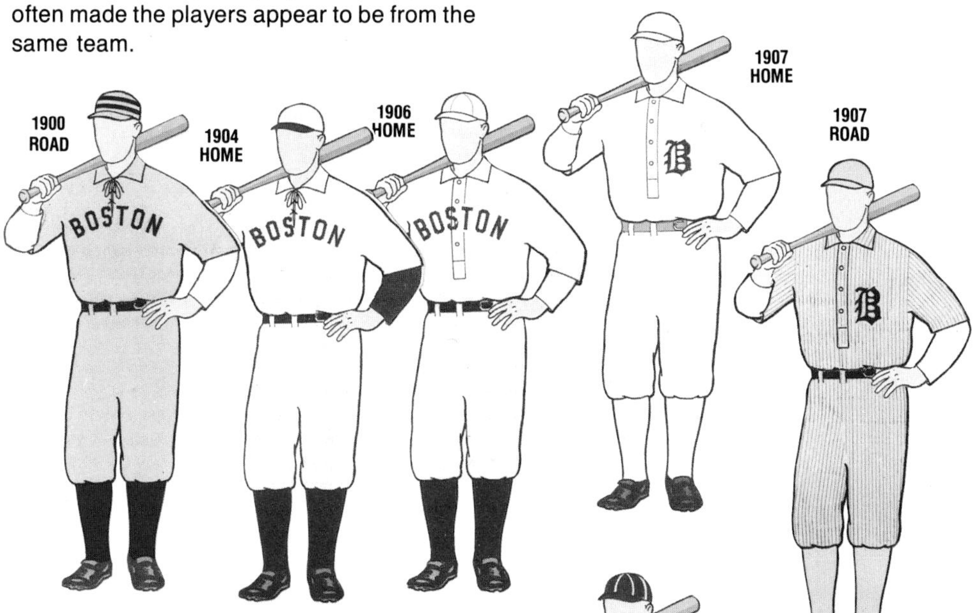

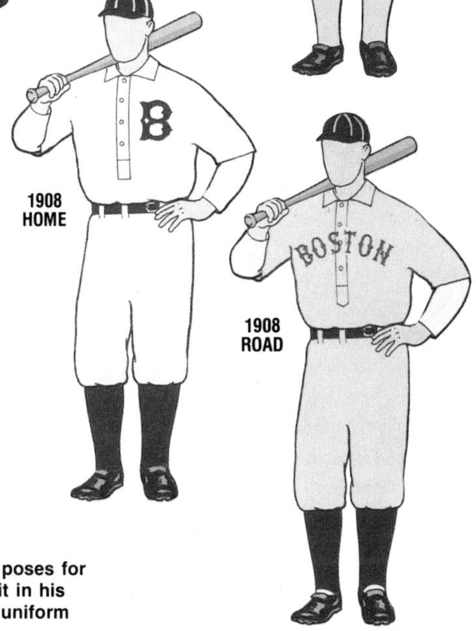

Fred Tenney poses for studio portrait in his 1897 Boston uniform

WHO ARE THE BOSTON RED SOX?

Apparently President Dovey, disenchanted with his 1907 uniforms, was determined to reclaim RED as the trim color of his new uniform sets for 1908. Bright red caps with white piping down the crown seams, solid red stockings, and even a red belt were featured on both home whites and road grays. A fancy red capital B appeared on the left breast of the home shirts while the name BOSTON was returned to the front of the road shirt, this time in fancy red capitals. The photographic similarity to the Americans' uniforms was not at issue for the time being, but the two Boston teams were now "Red Stockings" for most of the next several seasons. The similarity climaxed in 1910 when both teams used identical lettering on the shirts in the same color of red.

The new 1911 uniforms broke the "look-alike" pattern with another re-design by the Nationals. The fold-down style collar had already been replaced by the short stand-up "cadet" style in keeping with current trends. The Old English B was restored to the left sleeve of the home jerseys and the new road uniforms were a solid dark navy blue with the same B in white on the sleeve —a "negative" image of the home whites. A dark visor and seam piping were added to the caps. In 1912, new President John M. Ward elected to rename the team BRAVES after a series of forgettable nicknames had been tried (i.e. HEPS, RUSTLERS). Once again, the uniforms restored the block-lettered BOSTON to both home whites and road grays. RED was also resurrected as the sole trim color and a small Indian head profile patch was added to the sleeve as a symbol of the new nickname. With solid red stockings, part of the similarity to the other Bostons returned but by this time the Americans had abandoned the name BOSTON on their shirts in favor of RED SOX and their stockings were no longer solid red but a wide band of red around the calf. By the next season, the Boston Red Stockings identity crisis was history.

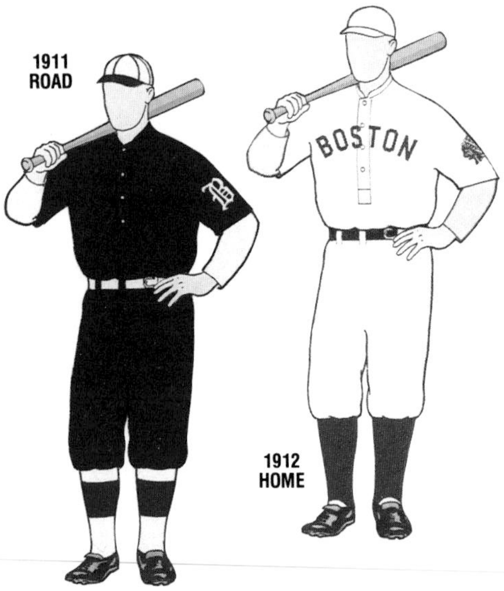

1911 ROAD

1912 HOME

WORLD WAR AND THE TWENTIES

As reigning world champions for 1915, the Braves uniforms were once again revamped to celebrate the occasion. The new home uniforms adopted pinstripes, a popular fad by this time. The home cap had a white crown (made of the same pinstriped fabric) with a navy visor and a red fancy capital B on the front. The road uniforms reverted to the traditional gray. Red and blue striped stockings were continued from previous years. The most unusual new design feature was the new emblem on the left front on both home and road shirts. The red Indian head profile was positioned on a circular blue field, reminiscent of an oversize Indian head penny. They repeated this uniform scheme through the 1920 season.

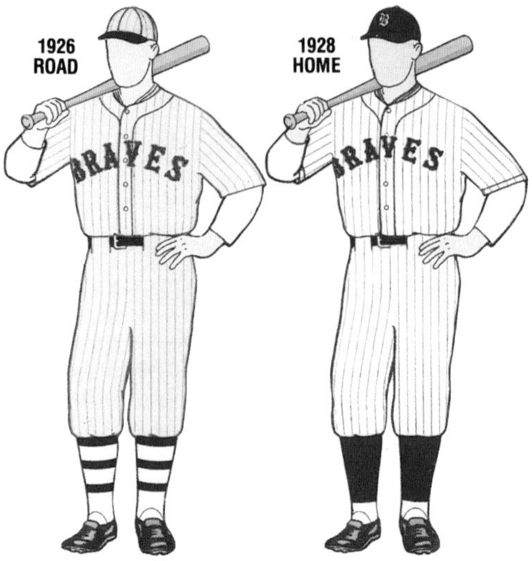

1926 ROAD

1928 HOME

THE MIRACLE BRAVES

The new BRAVES nickname proved a popular choice and the totally new uniforms for 1913 repeated the Indian head patch on the left sleeve for both home and road. Navy blue and red were combined as the new trim colors. Caps were solid navy with a thin red band around the base of the crown. Stockings were basically navy with a series of red stripes. A new red block capital B appeared on the left breast of the home jerseys. The new road uniforms were of a musty blue fabric with darker pinstriping and repeated the red B and Indian head patch. These uniforms set the stage for 1914 —the most incredible year in the history of the franchise.

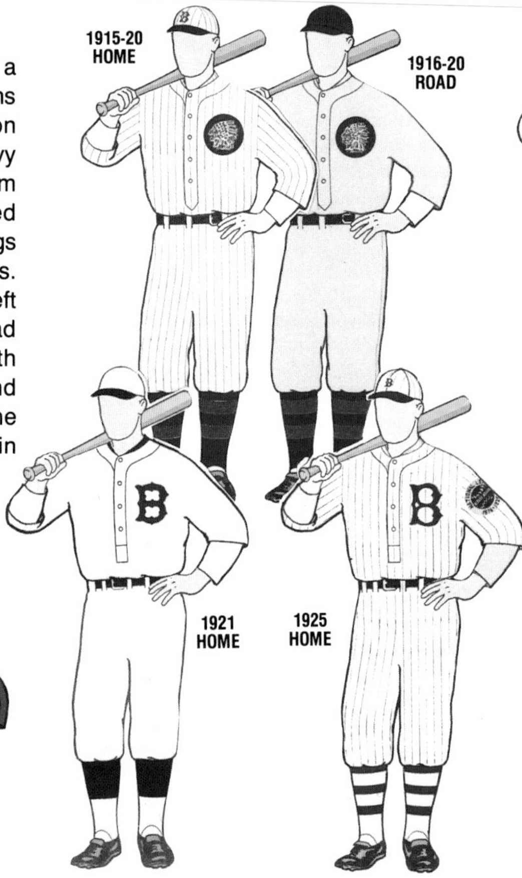

1915-20 HOME

1916-20 ROAD

1921 HOME

1925 HOME

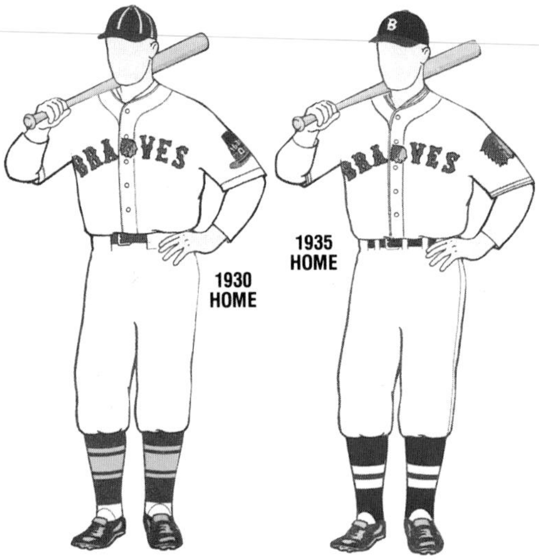

1930 HOME

1935 HOME

1913 HOME

1913 ROAD

Veteran baseball man George Stallings was hired to manage the Braves in 1913. Stallings was indeed a rare breed —one of the few managers who never donned a uniform and one of the most superstitious men in the history of the game. Last place in 1912, Stallings pulled the team out of the cellar in 1913 and acquired the scrappy veteran Johnny Evers to lead the team in 1914. Dead last on July 4th, these "miracle" Braves defied all logic by surging to a pennant and a world series upset of the legendary Philadelphia Athletics. The Braves were not seen again as a pennant contender for over three decades.

In 1921, the round Braves emblem was dropped in favor of a stylized fancy capital B, curiously similar to the B on the Brooklyn road suits. Caps had a solid white or gray crown with a dark visor and no B on the front. Stockings in the early twenties were various combinations of black and white striping. Pinstripes on the home whites were discontinued in 1921 but restored in 1924. In 1925, the B on the home jersey was modified to duplicate the form of the Brooklyn B. That same year, the road uniforms introduced some radically new features. Pinstripes were incorporated in the gray fabric and the name BRAVES was spelled out in fancy capital letters across the chest. This idea was also repeated on the home shirts in the late twenties. The caps were also changed to solid navy with a white Old English B on the front. The decade of the twenties were lean years for the Braves (and Red Sox as well), perennially mired in the second division and often dead last.

THE THIRTIES —MORE COLOR AND A NEW IDENTITY

Beginning in the late twenties, a surge of new innovations and extra color trim ideas appeared on major league uniforms and continued on through the thirties. The Braves participated in this renaissance and their new uniforms for 1929 were the talk of the league. With a startling combination of flaming red and yellow trim, they had once again restructured their image. Recalling that uniform numbers on the back were not just yet standardized, they displayed a large, blazing red Indian head profile in the middle of the back (an idea borrowed from the Detroit road shirts of '28). The caps were solid red with white seam stripes. Stockings were basically red with a yellow striped pattern at the calf. The BRAVES lettering of past seasons was repeated on the shirt fronts in red with gold outline trim plus a new twist —a smaller version of the Indian head was positioned smack in the middle of the BRAVES letters. The same combination was repeated in 1930 with a "Pilgrim hat" patch added to the left sleeve to observe the Boston Tricentennial year. This general uniform scheme was continued through the 1935 season with some modifications along the way —Sox striping was changed several times, when numbers were added to the shirt back the Indian head was transplanted to the sleeve, and navy blue was restored in the trim scheme by 1935. Babe Ruth was photographed repeatedly in this uniform —the last one he wore as a player.

THE TENURE OF THE "BEES"

Perhaps out of desparation to stimulate sagging attendance or to shake off an image of endless futility, the Boston National League Club re-christened themselves BEES to start the 1936 season. Once again it was a new look in uniforms —royal blue and gold the new trim colors. The first BEES uniforms were the conventional white at home and gray on the road with the name BOSTON in fancy capitals on the shirts for the first time since 1912. Piping trim was a mix of blue and gold, caps were solid blue with a gold B in front, and stockings were solid blue. For 1937 and '38, pinstripes were added to the home whites and separate versions of a capital B replaced BOSTON on the shirt front. Gold stripes were also added to the blue stockings. In 1939, the royal blue and gold trim theme was scrapped in favor of a return to red and navy. The name BOSTON was restored on the home shirts. Stockings were basically white or gray with a combination red and navy striping. Cap crowns were also white or gray with dark visors.

For the 1940 season, it was another new design but with a more conservative flavor. All piping trim was eliminated and navy blue was suddenly the predominant trim color. A new rendition of the Old English B appeared on the home jerseys as well as on the cap front. BOSTON in plain block arched capital letters on the road jersey was disturbingly similar to the latest Red Sox road uniform. The white stripes on the stockings were also dropped in favor of solid navy by '43. The home uniform of 1940 remained basically intact through 1944, but the 1941 road jersey introduced a slanted script BOSTON in place of the block letters. The BEES nickname was wearing thin by the WWII years and yielded to tradition as the Bostons were once again officially the BRAVES in 1945. The new '45 home uniform made it official, displaying the name BRAVES proudly across the front of the pinstriped jersey. The team was still struggling in the standings, but a 37-game hitting streak by Tommy Holmes focused some extra attention on this uniform.

A POST-WAR FLAG AND ADIEU TO BEANTOWN

In 1946, things were looking up for the Braves. A new manager, veteran Billy Southworth; a solid pitching staff paced by Sain and Spahn; and even a radical new uniform design that was destined to become a classic. To conservative tastes it was a gross overstatement with an abundance of color trimmings but it seemed to enrapture the fans who have since identified this image with success on the field. It was a generous balance of red and navy blue from top to bottom. A brand new slanted script version of BRAVES across the front was dramatically underscored with a tomahawk silhouette. The now familiar Indian head profile graced the left sleeve. Red and navy piping was everywhere you could put it on a baseball uniform. There was even a modified satin version for night games only. Meanwhile, back to the pennant wars, these post-war Braves finally captured a pennant in 1948 and the franchise had a new lease on life. The "Tomahawk" uniform design was here to stay for awhile.

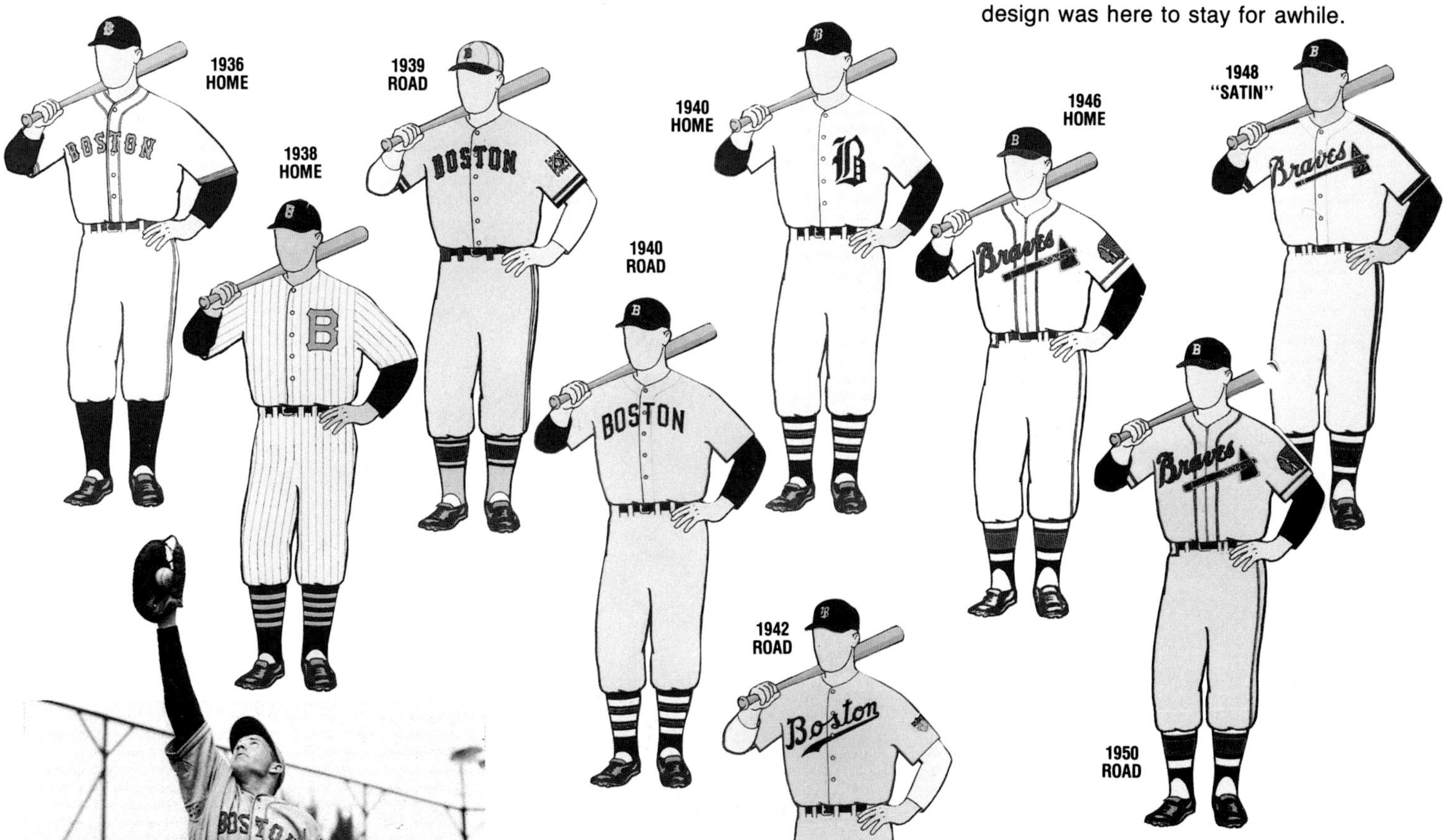

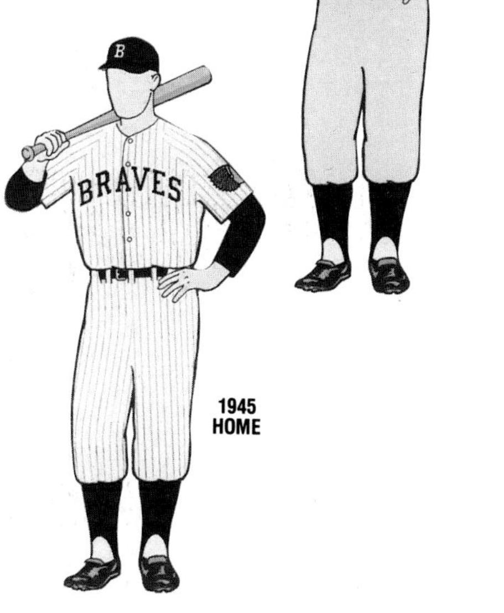

Elbie Fletcher reaches for a high one in spring training 1937 (1936 uniform)

Although a contender into the early fifties, the Braves couldn't quite recapture the needed momentum for another flag and as the phenomenal post-war attendance figures began to steadily dwindle, the question of Boston being a two-team town was beginning to surface. Major league baseball's stubborn resistance to any change in the status quo was likewise crumbling. Lou Perini was finally able to persuade the league fathers to allow him to transfer the Braves to Milwaukee for the 1953 season. And so the Boston Braves became the Milwaukee Braves and took their uniforms along. The only change for the maiden season in Wisconsin was to replace the white B on the cap to an M and to add the uniform number to the shirt fronts.

THE MILWAUKEE ADVENTURE

Beyond Mr. Perini's wildest dreams, attendance in Milwaukee was truly phenomenal — averaging over two million a year for the balance of the decade. And since success breeds more success, the Braves won pennants in 1957 and 1958 and missed by an eyelash in 1959. All this in those popular "tomahawk" uniforms, revised only by a new Braves "face" patch on the sleeve, replacing the profile Indian head. It all seemed too good to be true —a baseball "fairy tale" —and sure enough, it eventually began to sour. The team's performance began to slip, and so did the attendance. In 1963, the uniform was "cleaned up" and "quieted down". Piping was reduced to a minimum and the beloved tomahawk was removed. By 1965, the honeymoon was over and the Braves packed up their uniforms and headed south.

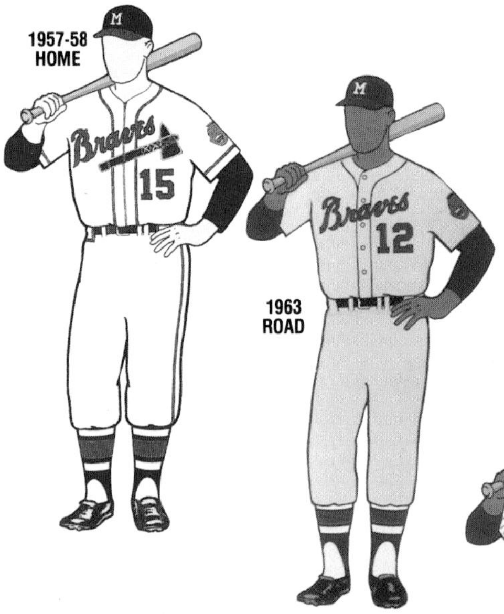

"Kiss it goodbye!" —Hank Aaron's record setting 715th home run in 1974

WELCOME TO THE SOUTHEAST

As before, the new Atlanta Braves opened the 1966 season with the same uniforms from Milwaukee except for a script A on the cap to replace the M. They stayed with this uniform set through the 1968 season. The new uniforms for 1969 were as much an understatement as the '46 suits were the opposite. Plain white pinstripes at home, plain gray on the road, solid blue stockings, no number on the front, simple script BRAVES with no underline —it was a soothing contrast to the golden years in Milwaukee, but it was not to last. With the advent of double-knit fabrics and their special new features, the Braves entered the 1972 campaign with another new look. The new pull-over jerseys offered a two-tone "softball" shirt appearance —white trunk with navy sleeves at home, navy trunk with white sleeves on the road. A colorful and highly conspicuous "feather" design blended into each sleeve. The BRAVES script was "awakened" with a double outline treatment and the stylized number was restored under BRAVES in the same treatment. The cap included a front white panel with a lower case stylized letter "a". In the only concession to tradition, the trousers retained the separate belt feature. Baseball history was made in this uniform when Henry Aaron finally eclipsed Ruth's career home run record in 1974.

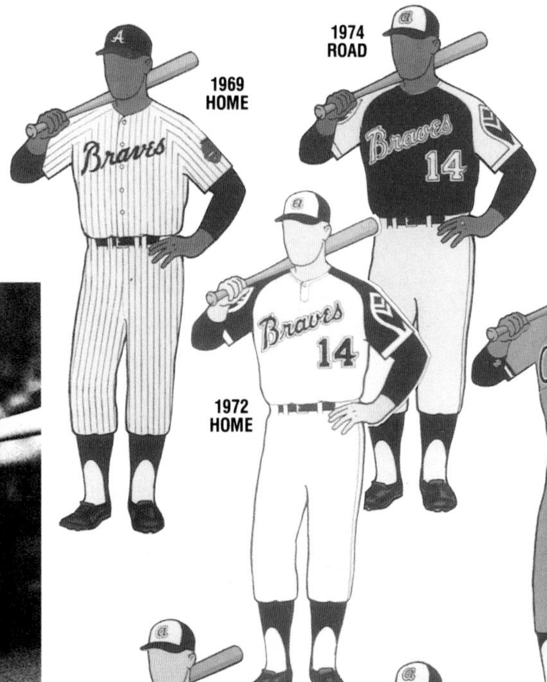

THE BICENTENNIAL YEAR & BEYOND

The new Braves home uniforms for America's bicentennial year (1976) were another breakthrough of color barriers —a spectacle of red, white and blue. If this was now "America's team", as owner Ted Turner labeled it, it was close to being draped in an American flag. With red pinstripes and red and blue trim, it was also comparable to a candy stick. The '76 road uniform restored gray to the trousers and torso part of the jersey, which repeated the decorative "feather" sleeves. The city name ATLANTA also appeared for the first time on this road jersey. This uniform set finished out the decade of the seventies.

For 1980, it was another celebration of the double knit uniform styles for the Atlanta Braves. The home suits were back to basic white but with generous red, white and blue striping on the collar, sleeve ends and the new beltless waistband. The '80 road uniforms went to the more trendy powder blue with navy blue and white trim —not a trace of red anywhere (except on the cap "A"). In 1982, the caps were changed to a solid blue with a white letter A in front. Also in '82, the ATLANTA on the blue road shirts was modified by changing the first letter A to a capital (vs. an enlarged form of lower case). This uniform set ran its course when, with an apparent yearning for past glories, the club decided to join the trend toward the traditional by introducing its 1987 re-issue of the "tomahawk" uniform —replete with buttons, separate belts, generous red and blue piping and even a return to standard gray color on the road. The public response to this concession to the past has been enormously favorable and it may be that the tomahawk is back for good.

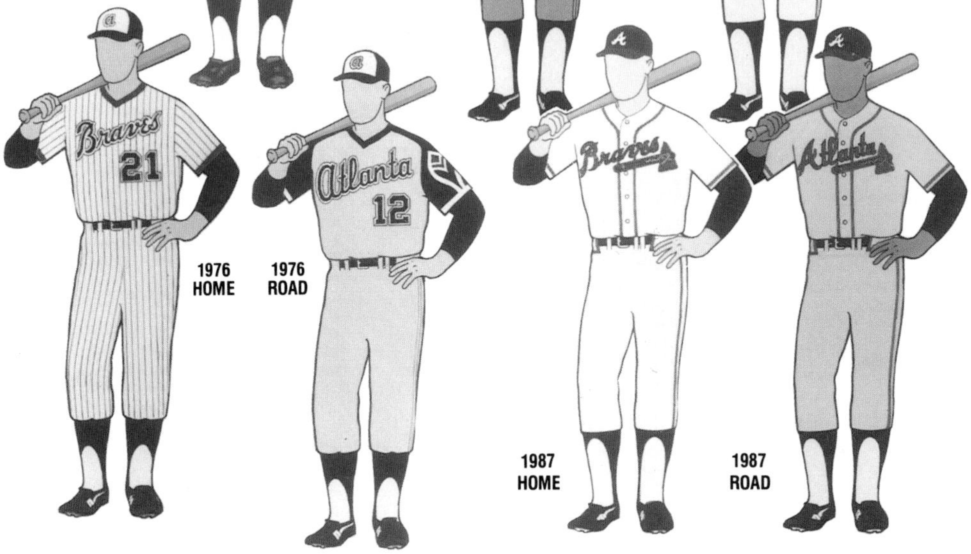

BALTIMORE ORIOLES

THE CHARTER MEMBERS OF 1901-02

When Ban Johnson decided to elevate his American League to "major" league status in 1901, it was important to establish a foothold in some of the major Eastern cities. Baltimore had a recent history of success with the legendary NL Orioles of the 1890's and was eager to re-enter the major league arena. The pugnacious ex-Oriole, John McGraw, was hired to manage the new Baltimore entry. Although the design features of the 1901 Oriole home uniforms are uncertain, the road suits were well documented and certainly extraordinary: All black caps, black shirts with a yellow-orange "O" on the left shirt pocket, black pants with a yellow belt and yellow & black striped stockings. Inspired by nature's coloring of its namesake, these uniforms were ridiculed in most of the AL cities they visited. McGraw had a passion for black uniforms but by the end of the 1901 season he had had enough. For 1902, the Baltimore uniforms were more conventional with a capital B on the left breast, similar to the uniforms of the legendary Orioles of the nineties. Unfortunately, attendance was disappointing and when the time was ripe for the new league to invade the lucrative New York City area it was decided to transfer the Baltimore franchise to the Big Apple. For the next fifty years Baltimore remained a minor league town (not counting their entry in the ill-fated Federal League of 1914-15). To their credit, the AAA Orioles were one of the most successful operations in the history of the International League.

1901
ROAD

1902
HOME

1902
ROAD

A NEW LEASE ON LIFE IN THE MAJORS

When the plight of the St. Louis Browns operation became clearly hopeless by the early fifties, Baltimore once again was considered part of a proposed franchise shift —only this time as the recipient. The first uniforms for the new major league Orioles in 1954 were a continuation of their AAA suits. Both the home whites and road grays were devoid of piping and featured a slanted script ORIOLES in orange & black across the chest. The black caps presented a silhouette Oriole bird on the front with the appropriate coloring of orange and black. The black stockings were accented by 3 orange stripes. The team lost 100 games that first season but thanks to the hapless A's they avoided a last place finish.

The second year provided some window-dressing to the same basic uniform design. White stripes were added to the orange & black stockings and piping was added to the collar and shirt front. A new Orioles cartoon-style patch was added to the left sleeve and a zipper front was introduced. The '56 road uniform replaced ORIOLES with the city name BALTIMORE in a slanted script with underline flourish. Except for the addition of the uniform number to the jersey front in 1958, this road uniform remained standard thru the 1962 season. The home uniforms also continued on thru the 1962 season. Consecutive third place finishes in 1960-61 signaled the Orioles' emergence as a legitimate pennant contender for the decade.

1954
HOME

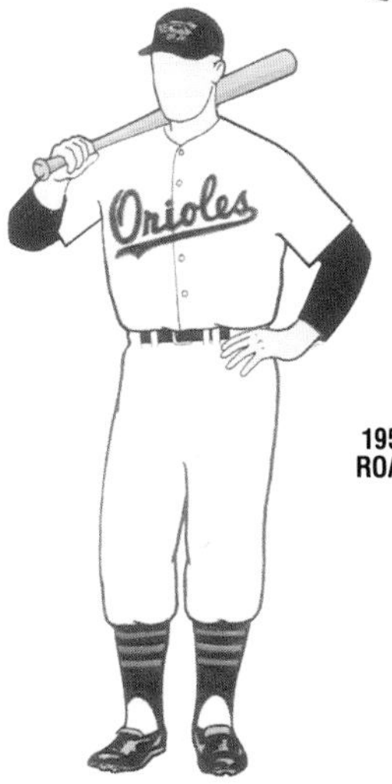

1954
ROAD

1955
HOME

1955
ROAD

Bullet Bob Turley —one of the "original" Orioles in 1954

1956
ROAD

1960
HOME

RESPECTABILITY —AT LAST!

The design of the home uniforms for 1963-65 represented a temporary detour in the steady evolution of the team's current graphics. The script form of ORIOLES was substituted for arched block capitals in black with orange border. Buttons also returned on the '63 shirts and the "cartoon" bird head patch "flew away" from the sleeve. Orange & black trim striping was used on the sleeve ends and around the collar edge but not down the button panel. 1966 was indeed a memorable year in Orioles history —the script ORIOLES was restored on the home jersey (minus the underline) but more importantly they captured their first AL pennant and stunned the baseball world by sweeping the favored Dodgers in the World Series. Names like McNally, Palmer, Robinson, Powell became instant household words and the Orioles had arrived as solid contenders for the next two decades. Also in 1966, a new version of the "cartoon" Oriole head appeared on the cap for the first time, replacing the full bird insignia.

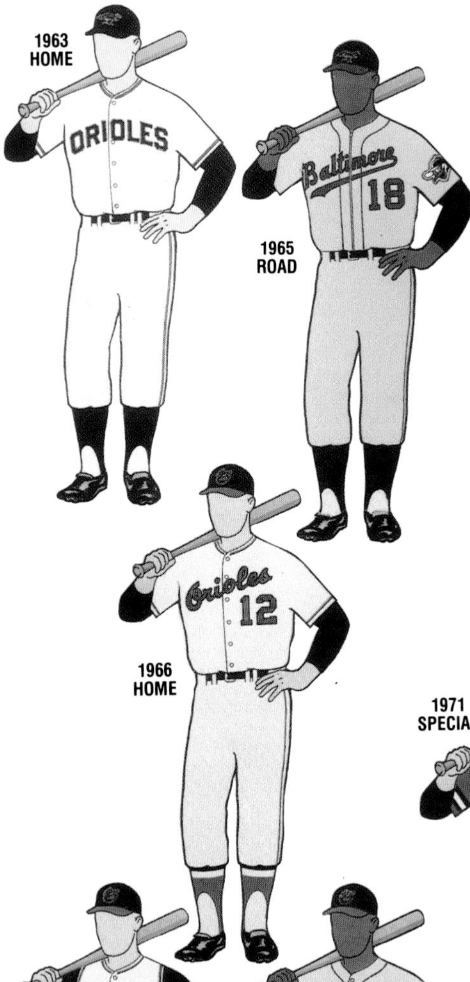

THE EARL WEAVER YEARS

The 1966 uniform theme continued on thru the pennant years of 1969-70-71 under Earl Weaver. On the eve of the conversion to the double-knits in 1972, an unusual all-orange uniform was tried out in 1971 —the season that produced an unprecedented quartet of 20-game winners (McNally, Cuellar, Palmer, Dobson). The first double knit home uniform in 1972 set the standard for the following seasons up to the present. For the first 3 years the cap crown was all black, then in 1975 the current model with a white front panel was introduced.Both home and road double knits utilized the built-in sash belt and incorporated orange, white & black stripes on the sleeve ends, sash belt and trouser legs. They opted for a button front rather than the pull-over style on the jerseys. The first double knit road shirts had the script BALTIMORE, but subsequent models were a gray copy of the home ORIOLES motif. A solid orange pull-over jersey with black and white trim was introduced in the mid-seventies and has been used as an alternate home uniform only occasionally. Boasting the best winning percentage in the majors during the seventies, the Orioles carried their winning tradition into the eighties with an impressive world championship in '83 under new manager Joe Altobelli. After a brief encore tenure by Earl Weaver, the Oriole fortunes became a family affair, with dad Cal Ripken Sr. managing and sons Cal Jr. and Bill in the lineup. The uniform designs seem to have stabilized into a solid tradition to complement the already established tradition of solid, winning baseball. Oriole fans are confident that the losing woes of 1987-88 are merely transitory. For 1989, the new uniform ensemble retains the basic Oriole look but with some conservative features —a belted trouser and solid black cap. The script ORIOLES has been enlarged and the cartoon bird face has given way to full-bird silhouette reminiscent of the fifties. Manager Frank Robinson should feel right at home in this outfit.

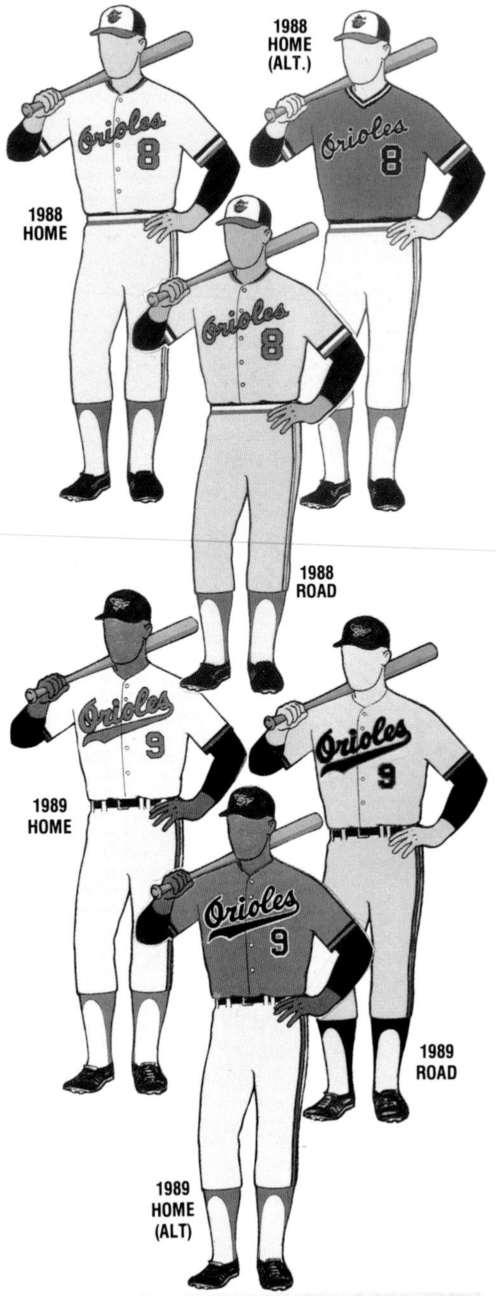

Pitching ace of the lates sixties, early-seventies —Dave McNally

BOSTON RED SOX

A SHAKY COEXISTANCE IN BEANTOWN

The first uniforms for the new 1901 Boston Americans were picked out by manager Jimmy Collins himself and purchased locally from Wright & Ditson. Nothing unusual about them —standard whites for home games and gray for the road. The jerseys had regulation turned down collars with lacing part way down the front. The trousers had built-in quilted padding for sliding protection —a carryover from the 1890's. The caps were so-called "Chicago" style —a pillbox shape with two stripes around the crown. A feature which may surprise the uninformed Red Sox fan is that all uniform trim, including the stockings, was not red but BLUE. Both home and road suits had the city name BOSTON in arched block capital letters across the jersey front. This lettering style was standard edition from uniform manufacturers of the day but is especially noteworthy for a couple of reasons. First, since this form of BOSTON letters is virtually identical to the current Red Sox road jersey, it represents the oldest antecedent trim feature of any surviving major league uniform. (The Reds might challenge this but, in truth, their current CINCINNATI is somewhat stylized to accommodate the arc of the letters). Secondly, it was identical to the rival Boston Nationals uniform lettering and practically impossible to differentiate in black in white photos of the period.

1901
HOME

1902
HOME

1903
HOME

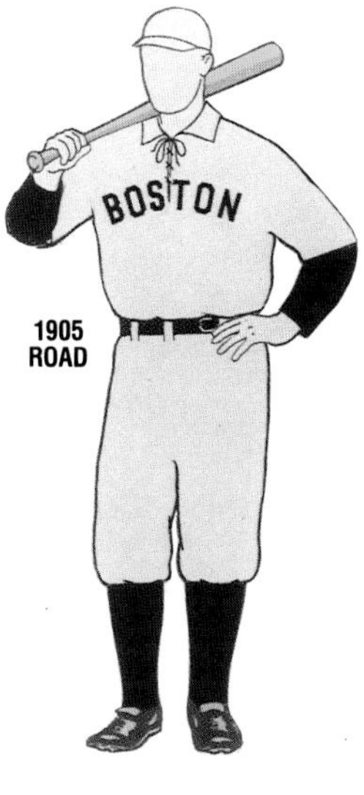

1905
ROAD

Perhaps to try to resolve this identity problem for 1902, the Boston Americans elected to change the front jersey trim to an Old English B and A on the right and left breast respectively (the two letters signifying Boston Americans). Since most team nicknames were not yet "official", (one exception being the Philadelphia ATHLETICS) "Americans" was the accepted name used to distinguish this team from the Boston Nationals. Unofficial nicknames for the club (used by newspapers) in the early years included "Pilgrims", "Puritans", and "Beaneaters". The decorative Old English letters were another common standard used on many team uniforms in this era —the only current survivor of this early century fashion being the "D" worn on the Detroit Tigers home uniform.

The 1903 was an important milestone in establishing the credibility of the new American League. For the Boston franchise it was a truly memorable season. Paced by future hall of fame legends Cy Young and Jimmy Collins, the Bostons captured the league pennant and challenged the National League winners, the Pittsburgh Pirates, to a post-season series to settle any claim to a "world" championship. The Pirates were the dominant team in the senior circuit and accepted the challenge as a sure means to demonstrate the inferiority of the upstart American Leaguers. But as fate would have it, the Bostons upset the mighty Pittsburghs led by Honus Wagner. The new league had "arrived" as a bona fide major league (or so it would seem). And, by the way, the uniforms for 1903 had reverted back to the BOSTON lettering of 1901. The only change was in the cap —a single wide stripe replacing the 2 narrower stripes.

Jimmy Collins, manager & third baseman of the original Boston Americans of 1901.

For 1904 (another pennant year) the Boston road cap was a plain gray standard rounded crown style. The BOSTON uniforms remained virtually unchanged through the 1907 season except for minor variations in the caps. The quilted trousers were abandoned but the laced collar was retained, even though they and the neighboring Boston Nationals were the only major league teams to cling to this 19th century feature as late as 1910. Coexistance of two Boston teams had become an accepted reality but the similarity of the two teams' uniforms was about to end.

WILL THE REAL BOSTON RED SOX PLEASE STAND UP?

A decision by the Boston Nationals in 1907 was the catalyst which ultimately gave the Boston Americans their Red Sox identity. After wearing red uniform trim in prior years, the Nationals (or "DOVES" as they were called, in reference to owner John Dovey) opened the 1907 season with all-white home uniforms. Manager Fred Tenney was determined to eliminate all red trimmings, especially the stockings, and the new appearance complemented the new nickname. Blue or navy blue was already the standard trim color for most of the other American League clubs and perhaps for this reason the Bostons were quick to adopt red as a new trim color, seemingly abandoned by their Boston neighbors. The new uniforms for 1908 made it abundantly clear that the Boston Americans were now officially the Red Stockings, or Red Sox. The abbreviated SOX spelling followed the precedent of the Chicago White Sox, who shortened the name partly to disclaim any association with the earlier National League Chicago White Stockings but more likely it was done to economize on space in newspaper accounts of the games. The 1908 jerseys were indeed unique —on the center of the chest was a slanted red stocking symbol with the name BOSTON in white capital letters inside the the stocking. This unusual graphic symbolization made no mistake about who this team was and it was the first pictorial reference to the team nickname on an American League jersey (the Detroit team had earlier displayed a small red tiger of their caps in 1901 and 1902).

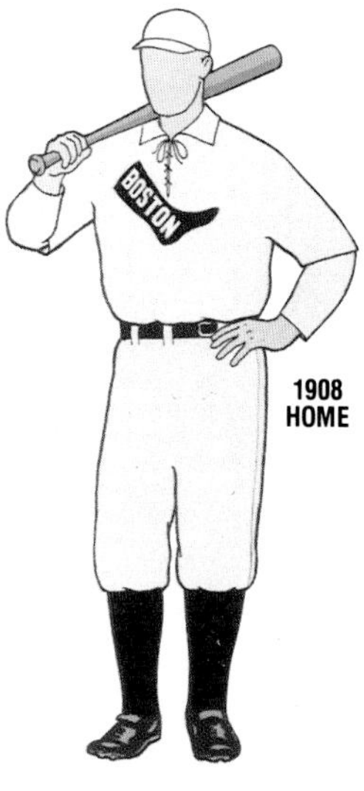

1908
HOME

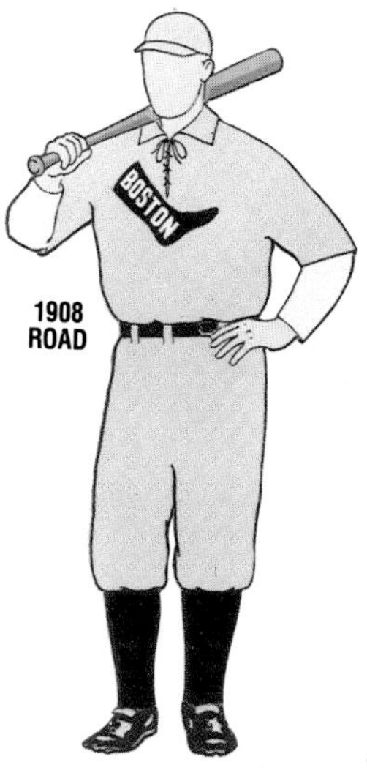

1908
ROAD

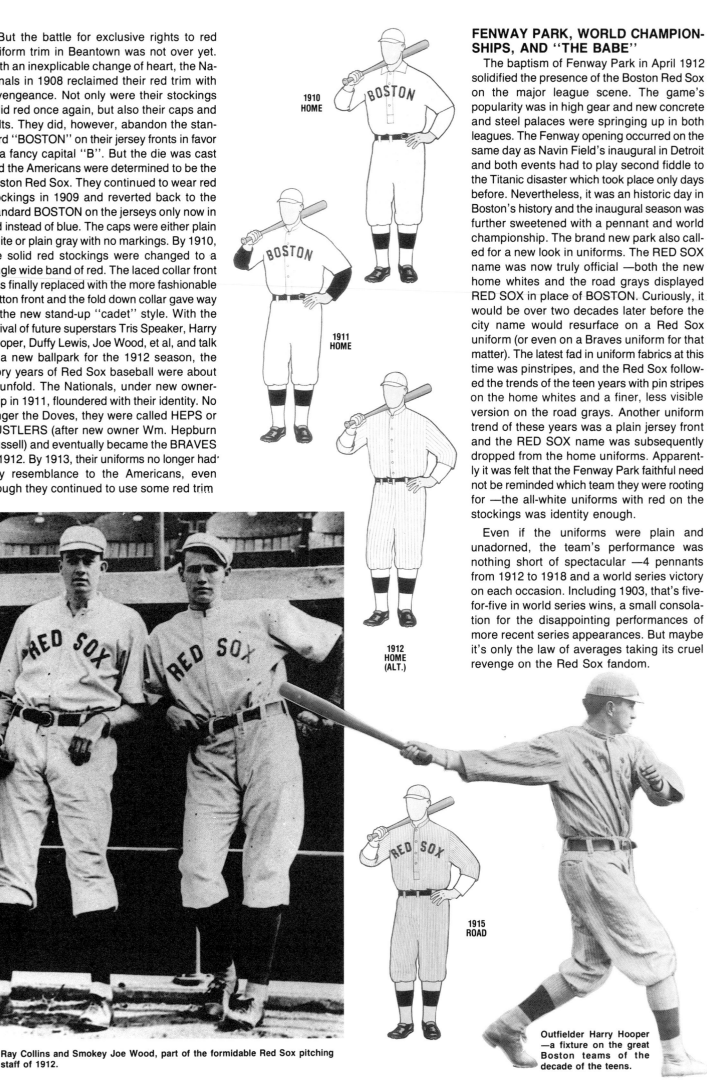

But the battle for exclusive rights to red uniform trim in Beantown was not over yet. With an inexplicable change of heart, the Nationals in 1908 reclaimed their red trim with a vengeance. Not only were their stockings solid red once again, but also their caps and belts. They did, however, abandon the standard "BOSTON" on their jersey fronts in favor of a fancy capital "B". But the die was cast and the Americans were determined to be the Boston Red Sox. They continued to wear red stockings in 1909 and reverted back to the standard BOSTON on the jerseys only now in red instead of blue. The caps were either plain white or plain gray with no markings. By 1910, the solid red stockings were changed to a single wide band of red. The laced collar front was finally replaced with the more fashionable button front and the fold down collar gave way to the new stand-up "cadet" style. With the arrival of future superstars Tris Speaker, Harry Hooper, Duffy Lewis, Joe Wood, et al, and talk of a new ballpark for the 1912 season, the glory years of Red Sox baseball were about to unfold. The Nationals, under new ownership in 1911, floundered with their identity. No longer the Doves, they were called HEPS or RUSTLERS (after new owner Wm. Hepburn Russell) and eventually became the BRAVES in 1912. By 1913, their uniforms no longer had any resemblance to the Americans, even though they continued to use some red trim

1910
HOME

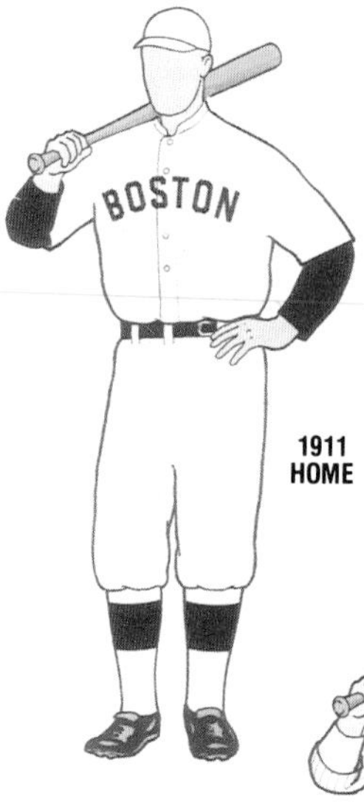

1911
HOME

1912
HOME
(ALT.)

Ray Collins and Smokey Joe Wood, part of the formidable Red Sox pitching staff of 1912.

FENWAY PARK, WORLD CHAMPIONSHIPS, AND "THE BABE"

The baptism of Fenway Park in April 1912 solidified the presence of the Boston Red Sox on the major league scene. The game's popularity was in high gear and new concrete and steel palaces were springing up in both leagues. The Fenway opening occurred on the same day as Navin Field's inaugural in Detroit and both events had to play second fiddle to the Titanic disaster which took place only days before. Nevertheless, it was an historic day in Boston's history and the inaugural season was further sweetened with a pennant and world championship. The brand new park also called for a new look in uniforms. The RED SOX name was now truly official —both the new home whites and the road grays displayed RED SOX in place of BOSTON. Curiously, it would be over two decades later before the city name would resurface on a Red Sox uniform (or even on a Braves uniform for that matter). The latest fad in uniform fabrics at this time was pinstripes, and the Red Sox followed the trends of the teen years with pin stripes on the home whites and a finer, less visible version on the road grays. Another uniform trend of these years was a plain jersey front and the RED SOX name was subsequently dropped from the home uniforms. Apparently it was felt that the Fenway Park faithful need not be reminded which team they were rooting for —the all-white uniforms with red on the stockings was identity enough.

Even if the uniforms were plain and unadorned, the team's performance was nothing short of spectacular —4 pennants from 1912 to 1918 and a world series victory on each occasion. Including 1903, that's five-for-five in world series wins, a small consolation for the disappointing performances of more recent series appearances. But maybe it's only the law of averages taking its cruel revenge on the Red Sox fandom.

1915
ROAD

Outfielder Harry Hooper —a fixture on the great Boston teams of the decade of the teens.

THE FORGETTABLE TWENTIES

Sadly, the nucleus of those fabulous teams of 1912-1918 were prematurely peddled away by 1920, including the great Tris Speaker and the one and only George Herman Ruth. Boston fans shall forever be tormented by this and "what might have been" had these star players remained in Boston to complete their careers in Fenway Park. Except for evolutionary changes in the collar design, the Red Sox uniform ensemble was basically the same throughout the entire decade of the twenties —all white (with or without pin striping) with no markings at home, all gray with the familiar RED SOX across the road jersey. The only red trim (besides RED SOX) were the stockings and sometimes the cap bill. The twenties were a forgettable period for Red Sox fans —dreary years in plain uniforms.

1921 ROAD

1922 HOME

THE THIRTIES—MORE DREARY YEARS BUT COLORIZED

After a decade of plain, repetitive uniforms by most of the major league teams, (can anyone truthfully say that the famous Yankee uniforms of that era were a sartorial classic?) the late twenties saw a resurgence of new graphics ideas and extra colors. Multi-colored piping was becoming fashionable along with 2-color, fancier lettering styles. Even the blank space on the back of the jersey was utilized —Detroit displayed a tiger head and the cross-town Braves featured their Indian Chief's profile in the years just before numbers on the back became standard. For 1930, the arched RED SOX was no longer basic block letters but a fancier lettering style. Both Boston teams that year displayed the same patch on their left sleeve —a large Pilgrim hat design symbolizing the city's tricentennial.

1926 ROAD

1930 ROAD

More new ideas were introduced for the 1931 season. The red block letters for RED SOX were restored but with an added outline trim of navy blue. For only the second time in the franchise history a graphic symbol of the team nickname was displayed on the uniform —a pair of red socks on the sleeve and a single small red sock on the cap front. The now familiar pin stripes were dropped in 1932 and the RED SOX lettering style was revised again to a "thick and thin" serif style. By this time, the wide red stripe on the stockings was extended to the entire sock except for white stirrups. The 1933-34 uniforms went a step further toward the familiar look of future decades. A solid navy blue cap was worn for the first time and a red letter B was introduced to the cap front —another first. Navy blue and white stripes were added to the upper half of the the stockings. Red piping was placed around the collar and down the button front. The red letters on the jersey front were once again a serif style but more condensed and with a navy outline piping. The city name BOSTON appeared in the same letter style on the gray road uniforms for the first time since 1911. For 1935, the home uniform temporarily returned to the plainer style, similar to 1932. The gray road suits were also toned down with BOSTON in the plain block capital letters of the early years. The socks were once again solid red.

1931 HOME

1935 HOME

1935 ROAD

Pitcher Howard Ehmke, one of the few bright spots for the Bostons in the mid-twenties —in his home whites.

1932 HOME

1934 HOME

1934 ROAD

New manager/infielder, the popular Joe Cronin in Spring training 1935.

The home uniform for 1936 was the original version of the long-running familiar look of the next 3 decades. The only differences in this early model were that the fancy red B on the cap did not yet have a white outline and the fancy lettering on the jersey front was rounder, less condensed. The 1936 road uniform repeated this lettering style for the BOSTON name. In 1938, the die was finally cast for the Red Sox uniforms of today. The RED SOX letters on the home uniforms were narrowed down and plain block capital letters BOSTON in solid navy were once again restored to the gray roads with red piping eliminated. This was the uniform first worn by rookie sensation Ted Williams in 1939.

1936 HOME

1936 ROAD

1940 HOME

1950's ROAD

TRADITIONAL LOOK

Except for a white outline added to the "B" on the cap in 1946, the Boston uniforms were as predictable and as certain as death and taxes up to 1970. Some great teams and some pretty pathetic teams represented Beantown during the 1940's, 1950's and 1960's. The post-war teams produced one pennant (1946) and a couple of losing dead-heats and featured an awesome collection of offensive stars: Williams, Pesky, Doerr, Dropo, Dom DiMaggio. The Bosox were pretty much a respectable first division team during the Yankee dominance of the fifties, but tailed off to an also-ran by the early 1960's. The "impossible dream" 1967 pennant team of Yaz, Lonborg, Harrelson, et al finally restored a touch of pride to the Bostons who wore this uniform. The approaching new decade would signal a temporary detour in the traditional design of the Red Sox uniforms.

The one and only "YAZ" in action at Fenway Park in his san-piping home whites, c.1970.

THE SEVENTIES—DOUBLE KNITS AND BACK TO BASICS

The first notable change in Bosox attire came on the eve of the double knit revolution of the early 1970's. For 1969, the familiar red piping on the home uniform was dropped and the BOSTON on the gray uniform now included a thin red outline. In 1973, the new double knit features of a pullover jersey and built-in sash belt provided even more radical changes. The new style home and road jerseys featured a red-navy-red striping on the V-neck collar and the same color combination was used on the new belt sash of the trousers. The cap crown was later changed to solid red with a navy bill and the "B" reverted to navy with a white outline. Other variations of this cap included a half-and-half navy/red combination. Red shoes were also introduced to complement the new double knit color scheme. The stockings never really changed but the new fad of stretching the stirrups fully up and under the trouser legs had by this time totally concealed the navy and white stripes on the upper part of the stocking. 1975 produced a pennant and a dramatic world series struggle with Cincinnati for the tenure of this uniform design. But the subtle pressures of a lingering nostalgia cried out for a restoration of the uniform of the Ted Williams/Carl Yastrzemski years.

In 1979, the familiar button-front jerseys and belt-loop trousers came back —the Boston Red Sox are the real Boston Red Sox once again. Sure, the fabric is still double-knit — no one wants to go so far as to resurrect the old flannels. The tailoring is in the tighter, closer-fitting style of the eighties. But tradition is synonymous with Boston and any Red Sox fan who can remember that "impossible dream" of 1967 and especially those who yearn for those wonderful years of the the Ted Williams generation can feel a tiny shiver go up their spine when the Red Sox of the eighties take the field. To watch them perform in anything else is comparable to going to a home game in some other park other than beloved Fenway —perish the thought!

1977 HOME

1989 ROAD

1990 ROAD

1960's ROAD

1970 HOME

1970 ROAD

1975 ROAD

1990 HOME

CALIFORNIA ANGELS

AT FIRST, "LOS ANGELES"

When the American League made the decision to add two new teams for the 1961 season, there was never a doubt that one franchise would be located in Southern California. With a natural climate for year-round baseball, it was already the prime breeding ground for future major leaguers. The instant success of the transplanted Dodgers in the vast megalopolis of 10 million people clearly indicated that there was an abundance of potential fan support for a second major league team. Retrieving the nickname of Angels from the defunct PCL club was an appropriate decision by new owner Gene Autry. In fact, they played their first few seasons in the old PCL facility, Wrigley Field. Forced to develop a competetive team overnight with has-beens and left-overs made the task far more difficult than the Dodgers —who brought an entire roster of established players with them from Brooklyn.

Navy blue and scarlet were the trim colors selected for the new uniforms. The home whites featured ANGELS in arched fancy capital letters across the chest —in scarlet with a navy outline. The same lettering style was used for LOS ANGELES on the road grays, except in navy blue with red outline. Modest piping trim of red & navy was used on both suits. The undersweaters and stockings were solid navy. The caps for the first season had a solid navy crown with a red visor and an L-A monogram in red edged with white. By the following season, they added a circular white "halo" stripe around the top of the caps to symbolize their "heavenly" origins.

1961 HOME

1963 ROAD

THE QUEST FOR A NEW HOME

Wrigley Field was an excellent minor league facility but far short of major league seating capacity. When the Dodgers completed their new Dodger Stadium, a temporary arrangement was made with the Angels to share the occupancy until a new park could be built for the American Leaguers. Dodger Stadium was AKA Chavez Ravine when the Angels were in town. In 1965, the new franchise was renamed CALIFORNIA ANGELS to appeal to more generic population base and because the new stadium would be built outside Los Angeles proper (in neighboring Anaheim). Accordingly, the L-A monogram on the cap was changed to C-A and the LOS ANGELES on the road uniform was replaced by the same ANGELS as on the home suits. At the same time, the navy stockings were changed to RED.

1965 HOME

1965 ROAD

The Angels opened the 1966 season in sparkling new Anaheim Stadium —a permanent home, at last! The uniform sets from 1965 were continued and remained unchanged thru the 1970 season. For 1971, the navy & scarlet colors also continued but the uniform graphics were completely overhauled. The shirts were still the button-front flannels and the trousers used belts. The caps retained the navy blue crown with red visor, but in place of the C-A monogram a red lower case "a" appeared with white outline and a little white halo floating off the top left of the letter. The name ANGELS was re-designed in a modern sanserif lower case style —in red with a navy outline. A red halo was positioned over the lower case "a" of ANGELS. The uniform number was placed on the left breast in red, just beneath ANGELS. A new shoulder patch design featured a red silhouette shape of the state of California encircled by another "halo" and with a small star in the lower corner of the "map". The same red & navy braid piping was carried over from the '70 uniforms. The new road uniform was a gray duplication of the home whites. The same uniforms were repeated in 1972.

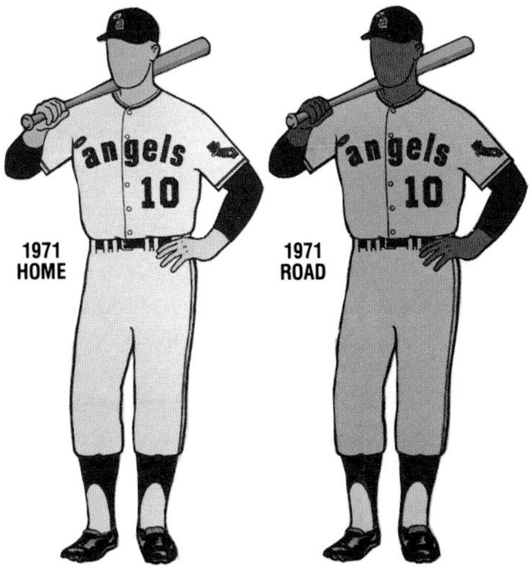

1971 HOME

1971 ROAD

DOUBLE-KNITS AND A TRADITION TAKES HOLD

The Angels adopted the new double-knit uniform for the 1973 season and converted the '71-'72 design to the pull-over shirts and sash-belted trousers. New blue/red/blue striping was incorporated on the V-neck, sleeve ends, belt sash, and trouser legs. The other significant revisions were: changing the "A" in Angels to a "haloed" capital A (emulating the huge "Big A" scoreboard structure at the stadium) and likewise on the cap front, changing over to red shoes to complement the red stirrup socks. This uniform set has remained intact to this day —it produced 3 division titles and is well on its way to become a full-fledged tradition. For 1989, the only significant modification is the return to a full-buttoned shirt and belted trousers.

1984 HOME

1988 ROAD

1989 HOME

1989 ROAD

CHICAGO CUBS

ENTERING THE NEW CENTURY

The Chicago Cubs, despite a prolonged drought of championships in recent decades, have a long & rich tradition as a charter member of the National League dating back to 1876. Cap Anson's White Stockings of the pre-1900 era were legendary and inspired Cormiskey's new AL franchise across town to quickly adopt the idea of white hosiery, since the National Leaguers had not used them for many years prior to 1900. The NL Chicago "Orphans" (or "Remnants" —they weren't the "Cubs" just yet) at the turn of the century wore the plainest of the plain in uniforms — no lettering or insignias of any kind. The jersey was strictly regulation —standard fold-down collar, buttons part way down the front, and a pocket on the left breast. Caps were the abbreviated "Boston" style with a close fitting round crown and a thin color band around the base of the crown. It was white at home and gray on the road with MAROON stockings and cap trim in 1900. The only change for 1901-02 was changing the socks and cap trim to BLUE. Because of the turmoil of widespread defection by players to the new American League, one Chicago writer wryly suggested that the plain uniform was a deliberate accommodation to those players who wished to abandon the NL ship and take their uniforms along.

For the 1903 season, the new uniforms added a simplified old-English C (in blue) to the shirt pocket of both home and road shirts. The stockings and trim color were still blue, but a lighter shade than in '02. The caps were solid white and solid gray. It was back to the plain, unmarked uniforms again for 1904 and at home in 1905. The name CHICAGO in arched block capital letters was added to the front of the the 1905 gray road jersey and continued on the road suits through 1907. A large circular C was added to the left breast of the home shirt in 1906 and was repeated (with a slight modification) for 1907. A special gray version of the 1906 home uniform with fine pin striping was made up for the '07 series. Since the Cubs had been upset by the cross-town White Sox in the '06 series by losing key home games, this gray suit was worn to open the '07 series in Chicago. The game ended in a tie, but the team was severely reprimanded by the National Commission for not wearing the traditional home whites. The attempt to break the "at home" jinx apparently worked as the Cubs had no trouble subduing the Detroits in the Fall Classic.

THE HEIGHTS OF GLORY

In 1908, the Chicago Cubs (the nickname was "officially" adopted by now) were the elite of the baseball wars. 2 straight pennants and a crushing defeat of Jennings' Tigers in the '07 series —it was the golden era of Cubs baseball. The uniform designs for the 1908 season were redone from head to foot. Both home and road caps featured a black visor and a small C in front. The C on the shirts encircled a small brown bear figure holding a bat —a visual confirmation of the new CUBS nickname. New stockings displayed alternate striping of black and gray. The gray road uniforms were of special significance in that they exhibited a narrow spaced fine dark stripe pattern —a fabric they had introduced for the first time in the 1907 world series. Even the new black coats sported a large white bear figure on each sleeve. They capped off this milestone season with third straight pennant and another humiliation of the Detroits in the world series. This unique uniform ensemble unwittingly celebrated the last world championship in the history of the franchise.

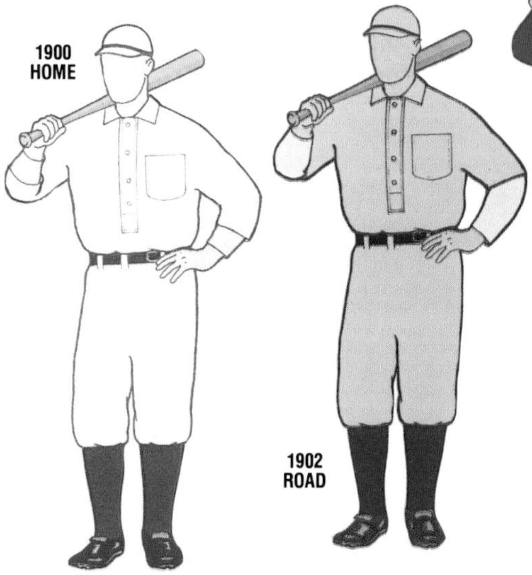

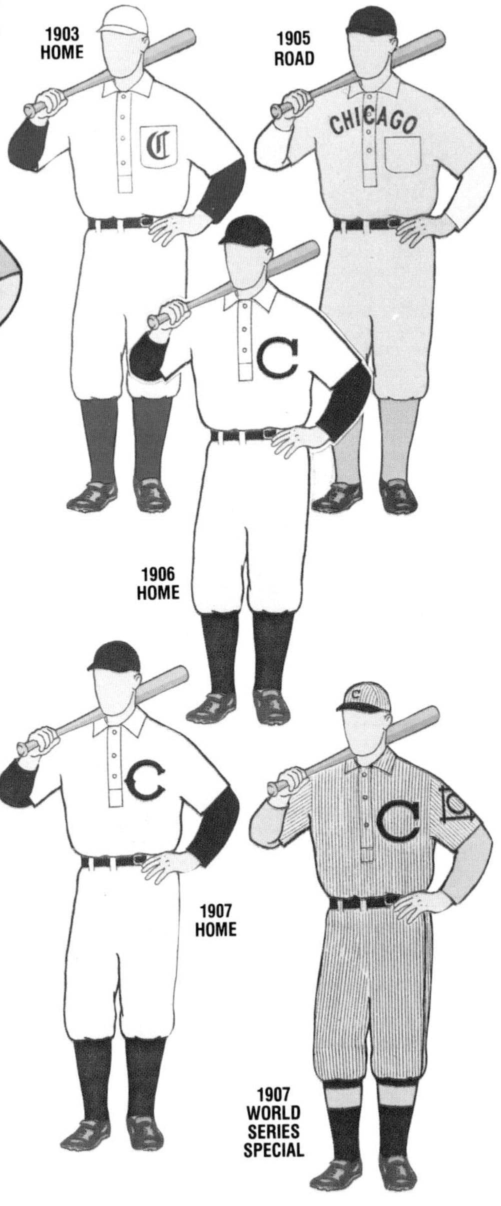

The Peerless Leader, Frank Chance, looking things over at the Polo Grounds c.1906.

The pitching bulwark of a great Cub dynasty, Mordecai Brown, at West Side Grounds in 1909.

The following season (1909), the home uniform of 1908 was repeated with only minor changes: a new "cadet" style stand-up collar on the shirt and solid dark stockings. The road grays repeated the pin-striped fabric but the jersey was dramatically remodeled. The new cadet collar and the button panel were solid navy and a thick navy stripe was added to the sleeve ends. The city name CHICAGO was added vertically to the button panel in white capital letters. But the most significant embellishment of all was the substitution of UBS inside the circular C, replacing the bearcub figure. This was the very first appearance of the famous Cubs emblem which has endeared itself to Cub fans for generations. It also marked first of rare occasions when the full team name (city plus nickname) appeared on a major league uniform. The following season of 1910 produced another pennant with a continuation of this uniform scheme (only the socks pattern changed and the "CHICAGO" trim feature was discontinued on the road uniform).

1913 HOME

1913 ROAD

1914 HOME

1914 ROAD

1909 ROAD

1910 HOME

1910 ROAD

1911 ROAD

1916 HOME

1917 HOME

1918 HOME

1918 ROAD

The unforgettable Johnny Evers in his new road uniform for 1913 (his last year as a Cub).

THE TURBULENT TEENS

The road uniforms in 1911-12-13 saw the abandonment of the pin-striped gray in favor of an all dark blue "negative" image of the home uniform. In "11 & '12, it was the now familiar C-with-bearcub and in 1913 it was a reverse of the totally re-designed home whites. The name CUBS was spelled out on the '13 shirt front in large capital letters. The home and road caps were solid white and solid navy, respectively. A fancier variation of the CUBS lettering followed in 1914 and 1915 on the home whites, while the road uniforms for those years reverted to a plain traditional gray with CHICAGO spelled out in the same lettering style as the home CUBS. The little bearcub figure re-appeared on the sleeve and cap of the 1914 road grays.

The 1913-16 period were troubling times for the franchise. The dynasty was gone —Tinker, Evers, Chance played out the string and the future of West Side Grounds was in doubt. Besides the advent of a world war, the major leagues were being threatened by the newly formed Federal League with a Chicago-based franchise. As luck would have it, the new league folded after the 1915 season and one Charles Weeghman, late of the defunct Chifeds, took over the Cubs operation. His first important move was to re-locate the team to his newly-built Weeghman Park (now Wrigley Field) on the North Side. The Cub uniforms also reflected the new order —a modification of the 1915 Whales uniform. On the left breast was a red & navy "wishbone" C encircling a walking bear (a substitution for the "whale" on the Feds '15 home whites).

With the country now at war, the new 1917 uniform sets displayed "old glory" on the left sleeve. For the second time, the full team name CHICAGO CUBS appeared on the front of both home and road suits. The patriotic fervor went a few steps further with the totally new 1918 uniforms. Pin striping was restored on both home & road suits and a conspicuous red, white & blue flavor was incorporated on the stockings and in the CUBS lettering. The Bruins captured another pennant in these uniforms but fell victim to the talent-laden Red Sox in the Fall Classic.

An ace pitcher for the Cubs in the WWI era, James "Hippo" Vaughn, posing in the new 1916 home uniform.

THE ROARING (?) TWENTIES

In the decade following WWI, Cubs uniform fronts went through a treadmill of variations of either the C-UBS emblem or CUBS spelled out in capitals. In keeping with the generally conservative uniform trends of the times, their trimmings were mostly one color only and devoid of decorative piping and sox stripes. 1926 saw the return of the city name CHICAGO on the road grays and also the introduction of more ornamental sox striping. A white block C appeared on the dark cap in place of the vertical white seam stripes of previous seasons. The 1927 uniforms heralded a rejuvenation of uniform trim and added color —part of a sartorial uplift that was occurring throughout major league baseball.

A generous use of red to complement the somber navy blue trim was the rule for the '27 uniforms: a red wishbone C on the navy caps, combination red & navy piping of the shirts and trousers, 3 red stripes on the navy stockings. The wishbone C on the home uniform front was solid red with a navy blue outline and the little bearcub-with-bat returned to replace UBS. With only slight variations in future versions (solid color belt tunnels, a solid color button panel in '33), this was to be the standard primary home uniform for the next 10 years. The gray road uniform of 1927 also included the additional red and it, too, became a standard thru the 1936 season. Another pennant year in 1929 featured this uniform motif.

THE THIRTIES —HOW MANY UNIFORMS?

From 1930-1936, the Cubs experimented with a series of alternate uniform designs for both home and road. The 1930-31 home alternates revived pin stripes and another variation of the C-UBS emblem on the front. The 1932-33 alternates continued to pin striping but in place of the usual insignia on the jersey a slanted script treatment of CUBS was displayed in navy and red. The red wishbone C on the cap was replaced by a white fancy capital C. The alternate road conterpart for these years had a slanted script CHICAGO across the chest and a smaller script CUBS on the left sleeve (once again the full team name spelled out). The 1934 home alternates used a refreshing new version of the team insignia on the left breast —the larger red & navy C embodied a serif style and the bearcub figure inside the C had abandoned the bat and assumed a pitcher's windup motion (or is it a gesture of triumph?). The same style C appeared in red with a white outline on the navy blue cap. The 1935-36 alternate road uniform displayed CHICAGO across the chest in straight horizontal fancy capital letters (not the usual "arc" alignment).

1919 ROAD

1921 HOME

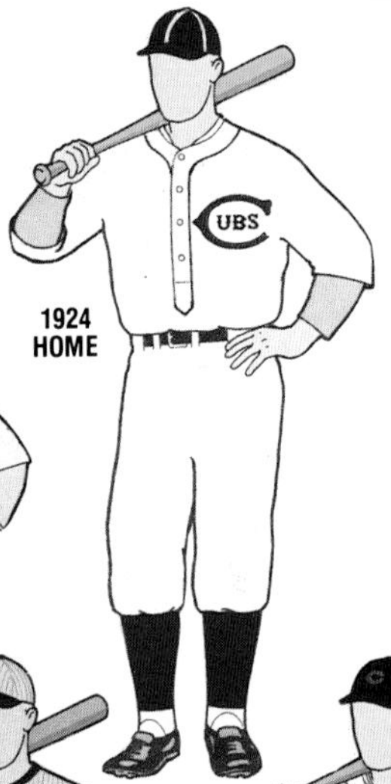
1924 HOME

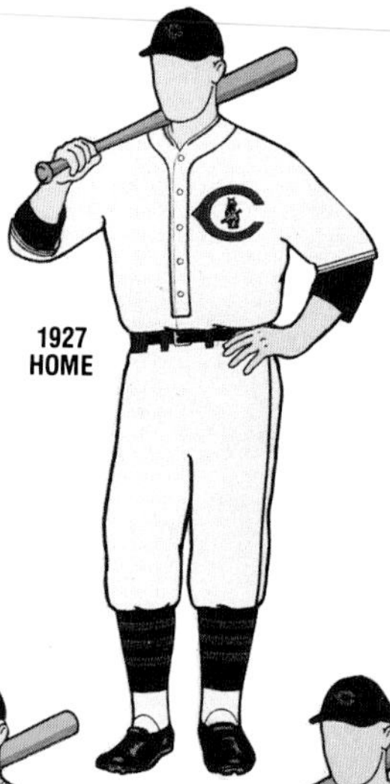
1927 HOME

1923 ROAD

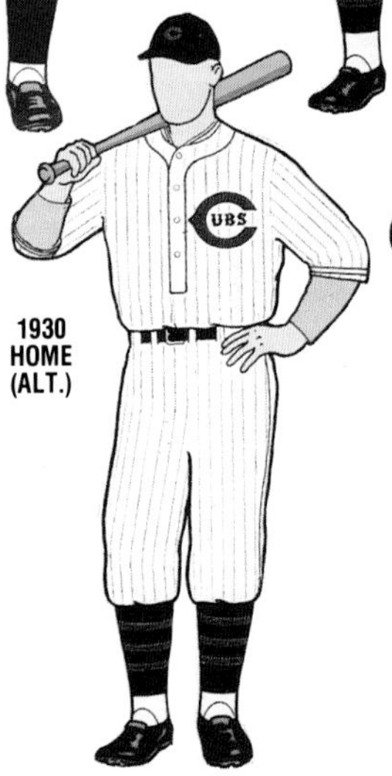
1930 HOME (ALT.)

1930 ROAD

1932 HOME (ALT.)

1932 ROAD (ALT.)

1933 HOME (ALT.)

1934 HOME (ALT.)

1935 ROAD (ALT.)

A fine Cub shortstop in the early-twenties, Charley Hollocher.

Riggs Stephenson, the hard-hitting outfielder, at Wrigley Field in the late twenties.

For the 1937 season, Mr. Wrigley decided it was time for a totally new image for the Cub uniforms. He delegated his own corporate design staff for the project and they responded with some novel ideas. Most importantly, the standard navy blue was replaced by a brighter "electric" blue. The new jerseys abandoned the buttoned front in favor of a ZIPPER —an idea that caught on quickly with other clubs and remained popular for over 2 decades. Instead of the usual thin beads of embroidered piping, thick striping of solid blue or red (on the road) was incorporated around the neck and parallel to the zipper as well as on the sleeve ends and trouser sides. The 3 red stripes on the stocking were lowered closer to the ankle for more visibility. On the home uniform, the original version of the C-UBS emblem (with a circular C) was resurrected from the distant past—except this time the C was solid red with a blue outline. On the travelling grays, the striping trim was RED and did not follow down the zipper line. The name CHICAGO was re-done in solid blue plain block capitals and was underlined with an arc of red striping. Except for the change in shade of blue, the cap theme stayed the same —a red C (not "wishbone" at first) on a solid blue cap. As if to "finish off" the new design idea for 1938, a shoulder stripe was added on both home and road suits. Also, the "wishbone" style C was restored on the cap. Despite hard times, the thirties were exciting years for Cub fans —3 pennants, but no cigar!

Catcher/manager Gabby Hartnett in the Wrigley Field dugout during the dramatic 1938 season.

THE FORTIES AND DOWNHILL

The Cubs began the 1940 season with perhaps the most dramatic innovation of the century in baseball uniform design —the sleeveless vest. It was a continuation of the novel ideas of 1937 and was adapted to complement the new vest. The C-UBS emblem and CHICAGO had to be lowered slightly and new emphasis was placed on the blue undersweater. The 3 red stripes on the stockings were duplicated on the forearms of the sleeves and on some versions a white crown was featured across the shoulders. For 1941 and 1942, the C-UBS emblem was redesigned to include an outline of blue. The CHICAGO lettering and underline arc on the 1941-42 road grays were changed to an outline style. The sleeveless vest uniform was abandoned after the 1942 season and never worn again by the Cubs, but enjoyed a revival with other NL clubs in the late fifties.

1940 HOME — 1940 ROAD — 1942 ROAD

For the 1943 season, the Cub uniforms drifted back to a more conventional plain look with a continuation of the same graphics. All piping was eliminated and buttons were returned on the shirt front. The club won its last pennant (1945) in these uniforms and they remained basically unchanged thru the mid-fifties. The zipper front returned after the war and remained a fixture thru the run of this uniform style. In the standings, the Cubs had drifted into permanent residency of the second division.

1957 HOME — 1957 ROAD

THE ERNIE BANKS YEARS

For the 1957-58 seasons, it was another "new look" for Cubs uniforms. On the home whites, pin stripes made a comeback and the C-UBS emblem was modified with a full circular outline. As if to recall 1917, the full team name CHICAGO CUBS was displayed across the chest of the new road uniforms. Red & blue piping was also restored to the road suits. The familiar red stripes on the socks were changed to white. The red C on the cap front was changed to a circular style with a white outline and vertical white piping was added to the seams of the cap crown —reminiscent of the mid-20's. This home uniform became the standard through 1971, the only modification being the little cub face patch added in 1962. Also, the white cap stripes were dropped and the zipper front was abandoned for good by 1960. The road uniform in 1959 dropped the word CUBS and then also became more-or-less the standard thru 1971 — CHICAGO in arched block capitals and no underline. Besides the cub face patch in '62, the uniform number was added to the front of the road jersey in 1969 (the high point of the Durocher years). Also, the stripes were dropped and the socks were solid blue during this long uniform run.

1938 HOME — 1939 ROAD

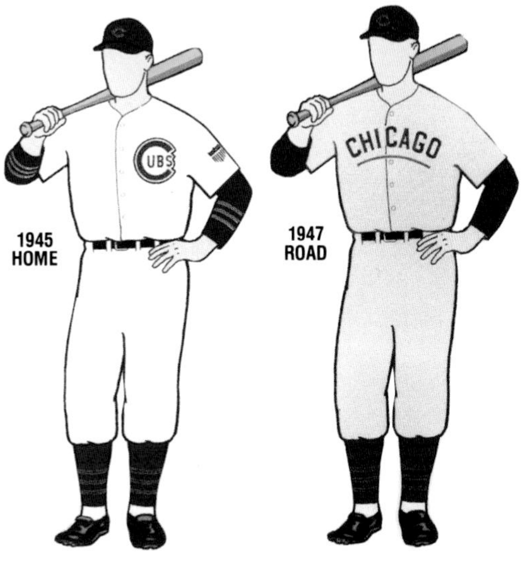

1945 HOME — 1947 ROAD

1965 HOME — 1969 ROAD

INTO THE MAINSTREAM OF DOUBLE-KNITS

In 1972, the Cubs joined the conversion from flannel fabrics to the revolutionary new double-knits. The same general uniform look was retained with special accommodations for the new style features of double-knit uniforms —namely pull-over jerseys and beltless trousers. On the new homes suits, solid blue trim was added to the collar, the sleeve ends, and on the new belt sash. The first double-knit road jerseys included red, white & blue trim on the collar and sleeve ends. With no buttons or zipper to interfere, the uniform number was placed dead-center under CHICAGO. Maybe because this idea was too much like football, the number was soon shifted back to the left side. The first road double-knits were the traditional gray color, but by 1977 a blue shade replaced gray —another popular trend of the color TV age. In 1978, the road uniform was made with an unusual reverse pin stripe pattern—white stripes on a light blue background. This unique fabric lasted thru the 1981 season. Meanwhile, in 1979, the home uniform incorporated some minor modifications —the blue circular outline on the C-UBS emblem was "beefed-up" considerably and the cub face on the sleeves now included a red circular outline. This home uniform has remained unchanged to date. In 1982, the road uniform was radically altered. A solid blue top and white trousers, no more CHICAGO (the C-UBS emblem instead) are the features which distinguish this still-current road combination. As any Die-Hard-Cub-Fan would tell you —ya gotta love it!

For 1990, the Cubs joined the trend to more traditional uniform sets by restoring buttons and separate belts. The road uniform also reverted to all-gray with the name CHICAGO across the chest.

A familiar sight at Wrigley Field in the sixties —"Mr. Cub" Ernie Banks crossing the plate after another four-bagger.

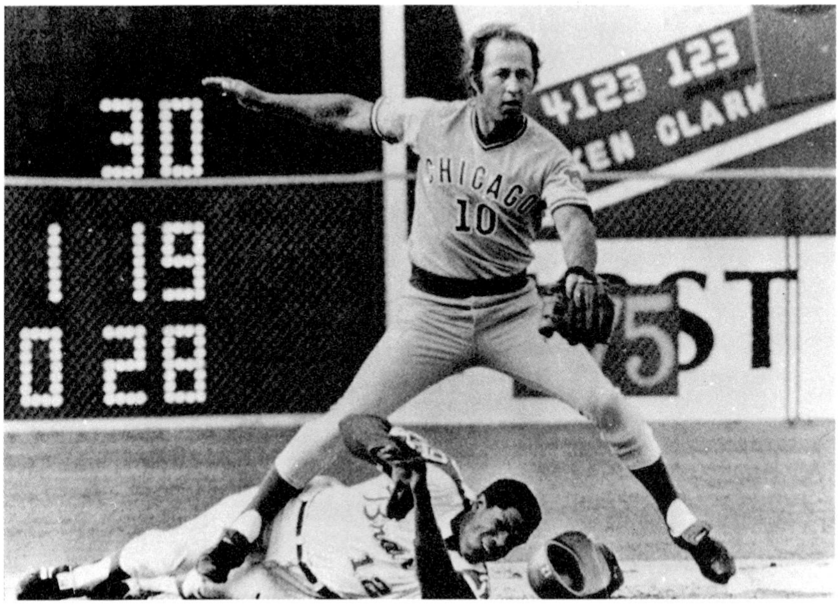

Popular third baseman Ron Santo in action at Atlanta's Fulton County Stadium in 1972, in the Cubs' first double-knit road uniform.

EVOLUTION OF THE BELOVED CUBS INSIGNIA

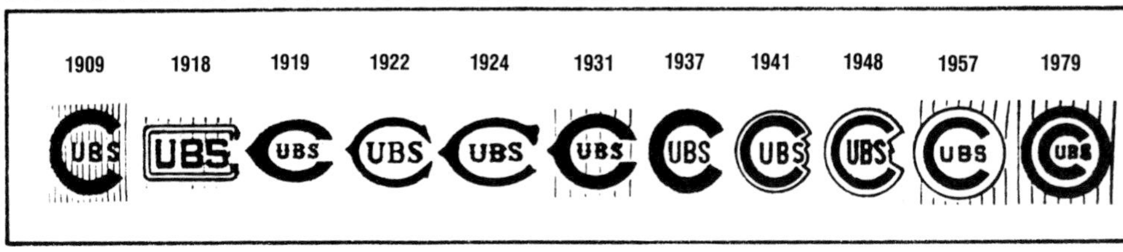

CHICAGO WHITE SOX

STARTING OFF ON TOP

The Old Roman, Charles Comiskey, transferred his Western League St. Paul franchise to the hallowed NL territory of Chicago for the 1900 season. The Chicago Nationals felt only mildly threatened by the competition since the renamed American League was still a minor league and the newcomers played their games on the distant south side of town. Comiskey agreed not to display the city name CHICAGO on his uniforms but he borrowed the abandoned nickname of White Stockings from an earlier dynasty of the NL Chicagoans. The invaders promptly won the AL pennant in 1900 and league president Ban Johnson boldly declared that the American League would elevate its status to major league for 1901. Comiskey's first uniforms were standard all-white and all-gray with a large square maroon C on the left breast. And, of course, the stockings were all white. The team won another championship in 1901 and since the West Side Orphans were strictly second division, Chicago fans began to pay more attention to the South Siders. They repeated the same home uniforms for 1902, but Comiskey reneged on his word (it was all-out war by now) and displayed the city name CHICAGO on his all dark blue road suits for 1902. The league and the franchise were in the Windy City to stay.

THE AGE OF THE "HITLESS WONDERS"

For 1903, some interesting changes were displayed on the White Stockings' game uniforms. The all-white stockings became a combination of blue with a 4-inch wide white stripe at the calf for both home and road suits. The home whites retained the white cap but added blue piping to crown seams. On the home shirt, the fold-down collar was now dark blue and the square C was changed to an ornamental style in BLUE instead of maroon. Except for the new stockings and a rounder cap style (w/blue visor), the 1903 road suits were a repeat of the '02 dark blues. The fancy lettering style of the white CHICAGO became a road uniform standard on thru the mid-teens. By this time ('03) the two leagues were settling their disputes and the West Siders even agreed to conduct a post-season series to settle the city championship (the Sox won the first meeting). The blue C on the home shirt was re-styled for 1904-05 and the all-white stockings were restored; otherwise the uniform was pretty much recycled thru the '05 season.

For 1906, the home C was modified again into a circular Roman style and the dark blue collar was dropped. Blessed with remarkable pitching (Doc White, Ed Walsh, Nick Altrock) and plenty of luck, the Sox stole a pennant with a team batting average of .231. These "hitless wonders" had the dubious task of facing the cross-town Cubs who set a major league record with 116 victories that season. The results are history and the new world champions commissioned a special patch to be worn on the sleeves of the 1907 road uniforms to proclaim their spoils. The 1908 uniforms were a basic "re-run" of 1906-07 except for the "Brooklyn" style plain white cap crown with blue visor. The road suits continued the all dark-blue tradition, accented with a white belt and white piping on the trouser legs. The home whites for 1909 had reduced all trim to a minimum —a small C on the sleeve, thin blue piping on the pant legs and a blue cap visor.

1909
HOME

1903
HOME

1903
ROAD

1901
HOME

1902
ROAD

1911
HOME

Manager
Hugh Duffy
at Hilltop
Park, New York
in 1910

1905
HOME

1906
HOME

A NEW SEASON, A NEW PARK

In June 1910, the White Sox had played their last game at old South Side Park and opened their new baseball palace, Comiskey Park. The all-white image was perpetuated on the 1910 home suits. The shirt style, however, was altered with the stand-up "cadet" collar (the latest trend) which contained a small W and S straddling the top button (denoting White Sox, of course). The only other identifying mark on the entire uniform was a small C on the front of the cap. For 1911, the home uniform jerseys were once again re-styled to incorporate a solid blue collar and button panel with S-O-X spelled out vertically in white capital letters. It was the first time the franchise nickname (or ½ of it) was displayed on a game uniform.

In 1912, the best known team emblem design in the club's history was first displayed on the new home uniforms. The large S encircling a small O and X was positioned on the left breast, along with a repeat of the small W & S on the cadet collar. The fabric was also a first for the Sox, in that it incorporated a pattern of thin narrowly spaced pinstripes. The dark blue road uniforms underwent only minor modifications in the years following —different collar style (including an occasional white W & S), different cap designs and no more white belt. The new S-O-X emblem underwent minor refinements in the following seasons but gradually established itself as the team's visual symbol for future decades. The dark blue road uniform was finally retired for the 1916 season in favor of a more conventional gray with pinstripes —a duplication of the home whites.

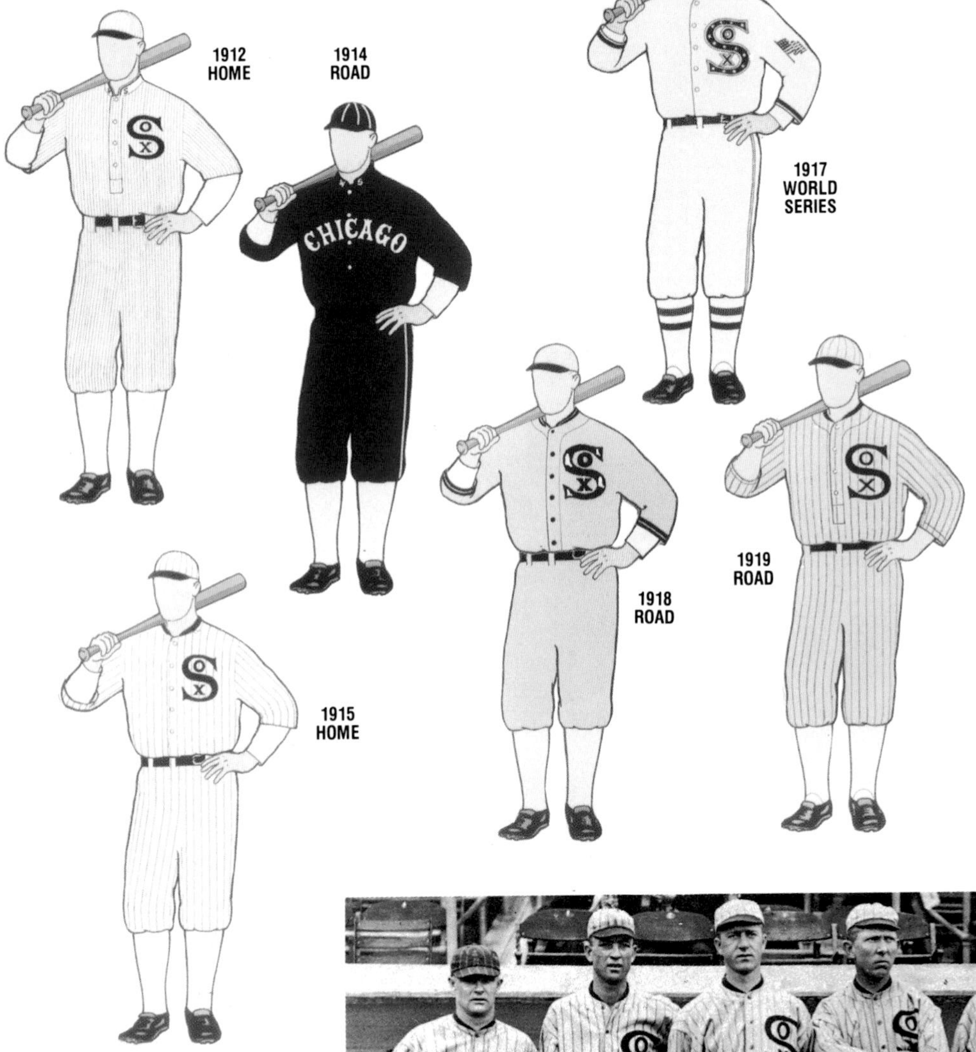

WAR, VICTORY AND SCANDAL

After a second place finish in 1916, the White Sox were once again a solid contender. By 1917, the home uniforms had standardized the team insignia and pinstripes. A small American flag was worn on the left sleeve to symbolize baseball's support of the war effort. Some double piping was added to the jersey and the S-O-X emblem was repeated on the cap front. The new '17 road uniforms deserted the gray color and went to a rather bizarre form of reverse pinstripes —white stripes on a dark blue fabric. The caps were constructed of the same fabric with a white vertical S-O-X on the front. The team insignia was displayed on the left breast in a white outline treatment. And, of course, the stockings were the usual all-white. Sure enough, they won the pennant and then showed up for the '17 world series (vs. McGraw's Giants) in a specially designed, star-spangled red, white and blue variation of their home suits. Even the sacred tradition of all-white sox was temporarily violated with a red and blue stripe. They came dressed in costume for the party and left with a world championship —the last one ever claimed by the Windy City. Those uniforms were subsequently retired for game use, but they came to symbolize the most glorious moment in White Sox history.

The Boston Red Sox were the Chicagoans' chief rivals for supremacy and they reclaimed the AL championship in 1918. In fact, the White Sox stumbled badly and finished under .500. The 1918 home uniforms eliminated the pinstripes (as did the '17 series suits) but they included an unusual added feature to the S-O-X emblem on the shirt front of both home and road. Small white "SOCKS" silhouettes were embodied in the large blue S. This was the first time a pictorial symbol of the team nickname was portrayed on game uniforms. They dropped this feature in 1919 and restored the pinstripes on both home whites and road grays. The magic returned and they once again met in the World Series with the Cincinnati Reds. The Sox lost the Fall Classic, but under a cloud of suspicion and rumors. The end result was the infamous "Black Sox" scandal and the budding White Sox dynasty was dismantled by Commissioner Landis.

The pitching staff for the 1917 world championship club

THE MEDIOCRITY OF THE TWENTIES

The decimated White Sox club plummeted to second division status for the entire decade of the twenties. For the first five seasons (1920-24) the uniform sets were the same combination: plain white at home with blue collar trim and blue cap visor, the standard S-O-X emblem in solid blue on the left breast. The road suits duplicated the home whites in GRAY. The home uniform continued the same thru 1926, but in 1925 the road uniforms returned to the white-on-blue reverse pinstriped fabric of 1917. This time around, the caps had no marking and the S-O-X insignia on the shirt was a solid white instead of the outline version of '17 (no flag on the sleeve, either). The new road uniforms for 1926 were the most creative design to date: solid navy blue from top to bottom (except for the white sox), this new design displayed a visual symbol of crossed white socks on both the cap front and sleeve. The city name CHICAGO was returned to the shirt front for the first time in a decade in clean, tasteful white block letters. White striping around the collar area, on the sleeve ends, and on the trouser legs completed the trimmings.

The only change on the home uniform for 1927 was a subtle addition of more pronounced serifs on the letters of the S-O-X emblem. The '28 road design restored a steel gray pinstriped fabric to the uniform and cap. The "crossed socks" graphics of '27 were dropped but the same lettering form of CHICAGO was retained in solid navy on the chest. The cap was once again a plain gray pinstriped crown with dark blue visor. The new 1929 home uniform design reflected the current trend for multiple-bead piping and a second trim color. The S-O-X insignia returned to the more "Roman" style and in a combination of blue and red. Dual white piping was added to the vertical seams of the all dark cap. The '29 road uniform was a bit more somber —plain gray with the CHICAGO letters slightly enlarged in solid navy. Solid navy trim was included on the sleeve ends as well as on the collar. The S-O-X emblem in white was placed on the front of the solid blue cap.

Hall-of-Fame pitcher Ed Walsh as a coach in 1928

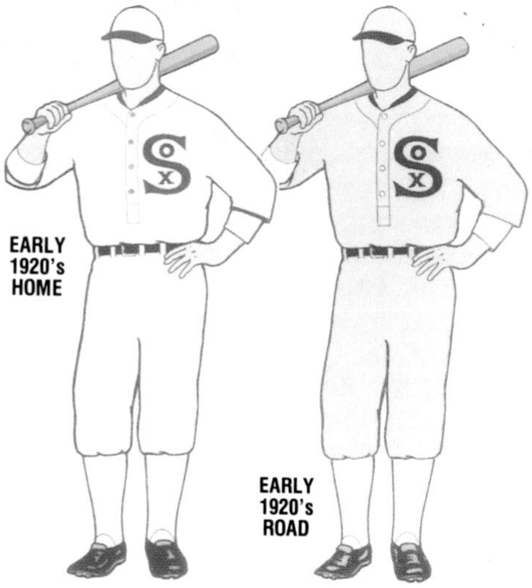

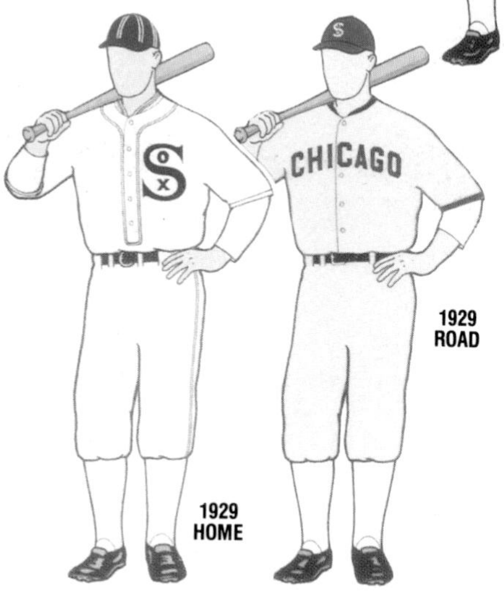

BRIGHTER UNIFORMS IN DARKER TIMES

The new decade of the thirties spelled double-depression for White Sox fans. Besides the economic hard times, the team continued its seemingly permanent residency in or close to the basement of the American League. A few stars like Luke Appling and Ted Lyons helped brighten the gloom somewhat and more eye-catching uniforms may have helped. The 1930 home suits were an encore of '29, but once again the road uniforms went back to the solid navy blue with white trimmings. The arched CHICAGO in white fancy capital letters harked back to old road suits of 1902-15. The white S-O-X insignia on the sleeve, the white belt and the solid blue cap with white seam stripes were also reminders of uniforms past. Another new re-design of the road uniform surfaced about 1932 with a blue and red treatment of CHICAGO on a plain gray fabric. This design became the standard road uniform thru the 1938 season.

Luke Appling, working out some "aches & pains" in his 1938 road uniform

Meanwhile the 1932 season introduced a total "new look" in home uniforms —in fact two versions. The primary design featured a fascinating new arrangement of the S-O-X letters, intertwined diagonally with a baseball and a bat worked into the design. The three letters were formed in a thick red pile outlined with blue and the background bat was yellow. The uniform itself was tastefully devoid of excess piping —a cream white with the collar and sleeve ends accented in solid navy. The cap was also solid navy. This uniform remained the home standard for the next four seasons and was featured in the first All-Star game at Comiskey Park in 1933. An alternate home uniform was also showcased in 1932 which incorporated novel ideas. Two interlocking horseshoes simulated the large S of the team insignia and the small O and X were represented by a baseball and crossed bats. This version was on a pinstriped material with only a navy blue collar as additional trim on the shirt. The long-standing tradition of all-white stockings was once again violated on this uniform scheme by addition of a single red stripe about half-way down. A feature which may have been a death sentence for both these designs was the use of a simulated baseball. This is technically a rule violation and may have been pointed out in the latter stages of its run.

In 1936, the home uniform was again re-designed and yet another variation of the S-O-X insignia was introduced. The letters were "fancified" somewhat and the color red was eliminated. Standard navy piping was returned to the jersey and the solid navy cap displayed a small white fancy capital C in the front. This uniform was worn through 1938 and set the stage for still further re-design of the uniform set with classical proportions. Not to be outdone by their cross-town neighbors, the Cubs, the Sox opened the 1939 season with totally new uniforms which, not coincidentally, had some similarities to new Cub suits of '37. The jerseys were the latest zippered front style and thick wide red striping edged in blue was generously used throughout. The new rendition of the S-O-X insignia used an extra-large squared S in solid red bordered with navy. The gray road uniform duplicated the abundant piping and displayed CHICAGO in square serif block capitals edged in blue. Both home and road caps were solid navy with a square C in front. This combination, with a few modifications and one clear exception, was the familiar standard for Sox fans in the forties. Gruesome or handsome, whatever your tastes, it endured for quite a long run and was to be the last Sox uniform design to incorporate all-white hosiery.

WWII, BOB ELSON, AND THE "GO-GO" SOX

In 1942, the first wartime season, the home uniform was dramatically altered (for reasons unknown) by substituting a script WHITE SOX on the shirt front in place of the familiar S-O-X emblem. The accompanying trimmings were retained as before, but the new marking was the first time the full team nickname appeared on the uniform. It was only a "hiccup" in the midst of a continuous run of a basic uniform theme. By the late '40's the piping was thinned down, the emblem size was reduced, and even some "unthinkable" striping was used on the road stockings. Besides these uniforms, another endearing symbol to Sox fans who remember the forties was the monotonous drone of the team's radio voice, Bob Elson.

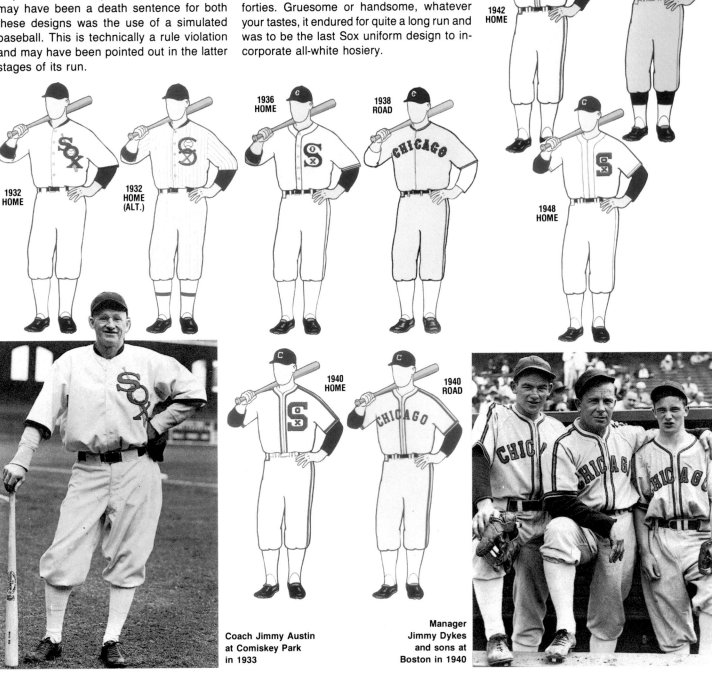

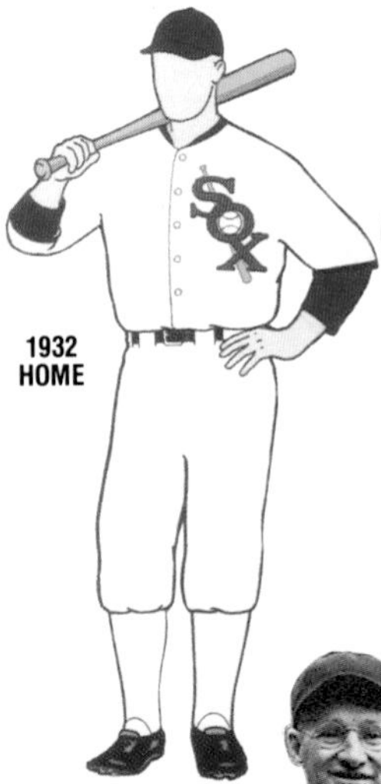

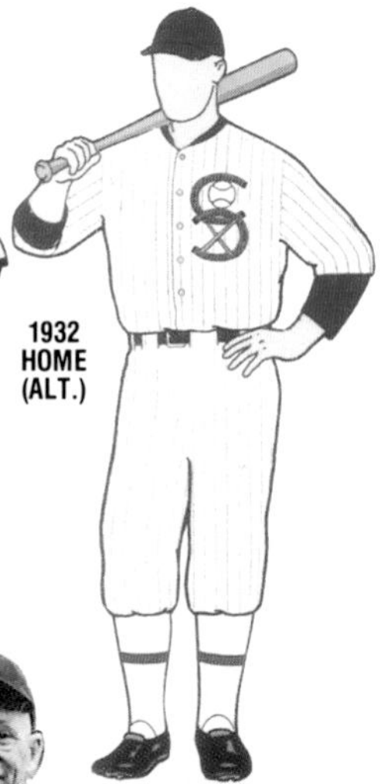

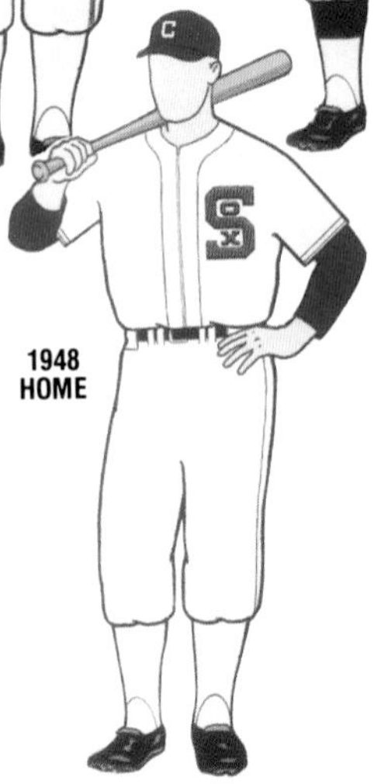

Coach Jimmy Austin at Comiskey Park in 1933

Manager Jimmy Dykes and sons at Boston in 1940

With "Trader" Frank Lane now in the front office, a new image was in order for the 1949 White Sox. The uniform re-design did away with all piping, and changed the primary trim color to BLACK. A brand new arrangement of the S-O-X insignia used a modified Gothic style for the letters and re-arranged them in an overlapping downward slope. The CHICAGO on the road grays was simplified with plain block capital letters. The socks were made black with a wide white stripe and the all-black cap had a white "fancy" capital C. This uniform was repeated in 1950. By 1951, Lane had assembled a whole new roster of exciting and talented players (Nellie Fox, Minnie Minoso, Billy Pierce et al) and hired Paul Richards to lead them into the first division. Speed and daring were the trademark of this new breed of White Sox and they were aptly referred to as the "GO-GO SOX". The tasteful and trendy new uniforms seemed to fit the new awakening.

WHERE HAVE YOU GONE, MINNIE MINOSO?

By the mid sixties, the uniforms still retained the look of the memorable fifties but the basic trim color was once again BLUE. In fact, the gray material of the road suits had even transformed itself to a powder blue, a new trend of the color TV era. In 1968, the new road BLUES featured the name CHICAGO in a slanted script lettering with a wide underline flourish that also incorporated the WHITE SOX nickname in small white lettering. It was one of the very rare occasions when the full team name was displayed on a major league uniform. The 1969-70 home uniform was without pinstripes for the first time in nearly two decades —and in fact a traditional treatment of piping was also re-instituted. In addition, the stirrup socks were actually white again with varied blue stripes and accented by a blue sanitary sock under the stirrups. The 1970 road uniform was once again GRAY with the CHICAGO script design in outlined white.

The sparkplug of the "Go-Go" Sox , Minnie Minoso at Comiskey Park in 1951

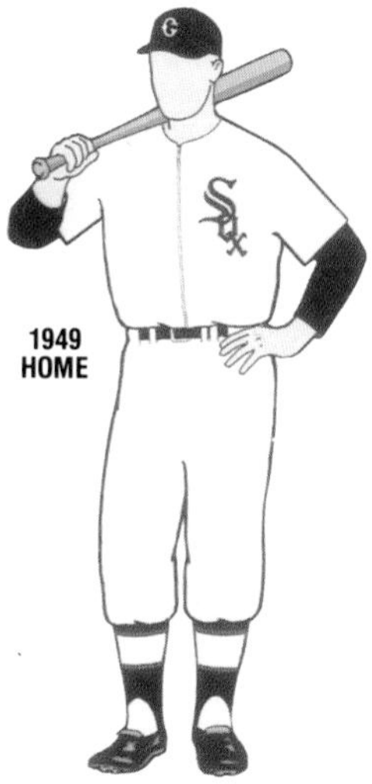

1949 HOME

1949 ROAD

1965 HOME

1965 ROAD

1971 HOME

1971 ROAD

LATE 1950's HOME

LATE 1950's ROAD

1970 HOME

1970 ROAD

For 1951, pinstripes were added to the home whites as well as a touch of red trim here and there. The C on the cap was replaced by an interlocking S-O-X and more stripes were included on the black stockings. This uniform ensemble was continued thru the decade of the fifties and reached its climax in 1959 with a long-awaited pennant. By this time buttons had returned to replace the zipper front, and in 1960 names were placed on the back of the shirts for the first time. Striping on the stockings was re-arranged almost annually during this uniform run.

In 1971, it was time for another new look and indeed it was new and dazzling! The zipper front, pinstriped theme of the early fifties was given new life but this time it was all bright RED from head to foot. The S-O-X emblem, the caps, the undersweaters, the stirrup socks and yes, even the SHOES and pinstripes were a vivid scarlet. The new road uniforms were even more colorful. Returning to a powder blue fabric, the all-red trim features were accented with white to set them off against the pale blue background. This combination remained thru the 1975 season and if you found it exciting or even disturbing, don't go away ... there's yet another new look just around the corner in 1976!

The most innovative idea in baseball uniforms since the sleeveless vest was commissioned by owner Bill Veeck for his 1976 edition of the Chicago White Sox. Gone was the red of past seasons, replaced by navy blue. But the dramatic change in trim color was of lesser significance than the radical new tailoring of the double-knit jerseys. The new shirts were strictly pullover style with a straight bottom to be worn pajama style outside the trousers. The V-neck collar included a simulated collar flap, recalling the fold-down collars of an earlier day. The shirts and trousers were made in white or navy blue and could be intermixed at home. The road version was usually all-navy. The CHICAGO lettering was a throwback to Sox road uniforms of bygone days. The home cap was solid navy with SOX in horizontal white letters. At first the road cap had a white crown, but later the all navy home version prevailed for both. The stockings were once again basically white with a continually changing navy stripe pattern thru the 6-year run of this uniform. Ever the showman, Veeck even presented a Bermuda shorts version briefly in 1976. When 56-year-old coach Minnie Minoso made a token game appearance in 1980, this avant-garde uniform must have made him wonder if the year was truly 1980 or maybe 2080.

Third baseman Kevin Bell wearing the much discussed short pants of 1976

THE EIGHTIES AND THE BEAT GOES ON

As if on an endless frenzy to introduce ever-newer uniform ideas, the 1982 edition of the White Sox donned another combination of totally new and unique uniforms. This time the new red, navy and white color scheme was an intelligent response to the new age of color television and the new potential provided by the double-knit tailoring features. It was clearly a forward-looking design statement, a near total denial of the traditional. With no need to accommodate a center row of buttons or zipper, the horizontal SOX lettering freely used the full expanse of the frontal area and carried it across to the shoulders.

The Houston Astros' burnt-orange "rainbow" design of the mid-seventies had the same good intentions, but somehow carried it too far for its day. If we could blank out our longing for the traditional look or earlier uniforms we could most certainly praise these purely contemporary uniform designs more. But, alas, our allegiance to the game is heavily immersed in its history and we refuse to forget. And thus the cycle of conservative preferences has carried us back to the new "old" look of the 1987 White Sox uniforms... slanted script lettering, buttons in front, a real belt, and even BLACK SHOES.

1976 HOME (ALT.)

1976 HOME (ALT.)

1983 HOME

1983 ROAD

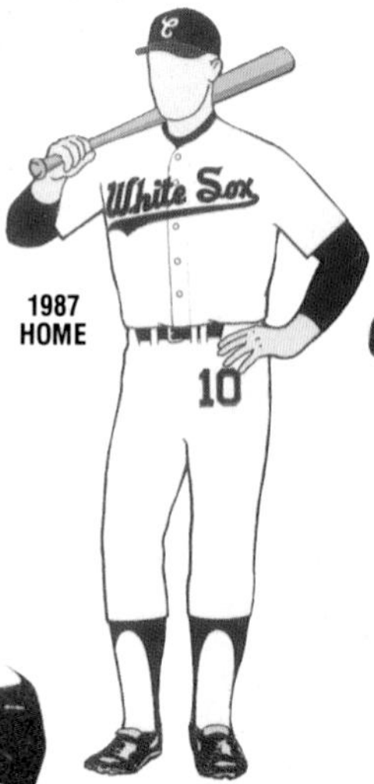

1987 HOME

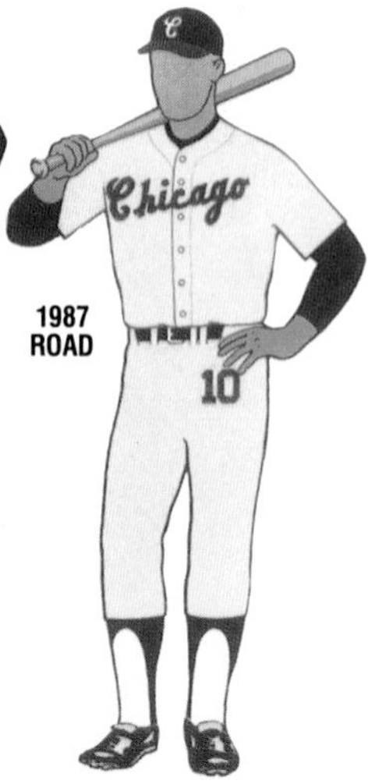

1987 ROAD

1981 ROAD (ALT.)

1981 ROAD (ALT.)

Harold Baines, the durable Sox superstar of the early eighties

CINCINNATI REDS

ENTERING THE NEW CENTURY

The Reds began the 1900 season with the oldest tradition in professional baseball, dating back to 1869. Their uniforms were basically a continuation of the 1890's while at home, and dark, musty blue on the road. The caps were the standard close-fitting round style with a short bill. Red piping was used on the seams leading up to the red top button and around the base of the crown. A red "C" was also added to the front of the cap around 1900. The home uniform in the first decade of the new century was always white and displayed either "CINCINNATI" or variations of a capital "C" on the left breast —a precursor of the standard emblem of future decades. On the road the city name "CINCINNATI" was continued on the chest in red capital letters on the gray or blue uniforms. By 1908, the standard block letters were replaced by a fancier style and the cap was a solid red with white piping and no "C". This cap was also worn at home along with a solid red collar. In 1909, the darker blue road uniform returned, but instead of "CINCINNATI", a large fancy style red "C" was positioned on the left breast as well as a smaller "C" on the sleeves and on the cap —a sort of "reverse" image of the previous white home uniform.

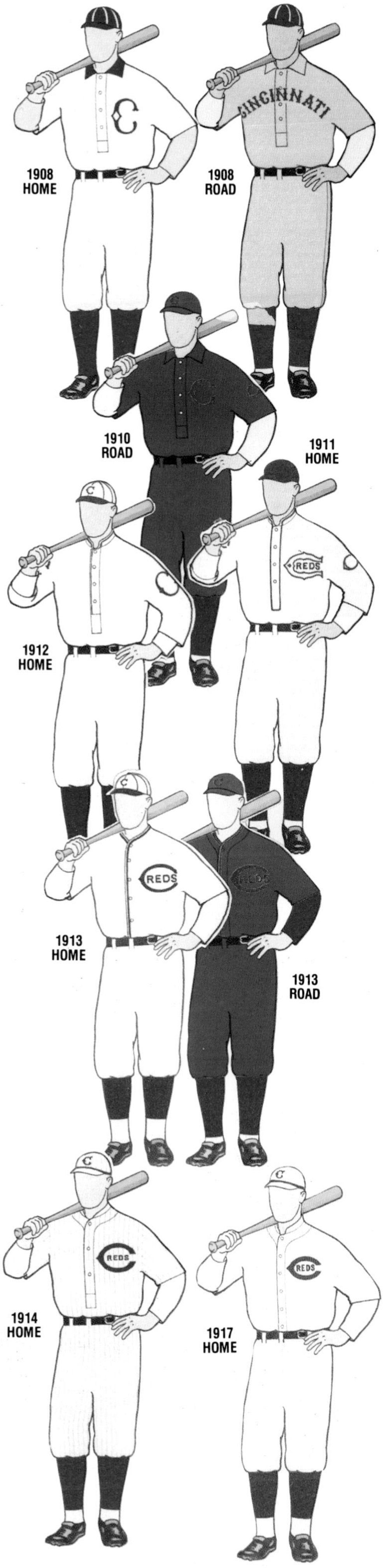

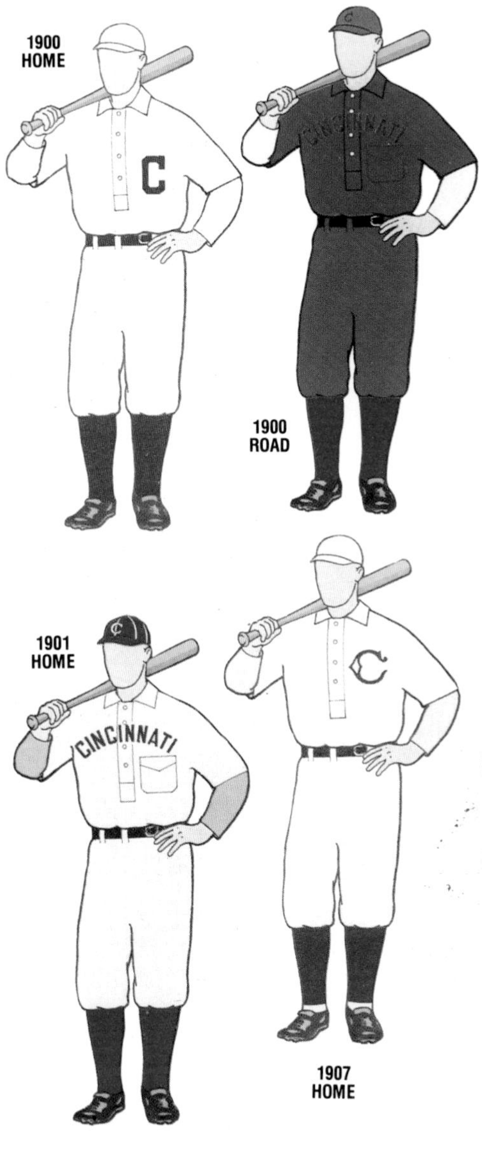

A LOGO TRADITION BEGINS

After 1910, several notable new trends in uniform design had become fashionable — the standard shirt collar was replaced by a short stand-up "cadet" style and subsequently by a tapered collar extension or no collar at all. Stirrup-type outer stockings were used in place of the one-piece color stockings — certainly a practical improvement in terms of daily laundering requirements. Pin-striped fabrics in various widths and color combinations became common. Team nicknames were being accepted as "official" by the clubs and began to appear on the uniform jerseys. The very first version of the now famous team logo made its appearance in 1911; the name "REDS" inside an ornate, scalloped "wishbone-style" capital C. Red striping was also introduced around the button lapel and along the edge of the "cadet" style collar. A smaller capital C was placed on the sleeve and the home cap was solid red. By 1913, the "cadet" collar was modified and the C-REDS logo was also included on the left breast of the darker road suits. This combination of red-on-blue has to be one of the homeliest outfits ever worn by a baseball team. Within a few years good taste must have prevailed because the road uniforms reverted to a more conventional gray version of the home whites. Those dark blue road uniforms never again appeared on a Red player. By the end of the decade the Reds logo had been established as a standard design and remained basically unaltered thru

Hard-hitting pitcher/outfielder Cy Seymour at home in 1902.

Catcher Bill Rariden, a member of the 1919 Reds championship team.

the entire decade of the twenties. About the only features that changed at all during this long run of uniform design were to be the alternate use of pin-striped fabrics, evolutionary modification to the collar shape and trim and the return to a dark solid cap in the late twenties. The team's first world championship in 1919 (tainted though it was by the infamous "Black Sox" scandal) must have convinced club management that they had a "winning" design, not to be tampered with in future years. The uniforms for most major league teams during the "roaring twenties" were, likewise, generally plain and conservative. Oddly enough, it took a stock market crash and the onset of a prolonged depression to trigger a new flurry of ideas and colorful innovations in baseball uniforms.

HARD TIMES, NIGHT BASEBALL AND PENNANTS

By 1930 the Reds, like most of the other clubs, were breaking out of the rut of repetitive, plain uniforms. Pin stripes were "out", and white or gray cap crowns with solid red bill were "in". The name "CINCINNATI" was restored to the gray road jerseys in red capital letters with a thin navy outline piping. By the mid-thirties, combinations of blue and white stripes were added to the solid red of the stockings and the piping trim in the uniform was embellished by multiple beads and combinations of red and navy blue. In 1935, "REDS" was added to the sleeve of the road jersey and marked one of the very few occasions when the full team name (city plus nickname) was displayed on any major league uniform. By 1936, the predominance of the color red on the uniform trimmings had given way to equal billing for navy blue. The cap bill, the undersweaters, the sox, and even the C-REDS logo incorporated navy. The overall appearance was brighter, in keeping with the multi-color trimmings of many of the other club uniforms. This inclusion of navy blue was to remain an integral part of the color scheme for the next twenty years.

The Reds' catcher in the Depression years, Hall-of-Famer Ernie Lombardi in 1936.

Cincinnati introduced night baseball to the major leagues in 1935. The following season, they experimented with a radically different uniform design referred to as the "Palm Beach" uniforms. All piping trim was removed and the C-REDS emblem was replaced by a REDS in script lettering on the left breast of the jersey. They wore this uniform only occasionally in 1936 and 1937 and for some night games they even included solid red trousers. This "orgy" of new graphics and extra color trimmings peaked out by 1938. The "CINCINNATI" on the road grays was still done in fancy style block letters but the socks were no longer multi-striped and the piping trim was somewhat toned down. The white or gray cap crown was replaced by solid navy with a red bill and a red "wishbone" C.

1931
ROAD

1934
HOME

1923
HOME

1928
ROAD

1936
HOME

1936
"PALM
BEACH"

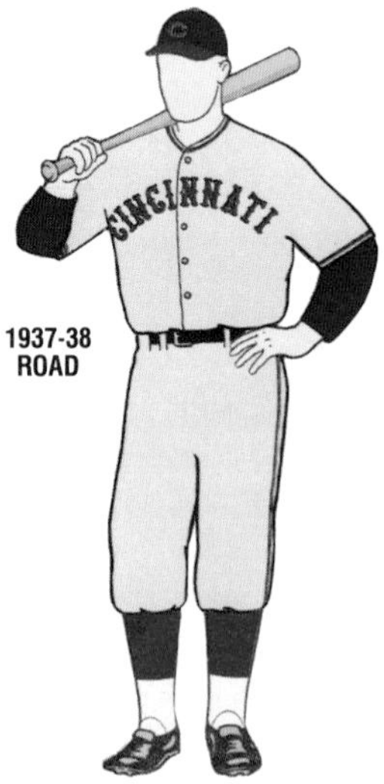

1937-38
ROAD

EVOLUTION OF THE REDS EMBLEM

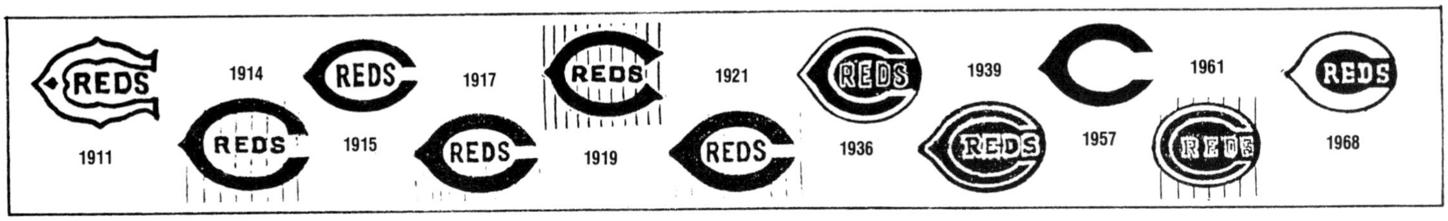

For the 1939 season, austerity made a dramatic comeback on the Reds uniforms. All piping was eliminated, the socks were a plain half-red, half-navy combination and "CINCINNATI" on the road grays was restored to plain block capital letters —all red with no outline trim. The navy blue background and white trim were retained on the C-REDS emblem on the home whites and remained constant thru the mid-fifties. Could the superstition of once again not wanting to alter a "winner" be the reason why this basic uniform motif remained unchanged for the next 16 years? A second and third pennant in 1939-40 plus a "bona-fide" world series championship in '40 would lend credence to this supposition. This long run of stable, conservative uniforms climaxed in the early fifties. The navy blue on the socks and sweaters was gone and the combination red and navy cap was replaced by your basic solid navy cap. The pendulum of design was ready to swing back to something more adventurous.

1940
HOME

1950
ROAD

Slugger Ted Kluszewski doing his thing on the road in the fifties.

THE "REDLEGS" AND BEYOND

The anti-communist hysteria of the McCarthy era contributed to what is, in retrospect, an embarrassingly silly descision on the part of the Cincinnati baseball club. After nearly 80 years of being identified as the Reds or Red Stockings —a fact which had absolutely no political or international overtones and is as purely and innocently American as Hotdogs and Crackerjacks —it was determined that the name REDS was detrimental to the organization and to baseball. To their credit, a thread of tradition was retained by compromising on a harmless corruption of the team nickname, Henceforth, they were to be called the REDLEGS. In cadence with this new image, the team uniforms for 1956 underwent the most drastic overhaul in nearly 20 years. Navy blue was abandoned entirely as red became the sole color of the uniform trim (another plus for the salvation of long tradition). The name REDS was no longer displayed on the home uniforms after 45 years. The most novel feature (not a first —the Cubs were the originals in 1940) was the sleeveless vest jersey. The stockings were still red, but with narrow white stripes. The caps were solid red with a white "wishbone" C and even the belts were red. The undershirt sleeves were solid red (when not cut off at the shoulder a la Ted Kluszewski). The gray road uniforms were identical to the home whites except for the baseball head cartoon face ("Old Red") which replaced the wishbone C on the left breast. The sleeveless vest won approval from the players (the Pirates "followed suit" in '57) and remained a uniform feature until the mid-60's.

1957
HOME

1956
ROAD

1960
HOME

As if to further underscore the all-scarlet theme, all red stockings were restored and red pinstripes were added to the home whites the following year. The solid red cap was also replaced by a white or gray cap crown (to match the jersey) for 1957. A touch of navy blue re-appeared in 1961 as piping trim on the vest sleeve holes and around the C on the cap. Also, as if to signify the end of the "Redlegs" era, a modified oval version of the C-REDS emblem returned to the home jersey front (with a navy blue background as in the last version). The city name "CINCINNATI" was also restored on the road gray uniform in arched red capital letters with a thin navy outline. The sleeveless vest era produced a 4th pennant (1961) but this time the uniform design was not destined for a long run.

1961
HOME

1961
ROAD

Popular outfielder Wally Post in the early sixties, his second tenure as a Red.

ROSE, BENCH AND THE BIG RED MACHINE

By the mid-sixties, a couple of future Cincinnati legends had arrived (Pete Rose and Johnny Bench) and the nucleus of the future Big Red Machine had its beginnings. The sleeveless jersey was displaced by a conventional short sleeved model and navy blue once again was eliminated as a 2nd color. The gray road uniform was basically a revival of the early fifties, except the cap was now solid red instead of navy, and a uniform number appeared on the jersey front. The first years of the revival of the short-sleeved home jersey retained the red pin stripes but by 1970 (Sparky Anderson's first pennant winner and the inaugural or Riverfront Stadium) the home uniform was plain white.

For 1972, Cincinnati joined the rest of the majors in adopting the new double knit fabric uniform with its revolutionary features. Lighter, cooler, more comfortable and easier to clean —it was the uniform of the future and the future for Cincinnati baseball spelled glory and championships. The famous C-REDS emblem was retained as was the all red trim motif. But with the new built-in sash belt and pull-over jersey, buttons and belts were no longer needed. Red and white striping trim was added to the sleeve ends and collar as well as on the new sash belt. Except for the red shoes of today, this is still the uniform of the "Big Red Machine" of the mid-seventies.

In spring training of 1978, the Reds jolted the baseball world by stepping on to the field with all-green uniforms for an exhibition game on March 17 (St. Patrick's Day, of course). After a century of basically red-trimmed uniforms, this novelty version had the same curious visual shock value as Andy Warhol's non-red Coca-Cola art. It was all in fun and the fans loved it. These hybrid uniforms were afterwards auctioned off for charity and have become prized collector's items. Another less bizarre departure from the norm was the addition of an optional solid red alternate jersey for occasional games use, both at home and on the road in the mid-eighties.

1967 HOME

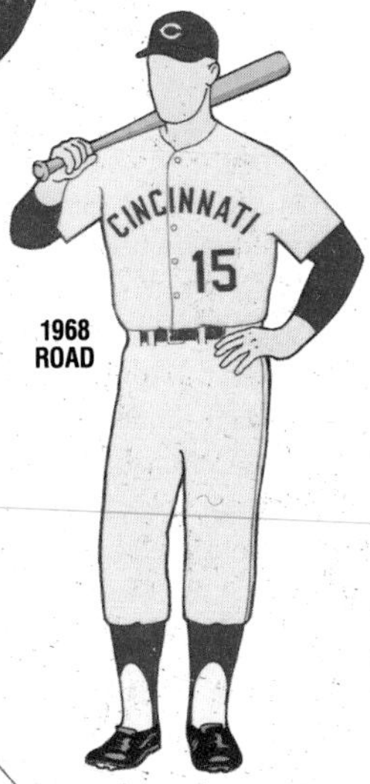

1968 ROAD

1970 HOME

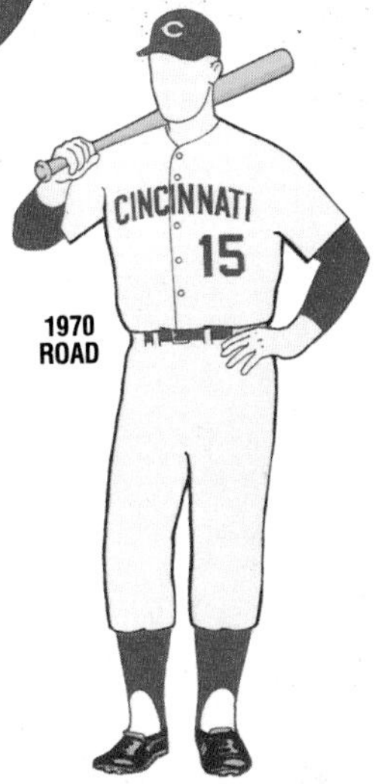

1970 ROAD

Pete Rose in his familiar home double-knits. Note the low-length trouser legs and the more traditional "no stretch" stirrups —a unique Reds' standard dress code.

Consecutive world championships in 1975 and 1976 exemplified the most successful teams in the long history of the franchise. Maybe the idea that the caliber of those winning years may never be surpassed of the superstition of not changing a "winner" has kept the current uniform standard for 15 years. Sooner or later, it will indeed be altered, but for this generation of Cincinnati fans, it is a heartwarming reminder of the glorious domain of the Big Red Machine.

"ST. PATRICK'S DAY" SPECIAL

1986 HOME

1986 ROAD

OPTIONAL ALL-RED TOP

1988 HOME

1988 ROAD

CLEVELAND INDIANS

OUT OF THE MAJORS AND BACK AGAIN

The Cleveland Spiders of the National League in the 1890's were one of the casualties when the league was reduced from 12 to 8 teams after the 1899 season. Cleveland then joined Ban Johnson's American League and the Forest City was back in business as a major league operation for the 1901 season. Blue was their uniform trim color and accordingly they were called BLUES for the first five or six years in the AL. Their first uniforms were standard stock — the city name CLEVELAND in block letters arched across the shirt fronts. They dressed up the uniform sets in 1902 by adding a dark blue collar on the white home shirts and adopting a dark solid blue material for the traveling suits. A large block C was displayed on the left breast —blue on the home whites and white on the blue road shirts. The dark blue stockings had a wide white stripe about halfway down and home caps had a blue visor to complement the white crown. Blue piping emanated from the button crown and was duplicated in white on the all-blue road caps. They repeated the same home uniforms in 1903 but replaced the white C on the road shirts with CLEVELAND. For 1904, the C was dropped from the home shirts but the '03 road suits were repeated.

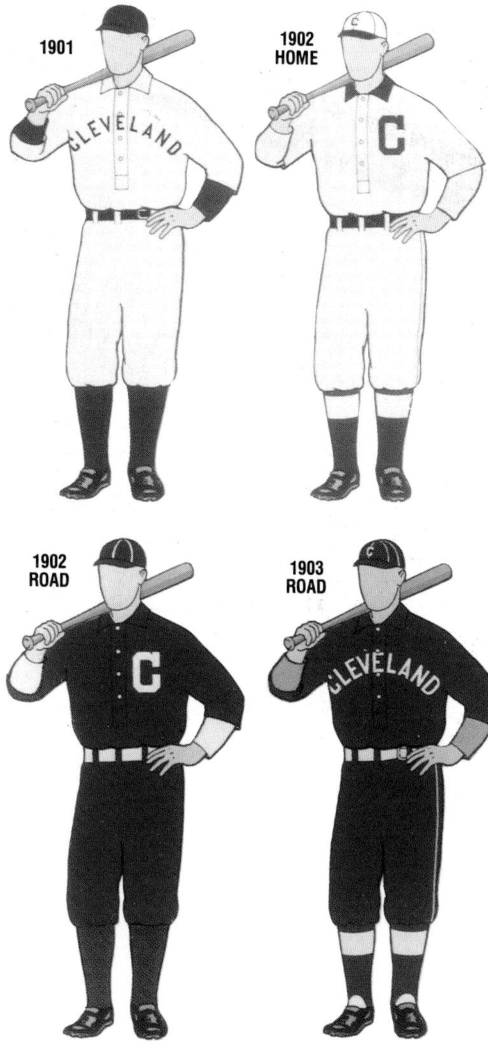

THE LAJOIE ERA

The Blues' great superstar second baseman, Napoleon Lajoie, was selected to also manage the team for the 1905 season. The new home uniforms for that season included an unusual form of the letter C on the left shirt front —an ornamental script style which was repeated with some modification through 1909. The new '05 road uniforms reverted back to the conventional gray with blue collar trim and the name CLEVELAND across the chest. This traveling suit was repeated for '06 and '07, except that the blue collar was changed to matching gray. The stockings were also modified to a basic white or gray with two blue stripes. By this time the fans were tiring of the nickname of BLUES and it was decided that NAPOLEONS, or NAPS, (in honor of their great leader) was a more suitable title. The new manager and the new nickname were acompanied by a surge in the team's fortunes including a razor-close second in 1908 but alas, no pennant.

The new road uniform for 1908 had a generally similar appearance to that of 1907 but with a few subtle differences that were more historically significant. The name CLEVELAND was repeated in a modified square serif style capital that would become the road standard for the next 13 seasons. The gray fabric material featured a narrow-spaced thin line pattern —a new idea in uniform design which would eventually evolve into the more popular pinstripes of the next decade. The Chicago Cubs had introduced the idea the year before. These uniforms were repeated for 1909, the popular Lajoie's last year as manager.

The legendary Napoleon Lajoie poses in his dark blue road uniform in 1903 or 1904.

Glenn Liebhardt, Sr. at League Park about 1909.

THE TEEN YEARS AND THE GRAY EAGLE

In 1910, the uniforms were revised again. Caps were now solid black with a white block C and the stockings were now solid dark. The fancy C on the home shirt was replaced by a standard block C and the fine striping was eliminated on the new blue-gray road suits. The new block C was retained for the entire decade as was the name CLEVELAND with some enlargement and condensation along the way. Pinstripes were introduced in 1915 on both home whites and road grays, but a couple of other items of historical trivia occurred about the same time. The NAPS were no more —INDIANS was the new team nickname in 1915. In 1916 the Cleveland club affixed player numbers on the left sleeve of the home jersey —an idea that didn't catch on and was shelved for another 13 seasons until the Yankees repeated the experiment on the backs of their shirts. Another important historical event took place in the spring of 1916 when the great Tris Speaker was purchased from Boston to replace Lajoie as the new home town hero. Spoke proved his worth by becoming player-manager in 1919 and leading the Indians to their first world championship in 1920. As a result of the tragic death of shortstop Ray Chapman during that pennant-winning season, the players wore black armbands on their left sleeves for the balance of the schedule.

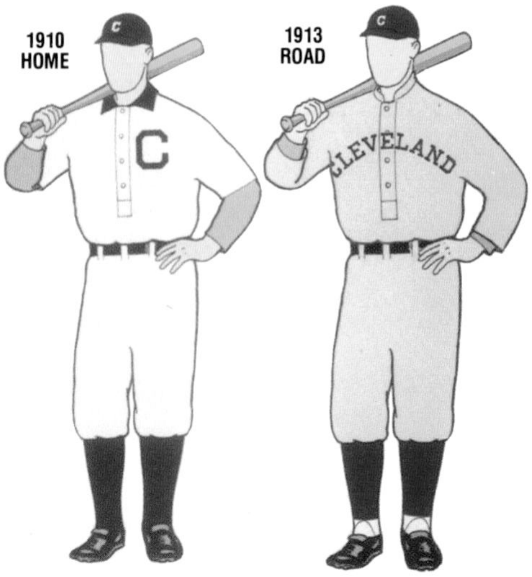

1910 HOME 1913 ROAD

1916 HOME 1918 ROAD 1920 ROAD

1922 HOME

1921 HOME

BRAGGING RIGHTS FOR A WHILE

The celebration of the series victory was carried over to the 1921 Cleveland uniforms —the words WORLDS CHAMPIONS were immodestly emblazoned on the front of both home and road shirts. An idea borrowed from John McGraw's 1906 Giants, it was not a hit with Mgr. Speaker or the players. Fortunately for their sake, they did not repeat in 1921 and conventional uniforms were ordered for 1922. Using the same fancy capital letters from WORLDS CHAMPIONS, the name CLEVELAND was displayed in an arc on the front of the 1922 gray road shirts. A large capital C in the same style appeared on the left front of the home shirts. The all-dark caps with a white C and the all dark stockings were repeated from 1921. This monochromatic uniform ensemble was repeated for the next six seasons. Speaker's leadership was not enough to secure any more pennants, only a respectable second place in 1926. Tris finally gave up the ship and moved on to Philadelphia in 1927 to finish out his great career.

1928 ROAD

1928 HOME 1930 HOME

SOME COLOR RETURNS FOR TRIBE BATTLE DRESS

Perhaps inspired by Detroit's "tiger head" uniform dress of 1927, the Indians' home uniforms for 1928 featured a colorful profile head of a full-bonneted Indian on the left breast. It was the first visual acknowledgment of the team's nickname on the game uniforms and represented the club's participation in a baseball-wide trend for more colorful uniforms. The road uniform remained as before except for the new stockings with two white stripes, which were worn also at home. For 1929, the Indian head was moved to the left sleeve on the home shirts and the block C from the 1920 season was returned to the left breast. The gray road uniforms were spruced up with pinstriping and double piping. This uniform set was continued through the 1932 season with virtually no changes. In 1933 the home uniform was restyled with some interesting color trim features. The button panel and collar were made solid red with thin navy blue edging as was the new "wishbone" style C on the left shirt front. The new home cap now included a "wishbone" C in red and the stockings were solid navy. The road uniforms did not change much for the next six summers; only the white C on the cap becoming "wishbone" style in 1937 and an extra white stripe added to the stocking. The solid red down the button panel was dropped in 1936 in favor of some red and blue combination piping but the Indian head patch continued on the sleeve. Ex-pitching great Walter Johnson managed some respectable tribe teams during this run and a future pitching great, Bob Feller, made his debut in these uniforms.

1930 ROAD

1933 HOME

1937 ROAD

THE FELLER-BOUDREAU ERA

Around 1938, red stripes were added to the home navy stockings and the Indian head patch was removed from the sleeve. But the red wishbone C remained as the dominant design feature of the home jersey through the WWII period. The gray road uniform was overhauled for the 1939 season —back to plain gray fabric, no piping, and the name CLEVELAND was redone in arched solid navy block capitals. In 1942 some red was introduced on the road suits. New red and blue piping, red and white stocking stripes, and CLEVELAND in red lettering were features of this new, brighter look. The navy home cap with red visor and red C was also now worn on the road. A young Lou Boudreau (25) was named player-manager in 1942 and the Indians eagerly anticipated the first post-war season of 1946. Some promising new talent was on the way and Rapid Robert, at the peak of his career, was due back from the war.

The stellar keystone combination of the 1948 championship club —Lou Boudreau and Joe Gordon.

Another new look for the home uniforms celebrated the arrival of the '46 season. The nickname INDIANS in red script with a navy border graced the front of the new home jersey and the following year an animated Indian face patch with a very toothy grin occupied the left sleeve. "Wahoo", as he was called, survived as a frivolous team symbol for five seasons until he too had a "face lift". The road uniform was retained from the previous summer and was kept intact for the entire post- war period. This uniform ensemble was about to become a big part of the history of the ball club.

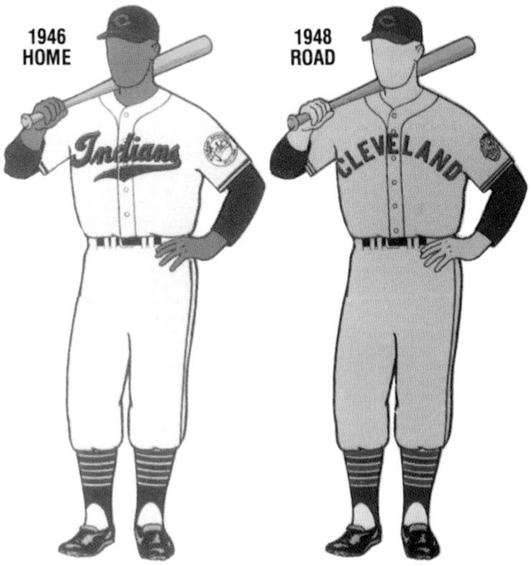

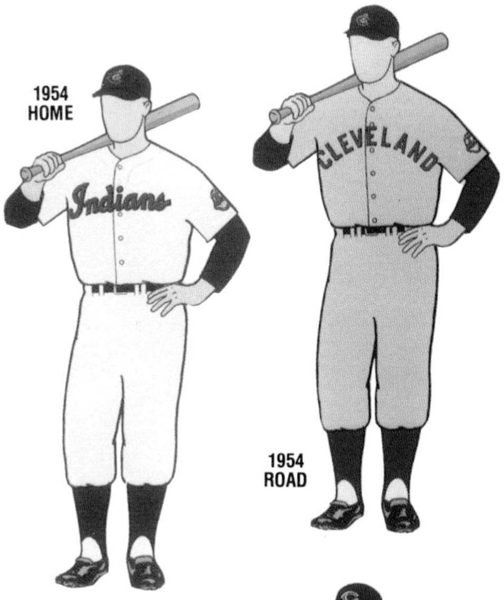

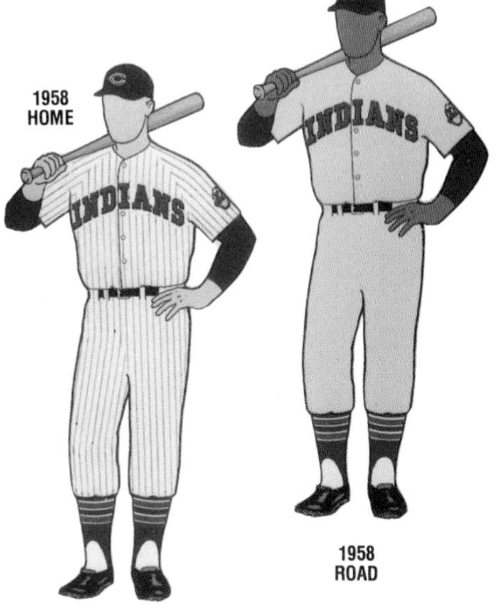

THE LOVABLE SHOWMAN, BILL VEECK

The war-weary public took to the return of top talent major league baseball with a fervor bordering on hysteria. Attendance figures were skyrocketing, especially in Cleveland. New owner Bill Veeck drew the crowds with imaginative promotional gimmicks and a steadily improving ball club helped sweeten the pot. In 1948 Cleveland drew 2.6 million fans into the stadium and then rewarded them with a world series victory. The home uniforms were designed "down" a bit in 1950 —piping was eliminated, the underline flourish was removed from the INDIANS script and the red striping on the socks was down to two, with no white accents. 1951 introduced new field manager Al Lopez and a few more uniform changes. Stripes were eliminated from the navy stockings and a new version of "WAHOO", the cartoon Indian face, was displayed on the sleeve and inside the C of the now all-navy cap. Another big season for the Indians (1954/110 wins) was played out in these costumes and Bob Feller finished out his great career in 1956, also the final season for manager Al Lopez. This uniform set was worn for the last time in 1957.

TOWARD THE SIXTIES AND MORE NOVEL GARMENTS

It was a new era in 1958 and it called for a whole new look in uniforms. Pinstripes were used on the home whites for the first time in decades. The name INDIANS was presented in red block serif capitals in place of script. A white outline was added to the cap C and "Wahoo" removed (he did, however, remain on the left sleeve). The white-accented red striping was restored on the stockings. The new road gray uniform repeated the graphics of the home suits. This combination remained the standard through the season of 1962. But this re-design was only a prelude to the "real" uniform of the sixties.

A smiling Bob Feller models the new 1958 home pin-stripes.

The sleeveless vest with a zipper front — an idea which had already had trials in the National League —was to be the dominant feature of the radically new uniform set of 1963. But equally as eye-catching was the abundance of RED on the caps, sweater sleeves and stockings —with just a touch of navy blue as an accent color. And the whimsical "WAHOO" took center stage on the left breast of the vest —across the zipper from the uniform number. These colorful new uniforms were a product of the new color TV age and endured through the 1969 season. But any theme of image continuity now discarded, one could say of the coming decade of the seventies: "You ain't seen nothin' yet!".

In the early seventies, every club was abandoning the flannel fabrics in favor of the new double knits and their unique new design features. Cleveland joined the trend in 1972 with another new look in uniforms. Now it was pullover jerseys with pronounced striping on the sleeve ends and around the V-neck collar. The new trousers incorporated this striping in the new beltless waistbands. "WAHOO" was discarded (temporarily) and the name INDIANS was displayed in a more conventional solid red block lettering on both home whites and road grays. This first double knit uniform set was only a one-year introductory trial for a more total commitment to the double knit designs of the seventies.

For 1973, the new double-knits introduced a truly unique lettering style for the name INDIANS on both the home whites and road grays. It resembled something from an ancient Greek tablet and even the C on the cap front was in the same mold. For 1975 thru 1977, the same lettering style was retained, but the uniform colors were re-arranged into a "mix-n-match" combination with a choice of either solid navy or solid red pullover top. In addition, red trousers were issued which could be worn with the red top —a gaudy all scarlet uniform which was not too favorably received. For 1978, a more conventional lettering style was restored for the names INDIANS and CLEVELAND and the red trousers were also history. It was still your basic double-knit look, but the optional navy blue home shirt was the only survivor of the "mix-n-match" features. In fact, the CLEVELAND road uniform was in the traditional gray fabric color of bygone years. By 1983, little "WAHOO" was returned to his perch on the left sleeve. The road uniform was a two-tone model: navy top and gray trousers, with INDIANS replacing CLEVELAND.

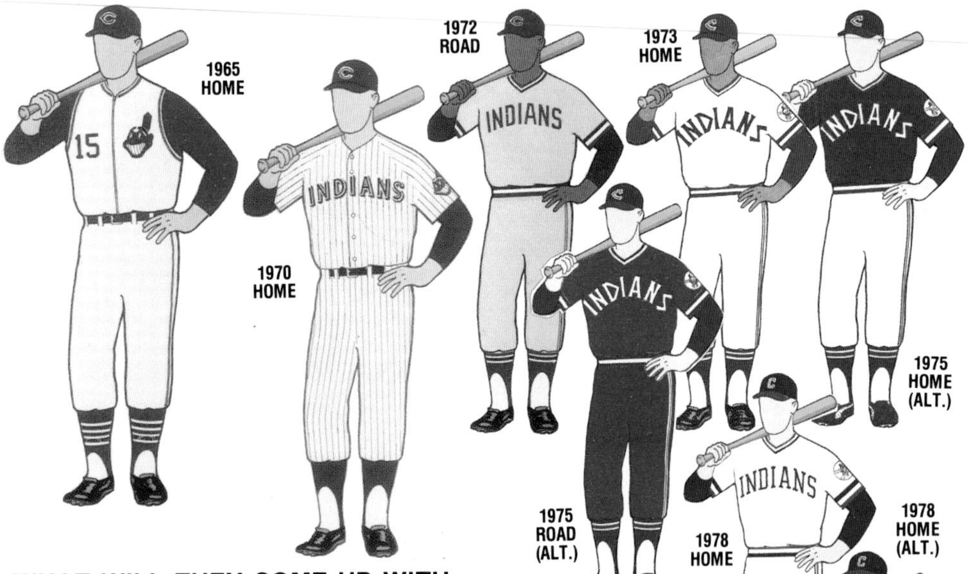

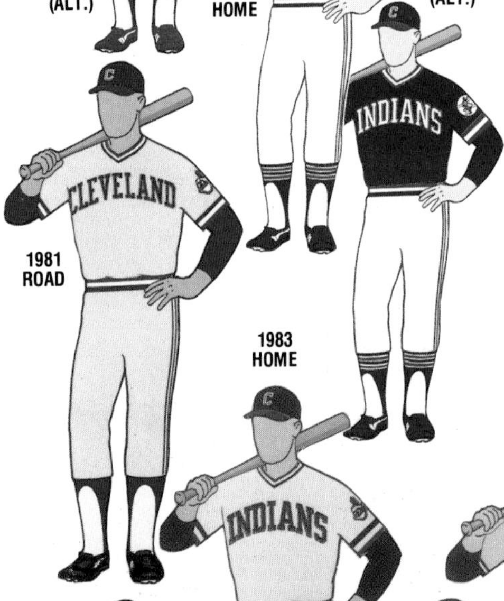

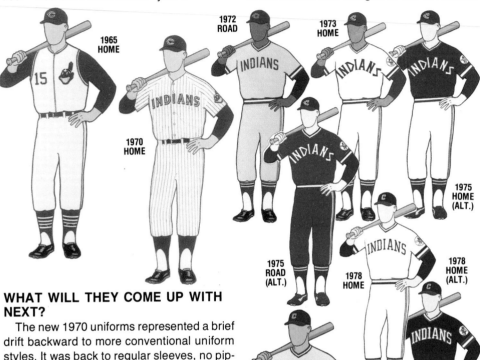

WHAT WILL THEY COME UP WITH NEXT?

The new 1970 uniforms represented a brief drift backward to more conventional uniform styles. It was back to regular sleeves, no piping (home pinstripes notwithstanding), buttoned shirts, and solid stockings. And, by the way, a comeback for the more somber navy blue as the dominant trim color. The name INDIANS on the home pinstripes was presented in an unusual outline-plus-shadow block lettering style. CLEVELAND on the road grays duplicated this lettering, only in a reverse of the color scheme. "WAHOO" had to return to his left sleeve mounting. This uniform set was modified with plain block lettering in 1971.

A SWING BACK TO THE TRADITIONAL

The bizarre colors of the double-knit craze had peaked in the late seventies and the trend throughout the major leagues in the eighties was definitely toward the more traditional look in baseball uniforms. One might say that the Cleveland Indians had finally rescued their sanity for the 1986 season and presented a non-controversial image in their new uniform selection. The same INDIANS lettering style was preserved from 1985, but now it was the basic all-white at home and all-gray for traveling. Buttons on the shirts and separate belts on the trousers were the new "old" look. Even little "WAHOO" had returned from near-extinction and made a solo appearance "front and center" on the new caps.

The 1989 season introduced another new variation in Indians' uniforms with some shoulder striping and the return of the city name CLEVELAND on the road grays.

DETROIT TIGERS

THE PRE-COBB YEARS

Although Detroit was an established member of Ban Johnson's Western League during the 1890's, its status as a big major league town was in jeopardy when the league went "major" in 1901. Mediocre attendance figures fueled ongoing rumors about shifting the operation to Pittsburgh or another more creditable major league city. Fortunately, the Tigers stayed in Detroit and wove a long and rich baseball tradition. They have been "Tigers" as far back as their minor league days in the 1890's —a name inspired by yellow and black stocking stripes. Their first home uniforms as a major league team in 1901 emphatically declared their feline identity with a red silhouette tiger on the front of their black caps. The black stockings also featured a red stripe. The rest of the white home uniform was standard stuff: fold-down collar, button front and the name DETROIT in arched block capital letters. The gray road uniforms wewre basically a duplication of the home suit except that MAROON was the trim color instead of black.

For 1903, the city name DETROIT was dropped in favor of a Roman-style D on the left shirt pocket of both home whites and road grays. The home caps were plain white with a black visor and the black stockings featured a white stripe about half-way down. On the road, they wore maroon stockings and an all-gray cap. The following season they opted for a plain white home uniform with no markings, and on the road grays they changed the D on the pocket to an Old-English style. This style of letter trim was common for the day —in fact, it was a revival of a similar D worn in the minor league days of the 1890's. Thus 1904 is an historically significant year in the history of Detroit Tiger uniforms —the Old English style D being the oldest major league emblem still in use today (unless the Athletics resurrect the A on their uniform shirts). Also, from an historical point of view, it was the last season without the services of one Tyrus Raymond Cobb —the famed Georgia Peach.

COBB, JENNINGS AND CHAMPIONSHIPS

The Old English D was repeated for the 1905 season, this time on the home whites as well as the road grays. The plain uniform was spruced up with a dark collar and the cap now included a dark visor, piping on the crown seams, and an Old English D in front. The new road uniforms were a dark "negative" duplication of the home suits with gray stockings and a gray copy of the home cap. Except for a modification to the D in 1908, the Tigers kept this home uniform thru the 1911 season. The dark reverse road uniform was used one more year ('06) and was replaced by a gray copy of the home suits in 1907. The '07 road cap was all dark with white D and white seam stripes. The years of these uniforms are especially noteworthy in the team's history for several reasons: the young Ty Cobb established himself as the game's new superstar and Hugh Jennings became manager to lead the Detroits to 3 straight flags in '07-08-09. Also, the Old English D had become a visual symbol of exciting and winning baseball and a permanent fixture in future Tiger uniforms.

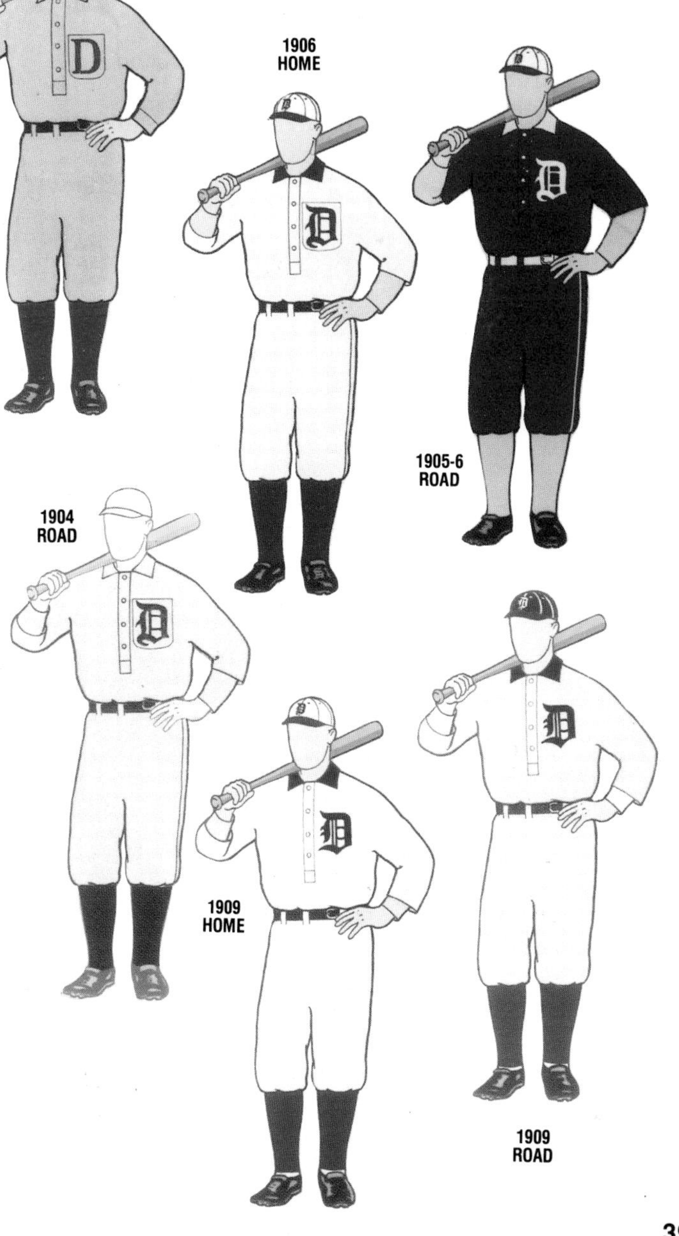

The Detroit Tigers of 1900, their final year as a minor-league team

THE NAVIN FIELD ERA BEGINS

The Tigers inaugurated their new Navin Field facility in April 1912 with the same uniforms as in 1911 except for pinstripes added to the home whites. They continued the Old English D motif thru the mid-teens with only minor variations. The white cap crown was dropped for 1913 as was the dark collar trim. The fold-down collar was replaced by a dark stand-up cadet style for 1914. The configuration of the decorative D underwent many subtle changes during these years, without losing its familiar identity. In 1915-16 a plain square D was displayed, but the Old English form was restored for 1917-18. The fold-down collar style also made its last hurrah on Tiger uniforms of 1917-18. Cobb's accomplishments were dazzling during these years but the team won no more pennants and the popular Jennings was near the end of the line. Yet another variation of the D design was displayed on the shirts and caps in 1919-20.

THE "TYGERS" UNDER MGR. COBB

After 14 years at the helm, Hugh Jennings was replaced by a reluctant Ty Cobb as field manager for the 1921 season. The newspapers even re-christened the team "TYGERS" in honor of the new leader. Tyger uniforms during Cobb's managerial reign (1921-26) were pretty standard —the Old English D on both home and road suits. The white home uniform was pin-striped while the traveling version was plain gray. Caps were solid dark navy or black with a white Old English D. Stockings were at first solid dark down to the ankle, then double-striped with white and finally a half dark, half white combination. The Cobb-led Tygers were exciting offensively (a .316 team BA in '21), but the defense and pitching failed them frequently. A golden era ended when Cobb resigned after the 1926 season to finish out his fabulous career with the Philadelphia Athletics. By this time the new hitting hero in the Motor City was 4-time batting champion Harry Heilmann.

GEHRINGER AND THE G-MEN DAYS

In stride with the sudden trend for more colorful uniforms, the Detroit team of 1927 donned the most imaginative uniform ensemble in franchise history. In place of the traditional D on the shirt front they displayed an orange and black tiger's head on both home whites and road grays. Two orange stripes were added on the stockings and the D on the cap was also orange. The following season the Old English D was restored on the home whites but the 1928 road uniform was another daring departure from team tradition. The team nickname TIGERS was spelled out across the chest in orange and black fancy capital letters (in a downhill slope, no less). And the colorful tiger's head from the season before was dramatically displayed in the middle of the back (uniform numbers were still a couple of years away). Charley Gehringer, the Fowlerville farm boy, was just hitting his stride as the premier second baseman of his time when these unusual uniforms appeared.

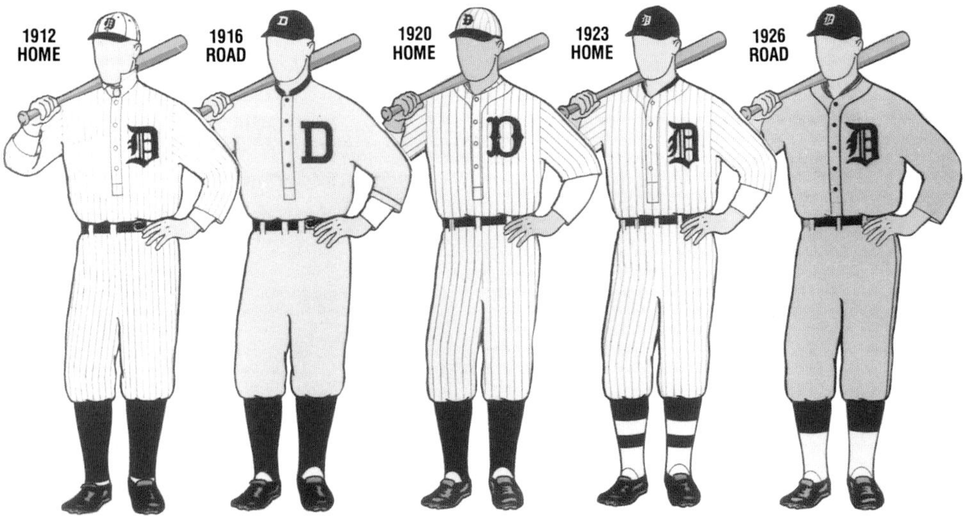

The immortal Ty Cobb in 1916, at the peak of his brilliant career.

Harry Heilmann, spring training 1929, wearing his 1928 road uniform.

THE EVOLUTION OF THE FAMOUS "D"

The 1929 uniform set continued the colorful innovation cycle with a hybrid version of the Old English D on home whites and road grays. The elements of this new D design were made thicker and included an orange outline. The belt tunnels were solid dark and the stockings were basically white (or gray) with a colorful stripe combination of orange and black (or dark navy?). The cap crowns for home and road were white and gray respectively with dark visors and a standard Old English D in front. Traditional team uniforms were once again ignored for the 1930 season. The city name DETROIT was presented on the shirt front at home as well as on the road in a slanted SCRIPT lettering style —a new idea which caught on with other clubs during the decade and is still a popular choice on many of today's uniforms. The "candy cane" stocking stripes theme and light cap crown encored on the 1930 uniforms but gradually evolved into more somber solid dark colors by 1933. The caps in '31 & '32 returned to the old standard all-dark but included an orange "square" D, reminiscent of the 1915-16 jerseys. Also for 1931-33, pinstripes made a brief comeback on both home whites and road grays. In December of 1933, fiery catcher Mickey Cochrane was purchased from the Athletics to be field manager for 1934. The Detroit Tigers, with new manager Cochrane and the memorable G-men (Gehringer, Greenberg, Goslin) had an appointment with destiny in 1934-35.

1933
ROAD

1934-35
HOME

1935
ROAD

1950
HOME

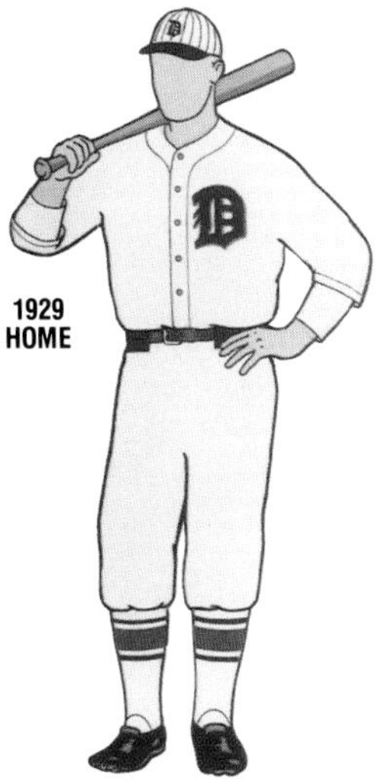

1929
HOME

1930
HOME

1957
ROAD

THE GLORY YEARS, 1934-45

For baseball fans (especially Detroit fans) who worship at the altars of tradition, a comparison of the home uniforms of the 1934 Tigers vs. the current home suits has to be heartwarming. Considering the differences in tailoring and fabrics, the common identity is unmistakable. The Old English D was restored on the home whites in '34, once again slightly modified but for the last time. It has not been tampered with for the last 50 years, and (except for one brief trans-gression in 1960) enjoys the longest continuous usage of any major league uniform insignia. The script DETROIT was continued on the 1934 road grays and became a road uniform standard for the next 25 summers. Piping trim was also restored on the '34 shirts around the collar and button panel. Consecutive pennants in '34 & '35 plus their first World Series win (1935) in this uniform set seemed to bury any further ideas for change. They continued to wear this same set of uniforms thru the entire era of the Briggs ownership (1936-59) with only minor trim changes along the way: a gray cap crown was worn on the road in '35 and '38, a white stripe was added to the stockings in 1937, orange stripes were reinstated on the socks in 1947 and the D on the caps was orange on occasion. Orange outline piping was added to the script DETROIT on the road uniforms in the mid-fifties. A young Tiger phenom by the name of Kaline earned his "stripes" during this uniform run.

Rookie Al Kaline at Comiskey Park, 1953.

Pete Fox, Jo-Jo White and Goose Goslin —the premier Detroit outfield of 1934-35.

A NEW ORDER IN MOTOWN

When the Briggs' family control of the club ended, the new president Bill DeWitt immediately proclaimed the new order for the 1960 season. Briggs Stadium was henceforth to be called Tiger Stadium, an idea which produced little resistance. The Old English D on the home uniforms was scrubbed in favor of a slanted script TIGERS —in the much admired mold of the Dodgers uniforms. On the new road uniforms, the script DETROIT was also scrubbed in favor of a conventional arched block capital letters form. Since the Tiger faithful are less attached to what the players wear outside of Detroit, the new road uniform was accepted and remained standard thru the decade. But the home uniform change was another story. Sure, it was a neat looking uniform but after 16 seasons of Greenberg, Newhouser, etc. and two world championships with the Old English D it was too late —the die was cast. Tiger management yielded to fan pressure and restored the Old English D to the home uniforms for 1961. As if in grateful response, the team won 101 games and challenged the power-laden Yankees for most of the season. Also the immortal Ty Cobb passed away that summer, but just maybe he too was relieved at the end to see the familiar D reinstated. Tiger fans were rewarded later in the decade (1968) with a memorable come-from-behind world series victory over the Cardinals, further cementing their love affair with the home uniform. A minor novel feature of the new '60's road uniforms was the inclusion of the uniform number on the right sleeve.

1960 HOME

1960's ROAD

1960's HOME

JOINING THE DOUBLE-KNIT BANDWAGON

In 1972 the Detroit uniforms abandoned the flannel fabrics in favor of the new double-knits. The home uniform design was not altered — only adapted to the new stretchy fabric. The gray road uniform was pretty much overhauled and catered to the new pull-over style jersey and beltless trousers. The DETROIT lettering was modified into a square-serif style with an orange border added. Orange, white and navy striping was included on the collar, sleeve ends, waistband and down the trouser legs. The D on the cap was made orange and included a white outline for a few seasons. In 1985, the pullover jersey was converted to a button front. The sacred home whites have endured, preserving a permanent historical link back to the G-men of the thirties and beyond.

1990 ROAD

1990 HOME

Mark "The Bird" Fidrych, dazzling the home fans at Tiger Stadium in 1976.

HOUSTON ASTROS

THE NATIONAL GAME BECOMES MORE NATIONAL

The abrupt departure of both National League clubs in NYC to the far West in 1958 opened the door for further expansion of major league baseball from the exclusive confines of the Northeast quadrant of the nation. New franchises in new territories were now inevitable with the coming of the Jet Age. The state of Texas, long isolated from the major league scene, was granted a National League franchise in October 1960 along with a new replacement franchise in New York City. The state's largest city, Houston, was the logical choice and the Houston Colt .45's were made operational for the 1962 season. Veteran baseball man Paul Richards was named general manager for the new team and they played their first three seasons at Colt Stadium.

A NICKNAME DRAWN FROM THE PAST

With more than a touch of regional pride in their frontier heritage, the new club appropriately adopted the name of Colt .45's—a reminder of the famous six-shooter that "won the West". Stocked with second-rate personnel extracted from the league's expansion pool, these Colt .45's hardly won the West—but the important thing was simply that they won the hearts of all Texans with an appetite for big league baseball. The team colors were to be navy blue and orange. The new home whites were devoid of piping trim but provided a dramatic graphic representation of their new name on their chests—a silhouette of a Colt .45 pistol with the word COLTS emanating from the gunsmoke of the barrel. The navy blue caps presented ".45's" in orange on the front. The socks were a combination of orange, navy and white stripes while the undersweaters were solid navy. The gray road uniforms were more conventional with the name HOUSTON in navy blue block capitals edged in orange. As to be expected from an expansion club, the Colt .45's shared the bottom of the standings with their counterpart, the Mets, for the first years of operation.

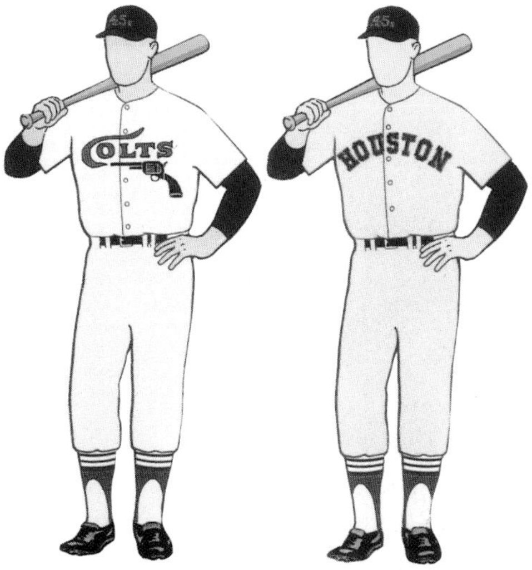

1962 HOME 1962 ROAD

A NEW NAME AND A NEW HOME

With the establishment of the new space center in Houston and a Texan in the White House plus the construction of a miraculous new enclosed stadium (the Astrodome), the Houston baseball club did an about face in team identity. After reaching into its past for a nickname, they now looked into the promise of the future and re-christened the franchise as the ASTROS for the 1965 season. The new home white uniforms now displayed a shooting star arched above the name ASTROS in a navy and orange combination. A modernistic, circular team insignia patch was worn on the left sleeve of both home whites and road grays. A white "H" over an orange star graced the front of the all navy caps. The stockings were now solid navy. The gray road uniforms repeated the HOUSTON lettering from the previous seasons. The new heroes were little Joe Morgan and the "toy cannon", Jim Wynn. Unfortunately, the team's performance continued to be sub-par for the balance of the decade. The ASTROS uniform remained unchanged through the 1970 season.

1965 HOME 1965 ROAD

The "Toy Cannon", Jim Wynn—Houston's first superstar c.1963.

1971 ROAD 1971 HOME

A BURST OF ORANGE AND THEN SOME

In step with the ever-increasing coverage of color TV and the advent of the new double-knit uniforms of the early seventies, the Astros modified their uniform designs for 1971. Orange was now the dominant color over navy blue as caps, undersweaters and stockings were solid bright orange on both home whites and road grays. Orange, white and navy stripes appeared on the new-fangled belt sash as well as on the sleeve ends and around the collar. The lettering graphics on the shirt fronts remained the same except for the color reversal to orange edged in navy. In an unusual retrieval of a long-dormant jersey feature, ZIPPERS were used to replace the buttoned fronts. If this brighter color scheme created some excitation for the visual senses, it would pale by comparison to what was to follow.

All-star second baseman Joe Morgan shows off the new ASTROS uniform motif.

THE UNIFORM OF THE FUTURE?

As if on a "feeding frenzy" of color exploitation and with a clamoring to cross new frontiers in uniform design, the Astros of 1975 jolted the baseball world with the most imaginative uniforms since the heyday of Charley Finley. With the entire lower half of the jersey enveloped in a horizontal "rainbow" effect of several hues of orange and the name ASTROS in a clean, modern, non-traditional (in terms of baseball uniform graphics) lettering style, this idea was a daring departure indeed. If the new double-knit features of buttonless pull-over jerseys and built-in sash belts were here to stay, this was the ultimate statement of how uniforms of the future ought to look. And since this generation and all future generations no longer tolerate black and white TV images, why not add to the visual appeal of televised games? These innovative ideas may ultimately survive but the forces of nostalgia and the preservation of traditions are ever-present with baseball fans everywhere and we are always looking back over our shoulder —too much so to readily accept new ideas without a struggle. Current trends in baseball uniforms reflect a resurgence of a more traditional look —buttons and belts, good old pin stripes, gray instead of powder blue on the road, etc. Even the Astros have yielded to this trend by abandoning the "rainbow" jersey in favor of their more modest alternate home uniform with a touch of the "rainbow" effect down the shoulders. We can scarcely wait to see how the Houston Astros of the 1990's will be attired.

For 1989, Houston joined the conservative trend in major league uniforms by introducing belted trousers and buttoned shirts.

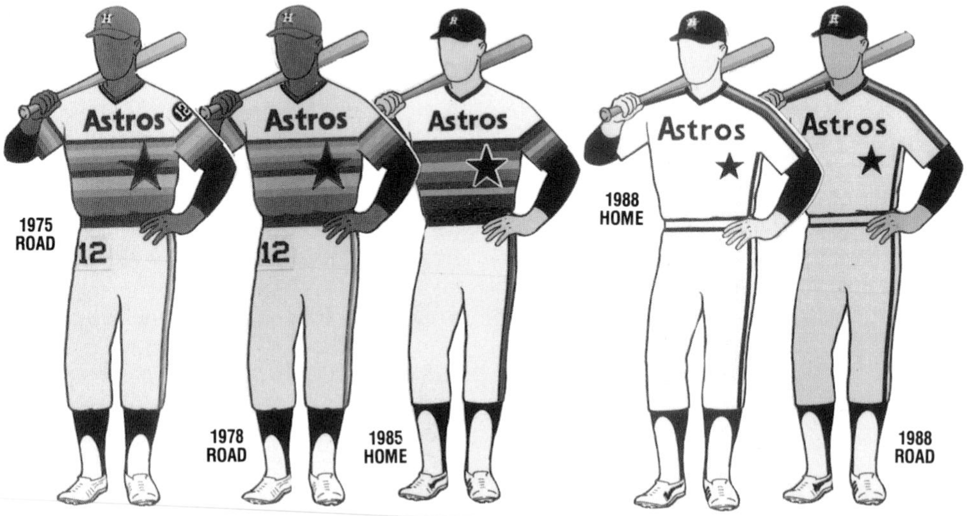

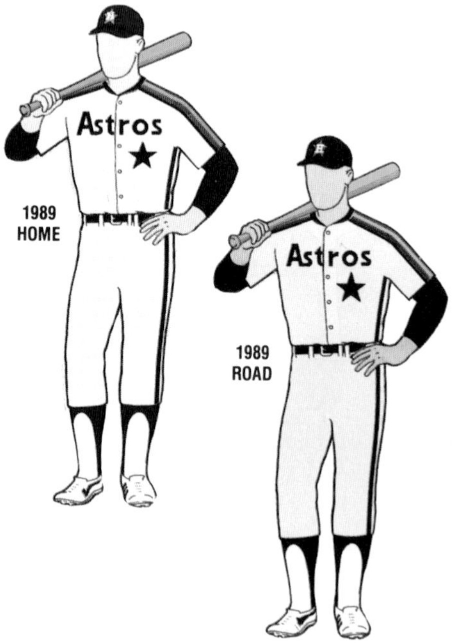

Stellar outfielder Jose Cruz in the first "rainbow" uniform. Note the unusual circled treatment for the jersey number.

The 1981 edition of the Houston Astros posing for the official team picture in the "Dome".

KANSAS CITY ROYALS

A QUICK RETURN TO THE MAJORS

When Charles Finley left town in a huff, Kansas City was abruptly without a major league team for 1968. Fortunately, the American League was poised for further expansion in 1969 and a replacement franchise was awarded to KC. A modern stadium complex was in the works and the new team was to be called ROYALS. Royal blue, appropriately enough, was chosen as the trim color for the new uniforms. The uniform designs were tasteful and conservative (a reaction to Mr. Finley's bizarre green and gold) with solid blue caps, stockings and undersweaters. The home whites displayed ROYALS in script while the gray road shirts had KANSAS CITY in similar script. An official team emblem patch in royal blue, gold and white was added to the left sleeve in 1971. For 1972, the KANSAS CITY on the road uniforms was changed to arched block capital letters.

ADAPTING TO THE DOUBLE KNITS

For the 1973 season, the Royals joined the trend for double knit fabric uniform styles. The white home uniforms kept the same general appearance except for the buttonless pull-over jerseys with a bit more striping trim and the new beltless waistband of blue and white stripes. The new road uniforms were more drastically redefined —a powder blue replaced conventional gray and the name KANSAS CITY was converted to WHITE (as was the number on the back). This uniform combination remained the same for the next ten summers. During this uniform run, the club jelled into a solid contender with several divisional titles and a world series appearance in 1980. Some new local heroes arrived on the scene in these uniforms —namely George Brett, Hal MacCrea, Frank White, Amos Otis and Dennis Leonard.

A SWING BACK TO THE TRADITIONAL

When the novelty of the new double knit features began to run its course, the Royals joined another trend toward more conventional uniform designs for the 1983 season. Buttoned jerseys and belted trousers were restored on both home and road uniforms. The player's number was also added to the left breast. The white KANSAS CITY lettering on the blue road shirts was replaced by a white duplication of the ROYALS script from the home whites. In 1985, the Kansas City Royals celebrated their first world championship wearing this combination so it figures that no changes will be in order for a while —at least as long as the flavor of victory lasts.

1969
HOME

1971
ROAD

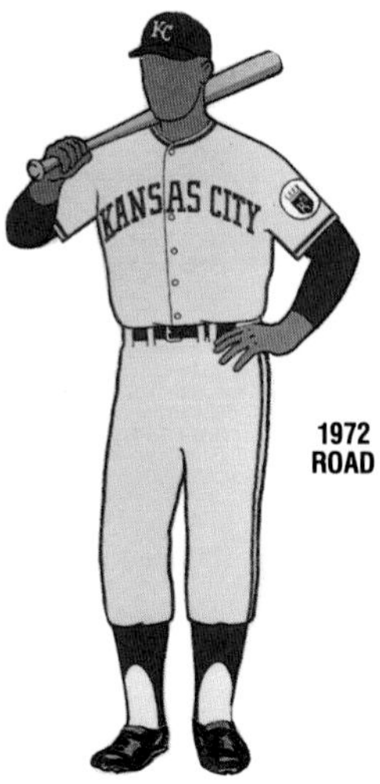

1972
ROAD

1973
HOME

1973
ROAD

1988
HOME

1988
ROAD

An early KC Royals standout, Amos Otis at home c.1971.

Future Hall-of-Famer George Brett demonstrates his classic swing in the tighter-fitting double-knit uniform style of the mid-seventies.

BROOKLYN/ LOS ANGELES DODGERS

CHAMPIONS OF THE NEW CENTURY

Manager Ned Hanlon's SUPERBAS (a nickname which mimicked a famous circus act of the time) started the new century as champions of the National League—in effect, World Champs since the American League was still a minor league. The Brooklyns of 1900 wore the standard white at home and gray on the road. Home caps were solid white with a rounded "pill-box" shaped crown. Road caps were the same in gray. Stockings were solid maroon at home, black on the road. Shirts were the standard buttoned front with a fold-down collar style. The road shirts displayed BROOKLYN in arched block capitals while the home shirts were plain or with an Old English B on the left breast. In 1902, the home trim color was changed to BLUE (probably navy shade) and the caps were now solid blue with a white B in front. The trim color on the BROOKLYN road suits continued to be black, but the cap color was solid gray with a black B in front about 1903. They kept this same overall uniform look through 1907, the only changes being a smaller Old English B at home and the dark blue cap replacing the gray model.

The uniforms were re-designed for 1907, retaining the blue as standard trim color throughout. At home, the Old English B was replaced by a fancy capital B—a letter style that was to be used repeatedly for the next five decades in Brooklyn. This style B in fact was still used on the Brooklyn caps in their final season in Flatbush (1957). But the new road uniforms for 1907 were daring indeed. Instead of the standard plain gray, they were made from a gray cloth with a fine blue "cross-hatch", or checked pattern. This material evoked comments throughout the league and even ridicule. Enough, perhaps, to dissuade the club not to repeat the unusual flannels for 1908. This fabric was historic in that it was one of the first attempts to dress up the monotonous gray of the road flannels and was an experimental forerunner of the more acceptable pinstripes of later years. And the cross-hatch idea itself would resurface in the later history of Brooklyn uniforms. The 1908 road uniforms were once again your basic gray with the BROOKLYN name in fancy capital letters. In 1909, a pair of stripes (gray or white) were added to dress up the solid navy blue stockings.

THE TROLLEY DODGERS ENTER THE TEEN YEARS

In keeping with the latest trend in uniform shirts, the 1910 uniforms replaced the fold-down collar with the short stand-up "cadet" style. The only trim feature on the new home whites was a letter B enclosed in a "diamond" design on the left sleeve. The new road gray shirts accented the new cadet collar in solid navy and the name BROOKLYN was displayed vertically in small capital letters down the button panel (another current trend). The following season (1911), fine, narrow pinstriping was used on the gray traveling uniforms—already an acceptable and popular alternative to plain gray. 1912 was the final season at old Washington Park and the Superbas celebrated the occasion with another new set of uniforms. Bold pinstriping was included on the home whites, even on the new cap crown. Cap visors were solid blue and the "B-enclosed-in-a-diamond" design was on the cap front. The road grays duplicated the pinstriping and included a solid navy cap with the same logo design in white. The stage was set for a new beginning in a brand new concrete and steel facility in 1913.

1901 HOME

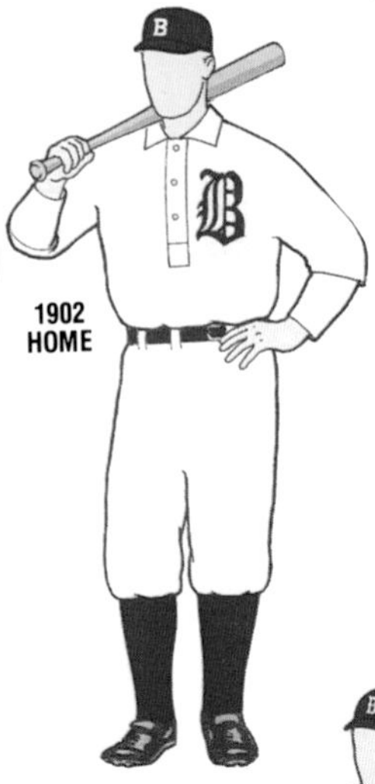
1902 HOME

1904 ROAD

1907 ROAD

1910 HOME

1910 ROAD

A studio shot of Bill Dahlen in his road uniform c.1905

1908 HOME

1909 ROAD

Nap Rucker, a fine hurler for the "Superbas", about 1909

1912 HOME

EBBETTS FIELD, "ROBBIE" AND PENNANTS

The Brooklyns opened Ebbetts Field in 1913 with spruced up new uniforms. The pinstriping was repeated, but the cadet collar, button panel and sleeve ends were in solid navy on both home and road jerseys. The name BROOKLYN in vertical white lettering was revived on the button area of the road shirt. The navy caps were the standard round crown by now and included a white trim stripe around the base of the crown. The white stripes on the blue home stockings were now wider and bolder, while the gray road stockings featured a single wide band of blue.

The popular Wilbert Robinson, the rotund ex-catcher and old Baltimore Oriole crony of John McGraw, was hired to manage the Brooklyns for 1914. The new uniforms were somewhat toned down —the extra navy trimmings were removed and the new V-neck collar style replaced the cadet version. It was pinstripes once again, but the cap was re-done in matching pinstripe material with a solid blue visor. The fancy capital B from 1909 was resurrected on both shirt fronts as well as cap fronts. Both home and road stockings featured the wide blue band about halfway down. "Uncle Robbie" acquired pitching ace Rube Marquard from the Giants in 1915 and catcher "Chief" Meyers a year later. The stage was set for a big year in Flatbush.

The "Robins" (as they were now being called) opened the 1916 season in a bold new version of the "cross-hatched" pinstriping of 1907. This time it was wider spacing and it was used on the new home whites as well as the road suits. Except for this unique pattern, the graphics were the same as 1915. The idea was more acceptable now —just another variation of the now widely accepted pinstripes. But also, this Brooklyn team was a pennant contender all the way, checked uniforms notwithstanding. The fans and the media seldom find reason to criticize a winner in any costume. Win they did, and met the Boston Red Sox in the world series. No cigar, but those unusual uniforms thus became a part of baseball lore. It was back to regular pinstripes in 1917 and the following seasons, leading up to another pennant in 1920. They lost again to Speaker's Indians but the pinstriped, plain look caught on as a standard for early years of the next decade.

THE DECADE OF THE TWENTIES

After wallowing in the dust of so many McGraw-led Giant teams, the "Trolley Dodgers" had finally achieved some respect and attention in the Big Apple. A couple of pennants can do wonders, and despite a solitary pennant threat for the decade (1924), Uncle Robbie put Brooklyn back on the baseball map for a while. The bland, pinstriped uniform set continued through the early '20's. The National League celebrated its 50th year in 1925 and Brooklyn spruced up their appearance to observe the milestone. As with all NL teams, a large circular blue and gold patch was displayed on the left breast of the home shirts and on the left sleeve of the road grays. Dazzling new red, white and blue stockings were introduced as well as some new piping trim. The road uniforms had a whole new look —plain gray with the name BROOKLYN in arched navy block capitals, the same as the infamous 1907 "checked" uniform. Piping trim was becoming quite fashionable and would be used on Brooklyn uniforms for the rest of the decade. The home uniforms were repeated in 1926-29 except for a dressier cap style with double piping down the crown seams. The road uniforms for 1926 reverted to the pinstripes (now with extra piping trim) and a version of the "B-inside-a-diamond" logo on the sleeve. The cross-hatch pattern was even revived briefly in the late '20's road uniform.

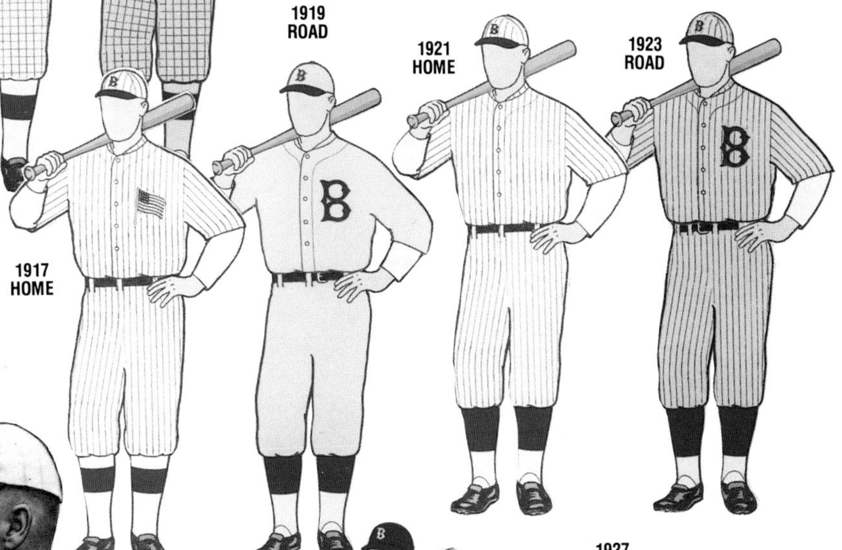

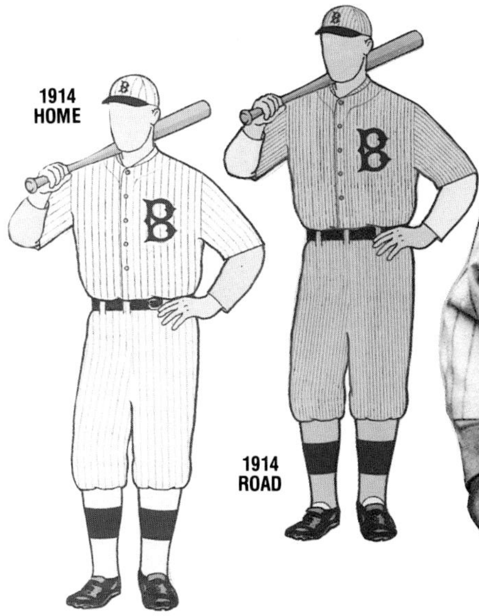

A Flatbush favorite, Zach Wheat in the early twenties.

THE "COLORFUL" THIRTIES

Hard times or not, the decade of the thirties produced the most dazzling and creative uniform designs in the history of the Dodger franchise. The Wilbert Robinson era was near the end and the Robins pretty much floundered in the middle of the pack for the entire decade, but at least they got some attention from their uniform ideas. The 1929 road uniforms had started it off with a return to the basic gray but with a generous amount of blue and red double piping trim. The old standard fancy capital B was displayed on the left breast, dressed up in piping trim outline. The following season, the name BROOKLYN reappeared on the front of the road shirt in two-color fancy capital letters. The home uniform through 1930 was still the plain pinstripes with extra piping trim.

1929 ROAD

1930 ROAD

Fire-balling Dazzy Vance near the end of his career in 1932

1931 HOME

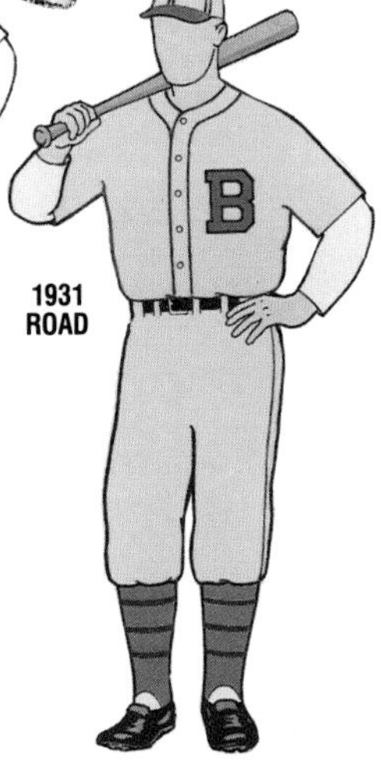

1931 ROAD

The uniforms for 1931-32 were a total redesign from top to bottom. The dominant trim color was BLUE (a lighter shade then navy) with some accents of red. Cap crowns were white or gray with blue visors, double blue piping and the familiar blue B in front. A new block capital B appeared on the sleeve of the home shirt and the left breast of the road jersey. Three thin stripes appeared on the stockings —in blue at home, in red on the road. With the Wilbert Robinson era ended, the Brooklyn club officially adopted the on-again, off-again sobriquet, (TROLLEY) DODGERS, as their team nickname. The restyled 1933 uniforms displayed DODGERS in fancy capitals across the chest of both home and road uniforms. The '33 home uniforms restored the pinstriping plus an abundance of piping embellishments and a large fancy B on the sleeves. Extra white striping was also added to the blue stockings. Caps were once again solid dark blue. From 1934-36 the name BROOKLYN replaced DODGERS on both home and road suits. Solid blue stockings appeared in 1936.

1933 HOME

1935 HOME

In an era of unprecedented experiments in new color combinations and excessive embellishments, the Dodgers took perhaps the boldest step thus far in the decade by introducing GREEN trimmed uniforms for 1937. No, it wasn't an April Fool's joke. It was a legitimate uniform design for the coming season. Except for the choice of a color which was considered "unthinkable" for baseball uniforms, the overall design was a bit conservative for the period —solid dark cap, BROOKLYN in plain block letters, minimum piping. In addition to the daring selection of green, the road uniforms also crossed a new frontier in baseball uniform schemes by using TAN in place of gray on the '37 road suits. This bold idea only survived one season but it had the equivalent impact of Charles Finley's green and gold uniforms in the sixties, even without the exposure of widespread color printing and color television coverage.

1937 HOME

1937 ROAD

THE BIRTH OF A MODERN TRADITION

Brooklyn management "came to its senses" in 1938 with yet another overhaul of their uniform designs. The more conventional ROYAL BLUE ("Dodger blue", if you will) was restored as the sole trim color. The new nickname DODGERS was worked into a slanted script (a new trend in the thirties) with an underline flourish and was displayed on both home and road shirt fronts. 1938 must be recorded as an historic milestone in the evolution of Dodger uniforms —this script DODGERS has remained intact through the years and is a permanent fixture on today's uniforms and no doubt will continue as far into the future as anyone can see. For '38 only, the home cap crown was white with blue piping. Other minor trim features from 1938 have also endured —solid blue stockings and undersweaters, no piping trim on the home whites and a consistent minimal piping on the gray road jerseys.

1938 HOME

1938 ROAD

A couple of minor changes were included in the 1939 uniform set. Zippered fronts (another trend) replaced buttons and an equivalent script BROOKLYN was displayed across the road jersey. The solid blue cap with fancy white B endured through the final season in Flatbush. With the advent of night baseball at Ebbetts Field in the forties, an unusual hybrid version of the familiar Dodger uniform was developed. Instead of the usual flannel, a highly reflective satin fabric was used with the idea that it would improve viewing the games under the arc lights. The home version included extra blue striping down the shoulders and on the sleeve ends. Also, the belt tunnels were solid blue and there was a heavy blue stripe down the trouser leg. The satin road suit was a bit more unique —the material color was a rich pale blue and the trim (including the script BROOKLYN) was added in WHITE. Curiously, some of these unusual trim characteristics would reappear decades later with the advent of double-knit fabrics. The basic uniforms remained constant through the forties and into the fifties with only one significant change —the name BROOKLYN was replaced by DODGERS on the road grays in 1946. Baseball history was written by Jackie Robinson in 1947, wearing the now familiar Dodger blue.

THE FIFTIES —THE LAST HURRAH ON FLATBUSH AVENUE

By the 1950's, the zipper front was history and buttons were once again standard. In 1952, the player's number was repeated on the left front of the home jersey in RED —the first major league club to do so. Many teams followed this precedent in subsequent years. After so many futile tries, the Brooklyn Dodgers finally captured the grand prize in 1955 with a thrilling world series victory over the hated Yankees. Despite another pennant in '56, owner Walter O'Malley was determined to seize the opportunity of a franchise on the West Coast and major league baseball in Brooklyn was no more after 1957.

TO THE CALIFORNIA GOLD FIELDS

Major league baseball was an instant hit on the West Coast in 1958. Sadly, Brooklyn fandom deserved a better fate, but the transfer was otherwise a glorious event and successful beyond O'Malley's wildest dreams. Attendance was phenomenal, aided by the enormous seating capacity of the Coliseum and the instant resumption of the rivalry with the Giants. The permanency of the move was sealed forever with a world championship in 1959, only their second season in Los Angeles. O'Malley was committed to continuation of team tradition, and the uniforms were repeated intact —except for the L.A. on the caps and the script LOS ANGELES on the otherwise familiar traveling suits. Also, the red player's numeral was now included on the front of the new road shirts.

When the Dodgers adopted the double-knit fabrics in the early seventies, changes were made on the road jerseys. Blue and white piping was added to the collar, down the shoulder line and on the sleeve ends. Also, with the team's West Coast identity now firmly established, the name LOS ANGELES was dropped and DODGERS was restored as before on the road shirt. A few seasons later the collar and shoulder piping were dropped and the road uniform of today's L.A. Dodgers was presented. Throughout the hectic years of bizarre color combinations and the double knit style features, the Dodgers image has personified the idea of a consistent tradition. The Dodgers of today look very much like the Dodgers of 1938 and most probably like the Dodgers of the year 2000.

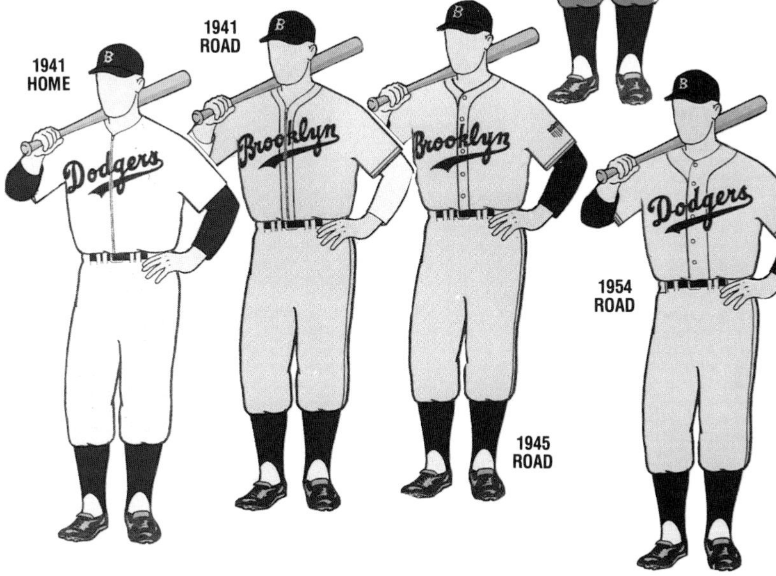

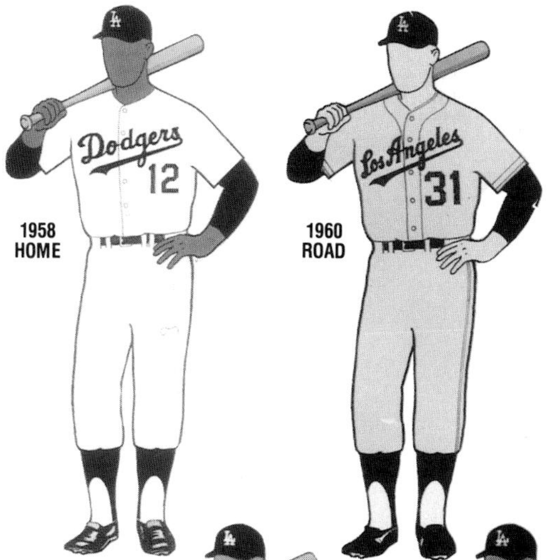

The "boys of summer" 1953 —Gilliam, Reese, Snider, Robinson

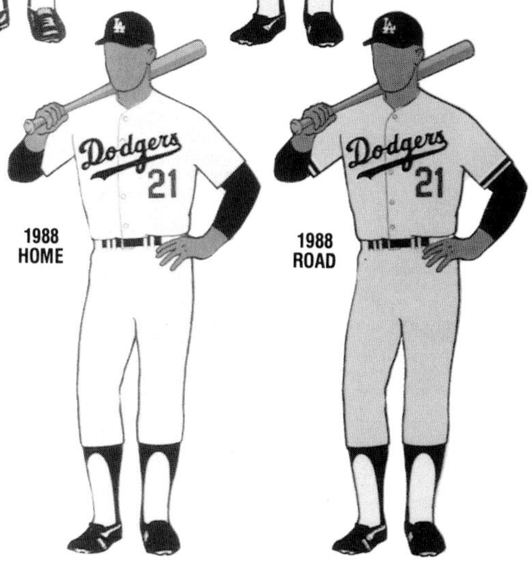

MILWAUKEE BREWERS

AN AMERICAN LEAGUE ORIGINAL

When Ban Johnson's Western League officially declared itself the American League and elevated its status to a competing "major" league in 1901, the Milwaukee Brewers were one of the teams carried over. Unfortunately, their status as a major league city was all too brief as plans were already underway during the 1901 season to relocate the franchise in St. Louis. Those "lame-duck" Brewers, under manager Hugh Duffy, finished dead last and the resulting poor attendance sealed their fate. Their uniforms were pretty much standard for the day —white at home, gray on the road and the name MILWAUKEE arched across the shirts in stock blue capital letters. Caps were the "pillbox" variety with thin bands of blue around the crown. The city of Milwaukee would have to wait another 50 years to host major league baseball again and almost 70 years to re-enter the American League.

Jim Slayton on the mound at County Stadium in the 1976 opener.

AT LONG LAST, BACK IN THE FOLD

After a glorious honeymoon with the National League Braves in the fifties and early sixties, the folks in Milwaukee had a difficult struggle in trying to re-enter the major league arena. After the Braves left in 1965, the Chicago White Sox tested the waters in Beertown by playing a handful of home dates at County Stadium. The Sox, of course, stayed in Chicago but the large crowds for those games convinced the American League that the potential was there for a healthy operation. When the ill-fated Seattle Pilots looked around for a new home after a disastrous maiden season in 1969, Milwaukee welcomed the franchise with open arms. The born-again Brewers opened the 1970 season with the same re-worked uniforms of the defunct Pilots. They kept the blue and gold trim colors and even repeated some of the unique uniform decorations from the Seattle suits. Both home whites and road blues repeated the gold and blue trim bands on the sleeve ends and the name BREWERS on the road shirts had a similar flavor as the replaced SEATTLE. Of course, the pilots emblem was eliminated as was the unique "scrambled eggs" trim on the blue cap. A gold M replaced the S on the cap front. The white home jerseys displayed BREWERS in arched blue block capitals with gold outline. For 1972, a number was added to the shirt front and blue and gold piping was introduced on the collar.

The Brewers uniforms switched over to the new double-knit styles for the 1973 season. The general appearance was about the same, but with the new V-neck pullover jerseys and built-in waistband on the trousers. New blue/gold/blue striping was incorporated on the sleeve ends, around the V-neck collar, on the belt sash and down the pant legs. The new powder blue road suit duplicated the graphics of the home uniform. The front panel of the road cap was changed to gold (or yellow) in 1974 —otherwise the uniform set remained the same through the 1977 season.

A NEW LOOK FOR THE EIGHTIES

The 1978 season saw a general re-design of the Brewer uniforms —still with the same color scheme and the double knit pullover shirt and beltless trousers, but with a new logo design for the caps (a clever "ball-in-glove" representation of M and B) and pinstripes for the home whites. Striping trim on the home suits was toned down to solid blue and eliminated from the sleeve ends. The combination striping was retained on the road uniform as before, but the city name MILWAUKEE in a sloping script style replaced BREWERS. Within four years (1982) these uniforms carried the Brewers into the world series and established the city as a solid major league baseball town. Not as spectacular as the wild "rollercoaster" ride with the Braves in the fifties, but a steady, determined corps of loyal fans to keep Milwaukee on the major league map for many years to come. Road uniforms changed from blue to gray in the mid '80's. The Brewers opened the new decade of the '90's with re-styled uniforms. Buttoned shirts, belts, and a script BREWERS at home were the most visible new features.

MINNESOTA TWINS

WELCOME TO THE BIG LEAGUES

In 1960, the American League announced its long-awaited formula for expansion to a ten-team circuit. A new franchise was awarded to Los Angeles and the Washington team was to transfer to the Twin Cities for the 1961 season. A replacement franchise in the nation's capital would continue the American League operation there. With a rich heritage of rival AAA minor league operations in both Minneapolis and St. Paul, a new single major league team had to consolidate fan support from both cities without favoring either. Thus, for the first time, an entire state was used to identify the new team, the MINNESOTA Twins —and the nickname was chosen to symbolize the solid support of the total metropolitan area.

Scarlet and navy blue were the trim colors for the new uniforms —a continuation of the color scheme used in Washington. In fact, the overall look of the new suits suggested an only slight alteration to the Senators' uniforms of 1960. The white home uniform carried over the pin stripes and the slanted script lettering of the team nickname. A special patch was designed for the left sleeve which portrayed two players shaking hands across the river —a representative symbol of Twin Cities allegiance. The navy blue cap displayed an interlocking white "T" and red "C" for Twin Cities —an "M" for Minnesota being avoided for fear of suggesting that it was a Minneapolis team. The undersweaters and stockings were solid navy and the gray road uniform was a duplicate of the home pin stripes. This uniform set remained unchanged for the next ten years. During the sixties, the team had jelled into a solid contender with a pennant in 1965 and a close second in 1967. This decade also provided some new heroes in slugger Harmon Killebrew and batting champ Tony Oliva.

JOINING THE DOUBLE-KNIT RAGE

Along with every other club in the early seventies, the Twins re-designed their uniform combination in 1972 to accommodate the new features of the double-knit styles. Pin stripes were dropped for the home whites. The new trousers for both home whites and road grays incorporated a red, white and blue striped sash in place of the standard belt. Additional red, white and blue striping was included down the trouser leg, on the sleeve ends, and around the collar. The new jerseys retained the buttoned front and the colors of the script TWINS were reversed to scarlet with a navy outline. A newly designed circular patch appeared on the left sleeve. The navy caps, undersweaters and socks were retained from 1971.

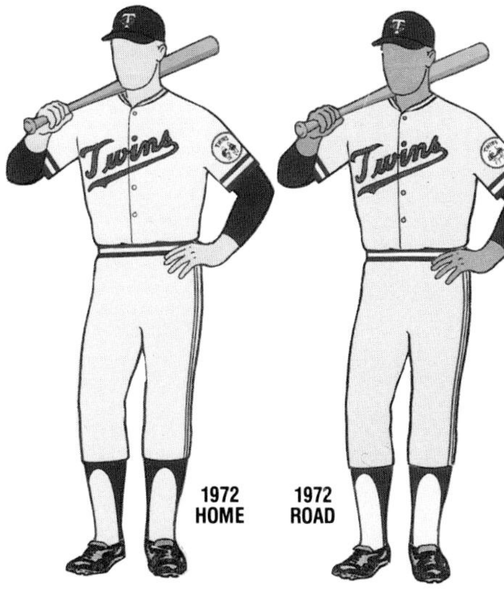

Further changes were introduced for the following season of 1973: the crown of the home cap was changed to scarlet, pull-over jerseys replaced the button fronts, the uniform number was added to the jersey front, and the sleeve patch was revised again into an outline shape of the state of Minnesota. Also, additional color was incorporated by making the home shoes red; and the gray road uniforms were now powder blue. The Twins in the seventies were pretty much perennially in the middle of the pack (after division titles in '69 and '70) but a new hitting phenom, Rod Carew, was the talk of the league. The uniform theme remained the same well into the decade of the eighties.

Slugger Harmon Killebrew, an early Twins favorite.

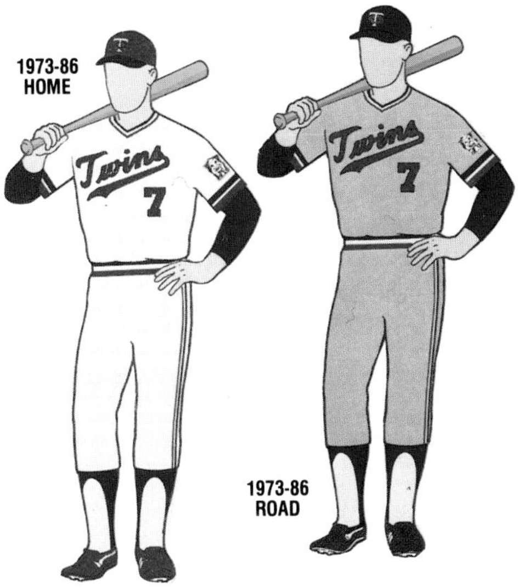

FINALLY, ALL THE MARBLES!

After the novelty of the new double-knit uniforms had begun to wear thin, the urge for a more traditional look in uniforms dictated another re-design for 1987. It was an encore for belts, buttons, pin stripes and gray uniforms for traveling. The franchise was now solidly established as a statewide (even regional) major league franchise and the inclusion of a stylized "M" on the cap could no longer offend the fans of St. Paul. The new uniforms were a classic blend of conservative uniform style with tasteful, modern graphics. The TWINS lettering on the home jersey was reminiscent of standard script, yet truly novel in typeface style. Pin stripes on the road grays added another touch of class to this new ensemble. The "M" from the cap was duplicated on the navy stirrup stocking but was seldom noticed because of the peculiar fads of the way players like to wear their trousers. The T-C monogram from the previous cap styles was repeated on the home shirt sleeve while a new "TWINS" patch was incorporated on the left sleeve of the road jersey. This handsome new uniform set of 1987 will forever be interpreted as a "uniform of destiny" as it provided the Twins fans with their first world championship. It will probably be with us for quite a few more seasons.

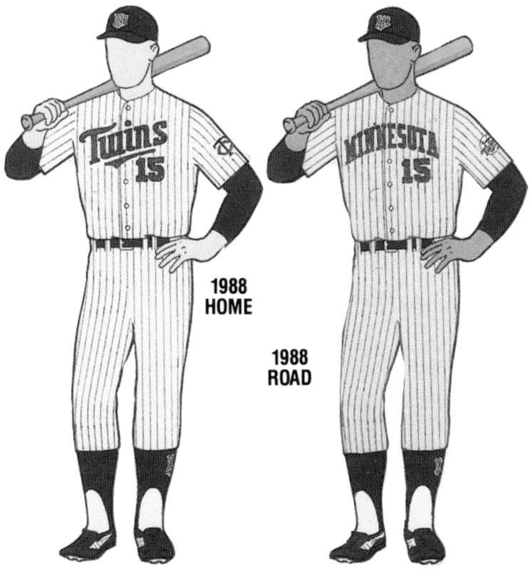

MONTREAL EXPOS

MAJOR LEAGUE BASEBALL INVADES THE PROVINCES

On May 27, 1968, the national game finally became international when the National League awarded the city of Montreal one of the two expansion franchises for the 1969 season. Inspired by the world's fair of the same name, EXPOS was chosen as the new team nickname and they were to play their home games at Jarry Park, the home field of their former AAA International League entry. Red, white and royal blue were chosen as the team colors, in keeping with the prevalent French-speaking influences in Quebec. A stylized M in these three colors was designed as the team emblem and would be displayed on the left breast of both home and road suits as well as on the front of the caps. The new home uniforms were the regulation white while a powder blue fabric was selected for the traveling suits. Undersweaters, socks, belt and most of the cap were to be solid royal blue. Even when the double-knit styles of pullover jerseys and built-in waistbands came along in the early seventies, the Expos kept the traditional look of buttoned fronts and separate belts on the trousers. Except for the addition of red and blue striping down the shoulder line and down the sides of the shirt and pants in 1981, the uniform theme has remained unchanged since the beginning of operation in 1969. With a long tradition of high level minor league baseball in the Canadian Metropolis behind them, the Expos' uniforms are well on their way to becoming a symbol of a new tradition —major league style.

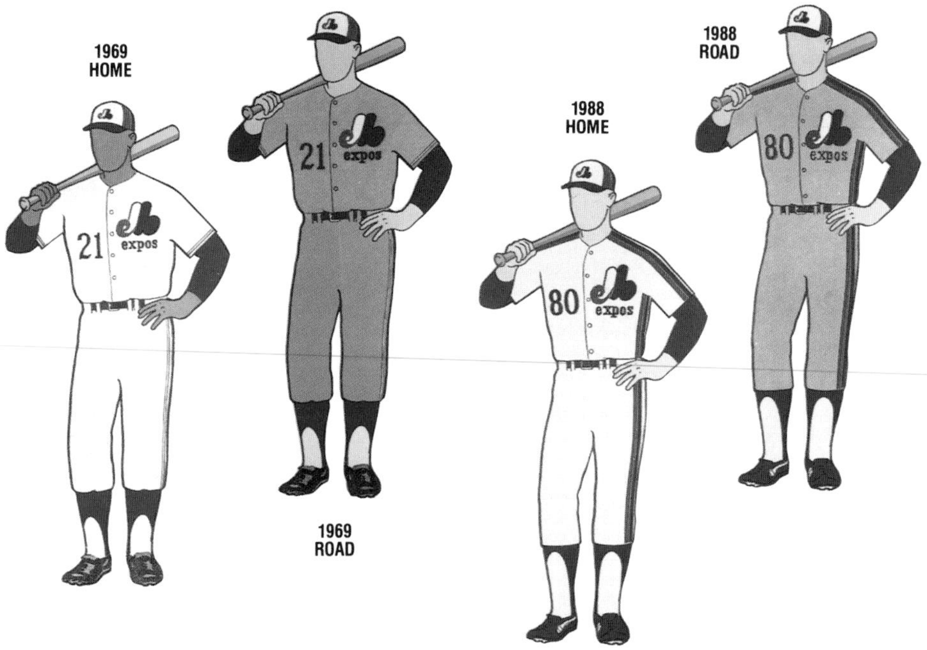

Perrenial all-star catcher Gary Carter swinging away in the double-knit Expos' uniform of the seventies.

"Le Grand Orange", Rusty Staub, an instant hit in Montreal's first year of operation —1969.

NEW YORK METS

THE NL IS BACK IN TOWN

The abrupt departure of both NYC National League clubs to the West Coast in 1958 made future league expansion a virtual certainty. The nation's #1 megalopolis was too lucrative a market to be denied National League baseball for very long after supporting two teams for so many years. When the announcement for 2 new franchises (Houston & New York) came, a poll was launched to select a nickname for the New Yorkers. The final selection was a resurrection of a 19th century NYC team name —the METROPOLITANS, or METS. The new team colors were to be Royal Blue and Orange. The new N-Y monogram was borrowed from the departed Giants and a circular team emblem patch was designated to be worn on the new uniform sleeves. The new home uniforms took a cue from the neighboring Yankees by including pinstripes. The overall effect was clean and classic —no piping and no sock stripes. A slanted script METS graced the jersey front in royal blue with an orange border. Socks, undersweater, and cap were solid Royal blue. The gray road uniforms employed thin piping around the collar and NEW YORK in arched fancy capitals —Royal blue trimmed with orange.

THE "AMAZIN' METS"

The first years at the Polo Grounds were nothing short of "black comedy". Casey Stengel's pick-up team was so inept in the early years (120 losses in '62 and 100+ for the next 3 years) they caught the immediate fancy of the New York fans —if for the wrong reason. The uniforms remained unchanged (except for a number added to the shirt front) thru the mid-seventies. It was the uniform of the 1969 "Amazin' Mets" world series victory. Yogi Berra's 1973 Met team (with aging superstar Willie Mays) surprised everybody by making an encore World Series appearance. The only other change in this original uniform set thru 1977 was on the road grays —NEW YORK was replaced by the script METS in 1975.

THE DOUBLE-KNIT AGE

For 1978, the Mets altered their uniform design to incorporate the new feature of double knit jerseys. The new shirts were pull-over style with a couple of buttons at the neck. Orange and blue striping trim was added to the sleeve ends and around the collar. They retained the belted trousers but added heavier striping down the leg of the road pants. This design continued into the early '80's, when the pullover jerseys were altered to a V-neck style. The new collars had solid blue trim on the home jerseys and new orange-blue-orange striping was added down the shoulder line and from the armpit all the way down to the trouser leg on both home and road suits. The last significant modifications were changing the METS on the travelling grays to a script NEW YORK and then to block letters in 1988. To celebrate their 25th year of existance, the Mets won it all in 1986. Their presence on the baseball scene has been so well received it is sometimes difficult to realize that they are a creature of expansion —their brief tradition belies their true age.

1975 ROAD

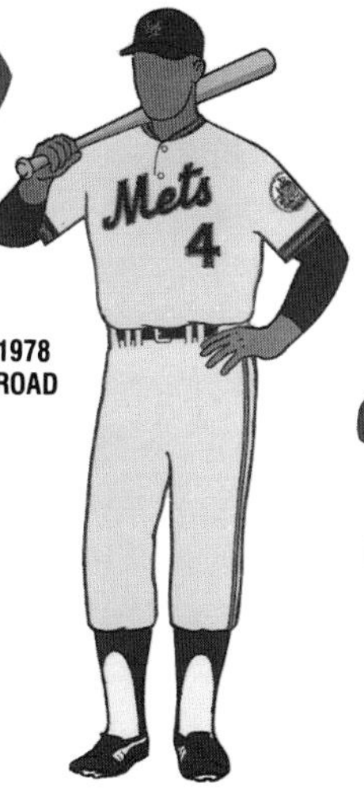

1978 ROAD

1962 HOME

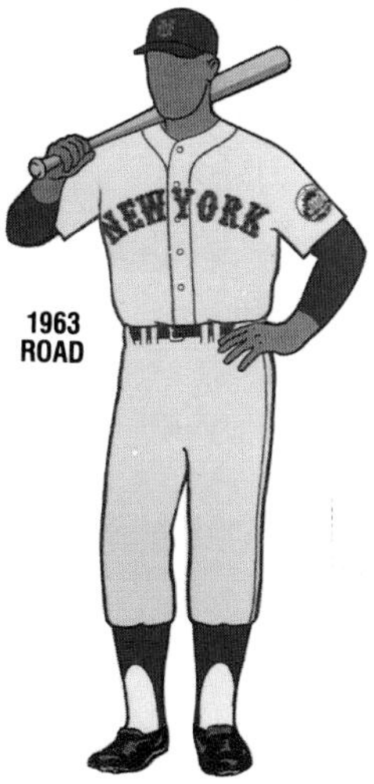

1963 ROAD

1973 HOME

Rusty Staub, a popular favorite in the Big Apple in the early seventies. His trademark was wearing his trousers and stirrup socks the "old-fashioned" way.

1988 HOME

1985 ROAD

1987 ROAD

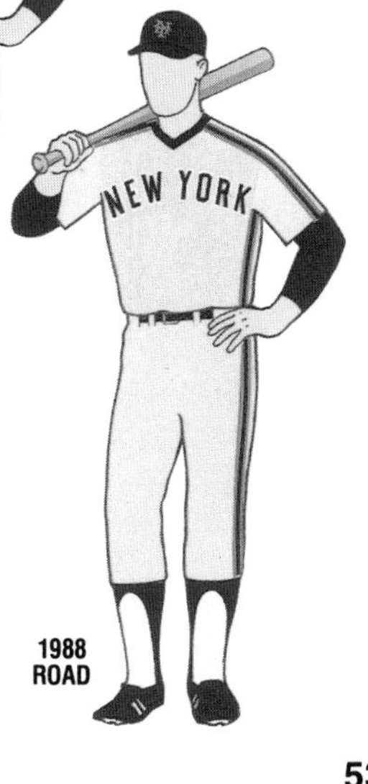

1988 ROAD

NEW YORK YANKEES

THE "HIGHLANDER" YEARS

After 2 years of disappointing attendance in Baltimore and the defection of John McGraw to the National League, the time was ripe for the fledgling American League to transfer the Orioles franchise to New York City. On April 29, 1903, the New York Americans (or "Highlanders") played their opening game at the hastily conceived Hilltop Park. The new home uniforms were the customary white with black trimmings. The caps had a white crown with black piping down the seams of the crown and a black visor. The stockings were solid black, as were the shirt collar and the large, overly decorative N and Y on the left and right breast of the jersey. The road uniform for this maiden season was a dark "reverse image" version of the home suits. This design was repeated for the 1904 season although the color was changed from black to a dark blue.

For 1905, the N and Y were simplified and merged into a monogram on the left breast —a forerunner of the famous emblem of later years. The road uniform reverted to a traditional gray and otherwise duplicated the home whites. For the following season (1906), the N and Y were once again separated and placed on the right and left breast. The road suits also reverted to the dark negative "reverse" of the home uniform. For 1907, the N and Y were modified to a straight square-serif style and the road uniform was once again the traditional gray, This pattern was repeated for 1908 except that the N and Y were restored to a more ornamental style. The home caps were changed from white to a solid black.

The new uniforms for the 1909 season incorporated some significant new features: red stripes were included on the navy blue stockings and the now legendary Yankee monogram made its first appearance on the front of the cap and on the left sleeve. By this time, the new nickname "Yankees" was used as often as "Highlanders" and was only a few more years away from becoming the "offical" team nickname. The new monogram caught on and remained on the left sleeve and cap the following season. By 1910, the old style regular collar was abandoned in favor of the short stand-up "cadet" style —a popular uniform trend of the period. The solid navy cadet collar also featured a small red "N" and "Y" straddling the top shirt button.

In 1911, another significant feature first appeared on the gray travelling uniforms —the full city name NEW YORK was spelled out in arched capital letters identical to the current style on today's Yankee road suits. The new stockings also featured a wide white band about half-way down.

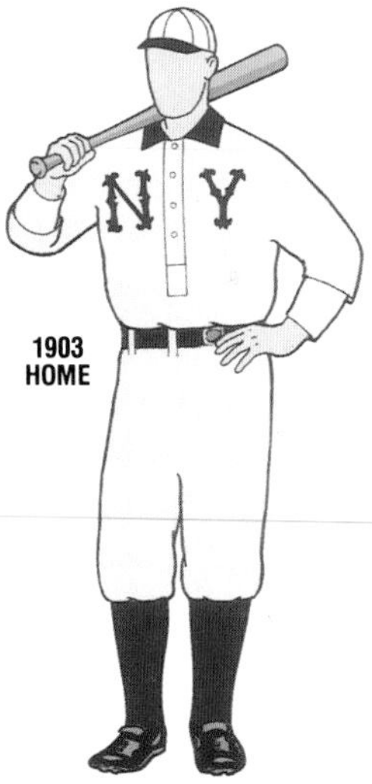

1903
HOME

1904
ROAD

Jack Chesbro "on the road" in 1903

1905
HOME

1906
ROAD

1906
HOME

1907
ROAD

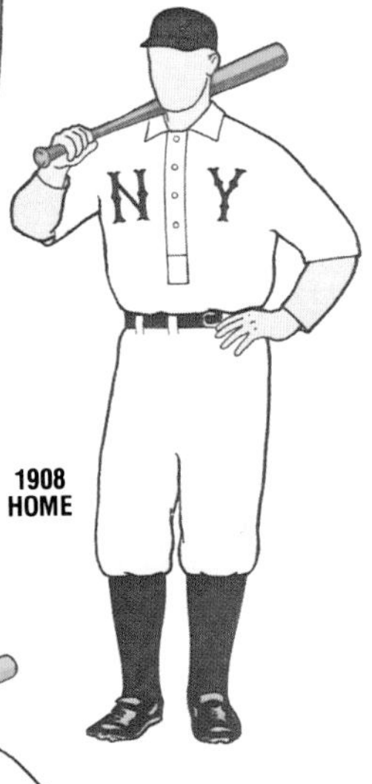

1908
HOME

Hal Chase in 1909
The prototype of the famous Yankee emblem on the sleeve.

1910
HOME

1911
ROAD

1912 HOME

1912 ROAD

1913 HOME

1914 ROAD

THE POLO GROUNDS ERA

The 1912 season was to be the last one played at old Hilltop Park, whose lofty location on upper Manhattan originally inspired the "Highlanders" name. By this time, the name "Yankees" was more or less the offical team name and the new home uniforms introduced an important precedent in establishing a great Yankee tradition. The season opener was reported by the New York Times:

"The Yankees presented a natty appearance in their new uniforms of white with black pin stripes"

Little did they realize that they were being introduced to the original version of the most famous baseball uniform design in the history of the game. The uniform itself had the baggy, wool-flannel look; a closer fitting cap crown made from the same pin-striped fabric as the jersey and pants; but it was the genuine article. The legendary NY monogram (albeit a bit larger than in later years) was emblazened on the left breast in all its glory.

In 1913, the Yankees abandoned old Hilltop Park in favor of a joint-tenancy arrangement with the Giants at the more commodious Polo Grounds. Resistance to the American League "Invaders" had long since given way to recognition. The new deal was also partly offered as retribution for allowing the Giants to use Hilltop Park temporarily after the disastrous Polo Grounds fire of 1911. For the first 2 seasons at Polo Grounds, the Yankees home uniforms temporarily excluded pin stripes but retained the NY logo on the left breast. The wide white stripe on the black stockings was also retained.

The NEW YORK lettering on the travelling grays went from the plain capital letters to "fancy" style capitals for 1914 and 1915, then returned to the same plain block letters by 1917 but with a new twist: pinstripes (the only time this was included on the "NEW YORK" road suits). When the plain gray material and the standard arched block letters were restored in 1918, the future standard for Yankees road uniforms was established (save for a few more years of white bottoms on the stockings). The pinstripes on the home whites were also retained as a permanent feature by this time but for reasons unknown, the NY monogram was removed from the home jersey in 1916. And speaking of pinstripes, the fact is that although this uniform feature is commonly identified with legendary Yankee dynasties of the past, the wearing of pinstripes was never an exclusive property of the New Yorkers and they did not introduce them to major league baseball. Pinstriped fabrics of various widths were already in vogue by the time they first appeared on a Yankee player.

Roger Peckinpaugh at the Polo Grounds in 1914

1915 HOME

1917 ROAD

Home Run Baker in his pin-striped 1916 road uniform

1921 HOME

1921 ROAD

THE BABE RUTH ERA

One of the other myths that seem to be eagerly consumed by the baseball public without factual support is the story that pinstripes were selected for the Yankee uniform by Owner Col. Jacob Ruppert because they tended to offset the portly appearance of his prize acquisition —George Herman Ruth. Of course the truth is that the New Yorkers were wearing pinstripes when the Babe was still in the orphanage. Considerations for the great one's appearance in uniform could only have perpetuated their use at most. The home uniform for Ruth's first years as a Yankee (1920-21) still had the white bottoms on the stockings and the cap crown had matching pinstripes with a blue bill and blue NY monogram on the cap front.

By 1923, the opening season at Yankee Stadium, both socks and cap were solid navy blue and the NY cap monogram was white. All during the twenties, the jersey collar had the tapered extension (as did most team uniforms of that decade) and the sleeves were often elbow length and longer. The now familiar grey "NEW YORK" road uniform also went to solid navy hose and cap, continuing through the 1926 season.

In 1927 (the Yankee team considered by many to be the mightiest of all time) the road uniform displaced NEW YORK with YANKEES in the same blue block letters. This road uniform lasted until 1930 and marked the only time in the franchise history that the team's nickname was spelled out on the uniform. In 1929, the Yankees established the precedent of permanent uniform numbers on the backs of the jerseys. The idea caught on quickly and became standard for all teams by 1932.

A pensive Lou Gehrig in his 1939 home pinstripes (note centennial patch)

The Babe in 1920 or 1921

For 1931, the standard NEW YORK was reinstated on the road grays and the tapered collar extension was subsequently dropped (by this time many players were surgically removing it anyway). The plain pinstriped home whites remained the same through 1935, a year after the Babe's final season as a Yankee. This fact brings out a curious (and probably useless) tidbit of trivia: Although the now familiar home pinstripes with Yankee monogram on the jersey front both preceded and followed Ruth's Yankees years, he never wore this uniform as a player.

FROM DIMAGGIO & MANTLE TO THE EIGHTIES

In 1936, the NY monogram was once again displayed on the jersey front. For the first few years of its resurrection, it was smaller than the current edition and the ends of the letters were somewhat more flared but it was the beginning of the still current run of continuous usage. Except for the normal evolutionary difference in style, fabric, tailoring, etc., the DiMaggios, Ruffings, Dickeys, et al could walk out on the Yankee Stadium turf today and practically blend in with the Mattinglys, Winfields, Guidrys—a fact that warms the hearts of baseball traditionalists in an era of sometimes constant changes and new design innovations. The same could be said for the Yankee road uniforms except for some white trim around the letters and added piping on the sleeve ends of today's uniforms. These trim features appeared in 1972 when the Yankees, along with all the other clubs, joined the "double knit" revolution.

PHILADELPHIA/KANSAS CITY
OAKLAND ATHLETICS

WHAT'S IN A NAME?

The team name ATHLETICS (be it from Philadelphia, Kansas City, or Oakland) has a unique status dating back to the earliest years of the American League's formation. All the other clubs seemed loathe to refer to themselves by their nicknames —after all, that was merely an invention of the writers who covered the game and was only a device to economize on space and break up the monotony of identifying the teams in their games stories. While all the other clubs were formally known as the Boston Americans, the Greater New Yorks, etc., the Athletics were called simply the ATHLETICS (or A's) without mention of Philadelphia and everybody knew what they meant. The story of the first 5 decades in Philadelphia has to also be the story of one man —the guiding hand of the team for all those years —Connie Mack. Mack was the father figure who had the last word on everything from the front office on down to the playing field.

THE FIRST DECADE

The standard Athletics uniforms for the first five or six years in the league were plain white at home and plain gray on the road, with a large blue A on the left breast. The stockings were solid blue on both versions and both home and the road caps occasionally included a thin band of blue around the base of the cap crown. The jersey was a pullover style with a regular fold-down collar and buttons half-way down the front. The sleeves were most often elbow length. Later in the decade, the trim on the road uniform was changed to maroon. Also, the plain cap crown later included piping trim down the seams of the crown. In 1909 (to coincide with the opening of Shibe Park), the round cap crown was replaced by a "Cap Anson" pillbox style with 4 thin horizontal bands of piping and the solid stocking gave way to a white version with 2 dark stripes. The standard "A" was retained on the left breast, but these 2 new uniform modifications became symbolic with possibly the greatest dynasty years of Connie Mack's long reign.

The great Eddie Plank about 1908. Note wrinkled shirt, wide belt, no belt tunnels

"BREAK UP THE WHITE ELEPHANTS"

The Mackmen's chief rivals during the early years of the century were John McGraw's Giants. McGraw had managed the Baltimore Orioles of the American League in 1901-02 before jumping back to the established National League to manage the New York team. McGraw and Mack were old cronies, both members of the clan of Irishmen which dominated the game around the turn of the century. After turning his back on the new league, McGraw disdainfully referred to Mack's Athletics as "white elephants" —a description which Mack adopted with more charity than its utterance had intended. The nickname stuck and when the the two teams met in the 1905 World Series, McGraw was ceremoniously presented with a small white elephant toy —which he good naturedly accepted. The Giants went on to capture the series in 5 games, but the white elephant nickname persevered and became a part of Athletics uniform history for many more decades to come. Its first appearance on team uniforms was on the team sweaters later in the decade.

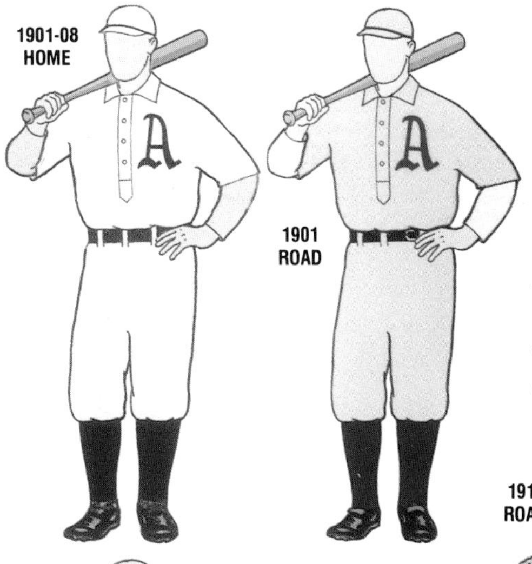

Although Mack's teams had won pennants in 1902 and 1905, the Athletics of 1910–1914 were legendary in their dominance of the game. Paced by future hall-of-famers Eddie Plank, Chief Bender, Eddie Collins and "Home Run" Baker, they won 3 world championships in 4 years. The Athletics uniform was probably the most photographed of the period and became identified with winning baseball. Sadly, this powerhouse team was prematurely broken up due to Mack's failing financial standing. His entire premier infield of McInnis, Collins, Barry and Baker were sold off for the then staggering sum of $100,000 and the team's fortunes went downhill accordingly. Even the famous uniform could not transform mediocrity into excellence. In keeping with general trends in uniform design, the turn-down collar was abandoned and pin stripes were standard on the home uniform by 1915. The famous "pillbox" striped cap was also history by the end of the decade—replaced by a basic round crown with piping up the seams. The standard "A" on the jersey remained virtually unaltered although the color was changed to black for a time. About 1918, the elephant symbol (albeit blue, not white) with a white "A" inside was worn on the left sleeve—its first appearance on a game uniform.

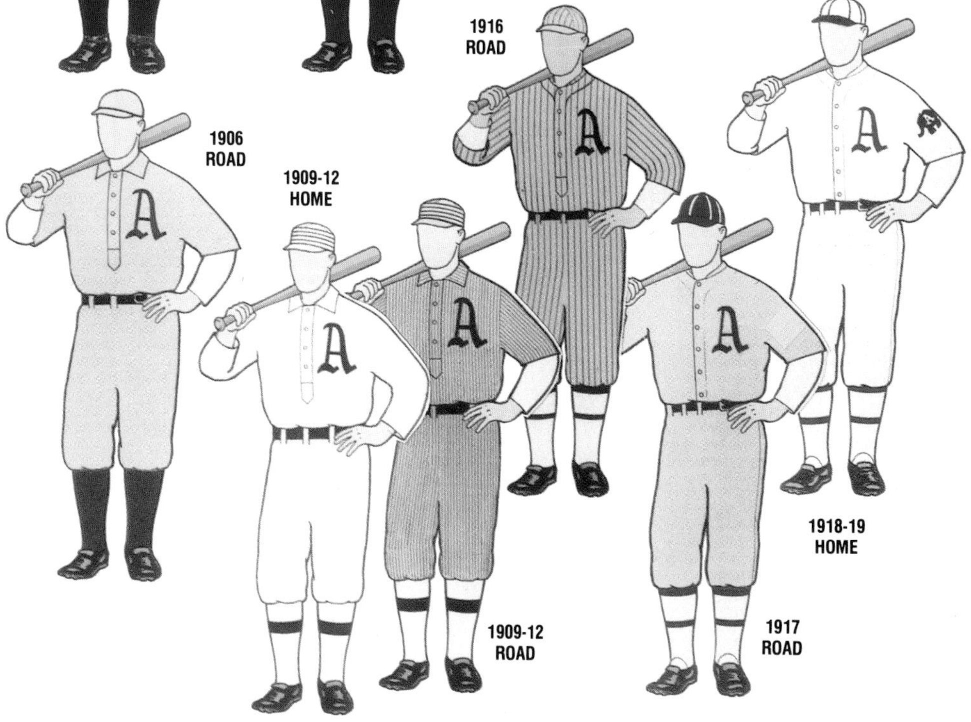

THE TWENTIES —MORE ELEPHANTS AND A RETURN TO GLORY

It has been said that Connie Mack's teams over the years were either unbearable or unbeatable—seldom in between. The decade of the twenties illustrates this axiom quite dramatically—last place in 1920-21, world championships in 1929-30. By 1918, Mr. Mack had fully adopted McGraw's unsolicited "elephant" label as a desirable graphic symbol for the team. The famous "A" was eventually removed from the jersey for the first time and replaced with a blue elephant. The famous 2 stripes-on-white stockings were also modified to solid blue on the upper half. In 1924, he made the blue elephant white to comply with McGraw's original dictum. If one can believe that Mack was at least mildly superstitious (as were most baseball men) he must have felt that the elephant signified better luck, as the team fortunes improved somewhat with the new pachyderm displayed. Fading legends Ty Cobb and Tris Speaker were added to the roster but the arrival of coming superstars Cochrane, Foxx, Simmons, Grove, et al, marked the emergence of a new dynasty. The elephant had seemingly served its purpose, as the familiar "A" was restored to the jersey front in 1928. The two stripes were also restored on the home white stockings (the road sox were a reverse version). The caps for 1928 were a plain white or gray crown with blue bill. An "A" was also added to the cap for the first time. For inexplicable reasons, the onset of the great depression seemed to spur a virtual rejuvenation of colors on major league uniforms after a decade of relative drabness and simplicity.

Connie Mack and pinch-hitter Eddie Collins at Comiskey Park about 1929

1920 ROAD

1922 HOME

1925 ROAD

1930 HOME

1930 ROAD

1940 HOME

1948 ROAD

MR. MACK SELF-DESTRUCTS AGAIN

Because of Mack's inability to bankroll the payroll demands of a team of superstars or even (as some say) his reluctance to hoard talent, once again an Athletics dynasty was prematurely dismantled. Hard times affected almost everyone, including winners, and one by one the likes of Grove, Foxx, Simmons, Cochrane, etc. were peddled off to other American League teams. By 1935, the once proud Athletics finished last and remained there for most of the last years of the thirties and on into the forties. The uniforms continued in the standard blue —the only difference between the road and home versions (besides white vs. gray) being that the home cap had a white crown with a blue bill while the road cap was solid blue. The same basic uniform prevailed throughout the '40's except that the home cap was also made solid blue.

THE END OF AN ERA

1950 was a milestone year for Connie Mack —5 decades at the helm —an incredible stretch that will probably never be matched (even the perennial John McGraw only lasted 30 years). To commemorate the occasion, the team uniforms were spruced up with gold trimming and a golden anniversary patch was worn on the left sleeve. After climbing up to the middle of the pack in '48 and '49, the team did its part in typifying the unbearable —losing 102 games and once again finishing dead last in the American League standings. It was the begining of the end for the Connie Mack era and the team's long residence in the city of brotherly love. Enough was enough, and after the Boston Braves shift to Milwaukee in 1953, the idea of seeking greener pastures was no longer unthinkable. Under new ownership, the team uniforms were totally redesigned for the waning days in Shibe Park. The long-standing blue "A" on the jersey front was dropped in favor of a script "ATHLETICS" on both home whites and road grays. Extra red trim piping was added to the blue from top to bottom — even a daring red, white and blue belt was issued. Unfortunately, the new ensemble was unable to avert the inevitable —103 losses and a last place finish for the final season in Philadelphia.

1950 HOME

1954 HOME

NEW FRONTIERS ON THE FRONTIER

With franchise shifts now acceptable, the team went West to open the 1955 season as the Kansas City Athletics. Their first uniforms were a carry-over from the last year in Philadelphia —a script "ATHLETICS" only with the red and blue colors reversed. The famous "A" was retained on the cap for a few more years and a second red & white stripe was added to the stockings. Another old tradition —the elephant —was kept alive in the team emblem which was worn on the left sleeve. Pin stripes were worn on the home whites briefly for the first time in many decades. By 1962, the road grays were totally revamped, erasing any links with their Philadelphia past. The city name "Kansas City" was inscribed across the jersey front in solid navy script and a K-C monogram was displayed on the cap front. The new uniform was definitely plain and conservative —no piping, no stripes, and only solid navy blue trim —but there was one new innovation. Besides the standard number on the back, the player's number was repeated on the sleeve —a hint of more radical innovations to come.

When Charles O. Finley purchased the Kansas City franchise in the early sixties, his presence was felt immediately. With more and more color television coverage of baseball, he saw fit to challenge the long-standing notion of basic white and gray uniform ensembles. Tradition be damned! —he jolted the baseball world by experimenting with heretofore unmentionable color combinations and various innovative devices. The sleeveless vest was introduced to the American League by the A's along with Cleveland (the idea actually began with the Cubs in 1940). The undershirts were red and navy at first, with the name "ATHLETICS" in arched fancy capital letters across the chest. Charley O. elected to distinguish his manager and coaches from the troops by assigning them white cap crowns. Next, the undershirts were made short-sleeved with white numbers on the sleeves.

But this was only the beginning. Soon the idea of an exotic blend of "Wedding Gown" white, "Kelly" green, and "Tulane" gold in various combinations became the new order from the desk of Mr. Finley. And, yes, even the shoes were white. In a solitary gesture for the sake of team tradition, he ressurrected the old capital "A" on the jersey front but there the conformity ended. The scheme of a single uniform theme for home and another for the road was discarded —much to the dismay of league fathers and traditionalists. The debate still rages over this today as many teams in the color TV age have drifted into some bizarre uniform ensembles and back again to the "basics".

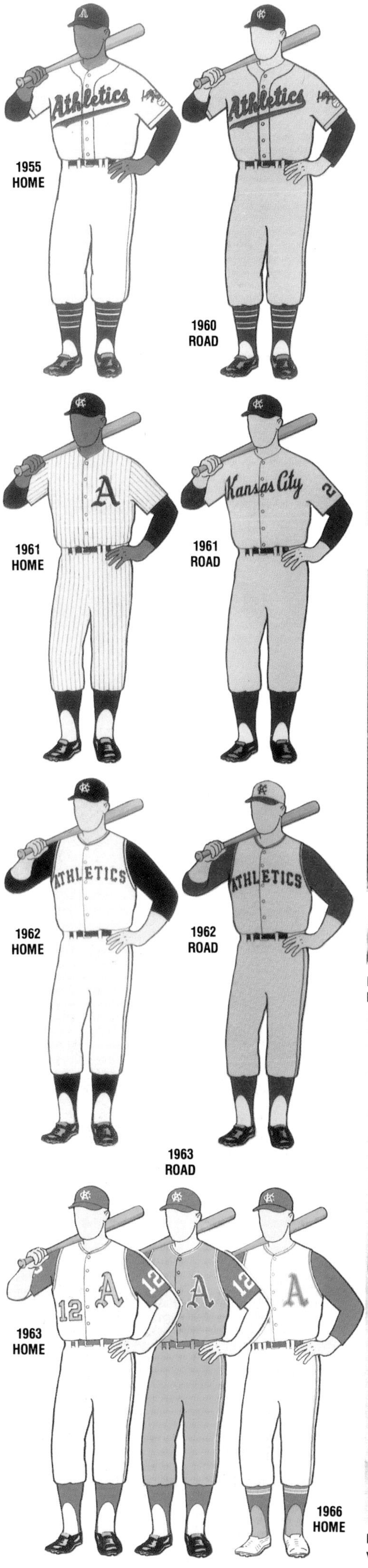

Pitcher Bobby Shantz in the first Kansas City uniform, complete with elephant patch.

Manager Hank Bauer accepting some "beef" at Municipal Stadium in 1961

Infielder Jerry Lumpe models the first A's sleeveless vest in 1962

OFF AGAIN TO THE WEST

By 1967, the rebellious Mr. Finley had had it with Kansas City. He thumbed his nose at the league and abruptly uprooted his KC franchise in favor of Oakland where a brand new coliseum was beckoning. The new Oakland uniforms for 1968 were still the same green, gold and white combinations except that the city name "OAKLAND" was displayed on the jersey front in fancy capital letters. In a sense, the traditional "A" was retained in that the letters used to spell OAKLAND were of the same style as the familiar A. As if to further flaunt tradition, he supplied ever-changing fanciful descriptions to his uniform colors —i.e. "FORT KNOX gold, "PACIFIC OCEAN" green, "POLAR BEAR" white, etc., etc..

By the early seventies, all major league teams were converting over to the new double-knit uniform fabrics and Oakland joined the parade. Closer-fitting, yet more comfortable, lighter and cooler, easier to launder and more durable —the change-over was irresistable. The important tailoring features of the double knits were the pullover style shirt and the built-in sash belt —no more buttons and no more separate belts. The new A's double knits retained the bright green and gold color combination with new striping around the collar, on the sleeve ends, on the belt sash and down the trouser leg. The old familiar capital A was returned to the left breast —with a small "s" added. This particular ensemble has a permanent place in the hearts of Oakland fans as it was the uniform of the Athletics third great dynasty —the world champs of 1972-73-74. The Charles O. Finley era had its finest hours in this uniform and was about to end.

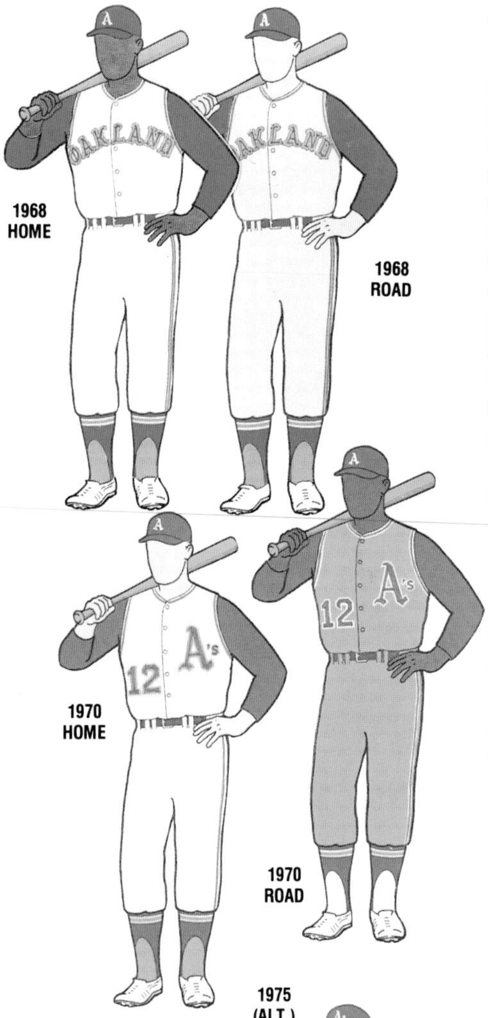

THE TREND REVERSES

By the end of the seventies, green and gold were firmly established as the identifying symbol of Oakland baseball. The myriad of uniform combinations continued but the pendulum was tilting back to more conservative tastes (as it has repeatedly done in the long history of baseball uniforms). The bright Kelly (or "Pacific Ocean"?) green was toned down to a more somber forest green shade by 1980. As an alternative home uniform, a button jersey and belt-loop trousers were restored in the early eighties. The city name OAKLAND was restored to the versions of the road uniform and also to the home uniform in 1986. Even the amount of possible uniform color combinations was reduced.

For 1987, the conservative trend had the last word...a single basic uniform scheme for home and likewise for the gray road uniform. Although an alternative pullover style jersey was worn occasionally both at home and on the road, it was buttoned shirts and belt-loop trousers in 1987. The old standard slanted script lettering was displayed across the chest —"ATHLETICS" at home, "OAKLAND" on the road. And the final stroke was that those beloved white shoes were to be discarded in favor of basic black, but a last minute players resistance preserved the whites. For the traditionalists, it was a partial victory —only fully complete when the famous "A" returns to the left breast (the elephant has already encored on the '88 sleeves).

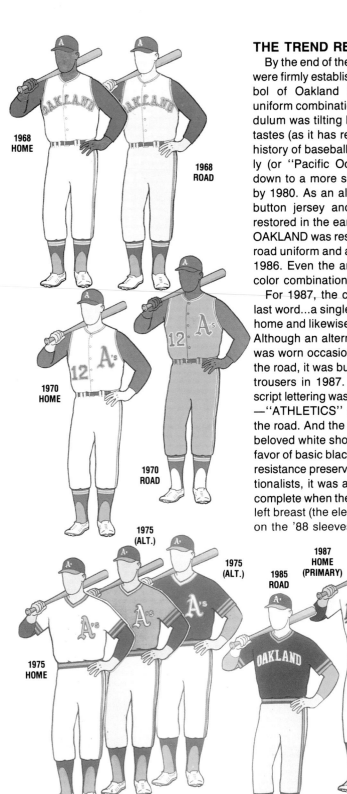

A key performer for Oakland's winning teams of the early seventies —Sal Bando

PHILADELPHIA PHILLIES

IN THE 19TH CENTURY

The Phillies joined the National League in 1883, only six years after the league was formed. Evidence of early Philly uniforms is indeed sparse but team photos from the 1890's show the abbreviated city name PHILA on the shirt fronts of some versions (possibly road uniforms) and either an Old English or standard capital P on others. Oddly, after the turn of the century the team uniforms never again displayed the city name —not even on road uniforms. The block capital P did, however, become a standard feature for several decades into the 1900's.

THE EARLY 1900'S

For almost the entire decade of 1900-1910, both home and road uniforms displayed the squared capital P on the left breast of the jerseys. Sketchy evidence suggests that the trim colors used during this decade were at times BLACK, RED, or MAROON. The P itself varied slightly in size and at times was without serifs. Home uniforms were always white (featuring a dark fold-down collar around 1900) with a standard buttoned front and turned-down regular collar. Traveling uniforms were the standard gray with similar trim features. Cap styles around 1901-2 were the "pillbox" style, either solid dark or with horizontal striping. From 1903-5 the white home caps had the close-fitting, round crown with piping down the crown seams and a trim stripe around the base of the crown. The road caps were solid dark with white piping emanating from the top button. In 1909, the capital P was removed from the shirt front and displayed on the left sleeve of both home whites and road grays. The caps were solid dark (presumably black) and with a higher, fuller crown.

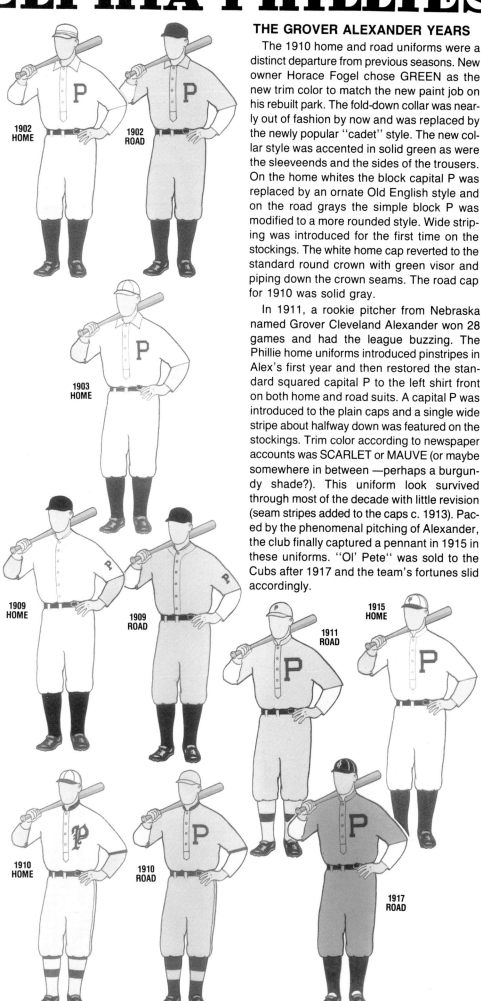

1902 HOME

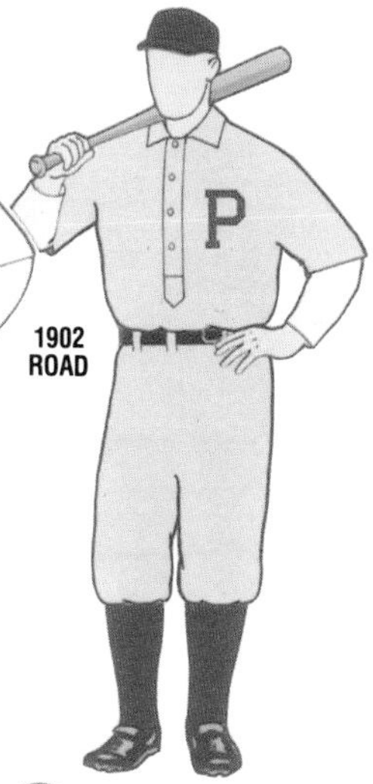

1902 ROAD

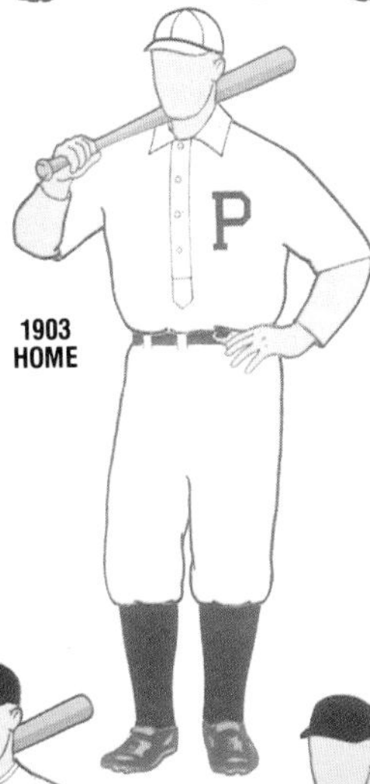

1903 HOME

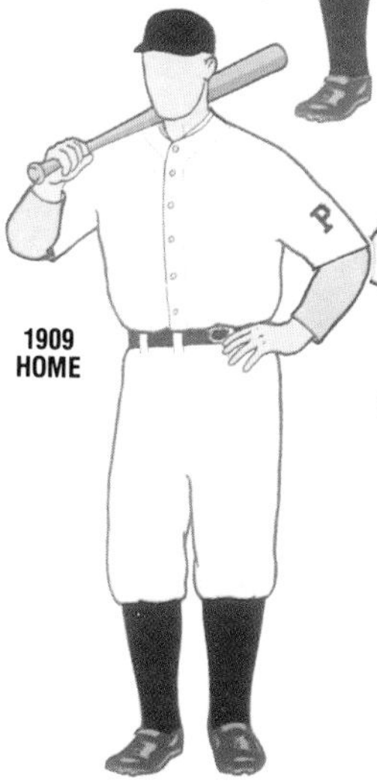

1909 HOME

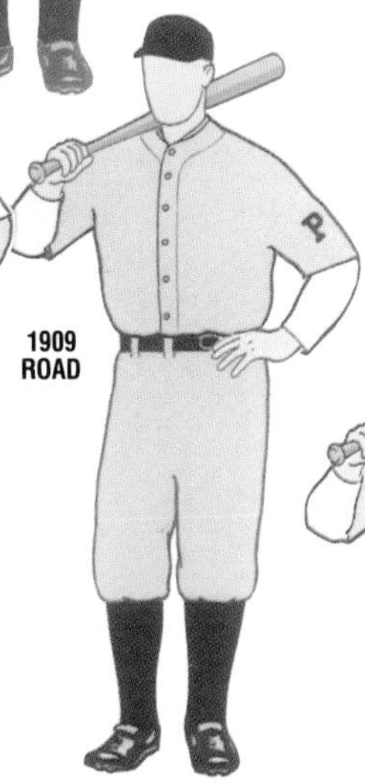

1909 ROAD

"Red" Dooin, solid backstop for the Phils from 1902-14, poses for Conlon's camera at the Polo Grounds in 1910.

THE GROVER ALEXANDER YEARS

The 1910 home and road uniforms were a distinct departure from previous seasons. New owner Horace Fogel chose GREEN as the new trim color to match the new paint job on his rebuilt park. The fold-down collar was nearly out of fashion by now and was replaced by the newly popular "cadet" style. The new collar style was accented in solid green as were the sleeveends and the sides of the trousers. On the home whites the block capital P was replaced by an ornate Old English style and on the road grays the simple block P was modified to a more rounded style. Wide striping was introduced for the first time on the stockings. The white home cap reverted to the standard round crown with green visor and piping down the crown seams. The road cap for 1910 was solid gray.

In 1911, a rookie pitcher from Nebraska named Grover Cleveland Alexander won 28 games and had the league buzzing. The Phillie home uniforms introduced pinstripes in Alex's first year and then restored the standard squared capital P to the left shirt front on both home and road suits. A capital P was introduced to the plain caps and a single wide stripe about halfway down was featured on the stockings. Trim color according to newspaper accounts was SCARLET or MAUVE (or maybe somewhere in between —perhaps a burgundy shade?). This uniform look survived through most of the decade with little revision (seam stripes added to the caps c. 1913). Paced by the phenomenal pitching of Alexander, the club finally captured a pennant in 1915 in these uniforms. "Ol' Pete" was sold to the Cubs after 1917 and the team's fortunes slid accordingly.

1911 ROAD

1915 HOME

1910 HOME

1910 ROAD

1917 ROAD

THE DREADFUL DECADE OF THE TWENTIES

The Phillies had plunged into the league cellar in 1919 and began a painfully long era of permanent residency in the second division—in last place more often than not. In 1921, the uniforms reflected the first significant redesign in a decade. The "cadet" collar was replaced by the now popular "V-neck" style—almost collarless with a brief tapered extension around the back of the neck. Pinstripes were introduced on both home whites and road grays. The familiar P on the left breast was now enclosed in a circle. Both home and road caps were the plain standard solid dark (BLACK or NAVY). The stockings were solid dark with two bands of maroon around the calf. For 1923, the circle around the P was dropped and the letter P enlarged to its earlier size. A small capital P was restored on the front of the caps. The stockings were now half white (or gray) from the calf down to the ankle.

The year 1925 marked the 50th anniversary of the National League and all teams observed the occasion by wearing a large circular blue and gold patch either on the shirt front or on the sleeve. The Phils opted for the left sleeve, as did most of the clubs. The uniforms for 1925 resurrected a version of the Old English style P on the shirt front and cap. By 1927, the P on the road grays was transplanted to the sleeve and was enclosed in a heavy diamond shape. The stockings by this time featured a simple wide band of red and caps had a red visor to complement the white or gray crown. This general trim theme persisted in the early years of the next decade.

Manager Art Fletcher at Ebbetts Field 1923.

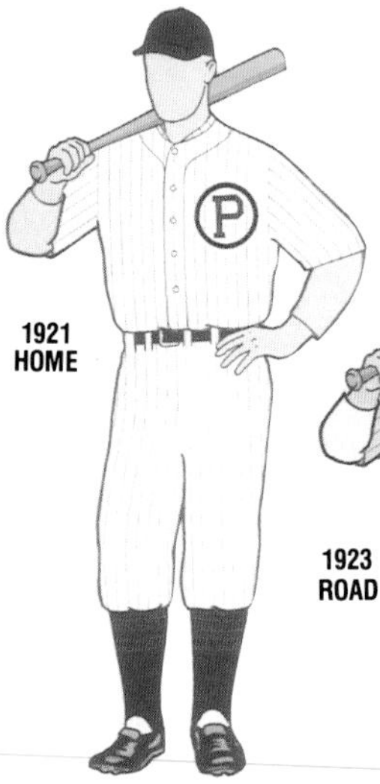

1921
HOME

1923
ROAD

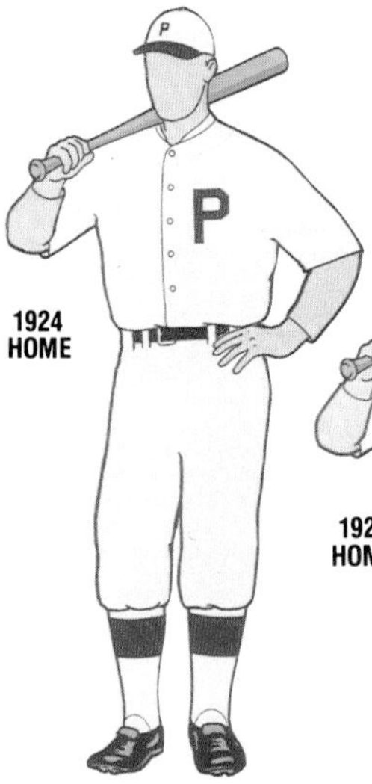

1924
HOME

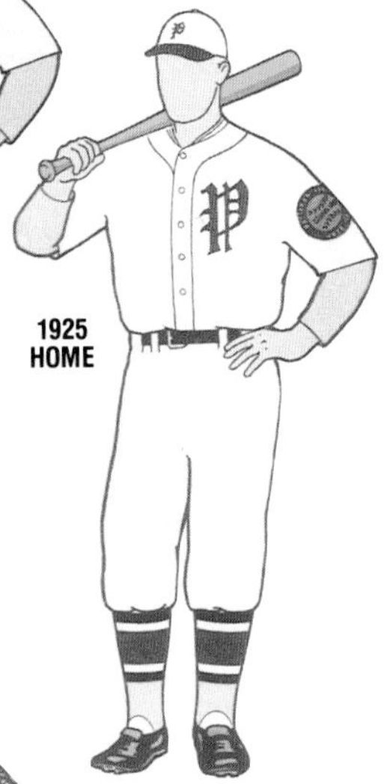

1925
HOME

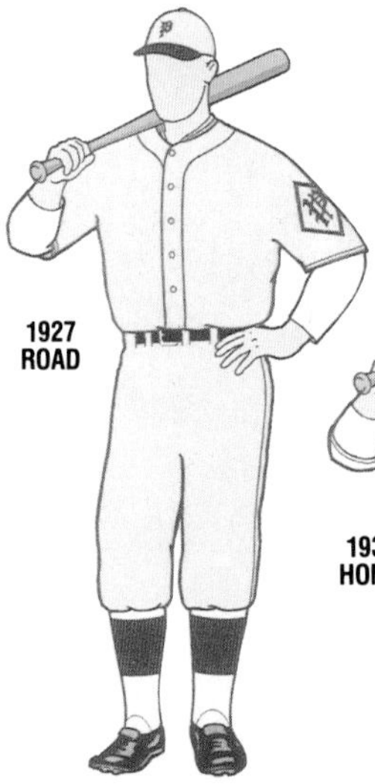

1927
ROAD

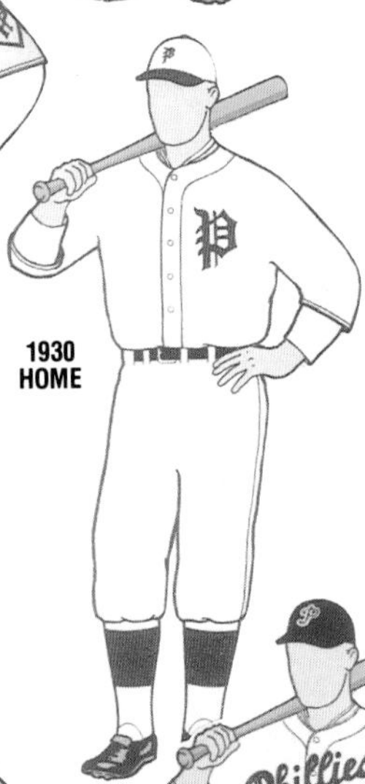

1930
HOME

DEPRESSION AND NEW COLOR SCHEMES

The Phillies entered the decade of the thirties still mired in the second division. About the only relief was to cheer the slugging feats of future hall of famer Chuck Klein. As was the practice then, black arm bands were worn on the left sleeve of the uniform during 1931 to commemorate the death of owner William F. Baker. For the 1933 season, the Phillies broke with long-standing tradition by introducing a slanted, full-script PHILLIES on their gray road uniforms for that year. Detroit had begun the practice in 1930 and the Cubs used it on their 1932 alternate road uniforms. It was just one of many new innovations in major league uniforms in that period but it was the beginning of a new pattern for Phillie uniforms in future decades. A new wave of more colorful uniform ideas was sweeping the major league scene and the Phillies jumped on the bandwagon. The following season (1934) they revamped their uniform look by mixing red, white and blue trim in contrast to the plain red trim of previous seasons. The script PHILLIES was embellished with an underline flourish and was now included on the shirts of the home uniforms. The home and road caps were now solid navy with a red script P outlined in white. This general design scheme (with some minor modifications) was continued through the 1937 season.

The first script-style PHILLIES lettering on the 1933 road shirts, modeled by Al Todd.

1933
ROAD

1934
HOME

1934
ROAD

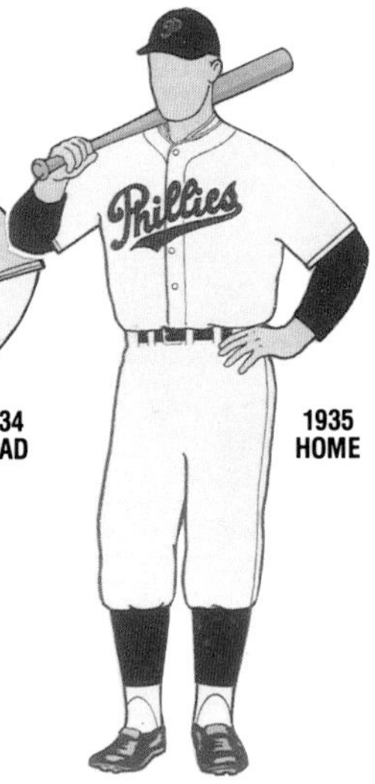

1935
HOME

For the 1938 season, the red, white and blue color trim was temporarily set aside for a combination of GOLD and ROYAL BLUE. The script PHILLIES was replaced on the home jerseys with a large block capital P in blue and gold. The block P was repeated in gold and white on the solid blue caps. The PHILLIES script on the pearl gray road jerseys was slightly re-styled and done in blue and gold. Stockings were solid royal blue. A circular blue and gold club insignia was placed on the left sleeve of both home and road uniforms. The year 1938 was also the end of the road for Baker Bowl as the Phils entered a joint tenancy agreement with the Athletics at Shibe Park. In 1939, the uniforms retained the same general graphics but reverted back to the red, white and blue color scheme. The uniforms remained basically unchanged through the 1941 season.

1938
HOME

1938
ROAD

1939
HOME

1940
ROAD

WWII AND THE ERSTWHILE BLUE JAYS

By World War II (perhaps weary with the perennial losers image of two decades) it was decided that the Philadelphia National League Club was to be re-christened BLUE JAYS (with apologies to the future Toronto franchise). For whatever reason, the new nickname failed to catch on (a similar fate for the Boston BEES) —nor was it ever implemented into the uniform graphics except for a brief appearance of a blue jay symbol on the sleeve. In fact, the name PHILLIES (or even PHILS) was displayed on the uniforms even while the new nickname was supposedly official. The 1942 road uniform dropped the red trim and went back to the basics —gray with navy blue trim. In place of script, the name PHILS in arched block capital letters was displayed on the shirt front.

1942
ROAD

1943
HOME

1945
HOME

1945
ROAD

The austere look of solid navy trim was continued in 1943 with a new version of the script PHILLIES on both home and road suits. For 1944-45, the plain image was spruced up somewhat with some extra piping and stars added to dot the "i's" in PHILLIES. Ironically, the only bright spot on these drab uniforms was the small patriotic shield which all major league clubs displayed on their sleeves during the war. The first postwar season was to include a distinct sartorial face-lift for the cellar-dwelling Phillies.

THE COMING OF THE WHIZ KIDS

The post-war era was a rebirth of hope for the Phils, as a bumper crop of new talent appeared on the scene —Del Ennis, Richie Ashburn, Robin Roberts, and Curt Simmons, to mention a few. The new uniforms for 1946 were a rebirth of the red, white and blue of the thirties and then some. Starting with the two-tone caps —a blue crown with red visor and a red script P with white outline —down to the red, white and blue striped stockings, it was a colorful dress-up of the plain uniform of the war years. Rich red and blue piping replaced the thin navy blue and even the belt tunnels were dressed up in red and blue. This colorful uniform scheme remained for the next three seasons and symbolized the resurgence of the Phillies as a legitimate pennant contender.

1946
HOME

1949
ROAD

Ken Heintzelman and Andy Seminick, a winning battery for the third place Phils of 1949.

1950 is a memorable year for Phillie fandom —finally securing a National League pennant after a 35-year draught. These were the fabled "Whiz Kids" who caught the fancy of baseball fans nationwide. Although they almost blew the pennant at the end and were destroyed in four games by the powerful Yankees in the Series, they endeared themselves to Philadelphia fans and provided plenty of optimism for the future. As if to anticipate a milestone season, the team uniforms were another totally new look. Gone were all traces of the familiar navy blue and RED was the new dominant color. Solid red caps, stockings and undersweaters plus daring red pinstripes on the home whites —this was the new look of the fifties. This uniform set remained the standard not only for the fifties but through the sixties as well. Despite its association with the success of 1950, it is also the uniform of the infamous collapse of 1964. By the end of the decade, it was time for a brand new stadium and a totally new uniform design to go with it.

The pride of Michigan State, Robin Roberts helped pitch the Phillies into contention in the fifties, popularizing the new all-red uniform style introduced in 1950.

Mike Schmidt in his familiar home-run trot on the road in the eighties. Note zipper front —the last major league jersey to incorporate this feature

GOODBYE SHIBE PARK, HELLO VETERANS STADIUM

For 1970, it was a brand new beginning for baseball in Philadelphia. The fans bid adieu to historic Connie Mack Stadium (nee Shibe Park) and entered the modern era of artificial turf and pillarless seats. The new uniforms also had the look of the future —a stylized new "P" logo, modern numerals, striping all the way up the sides (to the armpits) and a deeper burgundy shade of red for the trim color and pinstriping. It was basically a rejection of the traditional with the hope of planting the seeds of a new tradition for future generations. Even the conventional gray of the road uniform soon gave way to a more trendy bluish shade —a symptom of the color TV age. Except for a brief disastrous experiment with an all-burgundy edition in 1979, the new graphics have been accepted and indeed praised since their 1970 introduction. A world series victory in 1980 and another pennant in 1983 plus several divisional titles along the way have helped to solidify the popularity of the "new" traditional look. A major re-design is not likely in the immediate future. A slight concession to conservative trends by the Phils is reflected in the new GRAY shade of the 1989 road uniforms.

PITTSBURGH PIRATES

THE WAGNER YEARS

When the Louisville franchise dropped out of the National League in 1899, Pittsburgh had the good fortune of signing many of their star players. Among these were future legends Honus Wagner, Fred Clark, Tommy Leach and Deacon Phillipe. As a result, the only true "dynasty" in the club's history was formed as the Pirates won consecutive pennants in 1901-02-03. The Pittsburgh uniform of this era was awed much as was the Yankee uniform of the later decades. The dark blue stockings with red stripes were symbolic of the champions of the baseball world. The jersey was short-sleeved with no trim except for the dark blue collar. The same basic blue cap with a "P" was retained from the 1890's. The road uniform was simply a gray duplication of the home whites. The only blemish in this period of glory was losing the first world series ever in 1903 to the upstart Boston Americans.

1902
HOME

1902
ROAD

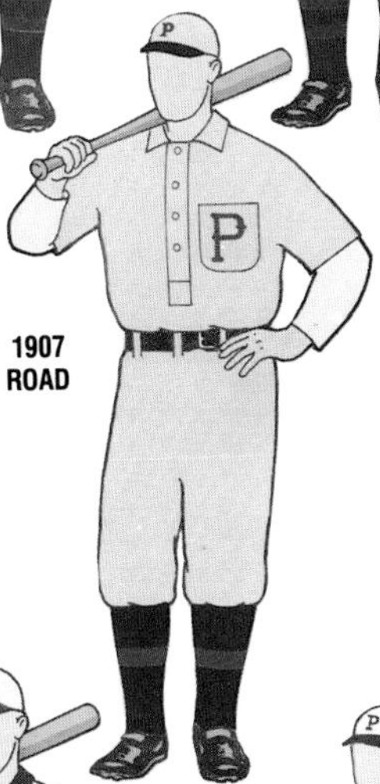

1907
ROAD

THE FORBES FIELD SAGA BEGINS

The Pittsburgh uniform changed very little during the years following 1903—an ornate capital "P" was added to the left front shirt pocket (front shirt pockets were eventually outlawed as a result of some "hidden ball" shenanigans) and the caps occasionally had white or gray crowns. The Chicago Cubs were the dominant team in the league from 1906-10, but in 1909 the Pirates put it all together with an incredible 110 victories (the Cubs won 104) and world series victory over Hugh Jennings' Detroit champions. Many feel that this was the greatest Pirate team ever, at least for a single season. The uniforms were still pretty much a carry-over from earlier in the decade—dark blue collar, red & blue stockings, a plain shirt front but with a new monogram added to the left sleeve: the "P-B-C" on the monogram signifying Pittsburgh Baseball Club. 1909 was a milestone year for another reason: the Pirates played their last game in old Exposition Park (after 18 years) and inaugurated their new Forbes Field in June of that year.

Tommy Leach, a mainstay of some great Pirate teams of the early 1900's. (c.1909)

The great Dutchman Honus Wagner, on the road in 1914 —the twilight of his phenomenal career as a player.

The years between 1910-1915 introduced many new innovations in uniform design and Pittsburgh abandoned tradition to conform to the trends. The regular collar was replaced by the short, stand-up "cadet" style. Pin-striped fabrics were now in vogue and the new collar and button lapel became a focal point of the jersey design. Team nicknames were becoming accepted as official by the clubs and the Pittsburgh Club joined this movement by displaying "PIRATES" in vertical capital letters down the button lapel. Later, the entire lapel and collar were solid dark blue. The cadet style collar soon gave way to a tapered collar extension but the button lapel remained solid dark blue with white buttons and a "P-P" straddling the top button. The latter half of the decade saw the solid blue lapel replaced by an outline trim in piping of various widths. During this period, the cap design included a "P" of white, red or a combination of the 2 colors. The capital "P" on the left breast periodically appeared in various styles and sizes throughout the decade.

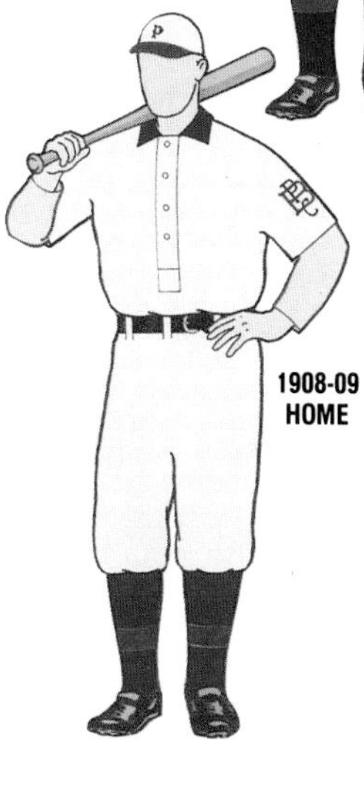

1908-09
HOME

1911
HOME

1912
ROAD

1913
HOME

1914
ROAD

1916
HOME

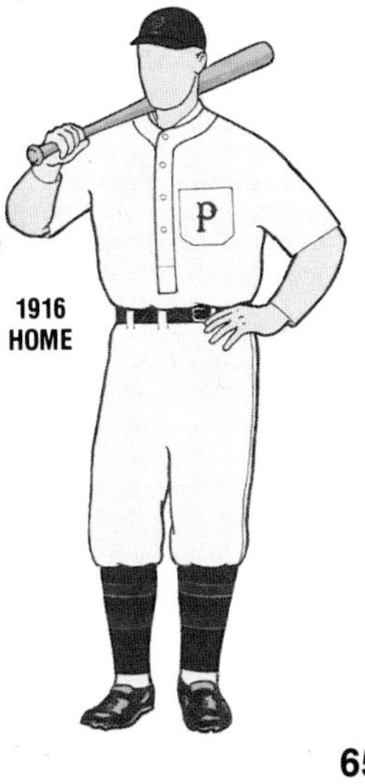

THE ROARING TWENTIES AND THE WANER ERA

Baseball uniforms of the 1920's, perhaps because of uncertainties following World War I and the Black Sox scandal were, by and large, somber and conservative. The Pirate uniforms of this decade exemplified this retreat to austerity. Standard whites at home, standard grays on the road, simple graphics and solid colors were the rule. Except for an Old-English style "P" in the early twenties and some double-piping trim later on, the uniforms were generally dreary. The 1925 and 1927 championship teams had the standard capital "P" on both sleeves. This was the uniform for most of the decade and the only embellishment which added any color at all was the large circular blue and gold patch which all National League teams wore in 1925 to commemorate the leagues' 50th year.

If the prosperous era of the twenties reflected drabness in uniforms, the hard times of the thirties gave birth to a virtual renaissance of added colors, trim features and graphic innovations. About 1933, the Pittsburgh uniform brightened up considerably —the team name PIRATES was placed across the chest of the road jersey in an arc of fancy red and blue capital letters. The home whites displayed a large, capital P in the same fancy red and blue lettering style. Solid blue belt tunnels and loops were included and piping trim incorporated both blue and red and was often double-striped. A wide, bold red stripe dressed up the stockings and the "P" on the blue cap was also red. In 1936 & 37, the PIRATES lettering was also displayed on the home jersey, replacing the P. As if on an "orgy" of uniform revitalization for the decade, the new trend of script lettering of the word PIRATES with underline flourish was introduced in 1938. By 1939, a zipper front replaced the buttons, following the lead of other major league teams. Except for contending teams in 1932 and 1933, the Pirates of the thirties were pretty much in the middle of the pack despite their sartorial uplift.

First baseman Elbie Fletcher in the zipper-front script lettered PIRATES jersey style of 1939.

1921
HOME

1922
ROAD

1932
HOME

1934
ROAD

1920's
HOME

1934
HOME

THE WAR YEARS AND ON TO OBLIVION

Continuing the cycle of ever-changing graphics from the last decade, 1940 and 1941 saw the introduction of the most innovative feature on Pirates uniforms to date. In place of "P" or "Pirates", a colorful emblem depicting the head of a typical buccaneer in appropriate headdress, earring, bandana, etc. was displayed on the left breast of both home and road jerseys. Extra red, white and blue stripes were added to the stockings and a narrow band of red or white trim was included around the base of the cap crown. This pirate-head emblem was the only graphic representation of the team nickname on a game jersey in the team's history and provided inspiration for the 1987 centennial logo.

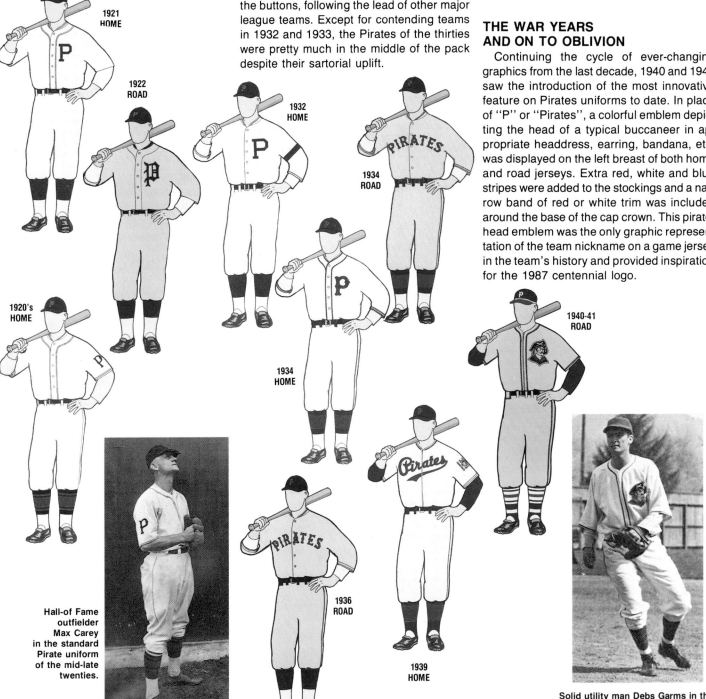

1940-41
ROAD

Hall-of Fame outfielder Max Carey in the standard Pirate uniform of the mid-late twenties.

1939
HOME

1936
ROAD

Solid utility man Debs Garms in the unusual Pirate uniform of 1940-41.

1942
HOME

1946
ROAD

For the WWII years, "PIRATES" and "PITTSBURGH" were restored to the home and road jerseys respectively. Although fairly colorful, this seemed to signal another trend back to the more conventional uniform design. For the year of Hank Greenberg (1947), the uniform trim was reduced to navy blue only and the "Pirates" and "Pittsburgh" were re-done in a simple script style. 1947 was the final year of navy blue (and/or red) as the basic trim color on Pirate uniforms.

1947
HOME

1947
ROAD

1947 at Forbes Field —Hank Greenberg in his "last hurrah" as a player.

A new era of team colors was reflected in the total re-design of the uniforms for 1948. Black and gold replaced blue (and red) forever and the clean, simple design of the home whites and road grays represented a full swing back to the traditional. The only decorative aspects of the new designs were the gold trimming on the black and the fact that the lettering style was at least moderately ornate. The piping down the edges of the button lapel was removed with only modest piping used around the collar, sleeve ends and down the sides of the trouser legs. The gold "P" on the cap matched the jersey lettering. This uniform set the standard for the fifties and although it was handsome and attractive, the teams who wore it were anything but. The early fifties were the "pits" for the Pittburghs —7th or last place every year fron '50 to '55. One interesting innovation in uniform caps did occur in the mid-fifties with the Pirates. A fiberglass cap was used for regular game duty (not just a batting helmet). Apparently, it was not practical as a full-time playing cap and was discarded after a couple of years.

1948
HOME

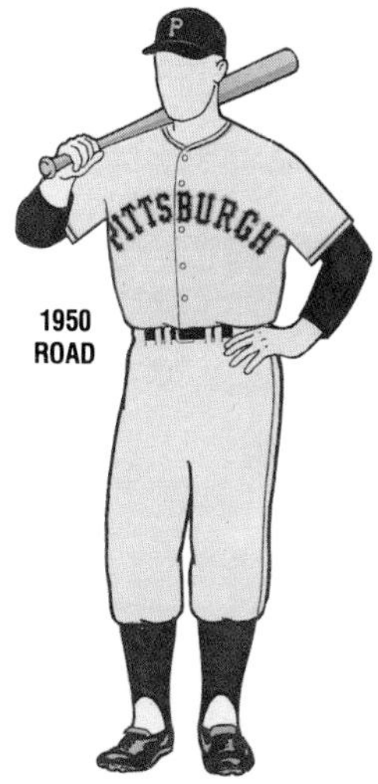

1950
ROAD

The home run king of the forties & fifties, Ralph Kiner, models the Pirate road uniform of his peak years.

OUT OF THE DEPTHS

By 1957, the team's fortunes were on the upswing and another experiment was introduced in the Pirate uniforms —sleeveless jerseys. The Cincinnati Reds had used the idea the summer before (actually, the Cubs first introduced the "vest" style in '40-'42) and apparently impressed Pittsburgh management enough to follow suit (no pun intended). The basic graphics and color scheme of the prior design were not changed —only adapted to the sleeveless format. This uniform style is, in truth, more historically significant for what the team accomplished while wearing it. A young Puerto Rican named Clemente had arrived and the team surged out of the depths to become a solid pennant contender. Who can forget Bill Mazeroski pouncing on home plate in his sleeveless jersey, giving Pittsburgh their first championship in over 30 years!

Popular second baseman Bill Mazeroski in the new sleeveless vest jersey.

1960
HOME

1962
ROAD

Apparently feeling that this particular uniform style was a good omen, the club stayed with it throughout the decade of the sixties. The only noteworthy modification was the introduction of numbers on the jersery front in 1962. This uniform produced no more championships but the association with the incredible year of 1960 by those who remember gives it a special place in the hearts of Pittsburgh fandom. It was also to be the last Pirate uniform worn at Forbes Field.

DOUBLE KNITS AND THREE RIVERS

When the time came to inaugurate the new Three Rivers Stadium in mid-1970, it was also time for a change in uniforms. Just as the new structure represented the march of progress, the newest trend in uniforms was the double-knit fabric; lighter, more durable, and more comfortable than the traditional flannels. It was another important innovation and the Pirates were the first major league club to adopt them. The color scheme of gold and black was retained and so was the basic lettering style of "PIRATES". The jersey was a pull-over (no more buttons or zippers) and the trousers had the built-in sash belt (no more separate belts). The piping and socks stripes were replaced by yellow, black and white bands, and the cap crown was yellow with a black bill. The advantages of the new double knits proved irresistable and within 2 years almost every other major league team had them.

To commemorate the 1976 bicentennial, many clubs decided to occasionally wear the old striped, "pill-box" style cap —a reminder of earlier days in baseball history. The Pirates participated and elected to retain this cap style for future years. Although its sartorial aesthetics may be argued, its use has certainly created a unique identity for all Pittsburgh teams thru the mid-eighties. In 1977, the club presented a daring departure from the tradition of one uniform theme at home, and another single theme for travelling. The Pirates introduced several color schemes in various combinations. Using sets of both shirts and pants in either striped or plain white, gold, or black and mixing them indiscriminately, no one could predict which ensemble the team would wear from one game to the next. To further complicate this mix, caps, undershirts and socks (both the outer stirrup sock and the full-length undersock) were also issued in different color combinations. The specifications for this dizzying mixture of color coordinates is really too complicated to fully explain in words. By 1985, sanity prevailed and the basic white and gray formula returned, signalling another general trend to the more traditional. The final stroke in the return to the traditional was the abandonment of the striped cap in favor of a standard black round crown type for the 1987 season. Perhaps it is fitting and proper to remember the striped cap as a symbol of the last world championship of 1979 —Wilver Stargell and the "family".

1970 HOME

1970 ROAD

1976 ROAD

The "father" of "the family", newly elected Hall-of-Famer Willie Stargell in the all-pinstriped version of the home uniform c.1980.

The city name PITTSBURGH was displayed on the 1990 road grays for the first time in a quarter century.

1980 "MIX-N-MATCH" COMBINATIONS

1988 HOME

1988 ROAD

1990 ROAD

SAN DIEGO PADRES

THE BIG TIME, AT LAST!

The dream of a major league team in San Diego became a reality on April 8, 1969 when the new Padres defeated Houston 2-1 in the season opener. Former Dodger exec Buzzy Bavasi was the principle architect of the new franchise. In some ways it was a continuation of the PCL Padres, merely elevating the operation to major league level. The nickname and color scheme of PADRE BROWN and GOLD were carried over from the AAA Padre uniforms. The uniform set for the first three summers was standard stuff —solid brown caps, undersweaters, and stockings (with some gold striping), buttoned shirts and belted trousers. The home flannels were white with the name PADRES arched across the front in brown capital letters. Road uniforms broke with an old tradition by using a TAN color instead of gray or blue/gray. The tan shirts displayed SAN DIEGO in the same lettering format as PADRES.

AN ENDLESS CYCLE OF CHANGE BEGINS

With the advent of the double knit uniforms in the early seventies, the Padres overhauled their uniforms to accommodate the new double knit tailoring in 1972. For the balance of the decade, the club established some sort of record for the most changes in uniform designs over an 8-year period. The only consistency throughout this continuous merry-go-round was the retention of the team colors, BROWN and GOLD. The first double-knit sets were made of a dazzling solid gold material with brown lettering and striping trim. The home and road uniforms were identical except for the name PADRES vs. SAN DIEGO. About 1974, they temporarily reverted to something a bit more conventional by restoring white and gray for home and road suits respectively. The name PADRES was redone in "Dodger style" slanted script, while SAN DIEGO on the road shirts was repeated as before. The brown caps now featured a triangular gold panel on the front with the interlocking S-D monogram in brown. Gold sanitary socks were now worn under the brown stirrups. About 1977 the road uniform was once again restyled in a two-tone (or three-tone?) format. The new "softball" style jersey had a solid brown torso with gold raglan sleeves and the name SAN DIEGO in gold capitals. Both trousers and shoes were now WHITE.

For 1978, the two-tone raglan style jersey was re-styled again and used on both home and road combinations. The home whites incorporated brown raglan sleeves while the road browns repeated the gold sleeves. The lettering graphics on the jersey fronts were the same for both versions and were another significant departure from the traditional. The name PADRES was presented horizontally (not arced) in a custom-designed all-lower case modern lettering style. The city name SAN DIEGO in small capital letters was included just above the first three letters in PADRES. This combination was indeed a rarity —one of the very few times in major league history when the full team name (city and nickname) was displayed on the uniform. The following year, the graphics were reworked again. The PADRES lettering on the home shirts was reformed in an arc and the small SAN DIEGO was scrubbed. SAN DIEGO in full size modernized letters was likewise arced across the front of the brown road shirts. To paraphrase an old joke about the weather in some regions, "If you don't like this year's uniforms, wait 'til next year!" —that mentality would apply to the Padres' uniforms of the seventies. Certainly there must be room for some innovation here and there, but sooner or later a more monotonous tradition is required to nurture fan loyalty for a baseball team. This embarrassing spectacle of ever-changing uniforms was finally near its end. By contrast, the sister expansion team in Montreal has established a firm visual identity by retaining the same basic uniform look throughout the full life of the franchise.

1969 HOME

1972 ROAD

1977 HOME

1977 ROAD

1979 HOME

1974 ROAD

1973 HOME

Randy Jones, the Padres premier pitcher on the road in 1977.

1978 HOME

1978 ROAD

1979 ROAD

THE EIGHTIES —FINALLY, SOME RESPECT!

The new uniforms for 1980 were once again revamped but finally showed some signs of a drift back to the more conventional. The two-tone raglan jersey was discarded in favor of solid white at home and solid brown on the road. The built-in waistband trouser was also restyled to accommodate a separate brown belt. The avant-garde lettering style of PADRES was tastefully dressed up in burnt orange with a double outline of brown and gold. An added touch of burnt orange to the striping trim seemed to improve the overall color scheme. This ensemble was still a creature of the double-knit color craze but at least it was kept intact for five full seasons. Its tenure was climaxed with a pennant-winning season in 1984. A huge world series audience gave it national exposure and perhaps its eventual death sentence.

The Padres opened the 1985 season with a totally new image and a resounding triumph for the more traditional look in baseball uniforms. It was a sublime blend of modern graphics (using non-traditional colors) and the conventional, familiar tailoring of decades past. No piping anywhere, solid brown accessories and even good old pinstripes (in brown, no less). It was back to all white buttoned uniforms at home, and gray on the road. This combination has done its best to please everyone —fundamentally conservative, yet trendy in its graphics. The franchise has come full circle in its uniform evolution and it looks like they've ended up with a winner —the only thing left is to establish a new winning tradition in the standings.

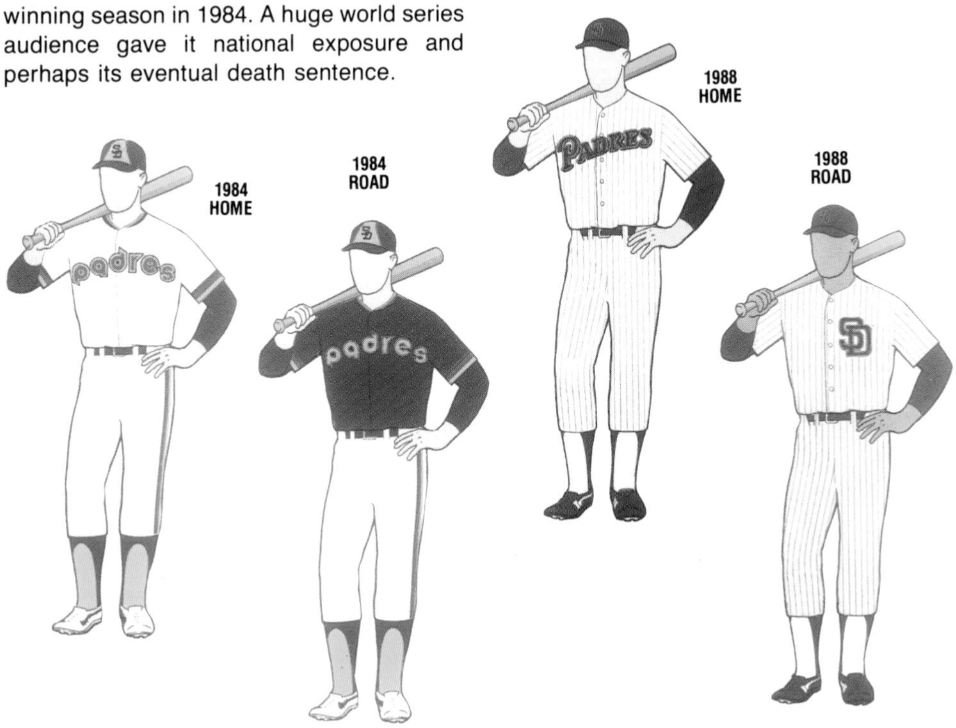

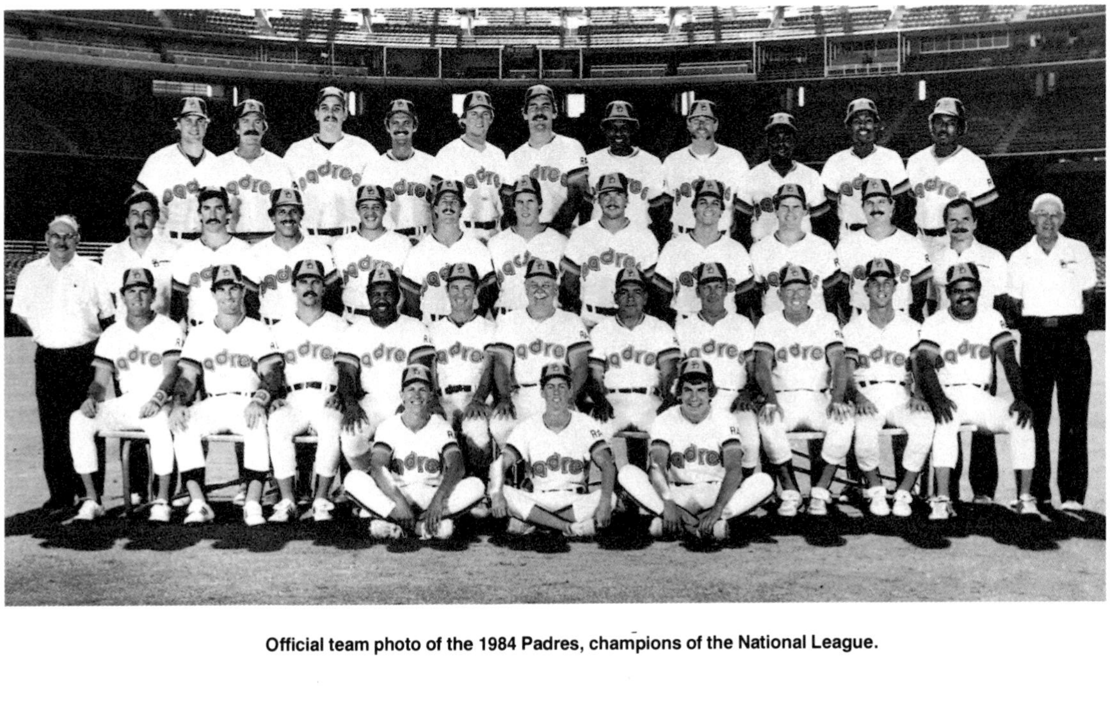

Official team photo of the 1984 Padres, champions of the National League.

NEW YORK/ SAN FRANCISCO GIANTS

THE DAWN OF THE McGRAW ERA

At the turn of the century, the New York Giants were one of the solid franchises in the league despite their low position in the standings. With the huge population base of metropolitan New York and the spacious Polo Grounds as the premier park in baseball, they survived the league's contraction from 12 to 8 teams after 1899. Hated rival Brooklyn was the class of the league at that time but before too many years, the tables would turn. Fiery John McGraw was lured away from the new American League in 1902 to become the Giants' player-manager and an illustrious winning tradition would soon follow. Giant uniforms for the early 1900's were pretty standard —white at home, gray on the road, and the name NEW YORK in arched block capitals on the chest. Trim colors were either BLACK or BROWN. Caps were standard round crown at first, but evolved into a modified "pill-box" crown with fine horizontal striping trim. By 1905 (McGraw's second pennant year) the NEW YORK was replaced by a large capital N and Y on the right and left breast respectively of the uniform shirts. After refusing to participate in a post-season series with the American League champs in 1904, the Giants relented in 1905. Connie Mack's Athletics were the AL opponents and McGraw procured special all-black uniforms for world series play. The large N and Y were duplicated in white on the black shirts. The psychology worked as the Giants were victors, a fact which would not be neglected in the new uniforms of 1906.

Still gloating over their spoils, the 1906 New Yorkers opened the season with WORLD'S CHAMPIONS displayed across the shirt fronts of both home whites and road grays. These uniforms had another unusual feature that is overlooked because of the boastful lettering message. The traditional fold-down regular collar was eliminated and in fact the jerseys were COLLARLESS. It was a daring innovation and set an important precedent for future uniform trends. The Giants failed to repeat in 1906 (the Cubs won an extraordinary 116 games) and the 1905 uniform designs were taken out of mothballs for the 1907 season (sans collars).

1905 WORLD SERIES

1906 HOME

A LOGO TRADITION BEGINS

The Giant uniforms of 1908 were a general redesign. Plain, round-crown caps were returned and a wide dark band was introduced on the stockings. The "collarless" collar was modified with a tapered extension around the neck. The shirt fronts were blank but a new N-Y monogram was displayed on the sleeve. This prototype rendition of the monogram simply attempted to merge the same block N & Y from the previous uniforms. The following year (1909) the uniform trim was dark brown and the N-Y monogram was reworked using a fancier letter style. This version was to become a traditional ingredient for Giant uniforms in future decades. In 1911, the trim color was once again black and fine blue pinstripes were present in the fabric for the first time. The new logo was also displayed on the black caps for the first time. The New Yorkers won the pennant and were to face the same Athletics in the Fall Classic. Once again, McGraw ordered special all-black suits (this time with the new logo on the sleeve) for the series. Unfortunately, the Mackmen prevailed this time and the all-black uniforms were permanently retired.

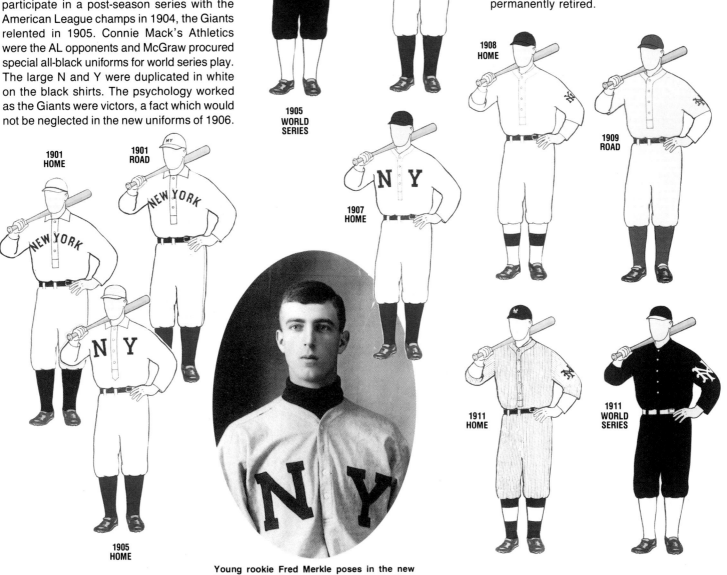

1908 HOME

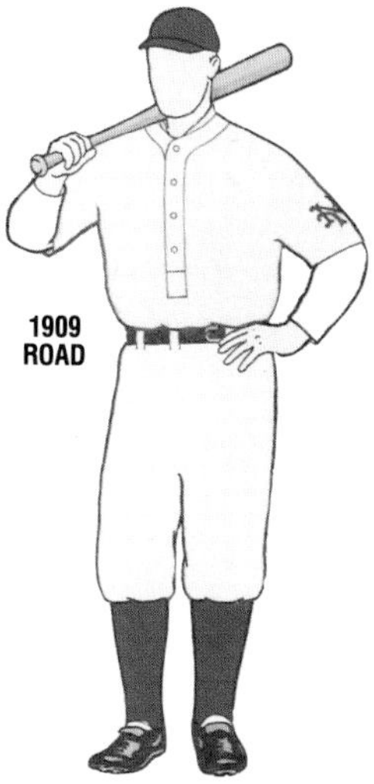
1909 ROAD

1901 HOME

1901 ROAD

1905 HOME

1907 HOME

Young rookie Fred Merkle poses in the new "collarless" shirt in a 1907 studio portrait.

1911 HOME

1911 WORLD SERIES

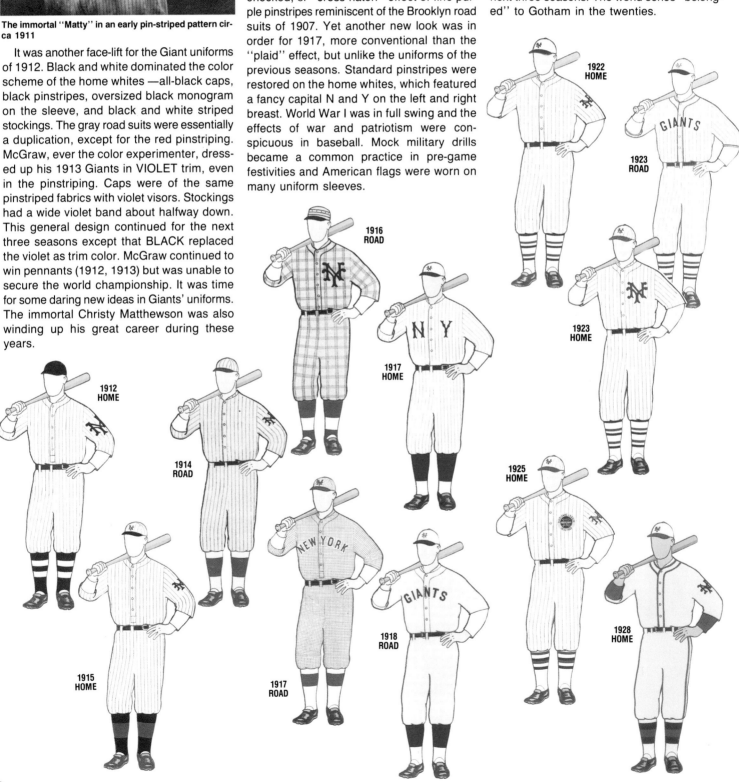

The immortal "Matty" in an early pin-striped pattern circa 1911

It was another face-lift for the Giant uniforms of 1912. Black and white dominated the color scheme of the home whites —all-black caps, black pinstripes, oversized black monogram on the sleeve, and black and white striped stockings. The gray road suits were essentially a duplication, except for the red pinstriping. McGraw, ever the color experimenter, dressed up his 1913 Giants in VIOLET trim, even in the pinstriping. Caps were of the same pinstriped fabrics with violet visors. Stockings had a wide violet band about halfway down. This general design continued for the next three seasons except that BLACK replaced the violet as trim color. McGraw continued to win pennants (1912, 1913) but was unable to secure the world championship. It was time for some daring new ideas in Giants' uniforms. The immortal Christy Matthewson was also winding up his great career during these years.

A BASEBALL WAR FOLLOWED BY GLOBAL WAR

The status quo of major league baseball was challenged again during 1914-15 by the new Federal League, a third "pretender" to major league status. Player threats ran amok and salary demands were escalating. The new league collapsed after 1915 and stability was restored. The new Giant uniforms of 1916 were another provocative new design. Violet was the trim color once again, but the real surprise was the fabric. It was a cross-hatch effect of fine purple stripes that provided a "plaid" look. An oversize version of the N-Y emblem graced the left shirt fronts. An optional cap made in the Athletics "layer-cake" mold was sometimes used. Another unusual road uniform was also worn in this period —a checked, or "cross-hatch" effect of fine purple pinstripes reminiscent of the Brooklyn road suits of 1907. Yet another new look was in order for 1917, more conventional than the "plaid" effect, but unlike the uniforms of the previous seasons. Standard pinstripes were restored on the home whites, which featured a fancy capital N and Y on the left and right breast. World War I was in full swing and the effects of war and patriotism were conspicuous in baseball. Mock military drills became a common practice in pre-game festivities and American flags were worn on many uniform sleeves.

WAR'S END AND A NEW YORK MONOPOLY

The gray 1918 road uniforms displayed the team nickname GIANTS for the first time in arched block capitals. This idea became a road uniform standard for the entire decade of the twenties. By 1920, the home uniform theme had also acquired a standard look — pinstripes (including the cap crown) with the N-Y emblem on the sleeve. The trim colors changed from time to time and in 1922 new white stockings with pairs of red and blue bands appeared. These "candy cane" stockings were also standard through most of the decade. The New York area seized center stage in baseball's Fall Classic from 1920-24. Brooklyn won the pennant in 1920, then the Giants and Yankees repeated together for the next three seasons. The world series "belonged" to Gotham in the twenties.

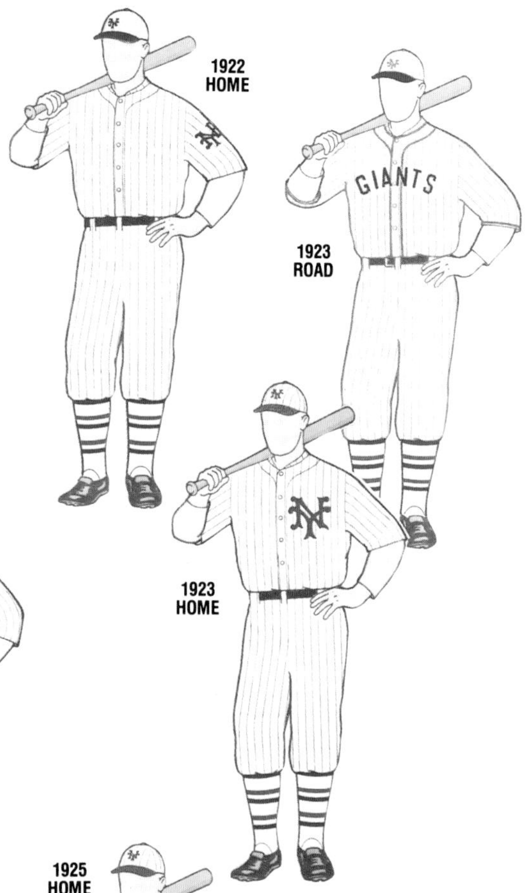

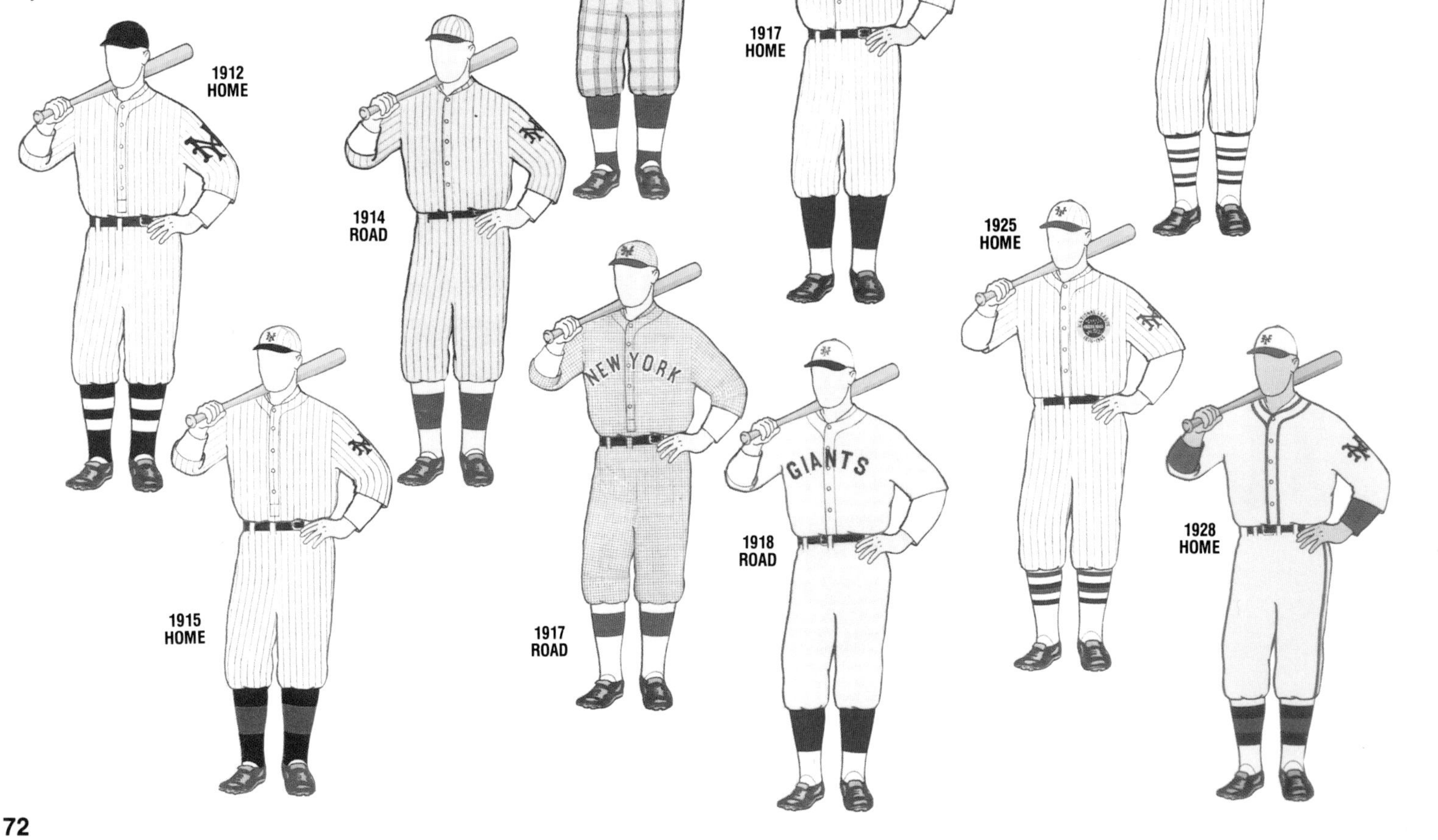

By the late twenties, the generally somber monochrome look of major league uniforms was becoming "awakened" with new color combinations and multi-colored piping. The new Giants' road uniforms of 1926 reflected this trend. The GIANTS lettering was made in "fancy" style red, bordered with blue piping. In addition to the two-color piping, even the pinstriping was now double striped. The new home whites for 1928 finally dropped the familiar pinstripes but dressed up the piping trim. The "candy cane" stockings were also modified to a solid band of red and blue stripes. This motif was more or less repeated (with and without pinstripes) on into the early thirties.

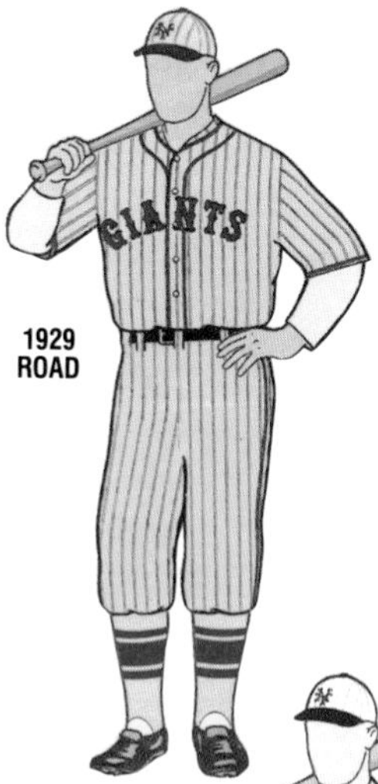

1929 ROAD

1930 HOME

1932 HOME

"MUGGSY" FINALLY CALLS IT QUITS

1932 was John McGraw's final season as the manager of the New York Giants. Bill Terry, a player of the McGraw mold, took over in '33 but for Giants fans it would never be the same team again. The new uniforms for 1933 included some new changes —ORANGE and BLACK were selected as the new trim color combination. Symbolically, the famous N-Y emblem was retired from the home jersey and the name GIANTS was transferred over from the road shirts. The name NEW YORK was now displayed on the gray road jersey for the first time in many seasons. The N-Y emblem was retained in orange on the front of the black caps. This uniform set lasted through the 1935 season, the only revision being the switch to white stockings with orange and black stripes in 1935. A world series victory in 1933 helped to offset the departure of John McGraw. The era ended officially when McGraw passed away in February 1934.

1933 HOME

1935 ROAD

BLACK IS OUT, BLUE IS IN

The mania for multi-color trim subsided temporarily in the design of the 1936 uniforms. ROYAL BLUE was the new solo color scheme. GIANTS on the home whites and NEW YORK on the road grays was still the fancy lettering, but in solid blue. Caps were solid blue with white monogram, stockings were likewise solid blue with three white stripes. The new uniforms brought consecutive pennants in '36 and '37, but destruction by the Yankees in the world series both years. Carl Hubbell and Mel Ott had some great seasons in these uniforms. In 1938, the stockings were changed to a half-blue, half-white combination. A patch publicizing the coming NY World's Fair in '39 was worn on the sleeves in 1938. Baseball's centennial patch occupied the same spot on the '39 uniforms. By 1940, the trend for more colorful piping had returned and the Giants' uniforms were embellished with touches of red piping. The stockings also included multiple bands of red and white accent striping. Zippers also replaced buttons on the shirts. This uniform theme lasted through the first wartime season of 1942.

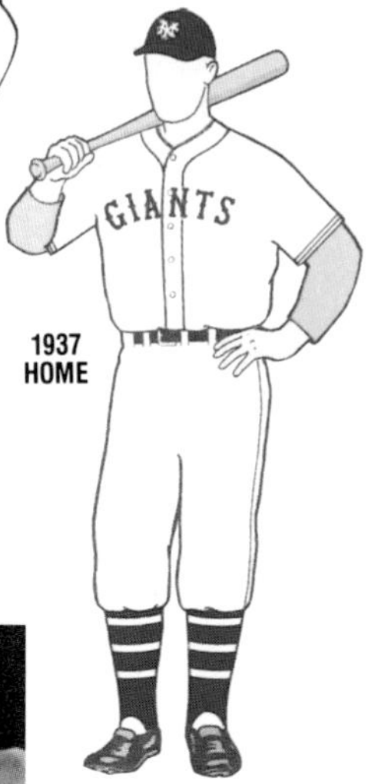

1937 HOME

1939 ROAD

Travis Jackson at the Polo Grounds in 1931

Carl Hubbell at Yankee Stadium —1936 world series

1940 HOME

1942 ROAD

THE POST-WWII PERIOD AND THE "MIRACLE"

About 1943, the lettering style was subtly but distinctly reworked on the names GIANTS and NEW YORK —still "fancy" but a different form of fancy. The color scheme and general appearance was the same and remained so through the 1948 season. For 1949 it was the end of the line for red and blue trim. The letter style of GIANTS and NEW YORK was retained but now in BLACK with an ORANGE border. Caps, undersweaters, and stockings were solid black. The N-Y emblem on the cap was now orange. Piping was an orange and black mix and was limited to the collar, sleeve ends, and trouser legs. This uniform set enjoyed the longest run in the club's history and some of the most glorious moments of Giants lore occurred in these years; the incomparable Willie Mays made his debut in 1951, Bobby Thomson's incredible pennant-winning homer also in 1951, and the 1954 series upset of the Cleveland Indians. And, sadly, it was the last Giant uniform worn at the Polo Grounds in 1957.

A NEW HOME, BUT STILL THE GIANTS

As did the Dodgers, the Giants retained the same uniform look as the now San Francisco Giants. Of course, SAN FRANCISCO (in block letters) replaced NEW YORK on the road shirts and an S-F logo was displayed on the cap fronts. But they still were the GIANTS, and a pennant in '62 paced by new heroes Marichal and McCovey solidified their West Coast identity. Finally in 1973, a barely noticeable modification was made in the lettering —the black and orange arrangement was reversed. This version lasted through the bicentennial year of '76. The advent of the double knit uniforms determined a whole new image for 1977.

The pull-over jersey and beltless trousers dictated a new order in the way baseball uniforms were to be decorated. Bold stripes replaced thinner piping and the graphics on the shirt front no longer needed to be split in half and matched up. With this new design criteria, the Giants introduced for the first time (on the uniform) their script version of GIANTS in orange and black. The uniform number was also displayed on the shirt front for the first time. An alternate home jersey in BLACK with orange graphics was worn on occasion. The 1977 road jersey consisted of an ORANGE top with SAN FRANCISCO in black lettering. Striping mix was orange/white/black on all three uniform sets. An orange bill was added to the black caps. In 1978, the script GIANTS replaced SAN FRANCISCO on the orange road shirts. This uniform set was used through the 1982 season.

The double knit honeymoon was over by the early eighties and the new trend in baseball uniforms was decidedly conservative. The new '83 Giant uniforms restored the buttons and belts, but with a touch of avant-garde graphics. It was also back to the basics — white at home, gray for traveling. This uniform has been well received by the players, fans, and media alike and may well have set the standard for re-designed uniforms of the nineties.

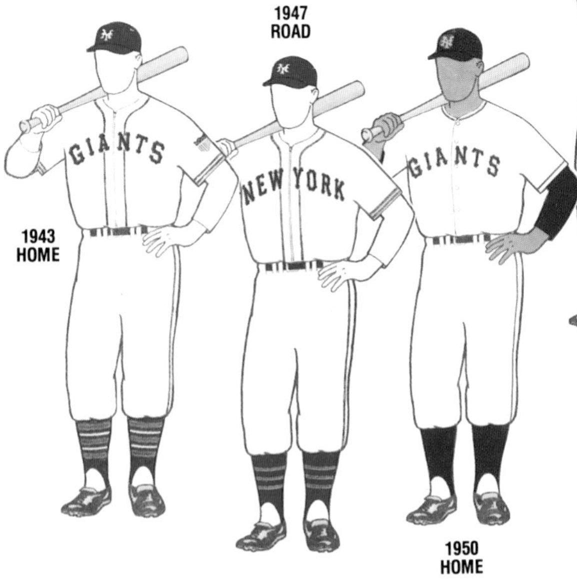

The "Say-Hey" kid, Willie Mays, hits one on the road in the sixties

SEATTLE PILOTS/MARINERS

A "CUP OF COFFEE" IN THE NORTHWEST

When the American League decided to add two expansion franchises for the 1969 season, Seattle was selected to represent the great Northwest. Temporary pre-season uniforms with the new team nickname PILOTS across the chest in blue block letters were hastily ordered. These first practice uniforms were standard stuff —no piping, solid blue socks, cap and undersweater, etc. BLUE and GOLD were the official trim colors chosen and when the Pilots opened the '69 season they presented one of the most unique uniform designs ever seen in the majors. With a maritime flavor, the blue caps featured a gold S with a gold braid underline across the front panel of the crown and a gold "scrambled eggs" decoration on the visor. The white home set continued the solid blue socks, belt and shirtsleeves. On the sleeve ends of the jersey was a wider band of thin combination gold and blue striping. The name pilots was displayed on the left breast in lower case block italics, in blue with a gold outline. Directly above PILOTS was a stylized pilots emblem, a small baseball framed in a pilots' wheel with wings. The player number appeared on the right breast. The road uniforms were done in a light blue material, repeating the piping on the caps and shirt sleeves. The city name SEATTLE in stylized gold lower case letters arched across the chest and the pilots emblem appeared above it on the right breast. In a strange twist of fate, the Pilots were doomed to play only one season and then would relocate in Milwaukee as the new Brewers. It was the second time in American League history (as a major league) that a franchise lasted only one season, the other occasion being the transfer to St. Louis in 1902 of —you guessed it —the Milwaukee Brewers.

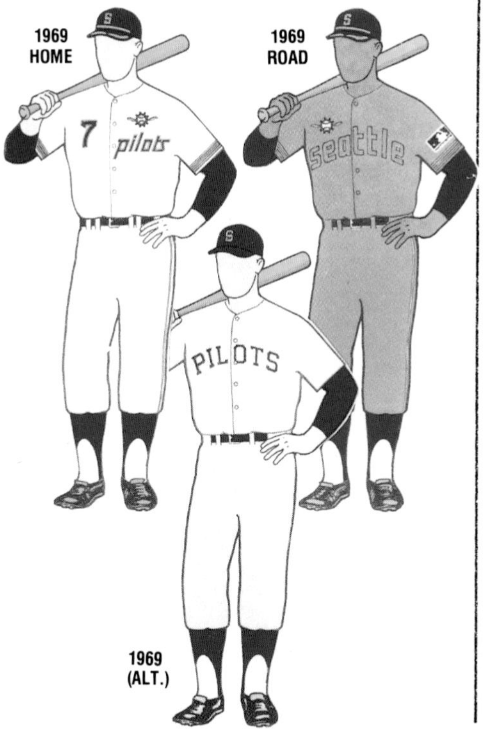

1969 HOME

1969 ROAD

1969 (ALT.)

A SECOND CHANCE

When two more teams were to be awarded American League franchises for the 1977 season, Seattle was given another opportunity to prove that it was indeed a major league city. The new franchise elected to continue the Pilots' blue and gold trim colors and even stuck with the nautical flavor in selecting the nickname MARINERS. The new uniform sets were also white at home and light blue for travel but there the similarity ended. By now, the double knit styles had become standard and the new Mariners' uniforms included the V-neck pull-over jerseys and the built-in waistband on the trousers. The caps were once again solid blue, but with a "trident" M insignia on the front in gold. Arched across the front of the white home blouses was the name MARINERS in a stylized lower case using the trident symbol as the capital M. This lettering as well as the uniform number was blue with gold edging. Blue/gold/blue striping appeared on the waistband, sleeve ends, and around the V-neck collar. Stockings and undersweaters were solid blue. On the blue road shirts the name SEATTLE was across the chest in a contemporary type style, in solid blue with a white outline. The striping trim on the road blues was a combination of gold, white and blue. This uniform set was repeated for 1978. In 1979, the road uniforms were slightly modified by adding gold trim to the front lettering and a rework of the striping accents. No further changes were made through 1979.

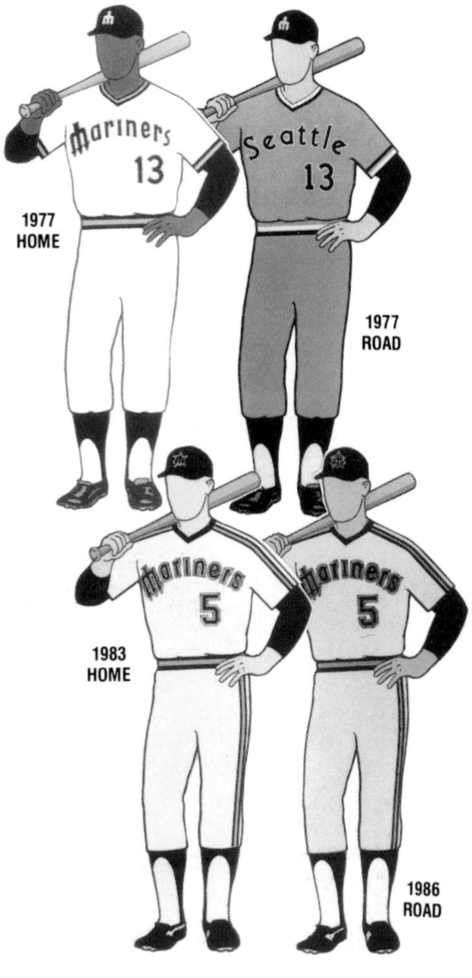

1977 HOME

1977 ROAD

1983 HOME

1986 ROAD

A NEW LOOK FOR THE EIGHTIES

Some new uniform embellishments were introduced for the 1980 season. A new trident insignia was designed for the cap fronts which added a star to the background. New striping was added to the trouser legs and down the shoulders of the jerseys, in keeping with the current trends in double knit uniform trimmings. Both MARINERS and SEATTLE on home and road shirts respectively were reworked to include a thin blue outline. The powder blue road uniform color was changed to a more traditional GRAY a few seasons later. Also, SEATTLE was dropped on the traveling shirts in favor of repeating MARINERS from the home whites. This uniform ensemble was retained through the 1986 season. The Mariners' first decade of existence was fairly successful attendance-wise (with the help of the new Kingdome) but on the field the team was unable to emerge as a serious contender.

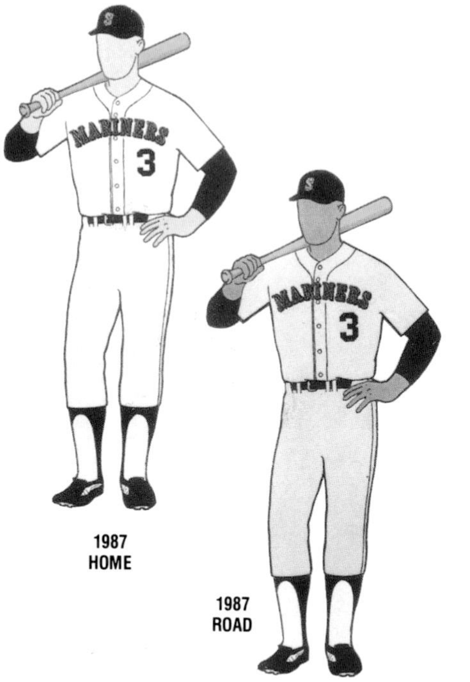

1987 HOME

1987 ROAD

A MORE TRADITIONAL UNIFORM CHANGE

For 1987, it was a totally new image for the Mariners' uniforms —and clearly a return to more conventional styles. It was back to buttoned jerseys and belted trousers with fine blue piping along the button row and down the sides of the pantlegs. The name MARINERS was redefined in three-dimensional Roman style capital letters. A gold S in the same style replaced the trident M emblem on the caps. The gray road uniform was an exact duplicate of the home suit. Those who resist the new design features of the double knit suits react favorably to this new Seattle getup —a typical comment being: "Now that's a real baseball uniform!". Maybe it will also transform the hapless Mariners into a real contender —after all, look what a restyled uniform did for the Twins in 1987.

ST. LOUIS BROWNS

THE FIRST DECADE

It was common knowledge throughout the American League's first season in 1901 that the Milwaukee franchise was a "lame duck", destined for transfer to St. Louis. Since the existing NL entry was firmly established as "Cardinals", the new AL franchise in the Mound City for 1902 was christened "Browns", recalling the great American Association dynasty of a decade or so earlier. Accordingly, the color brown was the primary trim feature for the team uniforms for the 52 year life of the franchise. Only the Giants on rare early occasions and the Padres of modern times were to use brown as a uniform trim color.

St. Louis team uniforms in the first years were the plain standard of white at home and gray on the road with little or no additional graphics required to identify the team. Only a large ST.L on the jersey front —first on the road grays, then also on the home whites, was used through the 1903 season. Caps and stockings were solid brown and the uniform shirts had the regulation fold-down collar. In 1904, the city name ST. LOUIS was displayed in standard, arched black capital letters across the chest of the road uniform. For 1905, a pair of white stripes were added to the brown stockings. These plain uniforms were about to be transformed dramatically.

When the 1906 edition of the St. Louis "Browns" appeared on the AL playing fields, their radical new uniform design was the talk of baseball. Abandoning the customary brown trim color in favor of BLACK (indeed, one St. Louis paper dubbed them "RAVENS"), new embellishments were incorporated from top to bottom. The cap had a white crown accented by heavy black piping on the seams and a solid black visor. The uniform jersey included thick black striping along the shoulder seams, around the edge of the collar, down the button lapel, and even around the shirt pocket. A newly designed "ST-L" monogram was displayed on the left sleeve, enclosed in a diamond-shaped frame. Black piping appeared down the sides of the trouser legs and 3 thin stipes dressed up the stockings. The gray road uniform for 1906 duplicated the home whites except that the stocking stripes were "reversed" —that is, 3 light stripes on a solid sock. This uniform ensemble was the first of a series of highly ornamental uniform designs in the next several seasons.

For 1907, the jersey design was modified by changing the collar to solid black, eliminating the piping on the shirt pocket, and re-designing the sleeve emblem to a solid black "reverse" version. The stocking stripes were changed to a more or less half-and-half black and white combination. Still further changes were made in 1908. The home cap was modified to include the city's "fluer-de-lis" symbol in front and the visor changed from solid dark to an unusual wide dark striping around the edge. Piping was eliminated from the jersey and the ST-L monogram style of 1906 was displayed on the left breast. The "Fluer-de-lis" symbol replaced the monogram on the sleeve. A re-design of the road uniform of 1908 ended the home uniform duplication and restored the unique identity of the travelling suits. The city name ST. LOUIS reappeared in fancy capital letters on the shirt front. The "Fluer-de-lis" symbol was positioned on the sleeve and in white on the dark cap.

The uniforms of 1909 & 1910 were pretty much a continuation of 1908 with some minor changes. The ST-L monogram on the home jersey was once again re-designed by separating the letters. The fabric of the gray road uniform was changed from a solid color to a thin, narrow-spaced pin striping material. This fabric pattern was just becoming popular at this time and was a forerunner of more pronounced pin-striped uniform fabrics of subsequent years. Some of the Browns' cap designs during these years were also a bit unusual, having a flat, "mushroom" shape on the crown —a throwback to pre-1900 styles.

1906
HOME

1907
HOME

1902
ROAD

1905
HOME

1908
HOME

1905
ROAD

1910
ROAD

Rube Waddell, on the road for the Browns in 1908

A RETURN TO "UNIFORMITY"

Important innovations in the manufacture and design of baseball uniforms occurred around 1910 and the new Browns' attire for 1911 reflected this. Socks stirrups were replacing the full stocking, shirt pockets were disappearing and more importantly, the regular fold-down collars were being discarded in favor of "collarless" or the short stand-up "military cadet" style. The Browns drifted from the heavily ornamental trim toward a more austere appearance. The stockings were solid brown (except for some white around the ankles). The caps reverted to the more standard style of the earlier years: solid brown visor, white cap crown with brown piping. The collar on both the home and road jersey was a solid brown "cadet" style. The home uniform introduced a newly designed version of the ST-L monogram on the left breast while the road grays restored ST. LOUIS to the regulation block capital letters. This style of home and road uniforms remained the standard for the next five seasons, except for the dropping of the brown color on the collar about 1915.

The trend toward uniform simplicity and stability continued by 1916 and expressed itself in the new home uniform for that season. Piping was removed from the cap seams and the S-L monogram was removed from the shirt front. The only graphic embellishment to the jersey was an S-L monogram on the sleeve (in black, no less) and some piping around the collar and button lapel. The "cadet" collar was, by this time, modified to the more popular "V-neck" —almost collarless, but with a brief tapered collar extension. The gray road uniform for 1916 included the plain gray cap with brown visor and the same shirt piping trim as the home jersey. The ST. LOUIS on the jersey front returned to a more ornamental lettering style. The stockings had evolved to basic half brown/half white (or gray) styles. This basic uniform appearance signalled a long stable period in Browns uniforms that lasted through the decade of the twenties and into the early thirties. The only changes during these ensuing years would be minor ones: narrower lettering style on ST. LOUIS, changes in piping trim, occasional striping on the sox, and some differences in the cap design (including the first appearance of an S-L logo about 1924).

A RENAISSANCE OF THE ORNAMENTAL

For whatever reason, the depression years of the thirties generated a virtual "explosion" of new ideas and added color trim features to major league uniforms. In 1934, the St. Louis Browns joined this movement and introduced the most innovative and colorful uniforms to date for the franchise. Among the more noteworthy changes were the introduction of orange as a secondary trim color and the display of the team nickname BROWNS on the home jersey for the first time. The new caps were solid brown with an orange ST-L monogram on the front. New multi-color (brown & orange) piping was generously used on both shirt and trousers, including around the belt tunnels. The wide brown stripe on the socks included an orange border stripe above and below. The brown fancy lettering of BROWNS and ST. LOUIS on the jersey front also incorporated an orange outline piping.

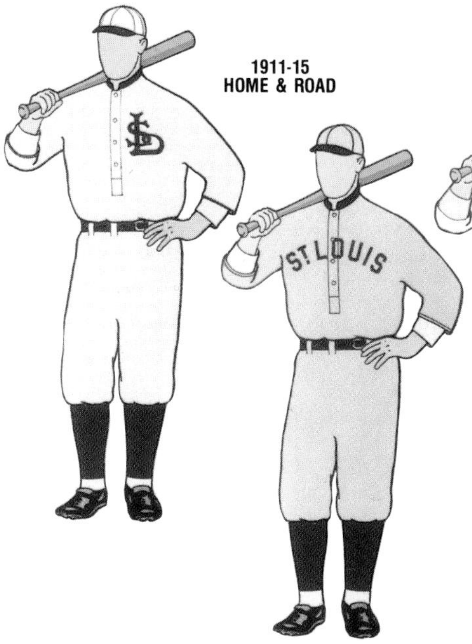

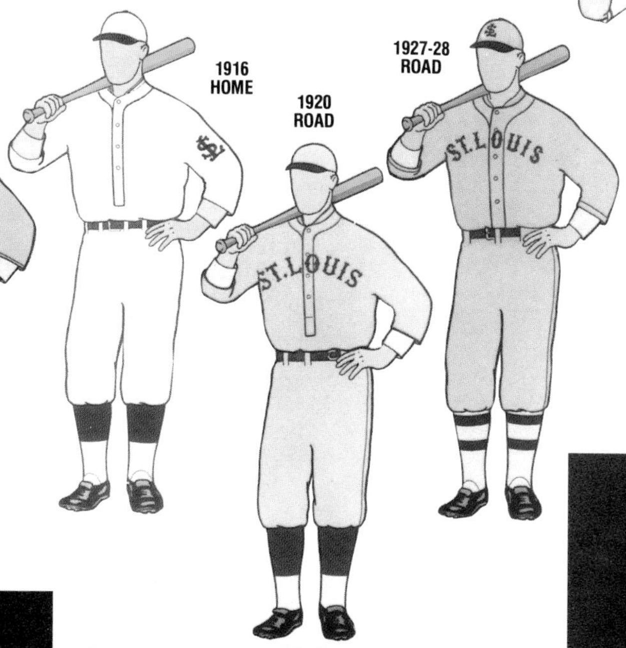

Del Pratt relaxing at Sportsman's Park c.1914

The immortal George Sisler in the early '20's

Rookie Harlond Clift at Comiskey Park in 1934

This general theme continued through the 1938 season except for some significant variations. In 1937, the color scheme of BROWNS and ST. LOUIS was reversed to orange letters with a brown outline and a newly designed team crest patch was added to the left sleeve. The piping on the button lapel was eliminated in '36 and '37 but was reintroduced in an unusual way in 1938. Instead of bordering both sides of the row of buttons, a single heavy orange & brown stripe passed directly through the buttons and up around the collar. Also in 1938, the belt loops and tunnels were made solid brown with orange trim around the edges of the tunnels.

For 1940, the brown cap was replaced by a white (or gray) crown (no ST-L emblem) with the brown & orange striping down the seams and a brown visor. This cap style remained through the 1945 season. Besides the WWII shield patches added to the left sleeve (the club crest patch was dropped after 1939), the only other modification to this run of uniforms was elimination of trim on belt loops & tunnels and reverting back to a buttoned version jersey in '44 and '45. This heavily trimmed uniform style lasted for 7 seasons (1939-45) and is best identified with the only pennant year (1944) in the club's history.

THE ROAD TO OBLIVION

The Browns opened the first post-war season (1946) with new uniforms that retained some of the trim features of previous years but much plainer and cleaner. The unique "reverse shadow" lettering of BROWNS was retained on the home whites and was also displayed on the new road grays replacing ST. LOUIS, but with the colors reversed (orange with a brown shadow edge). The zipper-front shirt style returned but the heavy striping was toned down to more modest conventional piping. The solid brown of the socks was extended down to include the stirrups and the cap was redesigned to include a plain white (or gray) crown with an orange ST.L monogram in front and a brown visor. This uniform style was retained without change through the 1949 season. In contrast to 1944-45, these uniforms symbolized dreary years of last place (or near last) finishes. The end of an era was only a few years away.

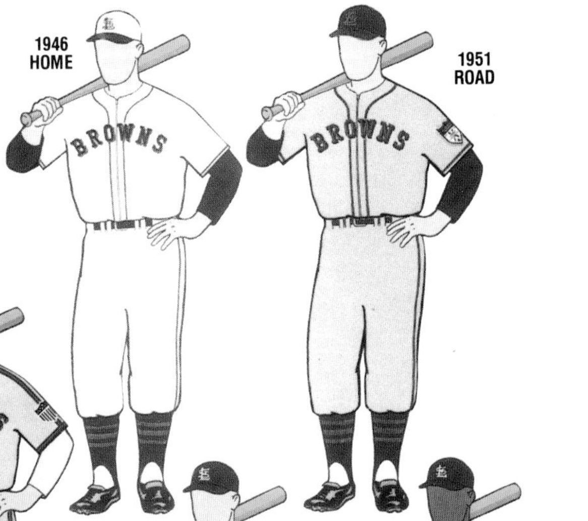

THE BEST IS YET TO COME

1939 was a landmark year for baseball — all professional teams observed the accepted centennial of the "invention" of the game by wearing the square centennial patch on the left sleeve (or right sleeve, as was the case with the Browns, since they opted to continue the display of their team crest on the left sleeve). But 1939 was also a landmark year for the Browns in particular since it marked the introduction of the best known uniform design in the club's history. This new uniform motif marked the climax of the color craze of the thirties. Zipper-front jerseys were the latest rage and the new ultra-wide brown & orange striping accented the cleaner lines of the zipper front. This wide piping also followed the shoulder lines, down to the sleeve ends, etc., etc.. The lettering style of BROWNS on the home whites and ST. LOUIS on the road grays was especially novel: a block "reverse shadow" lettering in brown and orange, not seen before on a major league uniform. The brown stockings were spruced up with 3 orange stripes and, for 1939 only, the brown cap included orange striping on the seams.

Bobo Newsom modeling the 1943 home whites

The only change made for 1950 & 1951 was in the cap —solid brown replaced white or gray as the crown color. When ownership of the franchise was turned over to Bill Veeck, he implemented the last total redesign of the Browns uniform. For 1952 and 53 (the final years of the franchise) the Browns uniform was a classic example of the no-frills, no nonsense (save the little "brownie" face on the sleeve) modern baseball uniform in the Brooklyn Dodger mold. A clean script BROWNS or ST. LOUIS slanted across the chest with an underline flourish and an absence of piping. Solid brown cap and stockings complemented this uniform which deserved a better fate...*RIP*.

ST. LOUIS CARDINALS

THE END OF THE HORSE & BUGGY ERA

Of the 16 major league franchises right after the turn of the century, only 10 have remained intact —that is to say 10 clubs among the current 26 have kept a team in the same city continuously since 1903. St. Louis has not only represented the National League since 1892 but has also been always identified as the CARDINALS, although it is said that the original meaning of the nickname had to do with its designated team colors rather than any association with birds. No matter, they have been the Cardinals as long as anybody can remember and red has always been the principal color for decorating their uniforms.

From the gay nineties on into 1900, the uniform was typical for its day —somewhat baggy with a wide belt, a full-length sleeve jersey with a regular fold-down collar and laced in the front. The city name ST. LOUIS was displayed across the chest in arched block letters. The cap was sometimes all white with a thin red band around the crown or more often a solid red with an S-T-L monogram on the front, much like today's cap. The stockings were solid red or a wide band of red with no stirrup design. This uniform design remained basically unchanged thru most of the first decade of the century except for the laced front being replaced by buttons and red trim added around the edge of the collar. Laced fronts were pretty much out of fashion by this time anyway except for the two Boston teams which continued to use them occasionally as late as 1910.

First baseman Ed Konetchy wearing the new Cardinals' uniform for 1909.

1909 HOME

1912 ROAD

1900 HOME

Patsy Donovan Cards' manager from 1901 to 1903.

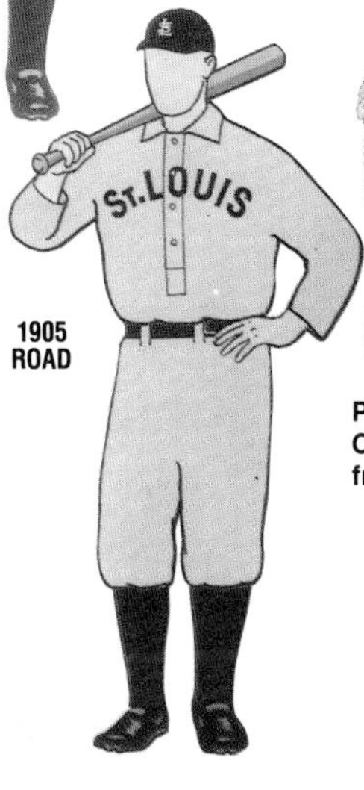

1905 ROAD

The young phenom Rogers Hornsby in 1917, his third season in the majors.

THE TEENS & INTO THE TWENTIES

The first radical change in the Cardinal uniform occured in 1909 when ST. LOUIS was removed from the jersey front. The only graphic identification with the home city was the S-T-L monogram on the sleeve. The new cap design had a white crown with red piping down the seams and a solid red bill. The stockings went from solid red to a single wide red stripe. This relatively plain uniform version remained standard for most of the next decade except for sometimes shorter sleeves and a switch to the "collarless" collar —another common trend of the times.

Since team nicknames were often inventions of the media and not always offically accepted by the clubs themselves, these nicknames were slow to appear on most team uniforms well into the century. St. Louis became the 4th team in the league (after the Cubs, Reds & Pirates) to include their nickname on the home uniform in 1918. This brand new design, replete with pin striping, represented the third major overhaul in the team's playing apparel. The significance of this is that it was the forerunner of a more famous design to come and the name CARDINALS has been displayed on every home uniform since then (except for a few interruptions). In the spirit of WWI patriotism, an american flag patch was added to the left sleeve. The home cap for 1919 was a "pillbox" style with two red stripes and a red visor. The home uniform for 1920-21 was plain white with no markings. The road uniform for these years was plain gray with ST. LOUIS restored to the jersey front in fancy style arched capital letters.

1919 HOME

1919 ROAD

1920 HOME

1921 ROAD

THE TWENTIES— FINALLY, A CHAMPIONSHIP!

In 1922, the most unique combination of graphic team symbol and team nickname made its maiden appearance on National League playing fields. The first version of 2 redbirds perched on a sloping bat which passes thru the large capital C of CARDINALS won immediate approval by St. Louis fans and helped offset the routine dullness and conformity of baseball uniforms in the twenties. The lively-ball era was also characterized by livelier, more colorful uniform graphics by the end of the decade. This particular design motif on the Cardinals unform has endured to this day (with some brief absences) and has been firmly entrenched as a visual identification of the great winning tradition of the team.

Also in 1922-23, alternate uniforms were worn on weekends and special days which included some bizarre sox striping and even a bird on the sleeve —the first graphic association with the redbird symbol. In 1923, the Cardinals experimented with uniform numbers on their sleeves, a precursor of a future standard. The 2-birds-on-a-bat design was temporarily displaced on the home uniform in 1926 by a plain white jersey with a new version of the ST-L monogram on the sleeve. A good omen, as the Redbirds defeated the heavily favored Yankees to capture the world championship. After their stunning world series upset, the club apparently could not restrain from further relishing their first baseball championship into 1927. Accordingly, they broke again with a budding tradition and proudly displayed "WORLD CHAMPIONS" on the jersey front. The Giants had done this in 1906 as did Cleveland in 1921.

Player-manager Hornsby at the peak of his career in the mid-twenties.

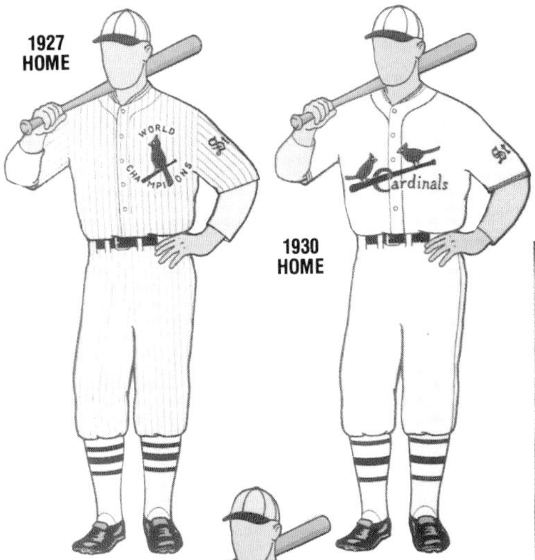

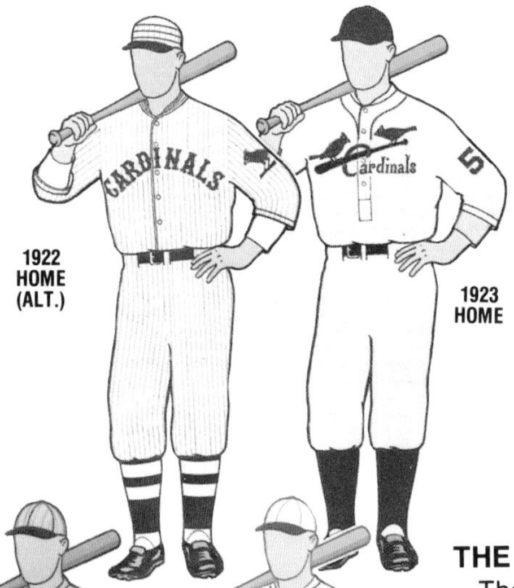

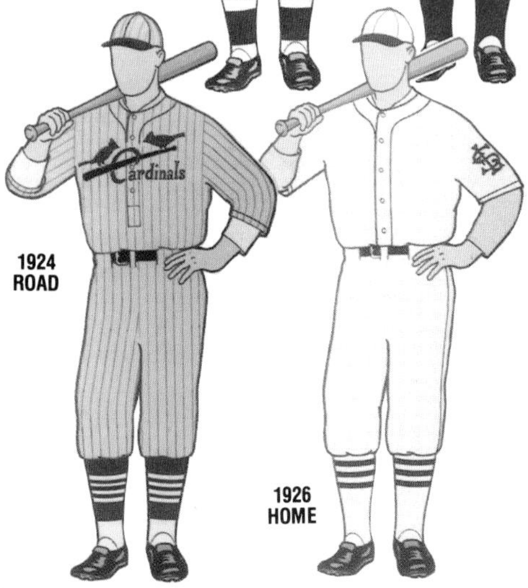

THE GAS-HOUSE GANG

The "birds-on-bat" design had been restored in 1928, but a variation of this theme appeared in the 1930 World Series —the city name ST. LOUIS supplanted the word CARDINALS. Both home and road uniforms displayed the ST. LOUIS version for the 1931-32 seasons. This Cardinal uniform symbolized the prominence of the infamous "Gas-house gang" —the Pepper Martin-Durocher-Frisch crew that stole the world championship from the powerful Philadelphia Athlethics in 1931. The only notable uniform changes thru the first half of the decade included extra white & blue stripes on the stockings and dropping the ST. LOUIS in 1933 in favor of restoring CARDINALS. By 1937, in keeping with colorful uniform trends of the thirties, extra piping was added down the button front, on the sleeve ends and around the belt tunnels. All this added piping (including on the cap) was double-striped. In 1939, again following the trends, a zipper front jersey was worn for the first time and the piping was changed again to a thicker, solid red stripe.

Young slugger Johnny Mize in the late-thirties version of the Redbirds uniform.

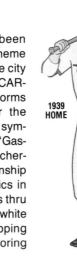

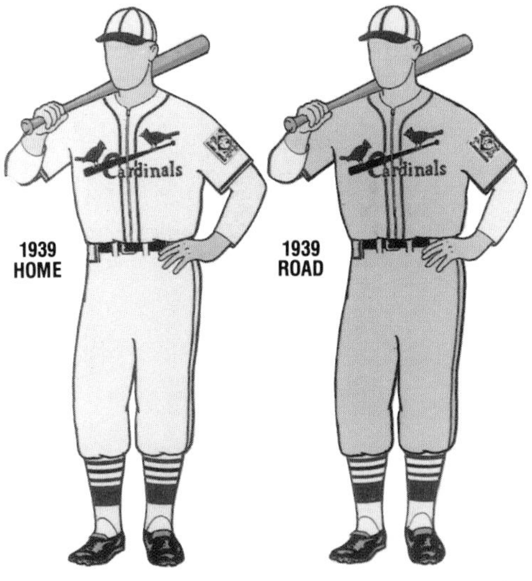

THE MUSIAL YEARS —A WARTIME DYNASTY

For the 1940 season the team dropped the white striped cap crown in favor of a solid navy blue crown with a return of the S-T-L monogram on the front and a solid red bill. An extra red stripe was also added down the shoulder. Except for a brief appearance of a redbird symbol on the cap front in 1942 and separate letters ST-L on the 1943 road cap, this was the basic uniform of the great Cardinal dynasty years of the Forties —4 pennants and 3 world championships. Appropriately it was the uniform first worn by "The Man" —Stanley Frank Musial. In the late '40's, the CARDINALS lettering was altered slightly and the capital C was elongated. The 2 birds were enlarged and changed to a more upright position on the bat. The red on the stockings was extended down to include the stirrups.

1940
HOME

1942
ROAD

A kid named Musial sparked the Cardinals to a wartime pennant in 1942.

In the early '50's, again following the trend away from excessive trim, the piping was thinned down and removed from the belt tunnels and shoulders. The bat color was changed from solid black to yellow. By the mid-fifties, club management decided once again to depart from tradition and subject the Cardinal uniforms to another major re-design from top to bottom. The cap was to be solid navy blue with the S-T-L monogram in red with a white outline. All piping was removed and the zipper-front jersey was restored to a button-front. Additional navy blue was added to the socks stripes and a red belt was issued to replace the traditional black. Navy blue sleeves were designated for the gray road uniform undersweaters. But the boldest stroke of all was to remove the long-standing 2 birds-on-a-bat from the jersey front in favor or larger, script CARDINALS —complete with the underline flourish already in vogue with many other clubs. To compensate for the absence of the birds on the chest, a new cartoon figure of a redbird in a batting stance pose was added to the left sleeve —an item still in use for jacket decoration and other club graphics. Even though this new uniform was indeed attractive on its own merits, it was to be short-lived —no doubt because of the public outcry by Cardinal traditionalists who felt that birds perched on a bat must be a permanent feature on the uniforms. By 1959, tradition had the last word and the familiar design was restored to the jersey with the "Cardinals" kept in a stylish script. To this day, this version has remained intact on front of all Cardinal jerseys.

Where have the birds-on-a-bat gone? Ken Boyer in the controversial 1956-57 uniform.

1949
HOME

1953
ROAD

1956
HOME

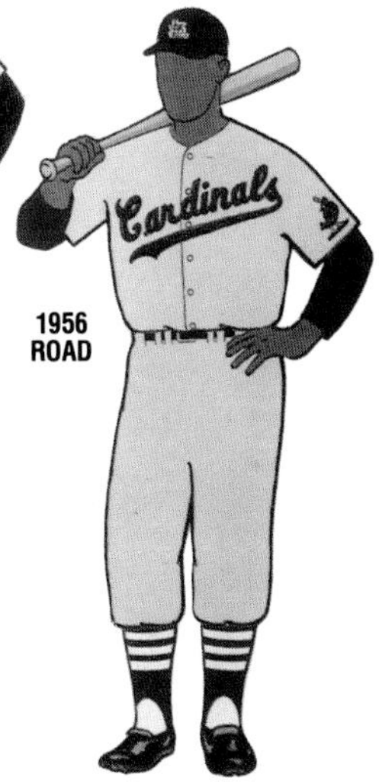

1956
ROAD

1960
HOME

1964
ROAD

THE SIXTIES AND ONWARD — A WINNING TRADITION CONTINUES

Throughout the decade of the '60's, this basic clean design was retained with only minor modifications. The solid navy cap was changed to solid red and a number was added to the jersey front by the mid-sixties. This uniform ensemble symbolized another "mini-dynasty" for the Redbirds —3 more pennants and 2 world championships from 1964-68.

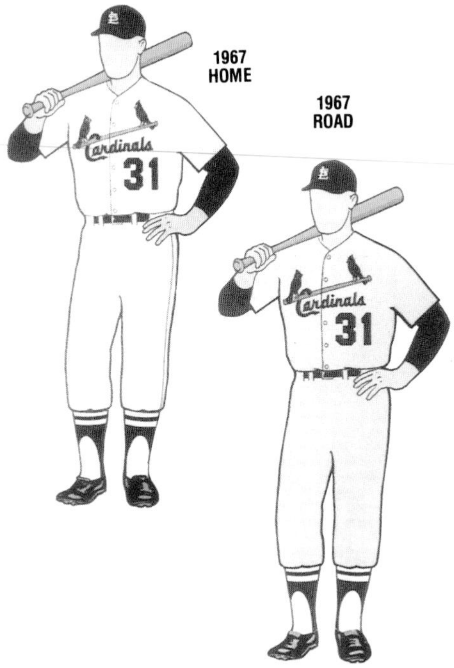

In 1972, the Cardinals jumped on the bandwagon along with all major league clubs by discarding the traditional flannels in favor of the new double-knit uniform fabrics. Lighter, more comfortable, more durable —this was the uniform of the future. Gone were the buttons & zippers on the jersey and the separate belt was discarded in favor of a built-in sash on the trousers. The Cardinal emblem design remained unaltered on the front of the new pull-over style jersey. Red, white & blue trim was added around the collar, on the sleeve ends, on the belt sash and down the sides of the trousers. This is still the basic design of today's Cardinals except for some running modifications along the way —the round "boat-neck" style collar was soon replaced by a "V"-neck, the pearl gray road uniform is now victory blue. The front uniform number was relocated to the sleeve for a year or two but was once again returned to the left front of the jersey in 1981.

History is destined to repeat itself and future changes in uniform materials, tailoring & graphics are inevitable whether they be minor or major. But after 65 years and more, certain elements of St. Louis Cardinal uniforms are so tradition-bound that they will most likely be incorporated in uniform considerations as far into the future as anyone can see... The predominant trim color will be RED and there will always be those 2 red birds perched there on that bat —perhaps contemplating how long they've been there, how many times they have symbolized championships, and gloating over their likely immortality.

Hall-of-Famer Bob Gibson mows them down in the flannels of the sixties.

Base-stealer supreme Lou Brock is off and running in 1976. Note the Bicentennial helmet and the NL 100th anniversary patch on the sleeve.

The powder blue shade for the road uniform fabric was dropped for 1985 in favor of a more traditional GRAY.

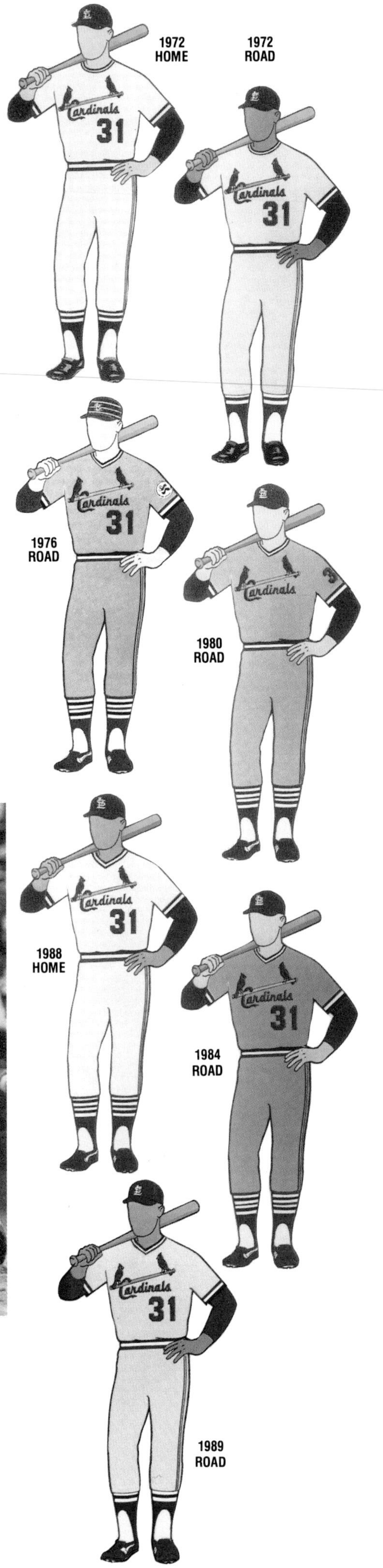

TEXAS RANGERS

SOUTHWESTWARD HO!

After a decade of dwindling attendance and mediocre team performance, the future of major league baseball in the nation's capital by 1971 was extremely precarious. The new expansion edition of the Senators fared no better than their predecessors —not even a new stadium, baseball legend Ted Williams at the helm, and more colorful uniforms could stave off the inevitable. With major league baseball Texas-style already established in Houston, the equally populous Ft. Worth-Dallas area was clamoring for representation in the Bigs. Further expansion was years away and franchise shifts provided a quicker method to attract new interest. The troubled Washington Senators seized the opportunity to relocate to greener pastures and the Texas Rangers of the American League became a reality in 1972. Faced with an identical twin-city identification crisis as the Minnesota Twins, the obvious solution was to use the state name for the official team designation.

With the double-knit uniform fabrics now in vogue, the Rangers became the first major league team to have never worn the old flannel fabrics. The nickname RANGERS was a natural —derived from a historic tradition unique to the Lone Star State. The lettering style of the name RANGERS which would appear on the chest of both home and road jerseys was also reminiscent of the old West — accented with a shadow effect. Defying originality, the team colors were to be red, white and blue —already over-used by other clubs but certainly "All American", "All-Texan", and not likely to be critized or ridiculed. The new uniforms utilized the new built-in waistband on the trousers but stayed with the traditional buttons on the jersey front. Blue was the primary trim color —caps, undersweaters and socks in solid blue. A white T edged in red was displayed on both home and road caps. Red, white and blue striping trim was used on the waistband, down the trouser legs, on the the sleeve ends and around the collar. The fabric selected for the road uniforms was gray or blue-gray for the first years of operation.

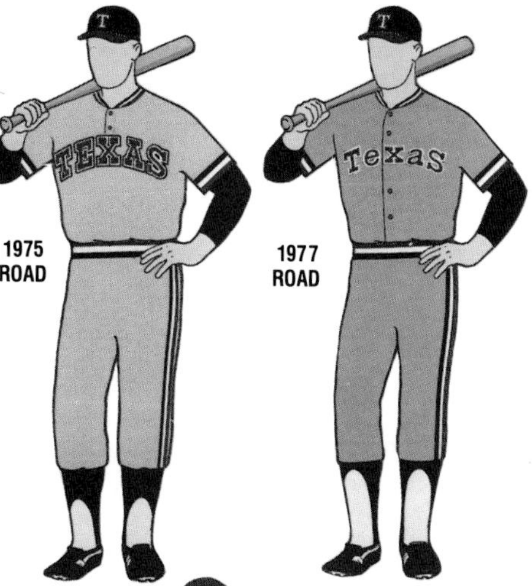

1975 ROAD

1977 ROAD

1983 HOME

1983 ROAD

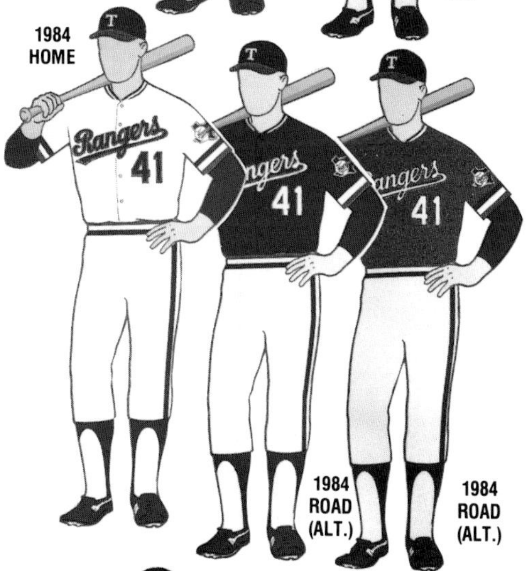

1984 HOME

1984 ROAD (ALT.)

1984 ROAD (ALT.)

1972 HOME & ROAD

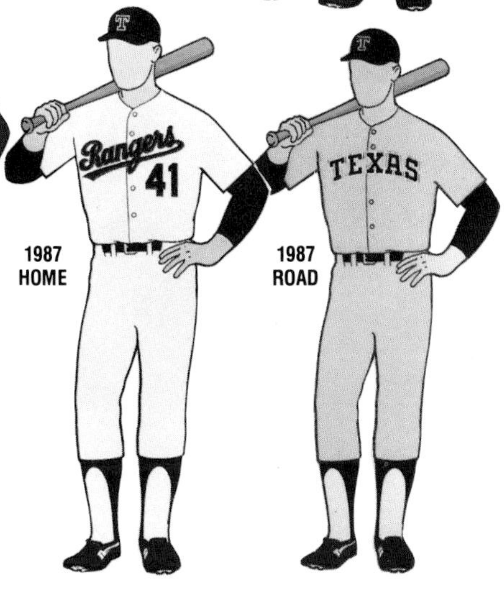

1987 HOME

1987 ROAD

The first modification to this uniform set occurred in 1975 when the name TEXAS in large red, white and blue capitals replaced RANGERS on the road suits. The following year the TEXAS name was trimmed down to duplicate the upper and lower case style of RANGERS (on the home whites) but using a white outline instead of the "shadow" effect. Also a bicentennial patch was added to the left sleeve of both uniforms. For the last years of the seventies, the jersey was changed to a pull-over style with a couple of buttons at the throat.

THE DECADE OF THE EIGHTIES

The Ranger uniform design of the late seventies continued into the early eighties. The only change was a full-button jersey style on the road uniform. With the 1983 season came a dramatic re-design of the jersey fronts. On the home whites, the RANGERS name was displayed in large blue capital letters edged in red. On the left breast, just under the lettering, was a version of the team insignia framed in an outline shape of the state of Texas. The road jersey for 1983 was solid blue with TEXAS in large white capital letters and the same team insignia underneath. This one-season uniform combination set the stage for a whole new look for the balance of the decade.

For the 1984 season, the uniform jerseys had a new look —the RANGERS name was restyled in a slanted script form, blue with a red outline. The player's number was displayed on the shirt front for the first time and the team insignia from the season before was made smaller and placed on the left sleeve. The road uniform had two versions — the primary version included a solid blue pullover jersey with the new script RANGERS and number on the front, a sort of "reverse" image of the new home jersey. A secondary road jersey of solid red with the same graphics was worn on occasion. They began the 1985 season with the same uniforms but later in the year they "jumped the gun" on 1986 by introducing their road uniforms of the future.

The Rangers joined the trend of more conventional and conservative uniforms for the '86 season. Perhaps inspired by the consistency and success of the "Dodger look", they reverted to a plainer, cleaner appearance —no striping trim and a belted trouser. They retained the RANGERS script lettering on the home jersey front, but dropped the number and sleeve emblem. The new road uniforms followed the cleaner pattern of the home whites and went to a standard all-gray fabric. The name TEXAS was revived in blue block lettering with a white outline. Will this uniform set become an enduring standard for future seasons? Not likely, unless an unexpected dynasty surfaces in Northern Texas —the trend for more futuristic uniform graphics will eventually make a comeback.

TORONTO BLUE JAYS

A SECOND CANADIAN FRANCHISE

On March 26, 1976, the American League voted to expand to 14 teams for the 1977 season. In addition to the Seattle area, Canada was awarded its second major league franchise to be located in Toronto. A "name the team" contest in the summer of 1976 produced the new nickname, the Blue Jays. Oddly enough, it was not the first time a major league club was called Blue Jays —the Philadelphia Phils attempted to adopt this name during WWII but it never really caught on. A striking team logo for the front of the jerseys was designed by Toronto-based Savage Sloan Ltd. The uniform trim colors were to be light and dark blue with a touch of white and red. The new uniforms were strictly contemporary, tailored to accommodate the features of the new double-knit styles. Both home whites and road blues utilized the pullover shirts and beltless waistbands with decorative striping of dark blue/white/light blue. Caps were dark blue with a white panel in front, displaying the new team emblem. Undersweaters and socks were solid dark blue.

In keeping with a fine Canadian reputation for tasteful graphic design (case in point: the Canadian flag), the lettering style for the name BLUE JAYS was uniquely modern with rounded corners and a thin white centered highlight line. The name TORONTO on the new powder blue road suits was in the same style without the white highlight line. A white outline was added later to highlight the solid blue lettering. For 1980, the BLUE JAYS lettering replaced TORONTO on the road suits except in a reverse form —that is, white letters with a thin blue center line highlight. This current uniform set has remained constant for the decade of the eighties and the Blue Jays have arrived as a solid contender.

A NEW STADIUM, A NEW LOOK

To celebrate a new domed stadium home, the Jays presented a redesigned uniform set for 1989 that retains the familiar graphics of past seasons. It's back to buttons and belts and the name TORONTO on the blue-gray road suits. The insignia is shifted to the left breast and a solid blue cap is to be worn on the road.

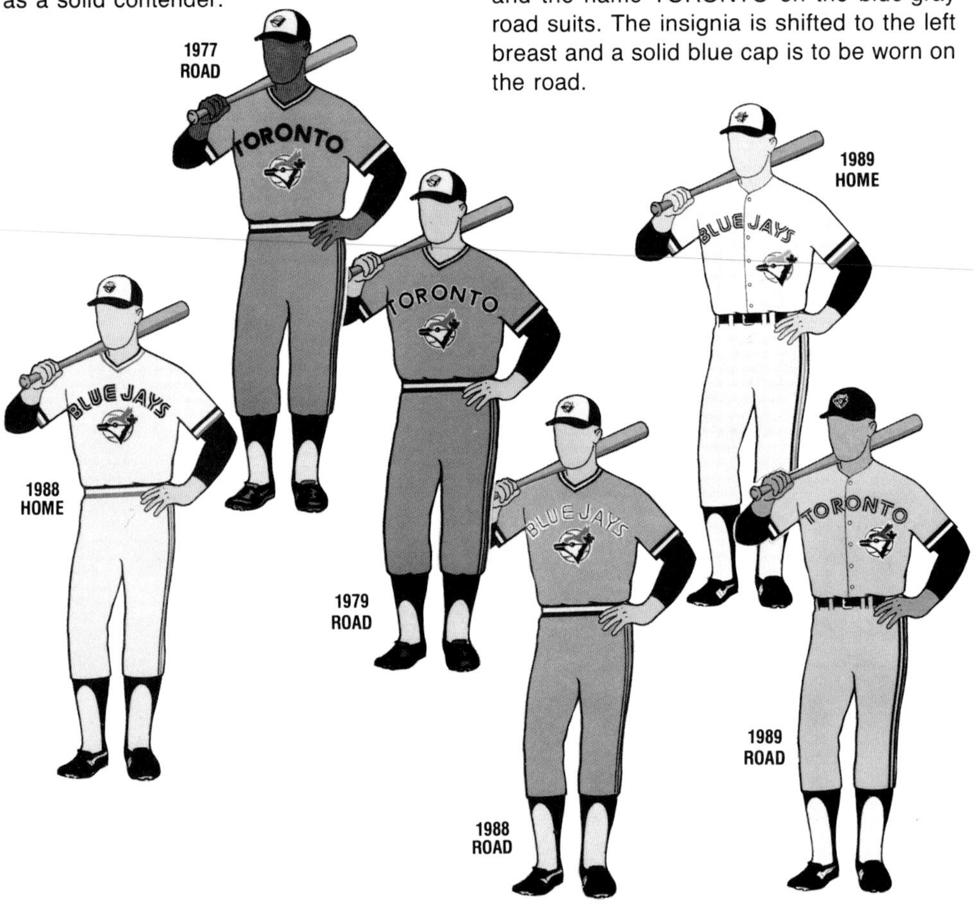

The 1984 Blue Jays, who finished a strong second place and emerged as a solid contender for the eighties

WASHINGTON SENATORS

ENDING A BRIEF ABSENCE FROM THE MAJORS

When the National League was reduced from twelve to eight teams after the 1899 season, the Washington club was one of the casualties. The American League decided to declare itself a second major league for the 1901 season and new franchises were set up in the major eastern cities, including the nation's capitol. A new park was hastily assembled in the northeast section of the district. The uniforms were selected in the standard styles of the day —white at home and gray for traveling. All trimmings were to be BLACK; including the stockings, two wide bands around the "pillbox" cap, and the city name WASHINGTON spelled out in arched block capitals. The 1902 uniforms were a bit dressier with a switch to BLUE trim. A large block W replaced WASHINGTON and solid blue was added to the fold-down collar and on the beaks of the new round-crown caps. The W was reworked in an ornamental style for the 1903 uniform shirts. It was back to the name WASHINGTON on the 1904 uniform shirt front.

A NEW IDENTITY IS IN ORDER

Apparently determined to disassociate itself with the defunct NL Senators of the 1890's, the club officially declared themselves the NATIONALS for the 1905 season. They had abandoned their NE park location the season before and relocated to the site of the former NL franchise just off Florida Avenue. The new uniforms returned to BLACK trim with the home whites strikingly similar to the first 1901 home suits, with one notable exception. The name NATIONALS was displayed across the front for one and all to see —the first time in major league history that the team nickname was spelled out on the game uniform. The gray road uniforms for 1905 displayed a large capital W on the left breast and the caps were the standard round crown —gray with black piping and a black visor. The "NATIONALS" theme was repeated on the 1906 home uniforms but the new traveling outfits for that season were a whole new image. Instead of the conventional gray, the whole uniform set was solid BLACK with WHITE trimmings — including buttons, belt, a wide stripe on the stockings and an Old English W on the shirt pocket. The new "Nationals" under Mgr. Jake Stahl fared no better than their predecessors and the club remained buried deep in the second division for the entire decade.

1907 HOME

1907 ROAD

As often seems the case with a perennial losing club, uniforms continued to be changed every year in an effort to escape the "hoodoo" of being a loser. The 1907 suits restored the capital W to the shirt fronts at home, and WASHINGTON on the dark blue road uniforms. It was back to the name WASHINGTON at home in 1908 and then the W again in 1909. The 1910 uniforms both retained the capital W on the front, but the shirts incorporated the new "collarless" look. A solid dark panel encircled the neck area and down the buttons. The road outfit was a gray duplication of the home uniform. The 1911 uniforms repeated the same general appearance but the collar was now the more trendy stand-up "cadet" style. On the road gray shirts, the trim on the button panel was changed to a heavy outline piping and the capital W was a square-serif block style instead of "fancy". The great Walter Johnson won 25 games in 1910 and 1911 and things began to look up for the "Nationals".

1901 HOME

1902 HOME

1905 HOME

1905 ROAD

1903 ROAD

'Long Tom" Hughes at home in 1909

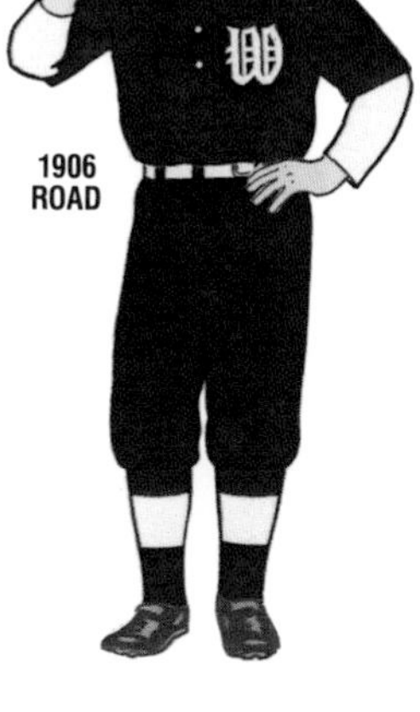

1906 ROAD

1908 HOME

1909 HOME

1909 ROAD

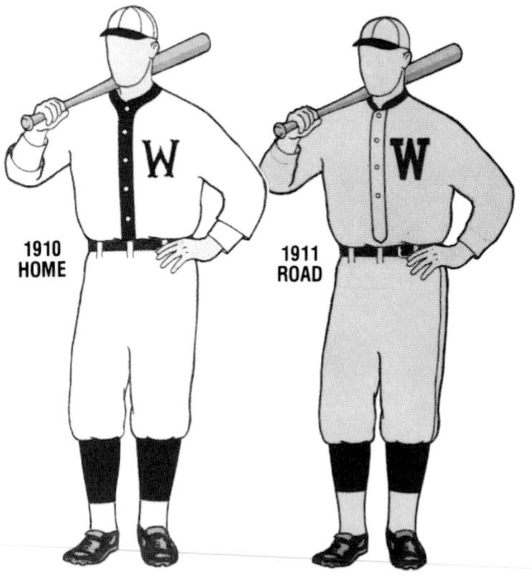

1910 HOME

1911 ROAD

THE CLARK GRIFFITH SAGA BEGINS

The "Old Fox", Clark Griffith, was hired to manage the Washington club for the 1912 season. One of his first directives was another re-design of the game uniforms —Griffith was determined to have his new charges well suited for the pennant wars. The fabric selected was the thin, finely spaced pinstriped material which had become somewhat popular by this time. The trim color was to be navy blue. The unusual caps were solid navy with a white accent trim around the base of the crown and also around the edge of the visor. The cadet collar and button panel were solid navy as was the trim stripe on the sleeve ends. The shirt fronts were otherwise plain with no markings, as the capital W was re-positioned to the sleeves. Stockings were half navy and half white (or gray). These striking new uniforms ordered by Mgr. Griffith seemed to work wonders, as the club skyrocketed to an incredulous second-place finish in 1912. They never could nail down a pennant in these outfits but at least they were a respectable first division club for most of the four-year run of this uniform set (1912-15). In 1916, those unusual caps were exchanged for a more conventional solid navy version with a white W in the front.

JOINING THE PIN-STRIPE BRIGADE

In 1917, the Nationals' uniforms were reworked into a more conventional "mainstream" look. The finer pinstriping gave way to the more common wider spaced, more visible stripes that were in vogue by this time. The navy trimmings on the shirt were gone and only the W on the sleeves was kept. An extra white stripe was added to the stocking pattern. As a by-product of WWI patriotism, a red, white and blue shield patch was placed on the left breast. This basic plain uniform look was repeated on through the 1925 season except for some minor changes along the way —a "V"-neck collar style in 1920 and a plain gray (no pinstripes) fabric for the road uniforms about 1922. Washington baseball history was made in these uniforms in 1924-25 as the team won two pennants and its only world championship in 1924. At the end of an illustrious career, "The Big Train" finally was able to capture a world series victory after performing annual miracles with mostly losing clubs. Boy manager Bucky Harris was also one of the heroes of the day in the Capitol city.

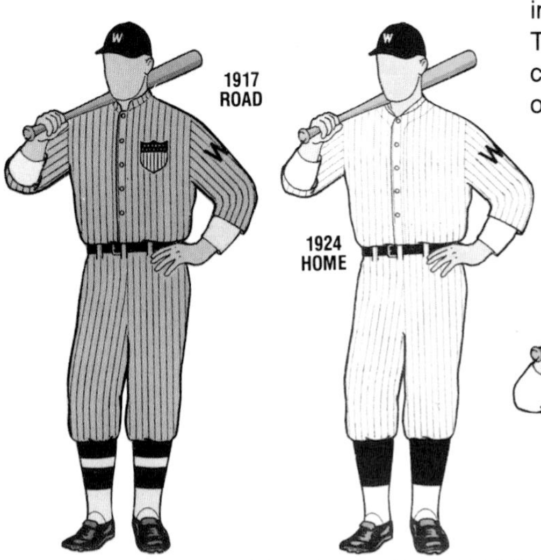

1917 ROAD

1924 HOME

SOME NOVEL IDEAS, THEN BACK TO THE NORM

The new uniform sets for 1926-27 were a refreshing change after nearly a decade of the "plain" look —a celebration, perhaps, of the fruits of recent pennant successes. The home suits were your basic plain white but with a touch of colorful piping on the sleeve ends and collar and a patriotic shield patch in place of the W on the sleeve. Cap crowns were now white (or gray) with a dark blue W in front and a dark visor. Stockings were solid white with narrow red and blue stripes at the calf. It was a brief participation in the "awakening" of baseball uniforms during the next decade, but in 1928 the uniforms drifted back to the plain pinstripe look of the early twenties. The block W was restored on the sleeves in a square-serif style and another white (or gray) stripe was added to the stockings, but otherwise the home uniform was back to "normal". The road suits remained plain gray or bluish-gray. By 1929 the early-20's look was back for good —for a while, at least. The stockings in 1933 were solid dark down through the stirrups and included a single white stripe about halfway. This particular uniform is also symbolic of a club milestone —another pennant, the last one ever in Washington.

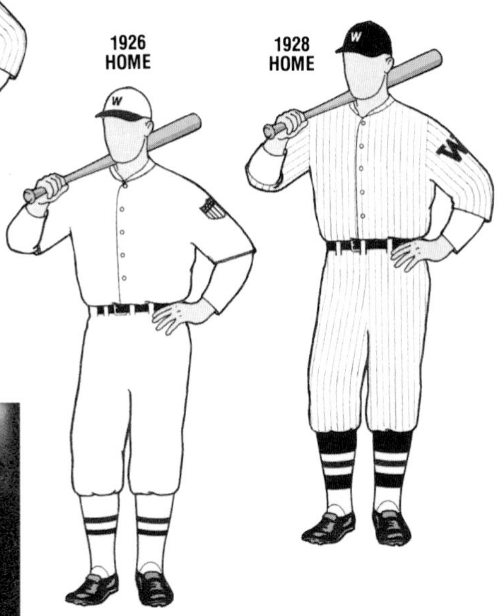

1926 HOME

1928 HOME

1912 HOME

1916 ROAD

Walter Johnson about 1913

The "Big Train" again in 1927

1930 ROAD

1933 HOME

A BIT MORE COLOR, BUT NOT FOR LONG

In a somewhat feeble attempt to join the trend of more colorful uniforms which was sweeping the major leagues in the thirties, the Senators (''Nationals'' just never seemed to catch on) added some touches of red to dress up the uniform starting in 1935. Red striping was added to the upper white of the stockings. Then in 1936, the W on the cap was done in red with a white outline. Red border piping was also included on the sleeve W and two red stripes were added to the upper blue of the stockings. If any team seemed historically and geographically entitled to wear red, white and blue, certainly it was Washington DC. But, for whatever reason, the club under Mr. Griffith was always reluctant to exploit this color combination and was forever destined to drift back to the somber predominance of navy blue trim. In 1938, the W was returned to the shirt front and edged in red piping, but after that it was no more red of any significance on the uniform trim.

''FIRST IN THE HEARTS ... LAST IN THE LEAGUE''

The 1939 uniforms were possibly the plainest uniforms ever worn by a major league team. Solid white at home, solid gray for the road —not a trace of piping trim anywhere. Caps, undersweaters and stockings were solid navy and the only markings were a plain W on the sleeve and on the cap. The only touch of color on this lifeless uniform was the red, white and blue 1939 centennial patch worn on the sleeve. The blank shirt fronts were made even more stark-looking by the new zipper front. This ''no frills'' look was repeated in 1940. In 1941, the block W was returned to the shirt front and new striping on the stockings provided some relief. This basic uniform design remained as the basic image of the Senators for the next ten seasons with only the addition of pinstripes at home during the war years and some piping added at the end of the war. The wartime teams of 1943 and 1945 under Ossie Bluege came close to winning the pennant, but it was to be the last time a Washington team would be a serious contender. They embarked on a long and dubious tradition as a tail-ender —''first in the hearts of their countrymen and last in the American League'' became a catch-phrase in the post-war era.

By 1950, some red trim was reinstated to give some relief to the dreary navy trim. Ironically, a losing tradition on the field in repetitive uniforms has the opposite effect of that of a winning team. Had those Washington teams of the forties been a winning dynasty, their uniforms would be considered untouchable classics. Case in point —the New York Yankees' uniforms during the same period were equally lifeless and colorless, yet no one dare suggest any sartorial overhaul for the New Yorkers then or now. Plain WINNING uniforms become a sacred tradition, plain LOSING uniforms a symbol of futility. The hit Broadway musical ''Damn Yankees'' was developed from this sense of futility. However, when the play was the talk of show business in 1956, the Washington uniforms worn by Joe Hardy et al had been considerably brightened up. A red stripe was added to the stockings and the cap W was also made red. The blue block W on the home jersey was made three-dimensional with red piping outline. The new road uniforms for that season resurrected the name WASHINGTON in blue block capitals trimmed in red —in an arc that stretched from armpit-to-armpit. This uniform set was kept intact through the 1958 season.

1935 HOME

1936 ROAD

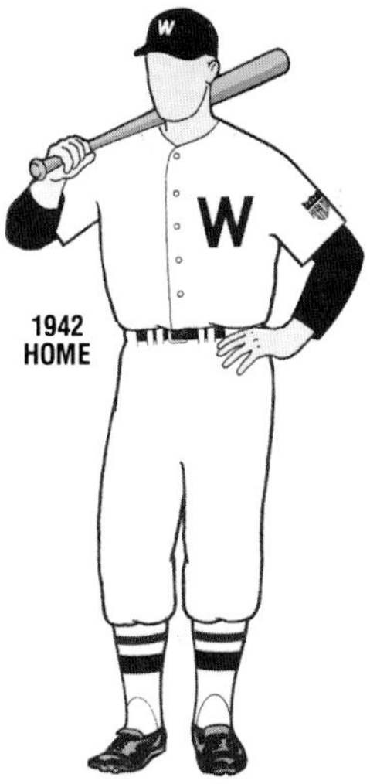
1942 HOME

1946 ROAD

1950 HOME

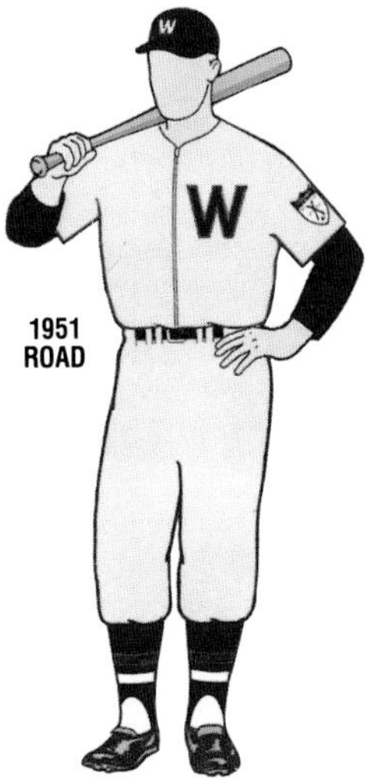
1951 ROAD

1938 HOME

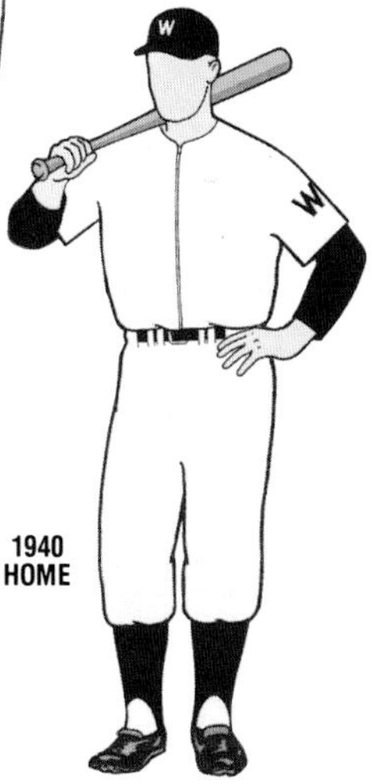
1940 HOME

Manager Bucky Harris and Clyde Milan in 1952

1956 HOME

1956 ROAD

A FACE LIFT FOR THE LAST HURRAH

After decades of losing teams and failing attendance, the handwriting was on the wall for the Washington club. Either turn the team's fortunes around or look for greener pastures. Relocation of franchises was no longer unthinkable. New uniforms for 1959 finally acknowledged the team nickname — SENATORS in navy and red script across the chest —but failed to avoid another last place finish. By 1960, Calvin Griffith had had enough and obtained permission from the league to transfer his franchise to Minnesota for the 1961 season. Happily, for the hard core of DC baseball fans, all was not lost as an expansion franchise was immediately formed to continue major league play in Washington. The departed club had also left the nickname SENATORS behind for continuity's sake.

The new Senators team was less reluctant to exploit red, white and blue as trim colors on the new uniforms for 1961. The W on the blue caps was now red with a white outline. The name SENATORS was displayed on the home pinstripes in a slight arc of fancy red capital letters. The new gray road uniforms were not unlike the traditional Red Sox road suits with WASHINGTON in solid navy block letters in a straight line across the chest. For 1963, the caps were totally re-styled with a new script W and red piping on the crown seams. The slanted script version of SENATORS was revived from 1960, this time in red with navy outline. The sock's striping was changed to individual red bands with white bordering in the last years of this uniform run. For the last three years of the Senators existence (1969-71), RED finally emerged as the primary trim color, reducing navy blue to merely an accent color. Caps, stockings, undersweaters and even the belts were solid red, both at home and away. With baseball legend Ted Williams at the helm, they played their last league game at RFK stadium in 1971 —destined to resurface as the Texas Rangers in 1972. The pain of the loss has remained and talk of another expansion franchise in the nation's capitol is a distinct probability by the 1990's.

1959 HOME

1960 ROAD

1961 HOME

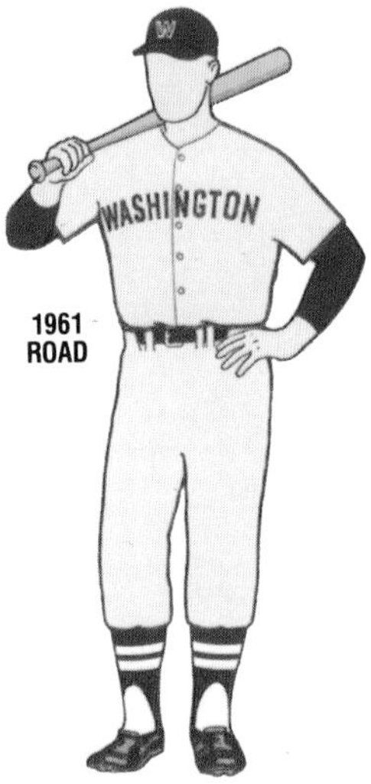

1961 ROAD

1963 HOME

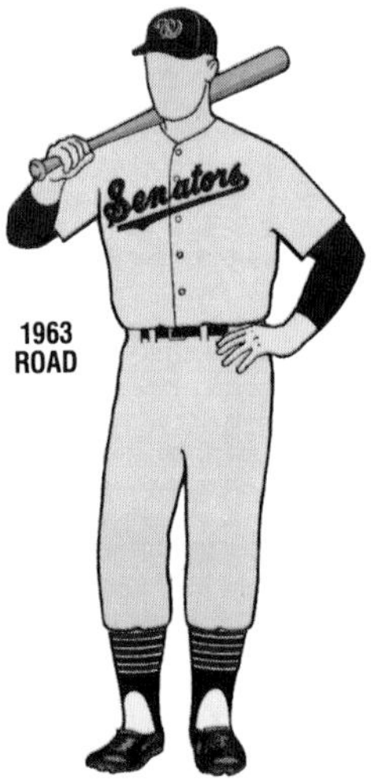

1963 ROAD

1971 HOME

1971 ROAD

Mike Epstein at home in the late sixties

NATIONAL LEAGUE 1900

BOSTON

BROOKLYN

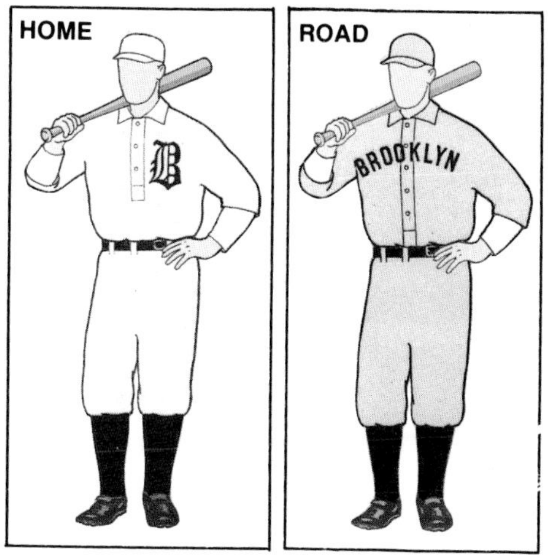

ST. LOUIS

PITTSBURGH

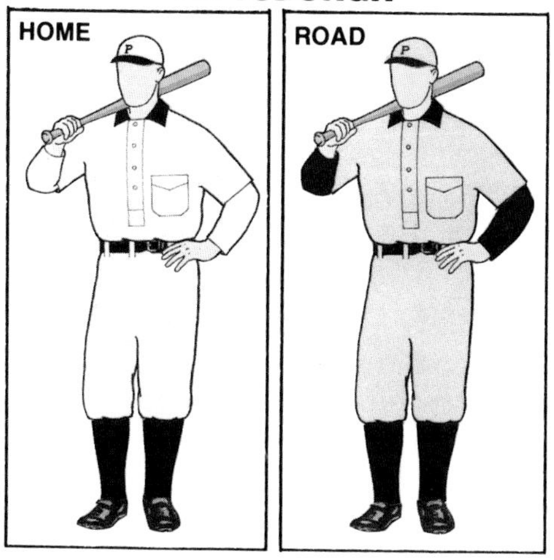

PHILADELPHIA

CHICAGO

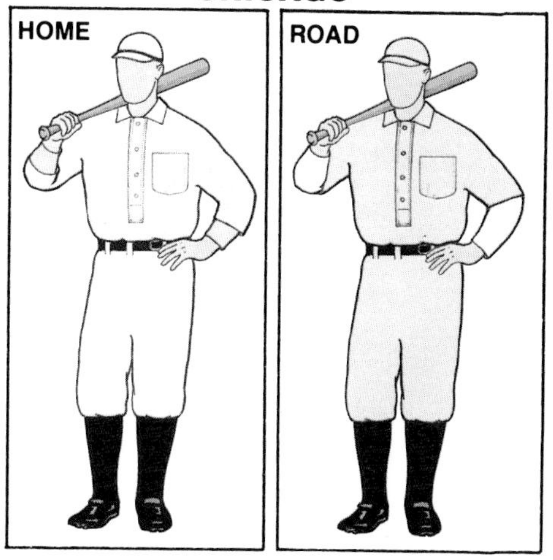

CINCINNATI

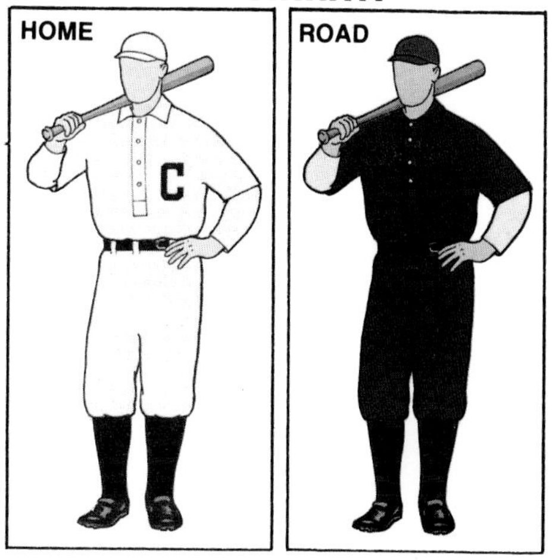

NEW YORK

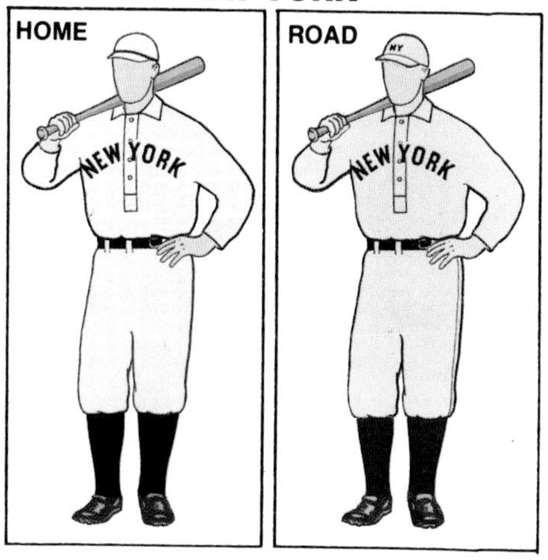

NIGHT EXTRA **Philadelphia Evening Item.** NIGHT EXTRA

FIFTY-THIRD YEAR. PHILADELPHIA, SATURDAY, MAY 12, 1900.—TEN PAGES. ONE CENT.

JEFFRIES WINS BIG FIGHT!

By Defeating Corbett, After 23 Rounds of Battle, He Retains the World's Championship.

FRIGHTFUI JAMES J. JEFFRIES JAMES J. CORBETT STRENGTH WINS

1901 AMERICAN LEAGUE

BOSTON

CLEVELAND

DETROIT

MILWAUKEE

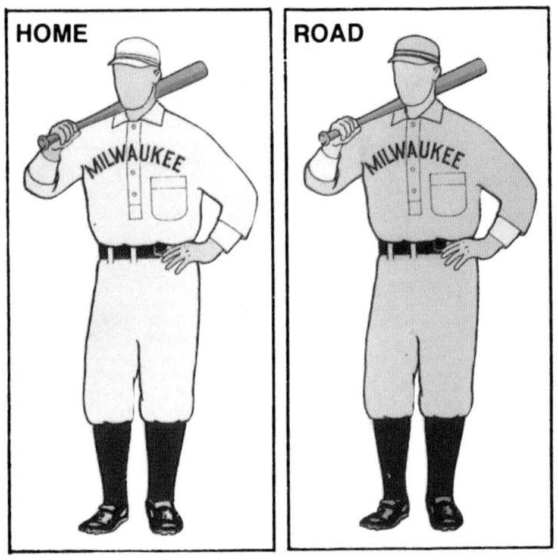

BALTIMORE

PHILADELPHIA

CHICAGO

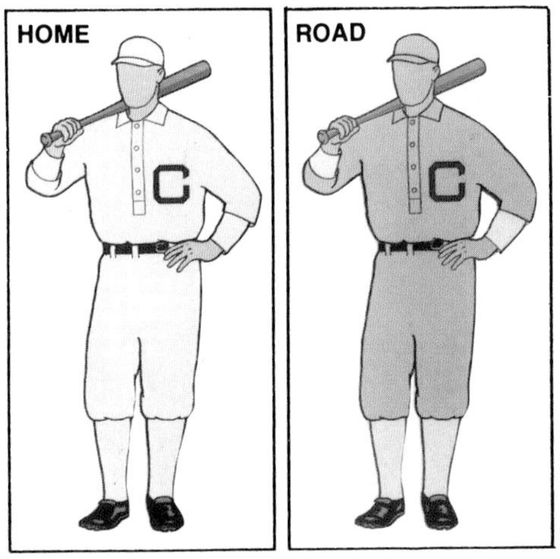

WASHINGTON

FIRST HOME GAME OF BOSTON AMERICAN LEAGUE TEAM WILL BE PLAYED TODAY.

Opening of the Huntington Avenue Grounds Eagerly Awaited by Enthusiastic Followers of the Game.

The first appearance of the Boston American League team at home and the dedication of the Huntington avenue grounds today makes this one of the beautiful ball park is putting it mildly. They are to be reckoned, location, also and convenience considered, among the very best in the country. Everything in connection with them will be in readi- pitcher to warm up after the batsman has taken his position.

The American League decided that as the baseball furnished by them last year was satisfactory, no change in the play- the Norwich team, and both he and Parent have been eminently satisfactory in their new company.

Young, the pitcher, is another old leaguer. He was long with the Cleveland

NATIONAL LEAGUE 1901

BOSTON

BROOKLYN

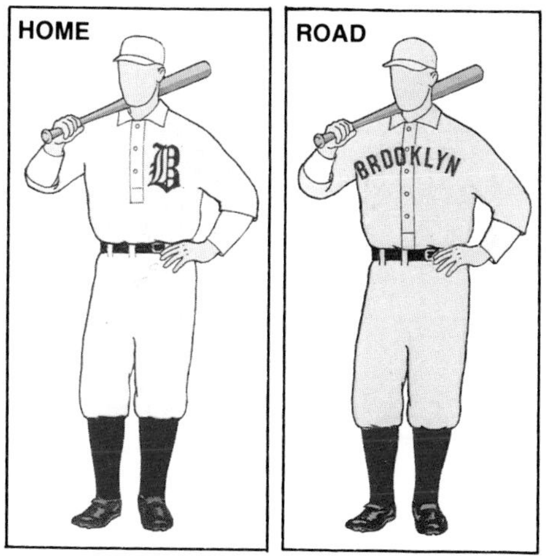

ST. LOUIS

PITTSBURGH

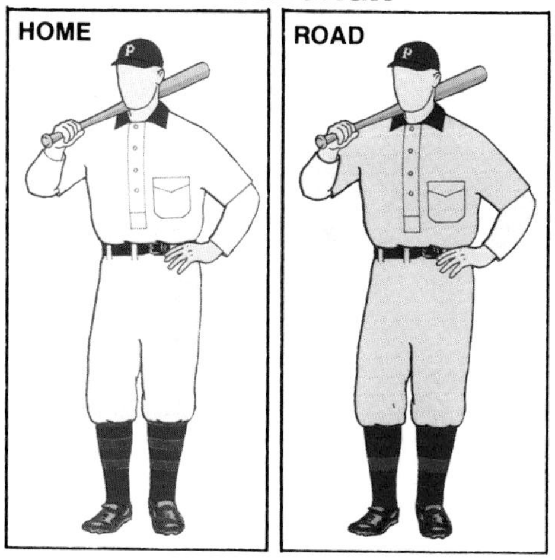

PHILADELPHIA

CHICAGO

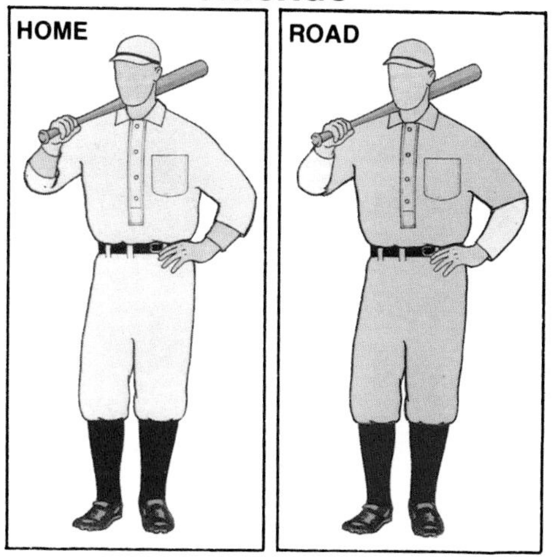

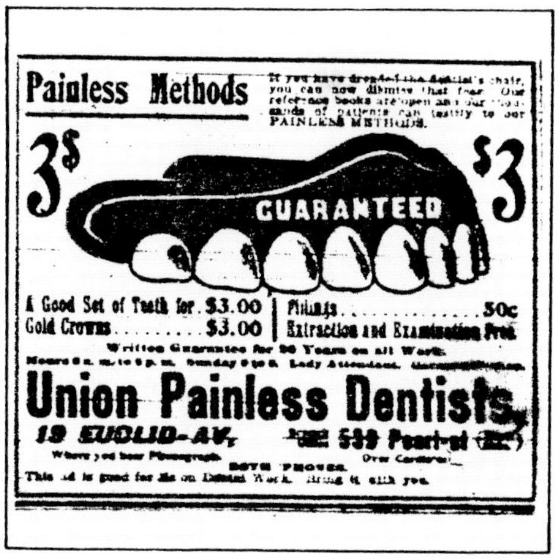

CINCINNATI

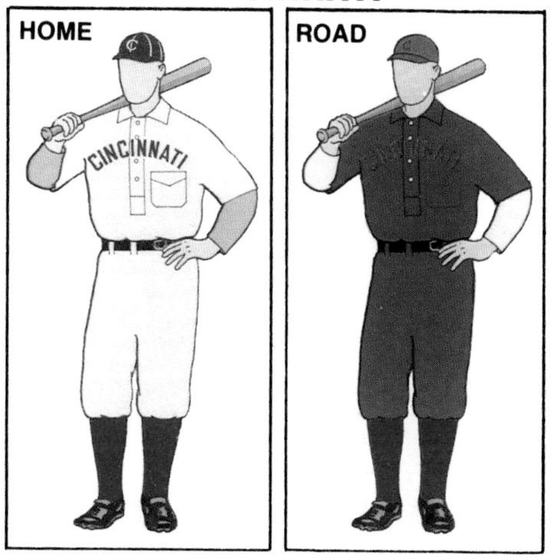

NEW YORK

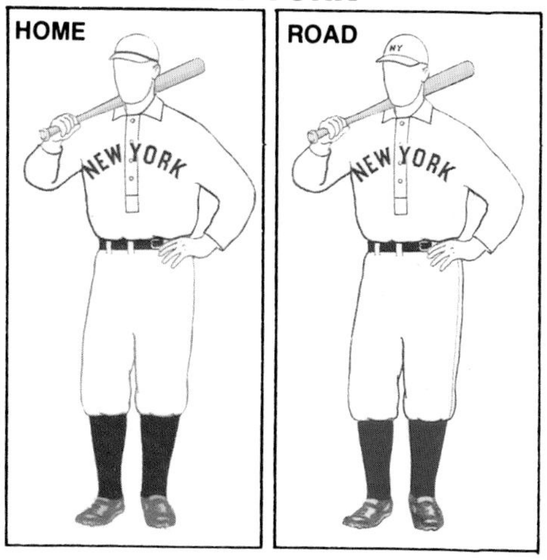

NEW YORK HERALD, SATURDAY, SEPTEMBER 14, 1901—TWENTY-TWO PAGES.

PRESIDENT M'KINLEY IS DEAD! HIS LAST WORDS WERE:---"IT IS GOD'S WAY---HIS WILL BE DONE"

1902 AMERICAN LEAGUE

BOSTON

CLEVELAND

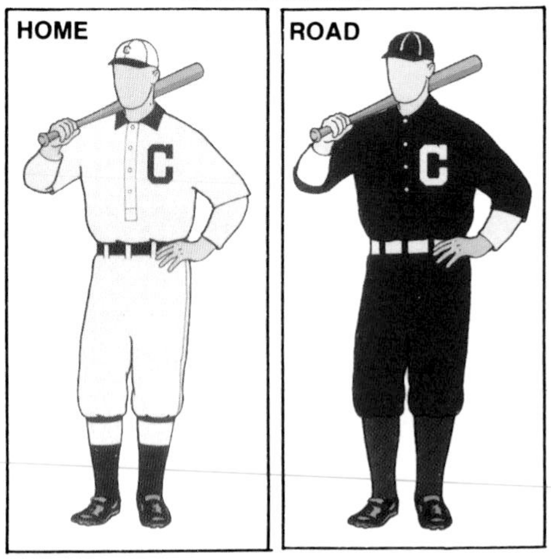

DETROIT

ST. LOUIS

BALTIMORE

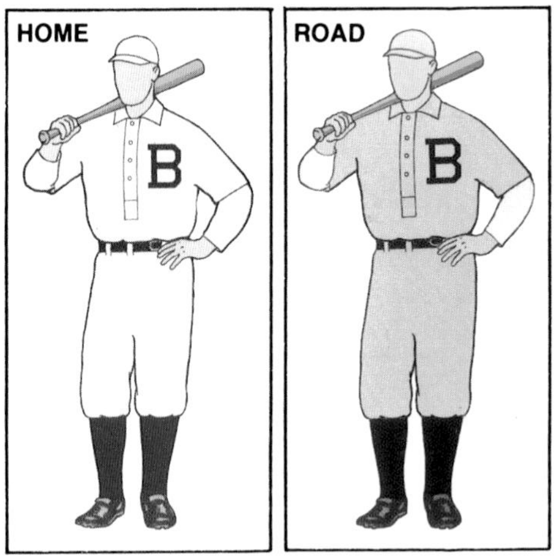

PHILADELPHIA

CHICAGO

WASHINGTON

1773 1902

Baltimore American.

ESTABLISHED 1773. VOL. CXCII. NO. 35,034. ★BALTIMORE, THURSDAY, APRIL 24, 1902.★ LARGEST SWORN CIRCULATION IN AND OUT OF THE CITY. PRICE ONE CENT.

Local Notes.

Special Notice to Carpenters.

FIRE SALE.

Local Notes.

GRACE GEORGE

"UNDER SOUTHERN SKIES"

ELITA PROCTOR OTIS

EAST LYNNE.

HENRY MILLER

D'ARCY OF THE GUARDS.

CHARLES DALTON in The Sign of the Cross

NEW PLANS FOR FRANCE'S NAVY.

STORMY DEBATE IN THE LANDSTHING.

BAD START FOR M'GRAW'S STARS.

PRIEST WAS KILLED BY WATER CURE.

A FEW MINUTES WITH THE NEWS.

NATIONAL LEAGUE 1902

BOSTON

BROOKLYN

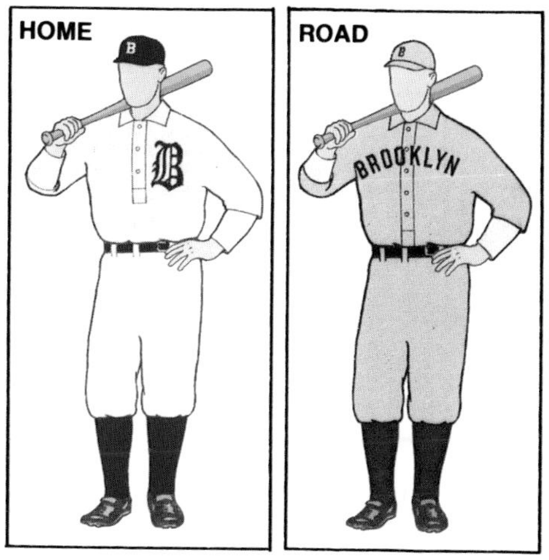

ST. LOUIS

PITTSBURGH

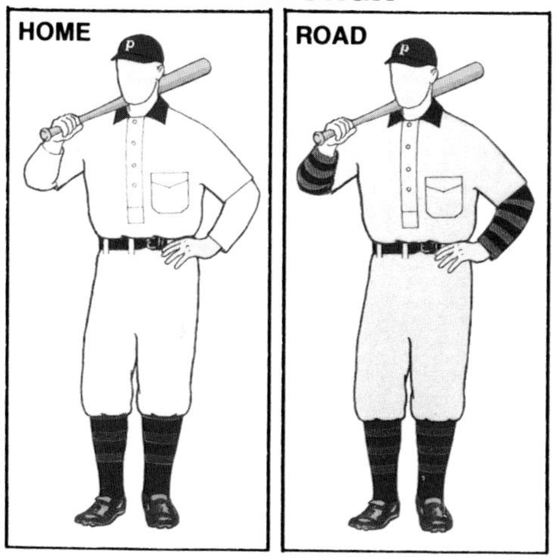

PHILADELPHIA

CHICAGO

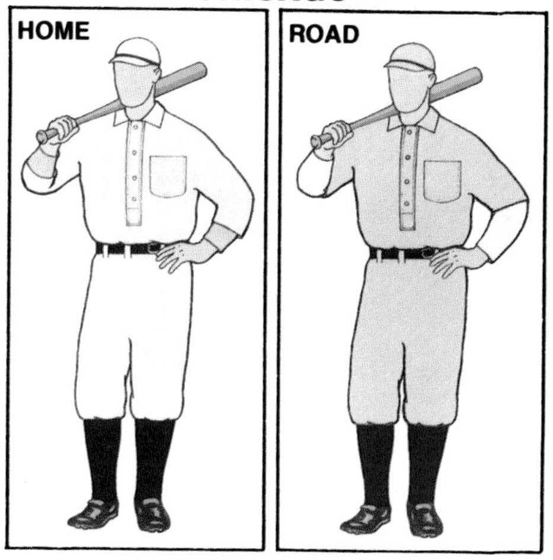

CINCINNATI

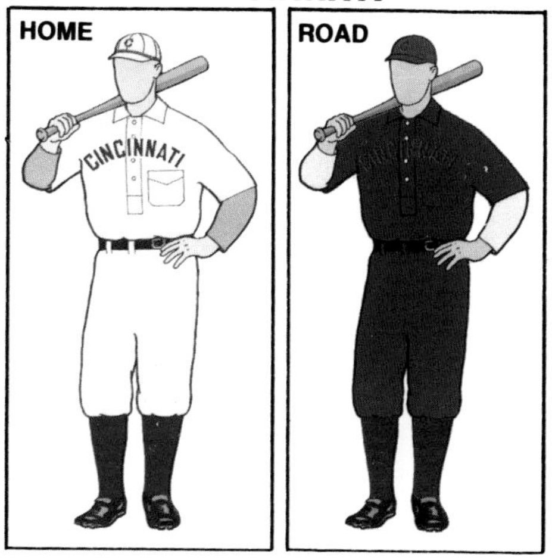

NEW YORK

THE PITTSBURG DISPATCH, TUESDAY, SEPTEMBER 8, 1903

PITTSBURG AGAIN CLINCHES THE PENNANT BY DEFEATING BROOKLYNS TWICE

CHAMPIONS AGAIN ARE THE PIRATES

TWO GOOD GAMES FROM BROOKLYNS

Pittsburg Wins Both by Sensational Ninth Inning Playing—Burke Batted Strongly.

EACH GETS A GAME

SAM STRANG GIVES ORIOLES THREE RUNS

Third Baseman Makes Misplays and Robinson's Wild Throw Puts Game to a Tie.

OTHER AMATEUR GAMES

BOSTON CAN'T SCORE

EDGEWORTH CLUB SCHEDULE

LABOR DAY ON THE LOCAL GOLF LINKS

1903 AMERICAN LEAGUE

BOSTON

CLEVELAND

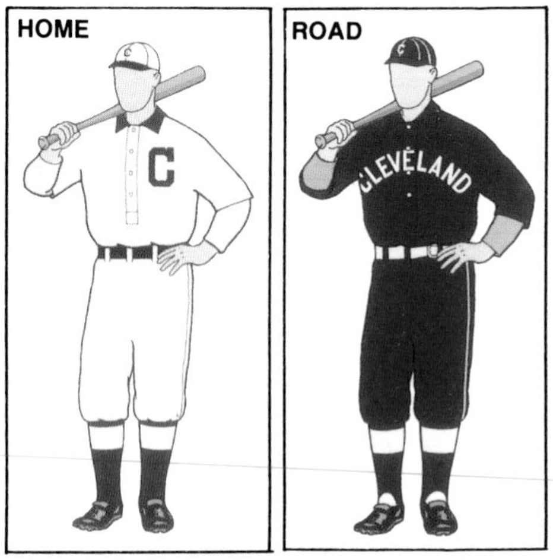

DETROIT

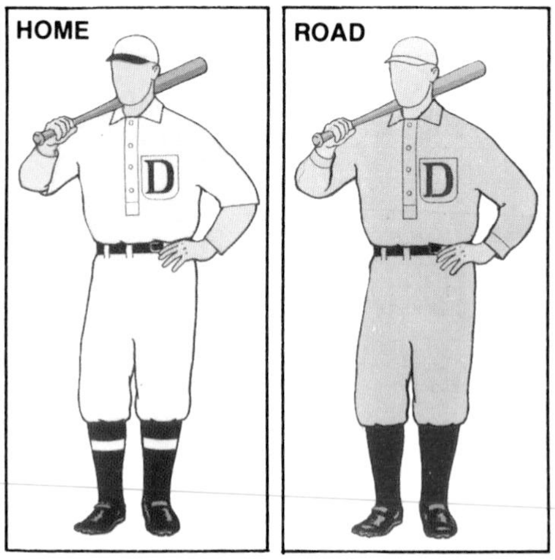

ST. LOUIS

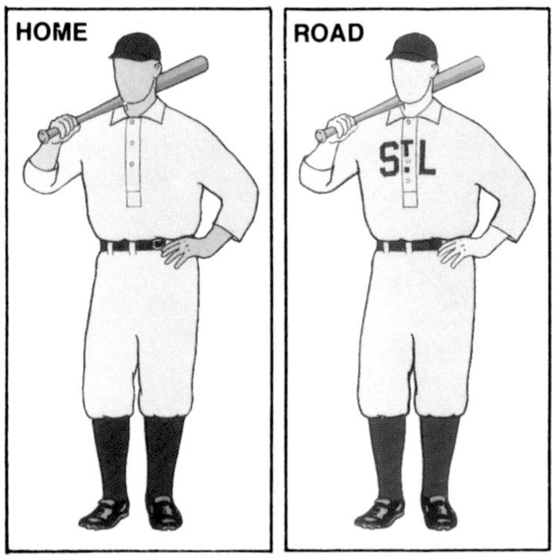

NEW YORK

PHILADELPHIA

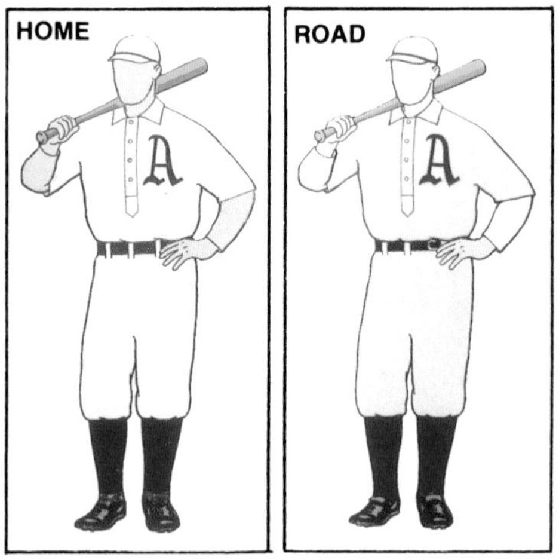

CHICAGO

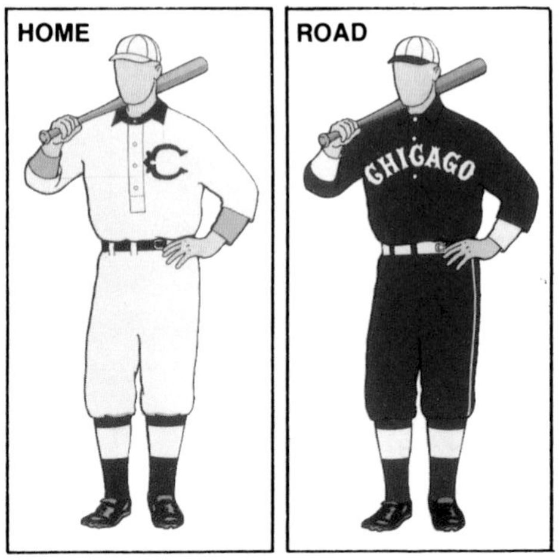

WASHINGTON

NIGHT EXTRA BASEBALL AND RACING

The Evening Telegram

NIGHT EXTRA BASEBALL AND RACING

VOL. XXXVI. NO. 21,648. NEW YORK, THURSDAY, APRIL 30, 1903.—SIXTEEN PAGES. PRICE ONE CENT.

SUN BAKED BASEBALL FANS CHEER AT AMERICAN'S OPENING

More Than 16,000 Enthusiasts Witness First Contest on New Grounds.

GRAND STAND IS STILL WITHOUT ROOF

Officials of New League from Many Cities Gather to Witness New York Debut.

WASHINGTON	000000110	— 2
N. Y. AMERICAN	11002020x	— 6

N. Y. NATIONAL

010000001 — 2

PHILADELPHIA

30210040 —10

BOSTON

0001003

BROOKLYN

010000

HARBOR TRAFFIC TIE-UP MAY YET BE AVERTED

Conferences in Progress May Result in at Least Deferring a General Strike.

MANY OWNERS ALREADY LET TUG BOATS STAY IDLE

NATIONAL LEAGUE 1903

BOSTON

BROOKLYN

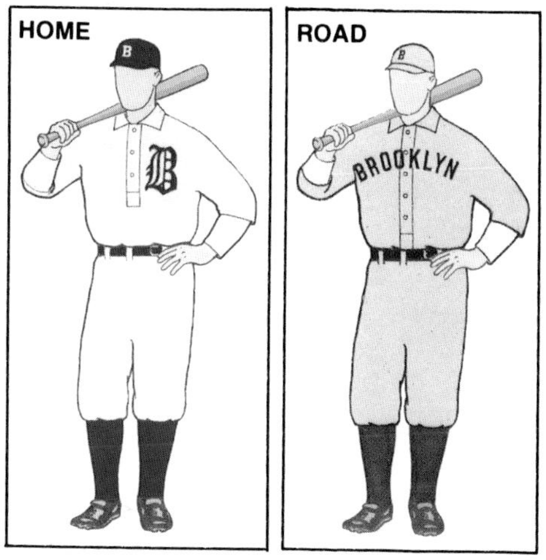

ST. LOUIS

PITTSBURGH

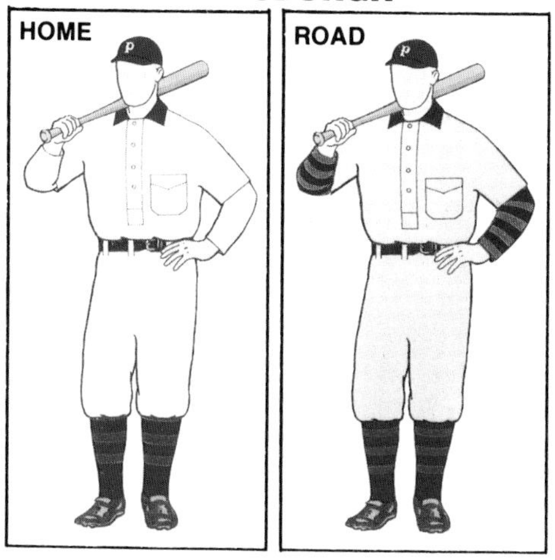

PHILADELPHIA

CHICAGO

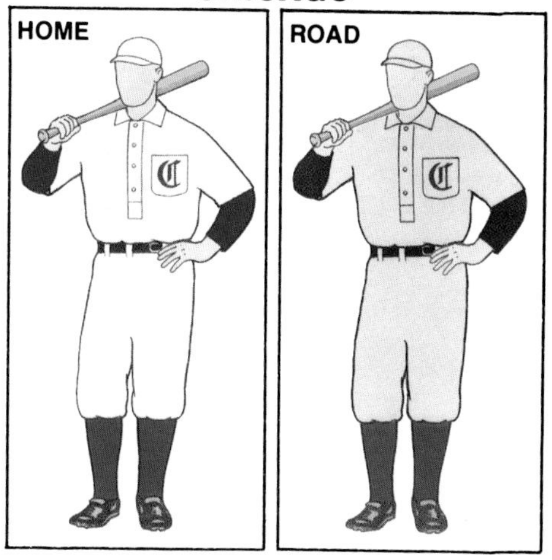

GARRICK THEATRE 35th St., near B'way. Evenings, 8:15. Matinées, 2:15.
CHARLES FROHMAN .... Manager
MATINEE TO-DAY & WEDNESDAY.
"Success for star and author."—Herald.
CHARLES FROHMAN PRESENTS
ANNIE RUSSELL
in Madeleine Lucette Ryley's Play,
MICE AND MEN.
"Annie Russell and 'Mice and Men' made an undeniable hit."—Sun.

NEW SAVOY THEATRE 34th St. & B'way. Evenings, 8:30. Mats., 2:15.
CHARLES FROHMAN .... Manager
MATINEE TO-DAY & WEDNESDAY.
100th Time March 23—Souvenirs
CHARLES FROHMAN PRESENTS
CLYDE FITCH'S GREATEST PLAY,
THE GIRL WITH THE GREEN EYES
With CLARA BLOODGOOD.

CINCINNATI

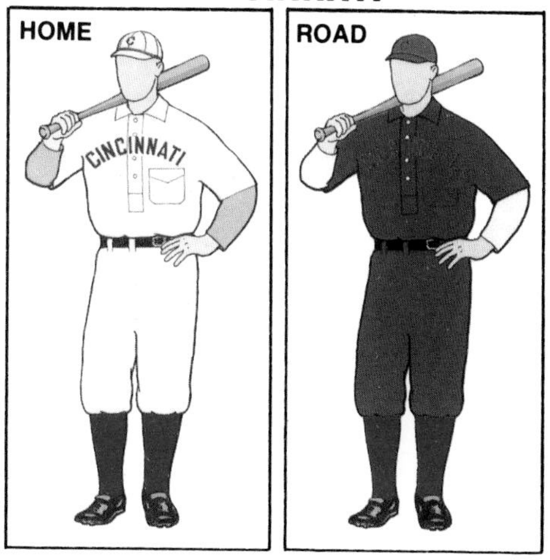

NEW YORK

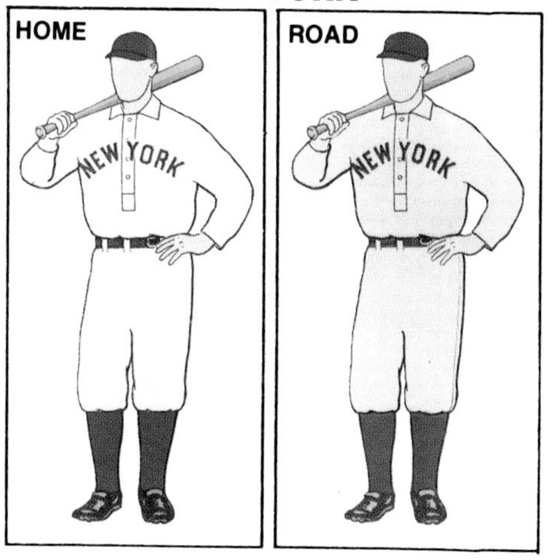

FIRST SECTION

PUBLIC LEDGER

20 PAGES TWO SECTIONS

XV.—NO. 21 PHILADELPHIA, SATURDAY MORNING, APRIL 18, 1903.—20 PAGES. ONE CEN

SUMMARY

CUP CHALLENGER'S MASTS TORN OUT

Yacht Shamrock III Completely Dismantled in a Squall in Weymouth Bay

SIR THOMAS SLIGHTLY HURT

Steel Mast Snaps, and Spars and Sails and Rigging Go Overboard

CAPTAIN'S RELATIVE DROWNED

CHICAGO MAY OWN TRACTION

Bill for City's Purchase of Street Railways Agreed Upon

PHILLIES LOSE THE OPENING CONTEST

Boston Wins the First Local Championship Game by the Score of 8 to 3

LOCALS WERE OUTCLASSED

Visitors Play Superior Ball in the Field and at the Bat

WILLIS PITCHES FINE BALL

JUDGE TAKES OATH AFTER SERVING FIVE YEARS

Curious Discovery Relative to Member of New Jersey Court of Appeals

STARTLING CHARGES OF POSTAL ABUSE

Men Alleged to Have Robbed Department Said to Have Been Shielded and Promoted

EXORBITANT PRICES ARE PA

One Contract in Which Thirty-... Times Proper Cost Was Given

MONOPOLY IN TIME CLOCK

1904 AMERICAN LEAGUE

BOSTON

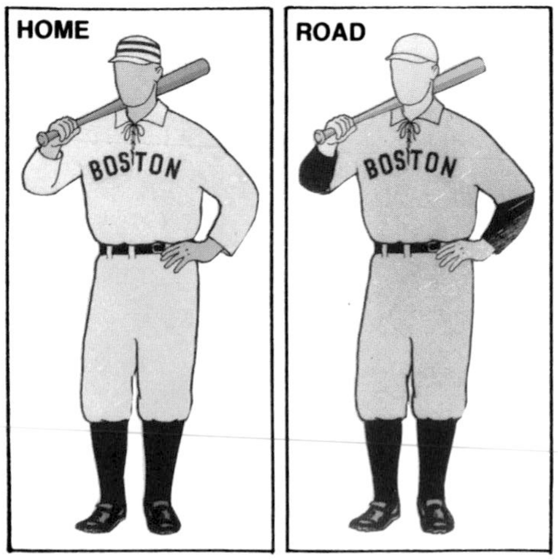

CLEVELAND

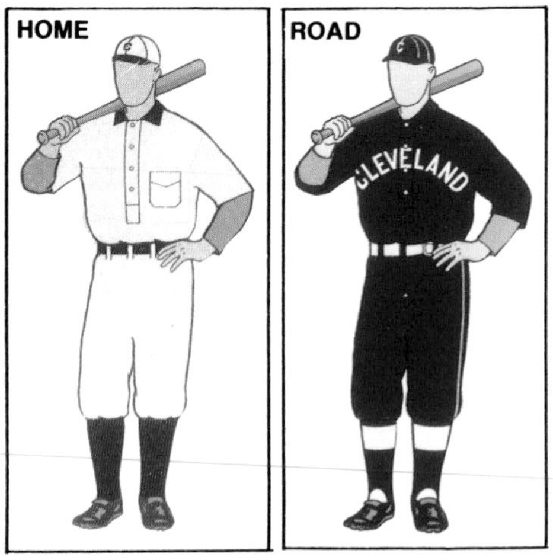

DETROIT

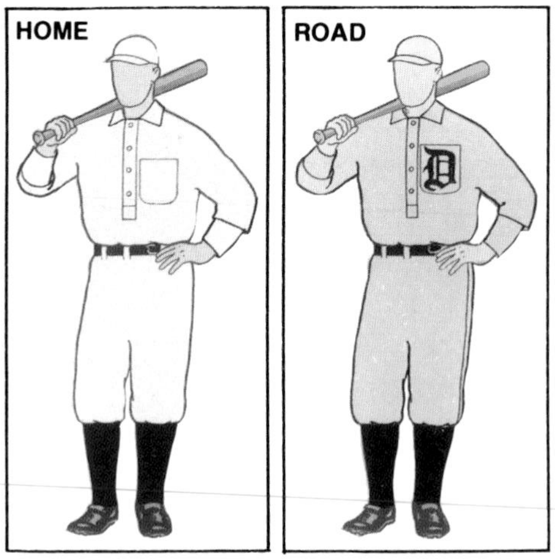

ST. LOUIS

NEW YORK

PHILADELPHIA

CHICAGO

WASHINGTON

BOSTON DAILY ADVERTISER.

LOCAL FORECAST. Showers and cooler Tuesday. Wednesday, fair; brisk northwest winds.

VOL. 186, NO. 88 — BOSTON, TUESDAY MORNING, OCTOBER 11, 1904 — PRICE TWO CENTS

THE PENNANT COMES TO BOSTON AGAIN

HIGHLANDERS OUTPLAYED IN DECISIVE GAME

Superior Steadiness Won for the Hub Team—Second Game Captured by New York After Close Struggle.

AMERICAN STANDING.

	Won.	Lost.	P.C.
Boston	[illegible]	[illegible]	[illegible]
New York	[illegible]	[illegible]	[illegible]
Chicago	[illegible]	[illegible]	[illegible]
Cleveland	[illegible]	[illegible]	[illegible]
Philadelphia	[illegible]	[illegible]	[illegible]
St. Louis	[illegible]	[illegible]	[illegible]
Detroit	[illegible]	[illegible]	[illegible]
Washington	[illegible]	113	[illegible]

A SENSATIONAL FINISH.

New York, Oct. 10.—Boston vanquished New York on the baseball field, winning the American League championship pennant for the second time. It was a sensational finish to a thrilling struggle.

RELIGION IS NOT A BAR

TO THE SUPPORT OF THE P. S. A.

Organization Has Therefore Disclaimed Any Affiliation With the Independent Women Voters—Positive Statement Issued.

The Public School Assn. has formally announced its divorce from affiliation with the independent women voters.

The announcement was made after a meeting of the Public School Assn.'s executive committee.

"The P. S. A. has striven from the outset to elect the best possible candidates to the Boston school committee regardless of sectarian issues. It has in accordance with this purpose, sought diligently the best candidates available and has urged the other parties—republicans, democrats, independent women voters—to unite in nominating them.

Last year, the P. S. A., having been fortunate in persuading some excellent citizens, who were Catholics, to accept its nomination, the issue with the independent women voters was made plain.

IMPRESSIVE SERVICE AT TREMONT TEMPLE

ARCHBISHOP DAVIDSON A POWERFUL MAGNET

His Last Public Appearance in This City Drew a Great Gathering—Aid for Missions Strongly Urged.

The final public appearance of the Archbishop of Canterbury, at the great Tremont Temple mass meeting was a fittingly dignified and impressive close to his eventful and important visit to America.

Long before the time set for the opening of the meeting the crowds that surged to the entrance to the building had to be turned away by the policemen and attendants. When at last the organ pealed forth the notes of Rev. C. LeV. Brine's sonorous hymn and 300 choir boys gave voice to the words "Wider and wider yet the gates of the nations swing," and 300 or more voices in the assemblage in the lofty hall took up the refrain, following the white-surpliced choir and the clear-throated cornets that blared from 2 galleries when the

JAPANESE OUTPOSTS RETIRE

RUSSIAN ADVANCE CONTINUES

St. Petersburg Military Experts Believe That Oyama Will Give Battle North of Liaoyang.

St. Petersburg, Oct. 11.—A battle upon which the fate of this year's campaign in Manchuria depends seems only a few days ahead. Advices from the front are meager. All that is positively known officially is that Gen. Kuropatkin has cast the die at last, [illegible] his army and is marching against the enemy as if resolved to do or die.

According to unofficial reports Field Marshal [illegible] at the first sign of Gen. Kuropatkin's taking the offensive, began drawing in his line and concentrating upon fortified positions north of Liaoyang. According to the latest reports, which are contained in a despatch from Mukden, dated at 6 p.m., the Japanese outposts are retiring all along the line.

All surmises as to where Kuropatkin intends to attack are mere guesswork.

It is not clear whether he contemplates an advance on the left, center or right of the Japanese army.

But the fact that stress is laid upon the

STATE PRISON BREAK A DARING PLOT?

AUTHORITIES TO HOLD A RIGID INQUIRY

Did Dansereau Sham Insanity for Years to Get a Good Chance to Break for Liberty.

Bridgewater, Oct. 10.—In spite of the most anxious search, the authorities have not yet found John Dansereau, the escaped convict, lately held in an insane ward—as in the "criminal insane" class. This dangerous character is now supposed to be at large in Boston.

Parties have scoured the woods in this neighborhood, but the convict seems to have vanished. The record of Bridgewater of not having lost a convict for many years is in danger of being broken. It will not be if Supt. Blackstone can help it. A general alarm has been sent all over the state.

Dansereau's every act shows that he

NATIONAL LEAGUE 1904

BOSTON

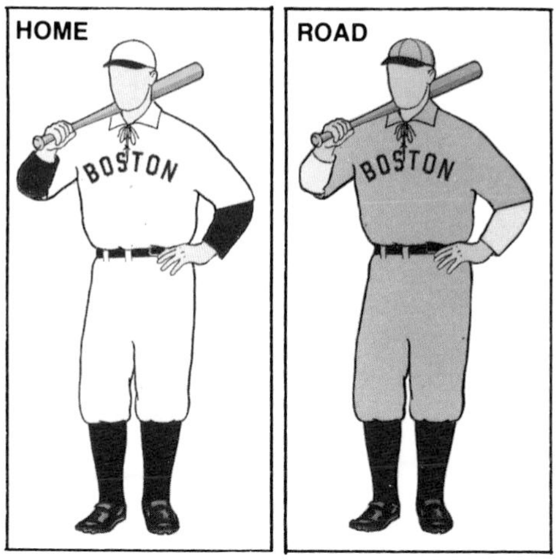

BROOKLYN

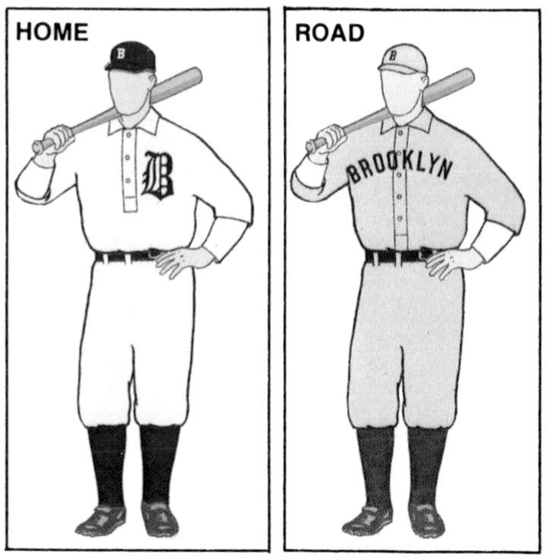

ST. LOUIS

PITTSBURGH

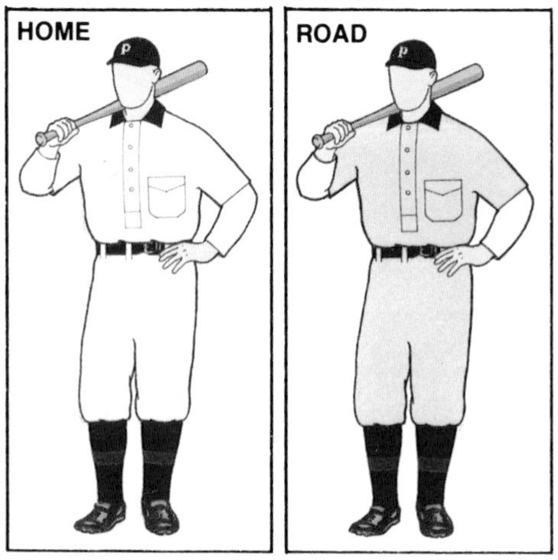

PHILADELPHIA

CHICAGO

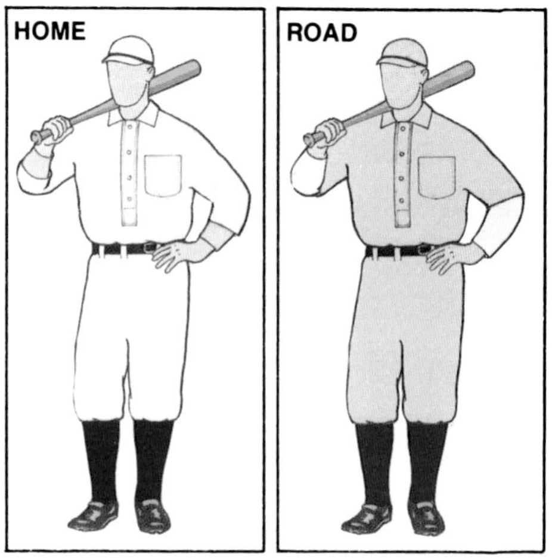

WORLD'S FAIR

AT ST. LOUIS.

The Best Way to Reach St. Louis from New York and New England is Without Question VIA THE

West Shore R. R.

OR VIA THE

New York Central

THE SIX-TRACK TRUNK LINE OF AMERICA.

COACH EXCURSIONS EVERY WEDNESDAY.

Via West Shore, $18. Via New York Central, $20.

FOR PARTICULARS APPLY AT THE TICKET OFFICES OF THESE ROADS.

CINCINNATI

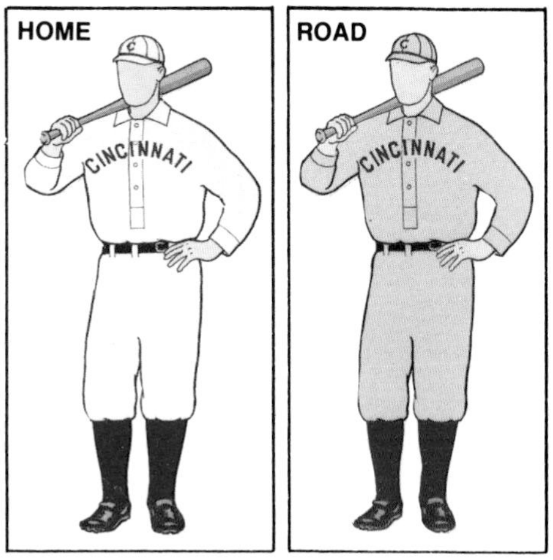

NEW YORK

THE COMMERCIAL TRIBUNE.

VOL. VIII. NO. 304. CINCINNATI, FRIDAY, APRIL 15, 1904. PRICE 3 CENTS

BASEBALL SEASON OPENS WITH CINCINNATI VICTORY

BY PRESIDENT PULLIAM.

The results of the first games of the season show that the players are fit to make the race interesting.

BY PRESIDENT BAN JOHNSON.

The American League is looking forward to great things. Baseball is on the boom and that's what we like.

BY PRESIDENT GRILLO.

The American Association opens its season next Wednesday and the indications are that our season will be successful.

1905 AMERICAN LEAGUE

BOSTON

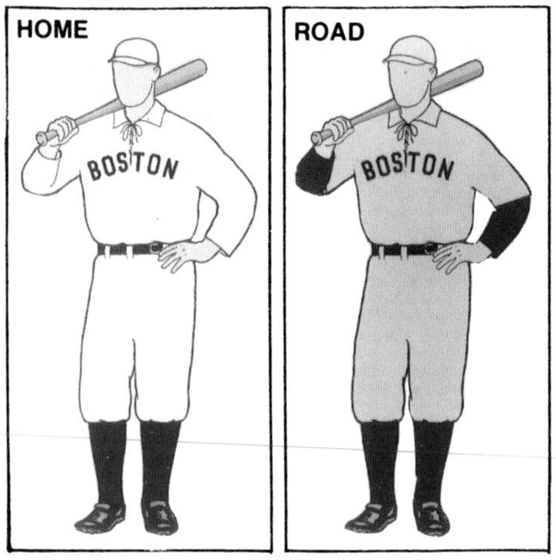

CLEVELAND

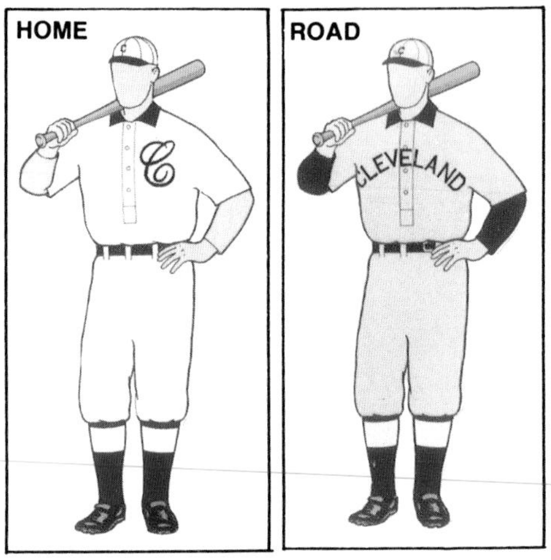

DETROIT

ST. LOUIS

NEW YORK

PHILADELPHIA

CHICAGO

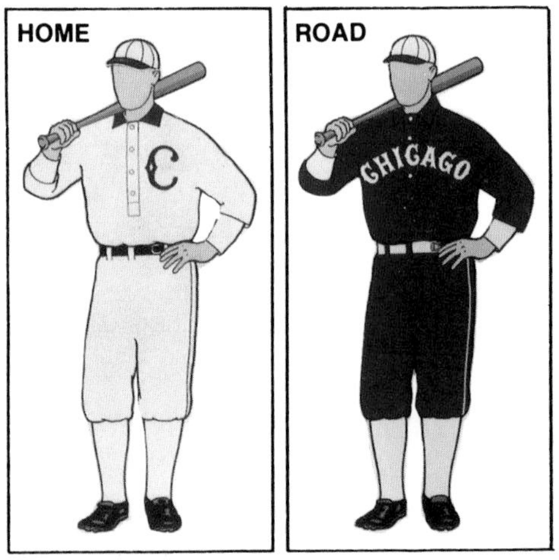

WASHINGTON

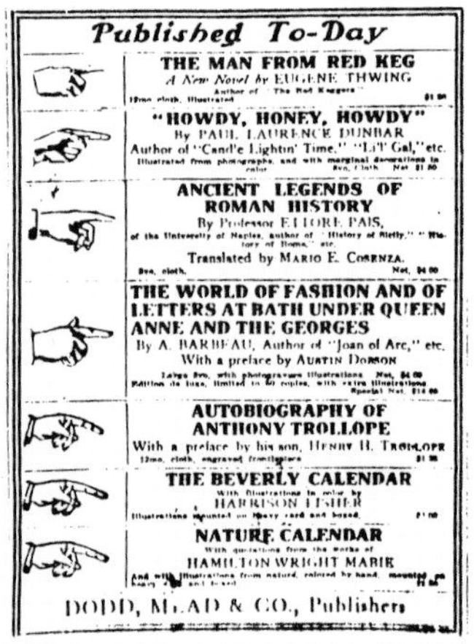

Published To-Day

THE MAN FROM RED KEG
A New Novel by EUGENE THWING

"HOWDY, HONEY, HOWDY"
By PAUL LAURENCE DUNBAR
Author of "Candle Lightin' Time," "Li'l' Gal," etc.
Illustrated from photographs, and with marginal decorations in color

ANCIENT LEGENDS OF ROMAN HISTORY
By Professor ETTORE PAIS,
of the University of Naples, author of "History of Sicily," "History of Rome," etc.
Translated by MARIO E. COSENZA.

THE WORLD OF FASHION AND OF LETTERS AT BATH UNDER QUEEN ANNE AND THE GEORGES
By A. BARBEAU, Author of "Joan of Arc," etc.
With a preface by AUSTIN DOBSON

AUTOBIOGRAPHY OF ANTHONY TROLLOPE
With a preface by his son, HENRY H. TROLLOPE

THE BEVERLY CALENDAR
With illustrations in color by
HARRISON FISHER

NATURE CALENDAR
With quotations from the works of
HAMILTON WRIGHT MABIE

DODD, MEAD & CO., Publishers

THURSDAY. — THE DETROIT JOURNAL

NEWS OF THE SPORTING WORLD

UNDER SPELL OF A SMILE

DONOVAN PUT IT ALL OVER WHITE STOCKINGS

FEATURE OF GAME WAS FIELDING OF TIGER INFIELD.

Manager Armour Has the Local Fans Pulling for Him

He is Popular With Players and is Trying Hard for a Winner.

BUSY DAY FOR BOWLERS

HEAVY SCHEDULE AT STATE TOURNEY.

A. B. C. STILL LEADS THE FIVE-MEN TEAMS.

NATIONAL LEAGUE 1905

BOSTON

BROOKLYN

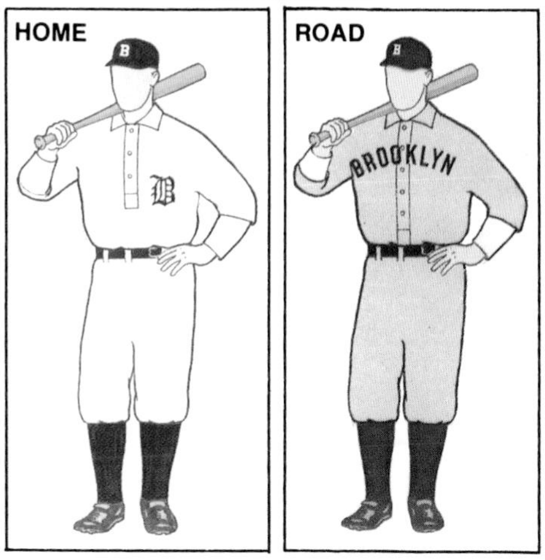

ST. LOUIS

PITTSBURGH

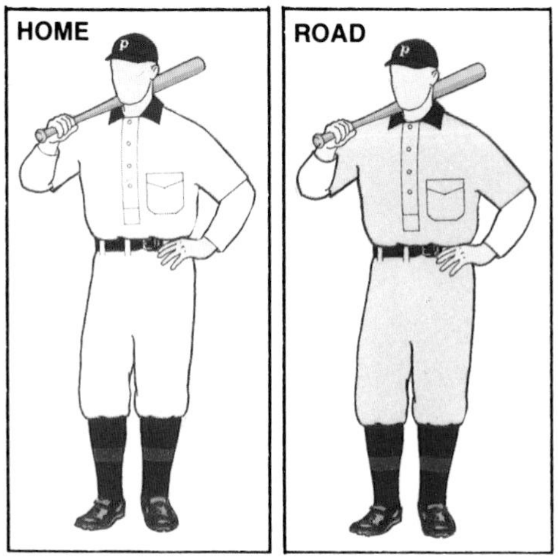

PHILADELPHIA

CHICAGO

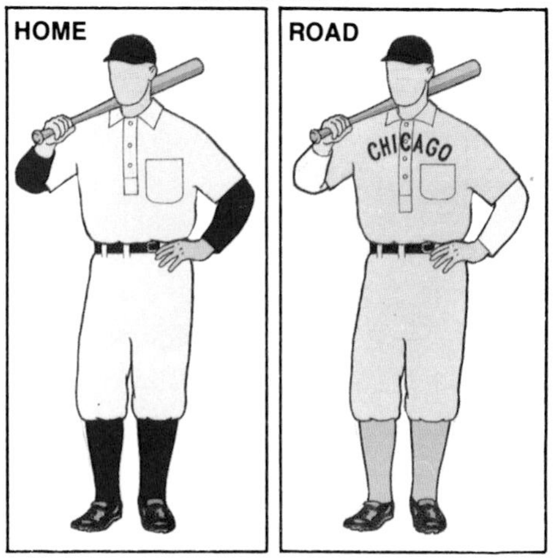

CINCINNATI

NEW YORK

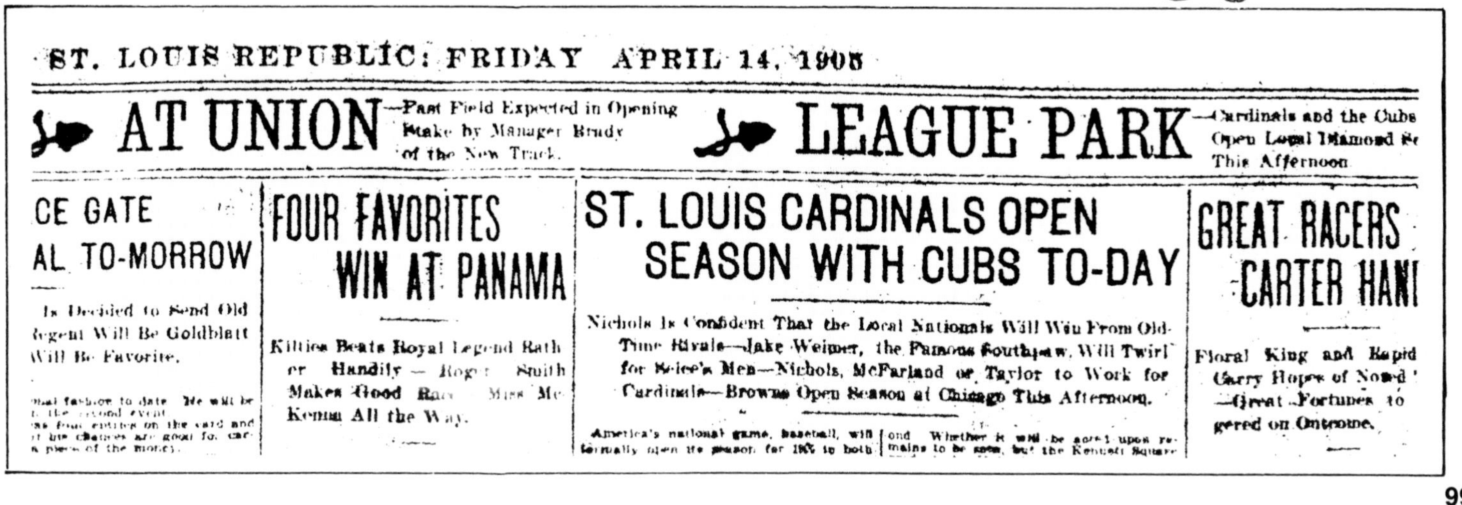

ST. LOUIS REPUBLIC: FRIDAY APRIL 14, 1905

AT UNION—Fast Field Expected in Opening Stake by Manager Brady of the New Track.

LEAGUE PARK—Cardinals and the Cubs Open Local Diamond Se... This Afternoon

CE GATE
AL TO-MORROW

...Is Decided to Send Old ...egent Will Be Goldblatt Will Be Favorite.

FOUR FAVORITES
WIN AT PANAMA

Kilties Beats Royal Legend Rather Handily — Roger Smith Makes Good Race — Miss Mc Kenna All the Way.

ST. LOUIS CARDINALS OPEN
SEASON WITH CUBS TO-DAY

Nichols Is Confident That the Local Nationals Will Win From Old-Time Rivals—Jake Weimer, the Famous Southpaw, Will Twirl for Selee's Men—Nichols, McFarland or Taylor to Work for Cardinals—Browns Open Season at Chicago This Afternoon.

America's national game, baseball, will formally open its season for 1905 in both ... ond. Whether it will be sorely upon remains to be seen, but the Kenosti Square ...

GREAT RACERS
CARTER HAN...

Floral King and Rapid ... Carry Hopes of Noted ... —Great Fortunes to ... gered on Outcome.

1906 AMERICAN LEAGUE

BOSTON

CLEVELAND

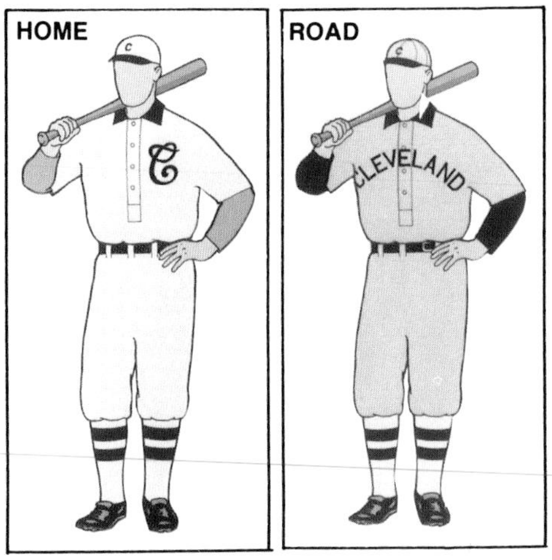

DETROIT

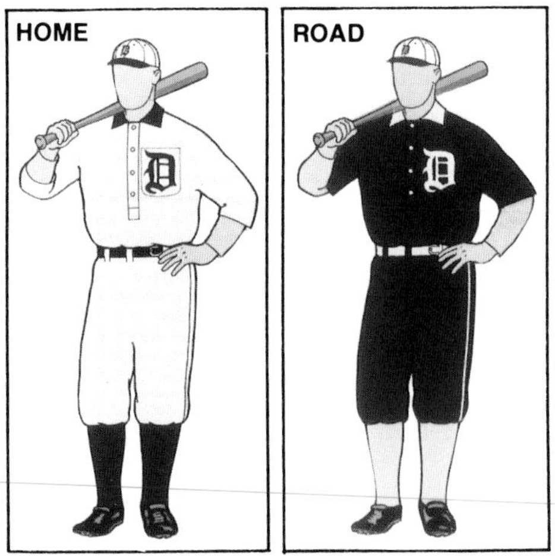

ST. LOUIS

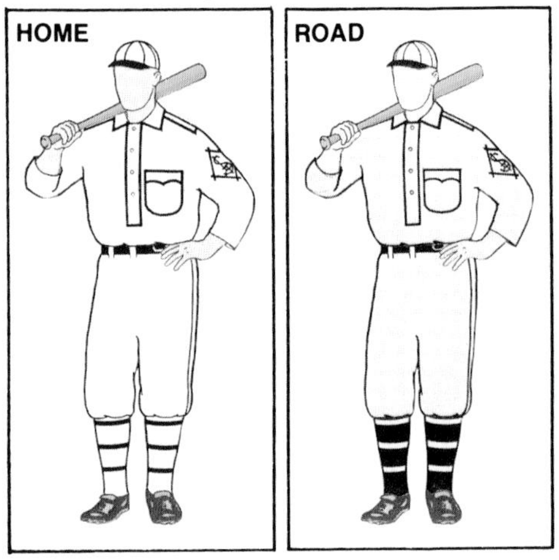

NEW YORK

PHILADELPHIA

CHICAGO

WASHINGTON

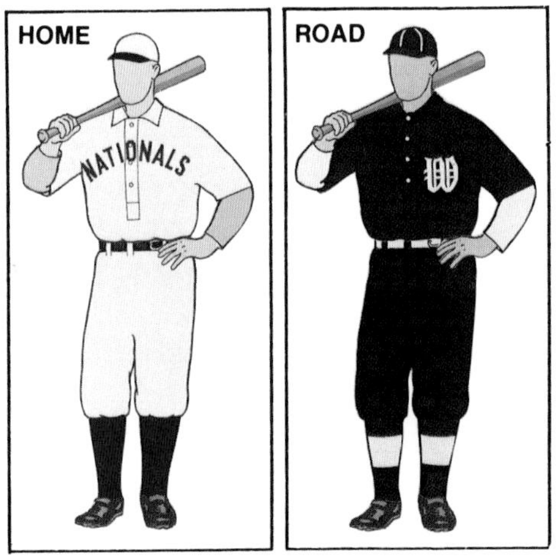

The New York Press

LARGEST REPUBLICAN CIRCULATION BY MANY THOUSANDS OF COPIES A DAY.

VOL. XIX.—WHOLE NO. 6,714. NEW YORK, THURSDAY MORNING, APRIL 19, 1906.—TWELVE PAGES. PRICE

FLAMES FAST DESTROYING SAN FRANCISCO;
GIANT EARTHQUAKE AND FIRE KILL 1,500;
PROPERTY LOSS IN STATE IS $250,000,000

Beautiful Leland Stanford University Wrecked and Two Persons Are Killed There and Several Students Injured by Crashing Walls—Institution with an Endowment of $30,000,000 Is

MAP SHOWING CHIEF SCENES OF DISASTER IN SAN FRANCISCO.

Terrific Early Morning Shock Demolishes Most of Business Section of Golden Gate City and Flames. Following Close Behind. Sweep Practically Unchecked Through Day and Night.

NATIONAL LEAGUE 1906

BOSTON

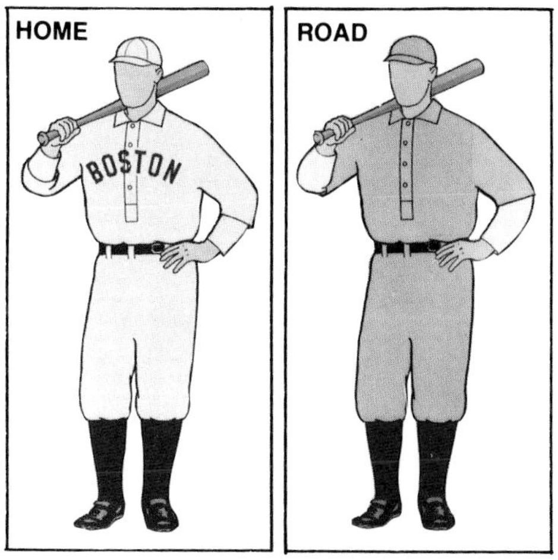

BROOKLYN

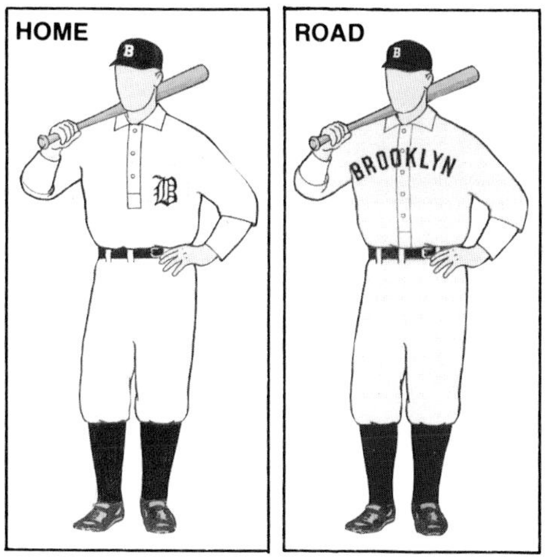

ST. LOUIS

PITTSBURGH

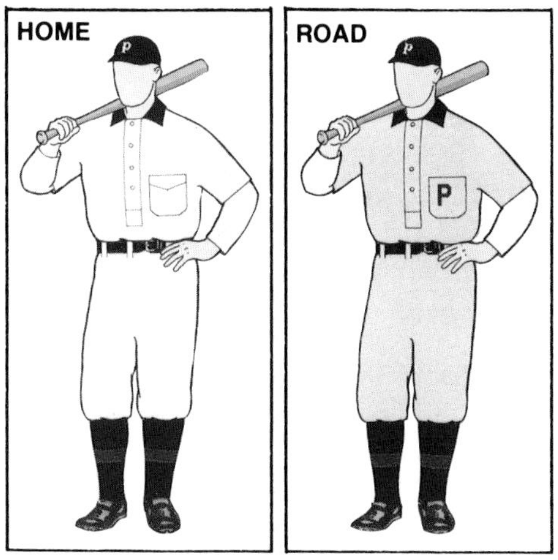

PHILADELPHIA

CHICAGO

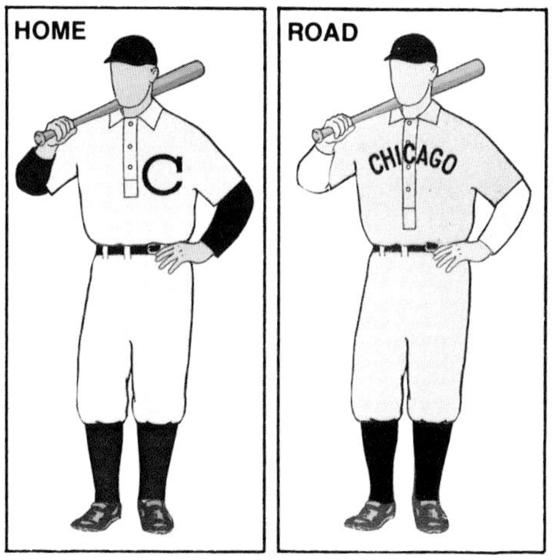

CINCINNATI

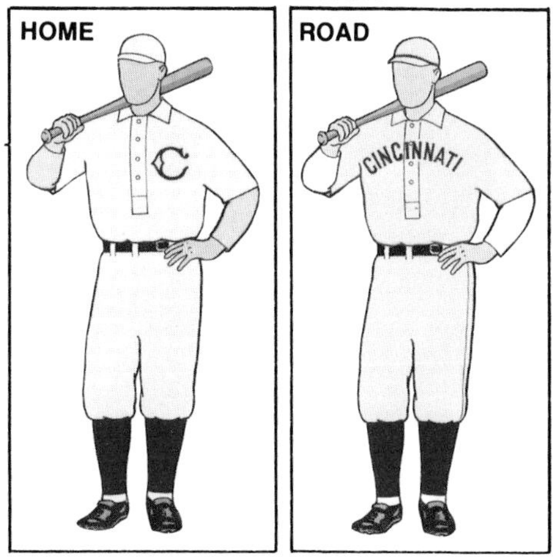

NEW YORK

THE INTER OCEAN, MONDAY MORNING,

NEWS OF THE SPORTING WORLD GATHI

WHITE SOX WIN CHAMPIONSHIP

Decisively Defeat Giant Killers in Sixth Game by Score of 8 to 3, Keeping Up Their

SCORE OF SIXTH AND FINAL GAME FOR WORLD'S CHAMPIONSHIP.

Comiskey, Murphy, Jones, Chance and Others Talk of Victory for World's Honors—Great

1907 AMERICAN LEAGUE

BOSTON

CLEVELAND

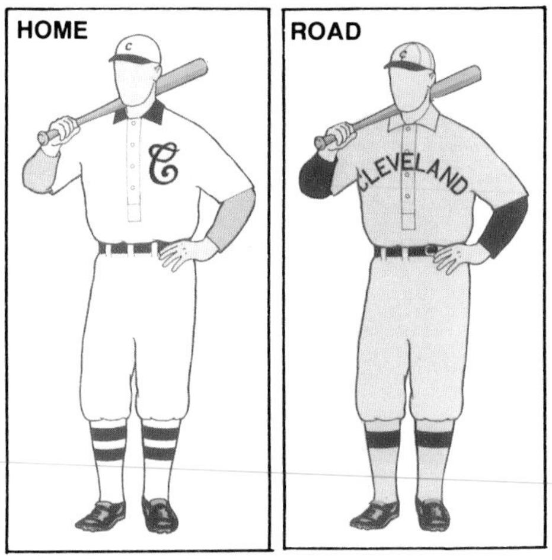

DETROIT

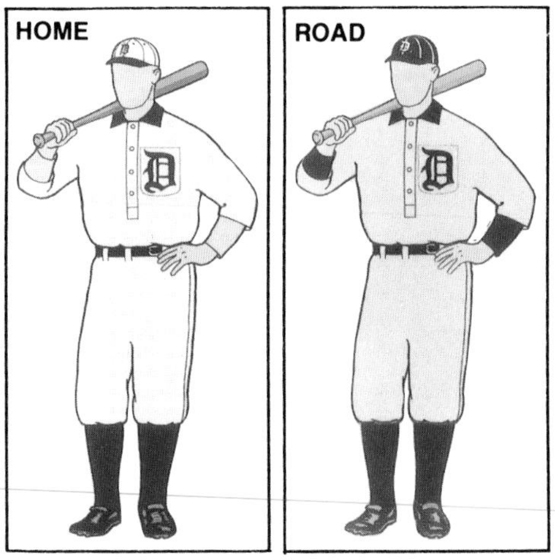

ST. LOUIS

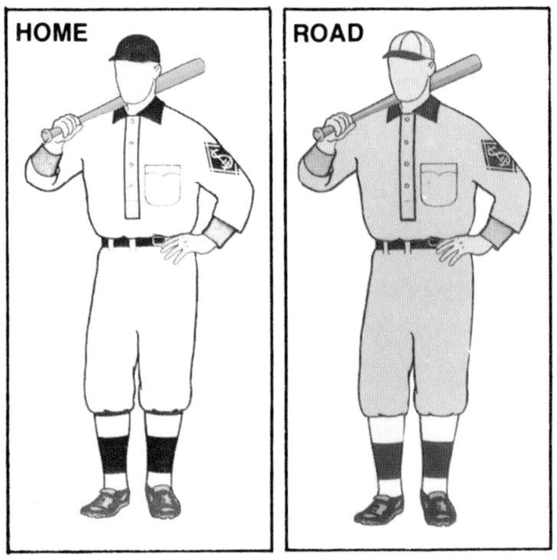

NEW YORK

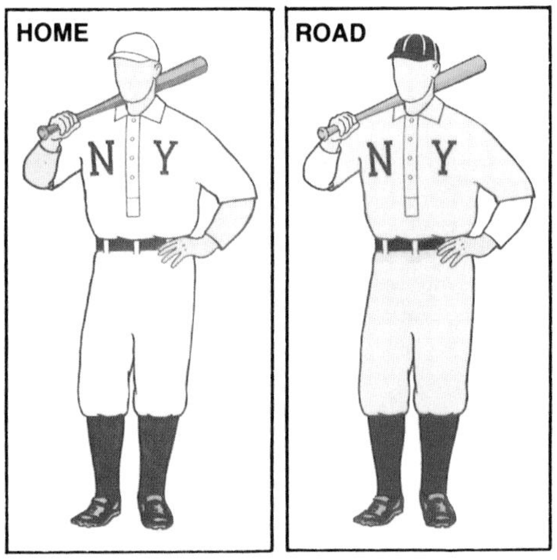

PHILADELPHIA

CHICAGO

WASHINGTON

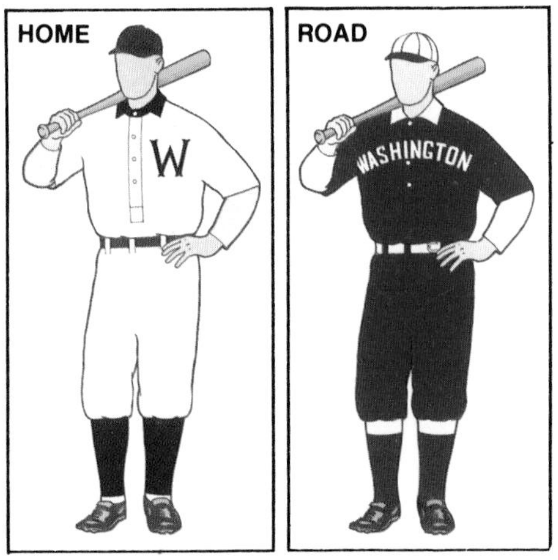

AMUSEMENTS.

POWERS'

"A SUCCESS"

JOSEPH BROOKS Presents

LILLIAN RUSSELL

In the New Racing Comedy "WILDFIRE"

ILLINOIS

LAST 2 NIGHTS

LAST MAT. SAT.

FRITZI SCHEFF

In Farewell Appearances in the Best of all American Comic Operas,

Mlle. Modiste

NEXT SUNDAY NIGHT

MARIE CAHILL

IN THE SUCCESSFUL MUSICAL PLAY

MARRYING MARY

THE DETROIT NEWS. FRIDAY, APRIL 12, 1907.

NEWS AND GOSSIP OF THE SPORTING WORLD

MULLIN SHOWED NAPS THE WAY

"Gingery" Base Ball at Bennett Park as Told by the Camera

SCHOOL PLAYERS DODGE PRACTI[CE]

NATIONAL LEAGUE 1907

BOSTON

BROOKLYN

ST. LOUIS

PITTSBURGH

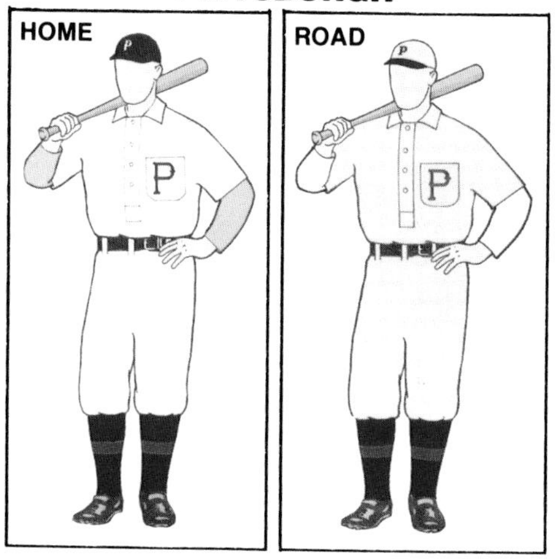

PHILADELPHIA

CHICAGO

CINCINNATI

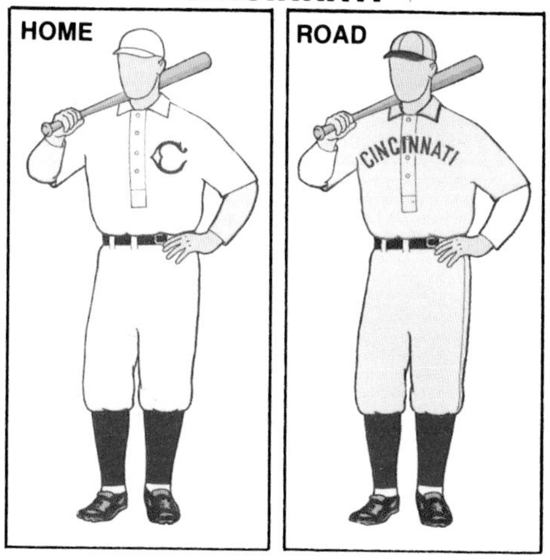

NEW YORK

THE CHICAGO DAILY NEWS.

SATURDAY, OCTOBER 12, 1907. LATEST SPORTING EDITION—ONE CENT.

CHICAGO CUBS ARE WORLD'S CHAMPIONS FOR 1908

SPORTING EXTRA

FINAL RESULTS

DORANTE IS A SURPRISE

Wins Nursery Race at Belmont Park Track at

CAPT. FRANK CHANCE IN A MERRY MOOD.

SPORTING EXTRA

FINAL RESULTS

WIN 4 STRAIGHT GAMES

Victory Over the Detroit American League Club

1908 AMERICAN LEAGUE

BOSTON

CLEVELAND

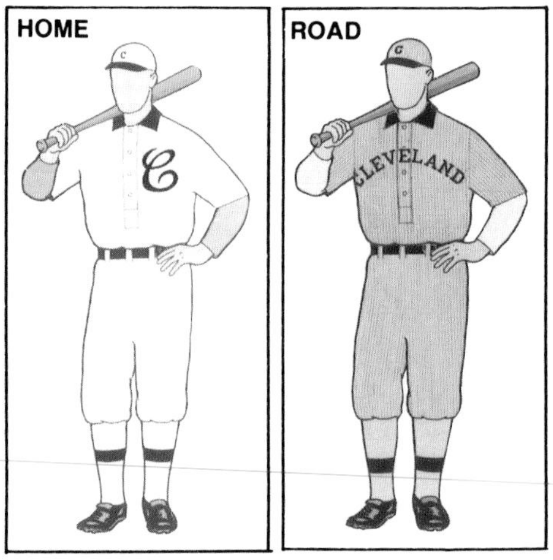

DETROIT

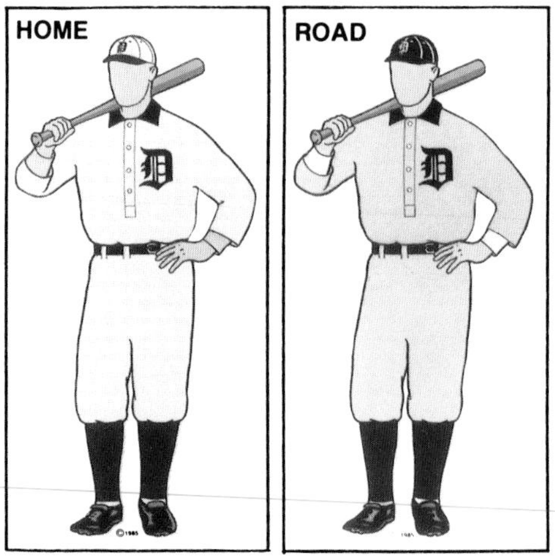

ST. LOUIS

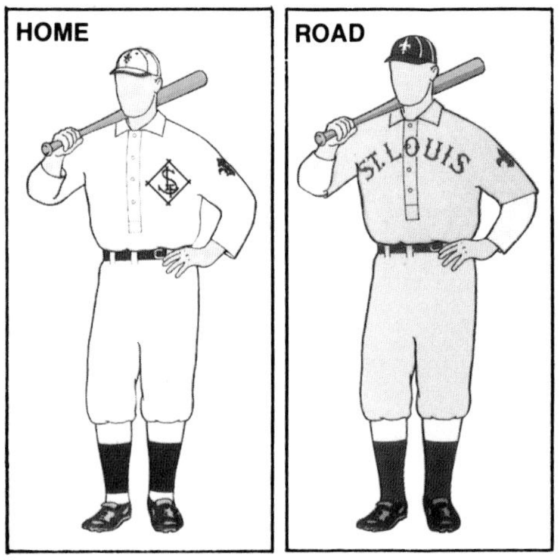

NEW YORK

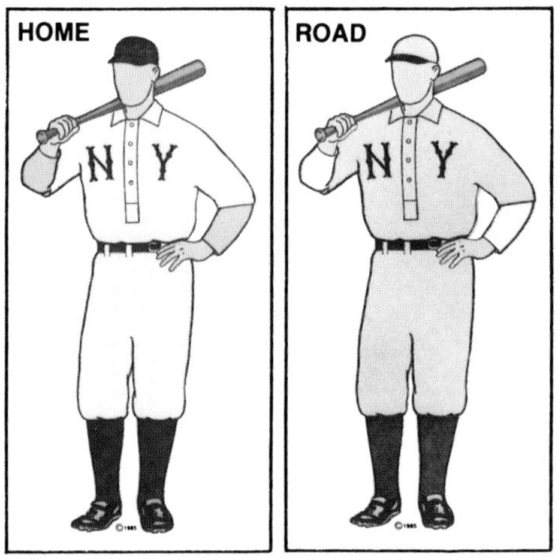

PHILADELPHIA

CHICAGO

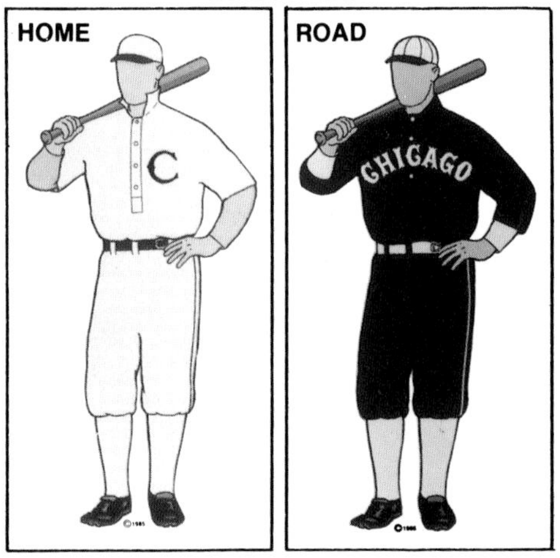

WASHINGTON

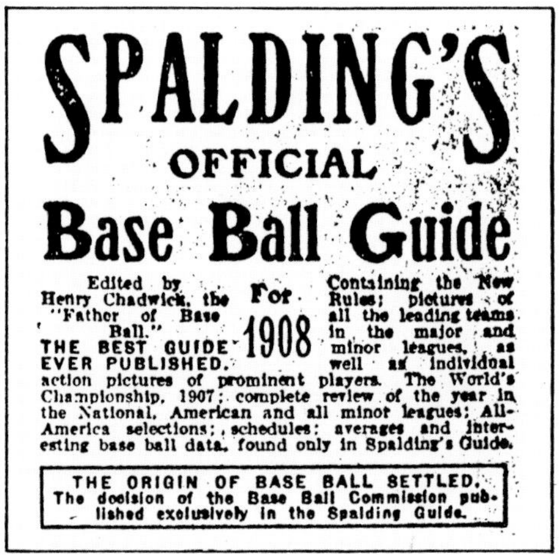

SPALDING'S OFFICIAL Base Ball Guide

Edited by Henry Chadwick, the "Father of Base Ball." THE BEST GUIDE EVER PUBLISHED.

For 1908

Containing the New Rules; pictures of all the leading teams in the major and minor leagues, as well as individual action pictures of prominent players. The World's Championship, 1907; complete review of the year in the National, American and all minor leagues; All-America selections; schedules; averages and interesting base ball data, found only in Spalding's Guide.

THE ORIGIN OF BASE BALL SETTLED. The decision of the Base Ball Commission published exclusively in the Spalding Guide.

The Evening Star.

Weather. Partly cloudy tonight and Friday.

No. 17,434. WASHINGTON, D. C., THURSDAY, JUNE 18, 1908 — TWO CENTS.

EXTRA!

TAFT IS NOMINATED ON THE FIRST BALLOT

THE REPUBLICAN STANDARD BEARER.

IN FEAR OF STAMPEDE

Roosevelt Sentiment Made Light of, But Respected.

"ANTIS" WERE TROUBLED

Yesterday's Demonstration Charges Situation With Electricity.

SCENE IN CONVENTION HALL

District Delegation Raises Laugh. Flather and Horner Get Compli-

THIRD TERM THREAT SAVES LABOR PLANK

Resolution Committee Whipped Into Line for Anti-Injunction.

ADOPTED BY VOTE 35 TO 16

"Taft on This Platform, or Man Who Can Win Anyway."

ORIGINAL DRAFT IS MODIFIED

NATIONAL LEAGUE 1908

BOSTON

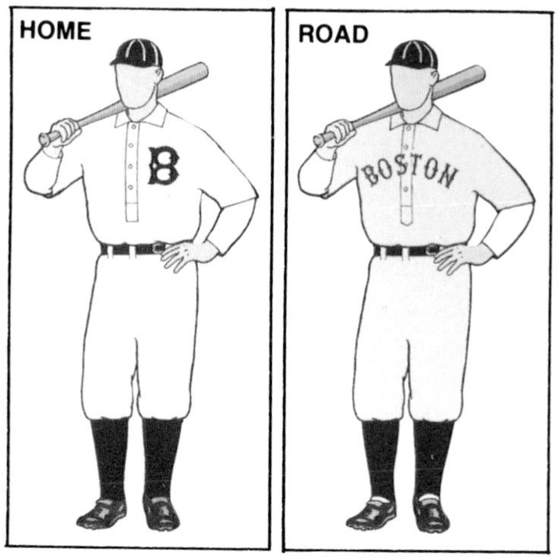

BROOKLYN

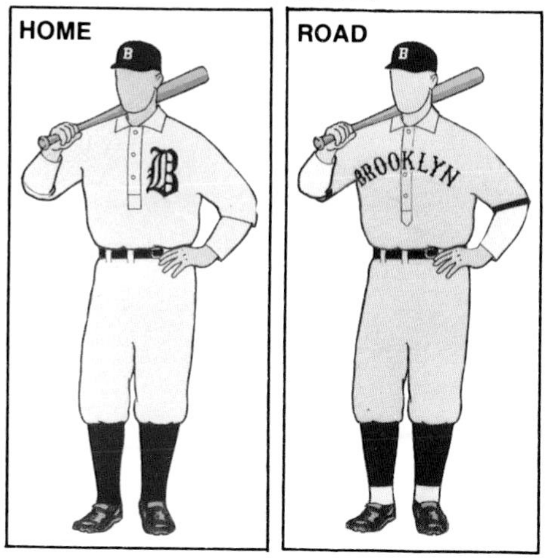

ST. LOUIS

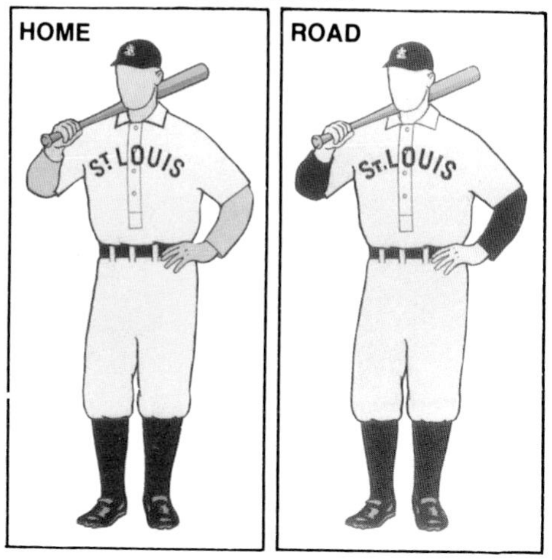

PITTSBURGH

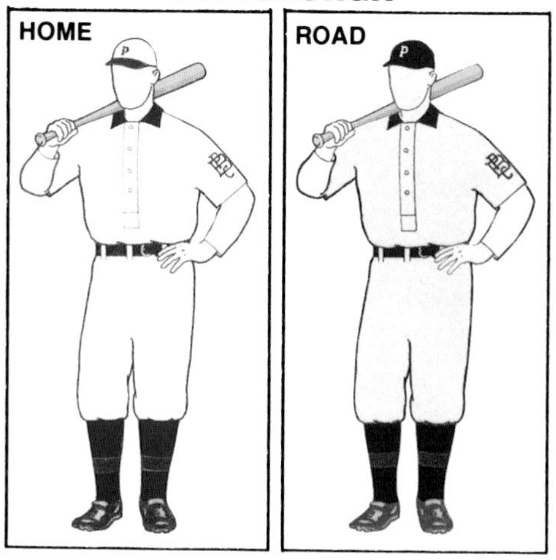

PHILADELPHIA

CHICAGO

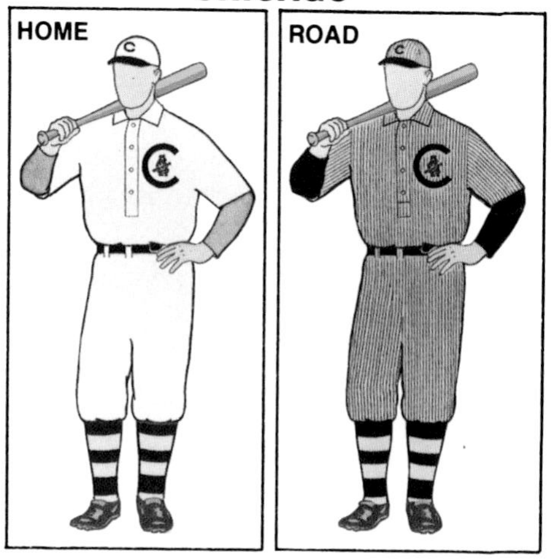

CINCINNATI

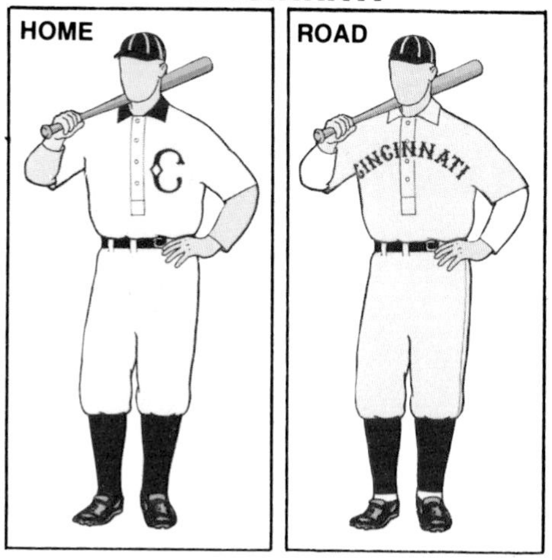

NEW YORK

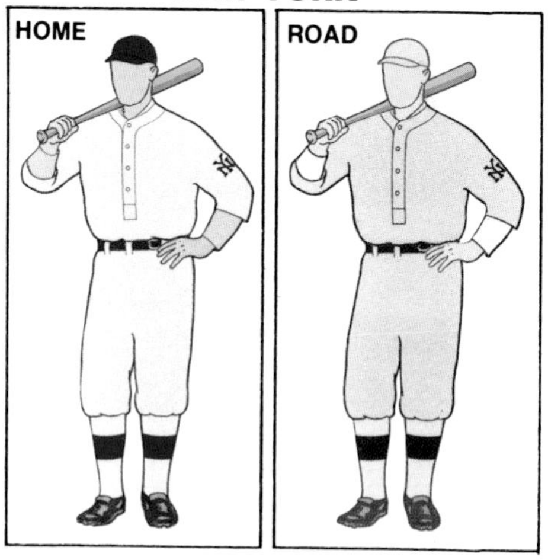

TTSBURGH'S MOST RELIABLE NEWS

The Pittsburgh Post.

UNQUESTIO
Sunday paper in
Ask your dealer
with other paper

THURSDAY MORNING, APRIL 23, 1908. TEN CENTS

Child
e Heir
ortune

Opening of the Baseball Season Here Is Marked by Victory Before Crowd of 13,081

Ch
I

1909 AMERICAN LEAGUE

BOSTON

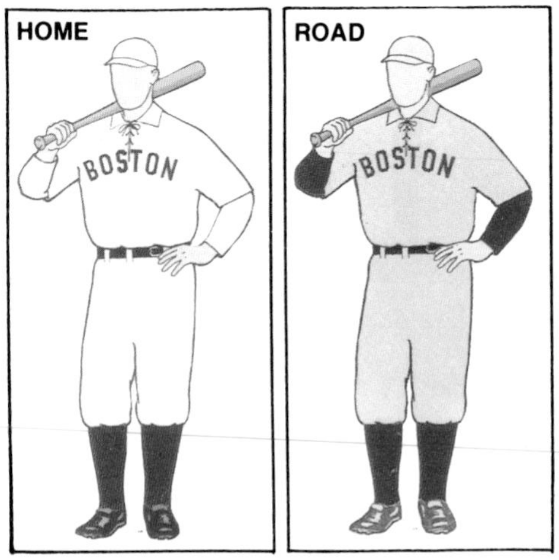

CLEVELAND

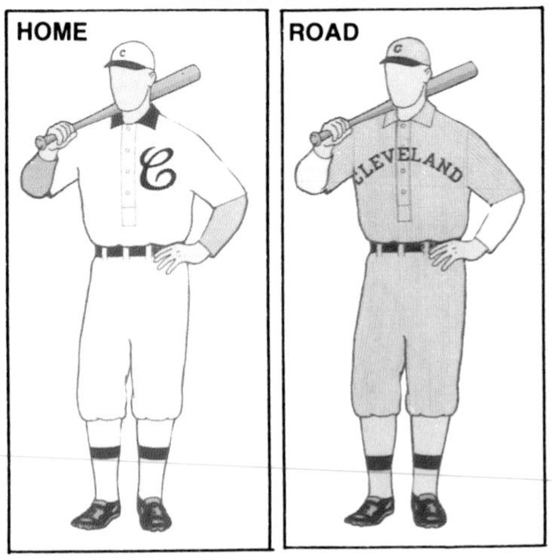

DETROIT

ST. LOUIS

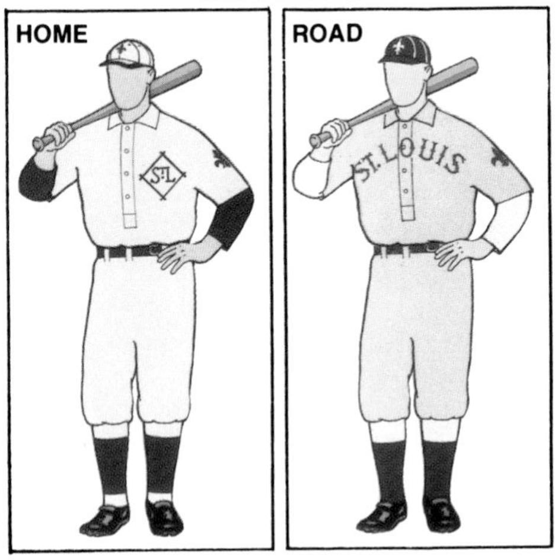

NEW YORK

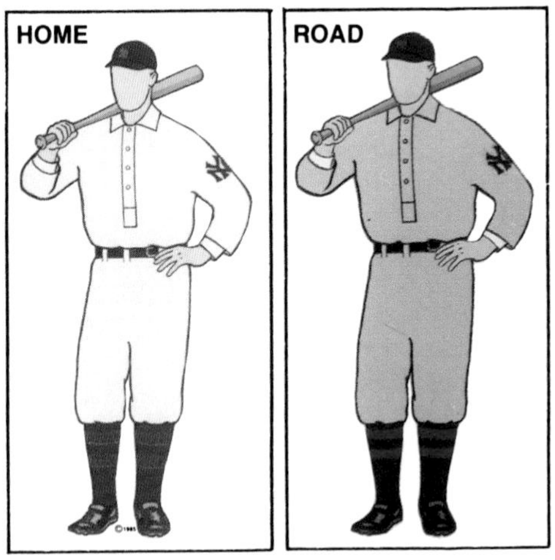

PHILADELPHIA

CHICAGO

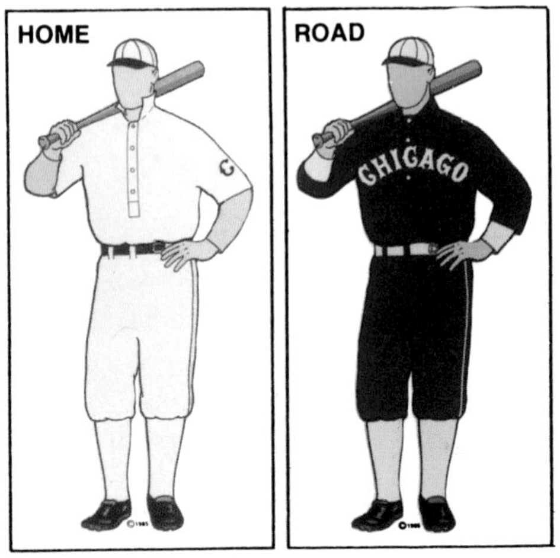

WASHINGTON

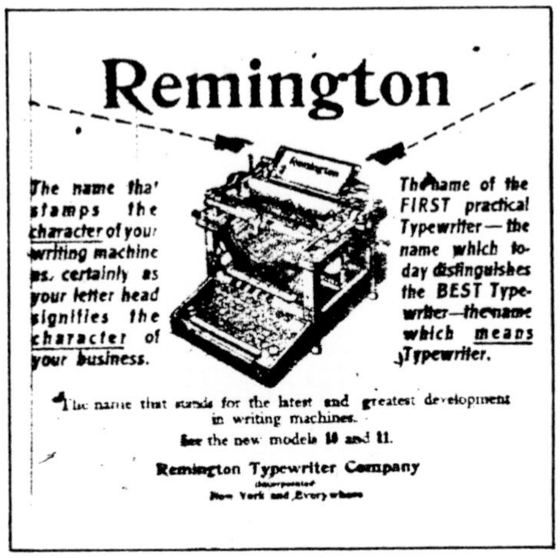

6 THE BOSTON JOURNAL—MONDAY, APRIL 12, 1909.

Shibe Park, Magnificent New Baseball Home Of The Athletics

NATIONAL LEAGUE 1909

BOSTON

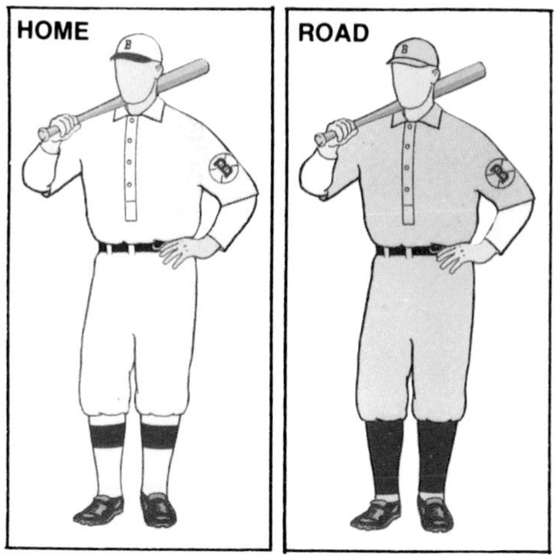

BROOKLYN

ST. LOUIS

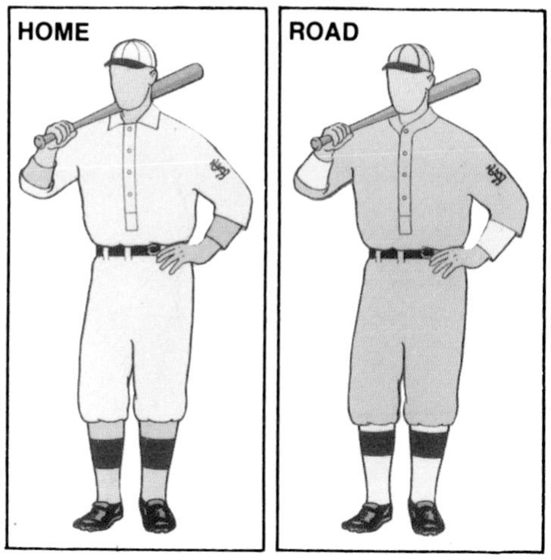

PITTSBURGH

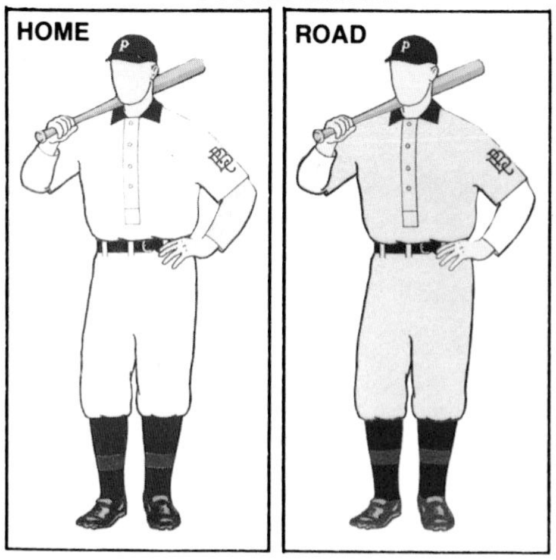

PHILADELPHIA

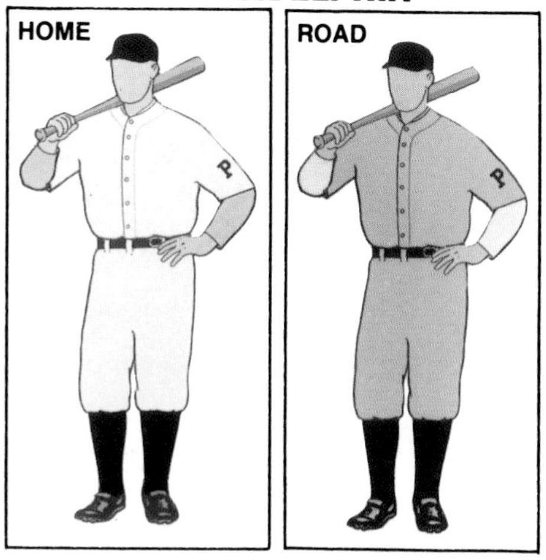

CHICAGO

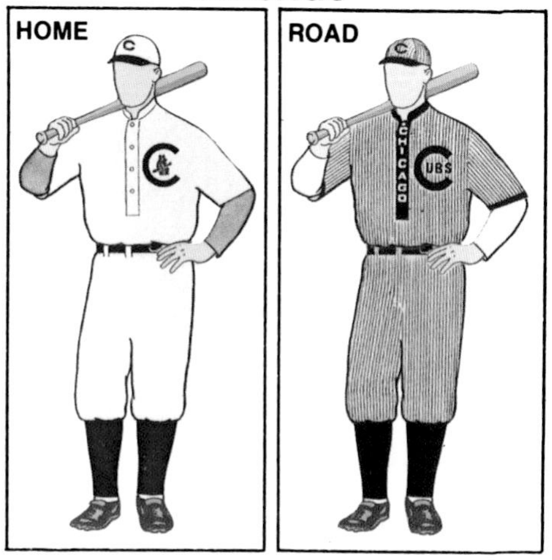

COLISEUM

TO-NIGHT AT 8:30

Dr. Frederick A. Cook

Will Lecture on His Discovery of the

NORTH POLE

Illustrated with photos taken by himself at the top of the world.

Seats Now on Sale. Prices 50 cents to $2, at the COLISEUM.

GRAND OPERA HOUSE

LAST MATINEE TO-MORROW

Liebler & Co.'s New Production.

FOREIGN EXCHANGE

by Booth Tarkington and Harry Leon Wilson.

CINCINNATI

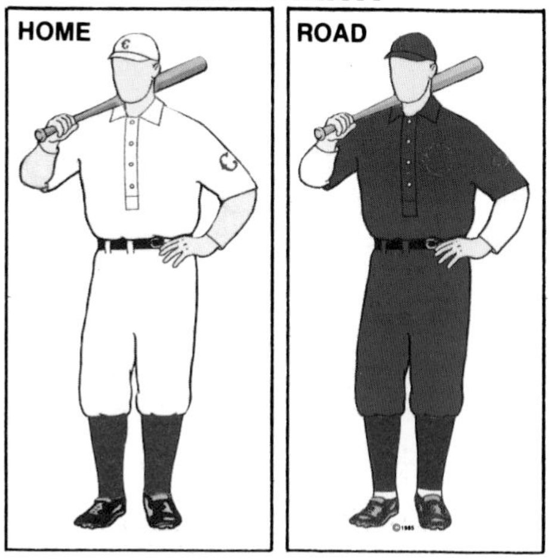

NEW YORK

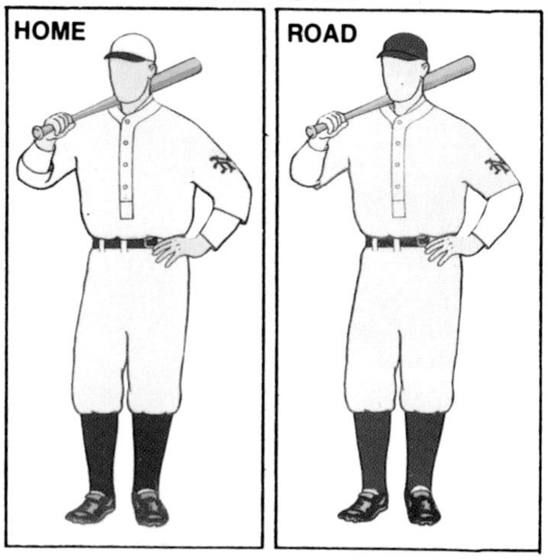

SPORTING SECTION

The Detroit News Tribune

SPORTING SECTION

DETROIT, MICHIGAN, SUNDAY MORNING, OCTOBER 17, 1909

PITTSBURG PIRATES WIN SEVENTH AND DECIDING GAME OF WORLD'S CHAMPIONSHIP SERIES FROM THE TIGERS, 8 TO 0

OUTCOME DOES NOT PROVE PITTSBURG IS BETTER THAN TIGERS

Clarke's Generalship and Pitching of Adams Gave Pirates the World's Championship.

THE MAN WHO BEAT DETROIT

"BABE" ADAMS TAKES HIS THIRD CONTEST OF SERIES, HOLDING DETROIT SCORELESS

THERE WERE WILD CHEERS BY CROWD

Jennings' Crew Unable to Get to Fred Clarke's Star Youngster From Louisville.

1910 AMERICAN LEAGUE

BOSTON

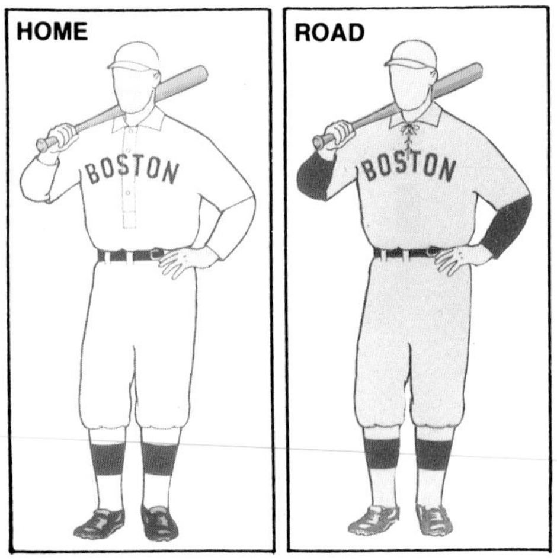

CLEVELAND

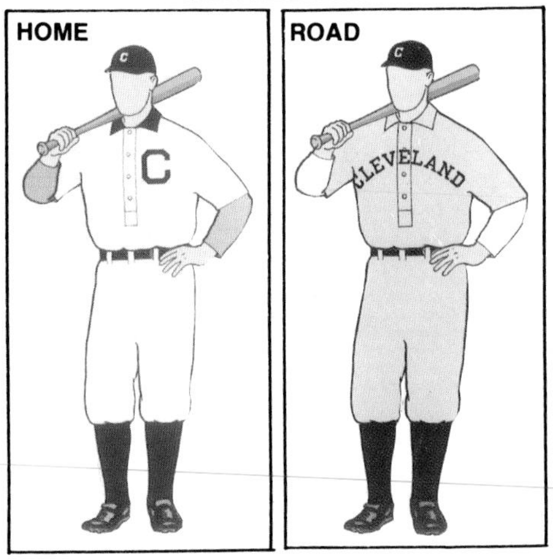

DETROIT

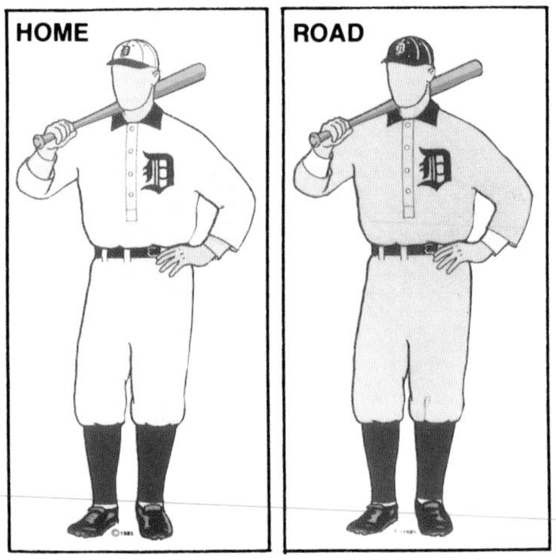

ST. LOUIS

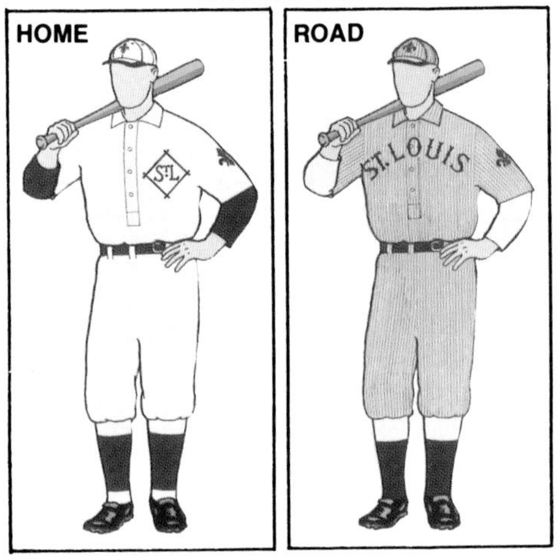

NEW YORK

PHILADELPHIA

CHICAGO

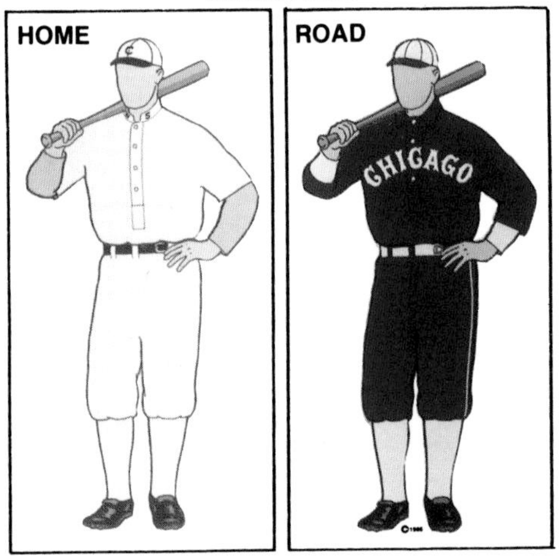

WASHINGTON

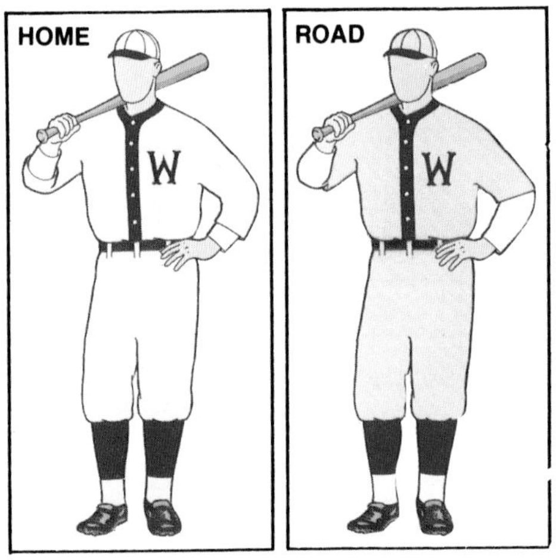

HERE'S THE NUMBER

The Cleveland Press

HOME EDITION

NUMBER [illegible] | THURSDAY, APRIL 21, 1910. | ONE CENT

LET NATIONS FALL. WHAT CARES MOSE? FOR IT'S OPENING DAY

Impulsive Everett True, Mr. Fuller Dope and Josh Wise Led Race to League Park.

OLD CY AND WILLETT FACE EACH OTHER AT GROUNDS' DEDICATION

FIRST GUN IN LAST WAR ON CANNON FIRED

Insurgent Introduces Resolution to Strip Speaker of Power to Name Committees.

ACTION ON IT DELAYED

Withdrawn After Point of Order to be Submitted Again in Regular Order.

Oh You Comet!

JUDGE MAY CALL FOR MILITIA TO GUARD HYDE MURDER TRIAL

Developments in the Case Have Stirred Kansas City and Public Outbreak is Feared.

DEFENSE GETS GRAND JURY'S NOTES, LOST BY PROSECUTOR

NATIONAL LEAGUE 1910

BOSTON

BROOKLYN

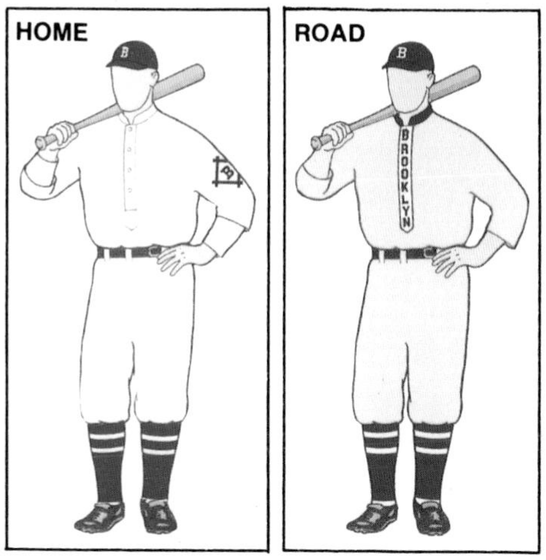

ST. LOUIS

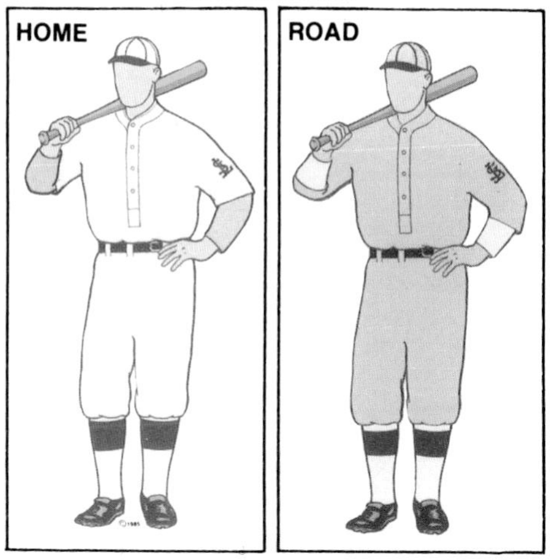

PITTSBURGH

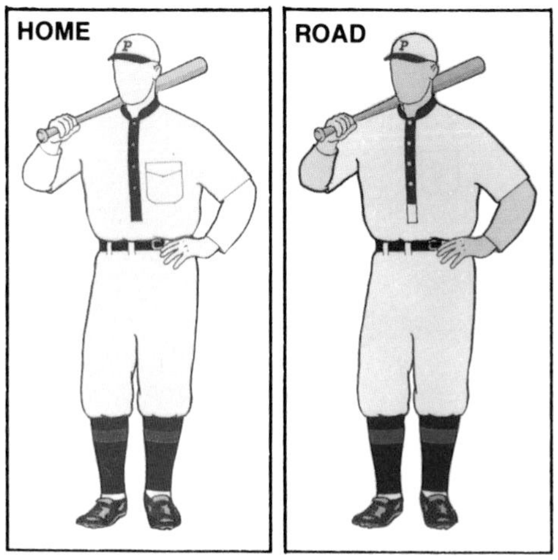

PHILADELPHIA

CHICAGO

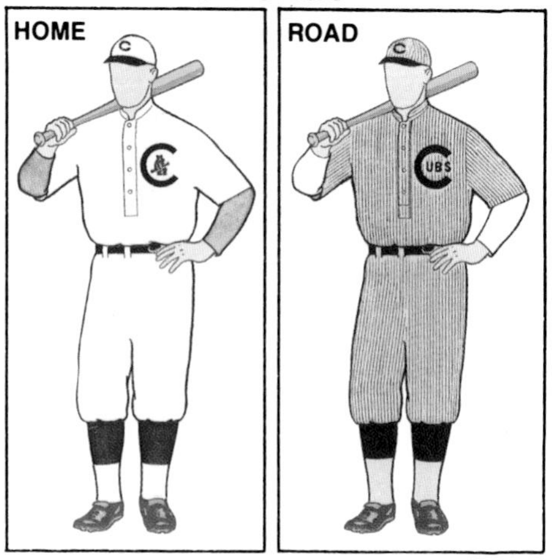

CINCINNATI

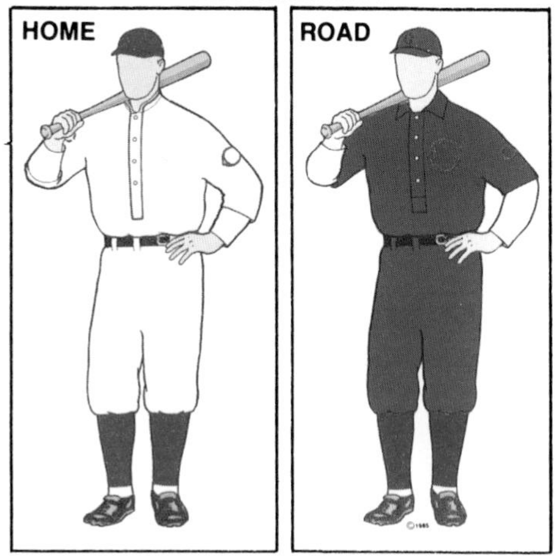

NEW YORK

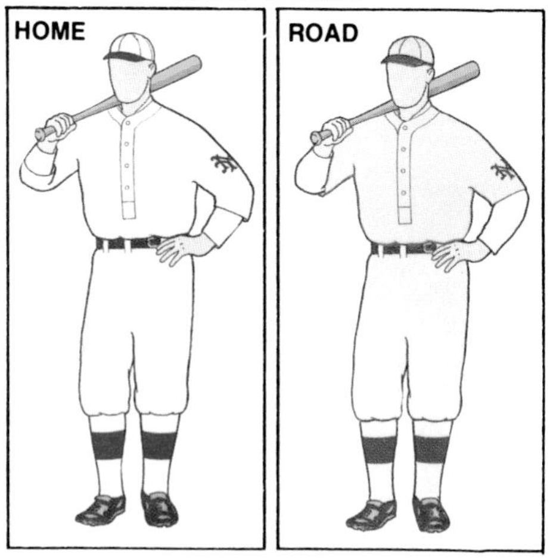

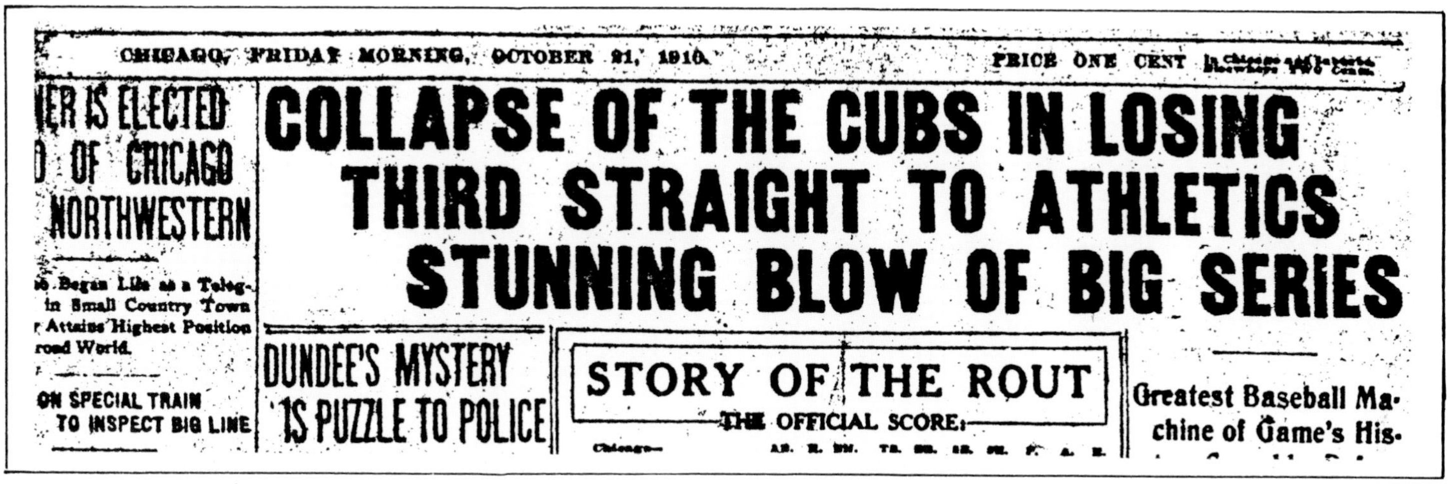

CHICAGO, FRIDAY MORNING, OCTOBER 21, 1910. PRICE ONE CENT

...ER IS ELECTED ...D OF CHICAGO NORTHWESTERN

...Began Life as a Teleg... in Small Country Town ...r Attains Highest Position ...road World.

ON SPECIAL TRAIN TO INSPECT BIG LINE

COLLAPSE OF THE CUBS IN LOSING THIRD STRAIGHT TO ATHLETICS STUNNING BLOW OF BIG SERIES

DUNDEE'S MYSTERY IS PUZZLE TO POLICE

STORY OF THE ROUT

THE OFFICIAL SCORE:

Greatest Baseball Machine of Game's His-

1911 AMERICAN LEAGUE

BOSTON

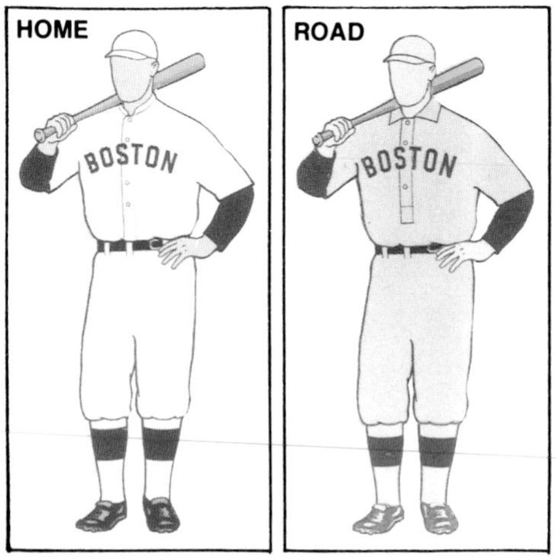

CLEVELAND

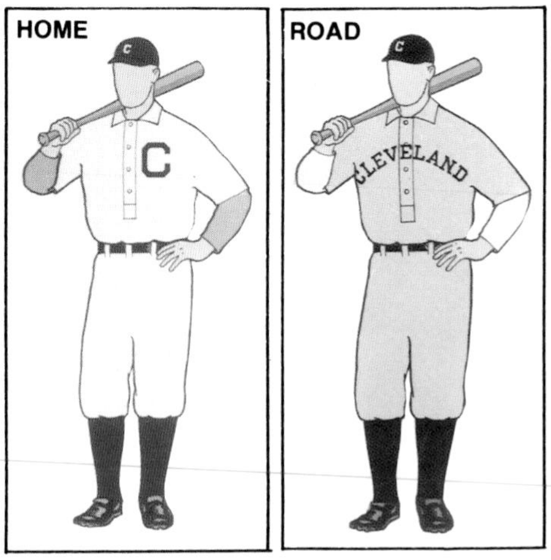

DETROIT

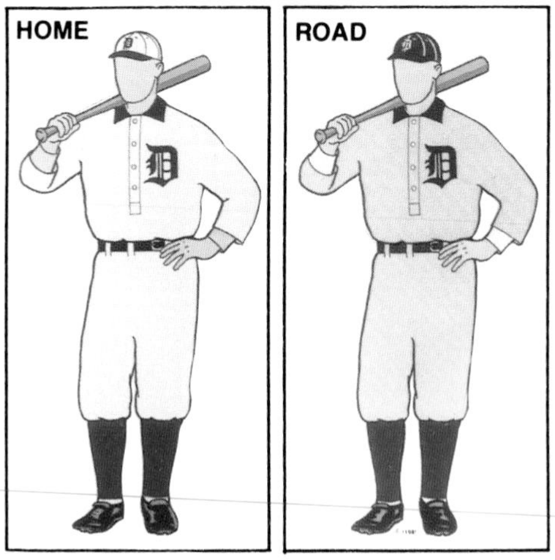

ST. LOUIS

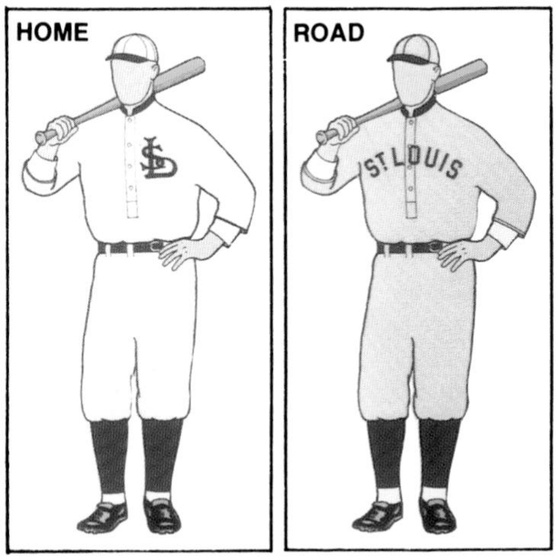

NEW YORK

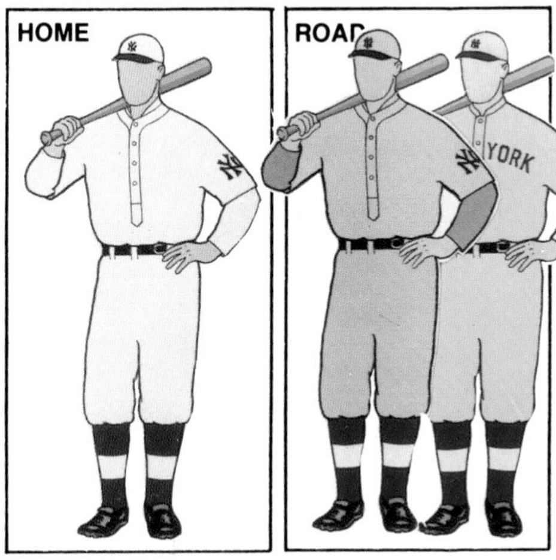

PHILADELPHIA

CHICAGO

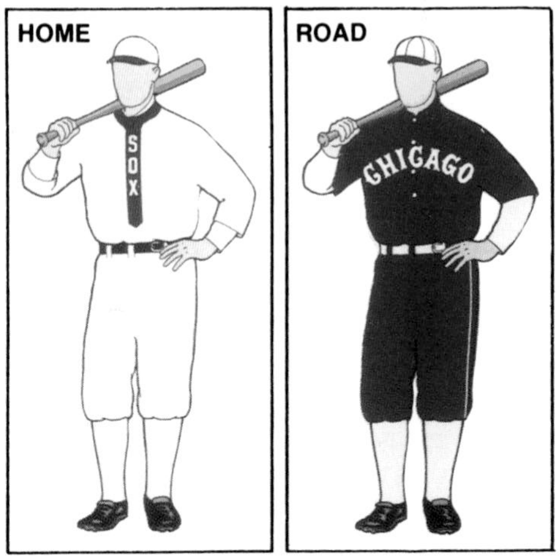

WASHINGTON

THE WEATHER TO-DAY.

The Press

EARLY EDITION

VOL. LIII. NO. 256. PHILADELPHIA, THURSDAY MORNING, APRIL 13, 1911. ONE CENT.

TITTERSVILLE COMMISSION BILL PASSES FINALLY

Ripper Bill Now Becomes a Law When Signed by the Governor.

VOTE IS UNANIMOUS

CURTIS GUILD, JR., AS AMBASSADOR TO RUSSIA

Washington, April 12.—President Taft will send to the Senate to-morrow the nominations of former Governor Curtis Guild, Jr., of Massachusetts, as Ambassador to Russia, and ... as Ambassador to Turkey.

Mr. Rockhill is at present Ambassador to Russia.

Governor Guild is an intimate personal friend of President Taft. He was appointed by the President as special ambassador to Mexico at the time of the centennial celebration of the foundation of that Republic.

Mr. Rockhill will succeed Oscar S. Straus, who was secretary of the Department of Commerce and Labor under former President Roosevelt. Mr. Straus resigned the ambassadorship to Turkey several months ago.

SCHWAB GIVES $800 TO HIS ORCHESTRA LEADER

Bethlehem, Pa., April 12 (Special).—The generous side of the many-sided Charles M. Schwab, president of the Bethlehem Steel Company, was shown in a new way to-day, when Andre M. ...

YANKEES BEAT ATHLETICS 2-1 BEFORE 20,000

Thrilling Scenes Mark Opening Basebr Game at Park World's "Champ

CLAY STARTS CON ST

Philadelphia's World's Cha... went through the formality of ... the 1911 American League championship season yesterday afternoon, the parade, the flag raising and all the other frills being religiously attended to. But ... Mack's team was defeated by the New ...

Scenes at the Opening Baseball Game at Shibe Park

THE FIRST BALL IS THROWN BEFORE 20,000 SPECTATORS

BLOODHOUNDS ON TRAIL OF MISSING GIRL

Vigorous Search of Country Being Made for Miss Mason, of Berwyn.

MOTHER IS TIRELESS

With only the ashes of a small fire of twigs amid the ancient, moss-covered tombstones of the old Friends' Cemetery near Willisville, as a clew, State police and scores of residents of the Main Line are continuing a minute and sweeping ...

NATIONAL LEAGUE 1911

BOSTON

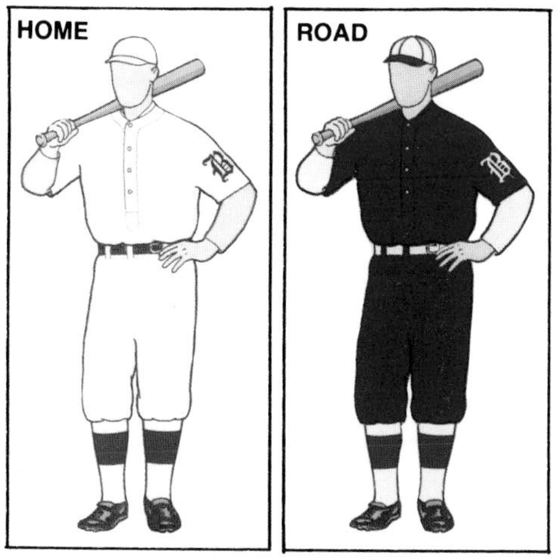

BROOKLYN

ST. LOUIS

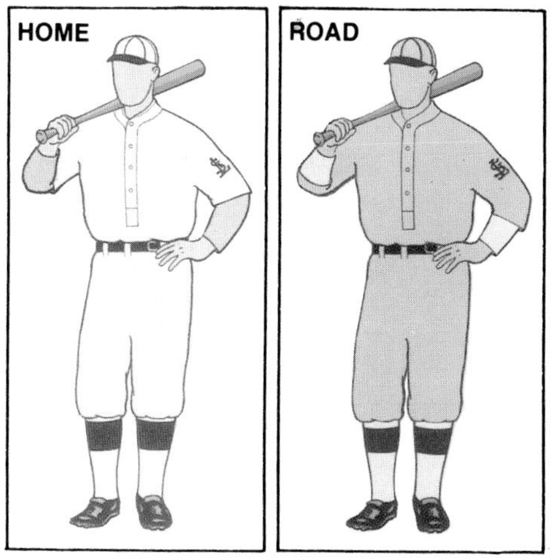

PITTSBURGH

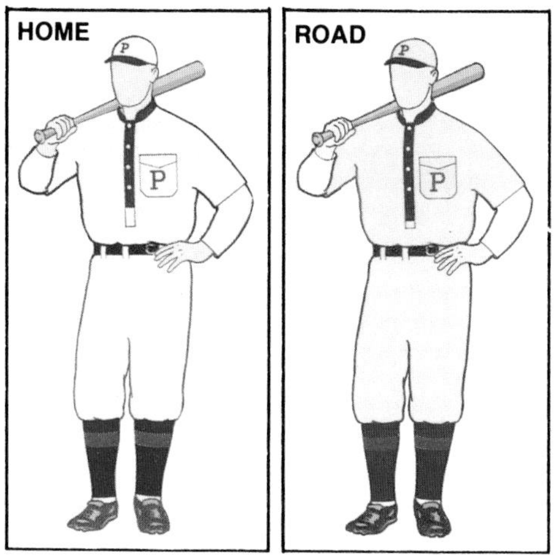

PHILADELPHIA

CHICAGO

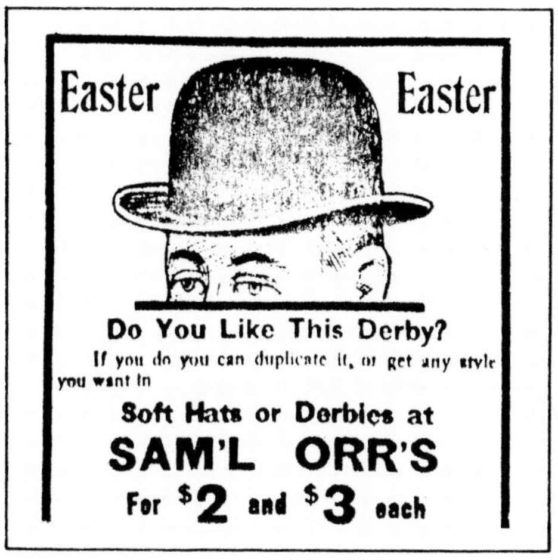

CINCINNATI

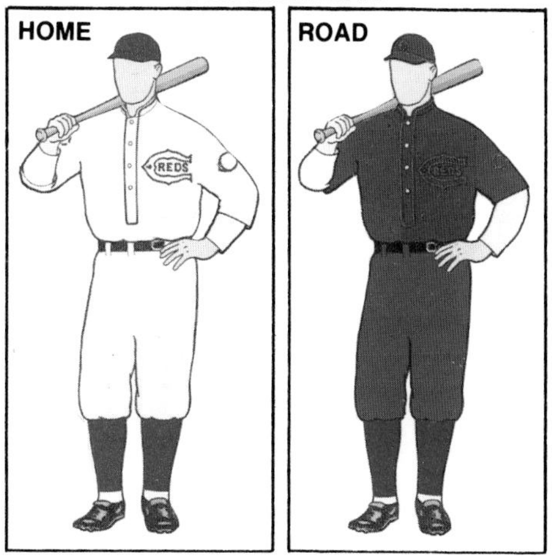

NEW YORK

FINAL ★★★★

The Evening Telegram

COMPLETE BASEBALL AND RACING RESULTS

VOL. XLIV. NO. 24,848. NEW YORK, FRIDAY, APRIL 14, 1911.—TWENTY PAGES. PRICE ONE CENT.

TEARS NEAR AS DANIEL O'REILLY IS HELD IN BAIL

Greatly Shaken, Faces Court to Answer Charge of Receiving Stolen Goods in the Bancroft Case.

GEORGE CONSIDINE GOES ON HIS BOND, PUTTING UP HIS HOTEL METROPOLE AS SECURITY FOR $5,000

DODGERS WIN THE THIRD, SCORE 15-2

Brooklyn and Boston Meet in Third and "Rubber" Contest in the "Hub."

National League Games To-Morrow.
Brooklyn at New York.
Philadelphia at Boston.
Pittsburg at Cincinnati.
St. Louis at Chicago.

American League Games To-Morrow.
New York at Philadelphia.
Boston at Washington.
Chicago at Detroit.
Cleveland at St. Louis.

GIANTS WILL USE HILL TOP FOR THE GAME TO-MORROW

Ruins at the Polo Ground After Fire Had Swept Through Stands

CITIZENS AIDING THE FIREMEN.

National League Owners Consent to Meet Brooklyn Team on "Foreign" Field.

MONTH BEFORE LOCALS HOME IS REHABILITATED

1912 AMERICAN LEAGUE

BOSTON

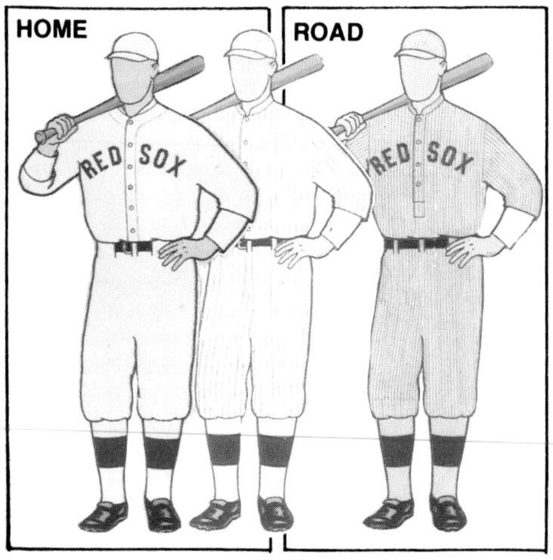

CLEVELAND

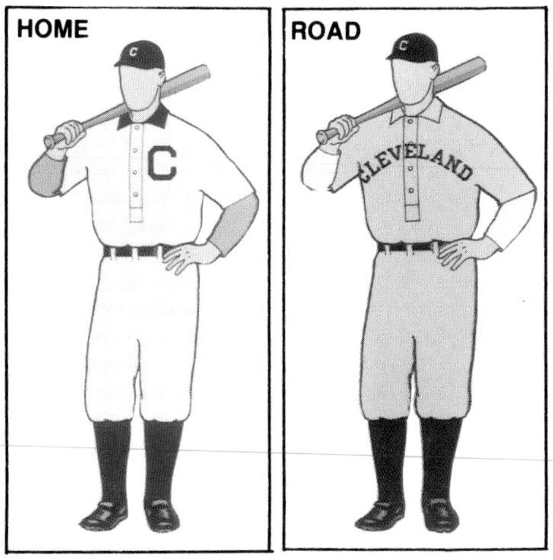

DETROIT

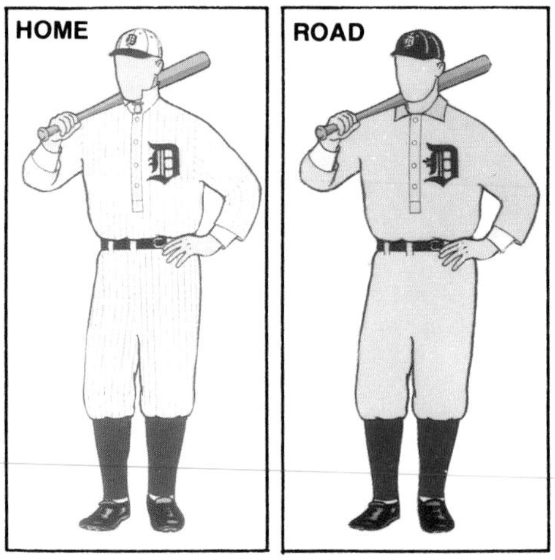

ST. LOUIS

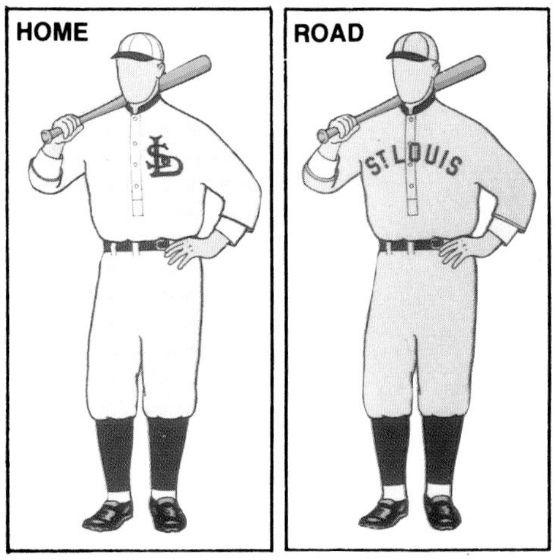

NEW YORK

PHILADELPHIA

CHICAGO

WASHINGTON

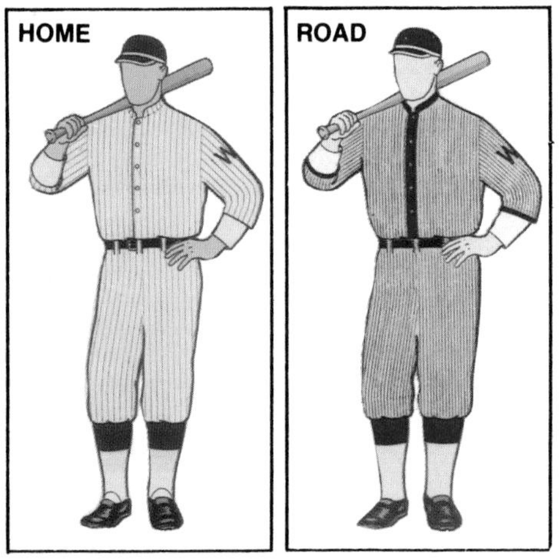

16 THE EVENING STAR, WEDNESDAY, APRIL 10, 1912.

From This On Everything the Nationals Do Will Affect the Pennant

HOW THE NATIONALS LOOK IN THEIR NEW ROAD UNIFORMS.

Waivers Asked on Nap First Sacker, Is Report

BUSH REPORTS

It's the cutting and polish the diamond which valuable.

NATIONAL LEAGUE 1912

BOSTON

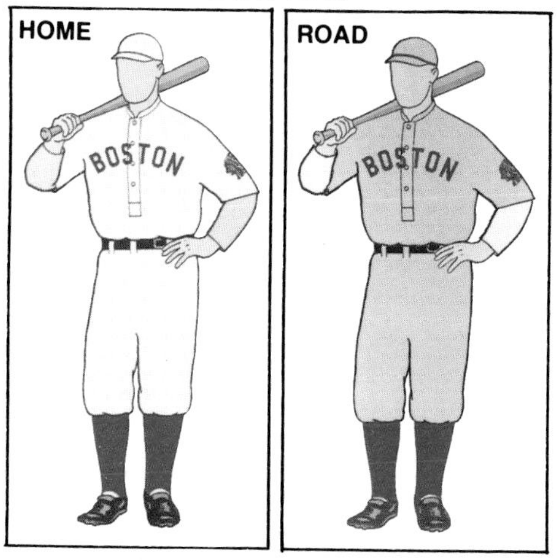

BROOKLYN

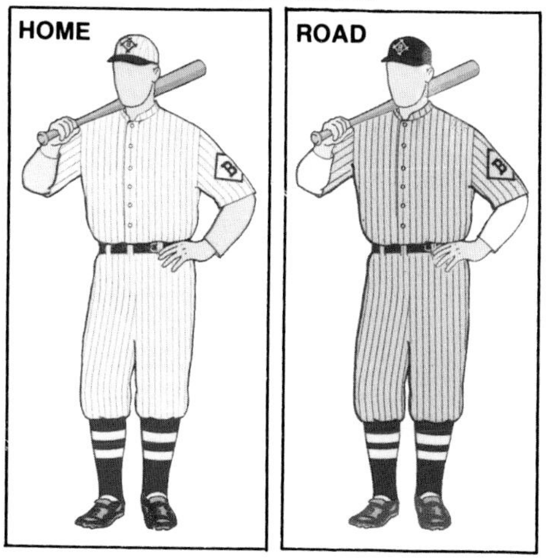

ST. LOUIS

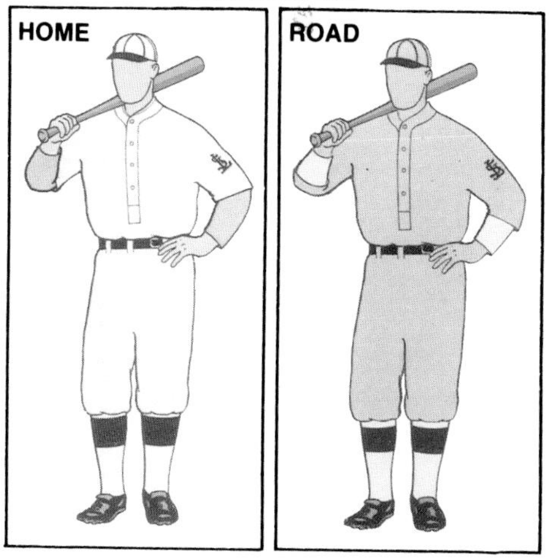

PITTSBURGH

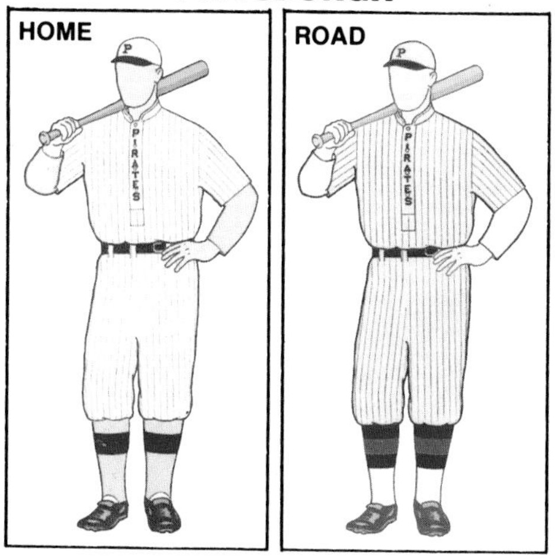

PHILADELPHIA

CHICAGO

CINCINNATI

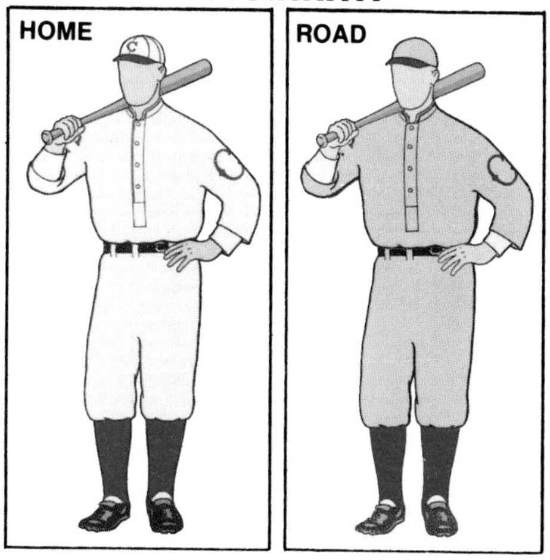

NEW YORK

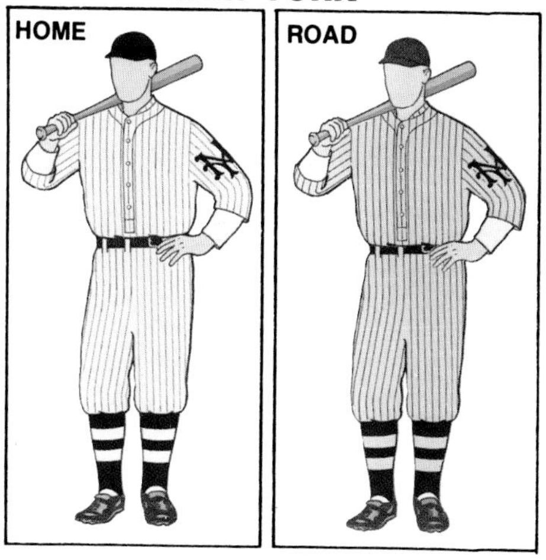

WEATHER.
Forecast To-day: Unsettled.
Temperature Yesterday:
Maximum, 65. Minimum, 42.

The New York Press

The Public's Newspaper.
Serving No Other Interest.
Fair and Square.

LARGEST REPUBLICAN CIRCULATION BY MANY THOUSANDS OF COPIES A DAY.

VOL. XXV—WHOLE NO. 8,903 NEW YORK, TUESDAY, APRIL 16, 1912—TWELVE PAGES PRICE

1505 MAY BE LOST ON STEAMER TITANIC;
GREAT LINER SINKS OFF CAPE RACE

WOMEN AND MEN IN TEARS SEEK NEWS OF RELATIVES AND FRIENDS IN TITANIC

Keep Long Vigil in White Star Office in Effort to Learn Whether Persons Whose Safety Concerns Them Were Carried Down When Giant Liner Sank.

AMERICAN WOMAN HAD ON BOARD $600,000 IN GEMS

LONDON, April 16. In addition to a valuable shipment of diamonds aboard the Titanic, it is said that among almost priceless jewels carried by the passengers are pearls belonging to an American woman valued at $600,000. The steamer also carried a large amount in bonds and a very valuable registered mail.

It is said the owners were unable to insure the Titanic to the full amount because the British

Meagre Wireless Reports Are That 675 Persons Are Saved, "Mostly Women and Children" Some of Others May Be Adrift in Lifeboats Among Field of Ice Off Cape Race First Reports That All on Board Were

1913 AMERICAN LEAGUE

BOSTON
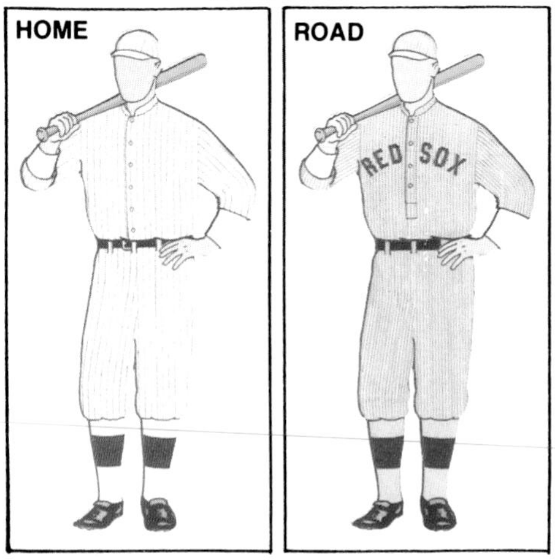

CLEVELAND
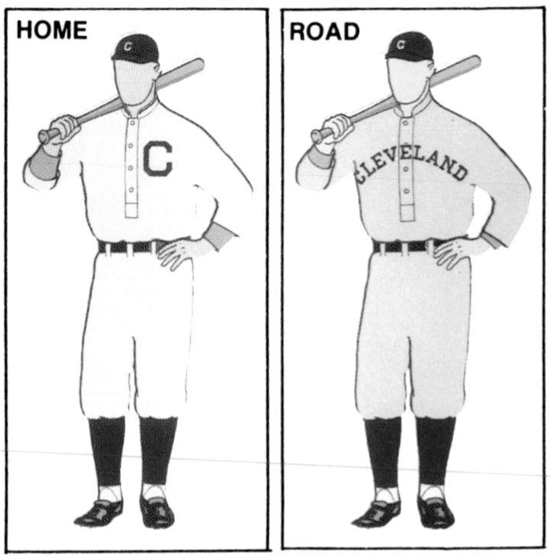

DETROIT
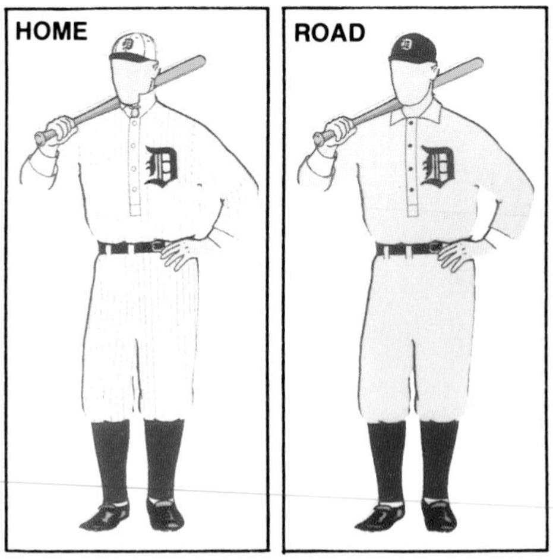

ST. LOUIS
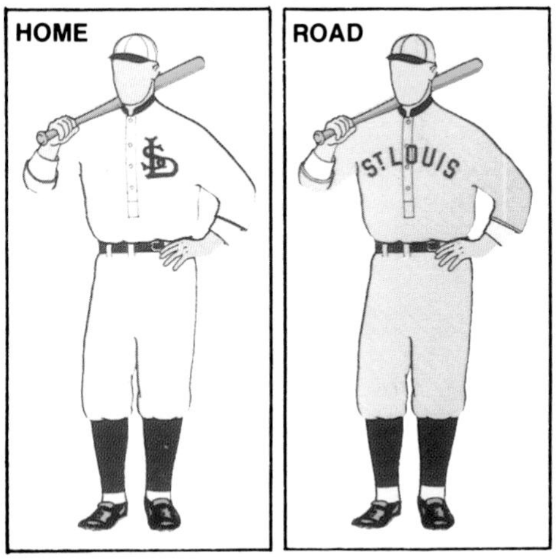

NEW YORK

PHILADELPHIA

CHICAGO

WASHINGTON
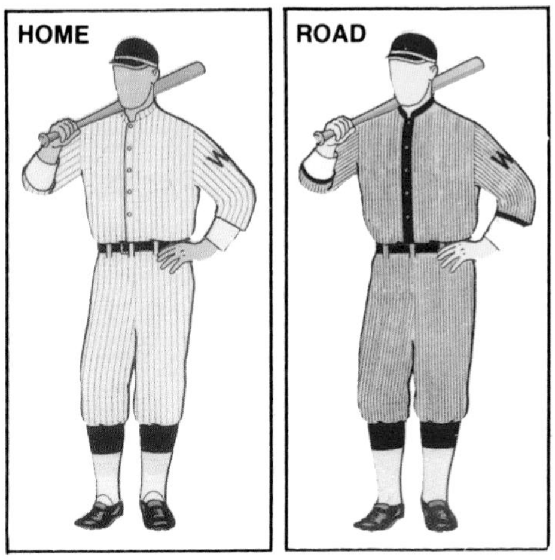

THE WEATHER TO-DAY
Fair.

The Press

EARLY EDITION

VOL. LVI. NO. 54. PHILADELPHIA, TUESDAY MORNING, SEPTEMBER 23, 1913. ONE CENT.

MACKMEN NAIL PENNANT FAST BY DUAL WIN

Clinch American League Flag by Twice Blanking Old Rivals, Detroit.

SCORES 4-0 AND 1-0

5th Championship Brought to Philadelphia by Connie Mack and Athletics.

Philadelphia will sport its fifth American League pennant this Fall. This fact was established beyond all doubt yesterday when Connie Mack's Athletics closed the doors of a burglar-proof safe on the 1913 bunting by using their old arch enemies—

Pennant-Winning Smile

POWDER PLANT EXPLODES AND 4 ARE KILLED

DuPont Mixing House in Gibbstown, N. J., Scene of Accident.

ONE MAN IS MISSING

Shock Closes Compartment Doors of Warships at League Island.

HOMES FLOODED IN SHENANDOAH

Families Flee in N— —Furniture Ruined by — Water

Self-Confessed Murderer as he Appeared before Detectives

CONFESSED SLAYER NOW DENIES GUILT

Wolfson Changes His Mind and Claims Innocence of Girl's Death.

POLICE INCREDULOUS

Take Little Stock in Second Statement — Rochester Despatch Aids Evidence.

NATIONAL LEAGUE 1913

BOSTON

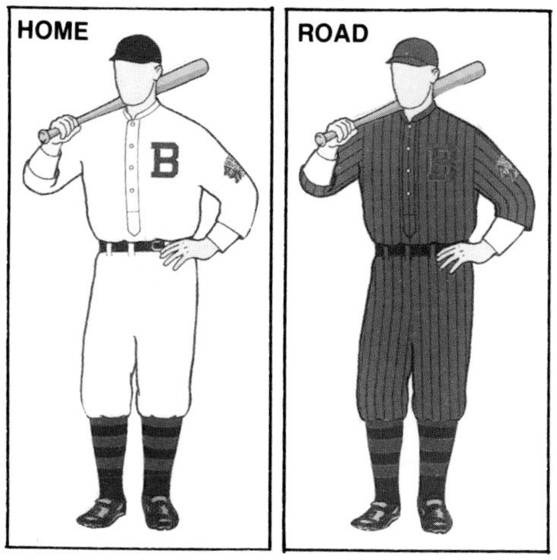

BROOKLYN

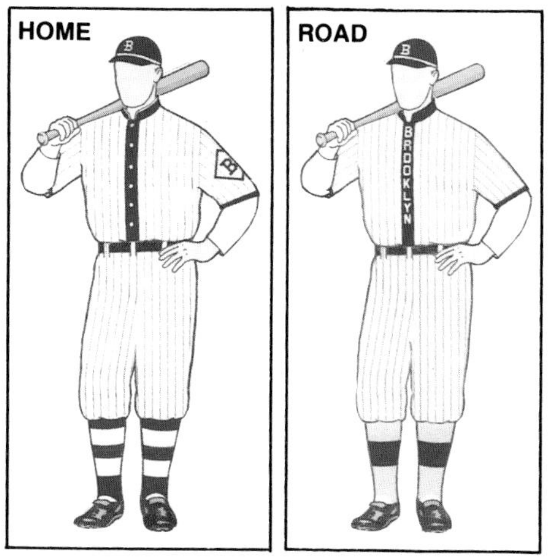

ST. LOUIS

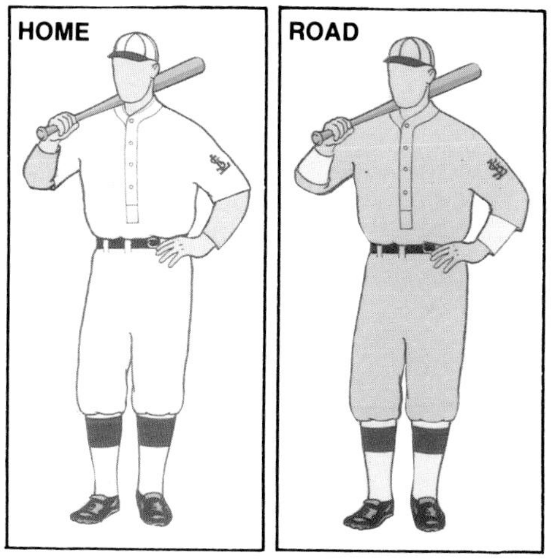

PITTSBURGH

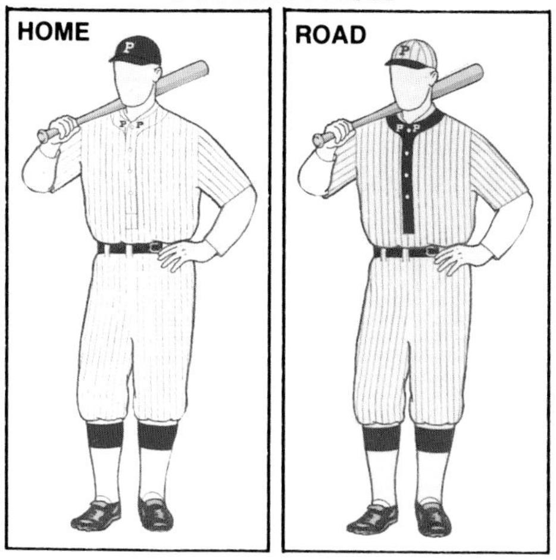

PHILADELPHIA

CHICAGO

CINCINNATI

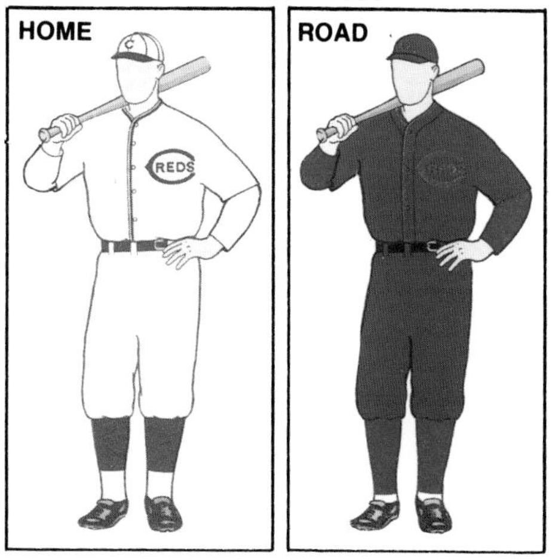

NEW YORK

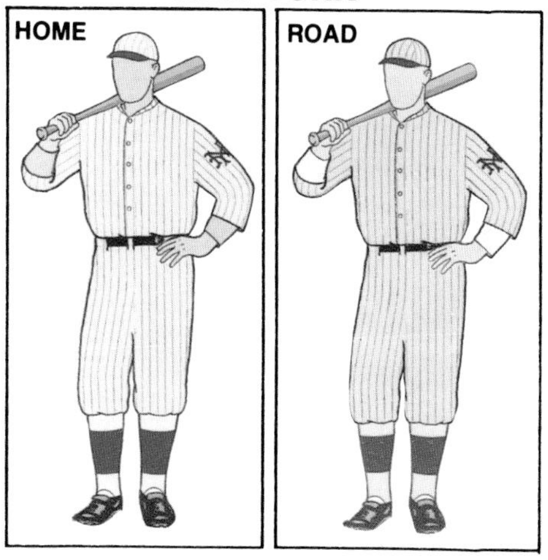

FINAL ★★★★★ **The Evening Telegram** COMPLETE BASEBALL and RACING

THE WEATHER:—UNSETTLED, PROBABLY SHOWERS TO-NIGHT OR SUNDAY.

VOL. XLVII. NO. 23,746. NEW YORK, SATURDAY, OCTOBER 11, 1913.—EIGHTEEN PAGES. PRICE ONE CENT.

ATHLETICS ARE CHAMPIONS

GIANTS LOSE THEIR FOURTH GAME IN WORLD'S SERIES BY A SCORE OF 3-1

1914 AMERICAN LEAGUE

BOSTON

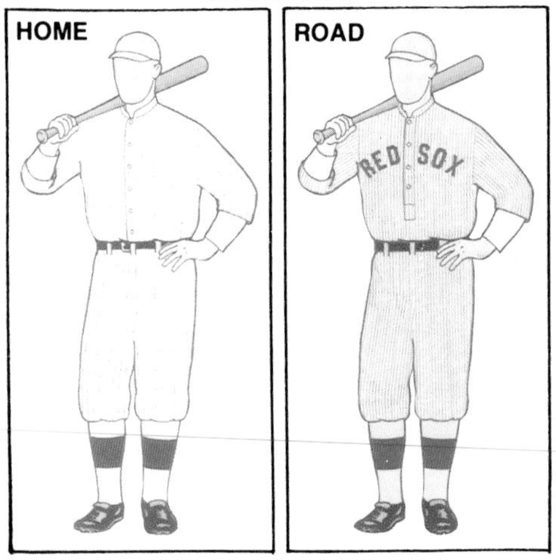

CLEVELAND

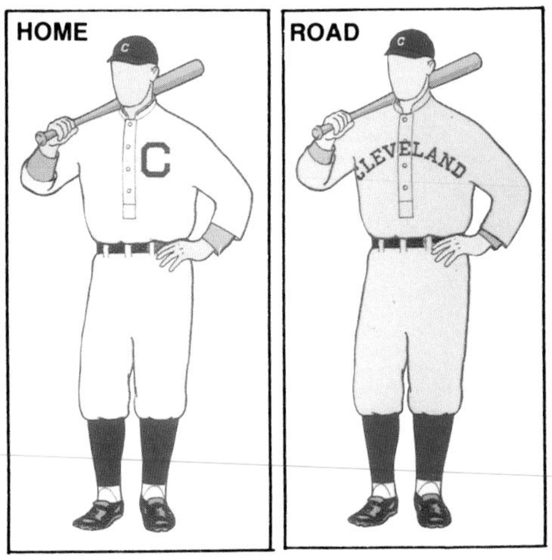

DETROIT

ST. LOUIS

NEW YORK

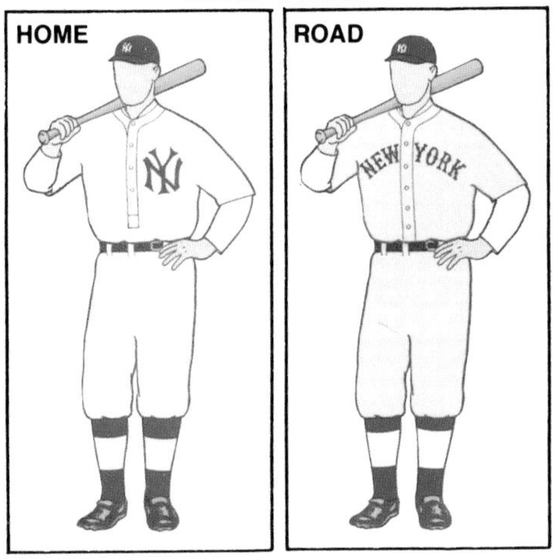

PHILADELPHIA

CHICAGO

WASHINGTON

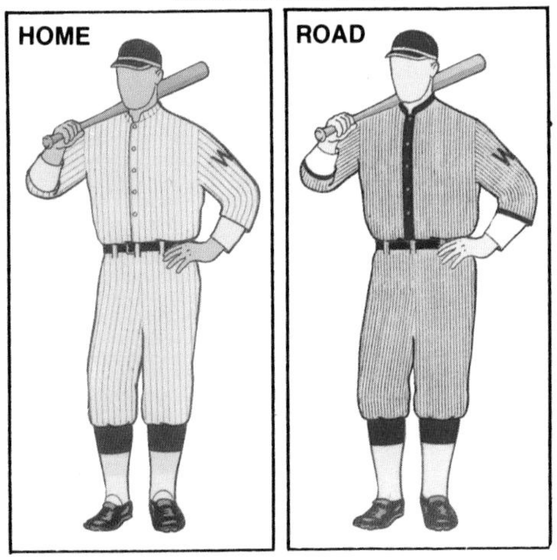

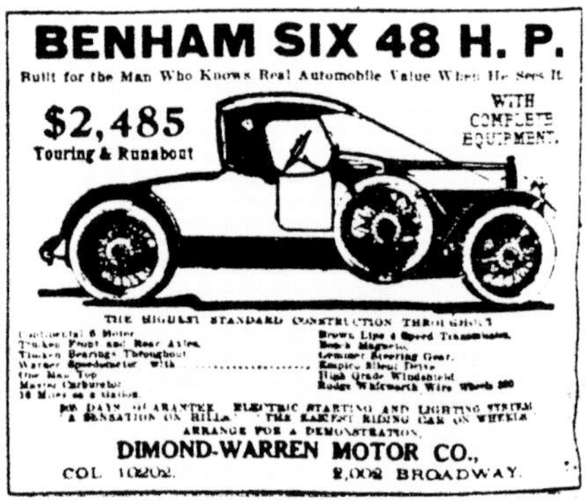

12 St. Louis Daily Globe-Democrat, Thursday Morning, April 23, 1914.

Local Federals Win Another; Detroit Defeats Browns

HOW THINGS LOOKED WHEN THE BROWNS HAD THEIR FIRST "AT HOME"

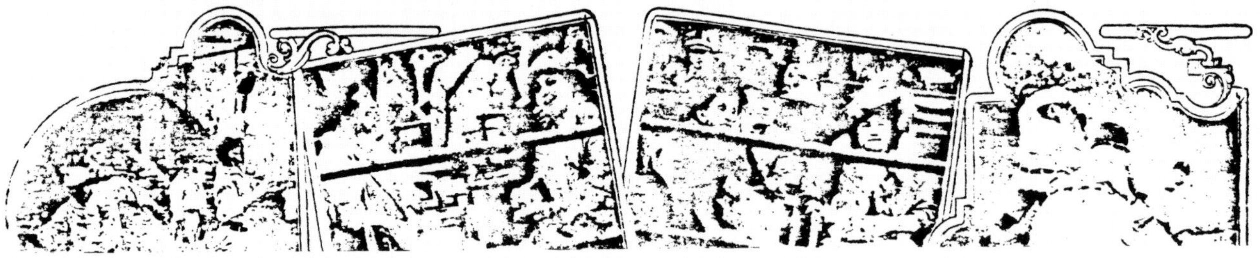

NATIONAL LEAGUE 1914

BOSTON

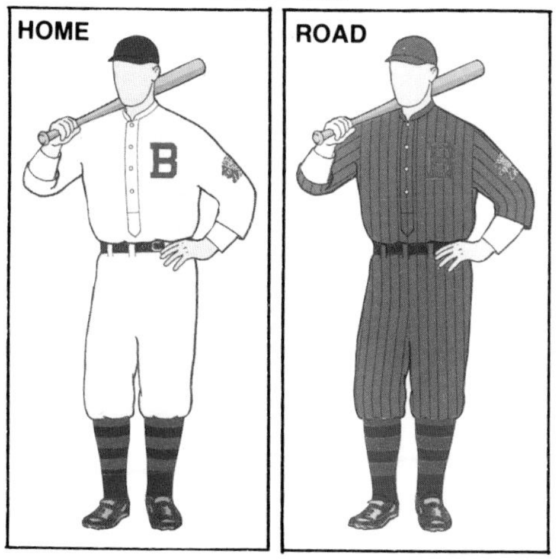

BROOKLYN

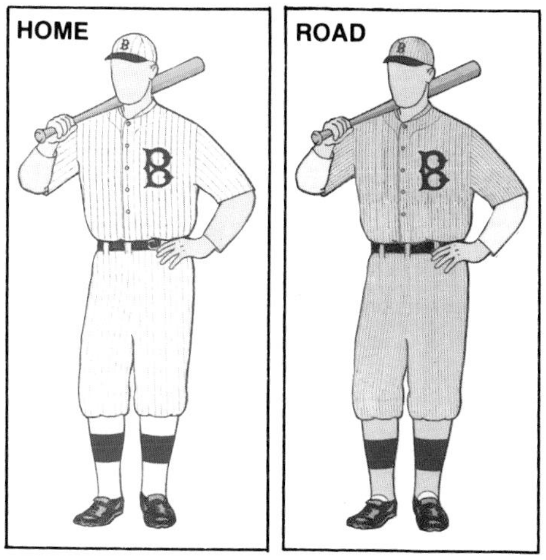

ST. LOUIS

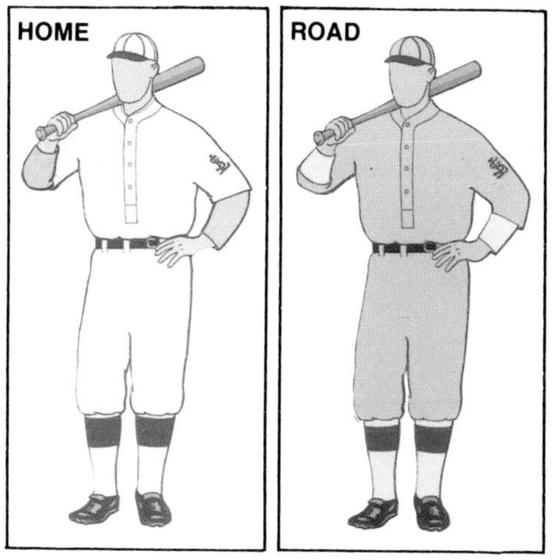

PITTSBURGH

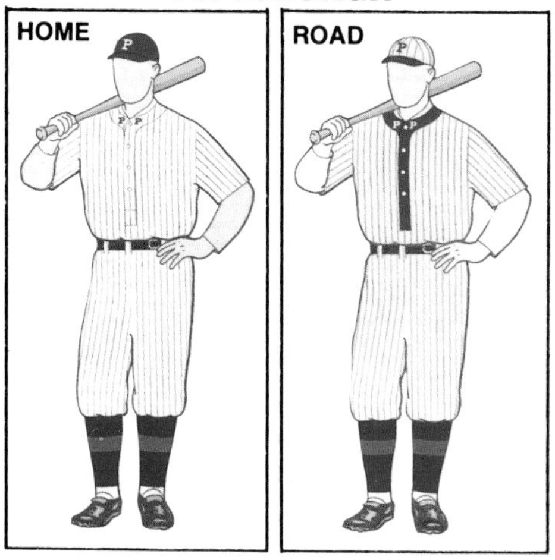

PHILADELPHIA

CHICAGO

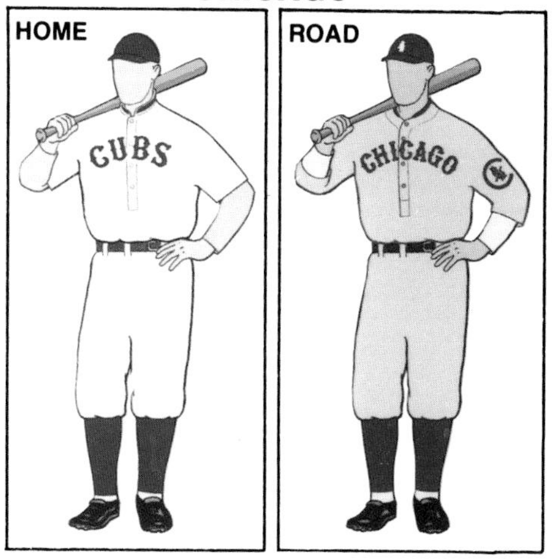

CINCINNATI

NEW YORK

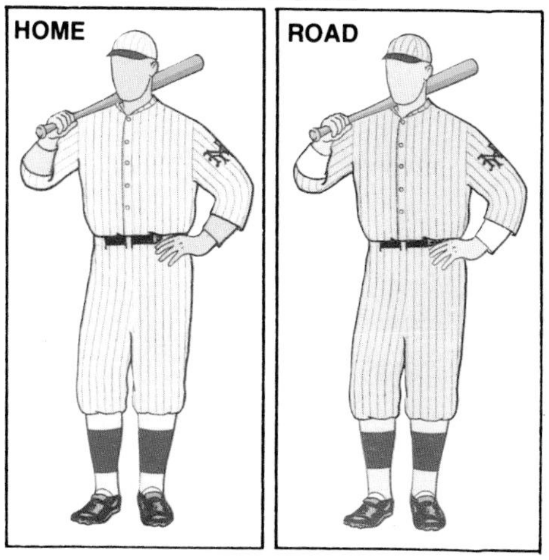

FINAL ★★★★★ **The Evening Telegram** FINAL ★★★★★

THE WEATHER:—RAIN, WITH SLOWLY RISING TEMPERATURES; MONDAY, CLOUDY.

VOL. XLVII. NO. 26,006. NEW YORK, SUNDAY, JUNE 28, 1914.—FOURTEEN PAGES. PRICE TWO CENTS.

ARCHDUKE FERDINAND ASSASSINATED; BULLETS KILL DUCHESS AT HIS SIDE; BOMB IS HURLED AT AUSTRIAN HEIR

1915 AMERICAN LEAGUE

BOSTON

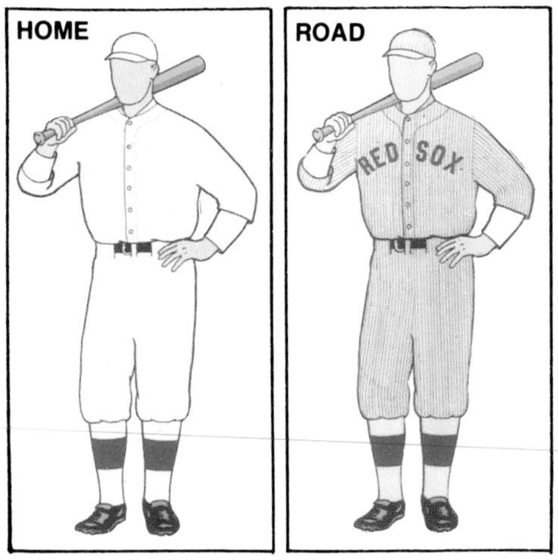

CLEVELAND

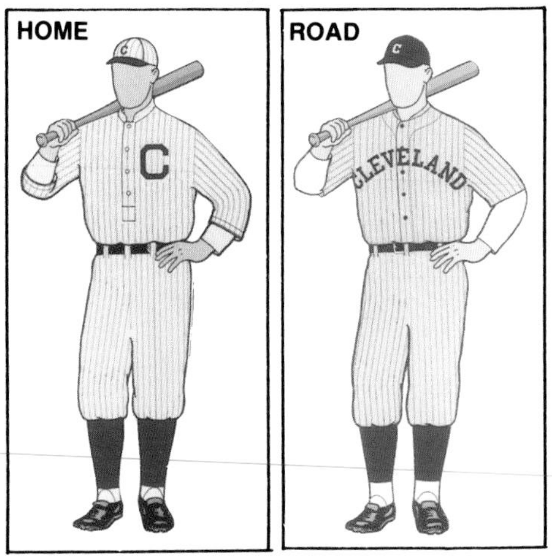

DETROIT

ST. LOUIS

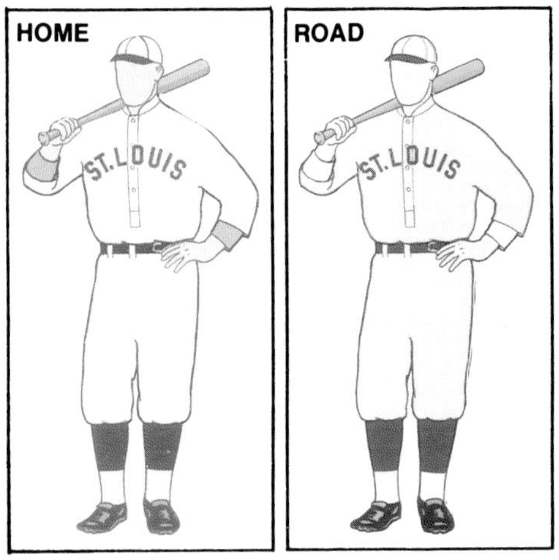

NEW YORK

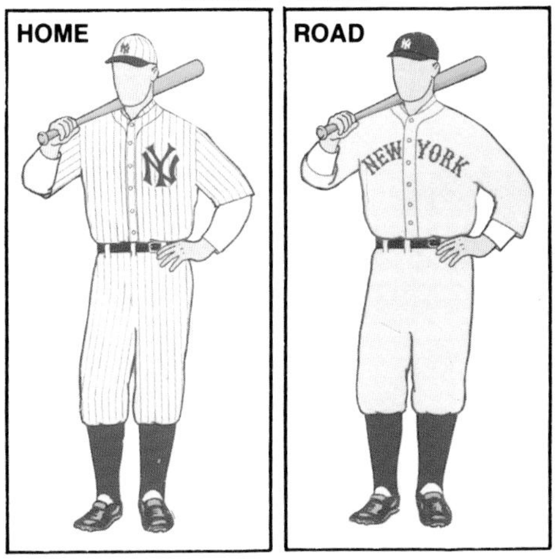

PHILADELPHIA

CHICAGO

WASHINGTON

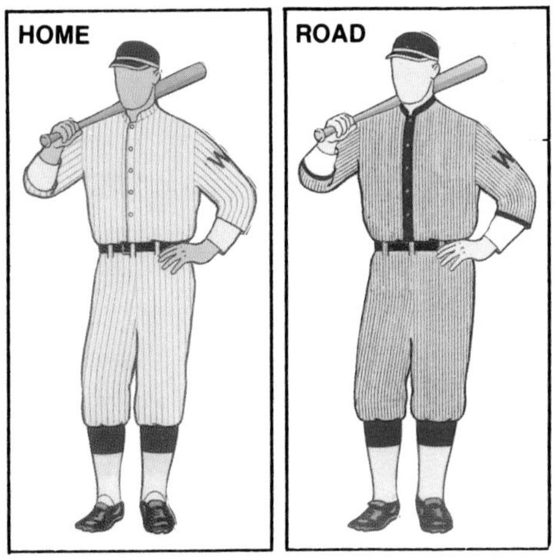

Sporting News Section

CHICAGO SUNDAY HERALD

Easy to Read and Worth Reading

Part Ei[ght]
Four Pag[es]

MAY 9, 1915.

WHITE SOX WIN, 5-0; CUBS WIN, 3-1; WHALES WIN, 2-1;
BENNY KAUFF KICKED OUT OF ORGANIZED BASEBA

RUSSELL PULLS TIGERS' CLAWS

Texan Lets Down Bengals With Two Hits and White Sox Win, 5 to 0.

OTHERS ALSO 'PRESENT'

Spring Batting and Pitching Phenoms Who Are Making History in Old Leagues

PIRATES BAFFLED BY STANDRIDGE

Timely Hits Also Help Cubs to Foil Buccaneers by Score of 3 to 1.

FINISH IN FOURTH ROUND

Where They Stand This Morning

American League

	W.	L.	Pct.	Win.	Lose.
New York	9	4	.692	....	....
Detroit	12	6	.667	.684	.632
Chicago	11	7	.611	.632	.579
Washington	8	6	.571	....	....
Boston	5	6	.455	....	....
Cleveland	7	10	.412	.444	.389
St. Louis	5	12	.294	.333	.278
Philadelphia	4	10	.286	....	....

TOTAL RUNS LAST WEEK.

Sox ....20 | St. Louis 13

National League

	W.	L.	Pct.	Win.	Lose.
Philadelphia	13	2	.867	....	....
Chicago	9	6	.600	.625	.563
Boston	8	6	.571	....	....
Cincinnati	9	7	.563	.588	.529
St. Louis	9	9	.500	.526	.474
Brooklyn	6	10	.375	....	....
Pittsburgh	5	10	.333	.375	.313
New York	5	10	.333	....	....

TOTAL RUNS LAST WEEK.

Cincinnati ....[illegible] | Philadelphia 24
St. Louis ....[illegible] | New York ....[illegible]

FIRST GAM[E] TO WHALE[S]

Prendergast H[olds] Run Margin D[espite] feds' Rally i[n]...

MANN STRANG[LES]

NATIONAL LEAGUE 1915

BOSTON

BROOKLYN

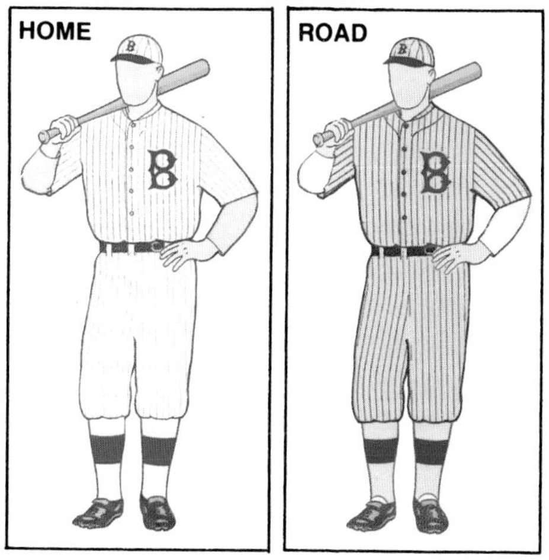

ST. LOUIS

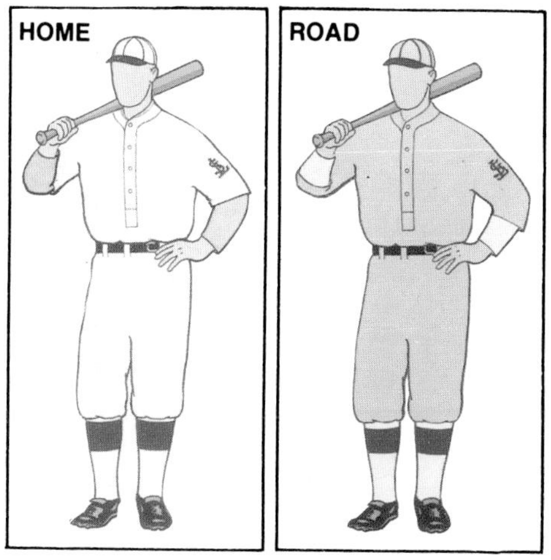

PITTSBURGH

PHILADELPHIA

CHICAGO

CINCINNATI

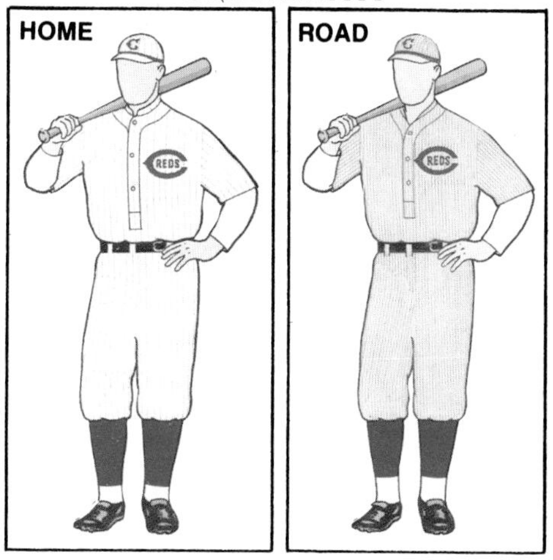

NEW YORK

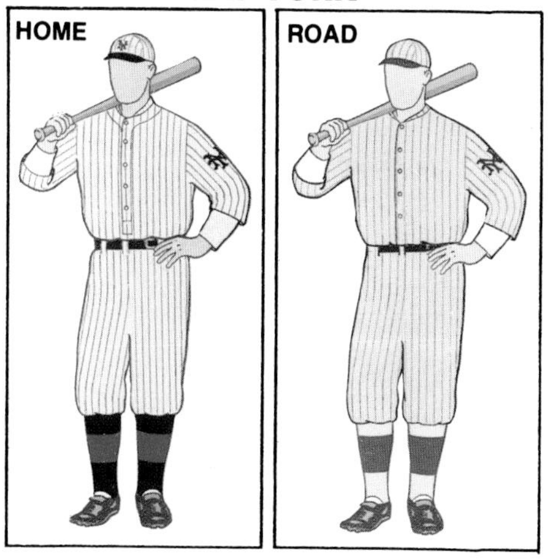

10 THE EVENING TELEGRAM—NEW YORK, MONDAY, APRIL 5, 1915.

WILLARD KNOCKS "JACK" JOHNSON OUT, WINNING THE WORLD'S CHAMPIONSHIP IN 26 ROUNDS

Cowboy Challenger's Youth and Strength Give Him Victory Over Opponent's Superior Skill and Ring Experience.

(CONTINUED FROM PAGE ONE.)

his balance and he wisely withheld the blow that he had been set to deliver.

Then Johnson advanced rapidly and scored lefts and rights to his opponent's jaw. Willard drove a slashing right to Jack's body, but in so doing left himself open for a left hook to his own [illegible] section. Johnson followed this advantage with three quick lefts to the body. Willard towered over Johnson, and it looked as if the champion was fighting for Willard's body in an effort to make him double up so that he could land more effectively on Willard's jaw.

WILLARD LAUGHS AT BLOWS.

Willard laughed as the body punches landed on his stomach,

THE NEW AND OLD CHAMPION

WALL SCALING EVENT AT SECOND BATTALION GAMES

When H. G. DeLoiselle and Walter Bursch broke the wall scaling record at the Twenty-third Regiment games on Saturday, a match was arranged between the Twenty-third regiment pair and the Bennet brothers, of the Second naval battalion, which will be held at the armory next Wednesday night. The open events will be half-mile Military Athletic League relay; three-mile bicycle race, scratch and a 600-yard run, scratch.

HUGGINS AND BESCHER FAIL TO AGREE ON TERMS

Little Rock, Ark., Monday.—Miller Huggins, manager of the St. Louis National League team, after a conference yesterday with "Bob" Bescher, said that

POLICE STOPPED THE MORNINGSIDE A. C. RUN

Acting on the complaint of clergymen in the vicinity of the Morningside Athletic Club, in West 128th street, the annual Harlem road run that was to have been conducted yesterday by the club was prevented by Arthur S. Woods, the Police Commissioner. The clergymen had protested that it was indecent for young men to run through the streets on Sunday clad in athletic costumes, and the club was served with a police notice on Saturday that the race would have to be called off.

MEYER AND CUTLER TO PLAY IN MATCH GAME

Joseph Mayer, who recently won the amateur billiard championship in Philadelphia, will play a match of 1,000 points balk-line 18.2, at Doyle's Academy during the week of April 12 with Albert G. Cutler,

1916 AMERICAN LEAGUE

BOSTON

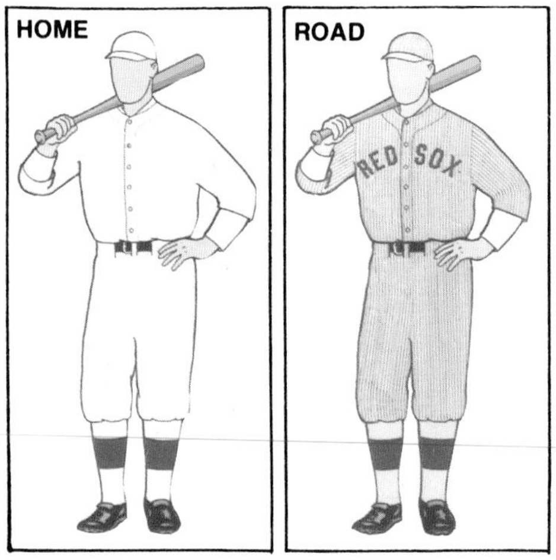

CLEVELAND

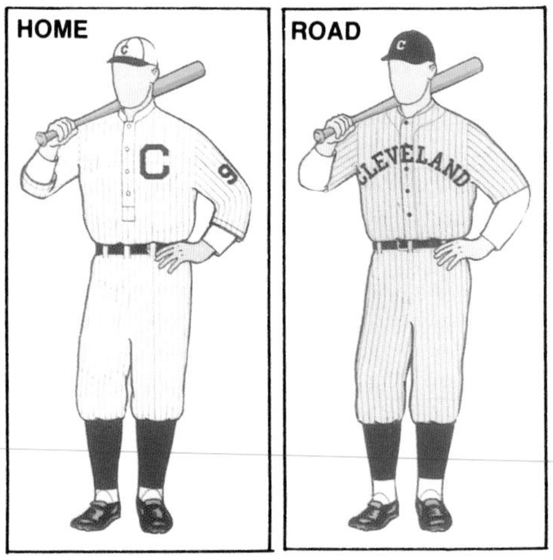

DETROIT

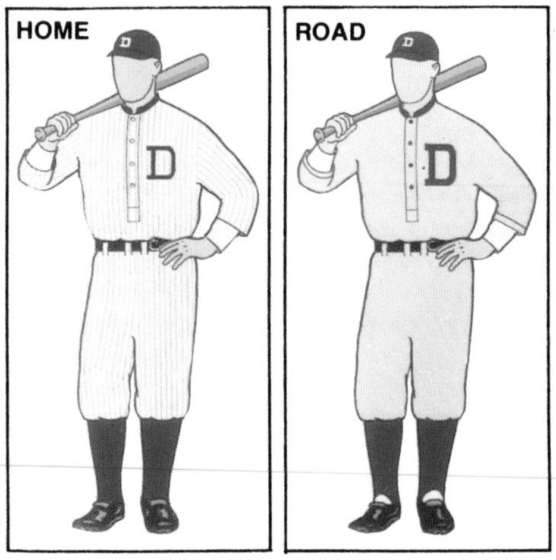

ST. LOUIS

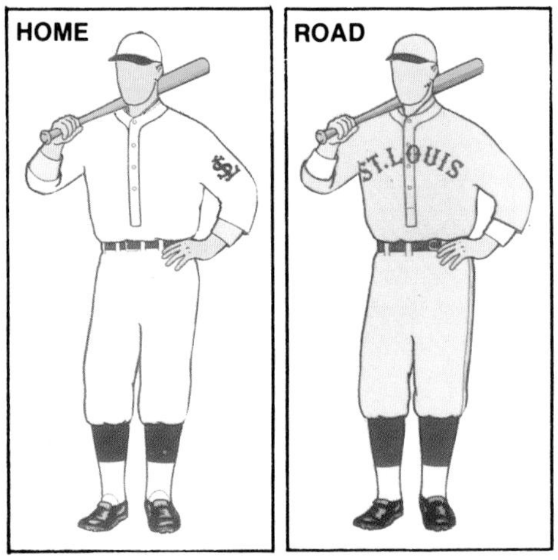

NEW YORK

PHILADELPHIA

CHICAGO

WASHINGTON

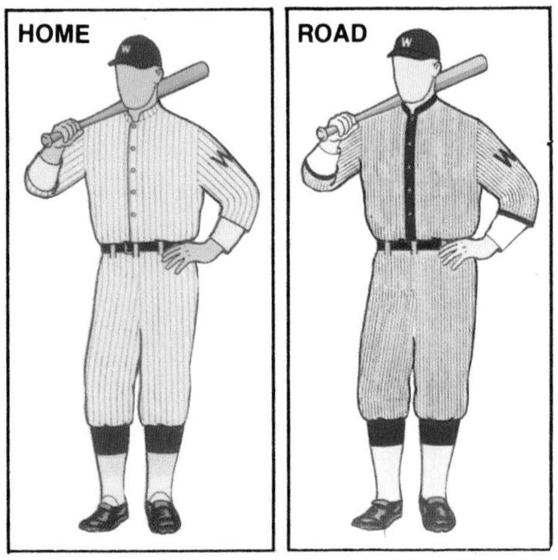

rowns and Cards to Play at Sportsman's Park—Meadows Vs. Weilman

SPORT SECTION

ARTLEY WOOD COLLINS LLOYD ESPY EVANS

THE ST. LOUIS REPUBLIC: SUNDAY, APRIL 9, 1916.

Boston Red Sox Sell Speaker to Cleveland

aseball Frapped, Highballs Popular, To-Day's Schedule

THREE MEN HUGGINS RELIES ON TO STAR FOR CARDINALS

NATIONAL LEAGUE 1916

BOSTON

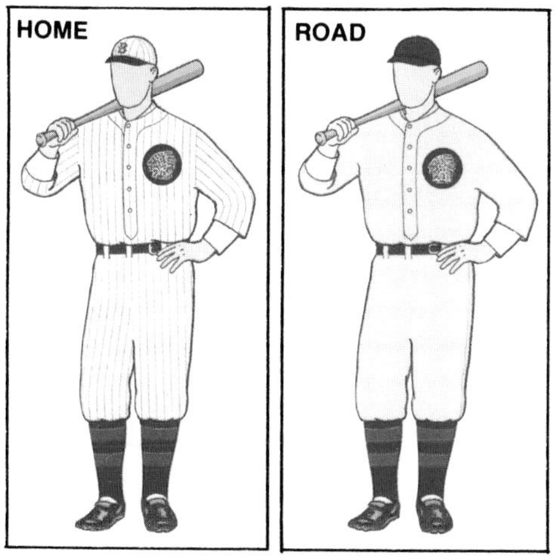

BROOKLYN

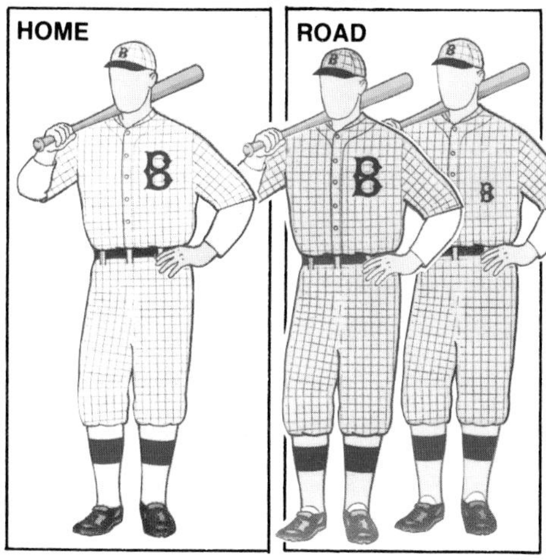

ST. LOUIS

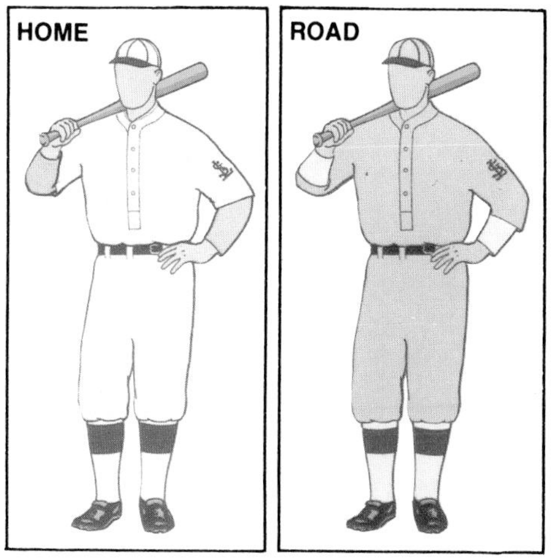

PITTSBURGH

PHILADELPHIA

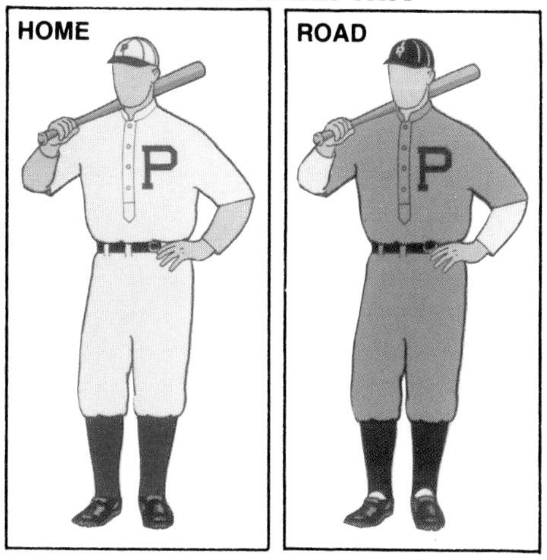

CHICAGO

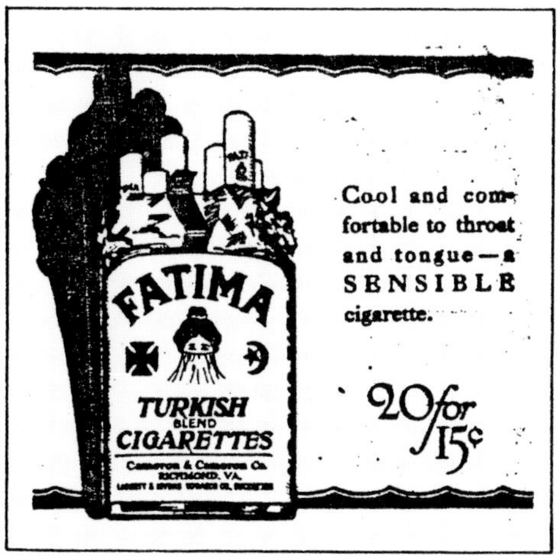

CINCINNATI

NEW YORK

18 * * CHICAGO HERALD, FRIDAY, APRIL 21, 1916.

CUBS OPEN NORTH SIDE PARK WITH 7 TO 6

SAIER'S WALLOP IN THE ELEVENTH ENDS BIG DOINGS

18,000 Fans Give Tinker's Team Great Reception and Are Rewarded With Thriller.

REDS TAKE EARLY LEAD

Sure, Old Man Cub Himself Was on the Job at Weeghman Park Yesterday
He's a Gift From J. Ogden Armour, but Didn't Come From the Stocky

AMERICAN LEAGUE

BOSTON

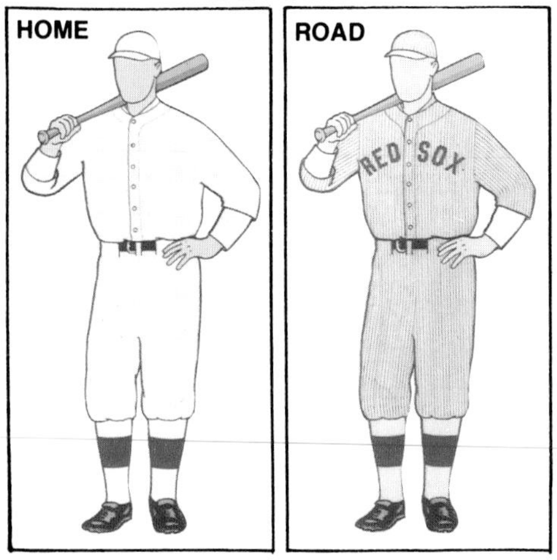

CLEVELAND

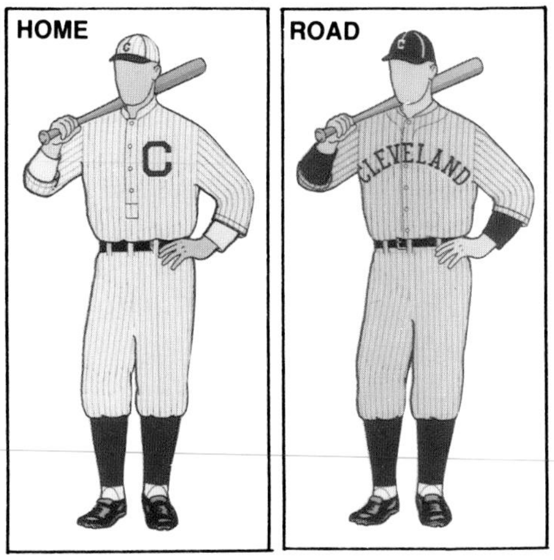

DETROIT

ST. LOUIS

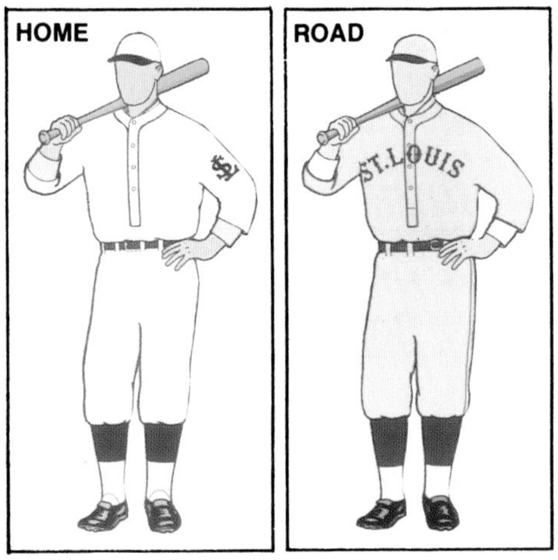

NEW YORK

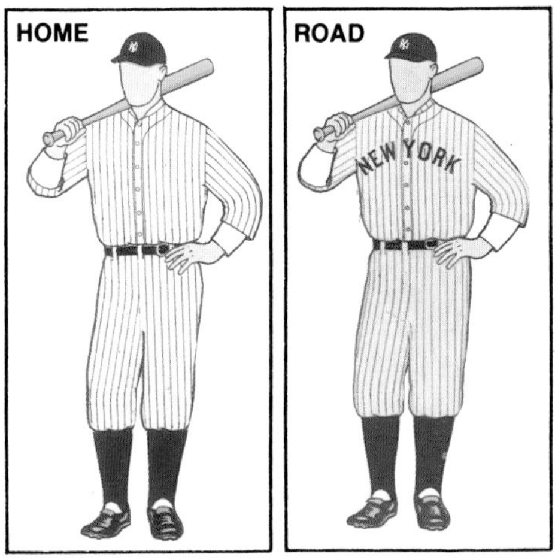

PHILADELPHIA

CHICAGO

WASHINGTON

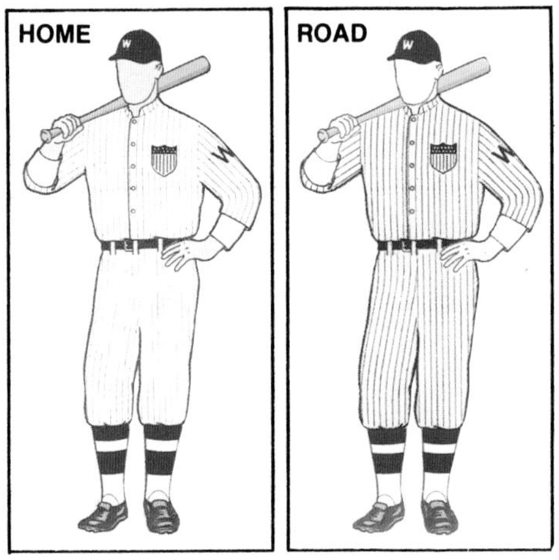

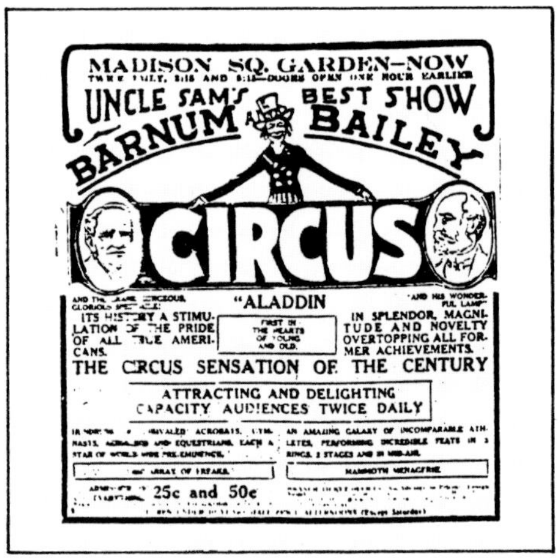

2 THE EVENING TELEGRAM—NEW YORK, FRIDAY, APRIL 6, 1917.

PRESIDENT SIGNS WAR DECREE WITHOUT CEREMONY

MR. WILSON GRAVELY, BUT AS SIMPLE DUTY, AFFIXES NAME TO ACT

Only Few Persons Present When Momentous Document Becomes Effective—Naval Militia and Reserve at Once Called Out.

(Special Despatch to the Evening Telegram.)

WASHINGTON, Friday.—At eleven minutes past one o'clock this afternoon President Wilson signed the joint resolution passed by Congress declaring war on Germany.

War Proclamation by President Warns All Enemies Within U. S. Against Plots, Spying or Use of Force

German Subjects Who Conduct Themselves Orderly and Obey Law Must Not Be Ill Treated by American Citizens, Says Mr. Wilson—State of War Formally Made Known to World.

WASHINGTON, Friday.—The full text of President Wilson's war proclamation follows:

"Whereas the Congress of the United States in the exercise of the constitutional authority vested in them have resolved by

States in the manner prescribed by sections [illegible] and [illegible] of the Revised Statutes and as prescribed in the regulations duly promulgated by the President.

within the jurisdiction of the United States."

FULLY APPROVES BIG ARMY SCHEME

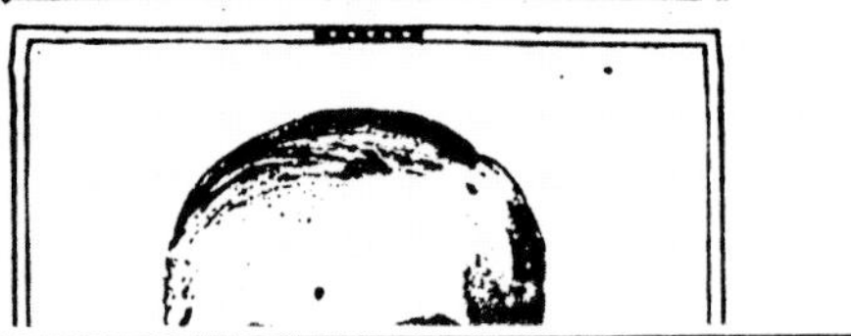

NATIONAL LEAGUE 1917

BOSTON

BROOKLYN

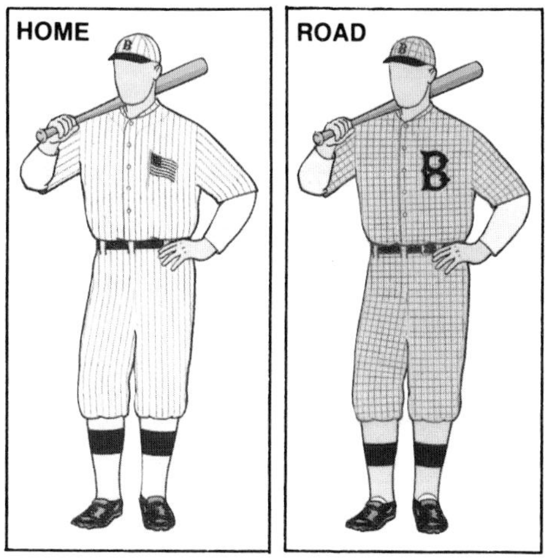

ST. LOUIS

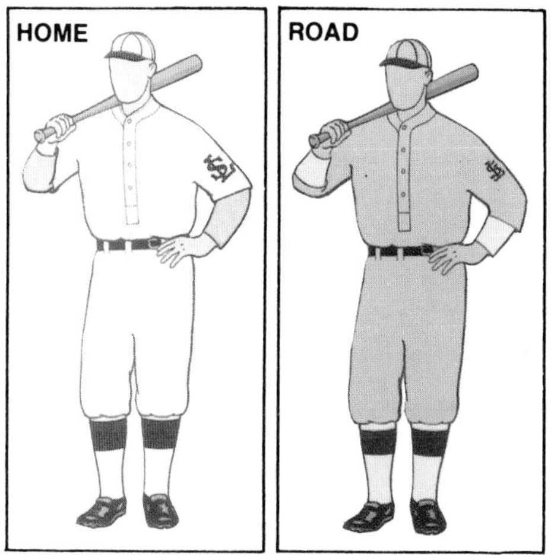

PITTSBURGH

PHILADELPHIA

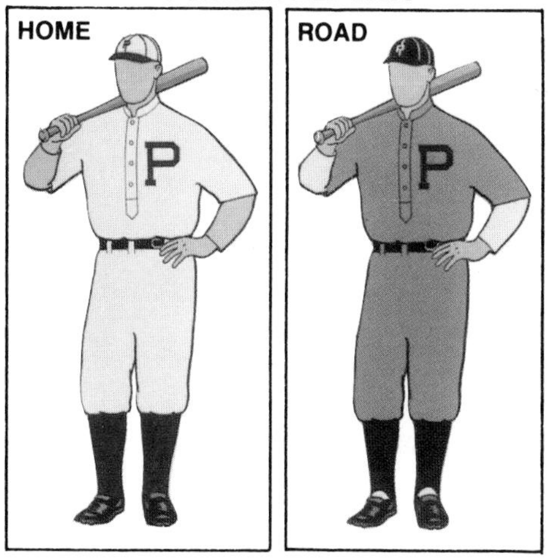

CHICAGO

CINCINNATI

NEW YORK

TWELVE The Pittsburg Dispatch

PROFESSIONAL SPORTS
By DAVID J DAVIES

Melancholy Home-Coming for the Bucs

Cubs Grab Opener By a 10 to 3 Score; Big Crowd on Hand

Cooper and Carlson Are Maltreated, While Hendrix Gets by With Some to Spare; Their Worst of the Season

AT YESTERDAY'S MASSACRE

WHEN THE CROWD CHEERED

1918 AMERICAN LEAGUE

BOSTON

CLEVELAND

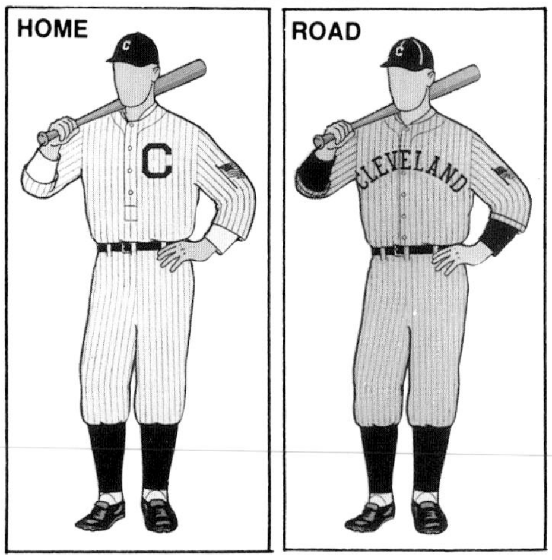

DETROIT

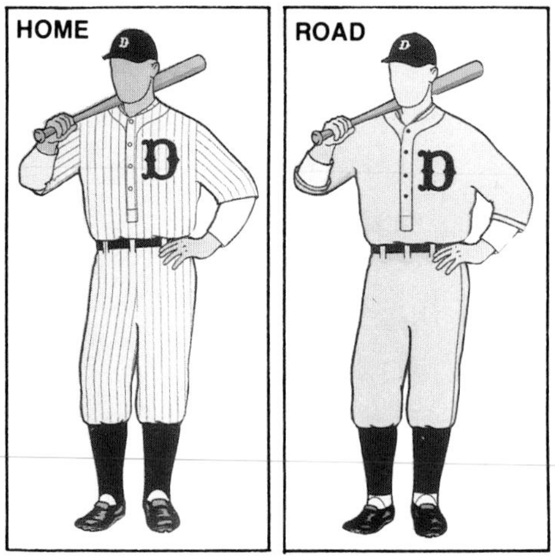

ST. LOUIS

NEW YORK

PHILADELPHIA

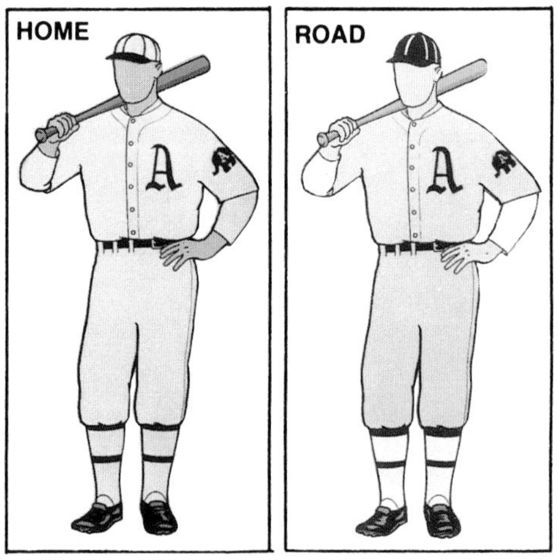

CHICAGO

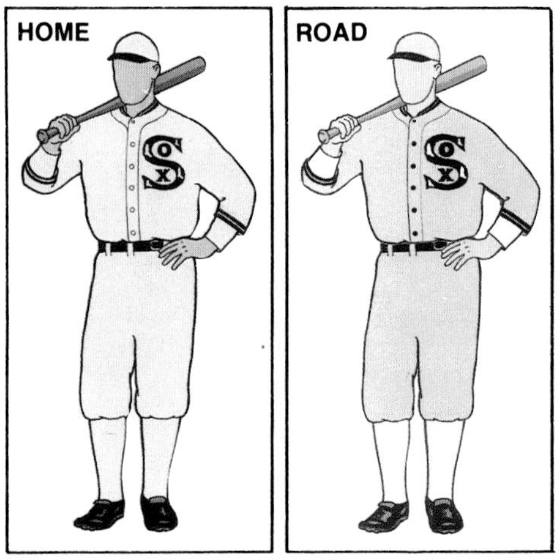

WASHINGTON

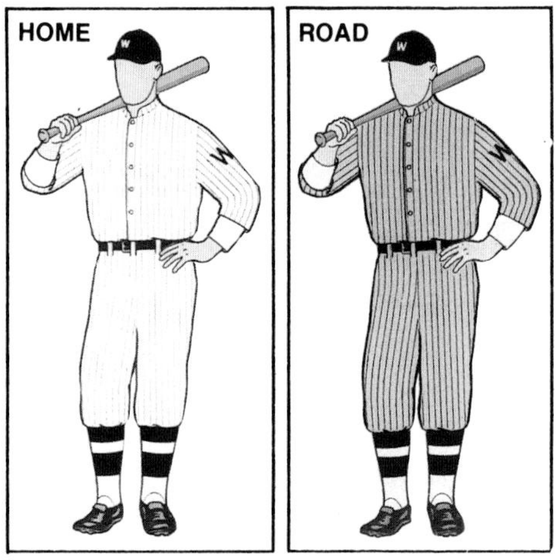

THE EVENING STAR, TUESDAY, APRIL 16, 1918.

NOTABLE FIGURES AT INAUGURATION OF BASE BALL CAMPAIGN.

BOTH BIG LEAGUES GET IN FULL SWING

Patriotism Plays Prominent Part in Chicago Inaugural. Twelve Clubs Open Today.

CHICAGO, April 16.—The champion White Sox planned to aid the third liberty loan drive today at the opening of the American League season in this city. Just preceding the game with St. Louis, according to program, the White Sox were to gather at the home plate and present to a flying squadron of aviators a check for $25,000 for bonds, every man in the club being represented in the check. Following the ceremony and between innings the liberty loan flying squadron was to canvass the grandstand for subscriptions to the bonds.

Manager Clarence Rowland expected to pick either Cicotte or Williams to do the pitching for the White Sox and Manager Fielder Jones said Lowdermilk or Shocker would be the selections for St. Louis.

Detroit Opens Minus Ty Cobb.

YANKEES VANQUISH GRIFFS IN OPENER

Pound Johnson for Eleven Hits. Shanks Is Local Star. Score, 6 to 3.

BY DENMAN THOMPSON.

Miller Huggins' new Gotham outfit yesterday lived up to all the nice things said of its slugging proposition, while some of the Nationals, Johnson and Foster particularly, failed to measure up to specifications, with the result that the Griffmen took a fine young trimming at the hands of the visitors in the initial clash of the season at American League Park—score, 6 to 3.

Johnson early encountered difficulties. As is the case with many other products in these times of war, Mr. Reach's base balls, although costing more than last season, are not of as good quality as formerly. Becoming rough and fuzzy on contact with the ground, the effect of the air resistance when propelled with the great speed used by Johnson was to make the sphere "sail"—jump

BOOST BY HALLEY FOR ALLEY SPORT

"Pop" Gives Points on Bowling and Tells Why He Has Been Rolling for 20 Years.

BY CURLEY.

SUNBEAMS OF BOWLING

The average man spends too much time paying somebody else to amuse him, instead of getting into some kind of play himself.

It's comfortable to sit in a shady seat in a base ball pavilion on a hot afternoon, but that doesn't get you as much as taking enough exercise yourself to get up a real sweat.

The trouble with a lot of people is that they expect to get health out of a bottle, taking medicine. Good health, like every other thing worth while, must be earned, and the best way to earn it is by exercise through play.

STATE MIDS

College P[illegible] to Anna[illegible] Game

NATIONAL LEAGUE 1918

BOSTON

BROOKLYN

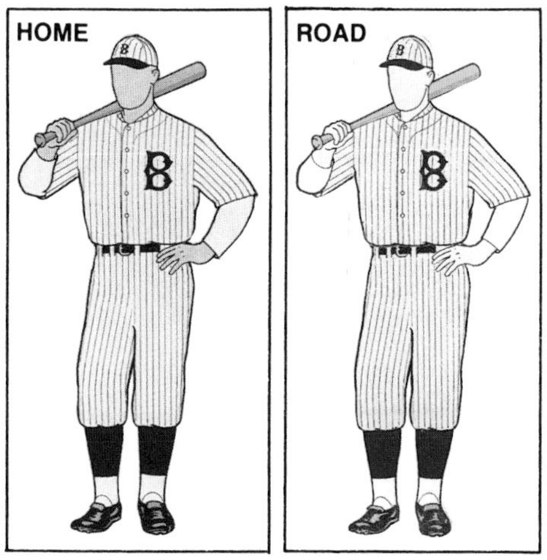

ST. LOUIS

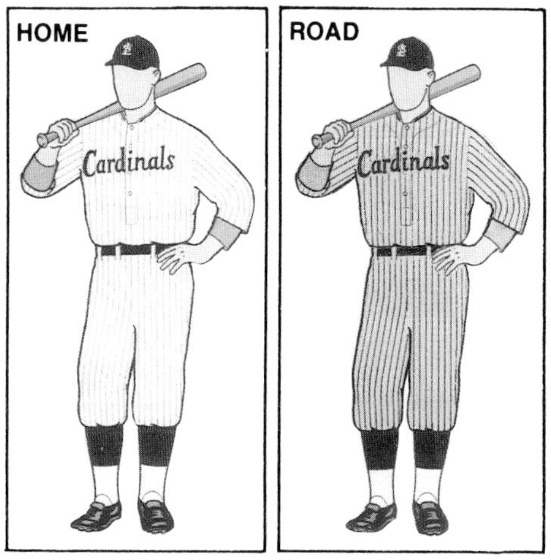

PITTSBURGH

PHILADELPHIA

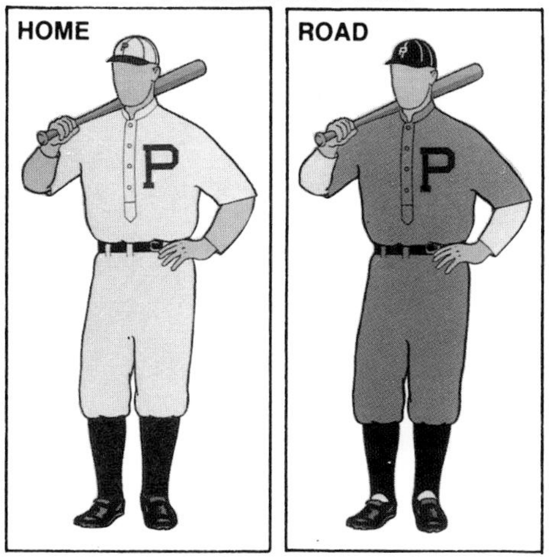

CHICAGO

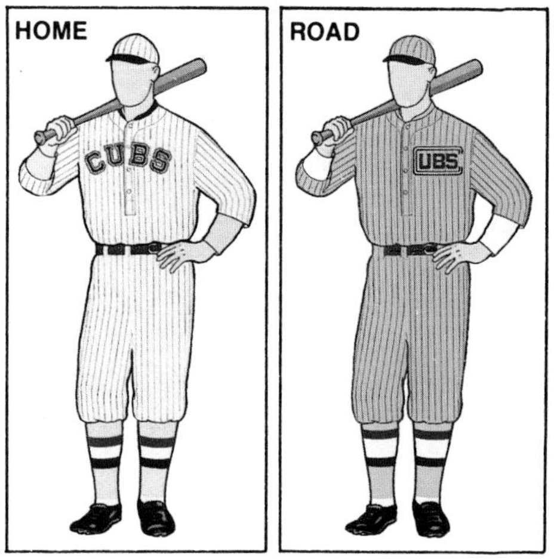

CINCINNATI

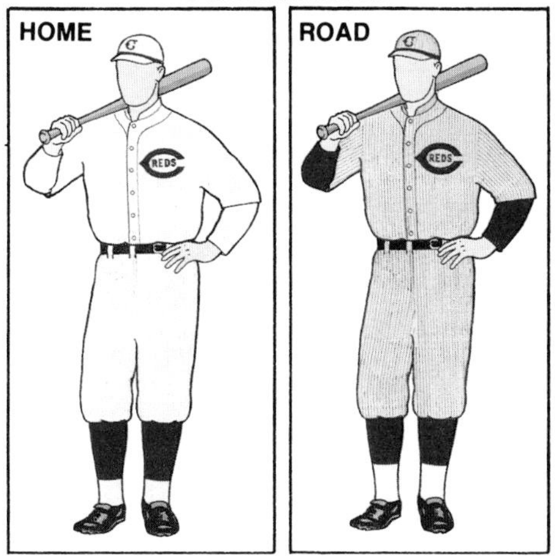

NEW YORK

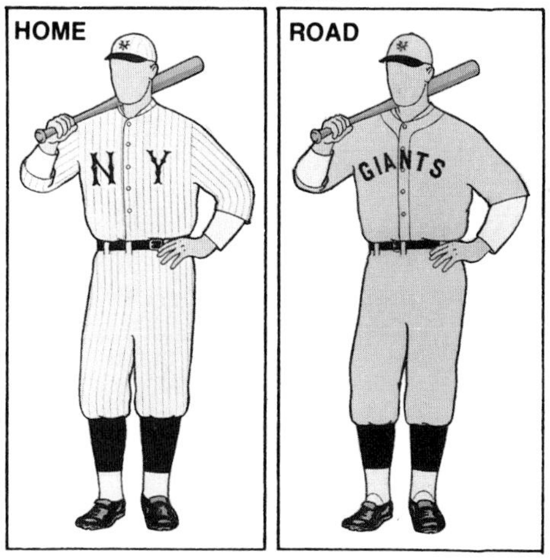

20 Pages Today — The Boston Post — EXTRA

TWENTY PAGES—ONE CENT · Established 1831 · FRIDAY, SEPTEMBER 6 1918 · Copyright, 1918, by Post Publishing Co. · TWENTY PAGES—ONE CENT

RUTH'S GREAT PITCHING GIVES RED SOX FIRST

Batting of Whiteman and McInnis Scores Boston's Lone Tally, Whitewashing Cubs

GERMANS IN HEADLONG RETREAT ACROSS AISNE

Driven Back Eight Miles in a Day by the French and American Forces—Mangin Driving Forward in Direction of Laon Threatens to Cut in Back of Chemin des Dames and

1919 AMERICAN LEAGUE

BOSTON

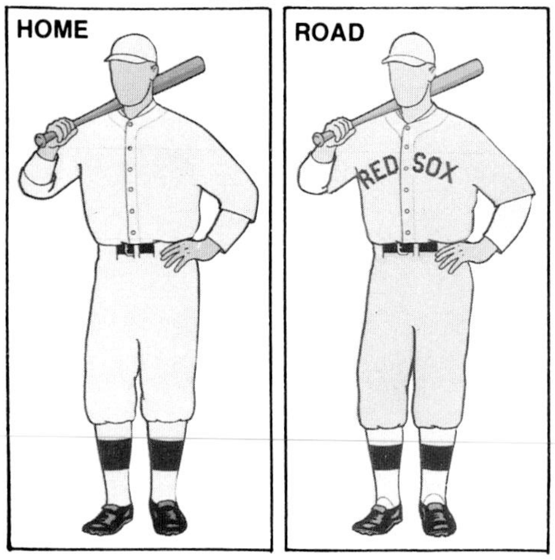

CLEVELAND

DETROIT

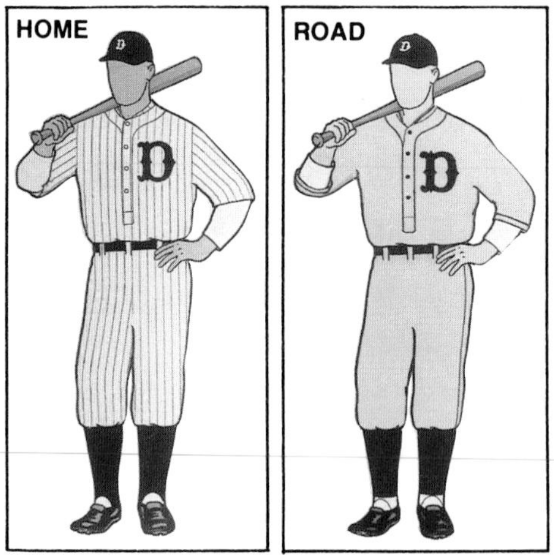

ST. LOUIS

NEW YORK

PHILADELPHIA

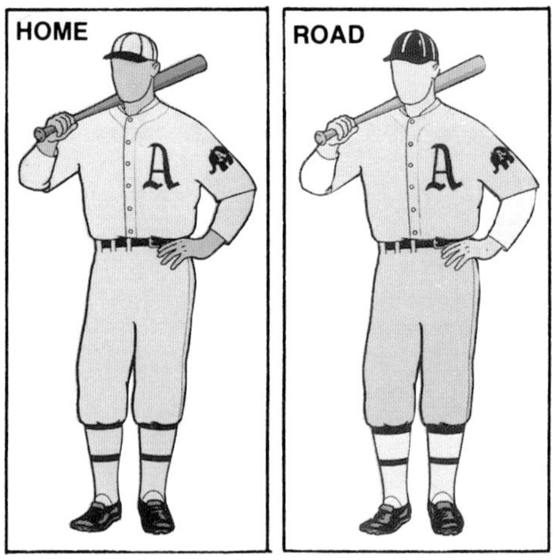

CHICAGO

WASHINGTON

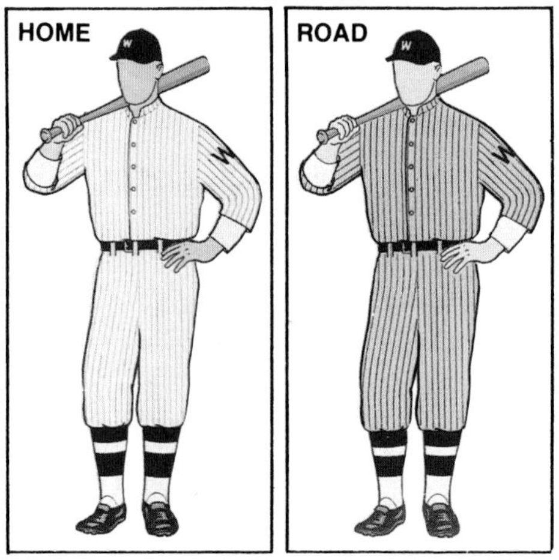

16 THE EVENING TELEGRAM—NEW YORK, THURSDAY, APRIL 24, 1919.

BASEBALL | BOWLING | RACING | ATHLETICS

The LISTENING POST
M. J. Wathey

WITH the parades, flag raising, speech making and presentations out of the way baseball can now settle down to its 140 game chase. Yearly the pennant pursuit becomes a testimonial to the survival of the fittest and invariably it is the strong that step to the front and the weak that are left straggling in the wake. While the opening games did not prove a great deal that would hold up to this assertion

Dignitaries and Celebrities Who Helped Make Opening of Baseball Season Memorable at the Polo Ground

SPRINTING ALONG with Francis

BASEBALL opened with a large bang yesterday, forecasting the greatest campaign in its history. Slowly but surely other pastimes in the curriculum of sport will stage revivals. Following closely on the heels of the crash of bat and ball comes the outdoor track and field combination which threatens to surpass the competition of pre-war days. Thanks to Generals Pershing and Foch, we are in the throes of the most exciting sport

NATIONAL LEAGUE 1919

BOSTON

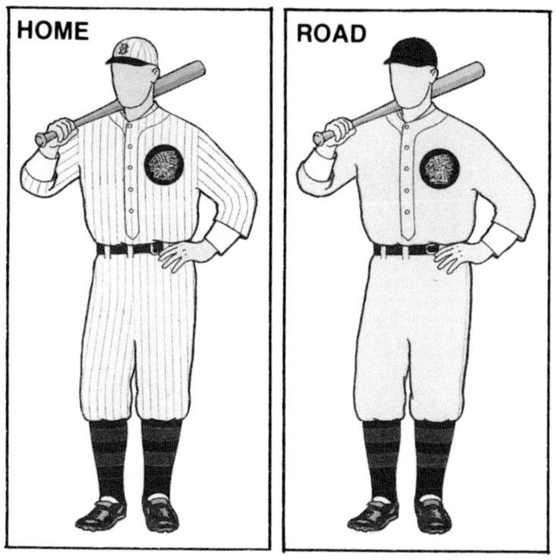

BROOKLYN

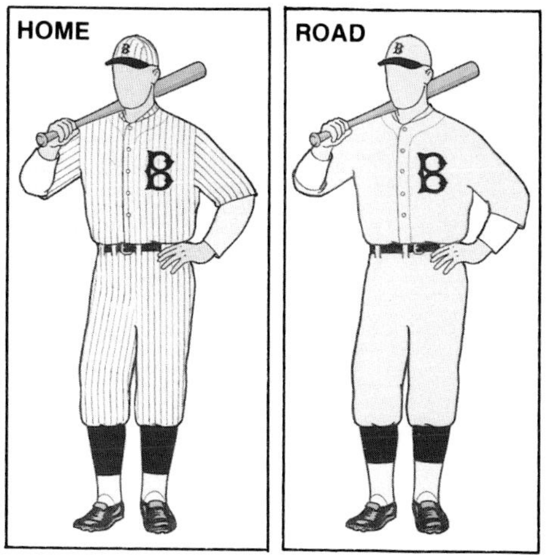

ST. LOUIS

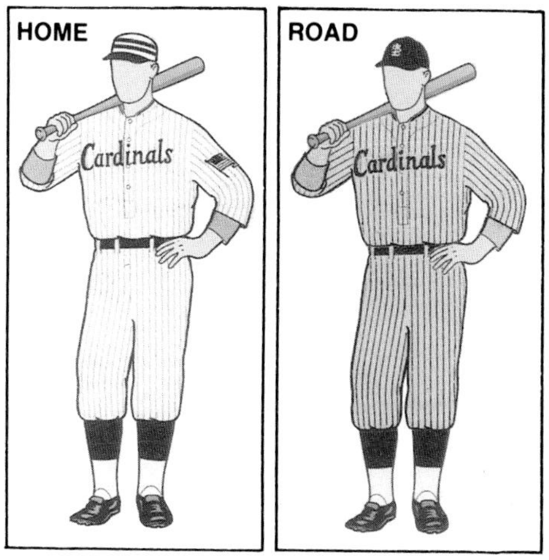

PITTSBURGH

PHILADELPHIA

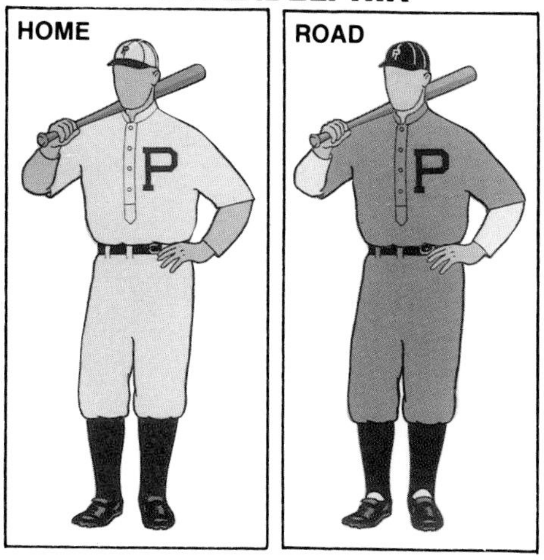

CHICAGO

CINCINNATI

NEW YORK

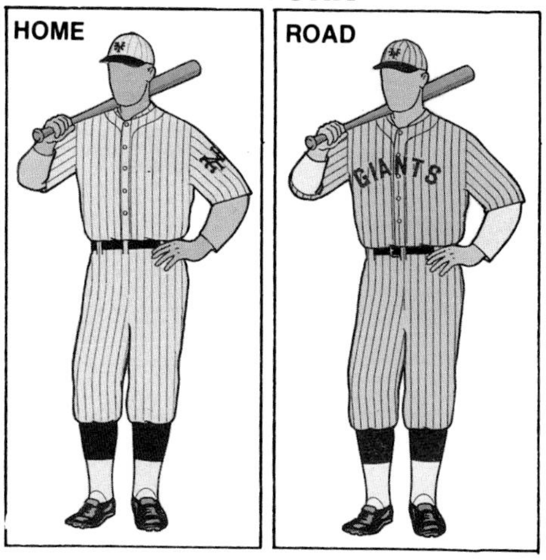

16 PAGES TO-DAY

THE CINCINNATI ENQUIRER

VOL. LXXVI. NO. 277 DAILY AND SUNDAY ENQUIRER ENTERED AT CINCINNATI POSTOFFICE AS SECOND CLASS MATTER AUGUST 1, 1879, UNDER ACT OF MARCH 3, 1879. SATURDAY MORNING, OCTOBER 4, 1919 PRICE FIVE CENTS

RENEWAL

Of Fighting Barred

In Wilson's Decisive Note, Prussian Chief Says.

Continuance of War Is Urged By Ludendorff

As Huns Learn Terms of Proposed Armistice.

PLEADS GUILTY OF FRAUD.

One of 36 Men Indicted Confesses Illegal Use of Mails.

SPECIAL DISPATCH TO THE ENQUIRER.

Indianapolis, Ind., October 3.—A plea of guilty was entered to-day before Judge Anderson in the Federal court by C. Myron Burch, Detroit, who was held under bond as an alleged member of a swindling band at Muncie which is said to have obtained several hundred thousand dollars from its victims. Burch is charged with being one of the men who piloted wealthy persons to where fake prize fights and wrestling matches were held in order that the victim might be induced to bet money on the results.

The plea of guilty was to the charge of conspiracy and use of the mails to promote fraud. ... Stansbury, James Whitney and Lucius Stillson, indicted on the same charge, pleaded not guilty.

Thirty-five men have been indicted on the charge of being implicated in the Muncie fraud case, but only 22 have been arrested.

CONDITION

Of Wilson Serious.

Members of ... Summoned

Two Consu... Called F...

Views Exchanged With Additional Specialists.

Kerr Stops Reds, Registering Shut-Out; Fisher's Wild Throw Gives Sox Two Runs

DIMINUTIVE YOUNGSTER CHECKS SURGING REDS

DICK KERR

SLANTS

Of Little Southpaw

Make Cincinnatians Look Foolish When at Bat.

1920 AMERICAN LEAGUE

BOSTON

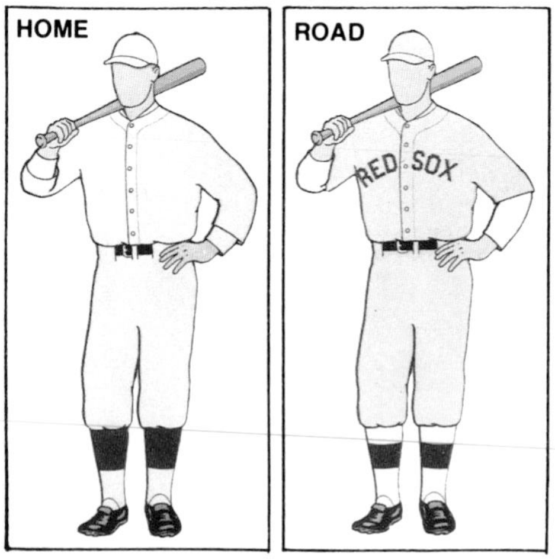

CLEVELAND

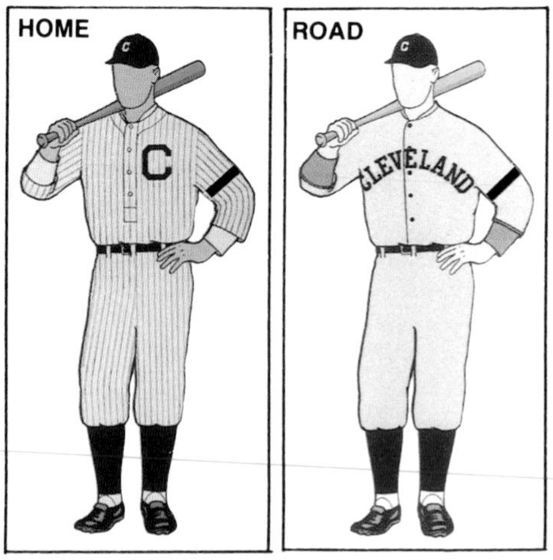

DETROIT

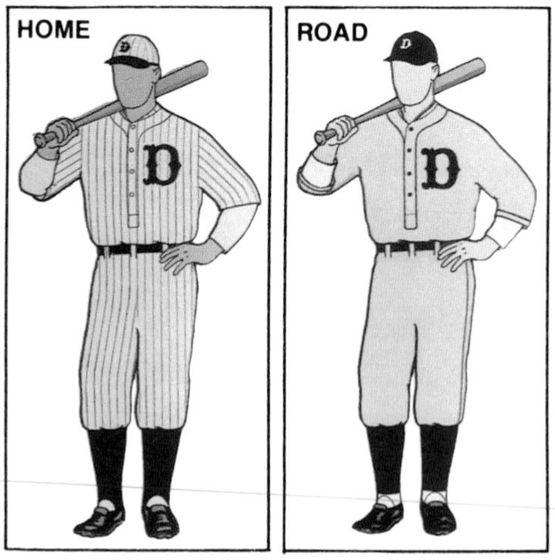

ST. LOUIS

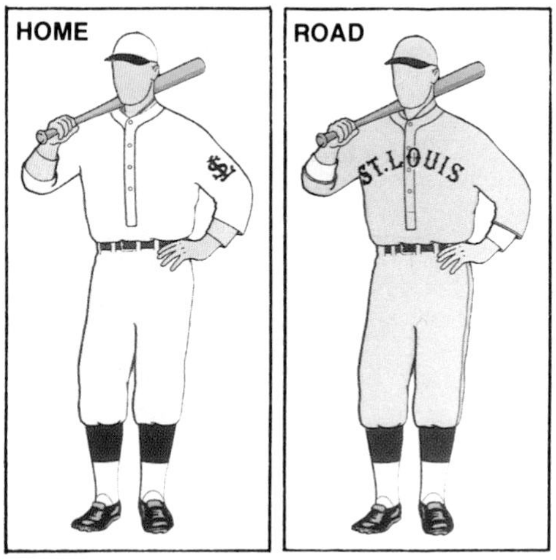

NEW YORK

PHILADELPHIA

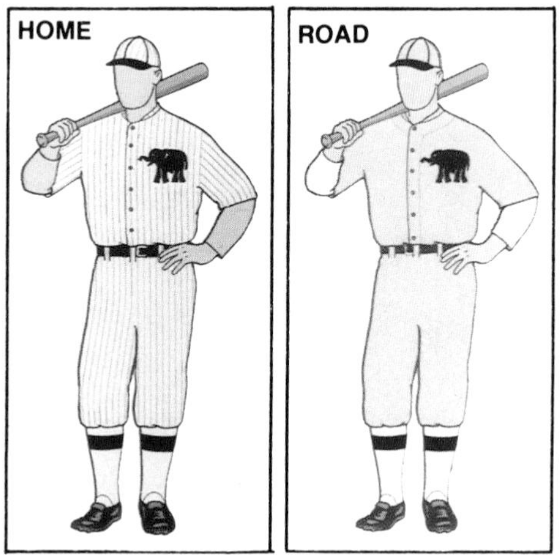

CHICAGO

WASHINGTON

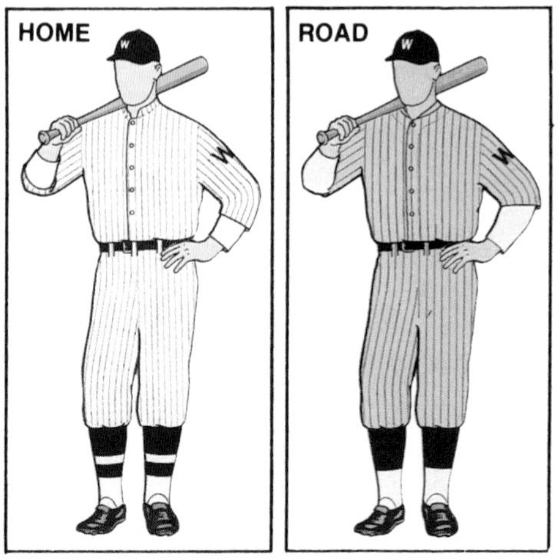

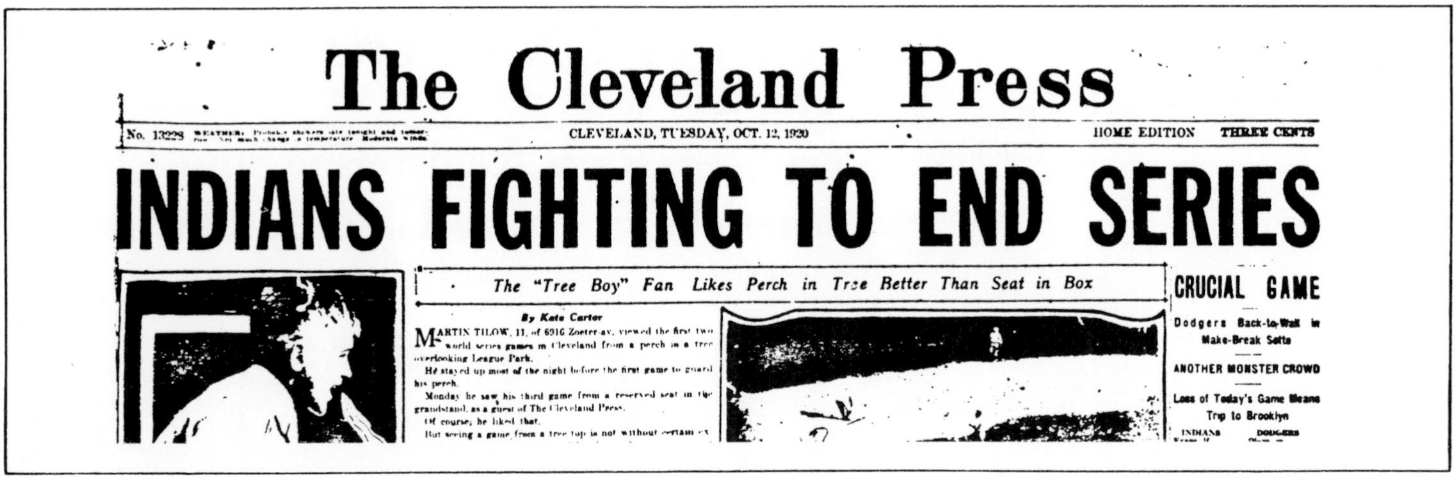

The Cleveland Press

No. 13228 | CLEVELAND, TUESDAY, OCT. 12, 1920 | HOME EDITION | THREE CENTS

INDIANS FIGHTING TO END SERIES

The "Tree Boy" Fan Likes Perch in Tree Better Than Seat in Box

By Kate Carter

MARTIN TILOW, 11, of 6916 Zoeter-av. viewed the first two world series games in Cleveland from a perch in a tree overlooking League Park.

He stayed up most of the night before the first game to guard his perch.

Monday he saw his third game from a reserved seat in the grandstand, as a guest of The Cleveland Press.

Of course, he liked that.

But seeing a game from a tree top is not without certain ex-

CRUCIAL GAME

Dodgers Back-to-Wall in Make-Break Setto

ANOTHER MONSTER CROWD

Loss of Today's Game Means Trip to Brooklyn

INDIANS DODGERS

NATIONAL LEAGUE 1920

BOSTON

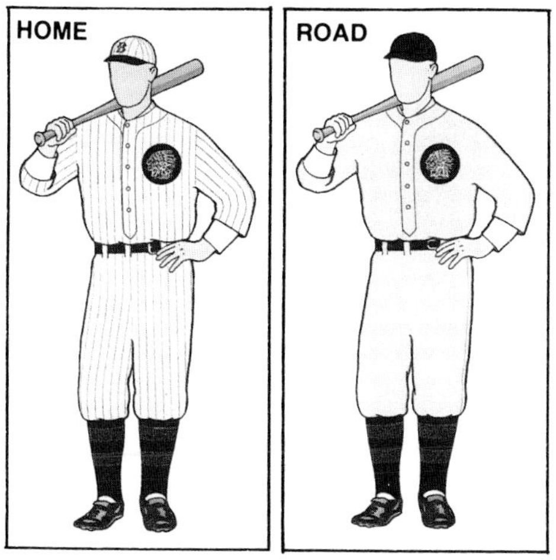

BROOKLYN

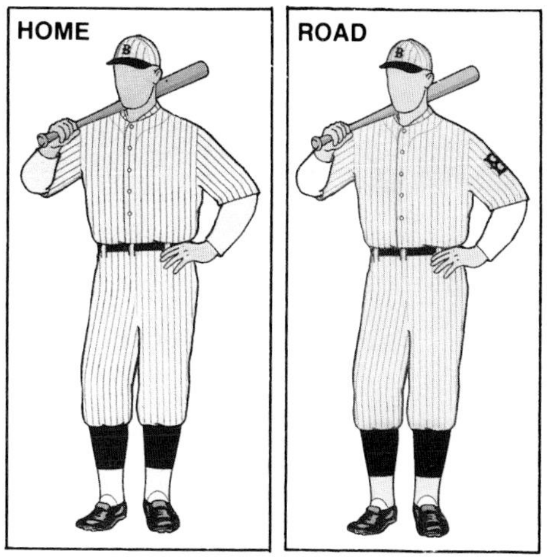

ST. LOUIS

PITTSBURGH

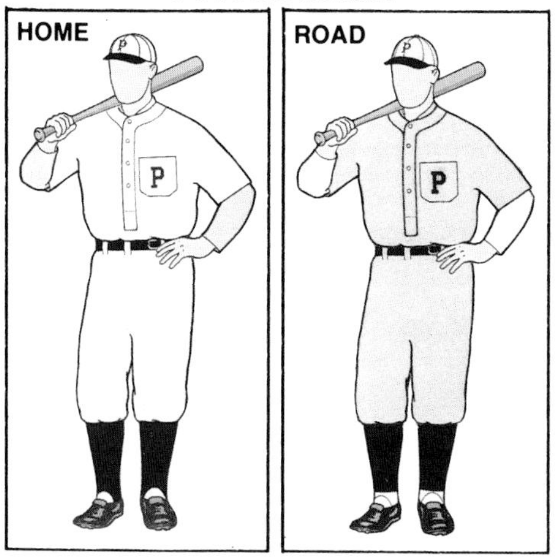

PHILADELPHIA

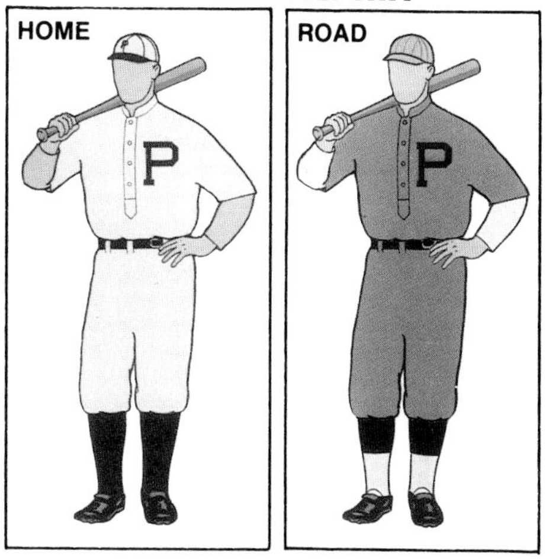

CHICAGO

CINCINNATI

NEW YORK

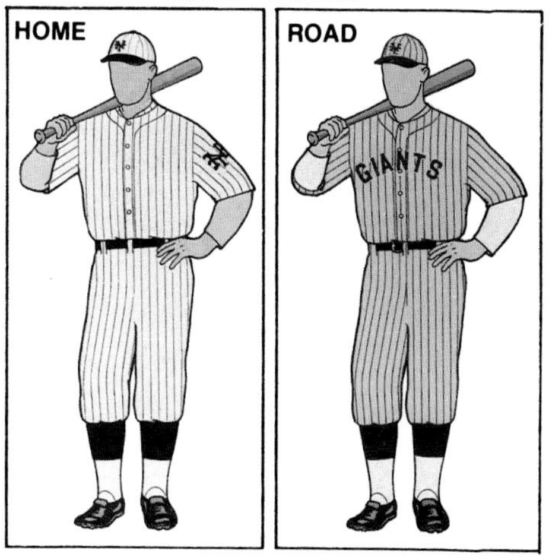

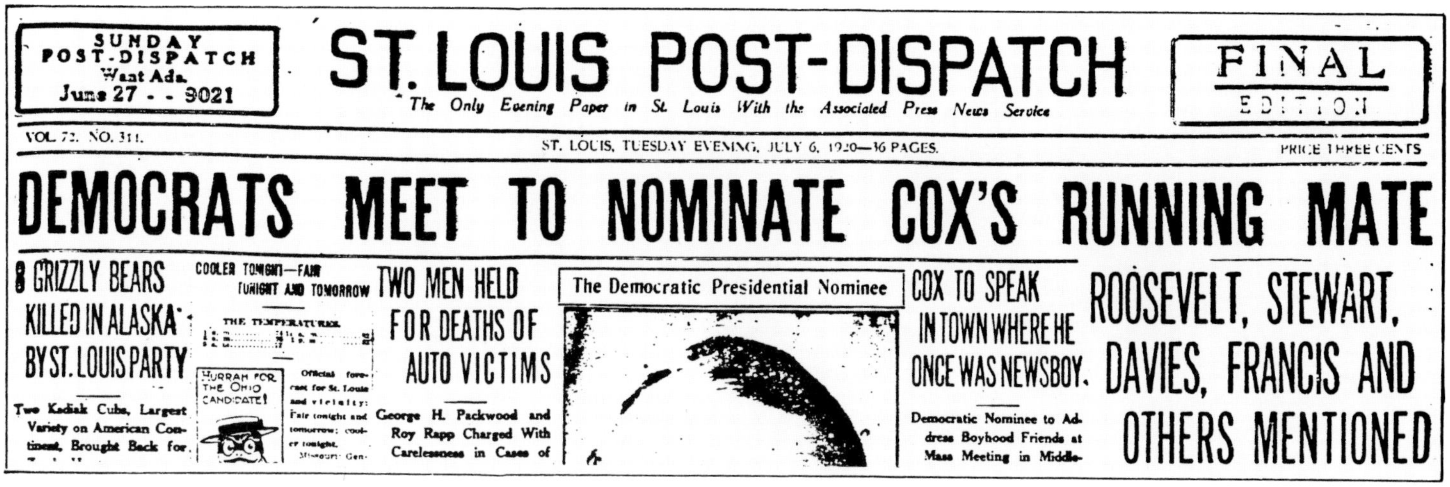

SUNDAY POST-DISPATCH Want Ads June 27 - - 9021

ST. LOUIS POST-DISPATCH

The Only Evening Paper in St. Louis With the Associated Press News Service

FINAL EDITION

VOL. 72. NO. 311. ST. LOUIS, TUESDAY EVENING, JULY 6, 1920—36 PAGES. PRICE THREE CENTS

DEMOCRATS MEET TO NOMINATE COX'S RUNNING MATE

8 GRIZZLY BEARS KILLED IN ALASKA BY ST. LOUIS PARTY

Two Kadiak Cubs, Largest Variety on American Continent, Brought Back for...

COOLER TONIGHT—FAIR TONIGHT AND TOMORROW

THE TEMPERATURES.

HURRAH FOR THE OHIO CANDIDATE!

Official forecast for St. Louis and vicinity: Fair tonight and tomorrow; cooler tonight. Missouri: Gen-

TWO MEN HELD FOR DEATHS OF AUTO VICTIMS

George H. Packwood and Roy Rapp Charged With Carelessness in Cases of

The Democratic Presidential Nominee

COX TO SPEAK IN TOWN WHERE HE ONCE WAS NEWSBOY.

Democratic Nominee to Address Boyhood Friends at Mass Meeting in Middle-

ROOSEVELT, STEWART, DAVIES, FRANCIS AND OTHERS MENTIONED

1921 AMERICAN LEAGUE

BOSTON

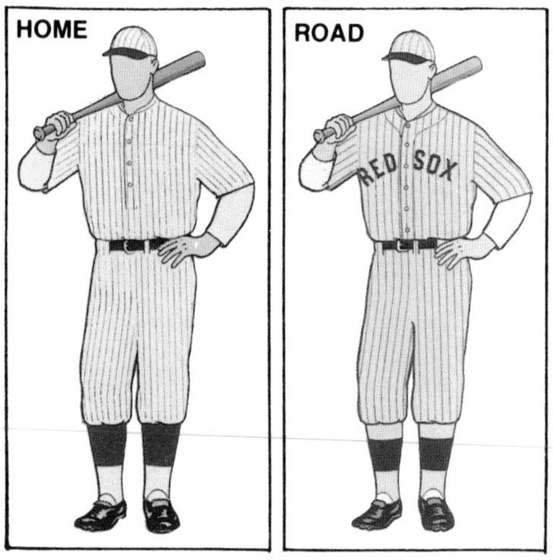

CLEVELAND

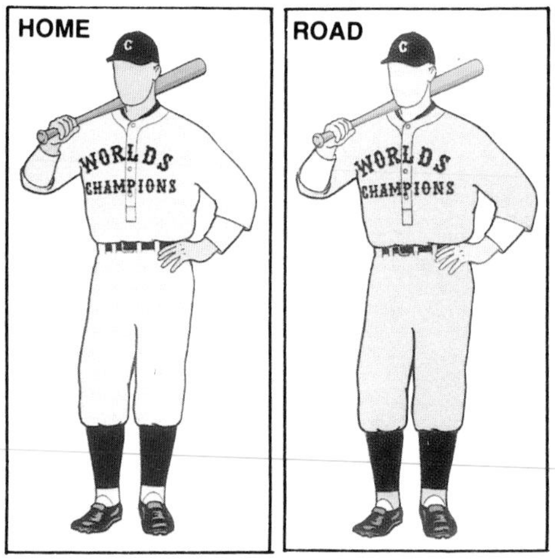

DETROIT

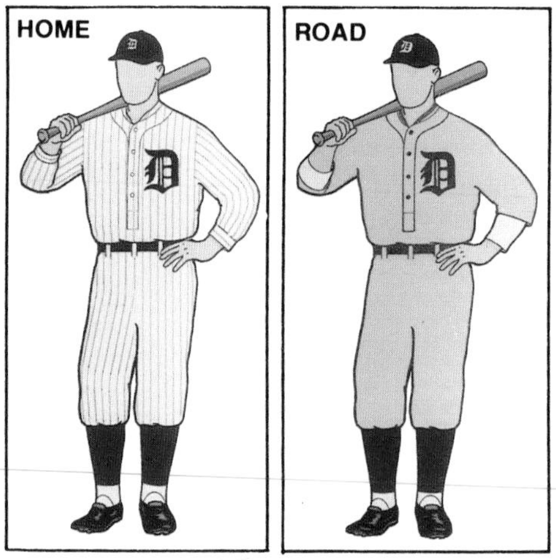

ST. LOUIS

NEW YORK

PHILADELPHIA

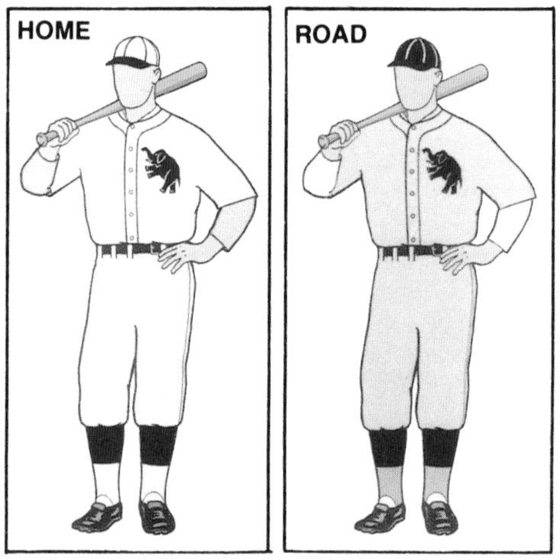

CHICAGO

WASHINGTON

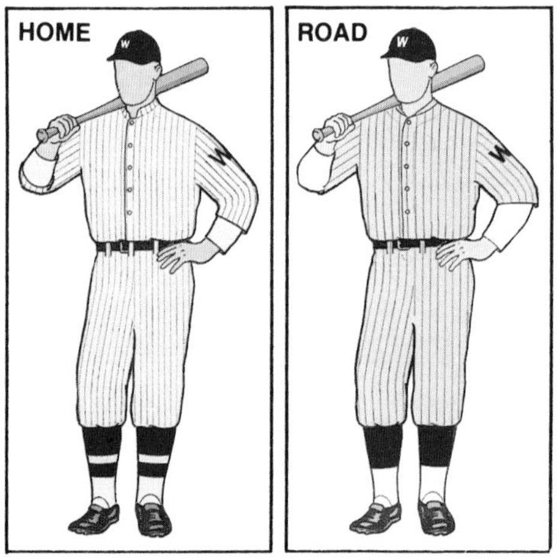

PAGE TWENTY — CLEVELAND PLAIN DEALER

Indians Defeat Tigers, 9 to 8, After American League Pennant is Raised

SPOKE USES 23 PLAYERS TO WIN "STRATEGY" TILT

Sets Record for Number of Men Used; Jim Bagby is Last of Six Hurlers to Get in Fray.

BY HENRY P. EDWARDS

Tris Speaker yesterday broke an American league record when, in celebrating the raising of the first baseball pennant in the history of Cleveland, he used twenty-three Indian players in defeating Detroit, 9 to 8.

Twenty-three—count 'em—six pitchers, two catchers, six outfielders, three first basemen, two pinch hitters and one pinch runner. The only Indians to play throughout the entire game were

Plays That Thrilled Fans at Indians' Pennant Raising

GARDNER SAFE AT HOME IN THE 3RD INNING

COLE SAFE AT HOME IN 2ND INNING

TRIS SPEAKER HAD PLANNED TO USE BAGBY

BAN JOHNSON SAYS GUILTY PLAYERS WILL GET STIFF SENTENCES

BULLETIN.

LOS ANGELES, April 26 —Arnold (Chick) Gandil, one of the former White Sox ball players indicted in connection with the alleged "throwing" of world series games in 1919, was arrested here tonight at the request of the state's attorney's office in Chicago.

NATIONAL LEAGUE 1921

BOSTON

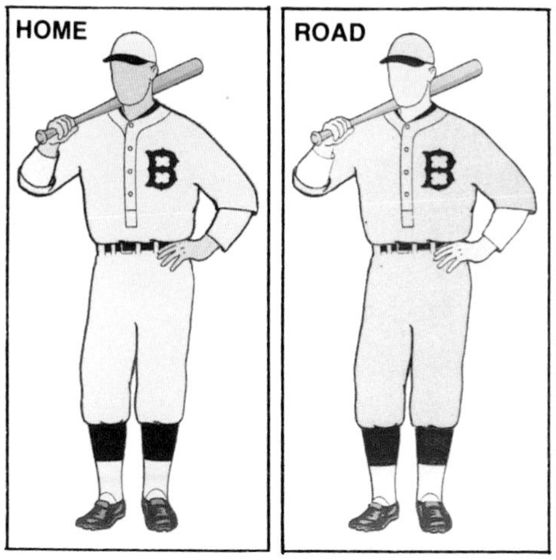

BROOKLYN

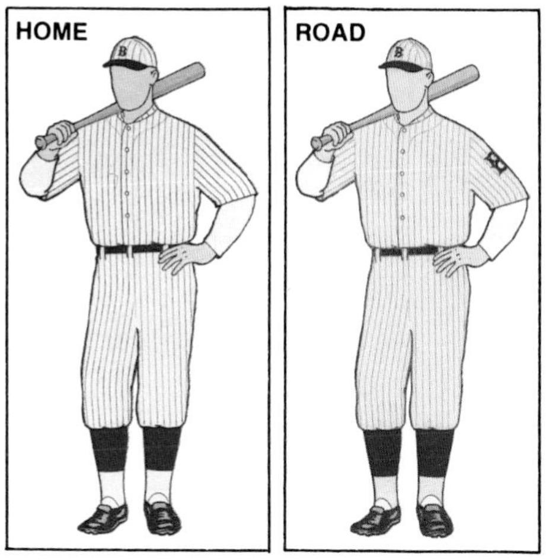

ST. LOUIS

PITTSBURGH

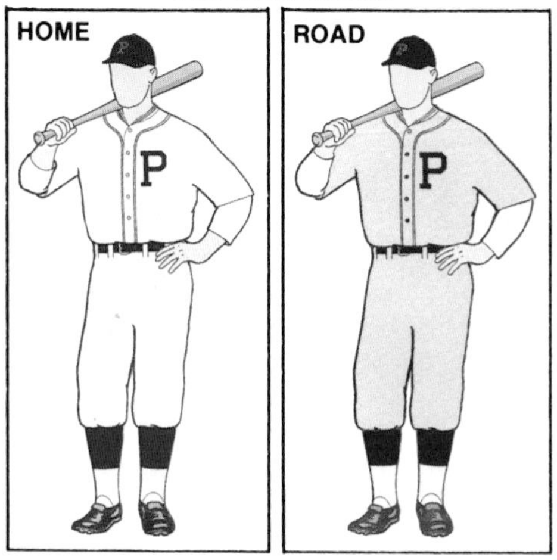

PHILADELPHIA

CHICAGO

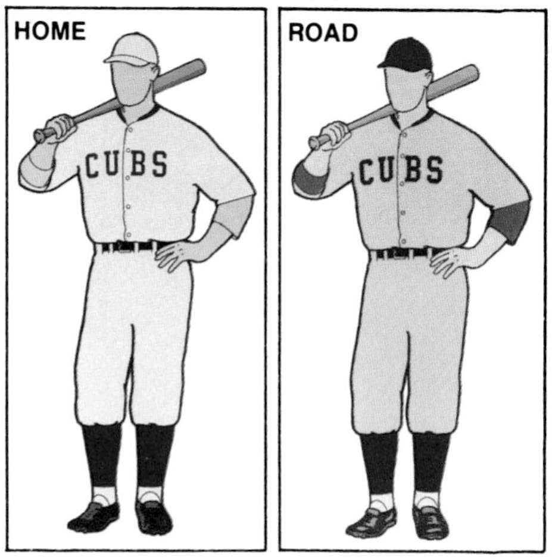

CINCINNATI

NEW YORK

THE BROOKLYN DAILY EAGLE. NEW YORK, THURSDAY, APRIL 14, 1921. 3

SUPERBAS GET AWAY FLYING WITH NINTH INNING RALLY

TOM McCARTHY PROVES HIS VALUE IN FIRST SUPERBA VICTORY

BOSTON, Mass., April 14—For several years the present writer has been advocating the signing by the Brooklyn club of a veteran ball player who could think quickly, knew the game and had the knack of teaching what he knew. Kid Elberfield was the only man of the sort who had been with the club except the managers, for a decade, at least. Jack Coombs was a smart exponent of baseball, but never was decorated with laurel wreaths for his work in beating base runners.

At last the Superbas have a quick-witted veteran of the old school in which a man had to keep his eye on his number or be kicked off the pay roll. He is Tommy McCarthy, who was playing left field for the Boston team of the old twelve club league before many of the present major leaguers were born. He joined the Superbas here yesterday morning and yesterday afternoon he was very largely responsible for the Superbas winning their opening game of the 1921 strife from the Boston Braves by 5 to 4 in nine innings, instead of having the game go into extra innings.

McCarthy's coaching and Uncle Wilbert Robinson's juggling of the material at hand, combined with a remarkable stickativeness displayed by the whole Brooklyn squad, not only overcame the lead of 4 to 0, which the Braves had at the end of the seventh inning, but made the final reckoning 5 to 4. It was

All's Well Once Again In Maryland Racing; Pimlico Won't Fight

By W. C. VREELAND.
(Special to The Eagle.)

Baltimore, April 14—That old game, "off agin, on agin, away agin—Finnegin," is being played here. The Pimlico officials and the Racing Commission are the opponents. First one side and then the other hurl verbal brickbats at each other. One side says, "I dare you," and the other says, "You daan't." Defiance meets defiance. Then presto! Everything runs smoothly. The dark clouds disappear. Heigh-ho! 'tis summer again. Merrily the adversaries embrace. All's well.

Just when turfmen were beginning to settle down on the sidelines with comfortable positions to witness the scrap between the Maryland Jockey Club and the Racing Commission, the bout is declared off because the Pimlico officials decline the issue. Gee whiz! All the sparkle of life seems missing these days. First its prohibition. Just when a man is trying to make up his mind whether he enjoys and the Jockey Club. It was an official slap in the face at the latter's authority in Maryland. But the victory for Bedwell may only be brief—until the middle of May, when racing ends in Maryland. After that—what? The deluge?

It's a thousand pities that the Maryland Jockey Club was forced—yes, that's the word, forced—to surrender to Bedwell. No fair-minded man blames the Pimlico officials for their about-face action. It was a case where they had everything to lose and nothing to gain by fighting the Jockey Club's battle except principle. The Maryland Jockey Club directors are strong advocates of clean racing. Its officers are sportsmen of high type. They have sought by all the means in their power to make racing popular and have spent money lavishly to improve the breed of thoroughbreds in America.

Political Pressure.

1922 AMERICAN LEAGUE

BOSTON

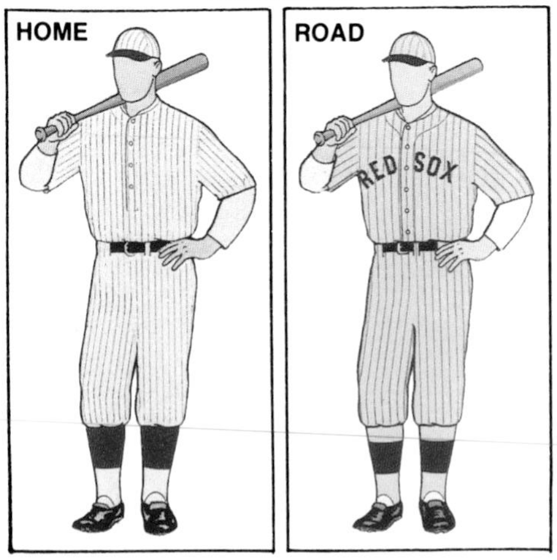

CLEVELAND

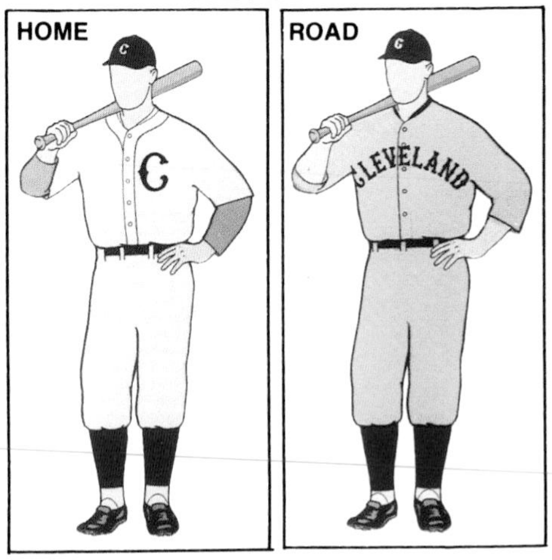

DETROIT

ST. LOUIS

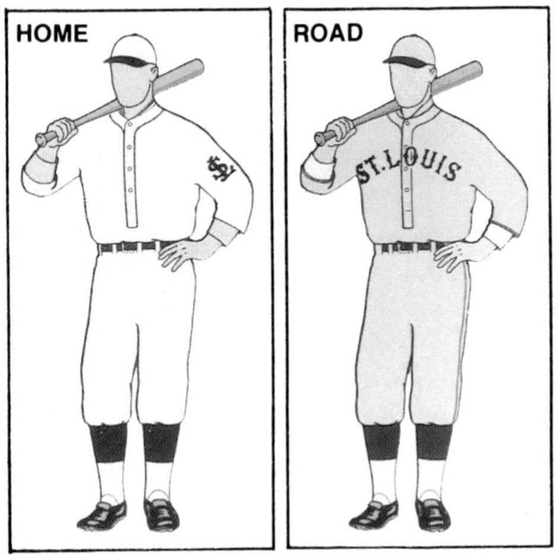

NEW YORK

PHILADELPHIA

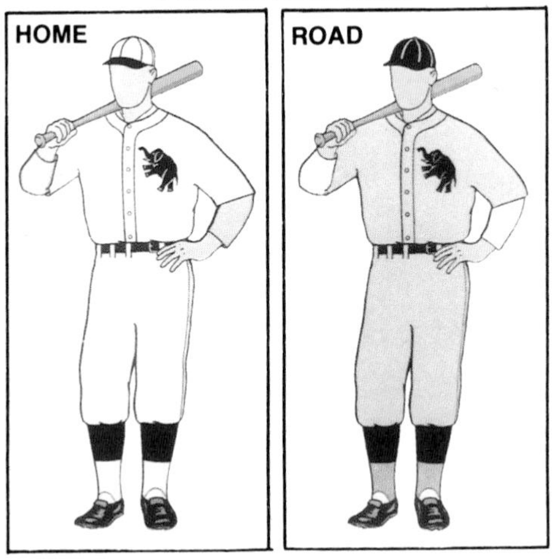

CHICAGO

WASHINGTON

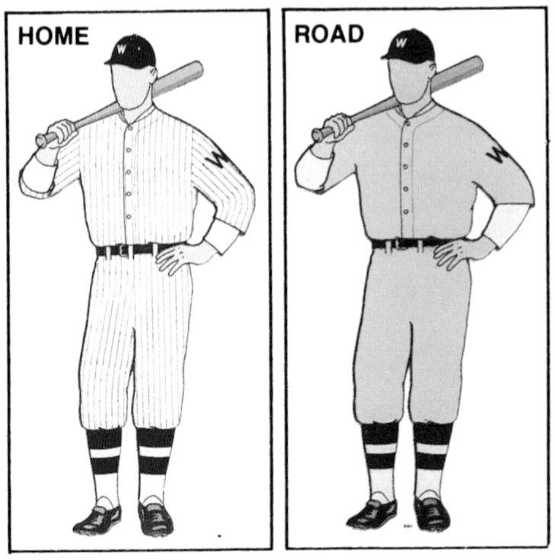

CHICAGO HERALD AND EXAMINER—MONDAY, MAY 1, 1922. 13

ROBERTSON TWIRLS PERFECT GAME FOR WHITE SOX; CUBS LOSE

PERFORMS FEAT EQUALED TWICE IN MODERN BALL

DETROIT, April 30.—Charley Robertson, a youngster who gained his baseball knowledge at the Texas A. and M. College, broke into baseball's hall of fame this afternoon by pitching a perfect game, while winning from the Detroit Tigers.

Just exactly twenty-seven men faced the young right-hander, and he set them down as fast as they walked up to the plate. His control was perfect, and when the Tigers

CHAS. ROBERTSON

As the Cubs Lost

HOLLOCHER

Charlie Hollocher beats Ainsmith in a race to second base. Hollocher won by a step and Ainsmith was called out. Big Bertha caught Ainsmith just as he was about to touch the bag.

Ainsmith beat the throw this time, getting back safe to first after Alexander had tried to catch him napping off the bag. The ball can be seen on the ground where Grimes dropped it after taking the throw.

Cub Box Score

CARD SLUGGERS FIND ALEXANDER AN EASY VICTIM

BY ED SULLIVAN.

Official Baseball

Standing of the Clubs

National League

NATIONAL LEAGUE.

AMERICAN LEAGUE.

Yesterday's Results

NATIONAL LEAGUE 1922

BOSTON

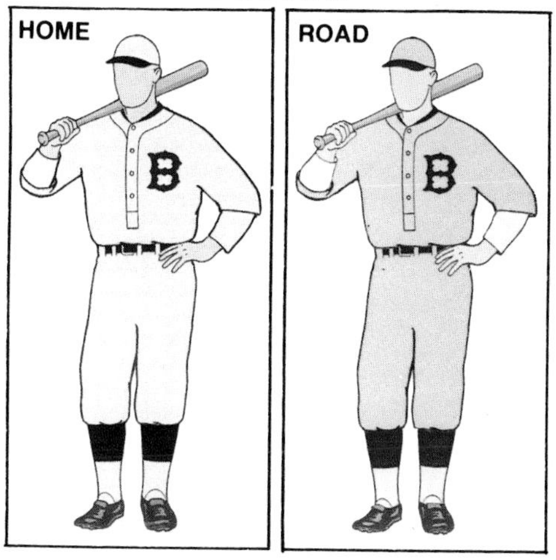

BROOKLYN

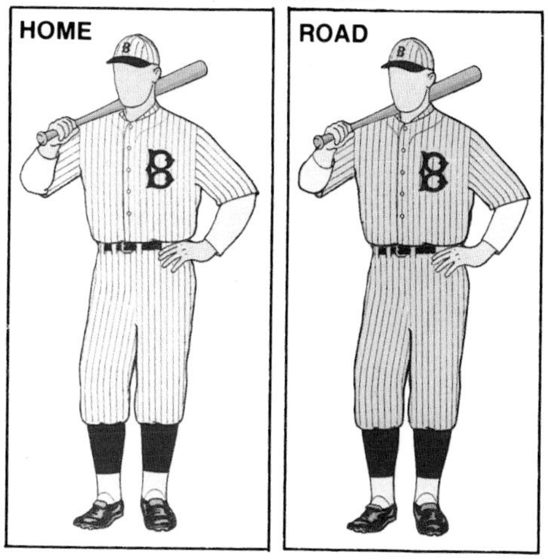

ST. LOUIS

PITTSBURGH

PHILADELPHIA

CHICAGO

CINCINNATI

NEW YORK

Classified Section

WEDNESDAY MORNING.

The Pittsburgh Post

Sporting Se

COOPER AND SHERDEL LIKELY HURLING SELECTIONS FOR OPENER

GOOCH, STEWART, TRAYNOR AND MOKAN CERTAIN TO START

Gibby Confident, But Ready to Make Changes If Conditions Warrant; Fournier Out of Cards' Lineup; Cold Weather May Mar Game.

GIBBY SATISFIED WITH TEAM; "EQUAL OF LAST YEAR"? HE SAYS

START TODAY—WHERE WILL THEY FINISH?

1923 AMERICAN LEAGUE

BOSTON

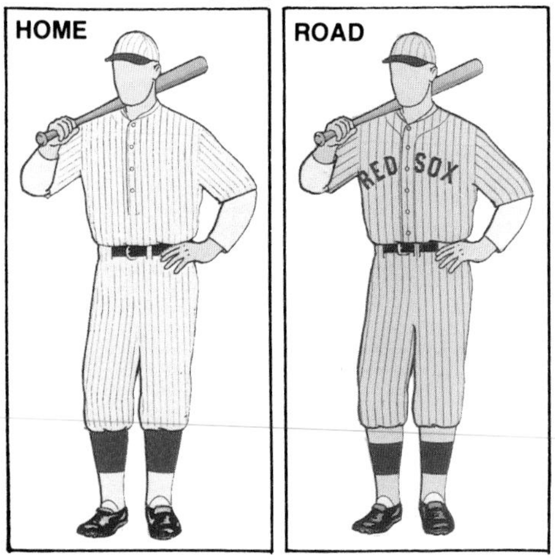

CLEVELAND

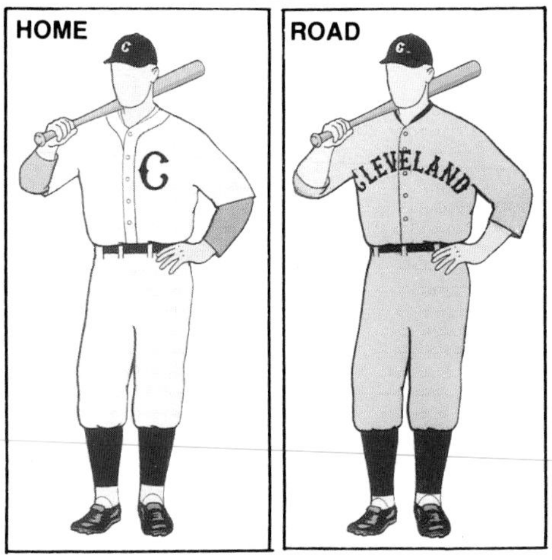

DETROIT

ST. LOUIS

NEW YORK

PHILADELPHIA

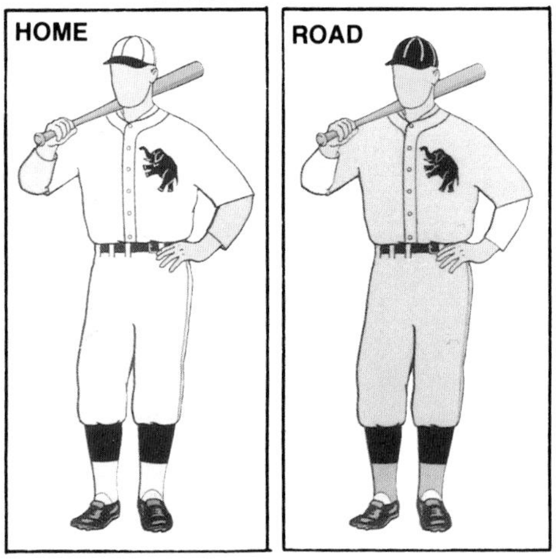

CHICAGO

WASHINGTON

PART 4
Sport, Financial, Real Estate

The Detroit News

"Home Sweet Home," Now Printed in 4 Colors, Will Appear Every Sunday in The News Comics. Watch for It Every Week!

"ALWAYS IN THE LEAD" SUNDAY, APRIL 1, 1923. "ALWAYS IN THE LEAD"

Muskegon Quintet Wins 1923 Michigan State High School Basket Ball Championship

TYGERS WILL NOT BE IN CONDITION FOR SEASON'S OPENER

NOR'WESTERN BEATEN, 36-24

Team Runs Up Early Lead on Detroiters and Maintains It.

Pick of the Recruits

ONE IS AN OUTFIELDER, THE OTHER AN INFIELDER

Only 3 Pitchers Ready, Others Far From Right

Early Weeks of Training Wasted on Rocky Fields Encountered on Circus Jaunt Now Ending.

NATIONAL LEAGUE 1923

BOSTON

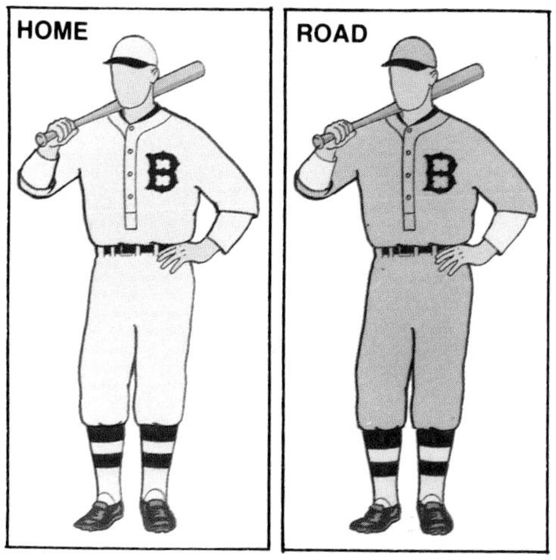

BROOKLYN

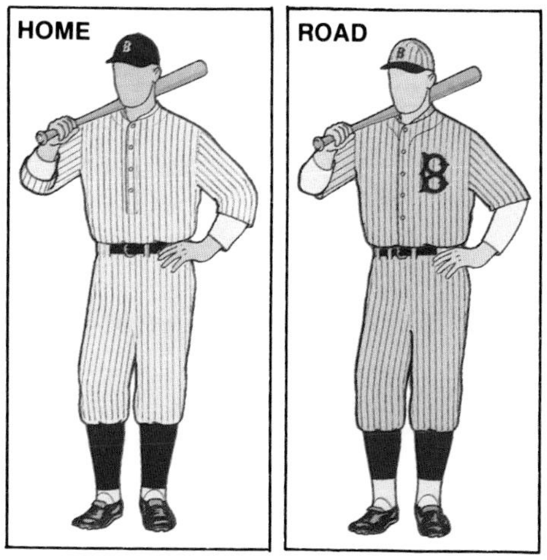

ST. LOUIS

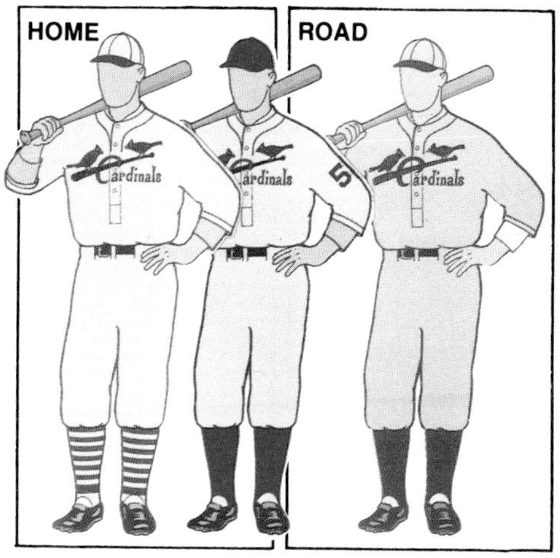

PITTSBURGH

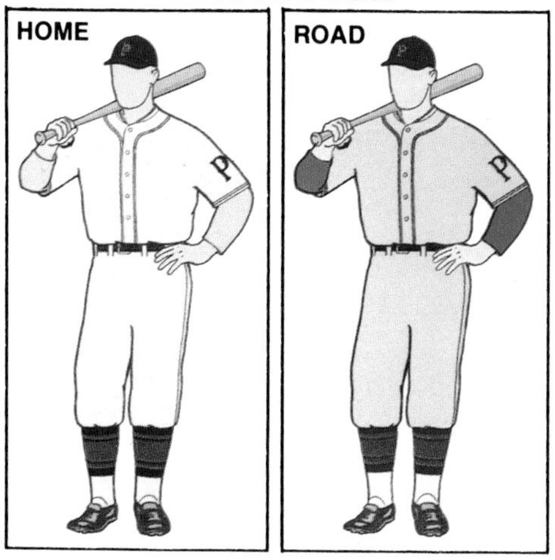

PHILADELPHIA

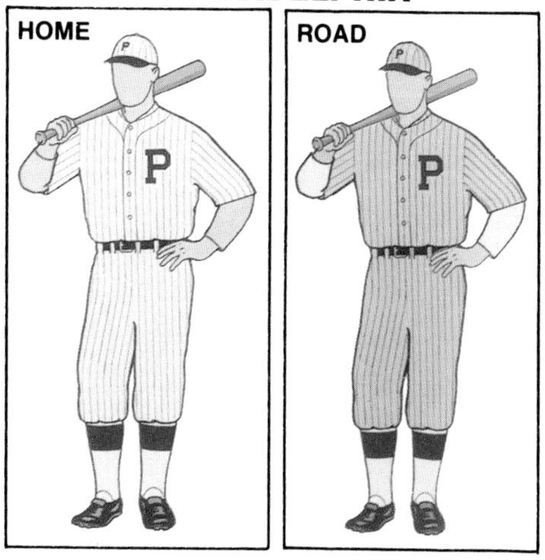

CHICAGO

CINCINNATI

NEW YORK

Herald and Examiner Sports

LATEST SPORT NEWS

Three Cents

WEDNESDAY, APRIL 18, 1923.

34,000 AT NEW CUB PARK OPENER

PIRATES DEFEAT BRUINS, 3 TO 2

BIG BERTHA' CATCHES THE CLOSE PLAYS

"Big Bertha," The Herald and Examiner's long range camera, was on the job yesterday to catch some close plays at the Cub-Pirate opening game. This play raised the first "beef" of the season. Carey was called out at first on Grimes' stretching catch, although he apparently had beaten the throw.

"Rabbit" Maranville showed plenty of speed throughout the day, but not quite enough in this play. Johnny Kelleher is shown catching him off second base on an attempted steal in the fifth.

CHICAGO GREATEST FIRST DAY CROWD AT

1924 AMERICAN LEAGUE

BOSTON

CLEVELAND

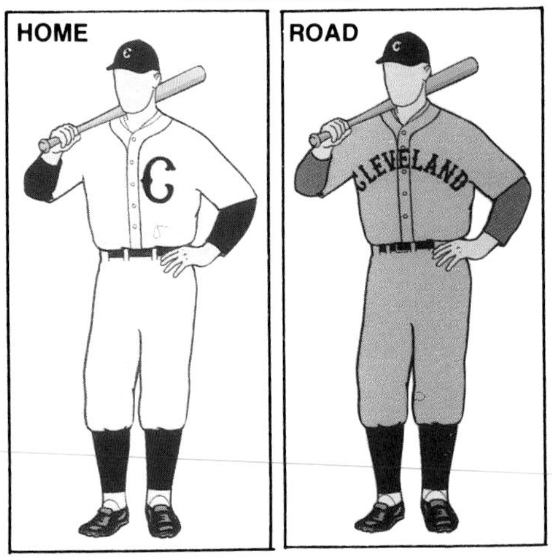

DETROIT

ST. LOUIS

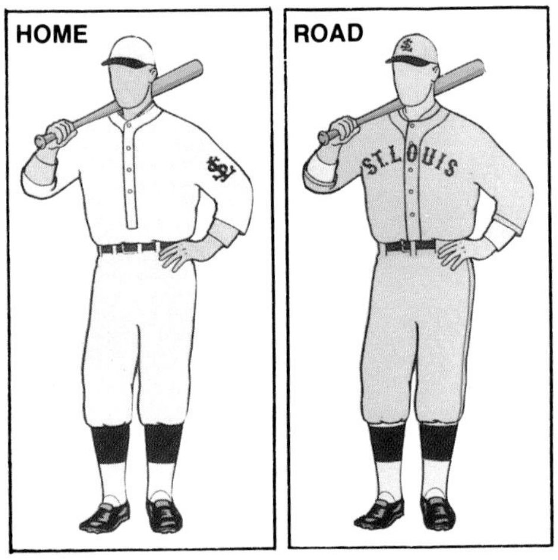

NEW YORK

PHILADELPHIA

CHICAGO

WASHINGTON

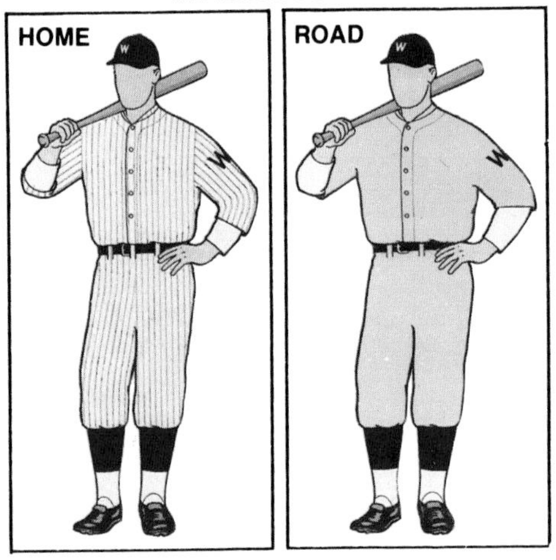

THE NEW YORK HERALD TRIBUNE, WEDNESDAY, APRIL 16, 1924 17

Shawkey and Hoyt Pitch Yankees to Victory Over Red Sox in Opening at Boston by 2-1 Score

World's Champions Drive In Both Runs in the Last Inning

Ruth, Quiet Up to That Time, Starts Trouble for Ehmke With Clean Single to Start Ninth; Fumbles by Wambsganss Settle Pitching Duel Issue

By W. B. Hanna

BOSTON, April 15.—A touch of winter was here to-day for the start of the American League baseball pennant race, but just a touch and not enough to prevent a successful beginning for the new baseball regime in the stronghold of the national game. And winter's snow or summer's sun the champion Yankees go on with their strong resourceful playing. The New Yorkers did all their scoring in the ninth inning this afternoon. They rose up with two runs and snatched victory, 2 to 1, from the rehabilitated Red Sox.

Won in the Ninth

Scenes at Opening of Baseball Season at Polo Grounds Yesterday

Giants' Party Was Gala Affair Aside From Score of the Game

Greatest National League Crowd Sees Mayor Hylan Parade, Sees Old Glory Hoisted, Sees New Uniforms and Everything—Also Sees Robins Win

By John Kieran

The grand gala opening of the baseball season on the old Polo Grounds lived up to the advance advertising in every little detail except the score of the game. The greatest crowd that ever witnessed a National League opening in any town was on hand.

NATIONAL LEAGUE 1924

BOSTON

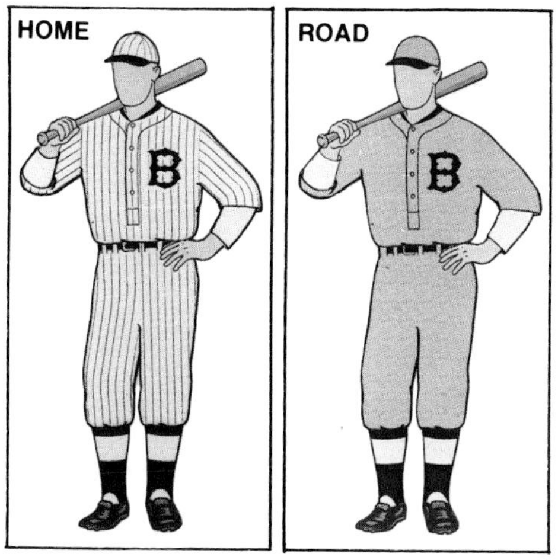
HOME
ROAD

BROOKLYN

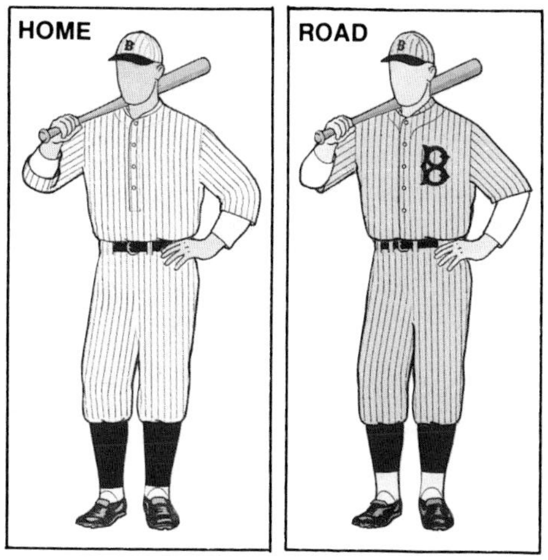
HOME
ROAD

ST. LOUIS

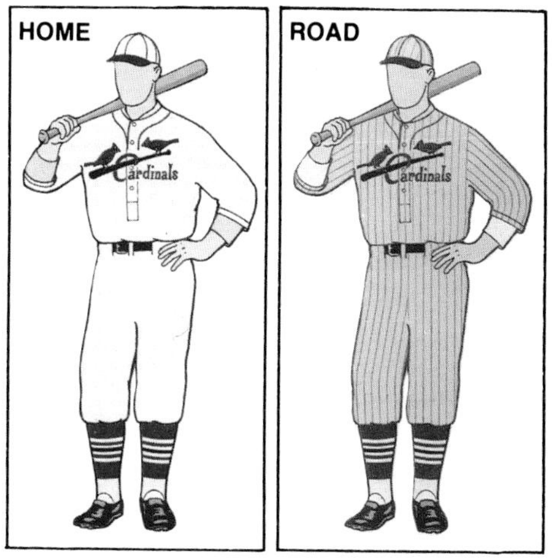
HOME
ROAD
Cardinals
Cardinals

PITTSBURGH

HOME
ROAD

PHILADELPHIA

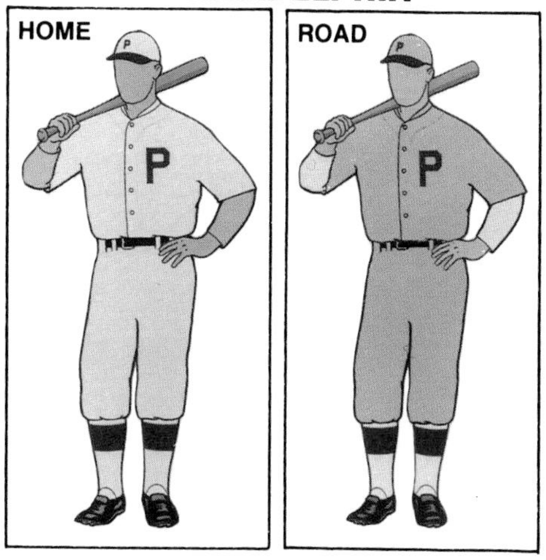
HOME
ROAD

CHICAGO

HOME
ROAD
CUBS
CUBS

We Service Your Tires
When You Stop For Oil or Gas
To get real tire service requires no special trips or long delays here. When you drive in for oil or gas, an expert is ready to look over your tires, inflate them, check your wheel alignment and repair small tread cuts if necessary.
We aim to make tires deliver maximum mileage. That's why it pays to deal here regularly.

CINCINNATI

HOME
ROAD
REDS
REDS

NEW YORK

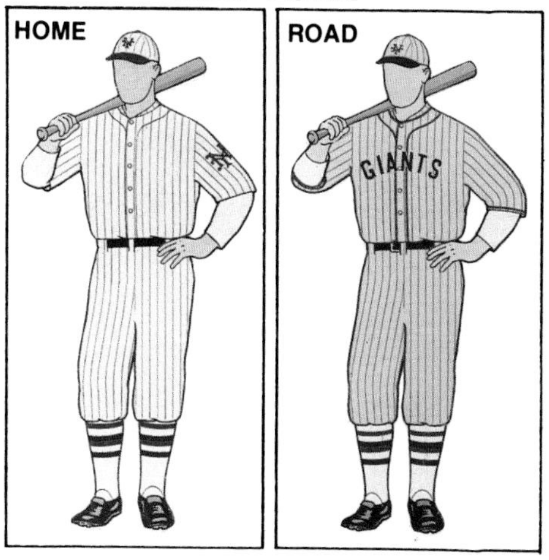
HOME
ROAD
GIANTS

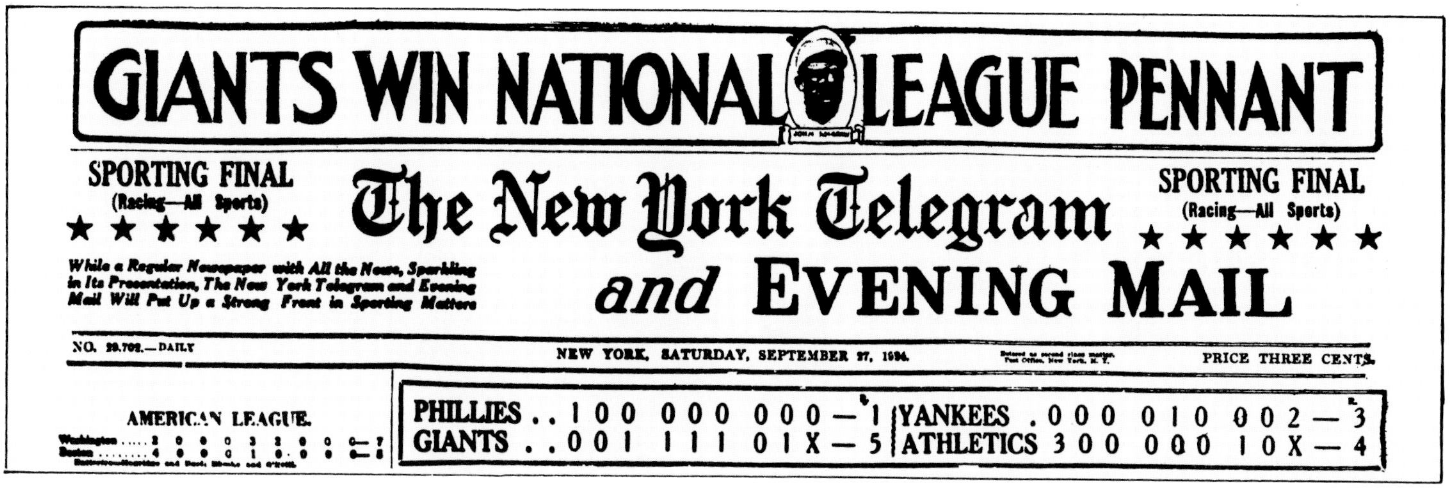

GIANTS WIN NATIONAL LEAGUE PENNANT

SPORTING FINAL (Racing—All Sports)

The New York Telegram and EVENING MAIL

SPORTING FINAL (Racing—All Sports)

While a Regular Newspaper with All the News, Sparkling in Its Presentation, The New York Telegram and Evening Mail Will Put Up a Strong Front in Sporting Matters

NO. 29,702.—DAILY | NEW YORK, SATURDAY, SEPTEMBER 27, 1924. | PRICE THREE CENTS

AMERICAN LEAGUE.

PHILLIES ..	1 0 0	0 0 0	0 0 0	— 1
GIANTS ..	0 0 1	1 1 1	0 1 X	— 5
YANKEES .	0 0 0	0 1 0	0 0 2	— 3
ATHLETICS	3 0 0	0 0 0	1 0 X	— 4

1925 AMERICAN LEAGUE

BOSTON

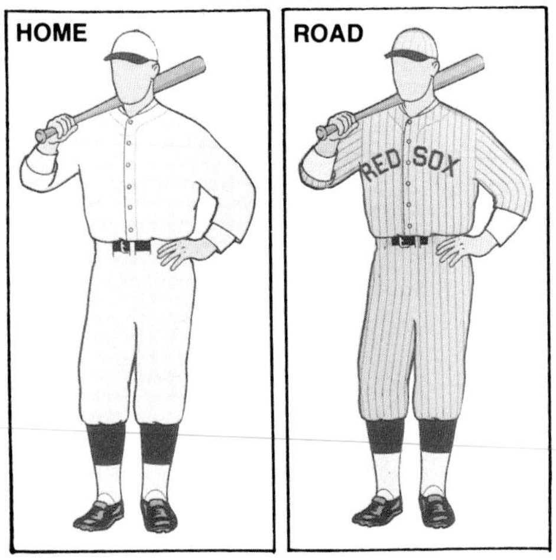

CLEVELAND

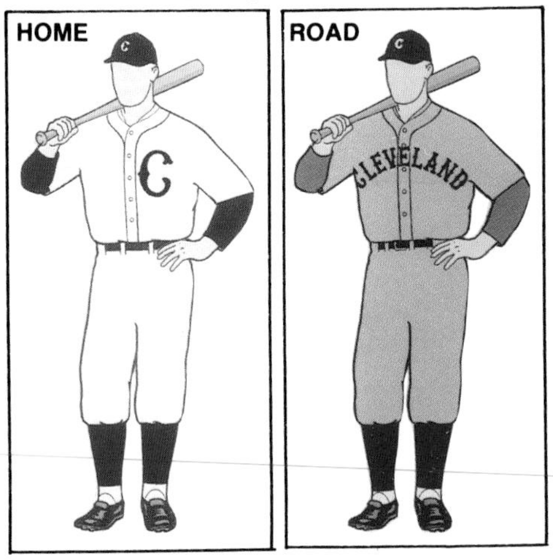

DETROIT

ST. LOUIS

NEW YORK

PHILADELPHIA

CHICAGO

WASHINGTON

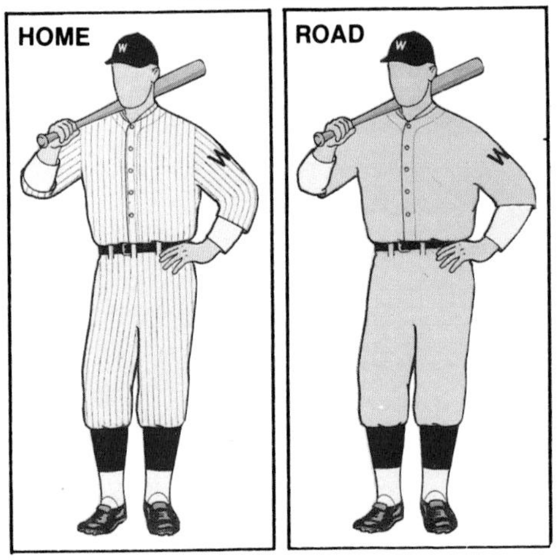

Closing N. Y. Stocks and Bonds, Page 30

The Evening Star.

WITH SUNDAY MORNING EDITION

"From Press to Home Within the Hour"

Yesterday's Circulation, 97,227

No. 29,744. — WASHINGTON, D. C., WEDNESDAY, OCTOBER 7, 1925–FORTY-EIGHT PAGES. — TWO CENTS.

CHAMPS HOLDING 3-1 LEAD OVER PIRATES; J. HARRIS HITS HOMER

Griffmen Increase Advantage by Terrific Attack in Fifth Inning.

JOHNSON AND MEADOWS GET OPENING PITCHING ASSIGNMENT

Brilliant Fielding Display Features Open-

NEED FOR JUSTICE BUILDING HASTENED BY ORDER TO MOVE

Present Quarters Far Too Cramped for Efficiency, Even if Retained.

NEW STRUCTURE PLANS WERE SPOILED BY SENATE

Mitchell Ordered To Report in Probe Here Tomorrow

NEW NAVY AIRSHIP ASKED BY MOFFETT

CONE LEAVES FLEET POST IN PROTEST OF PALMER'S REMOVAL

Vice President and General Manager Scores Action of Shipping Board.

SEES PRESIDENT DEFIED AND POLICIES IGNORED

NATIONAL LEAGUE 1925

BOSTON

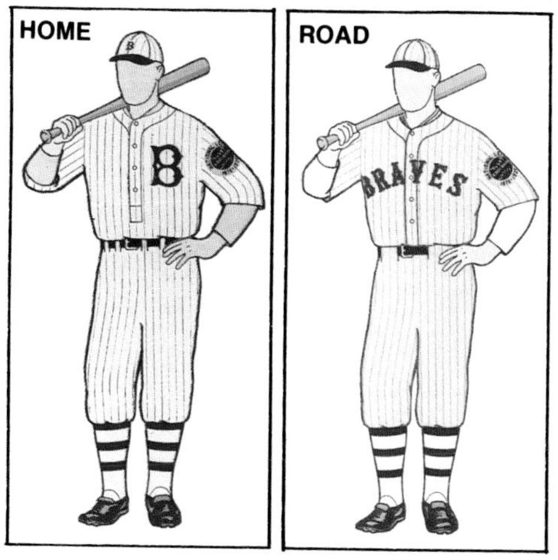

BROOKLYN

ST. LOUIS

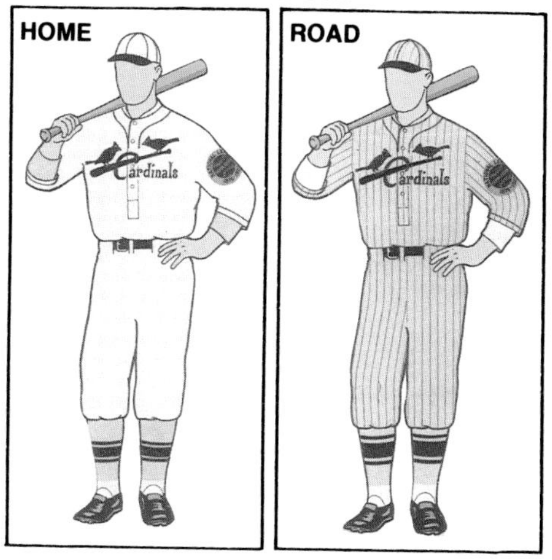

PITTSBURGH

PHILADELPHIA

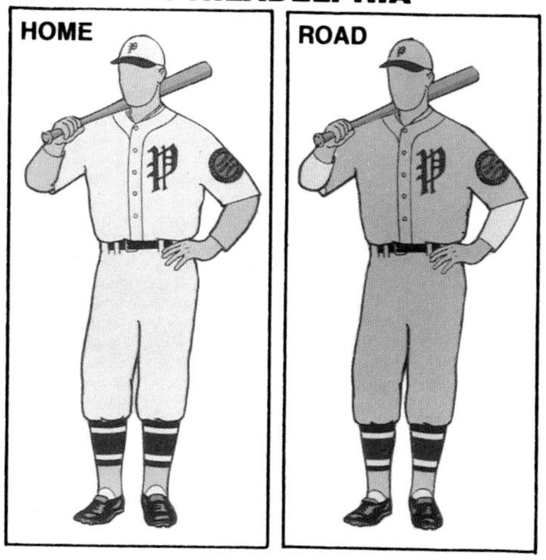

CHICAGO

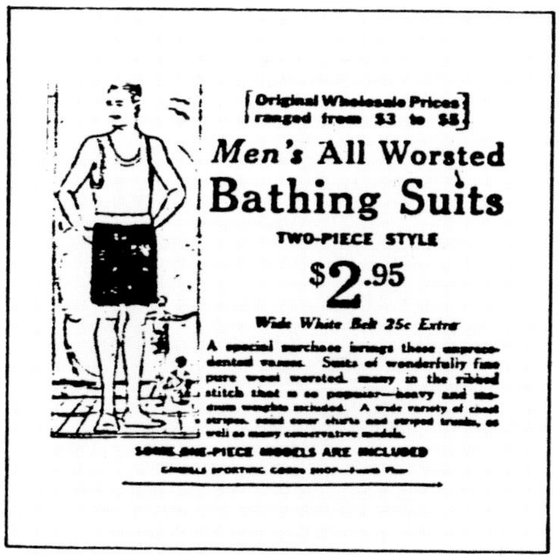

CINCINNATI

NEW YORK

8A THE BROOKLYN DAILY EAGLE, NEW YORK, WEDNESDAY, APRIL 15, 1925

VANCE HOLDS PHILLIES TO FIVE HITS AND SUPERBAS WIN

Jimmy Ring Has a Hunch That Is Borne Out by Events at Ebbets Field

By THOMAS HOLMES.

SENOR JIMMY RING of Maspeth, L. I., and Philadelphia, knows his stuff, as they say. After what happened at Ebbets Field yesterday afternoon the whole wide world can be informed to this effect.

A number of things occurred at Ebbets Field yesterday afternoon. First of all, there was a band concert. Following that came a more or less soul-inspiring parade across the field and after that an exhibition of how not to throw a baseball by Boro President Joseph Guider. Then a ball game was staged.

A crowd numbering some 20,000 specimens of baseball bugs sat under the bleakest of skies through the entire program. The bugs endured the

HIGH SPOTS IN THE OPENING GAME AT EB

1926 AMERICAN LEAGUE

BOSTON

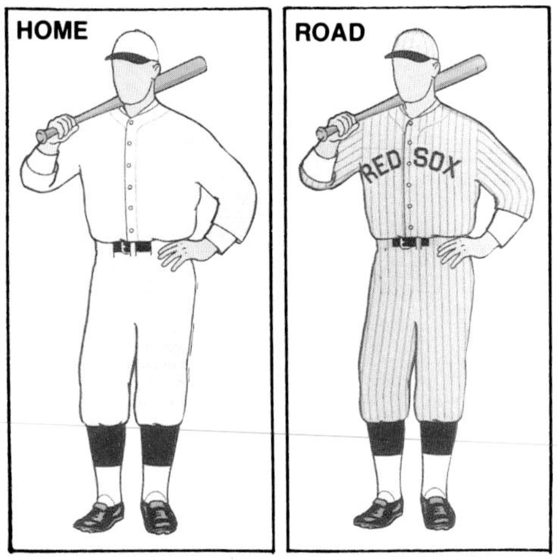

CLEVELAND

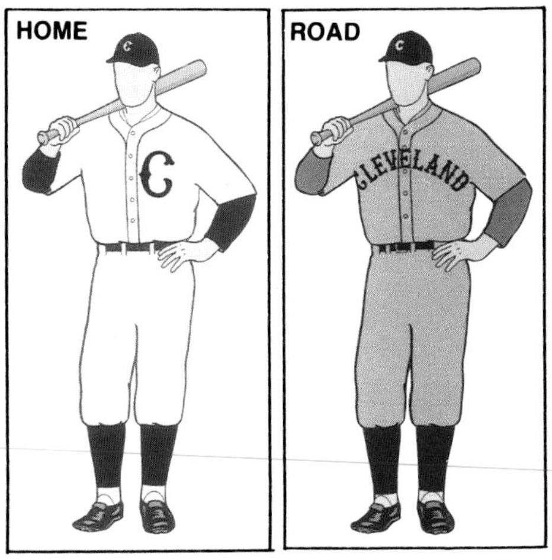

DETROIT

ST. LOUIS

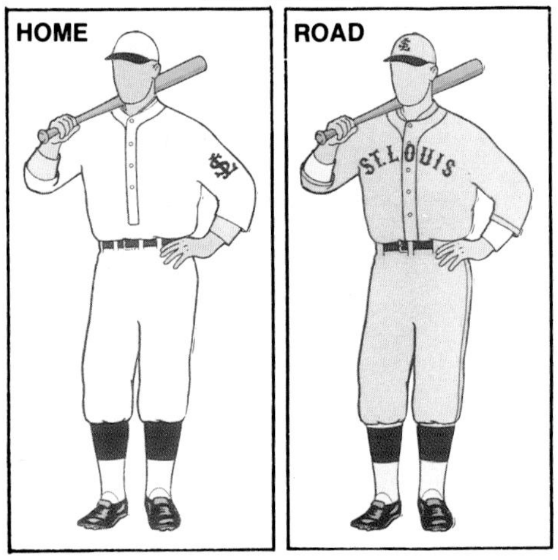

NEW YORK

PHILADELPHIA

CHICAGO

WASHINGTON

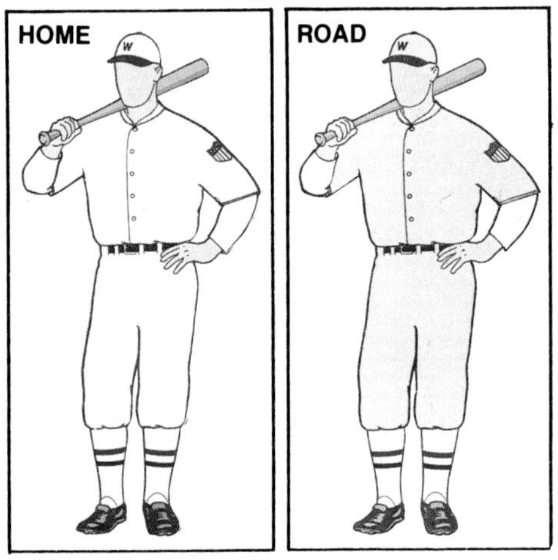

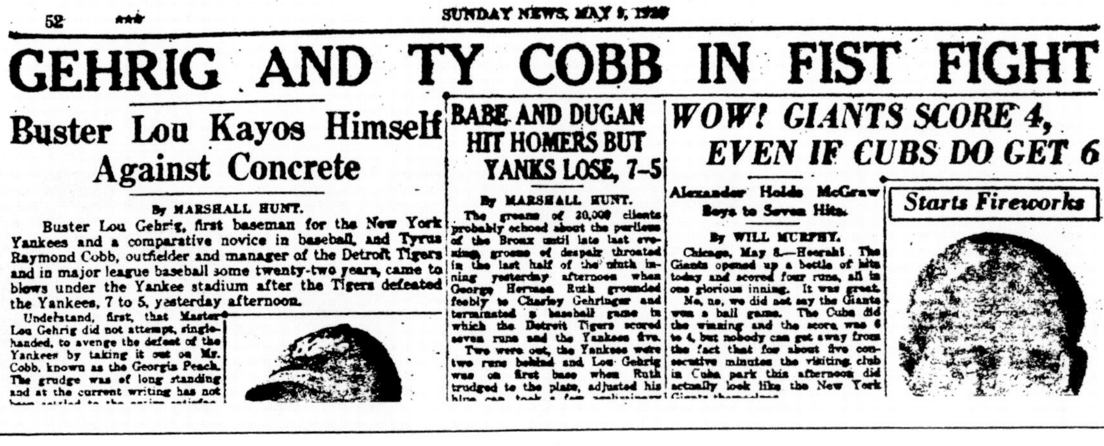

52 SUNDAY NEWS, MAY 9, 1926

GEHRIG AND TY COBB IN FIST FIGHT

Buster Lou Kayos Himself Against Concrete

By MARSHALL HUNT.

Buster Lou Gehrig, first baseman for the New York Yankees and a comparative novice in baseball, and Tyrus Raymond Cobb, outfielder and manager of the Detroit Tigers and in major league baseball some twenty-two years, came to blows under the Yankee stadium after the Tigers defeated the Yankees, 7 to 5, yesterday afternoon.

Understand, first, that Master Lou Gehrig did not attempt, single-handed, to avenge the defeat of the Yankees by taking it out on Mr. Cobb, known as the Georgia Peach. The grudge was of long standing and at the current writing has not

BABE AND DUGAN HIT HOMERS BUT YANKS LOSE, 7–5

By MARSHALL HUNT.

The groans of 20,000 clients probably echoed about the purlieus of the Bronx until late last evening, groans of despair throated in the last half of the ninth inning yesterday afternoon when George Herman Ruth grounded feebly to Charley Gehringer and terminated a baseball game in which the Detroit Tigers scored seven runs and the Yankees five.

Two were out, the Yankees were two runs behind and Lou Gehrig was on first base when Ruth trudged to the plate, adjusted his

WOW! GIANTS SCORE 4, EVEN IF CUBS DO GET 6

Alexander Holds McGraw Boys to Seven Hits.

By WILL MURPHY.

Chicago, May 8.—Hoorah! The Giants opened up a bottle of hits today and scored four runs, all in one glorious inning. It was great.

No, no, we did not say the Giants won a ball game. The Cubs did the winning and the score was 6 to 4, but nobody can get away from the fact that for about five consecutive minutes the visiting club in Cubs park this afternoon did actually look like the New York

Starts Fireworks

NATIONAL LEAGUE 1926

BOSTON

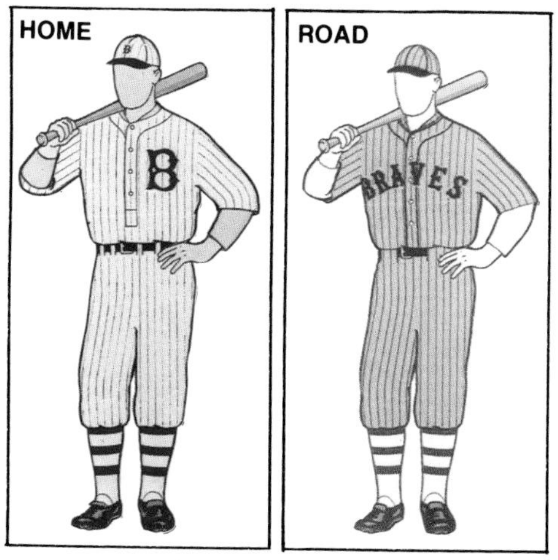

BROOKLYN

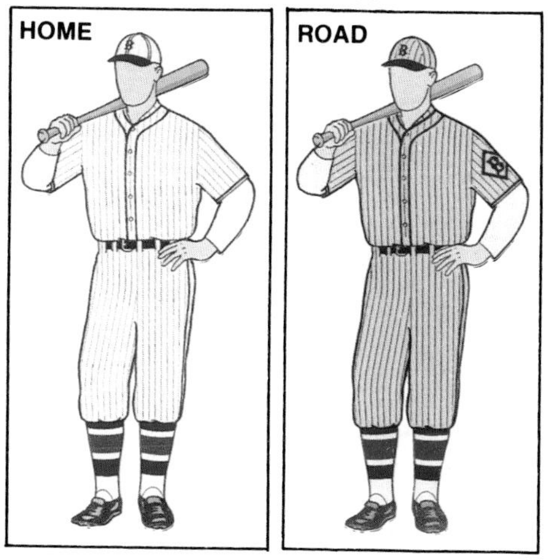

ST. LOUIS

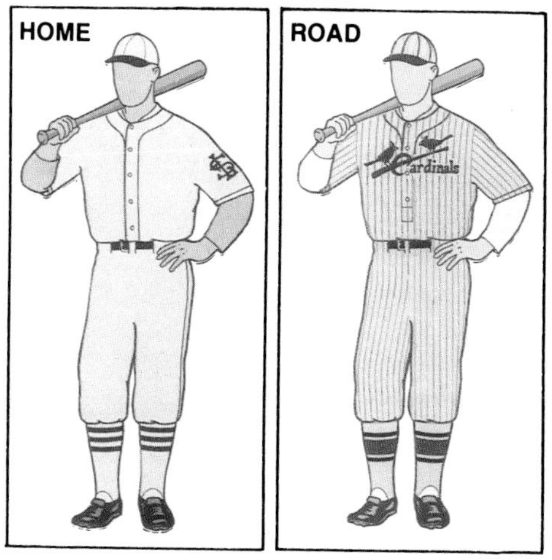

PITTSBURGH

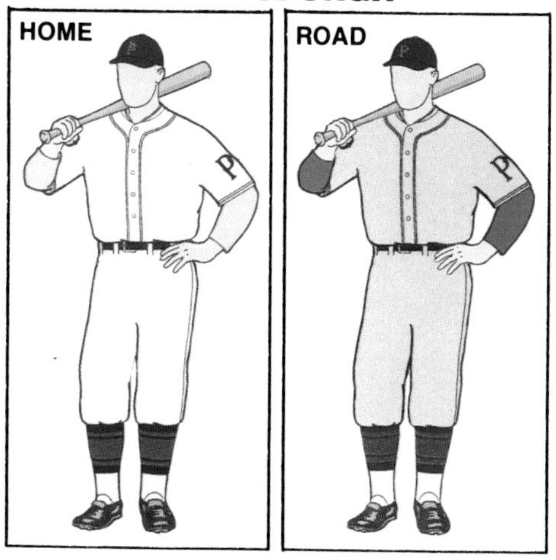

PHILADELPHIA

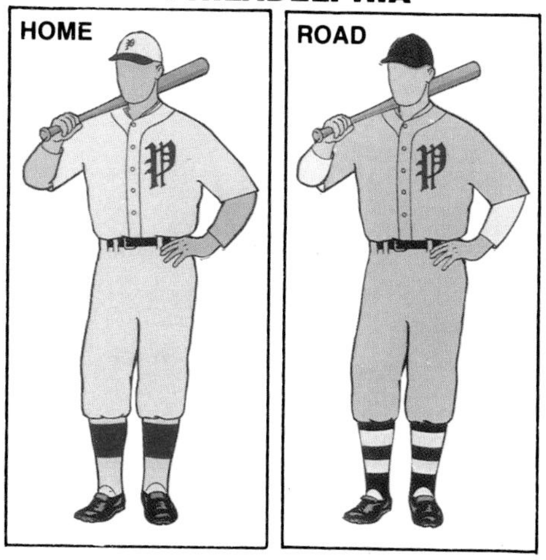

CHICAGO

CINCINNATI

NEW YORK

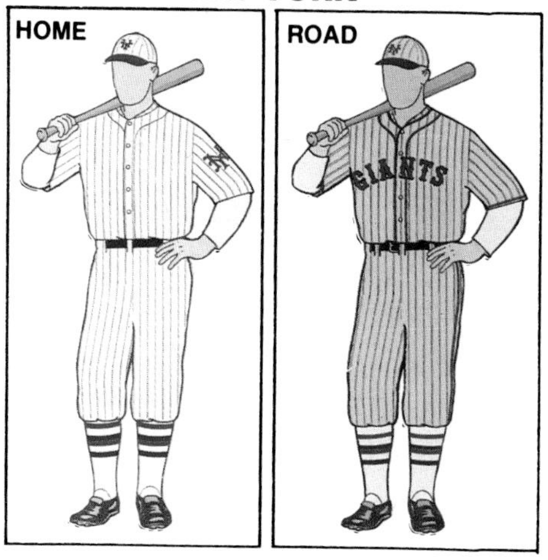

OCTOBER 14 THE SPORTING NEWS PAGE 3

INDOMITABLE SPIRIT OF CARDS CARRIES THEM TO VICTORY

AGE UPHILL FIGHT N LAST TWO GAMES

ANDER TAKES HERO ROLE IN DECIDING CLASH.

Master, After Pitching Two Victories, ... Yanks in Crises; Errors ... Chances of Yankees.

THE 1926 World's Series came to a close at Yankee Stadium, New York, Sunday, October 10 with the St. Louis Cardinals, champions of the National League, emerging victorious. The Series went to the limit of seven games with the American League

ROGERS HORNSBY AND HIS WORLD'S CHAMPION CARDINALS

WORLD'S SERIES DAT

FINAL STANDING.

	W.	L.
St. Louis	4	3
New York	3	4

FIRST GAME—OCTOBER 2.

Result—New York 2; St. Louis ... Batteries—Pennock and Severeid; Sherdel, Haines and O'Farrell.

Attendance—61,658, with money receipts of $186,776.

SECOND GAME—OCTOBER 3.

Result—St. Louis 6; New York 2. Batteries—Alexander and O'Farrell; Shocker, Shawkey, Jones and Severeid and Collins.

Attendance—63,600, with money receipts of $201,828.

THIRD GAME—OCTOBER 5.

Result—St. Louis 4; New York ... Batteries—Haines and O'Farrell; Ruether, Shawkey, Thomas and Severeid.

Attendance—37,708, with money receipts of $162,966.

FOURTH GAME—OCTOBER 6.

Result—New York 10; St. Louis ... Batteries—Hoyt and Severeid; Rhem, Reinhart, H. Bell, Hallahan, Keen and O'Farrell.

Attendance—38,825, with money receipts of $166,199.

FIFTH GAME—OCTOBER 7.

1927 AMERICAN LEAGUE

BOSTON

CLEVELAND

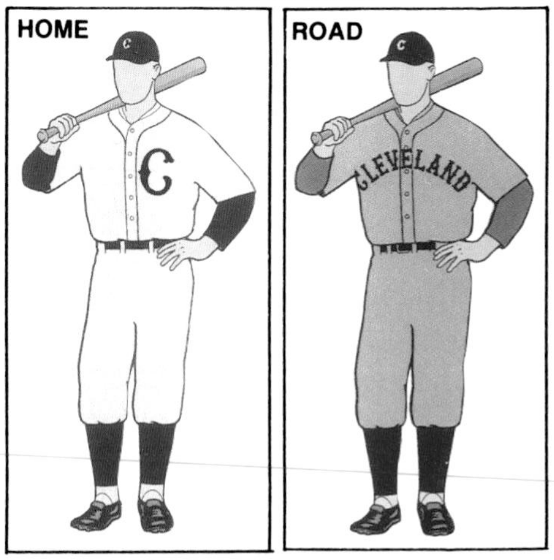

DETROIT

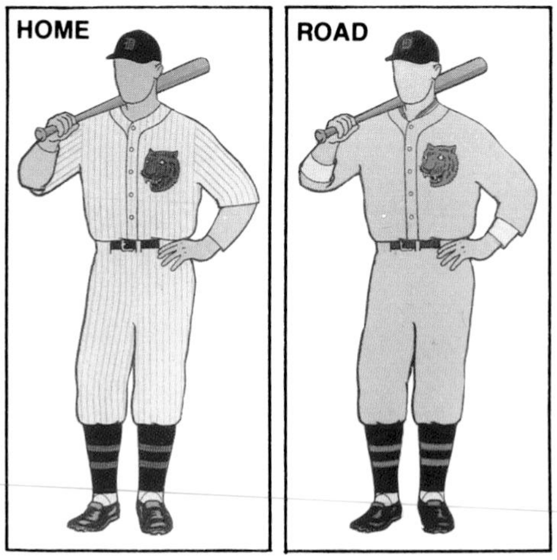

ST. LOUIS

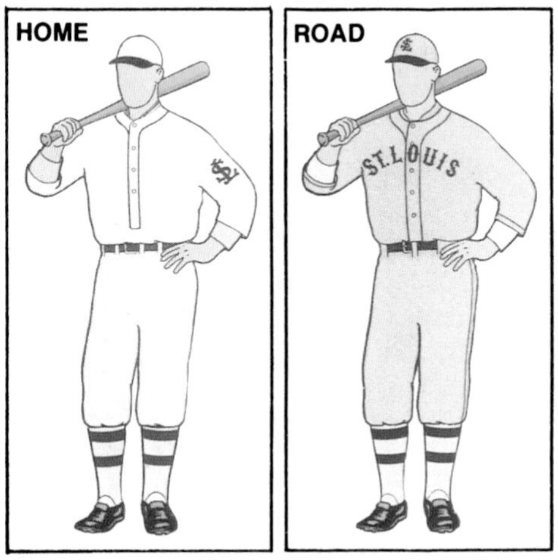

NEW YORK

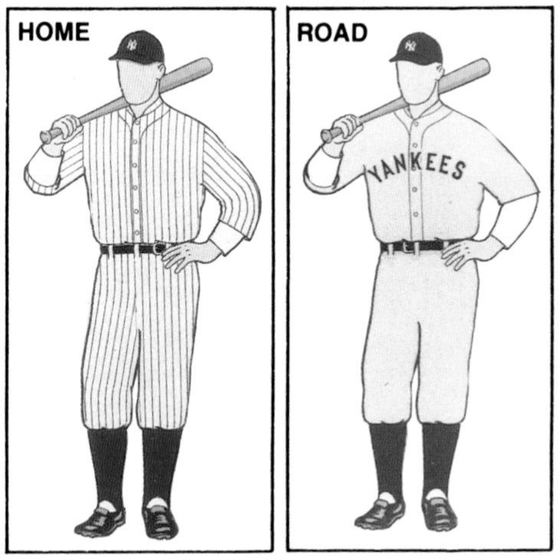

PHILADELPHIA

CHICAGO

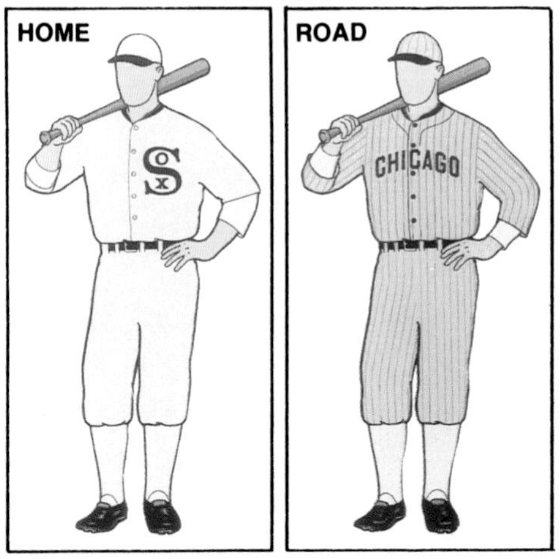

WASHINGTON

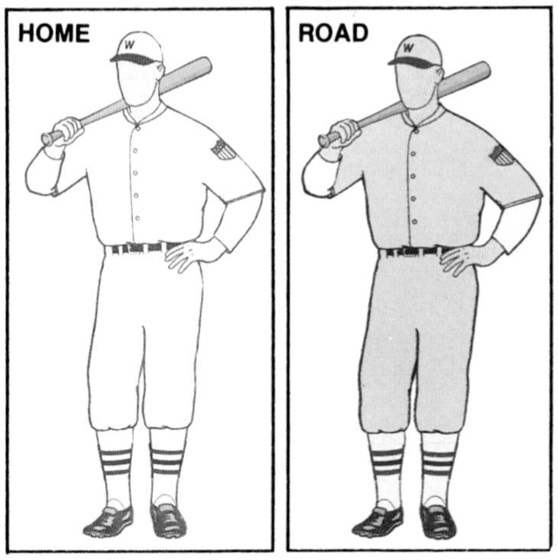

THE WEATHER.
Today: Generally fair; moderate southeast winds
To-morrow: Fair
Detailed weather report on Page 23

NEW YORK **Herald Tribune**

LATE CITY EDITION

Vol. LXXXVII No. 29,407 (Copyright, 1927, New York Tribune Inc.) SUNDAY, MAY 22, 1927—196 PAGES—Section One FIVE CENTS

Lindbergh Lands Safely in Paris at 5:21 P.M.; 3,800-Mile Flight in 33½ Hours Thrills World

New York Millions Hail His Triumph

'I'm Grateful' Says Mother As Son Wins

"Well, I Did It"

Paris Goes Wild: Flyer Only Tired

NATIONAL LEAGUE 1927

BOSTON

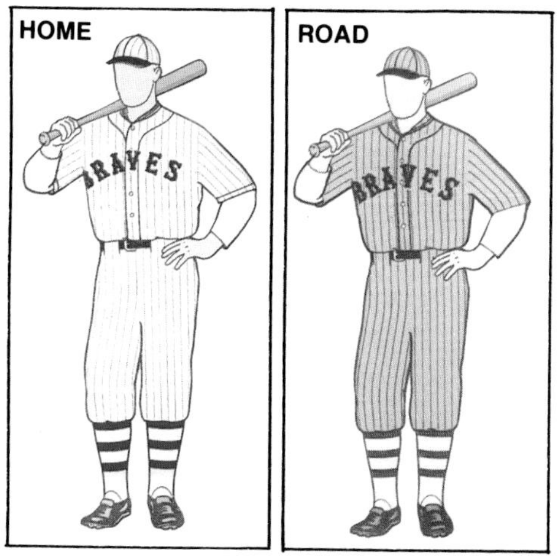

BROOKLYN

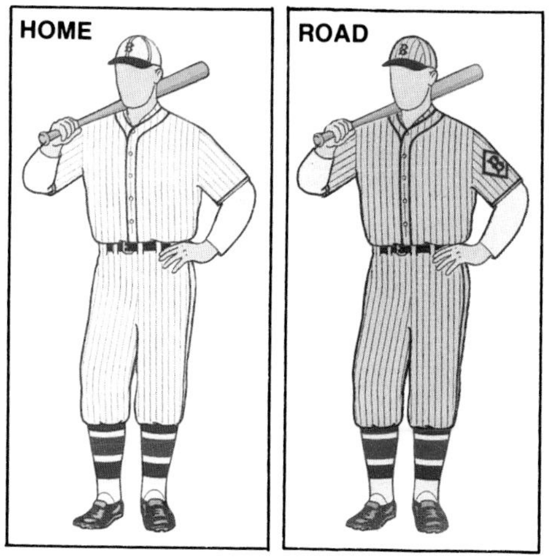

ST. LOUIS

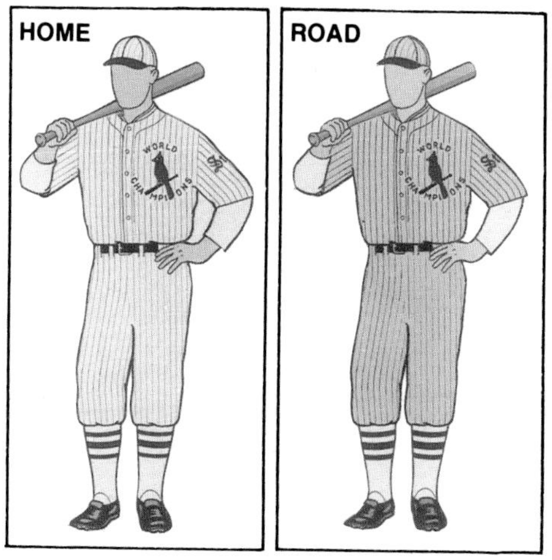

PITTSBURGH

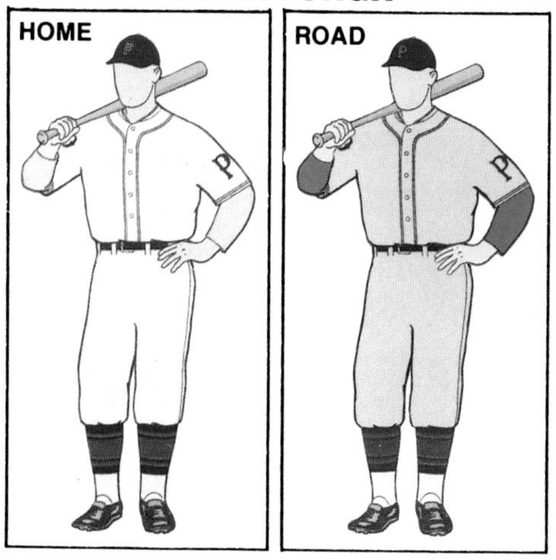

PHILADELPHIA

CHICAGO

CINCINNATI

NEW YORK

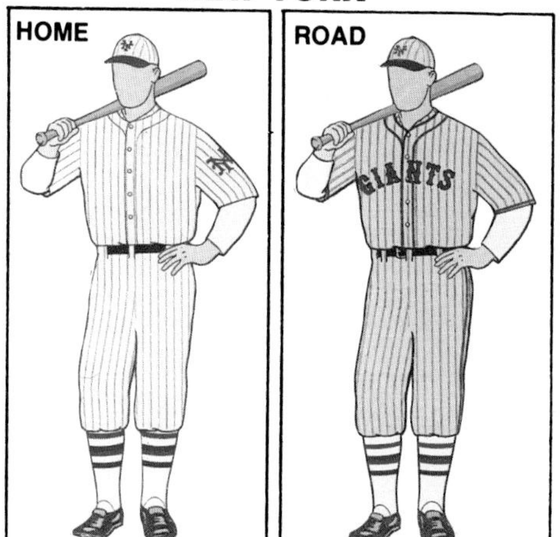

HAINES' 2-HIT GAME BLANKS CUBS, 5-0

Sox Beat Indians in Ninth Inning, 7-2

HOSE HAMMER OUT 6 RUNS IN RALLY AFTER TRAILING, 2-1

Levsen Holds Chicago to One Hit; Blankenship Yields Eight Safeties.

CHICAGO HERALD and EXAMINER SPORTS

THURSDAY, APRIL 14, 1927

'You're Out!'

Lester Bell out at the plate in the second inning, when Sparky Adams

7,000 FANS SEE CARD ACE STOP HEAVY-HITTING M'CARTHY CLAN

Heathcote and Cooney Get Bruins' Only Blows; Jess Walks One.

BY SAM HALL.

GROVER CLEVELAND ALEXANDER had to go to the rescue of Jess Haines to save the last game of the 1926 world series.

1928 AMERICAN LEAGUE

BOSTON

CLEVELAND

DETROIT

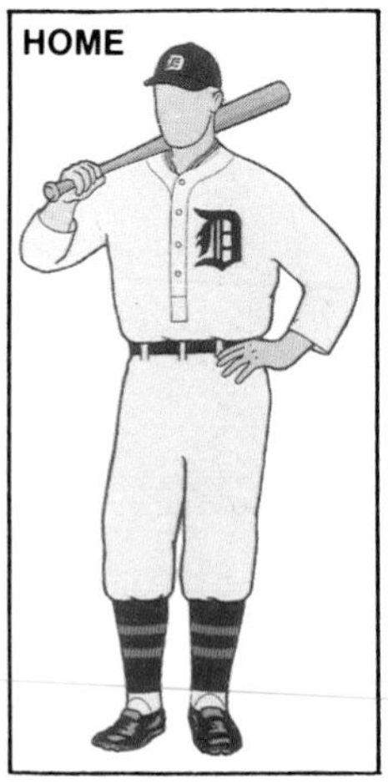

ST. LOUIS

NEW YORK

PHILADELPHIA

CHICAGO

WASHINGTON

14 NEW YORK EVENING POST, FRIDAY, APRIL 20, 1928

Miller Huggins Leads Baseball Circus Into Stadium for Season's Opening Today

RUTH AND COMPANY AT PEAK OF FORM FOR LOCAL DEBUT

Cobb, Speaker and Other Stars Make Inaugural Fray Real Attraction

JUDGE LANDIS TO PRESENT RINGS TO YANKEE PLAYERS

Some of the Actors in Baseball's Big Parade at Stadium Today

CONNIE MACK Athletics Mgr.

MILLER HUGGINS Yankee Mgr.

TRIS SPEAKER Athletics

FAILURE OF ROBINS DUE TO SHORTAGE OF FIRST SACKERS

Robbie Should Have a Half Dozen First Basemen Instead of Only Four

ANNOUNCER ENLIVENS PHILLY PROCEEDINGS

NATIONAL LEAGUE 1928

BOSTON

BROOKLYN

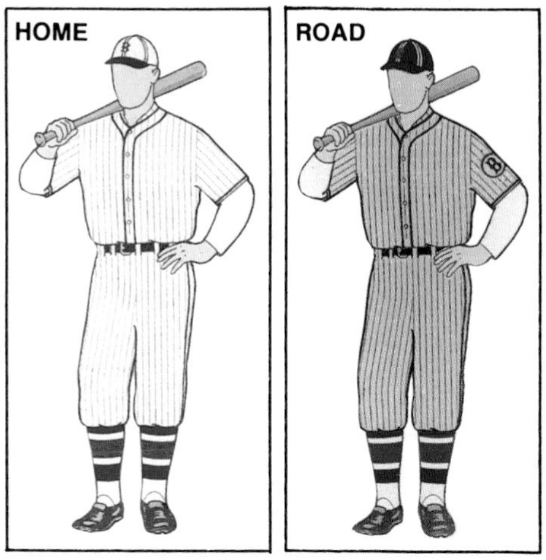

ST. LOUIS

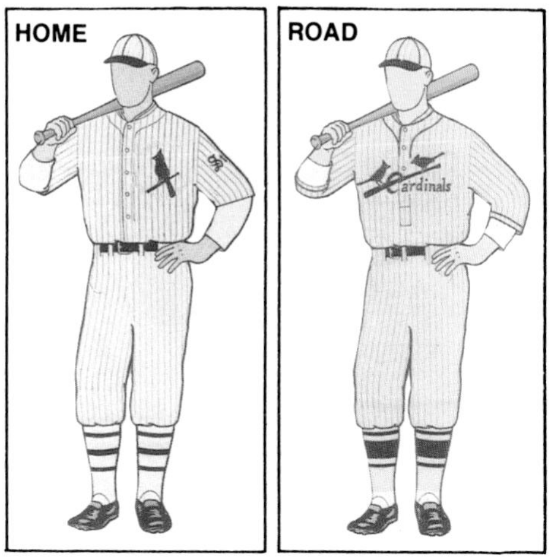

PITTSBURGH

PHILADELPHIA

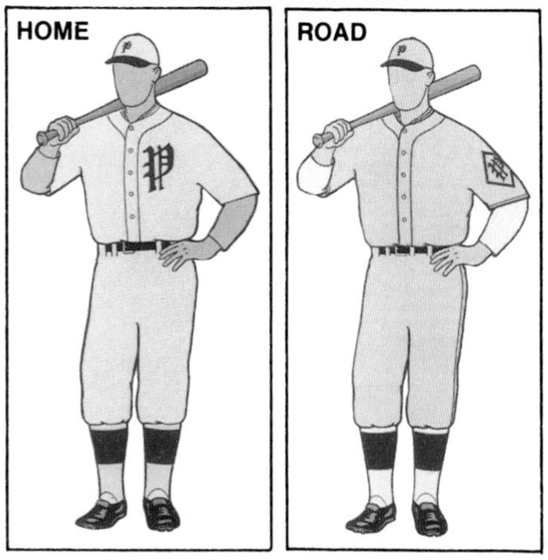

CHICAGO

CINCINNATI

NEW YORK

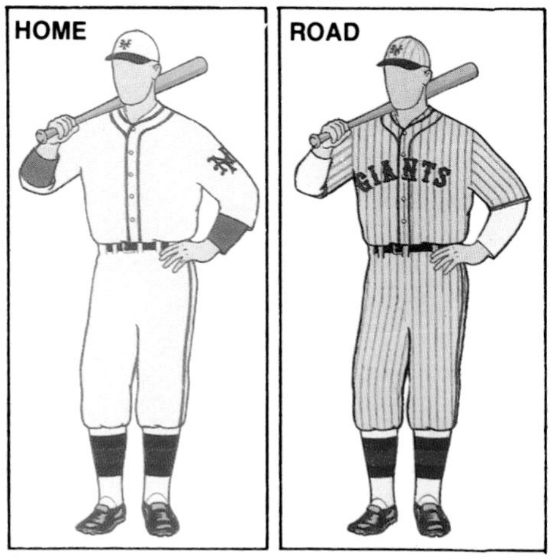

THIRTY-SIX Want Ad Headquarters, Court 4900 THE PITTSBURGH PRESS Other Departments, Court 5400 THURSDAY, APRIL 19, 1928

PIRATE FANS EAGERLY AWAIT OPENING GAME TODAY

RALPH DAVIS SAYS

St. Louis-Pirate Openers of Past Years.

Buccaneers Are Showing Splendid Spirit.

Hack Wilson Might Have Been Fistic King.

IF THE dope runs true to form, the Pirates should win over the Cardinals today. However, baseball dope is a fickle proposition, and one cannot delve into the past and ascertain definitely what will happen in the present.

ST. LOUIS teams have been the opening day attraction in Pittsburgh on 16 occasions, and of those games nine have resulted in victories for Pittsburgh, while the invaders have taken home the bacon on seven occasions.

SO THAT the dope does not give the Pirates such an enormous edge, at that. If the Cardinals should win today, they would be just one game behind the Pittsburghers in inaugural victories here, and it goes without saying that Bill McKechnie's boys will strive with might and main to knock over the champions, as they did twice last week in the Mound City.

THE FIRST opener here in which a St. Louis team ...

FANS, MEET NEW SPARK PLUG IN BUCCANEERS' INFIELD

Here Are Five Different Poses of "Sparky" Adams, New Pirate Second Sacker, Who Makes Debut As Bucco in Pittsburgh Today—Upper Left Is a Five-Facial Likeness, Next Comes His Batting Pose and Then He Is Shown Scooping a Grounder—Below Are Two Pictures of Him Fielding, One Taking an Easy Chance, the Other Spearing a High One.

Hill Is Picked For Mound Duty

Carmen to Be Opposed by Frankhouse in Opening Game With Cards.

GOOCH WILL CATCH

"Sparky" Adams Will Make First Appearance Here in Pirate Togs.

By LOU WOLLEN, Press Baseball Writer.

NICK ALTROCK CHIRPS

Philadelphia, April 19.—New York is tearing up its telephone books getting ready for the Bremen fliers. When those Germans and the Irishman land they will get the biggest reception New York has given since Andy Cohen made his first home run.

Well, the pennant race is settling down. The Bodies and Phillies have already picked out their lower berths. The surprise of the season so far is the way the Cleveland club has spurted along. The Clevelands don't

1929 AMERICAN LEAGUE

BOSTON

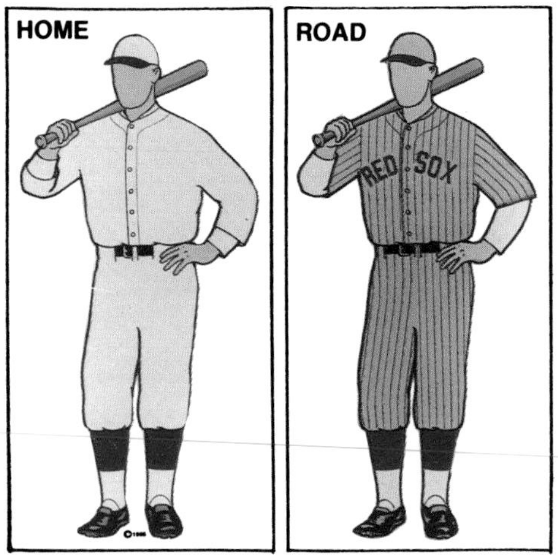

CLEVELAND

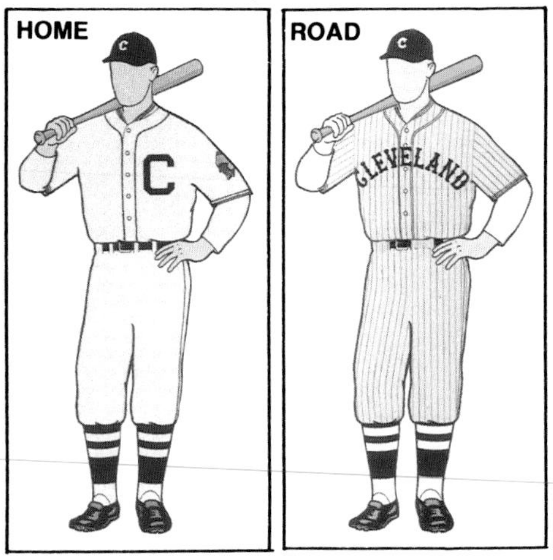

DETROIT

ST. LOUIS

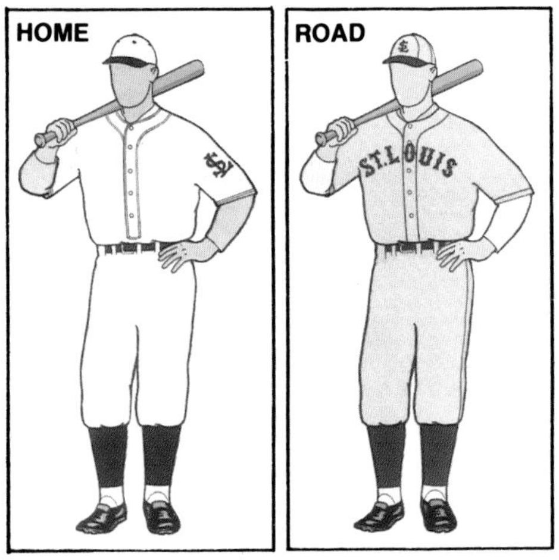

NEW YORK

PHILADELPHIA

CHICAGO

WASHINGTON

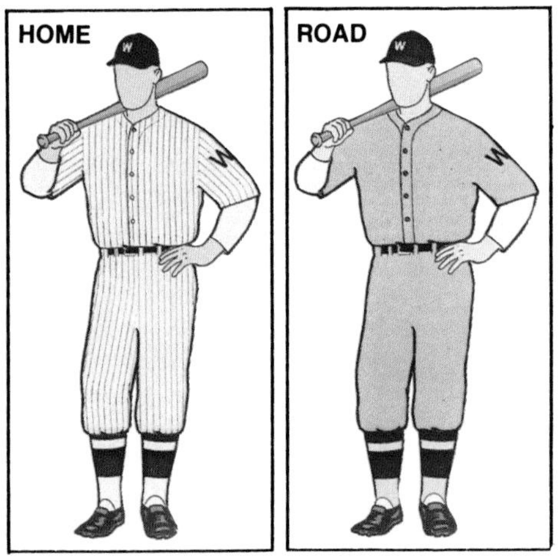

The Evening Bulletin

FINA

83RD YEAR, NO. 158 (SEPTEMBER CIRCULATION, 661,323 COPIES DAILY.) PHILADELPHIA, MONDAY, OCTOBER 14, 1929

A's World Champions, Beat Chicago, 3-2; Home Run and Double Crush Cubs in Ninth

HAAS' HOME RUN TIES SCORE, HIT BY MILLER WINS

President Hoover Sees Anoth-

PRESIDENT AND MRS. HOOVER AND A'S HEROES WHOSE HITS WON TITLE

LATEST NEWS AND SPORT

WORLD SERIES EXTRA

(Score by Innings)										Runs	Hits	Errors
CHICAGO	0	0	0	2	0	0	0	0	0	2	8	1
ATHLETICS	0	0	0	0	0	0	0	0	3	3	6	0

Chicago (N. L.)

	A.B.	R.	H.	O.	A.	E.
McMillan 3b	4	0	1	2	3	0
English ss	4	0	1	2	3	0
Hornsby 2b	4	0	0	2	4	1
Wilson cf	4	0	1	1	0	0
Cuyler rf	4	1	1	3	0	0
Stephenson lf	3	1	1	1	0	0
Grimm 1b	4	0	1	10	0	0

Athletics (A. L.)

	A.B.	R.	H.	O.	A.
Bishop 2b	4	1	1	2	0
Haas cf	4	1	1	1	0
Cochrane c	3	0	0	10	1
Simmons lf	4	1	2	0	0
Foxx 1b	3	0	0	8	1
Miller rf	4	0	2	5	0
Dykes 3b	3	0	0	0	1

NATIONAL LEAGUE 1929

BOSTON

BROOKLYN

ST. LOUIS

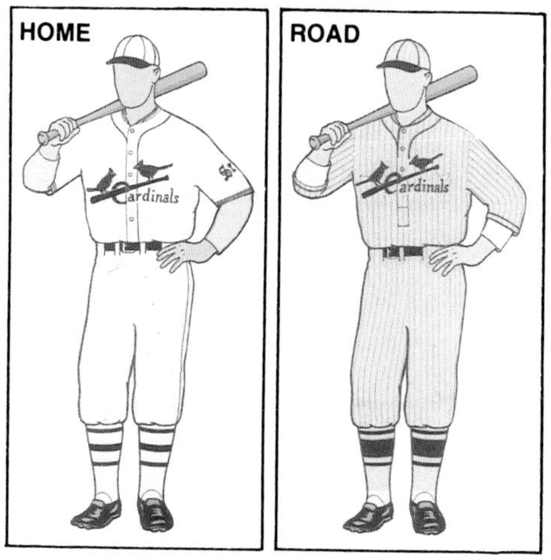

PITTSBURGH

PHILADELPHIA

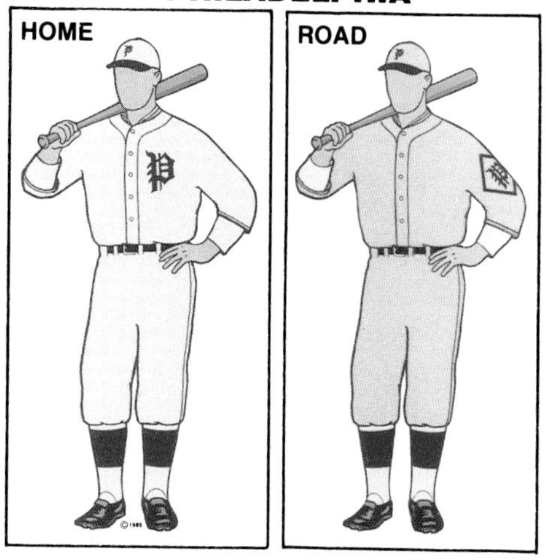

CHICAGO

CINCINNATI

NEW YORK

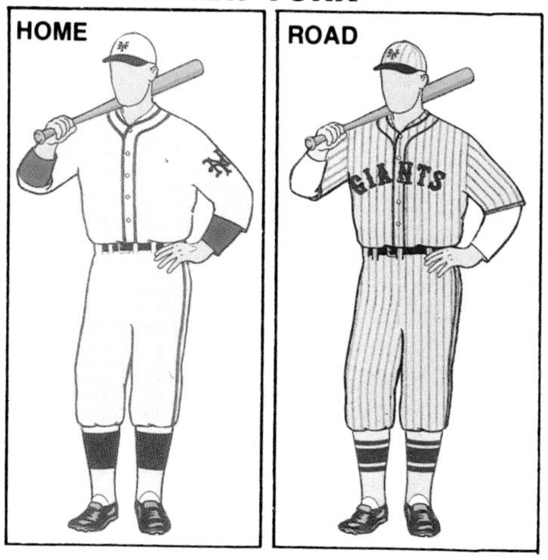

The Boston Post

FRIDAY, APRIL 19, 1929 — FORTY-FOUR PAGES—TWO CENTS

Post Man Goes With Cardinal's Party Today

BILL TO BUY EL ROAD IS FILED

BRAVES WIN SLUGFEST —YANKS BEAT RED SOX

Brooklyn Nosed Out 13-12--Cold Weather Causes Slim Crowd--40,000 See Sox Defeated 7-3--Ruth Hits Home Run First Time at Bat

MICHELSON CHOICE FOR MARATHON

1930 AMERICAN LEAGUE

BOSTON

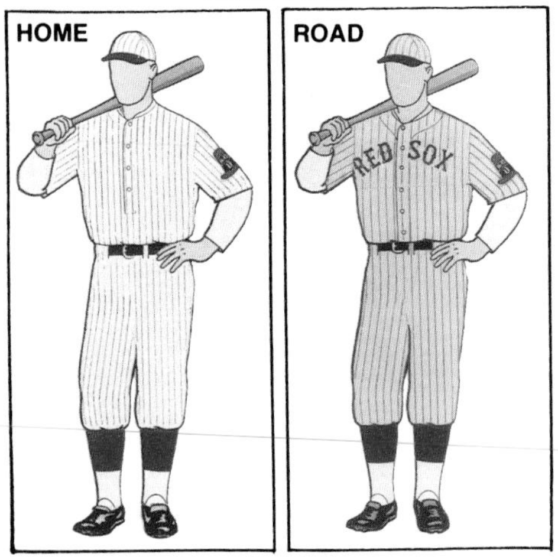

CLEVELAND

DETROIT

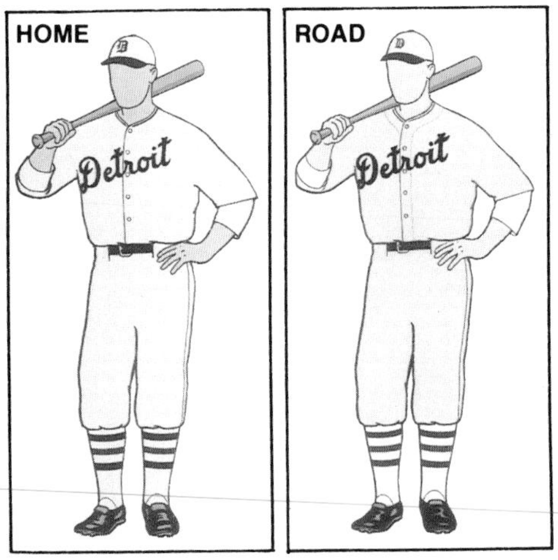

ST. LOUIS

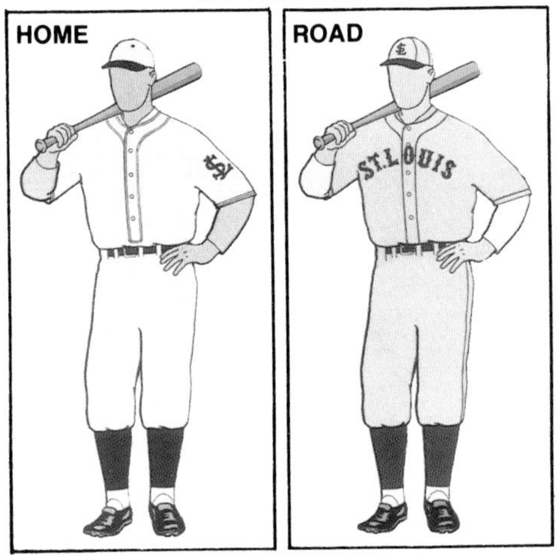

NEW YORK

PHILADELPHIA

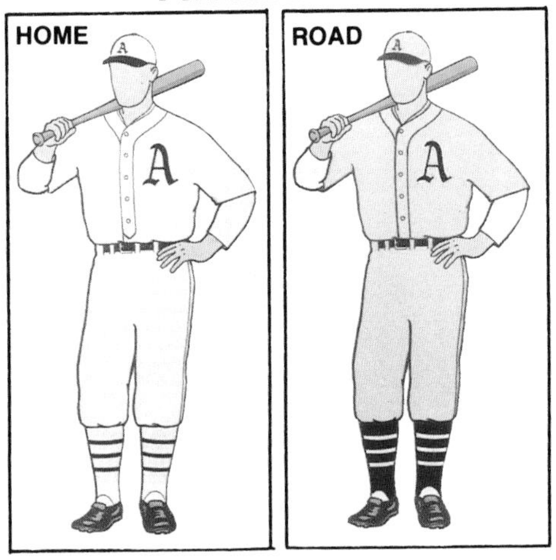

CHICAGO

WASHINGTON

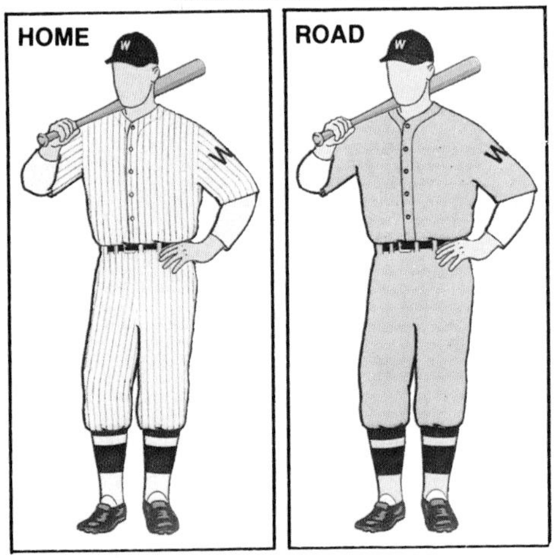

The Evening Bulletin

OCT -2 1930

SPEARED!

FINAL ★ ★

84TH YEAR, NO. 147 — (AUGUST CIRCULATION, 561,660 COPIES DAILY.) — PHILADELPHIA, WEDNESDAY, OCTOBER 1, 1930 — TWO

Athletics Beat St. Louis 5-2 in Opener; Simmons and Cochrane Clout Home Runs

5 RUNS ON 5 HITS DEFEAT GRIMES, CARDINALS' ACE

President Hoover Sees Lefty Grove Yield 9 Safeties but Turn Back National Leaguers

35,000 GO WILD AS A'S TAKE WORLD SERIES LEAD

AS THE PRESIDENT OFFICIALLY OPENED THE SERIES

HOOVER THRILLED AS SPECTATOR AT FIRST SERIES GAME

Shakes Hands With Connie Mack at Start and Asks Mayor to Congratulate Him on Victory After Game

TOSSES OUT FIRST BALL TO OPEN SPORTS CLASSIC

LATEST NEWS AND SPORTS

WORLD SERIES EXTRA

ST. LOUIS	0	0	2	0	0	0	0	0	0	—	2	9	0
ATHLETICS	0	1	0	1	0	1	1	1		—	5	5	0

St. Louis (N. L.) — Athletics (A. L.)

aBatted for Grimes in 9th.

SAW DAN... AS SON...

NATIONAL LEAGUE 1930

BOSTON

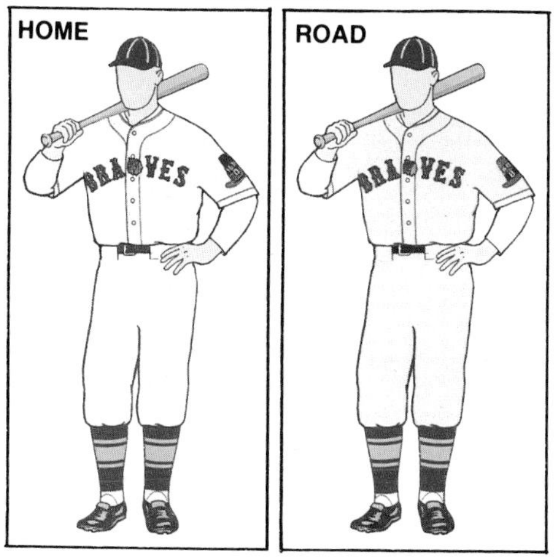

BROOKLYN

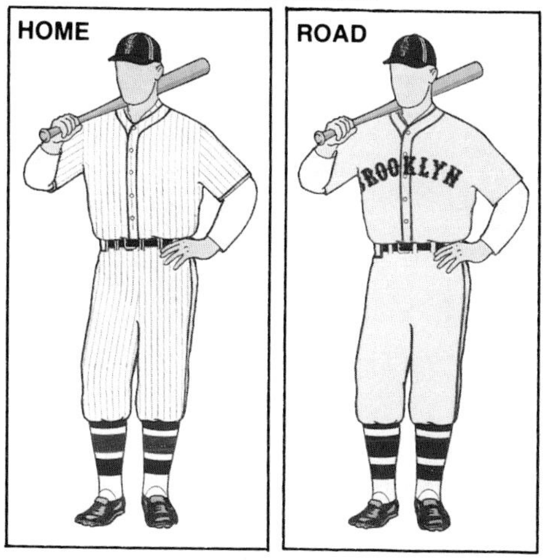

ST. LOUIS

PITTSBURGH

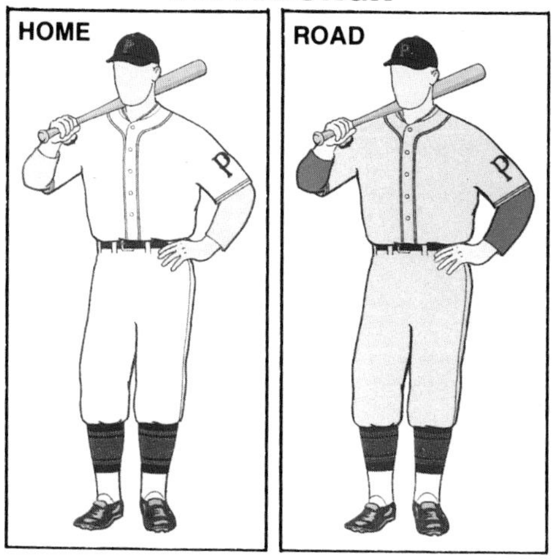

PHILADELPHIA

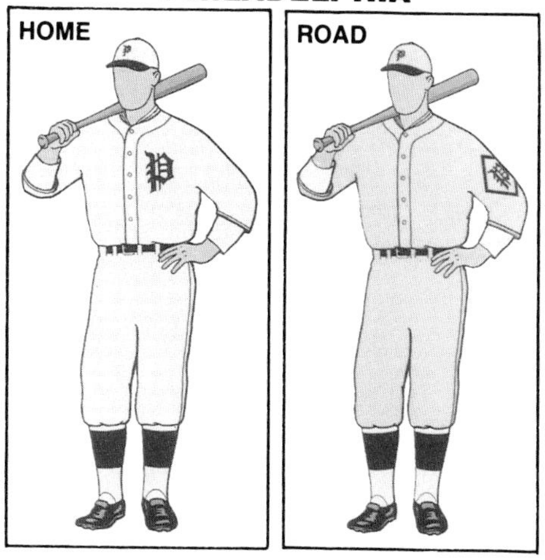

CHICAGO

CINCINNATI

NEW YORK

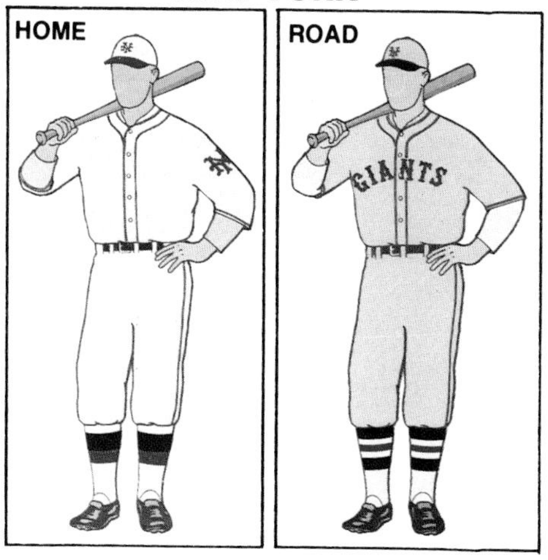

BOSTON POST, SATURDAY, APRIL 26, 1930 15

BRAVES HUMBLED BY DAZZY VANCE

Get Only 3 Hits Off Speed King to Lose, 5-1 --- Opening Home Game Ends Disastrously

BY PAUL H. SHANNON

Bitterly blew the wind over the Braves' battle ground yesterday afternoon as the Dodgers and the Tribe, led by the waddling Uncle Wilbert Robinson, trooped out to the flag pole in right field for the elevation of the colors and then hustled back to the dubious shelter of their dugouts. But the wintry blast had died away to a requiem toward the close, as the Braves went down in defeat in this opening game by the tally of 5 to 1.

DAZZLED BY VANCE

OFF ON WRONG FOOT

[illegible]

FLORAL PIECE FOR THE RABBIT

Before the game began Rabbit Maranville was called to the plate to acknowledge the receipt of a floral testimonial from some unknown admirer. Lieutenant-Governor Youngman on the left and Manager McKechnie on the right are shown holding the basket up for the Rabbit's inspection with the Braves grouped in the background.

SISLER AN EASY OUT

KREMER DOWNS

GOSLIN'S HOMER BEATS A'S, 6-4

Comes Across in 8th With Team One Run Behind

WASHINGTON, April 25 (AP)—Goose Goslin's homer in the eighth inning of the Senators-Athletics contest here this afternoon, won the ball game, 6-4, and sent the Washington club into the American league lead.

With the Athletics leading 4-3 entering the eighth, Goslin collected his third bingle in four tripe to the plate, a long four-bagger that climbed the right field fence. Washington stepped into an early three-run lead which they held until the sixth, when hits and boots put together four runs for the A's.

Lloyd Brown, Senator pitcher, was a trifle erratic and the Athletics collected 12 hits off his slants. The A's Waterloo was in the left on bases column with the 13 [illegible] pursuing them here. Sam West also homered for Washington.

The score:

[illegible]

Babe the Big Hero Beating Sox, 3-2

Bangs Out First Homer of Season to Tie Up Game--Chapman's Double in 10th Sews Up Decision

NEW YORK, April 25—It's a far-flung fact that you can't keep a good man down and that goes for good ball teams, too. The Yankees, being a good ball team, consequently started their upward climb from the depths of the American league cellar yesterday winning their first victory of the season.

And as the Yanks got started so Babe Ruth got underway. He hit his first home run of the current campaign after reaching for it and just missing several times. In fact it was the Babe's homer which made the 3-2 victory over the Boston Red Sox possible.

CAME JUST IN TIME

Babe Gets in His Work

[illegible]

1931 AMERICAN LEAGUE

BOSTON

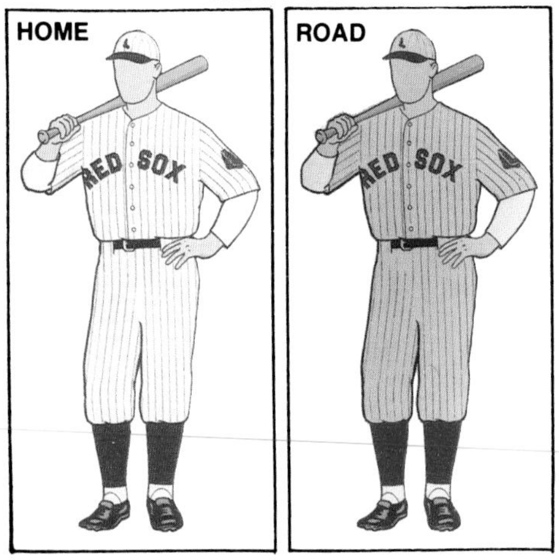

CLEVELAND

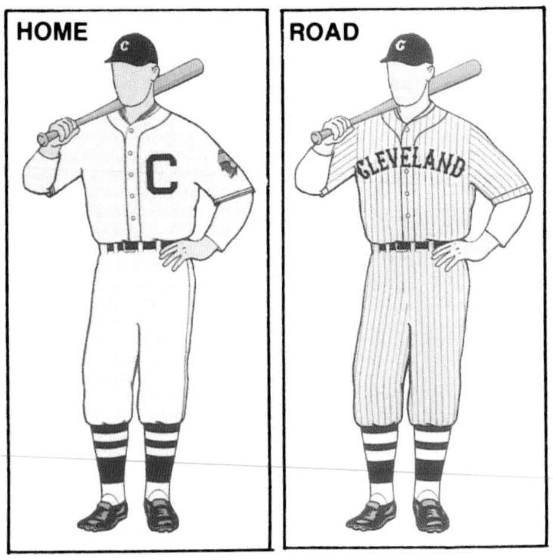

DETROIT

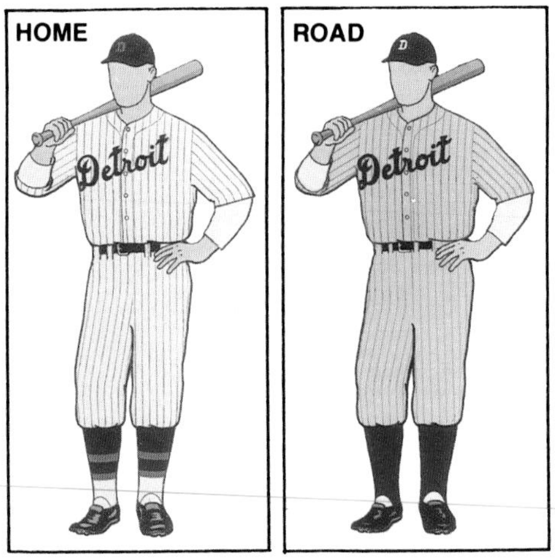

ST. LOUIS

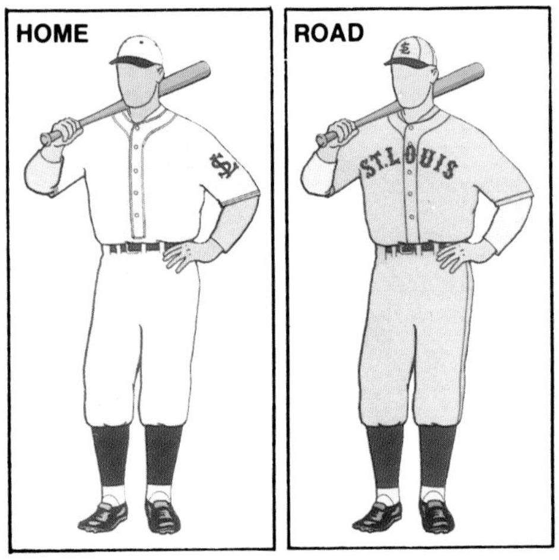

NEW YORK

PHILADELPHIA

CHICAGO

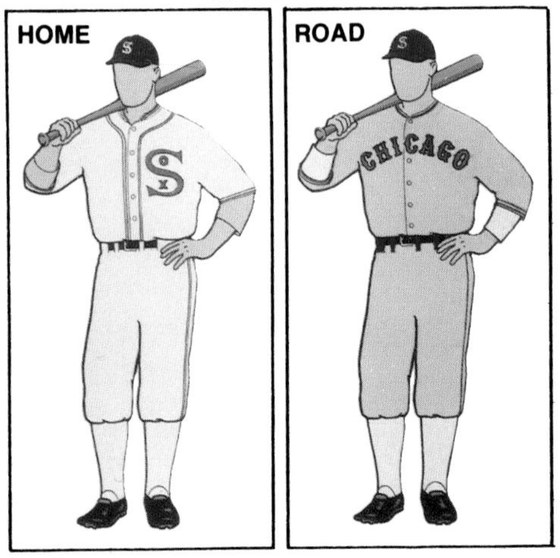

WASHINGTON

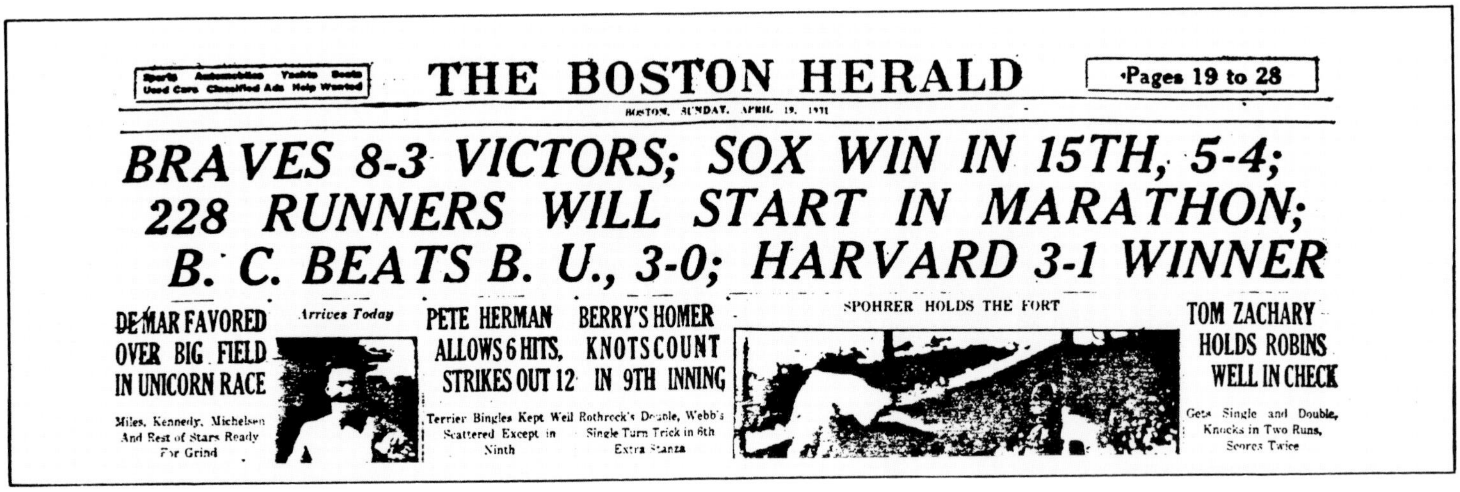

Sports Automobiles Yachts Boats Used Cars Classified Ads Help Wanted

THE BOSTON HERALD

·Pages 19 to 28

BOSTON, SUNDAY, APRIL 19, 1931

BRAVES 8-3 VICTORS; SOX WIN IN 15TH, 5-4; 228 RUNNERS WILL START IN MARATHON; B. C. BEATS B. U., 3-0; HARVARD 3-1 WINNER

DE MAR FAVORED OVER BIG FIELD IN UNICORN RACE

Miles, Kennedy, Michelsen And Rest of Stars Ready For Grind

Arrives Today

PETE HERMAN ALLOWS 6 HITS, STRIKES OUT 12

Terrier Bingles Kept Well Scattered Except in Ninth

BERRY'S HOMER KNOTS COUNT IN 9TH INNING

Rothrock's Double, Webb's Single Turn Trick in 6th Extra Stanza

SPOHRER HOLDS THE FORT

TOM ZACHARY HOLDS ROBINS WELL IN CHECK

Gets Single and Double, Knocks in Two Runs, Scores Twice

NATIONAL LEAGUE 1931

BOSTON

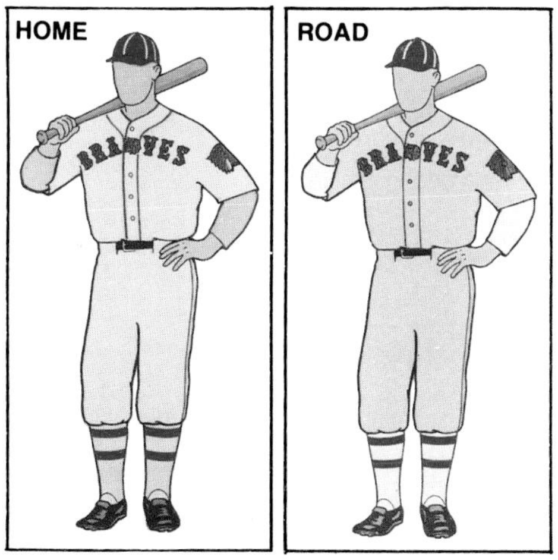

BROOKLYN

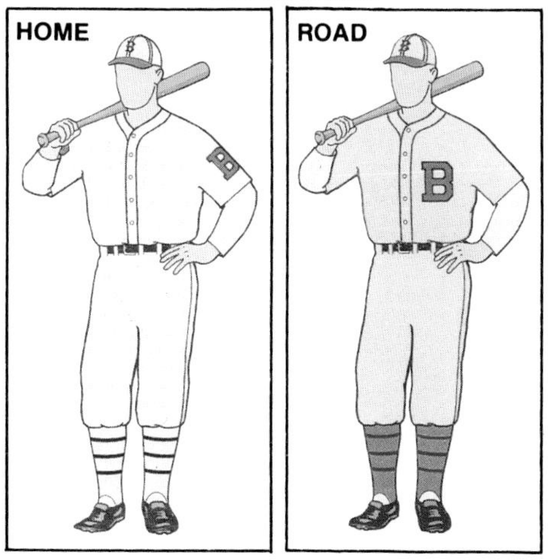

ST. LOUIS

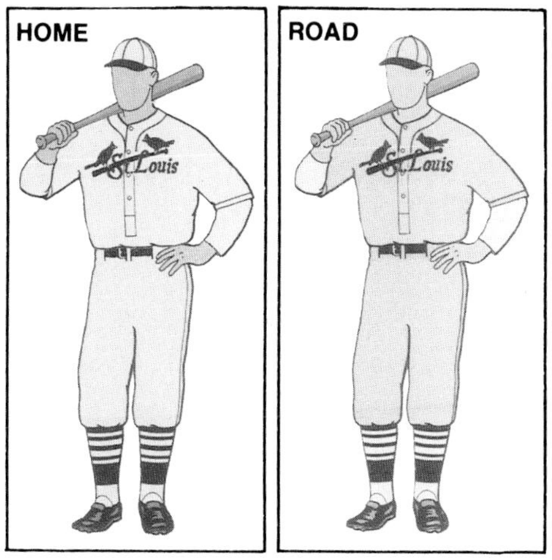

PITTSBURGH

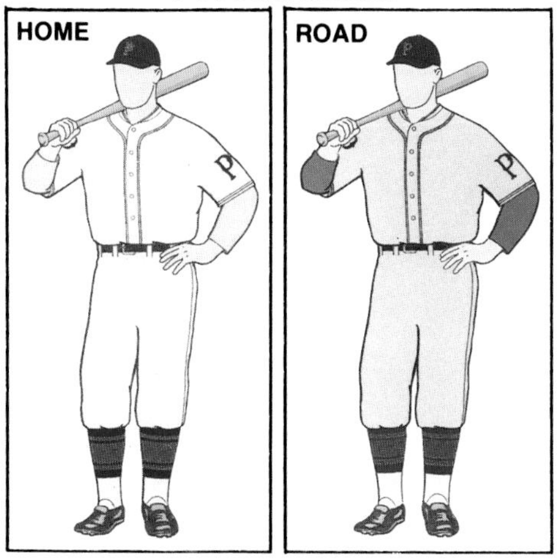

PHILADELPHIA

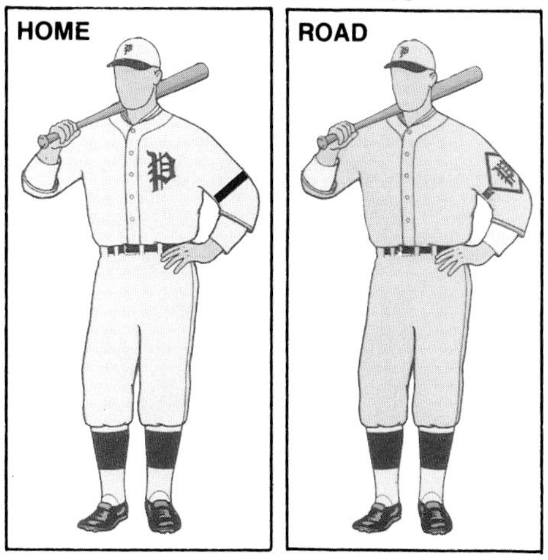

CHICAGO

CINCINNATI

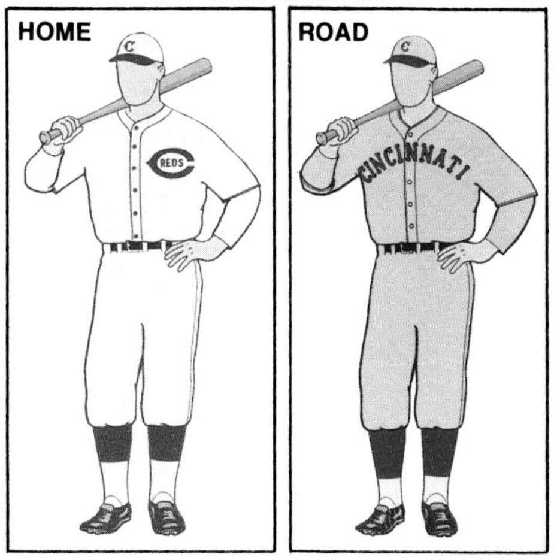

NEW YORK

Reports of UNITED PRESS, the Greatest World-Wide News Service

Pittsburgh Press

Baseball Extra
COMPLETE MARKETS

50 PAGES. PITTSBURGH, PA., FRIDAY, APRIL 24, 1931 THREE CENTS

CRAZED CONVICT STABS CHAPLAIN AT WESTERN PEN

Plunges Knife Into Rev. Alfred E. Fletcher Dur-

Part of Opening Day Crowd

HORNSBY CLOUTS THREE HOMERS AS CUBS BEAT PIRATES IN INAUGURAL

1932 AMERICAN LEAGUE

BOSTON

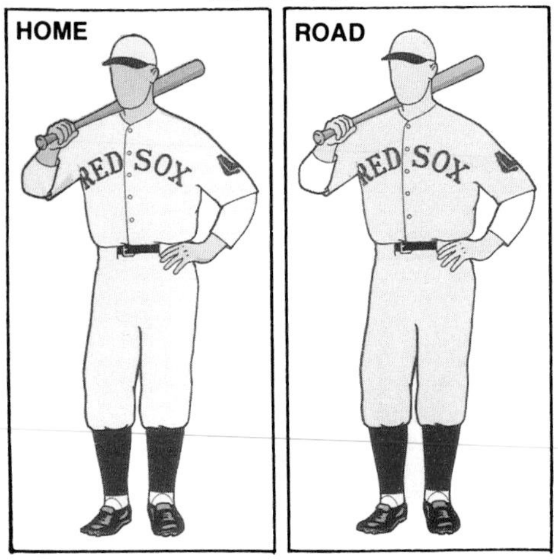

CLEVELAND

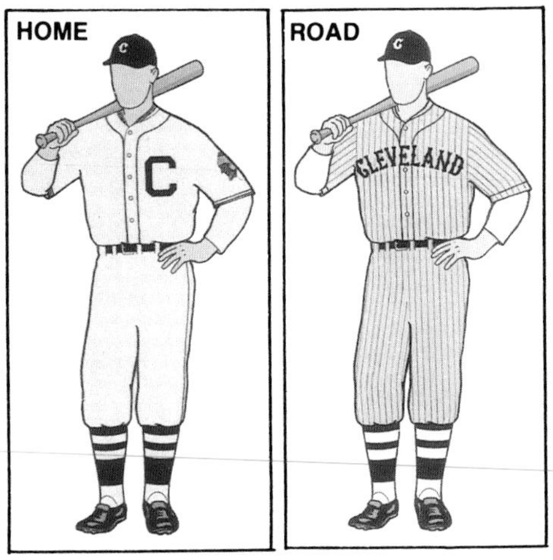

DETROIT

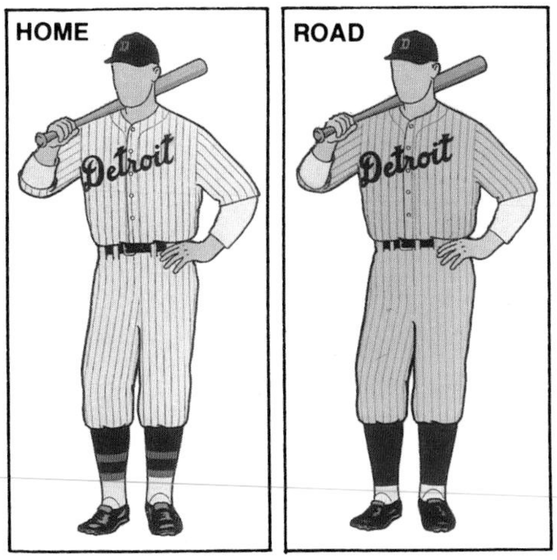

ST. LOUIS

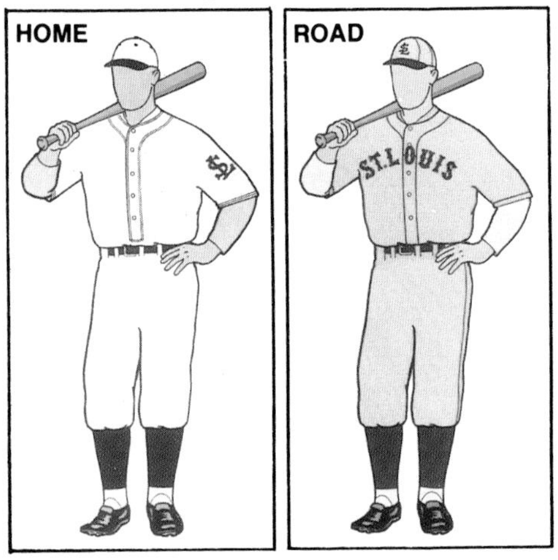

NEW YORK

PHILADELPHIA

CHICAGO

WASHINGTON

THE PHILADELPHIA INQUIRER, TUESDAY MORNING, APRIL 12, 1932

Manush's Double in 10th Gives Senators 1-0 Victory in First of Season; Earnshaw on Mound for A's in Opener With Yanks at Shibe Park Today

M'FAYDEN OF SOX LOSES KEEN MOUND DUEL IN CAPITOL

Bested by Crowder ... Each Hurler Al- ... Seven Swats

... Hoover ... in Serving First Ball of Year

Some Battle

Bang! And the 1932 Baseball Season is Under Way

PHILS SPRING AWAY FROM MARK PLAYING GIANTS IN NEW YORK

Connie Stands Pat on Line-up in First American League Engagement

Phil Collins Draws Assignment From Shottonmen to Face M'Grawmen

Continued From First Page

... American League flag. And their foes will be the New York Yankees, recognized throughout the country as their most formidable

Batting Order for Shibe Park Battle

NATIONAL LEAGUE 1932

BOSTON

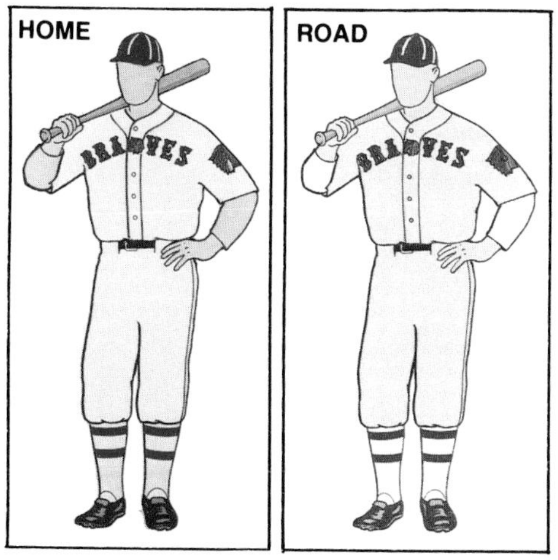

BROOKLYN

ST. LOUIS

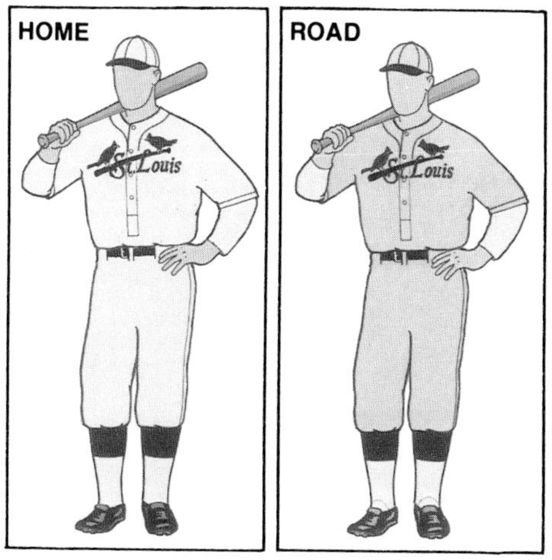

PITTSBURGH

PHILADELPHIA

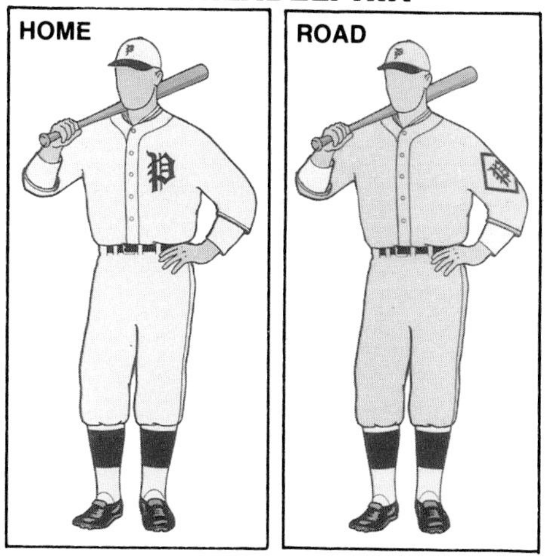

CHICAGO

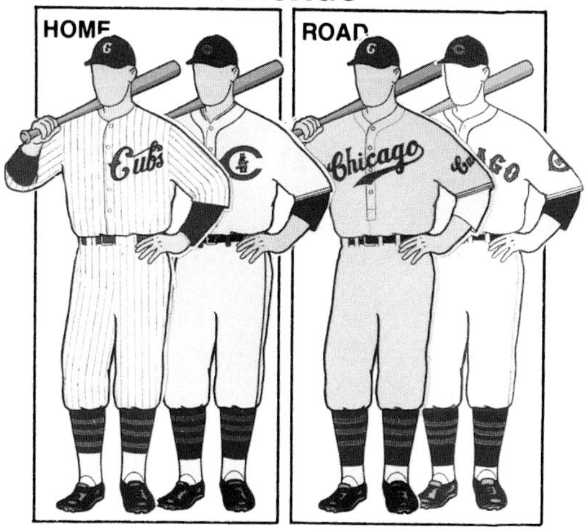

CINCINNATI

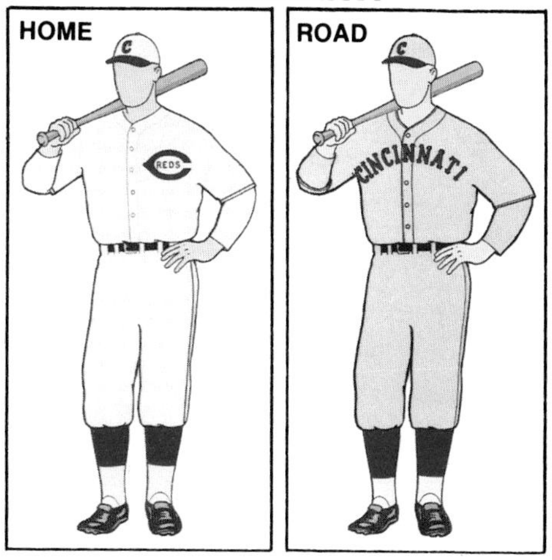

NEW YORK

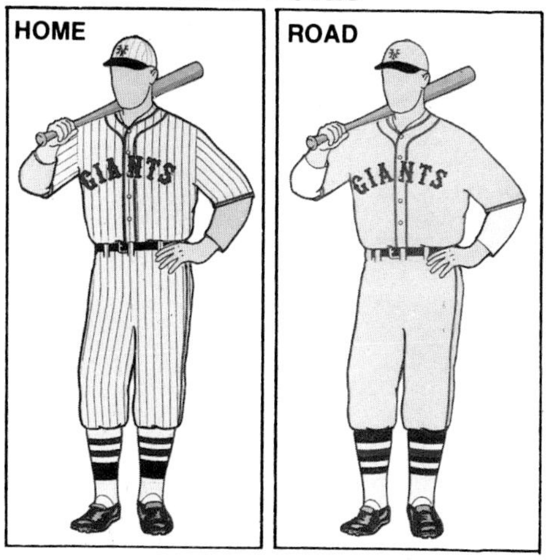

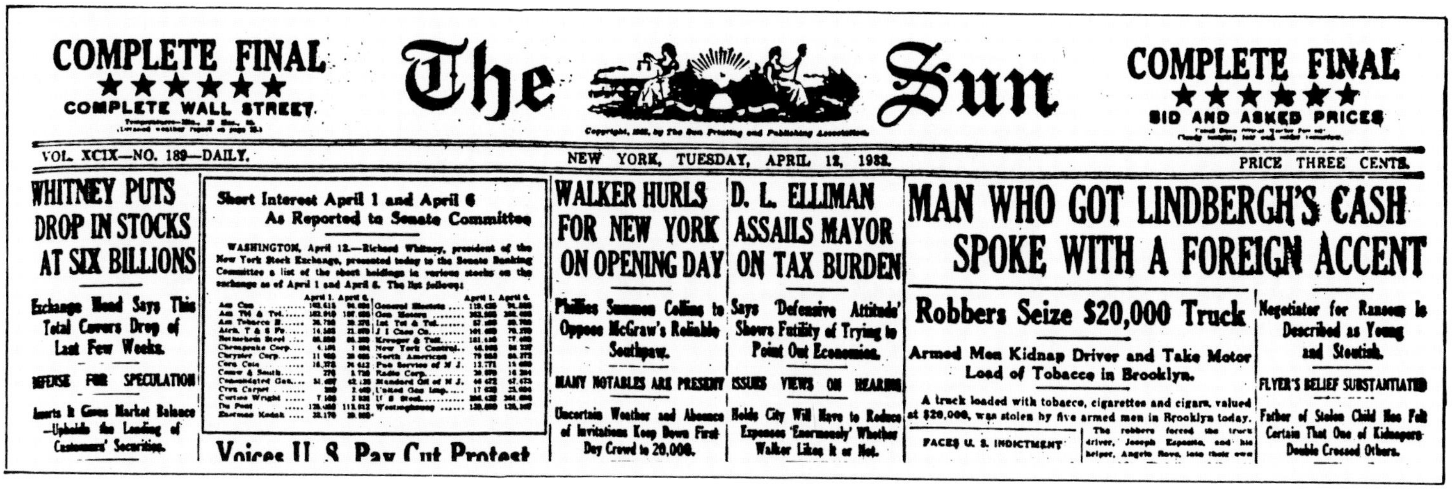
COMPLETE FINAL ★★★★★★ COMPLETE WALL STREET

The Sun

COMPLETE FINAL ★★★★★★ BID AND ASKED PRICES

VOL. XCIX—NO. 189—DAILY. NEW YORK, TUESDAY, APRIL 12, 1932. PRICE THREE CENTS.

WHITNEY PUTS DROP IN STOCKS AT SIX BILLIONS

Exchange Head Says This Total Covers Drop of Last Few Weeks.

DEFENSE FOR SPECULATION

Asserts It Gives Market Balance—Upholds the Lending of Customers' Securities.

Short Interest April 1 and April 6 As Reported to Senate Committee

Voices U. S. Pay Cut Protest

WALKER HURLS FOR NEW YORK ON OPENING DAY

Phillies Summon Collins to Oppose McGraw's Reliable Southpaw.

MANY NOTABLES ARE PRESENT

Uncertain Weather and Absence of Invitations Keep Down First Day Crowd to 20,000.

D. L. ELLIMAN ASSAILS MAYOR ON TAX BURDEN

Says 'Defensive Attitude' Shows Futility of Trying to Point Out Economies.

ISSUES VIEWS ON HEARING

Holds City Will Have to Reduce Expenses 'Enormously' Whether Walker Likes It or Not.

MAN WHO GOT LINDBERGH'S CASH SPOKE WITH A FOREIGN ACCENT

Robbers Seize $20,000 Truck

Armed Men Kidnap Driver and Take Motor Load of Tobacco in Brooklyn.

A truck loaded with tobacco, cigarettes and cigars, valued at $20,000, was stolen by five armed men in Brooklyn today.

FACES U. S. INDICTMENT

Negotiator for Ransom Is Described as Young and Stoutish.

FLYER'S BELIEF SUBSTANTIATED

Father of Stolen Child Has Felt Certain That One of Kidnapers Double Crossed Others.

1933 AMERICAN LEAGUE

BOSTON

CLEVELAND

DETROIT

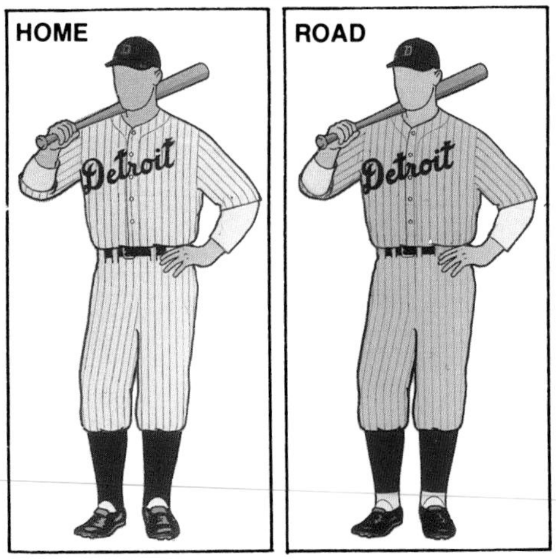

ST. LOUIS

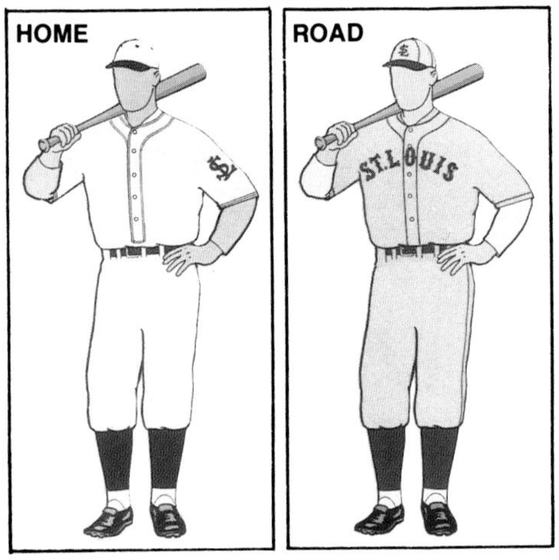

NEW YORK

PHILADELPHIA

CHICAGO

WASHINGTON

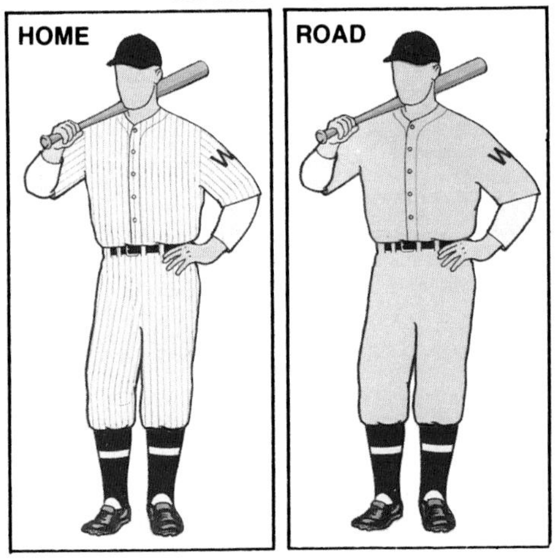

Deal That Brought Finn to Phillies a "Clean Steal" Admits Brooklyn L

SPORTS | The Philadelphia Inquirer | SPOR

PHILADELPHIA, THURSDAY MORNING, APRIL 13, 1933

ROOSEVELT SEES SENATORS BEAT A'S, 4 T

CUBS, PIRATES, INDIANS AND SOX SCORE W

CRONIN'S THUMPING AND STRATEGY SEND MACKMEN TO DEFEAT

Another Capital Inaugural - - - Baseball Back for Long Term

CAREY COUNTIN BENGE, BUT ASS HE WAS OUTSWA

NATIONAL LEAGUE 1933

BOSTON

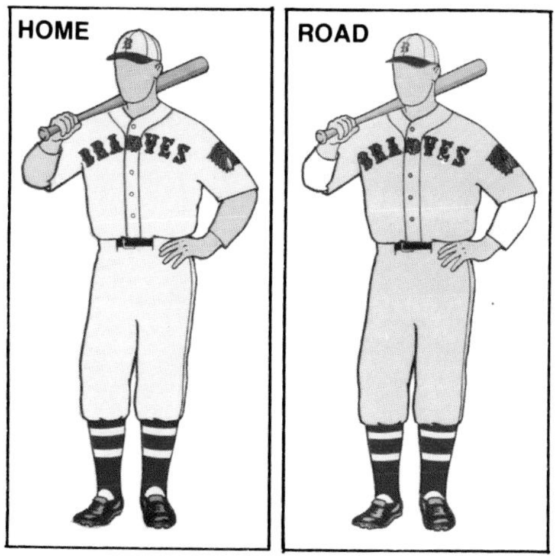

BROOKLYN

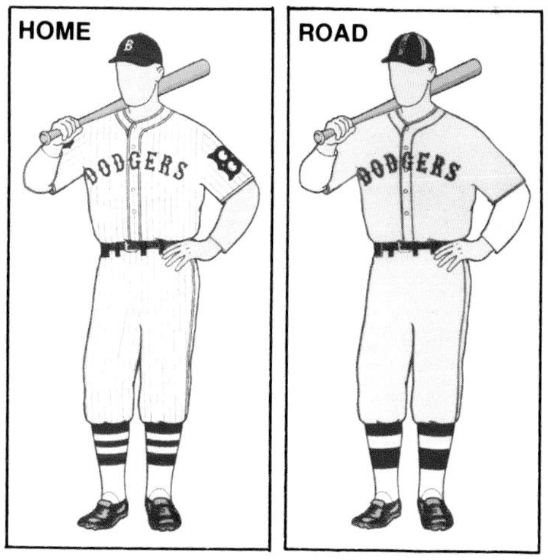

ST. LOUIS

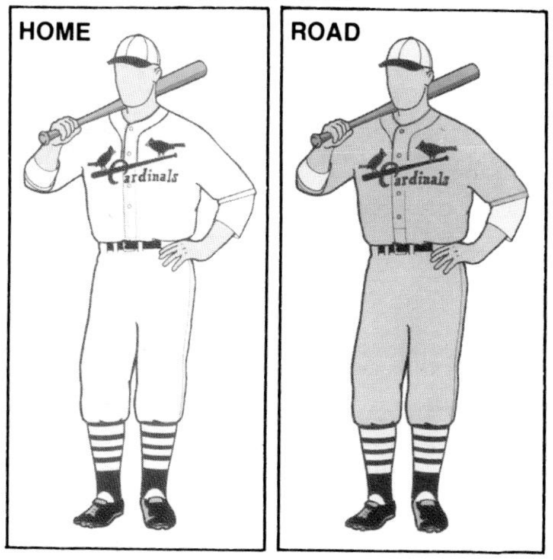

PITTSBURGH

PHILADELPHIA

CHICAGO

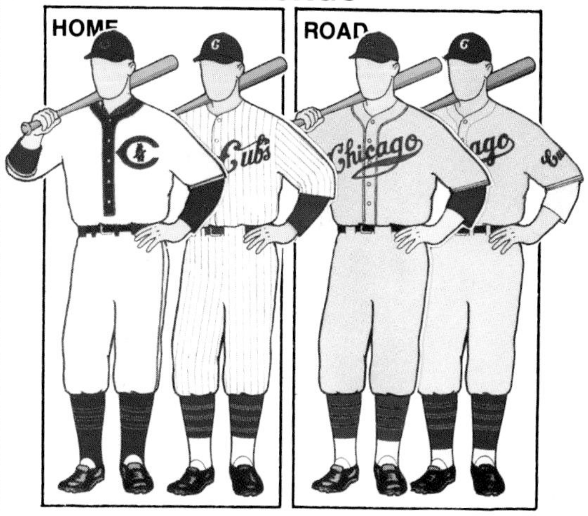

FIRST
ALL-STAR GAME
Comiskey Park
Chicago

CINCINNATI

NEW YORK

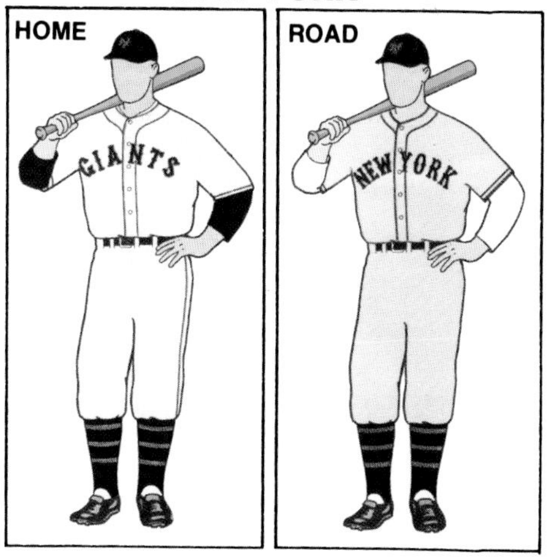

OCTOBER 12 — THE SPORTING NEWS — PAGE 3

Giants Outplay and Outgeneral Senators in Gaining World's Title

Pitching of New York Club Silences Washington Attack, With Hubbell Blazing Way

Batting of Melvin Ott Plays Important Part in Victory Which Leaves A. L. Adherents Groggy; National Leaguers Make Their Own Breaks in Winning

By DICK FARRINGTON

THE GIANTS did it! The same Giants who bulldogged their way to the National League pennant, who shook off the challenge of the Pirates, who smashed the Braves down when they reared up late in the campaign and then put the works on the Cubs, are the champions of baseball. With characteristic gameness and with bright, forward, aggressive playing they knocked the supposedly superior Washington team over in four games out of five to move into the purple throne room. Partisan fans, stunned by the quick defeat of the Senators, were inclined to charge the reversal to bad breaks. This could be expected. The Sena-

POLO GROUNDS RESOUNDS TO FIRST WORLD'S SERIES SINCE 1924

1934 AMERICAN LEAGUE

BOSTON

CLEVELAND

DETROIT

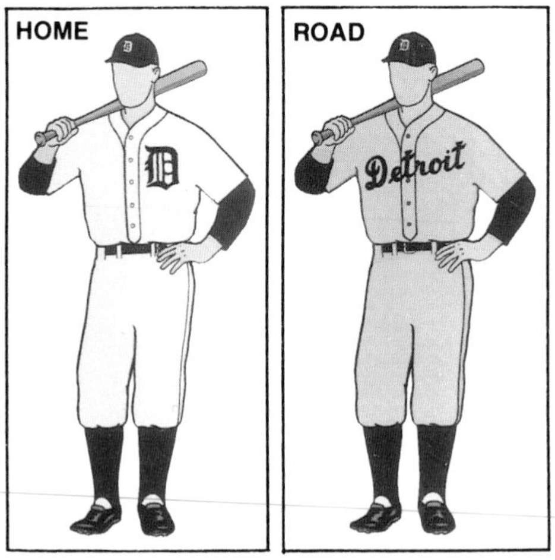

ST. LOUIS

NEW YORK

PHILADELPHIA

CHICAGO

WASHINGTON

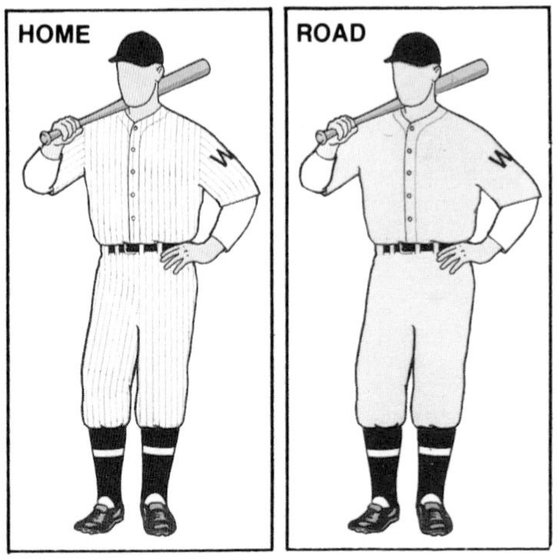

CHARLIE GEHRINGER
Announces the Official Opening of His Standard Service Station
WEDNESDAY, SEPT. 12

WRESTLING OLYMPIA
Fri. Sept. 14th.
The Prize Bout of the Year
McCREADY vs. ROMANO
ZAHARIAS vs. BRONOWICZ
GARIBALDI VS. ZELLER
MacDOUGALL VS. DeVITO

THE WEATHER

The Detroit News

—THE HOME NEWSPAPER—

-HOME-
EDITION
COMPLETE WANT ADS

FRIDAY, MAY 18, 1934, 61st Year, No. 269.

52 Pages—THREE CENTS

DILLINGER SOUGHT IN FLINT BANK RAID

BILLION-DOLLAR DEPOSITOR AID IS IN PROSPECT

Jam Blocking Payoff Broken and Steagall Bill Will Pass, Leaders Declare.

Danger of Splitting Measure Involving Bank Insurance Believed Ended.

Britain-Bound

SINGLE LICENSE SCHEME LEGAL

Lodge Plan Depends Only on Action by Board, Says Goldstick Ruling.

A Lifetime to Think It Over

$25,000 IN CASH TAKEN BY THUGS

Bandits Carry Machine Gun and Pistols; Woman on Guard Outside.

ABBOTT FACES INQUIRY BY SENATE AND HOUSE

Vandenberg and Weideman Act to Bring Investigation Into Charge Tighe Asked

NATIONAL LEAGUE 1934

BOSTON

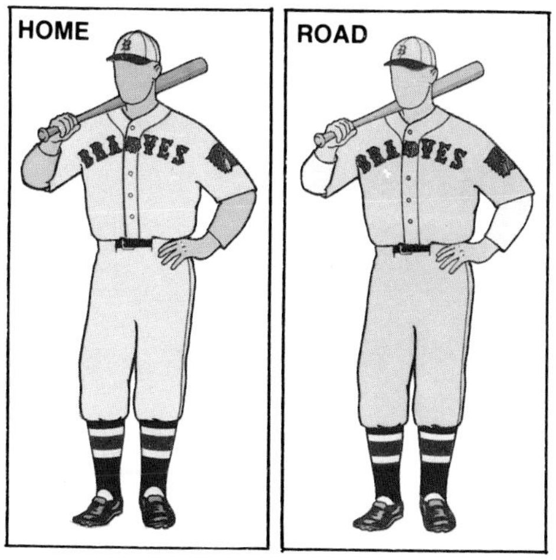

BROOKLYN

ST. LOUIS

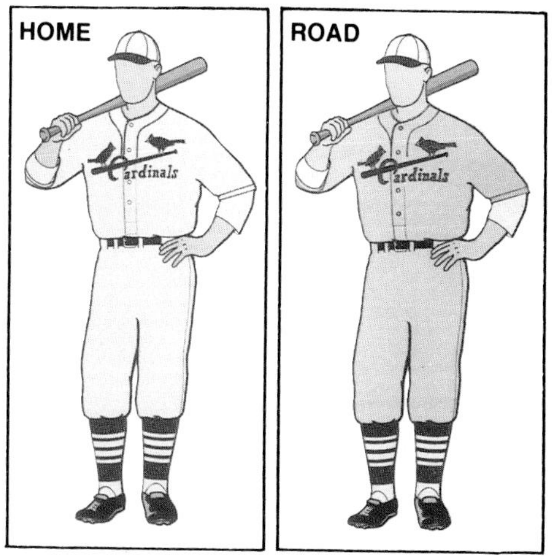

PITTSBURGH

PHILADELPHIA

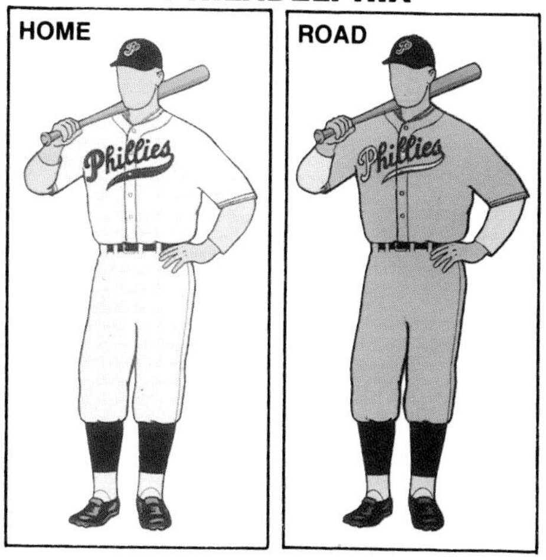

CHICAGO

CINCINNATI

NEW YORK

Medwick Exonerated

Apparently that rumor of the Cardinals' sale was the only thing spiked at Detroit.

POST-DISPATCH SPORTS

He Has a Slice of That

Detroit fans threw all kinds of fruit at Medwick except the world series melon.

PART TWO — ST. LOUIS, WEDNESDAY, OCTOBER 10, 1934. — PAGES 1—6B

CARDINALS' WORLD SERIES VICTORY A TRIUMPH OF DEANS

Landis Says Medwick Took Blame for Row at Third

Cardinal Would Not Accuse Owen of Giving Him Jolt With Knee

By W. J. McGoogan.

Cardinal left fielder, suffered the very unusual ... ordered out of a world series game in the final at ...

Landis Banishes Medwick—*and the Play That Caused It All*

DIZZY'S PITCHING AND BATTING POTENT FACTORS IN WINNING FINAL GAME

By J. Roy Stockton

Frankie Frisch's Cardinals are champions of the baseball world and a new dynasty is in the throne room in the great American game. The Yankees had Ruth and Gehrig and the Athletics had Foxx, Simmons and Grove and now the Cardinals have Dean and Dean.

And because Jerome Herman and his brother, Paul, will be in St.

FINAL GAME BOX SCORE

1935 AMERICAN LEAGUE

BOSTON

CLEVELAND

DETROIT

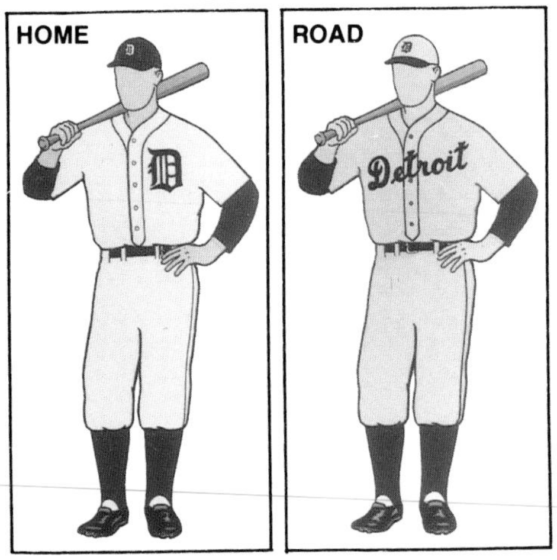

ST. LOUIS

NEW YORK

PHILADELPHIA

CHICAGO

WASHINGTON

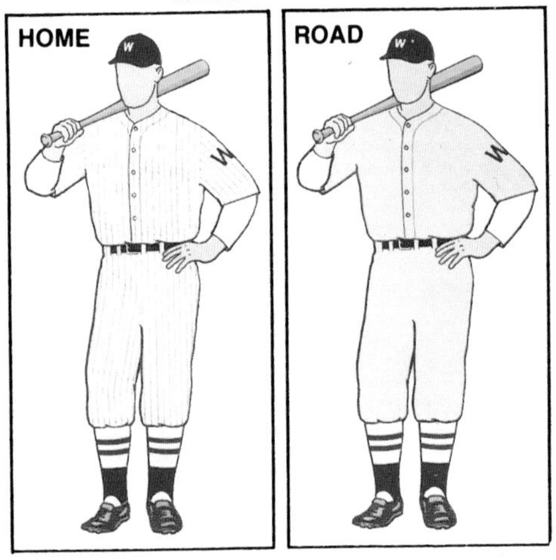

SPORTS FINANCIAL

The Detroit News

THE HOME NEWSPAPER

SPORTS RADIO

FOR BEST RESULTS—NEWS WANT ADS

SUNDAY, OCTOBER 6, 1935.

Tigers Win, 2-1, and Need Only One More to Take Title

State Gives Michigan Lesson in Foot Ball

Pass, Plunge and Run to Easy 25-6 Victory

Spartans Repeat 1934 Performance, Outrush Beefy Wolverine Line in Opening Game as 45,000 Look on

By JOHN E. McMANIS

Here It Is! The Run That All but Clinched the World Series!

Crowder Holds Lead Given Him on Errors

Clifton Circles Sacks in the Sixth on Two Misplays to Score Winning Run

By H. G. SALSINGER

CHICAGO, Oct. 5.—Detroit is tonight within one game of the world's base ball championship. The veteran Alvin Crowder realized a lifelong ambition when he pitched Detroit to a 2-to-1 victory over Chicago, giving the Tigers a 3-to-1 advantage over the Cubs, and tomorrow afternoon Tommy Bridges will try to

NATIONAL LEAGUE 1935

BOSTON

BROOKLYN

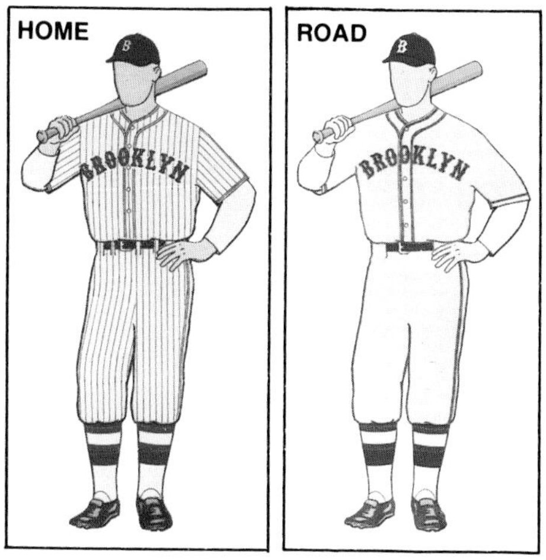

ST. LOUIS

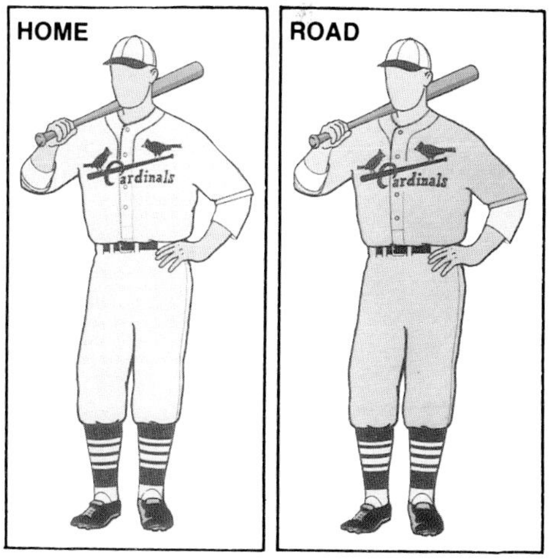

PITTSBURGH

PHILADELPHIA

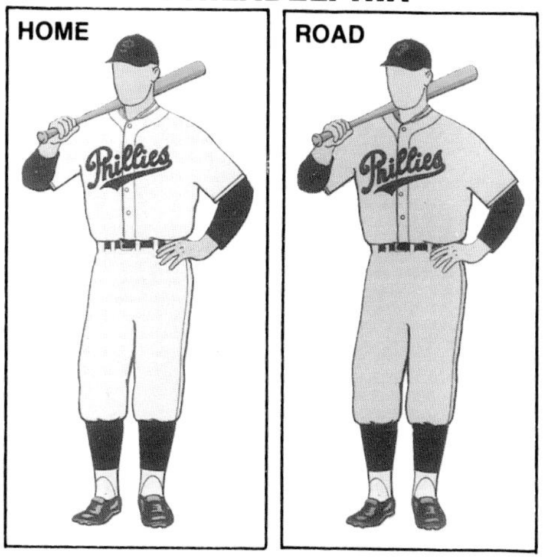

CHICAGO

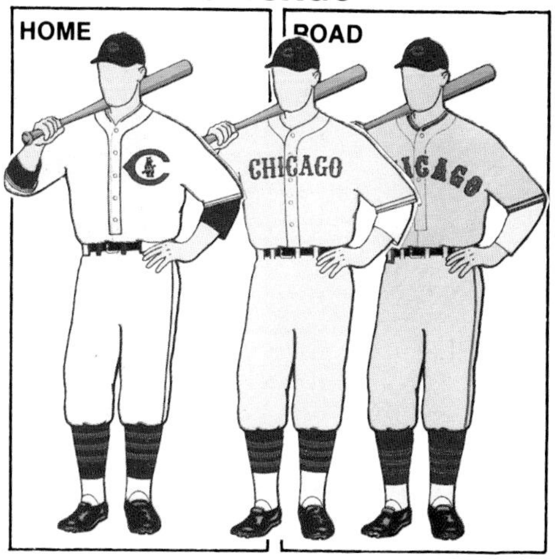

CINCINNATI

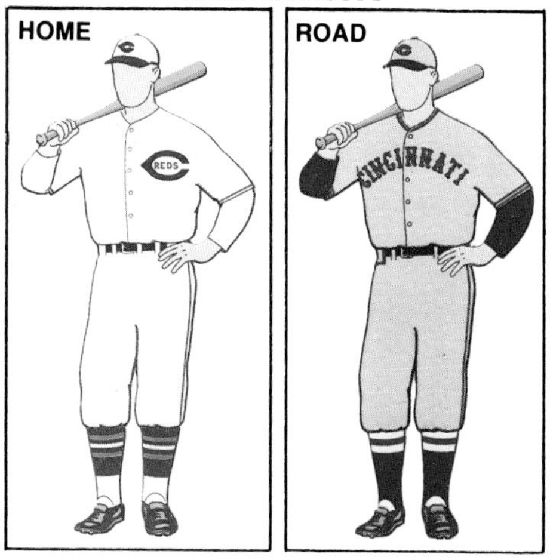

NEW YORK

FINAL EDITION

THE CINCINNATI ENQUIRER

WEATHER —

VOL. XCV. NO. 46—DAILY SATURDAY MORNING, MAY 25, 1935 24 PAGES THREE CENTS

REDLEGS DEFEAT PHILS IN NIGHT GAME

AIR WAVES

To Carry Music

Of Festival To All Parts Of World Today.

Composition By Cincinnatian

Today's Program

AFTERNOON CONCERT.

MERGING

Of Boards Waits.

Presbyteries To Study Proposal For Year.

Decision Due At Assembly

Scenes At First Night Game

BIG PAUL

Shoots 'Em Over.

Bowman Is Shaded In Mound Duel, 2-1.

Our Lads Make Four Blows

1936 AMERICAN LEAGUE

BOSTON

CLEVELAND

DETROIT

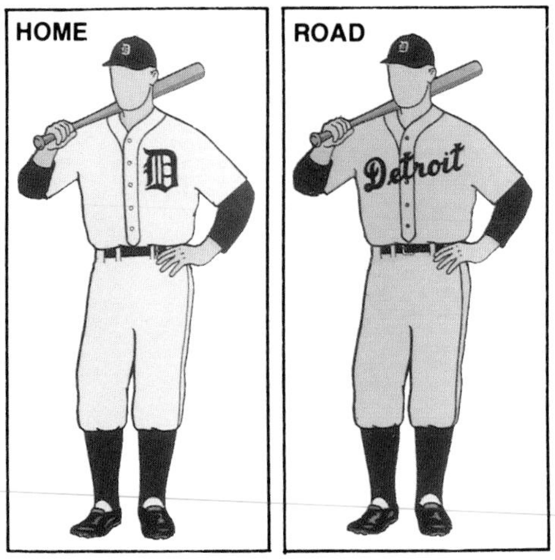

ST. LOUIS

NEW YORK

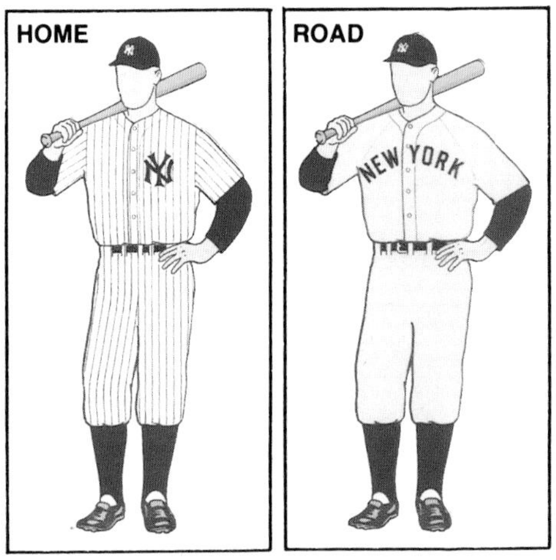

PHILADELPHIA

CHICAGO

WASHINGTON

THE NEW YORK SUN, WEDNESDAY, APRIL 15, 1936.

Both BarrelS

Primo Carnera Ready to Retire | *Former Champion Pretty Well Fixed*

By DAMON RUNYON

New York American Sports

WEDNESDAY, APRIL 15, 1936

Yanks Bow to Senators, 1-0

REYNOLDS' HIT IN 9TH BREAKS UP GAME

MEL HITS ONE!

Giants Rout Dodgers, 8 to 5, Before 55,592

BARTELL WINS OPENER WITH HOME RUN

NATIONAL LEAGUE 1936

BOSTON

BROOKLYN

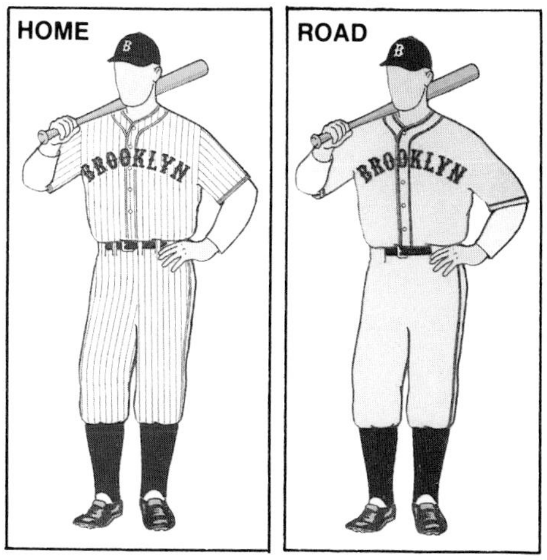

ST. LOUIS

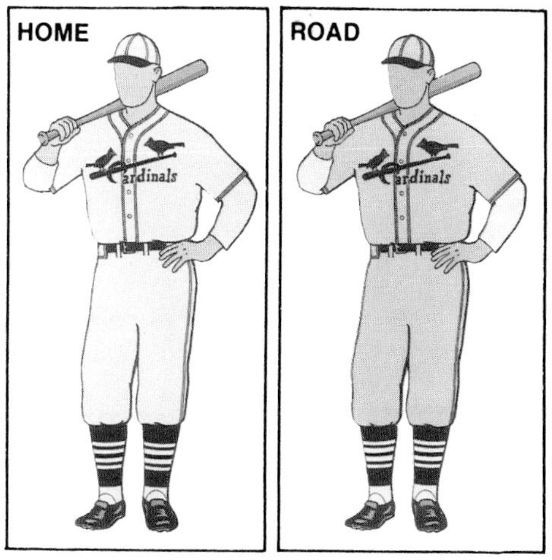

PITTSBURGH

PHILADELPHIA

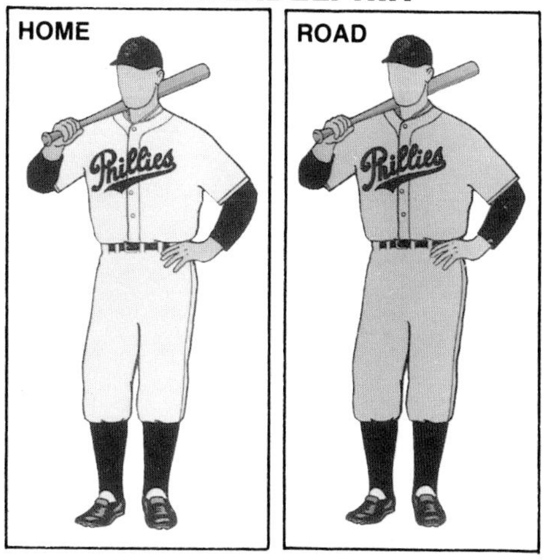

CHICAGO

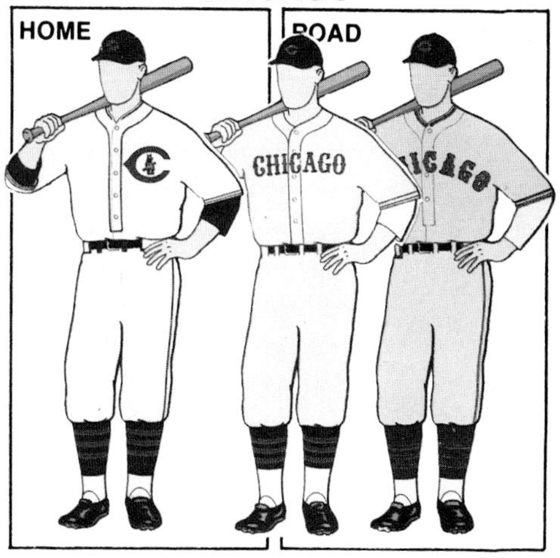

CINCINNATI

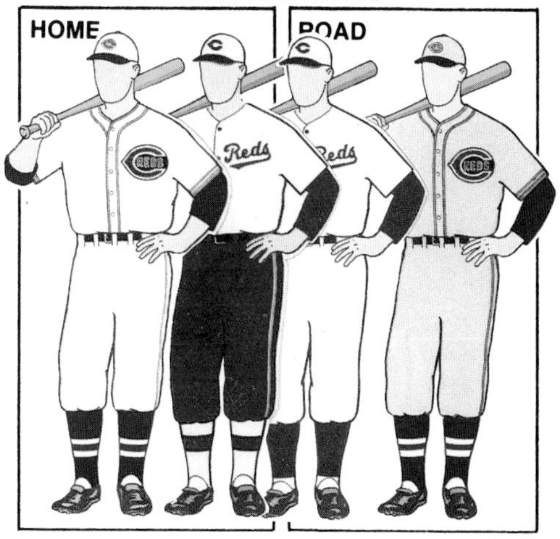

NEW YORK

MAJORS BOX SCORES MINORS

The Sporting News

THE BASE BALL PAPER OF THE WORLD

FROM ALL POINTS OF COMPASS BASEBALL NEWS-GOSSIP-COMMENT

VOLUME 101, NUMBER 15 — ST. LOUIS, MAY 28, 1936 — TEN CENTS

SHREWD DEALS NET PHILS $137,500 AND CHUCK KLEIN

MEDWICK PUTS WICK TO CARD FLAG FLAME

HARD-DRIVING OUTFIELDER STANDS GOOD CHANCE FOR BATTING TITLE

Sox Wins in 12 Road Games Rekindle Championship Hopes; Browns Fall Back After Catching Foothold

GAS ATTACK--Led by Gas House Gang Boss--Frisch Blows Off to Umps

TRAFFIC IN PLAYERS BRINGS BIG PROFITS

GERRY NUGENT GETS COIN WHETHER STARS ARE COMING OR GOING

Swaps for Three Davises, Whitney, Wilson Among Profitable Transactions; A's Bog Down When Hitting Fails

1937 AMERICAN LEAGUE

BOSTON

CLEVELAND

DETROIT

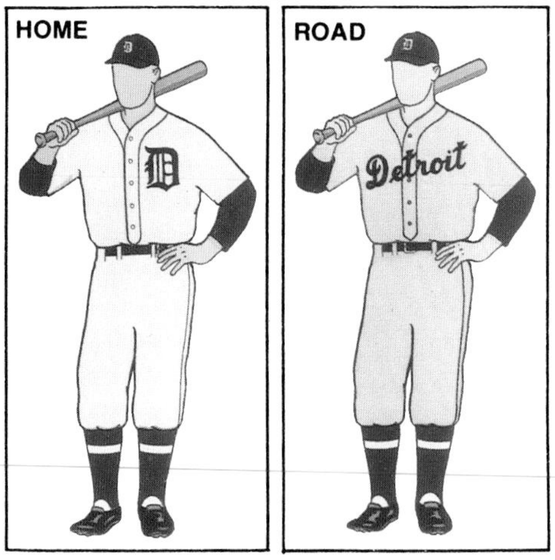

ST. LOUIS

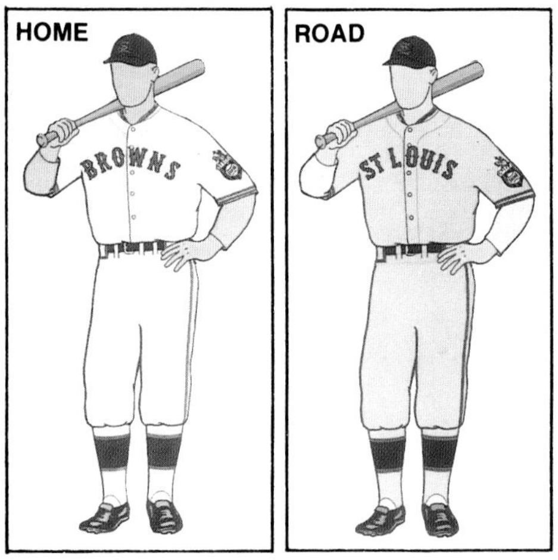

NEW YORK

PHILADELPHIA

CHICAGO

WASHINGTON

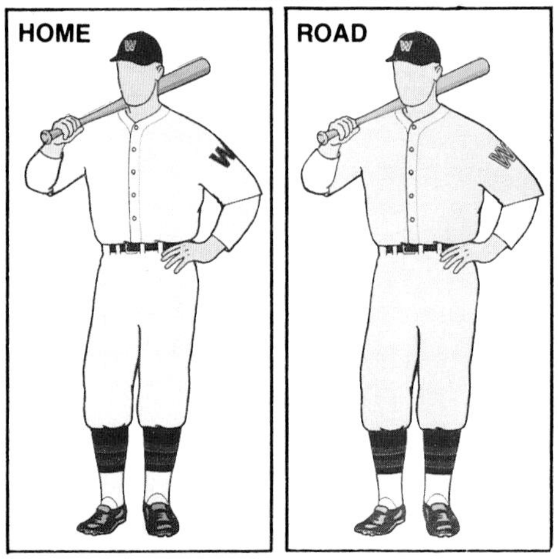

COMPLETE FINAL ★★★★★★ RACING—LATE SPORTS

The Sun

COMPLETE FINAL ★★★★★★ BID AND ASKED PRICES

VOL. CIV—NO. 195—DAILY. NEW YORK, TUESDAY, APRIL 20, 1937. PRICE THREE CENTS.

YANKS FACE SENATORS BEFORE 50,000 FANS

Dodgers and Giants Play Before 37,000 Crowd—Metropolitan Teams Open Season.

Eighty-seven thousand spectators helped the New York Yankees open the American League season at the Stadium and the Brooklyn Dodgers and New York Giants began the National League campaign at Ebbets Field today. There were 50,000 persons at the Stadium.

FATHER DIVINE MISSING AFTER CUTTING SCRAPE

Harlem 'God' Disappears and Police Alarm Is Out for Him.

THREE NEGROES ARRESTED

'Kingdom's' Leader Accused of Assaulting Process Server—Sermon Interrupted.

FRAUD CHARGED IN MOVE TO GET NEW VICE TRIAL

Supreme Court Summons Luciano's Attorneys to Answer Accusations.

DEWEY QUESTIONS LAWYERS

They Deny Affidavits Are False—One Accuses Justice McCook of Bias and Unfairness.

PRESIDENT HINTS NEW TAXES IN 1938; REQUESTS $1,500,000,000 FOR RELIEF

INJUNCTION HALTS MAINE SHOE STRIKE

Judge Finds Union Lacked Requisite Membership.

LEWISTON, Me., April 20 (A. P.)

British Income Tax Increased To 25 Per Cent in New Budget

Chamberlain Presents $4,314,240,000 Plan to Commons—Armament Expenditures Are Blamed for Rise.

Message to Congress Says Treasury Will Report on Tax Study in November.

1937 DEFICIT $2,557,000,000

Roosevelt Figures Bring Debt to $35,500,000,000—New

NATIONAL LEAGUE 1937

BOSTON

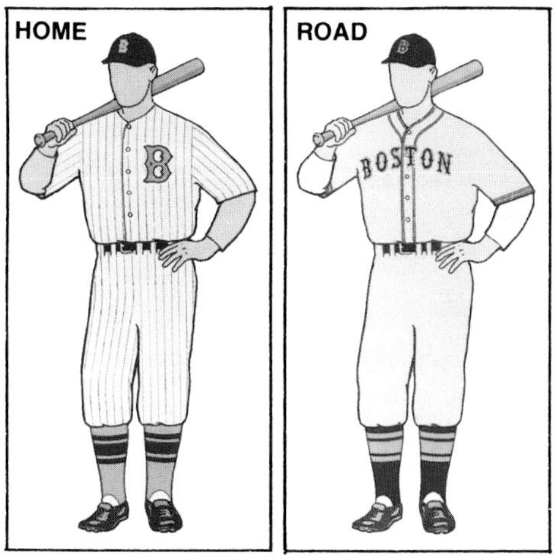

BROOKLYN

ST. LOUIS

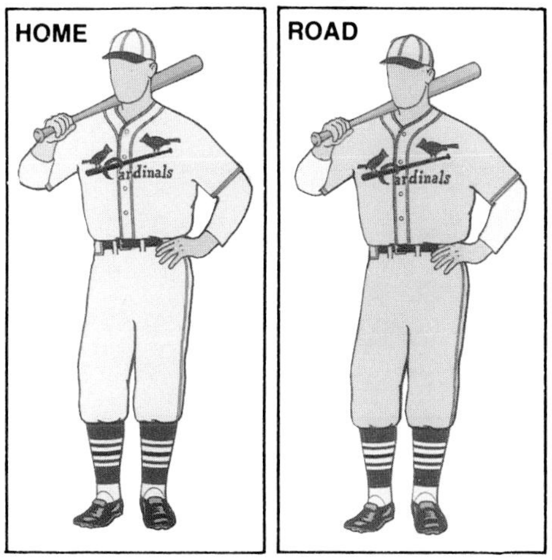

PITTSBURGH

PHILADELPHIA

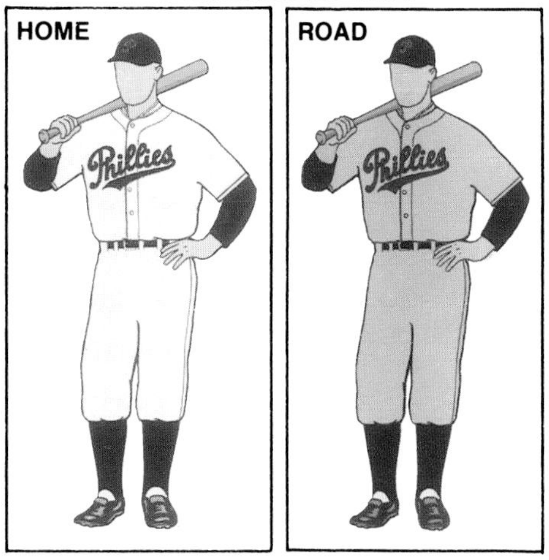

CHICAGO

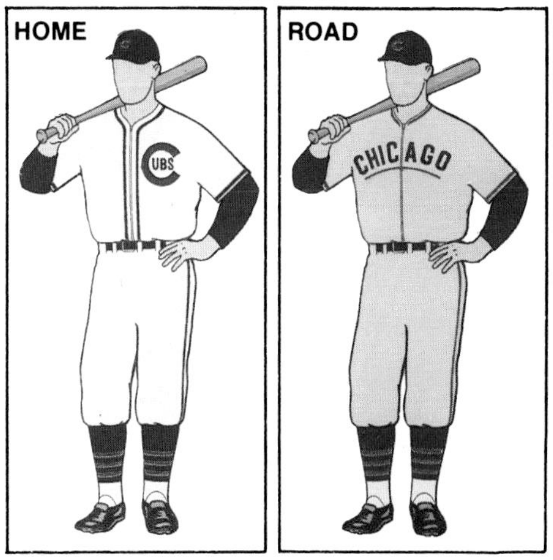

On the Radio Today

(Saturday, April 17)
EASTERN STANDARD TIME

In the Spotlight

1.30 P. M.—WCAU, WABC—Al Smith, others.
2.00—KYW, WEAF—"Carmen," by Metropolitan Opera Company.
2.30—WIP—Clyde Pangborn, Clarence Chamberlain, others.
4.00—WABC—Columbia-Oxford debate.
8.00—WFIL, WJZ—Ed Wynn, Graham McNamee.
KYW, WEAF—James Melton, others.
8.30—WIP—"Philadelphia Parade of Events"
9.00—WCAU, WABC—Songs by Grace Moore.
9.30—KYW, WEAF—Joe Cook, Carl Hubbell, Albert Spalding.
10.00—WCAU, WABC—Hit Parade; Lanny Ross.
11.00—WABC—Benny Goodman's Orchestra (WCAU at 11.10).

SUNDAY

10.00 A. M.—KYW, WEAF—Radio Pulpit.
2.00 P. M.—WFIL, WJZ—Stokowski, Iturbi, Ormandy, O'Connell conducting Philadelphia Orchestra.
3.00—WCAU, WABC—New York Philharmonic.
5.30—WCAU, WABC—Guy Lombardo's Orchestra.
6.30—WCAU, WABC—Rubinoff, Eddie Cantor.
7.00—KYW, WEAF—Jack Benny.
8.00—WCAU, WABC—Victor Moore, Helen Broderick.
WFIL, WJZ—Richard Crooks, others.
8.30—WCAU, WABC—Eddie Cantor.
9.00—WFIL, WJZ—Frank Parker, Shep Fields' Orchestra.
WCAU, WABC—Nelson Eddy.
10.00—KYW, WEAF—Gladys Swarthout.

WHERE TO TUNE

WFIL WIP WABC WCAU KYW WJZ WEAF

CINCINNATI

NEW YORK

THE WEATHER

NEW YORK **Herald Tribune** LATE CITY EDITION

Vol. XCVII No. 33,045 FRIDAY, MAY 7, 1937

Hindenburg Explodes at Lakehurst, 34 Die; Dirigible, Landing, Falls 500 Feet in Flames

Horror Dazes Field Crowd Unable to Aid

63 Survive in Plunge Of Burning Zeppelin

1938 AMERICAN LEAGUE

BOSTON

CLEVELAND

DETROIT

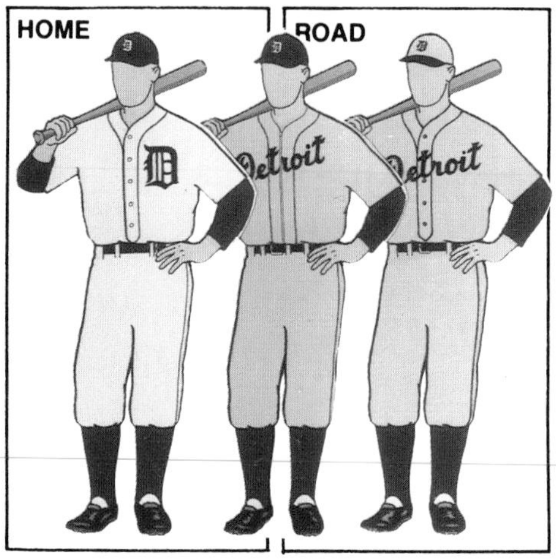

ST. LOUIS

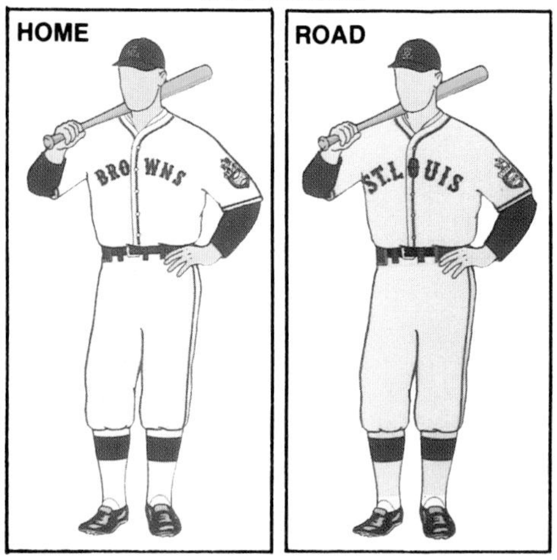

NEW YORK

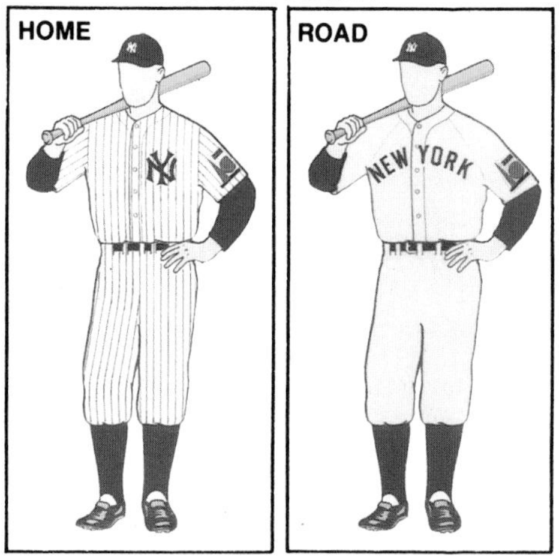

PHILADELPHIA

CHICAGO

WASHINGTON

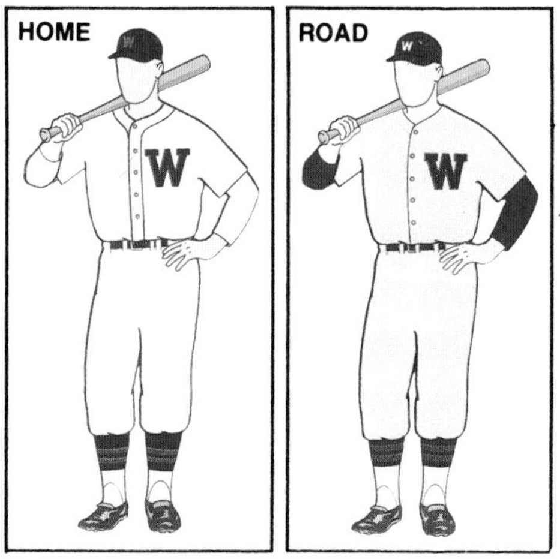

Stuart Bell

Ruminations on Master Bob Then He Pitches One-Hitter Not Just Another Hurler Now

Even before Bob Feller had completed his sensational pitching against St. Louis yesterday I had been thinking about the spot this young man was in. It had occurred to me that now he was just another pitcher.

I wasn't thinking that he was just another pitcher in the matter of ability, but that he was in the matter of earnings.

Feller, though his salary hasn't been announced, is getting more money this year than Mel Harder, who has been an Indian ace for eight years and who won six more games than Bob in 1937. Feller is the best-paid Cleveland pitcher next to Johnny Allen, who signed a two-year contract that calls for something like $19,000 a season.

Stuart Bell

Peak of Earning Power Reached at 19—

My ruminations on Feller were to the effect that, unless he turned out to be a steady winner of games, he was, at 19, at the peak of his earning power despite the fact he was no more than getting started in baseball.

Certainly, on his won and lost record of 1937 he wasn't worth the

Dean and Di Mag Were 'All Set for Headlines When 'Along Came a L'il Feller

The Press Sports

28 CLEVELAND, THURSDAY, APRIL 21, 1938 28

"HEAVYWEIGHT THINKER"

ATLANTA, April 21—Declaring himself to be a "heavyweight thinker," Man Mountain Dean today began his campaign for the Georgia General Assembly. The 300-pound retired wrestler would be Representative Frank S. Leavitt if elected. His first athletic ventures were under the name of Soldier Leavitt. His bulk and whiskers are well known about the country.

Feller's Pitching Makes One-Hitter Look Too Easy

Back in the Headlines

Bob Exhibits "Spot" Control

Crowd Stays Cold, Even on Sullivan's Safe Bunt

By FRANK GIBBONS

Bob Feller, the kid with the big feet, big heart and big ambition to be a completely polished big league pitcher, today had arrived in the ranks of those hurlers who make a one-hit performance look routine.

We know you're tired of hearing this bashful country boy termed a blaze ball king, a fast ball phenom,

Di Mag Speeds to Yanks

By United Press

ABOARD STREAMLINED TRAIN CITY OF SAN FRANCISCO EN ROUTE TO CHICAGO, April 21—Joe Di Maggio, team's highest paid baseball player, who is losing $162.35 for every game he does not play with the New York Yankees, sped eastward to join his team today after ending one of the most stubborn holdouts in the game's history.

This time yesterday the dark-haired Italian youth was lying in bed figuring the receipts of his cafe in San Francisco. Only Monday he had denied vehemently that he had any intention of accepting the $25,000 offer of Owner Jacob Ruppert. Yet, today he is 1800 miles away from his cafe. He will be in uniform at Yankee Stadium Saturday.

"It just came to me like that," Joe said when asked why he gave up his demands for $40,000 and accepted $25,000 so suddenly. He snapped the fingers of his powerful right hand to indicate just how suddenly the decision was made.

NATIONAL LEAGUE 1938

BOSTON

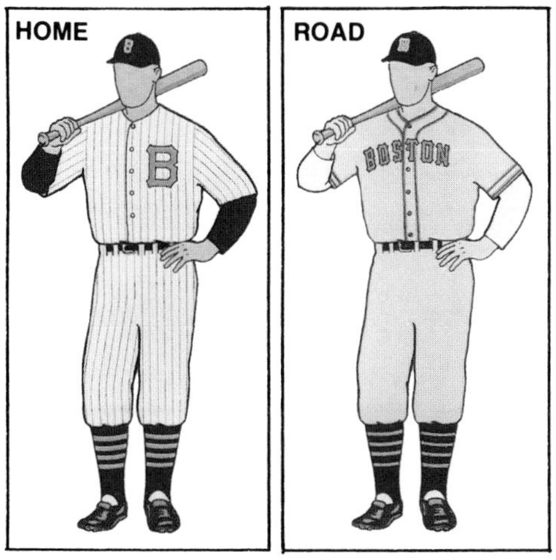

BROOKLYN

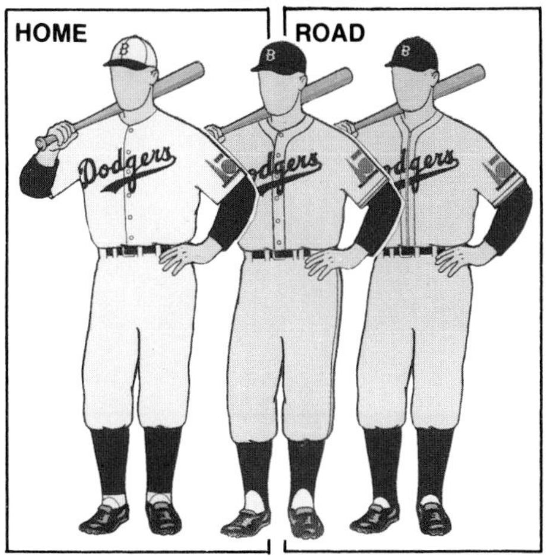

ST. LOUIS

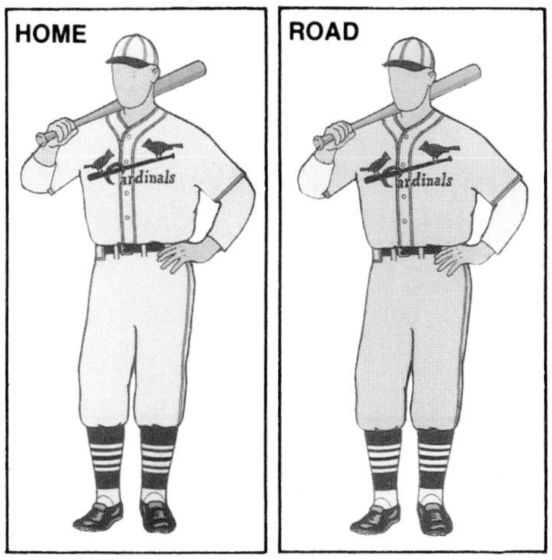

PITTSBURGH

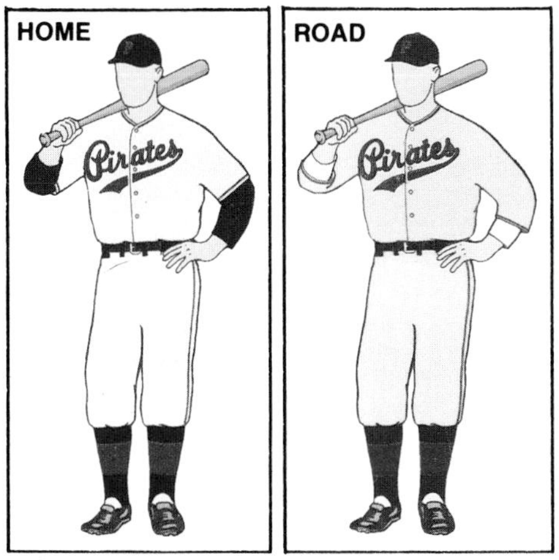

PHILADELPHIA

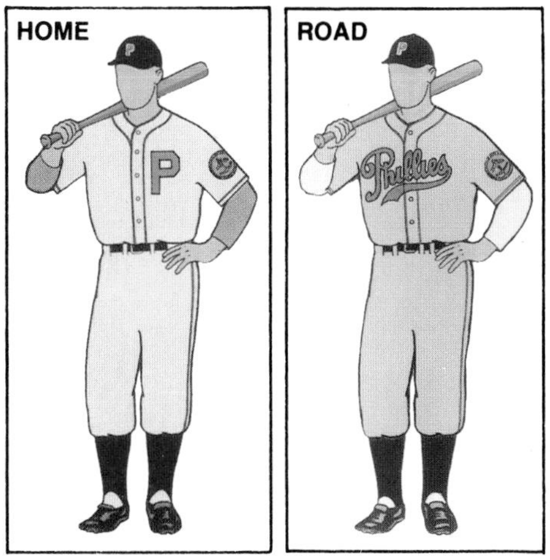

CHICAGO

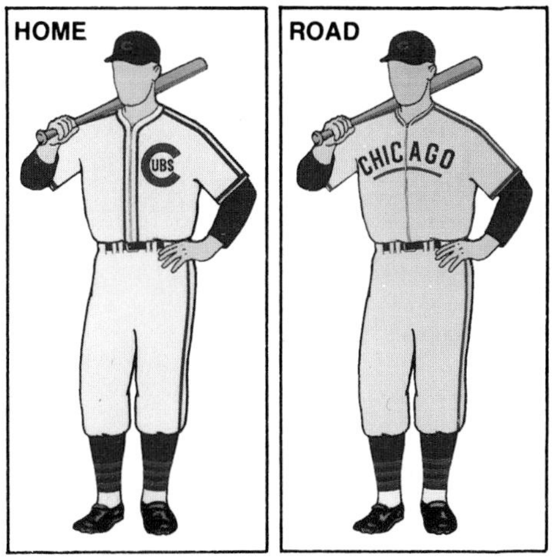

CINCINNATI

NEW YORK

Complete MARKETS THE CHICAGO DAILY NEWS FINAL Edition

THURSDAY, SEPTEMBER 29, 1938—FORTY PAGES. THREE CENTS

POWERS AGREE, AVERT WAR

★ ★ ★ ★ ★ ★

Cubs Jump Into Lead Over Pirates

BASEBALL SCORES | GET TO BAUERS | KEY MEN IN EUROPE'S PLIGHT | PRAGUE ACCEPTS | 4 Leaders Ready

1939 AMERICAN LEAGUE

BOSTON

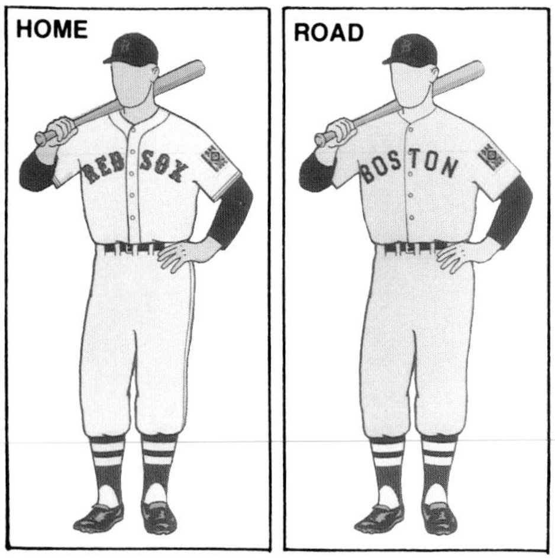

CLEVELAND

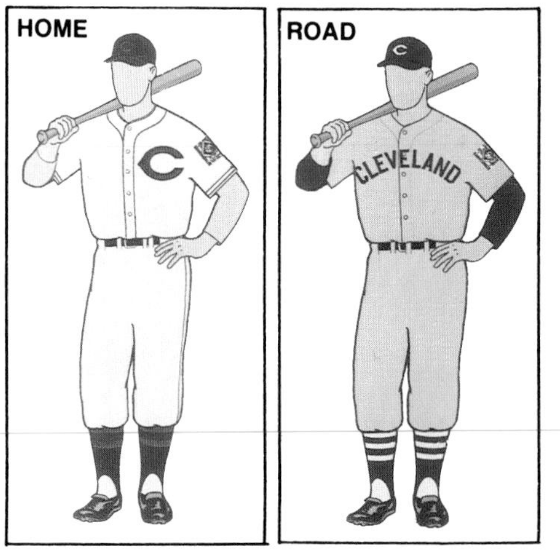

DETROIT

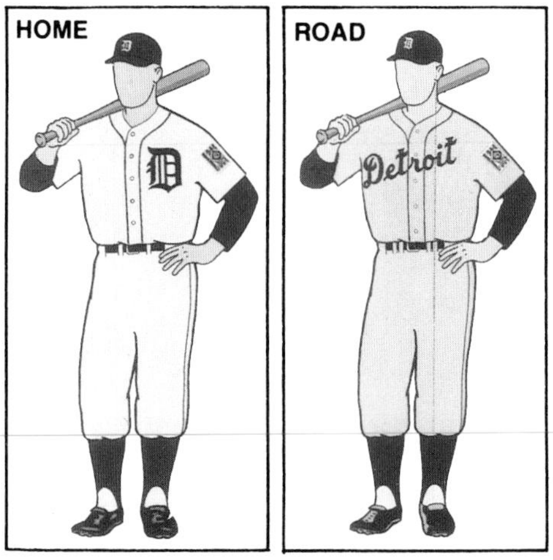

ST. LOUIS

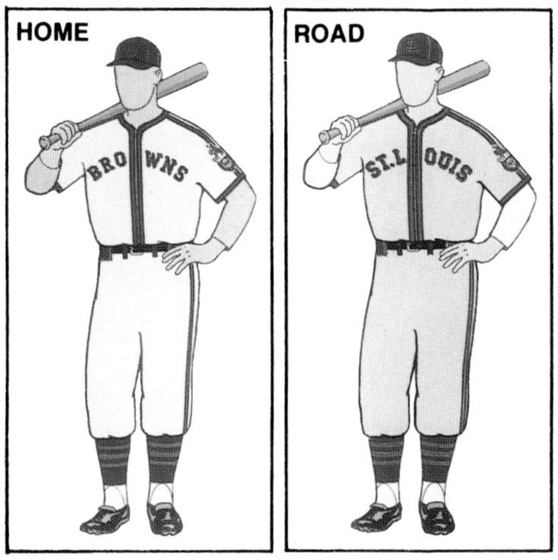

NEW YORK

PHILADELPHIA

CHICAGO

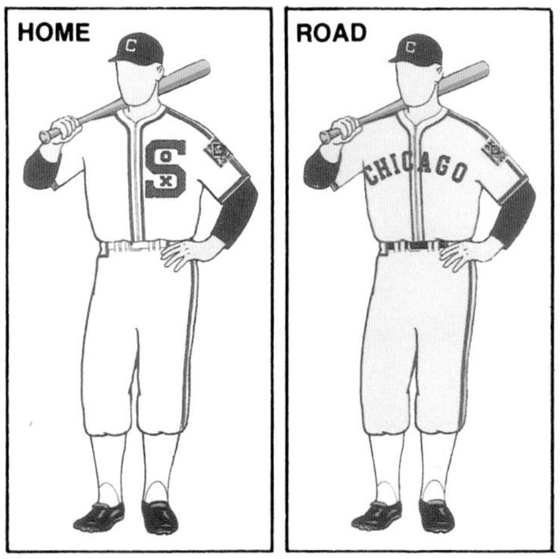

WASHINGTON

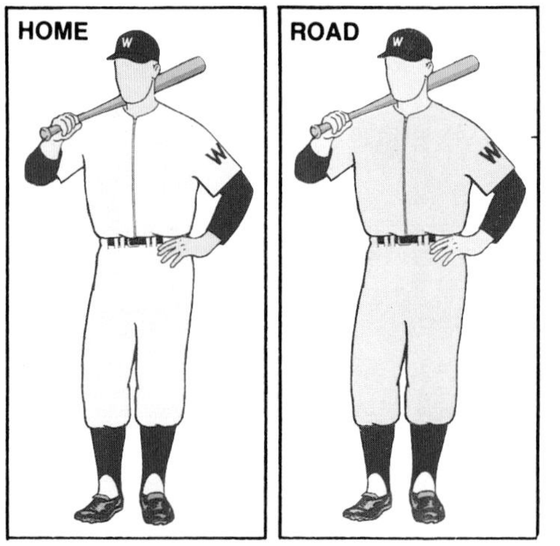

THE NEW YORK SUN, MONDAY, OCTOBER 9, 1939 — SPORTS — 25

Setting the Pace

By FRANK GRAHAM

The Yankees Just Wore Them Down.

CINCINNATI, Oct. 9.—The story of the world series is simple. The Yankees wore the Reds down and then knocked them out. The Yankees didn't hit as they can hit. Charlie Keller and Joe DiMaggio were the only players on their side to hit .300 or better. But the weight of their scattered blows was terrific and finally the Reds collapsed and went down with a soggy thud.

Through three games the Reds, although beaten, held up and fought back. Through part of the fourth game they not only fought back but actually seemed to be about to win. Then the Yankees bore down again and the Reds began to give all along the line. Their finish was rather pitiful. They wound up—so far as the actual outcome of the game was concerned—with Ernie Lombardi lying on the ground at the plate wondering what had become of the ball, while Yankee base runners skipped around him to score.

It was an unfortunate finish. Perhaps it was inevitable. Certainly no team reasonably could be expected to go on taking a physical and mental beating day after day without bogging down. The Reds against the Yankees were like Bob Pastor against Joe Louis. They looked all right, in spots. They . . . in a manner of speaking . . . won a round here and there. But it was only a question of time when the Yankees were going to catch up with them and flatten them—in four games, in five games, in six. It was incredible the series could go to seven games. Incredible that a team could withstand so long pressure such as the Yankees were putting on the Reds.

No Excitement in the Clubhouse.

The frayed and soggy finish of the final game had a reaction, curiously enough, in the Yankees' clubhouse. Maybe—although they are an unemotional lot—the Yankees would have been excited if the game had gone to a break-neck finish. As it was, they were about

Joe McCarthy Equals Connie Mack's World Series Winning Record

BULLPEN JINX DOGS WALTERS TO BITTER END

Pursued Major Leagues' Leading Pitcher Even Into World Series.

By THE OLD SCOUT.

Bucky Walters, a likable fellow with a wistful look in his eyes and a pointed chin, probably won't sleep nights trying to figure it out. Bucky this year was the best pitcher in his league and probably the most valuable player. But every time he carried his bowed legs out of the bullpen and onto the mound, trouble stalked him and delivered a death blow to the Reds.

It happened on opening day. It happened one cold, dark day at the Polo Grounds. It happened as the campaign closed like a

SITTING PRETTY AS HE RINGS UP THE TYING RUN

Wins Five Times Since 1932

Philadelphian Needed Twenty Years—Yanks Make It Four in Row on Schedule.

By EDWARD T. MURPHY.

CINCINNATI, Oct. 9.—Winners and still world champions, with their position on top of the baseball world more secure than ever before, Joe (Four Straight) McCarthy's awe-inspiring Yankees today must be proud of their rapid conquest of Bill McKechnie's National League pennant-winning Reds.

The Yankees achieved the unprecedented feat of capturing four world series in a row, attaining the distinction in the shortest time possible. Taking over his newest laurels McCarthy now shares with Connie Mack, manager of the Athletics and patriarch of the American League, the honors of having captured five world series championships.

No manager has directed six teams to victory in world series competition. Mack's world series successes were reaped over a twenty-year span, starting with his 1910 champions who vanquished the Cubs and ending with his triumph over the Cardinals in 1930.

McCarthy has crowded his five world championship emblems into

Yankee outfield functioned smoothly, with DiMaggio demonstrating his remarkable skill. Joe made one of his best catches in the series yesterday when he went far back and pulled down Ernie Lombardi's hard hit drive in the second inning. Joe almost made a sensational shoestring catch of Willard Hershberger's pinch hit single in the seventh. The ball sank sharply as Joe, after a long sprint towards the infield, tried to snare the pellet in his outstretched gloved hand.

"The ball just tipped the end of my gloved hand," explained Joe. "That was the first bit of acrobatics I ever went in for in the outfield. What did I look like when I was tumbling?"

NATIONAL LEAGUE 1939

BOSTON

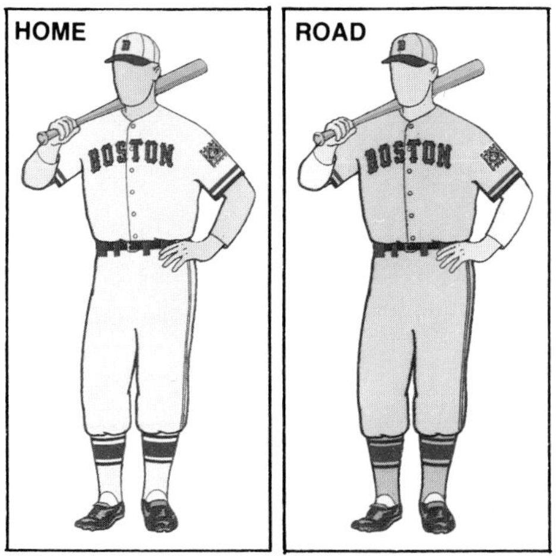

BROOKLYN

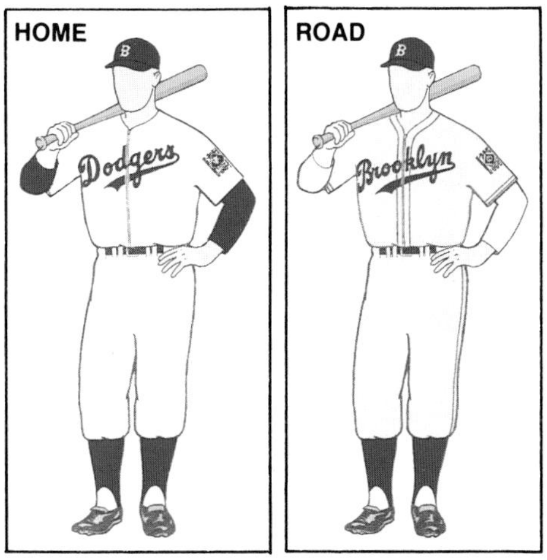

ST. LOUIS

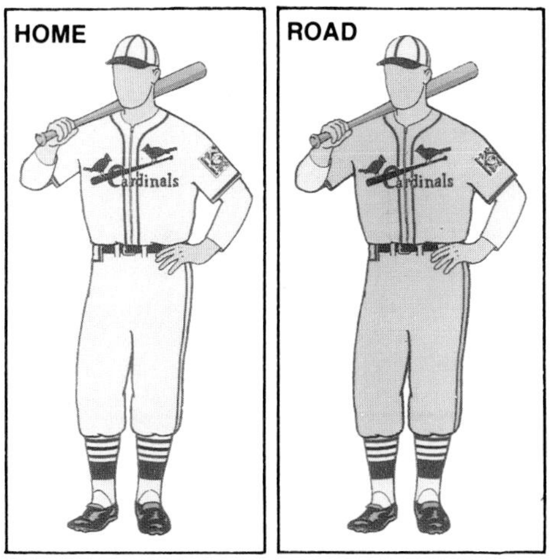

PITTSBURGH

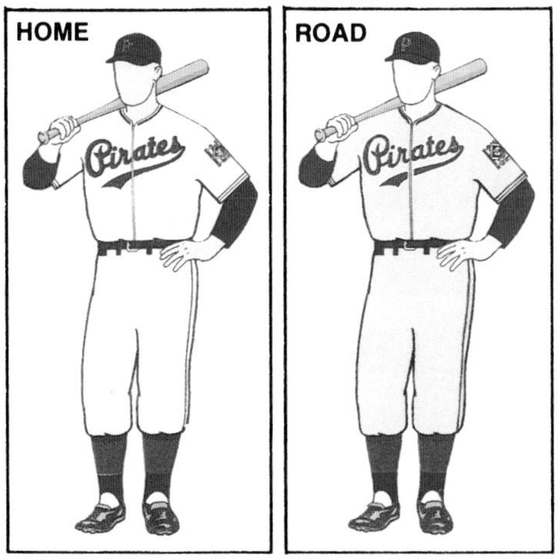

PHILADELPHIA

CHICAGO

CINCINNATI

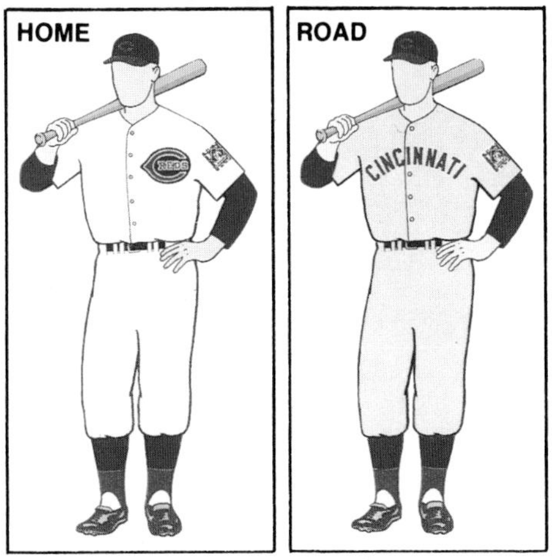

NEW YORK

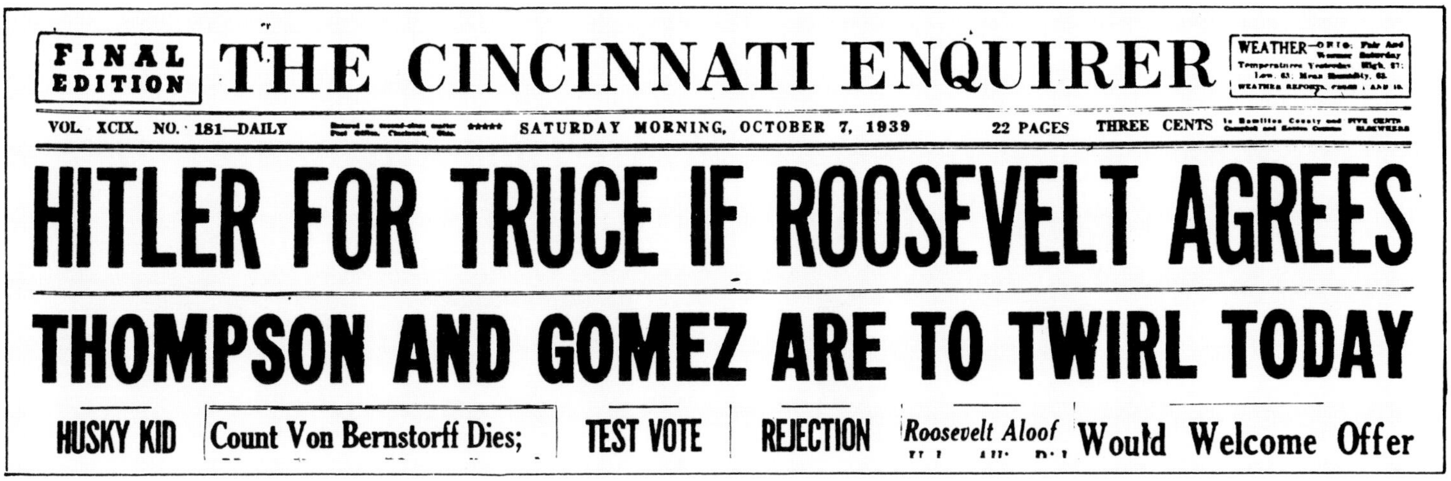

FINAL EDITION **THE CINCINNATI ENQUIRER**

VOL. XCIX. NO. 181—DAILY ★★★★★ SATURDAY MORNING, OCTOBER 7, 1939 22 PAGES THREE CENTS

HITLER FOR TRUCE IF ROOSEVELT AGREES

THOMPSON AND GOMEZ ARE TO TWIRL TODAY

HUSKY KID | Count Von Bernstorff Dies; | TEST VOTE | REJECTION | *Roosevelt Aloof* | Would Welcome Offer

1940 AMERICAN LEAGUE

BOSTON

CLEVELAND

DETROIT

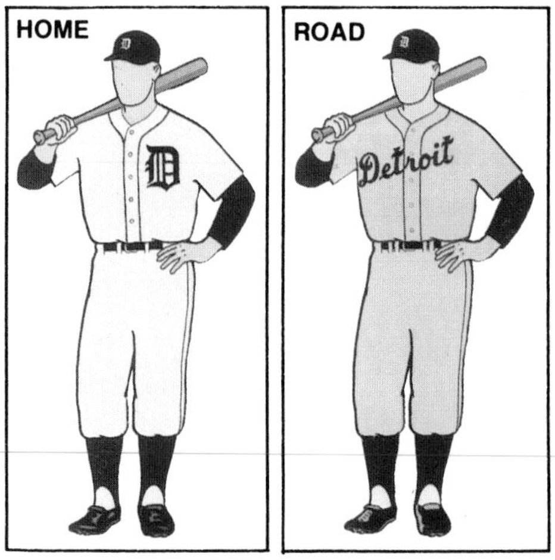

ST. LOUIS

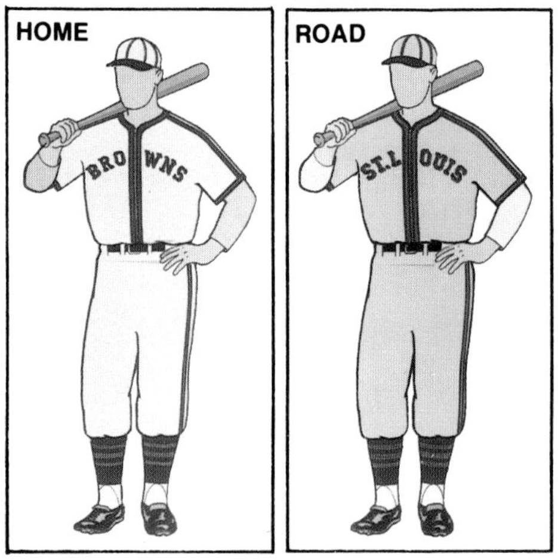

NEW YORK

PHILADELPHIA

CHICAGO

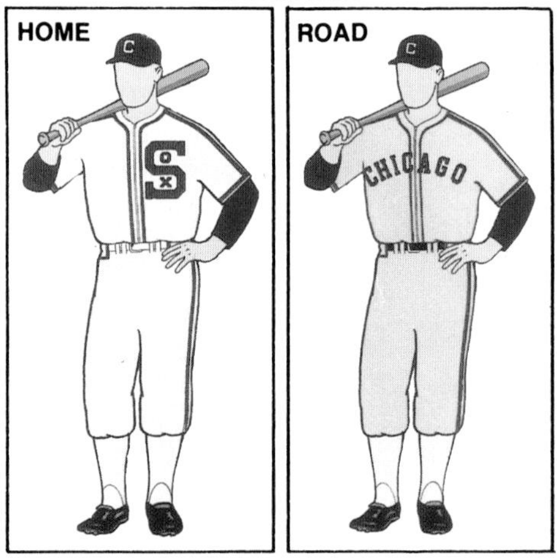

WASHINGTON

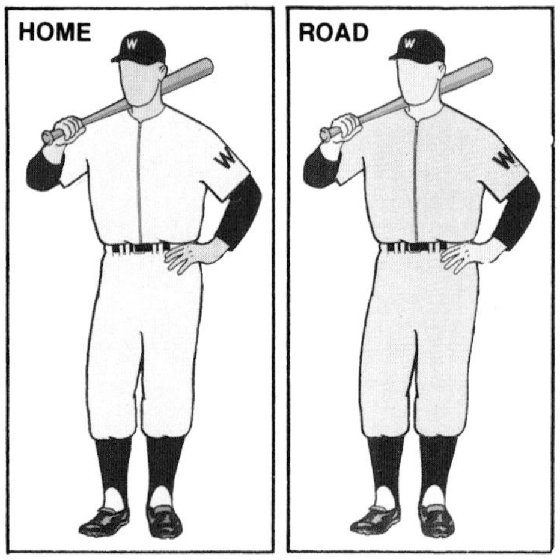

AMUSEMENTS—PAGE 18
RADIO PROGRAMS—Page 9

The Detroit News

COMPLETE SPORTS

MONDAY, OCTOBER 7, 1940—THE HOME NEWSPAPER — Page 17

Newsom's Victory Belongs With All-Time Pitching Classics

ALL SORTS

EACH World Series victory has been scored with an umpire from rival league of victors working behind plate . . . Bill Klem of the National Circuit called balls and strikes as Detroit won the first and fifth contests and Lee Ballanfant, of same circuit, was arbiter in Detroit's third game triumph . . . Emmett Ormsby and Steve Basil, of American League, umpired at plate in Cincinnati's

4 Tigers Batting Above .350 in Series

Campbell's .474 Leads

Explains Fox's Absence From Lineup

CINCINNATI, O., Oct. 7.—Back in Cincinnati to wind up the World Series, for better or for worse, the Tigers boasted four hitters with batting averages above .350 for the four

Action Studies (of a Serious Man at Work) Flanking a Finished Product—the Box Score

CINCINNATI

	AB	R	H	O	A
Werber, 3b	4	0	1	0	0
M. McCormick, cf	4	0	1	5	1
Goodman, rf	4	0	0	1	0
F. McCormick, 1b	4	0	1	5	0
Ripple, lf	2	0	0	4	0
Wilson, c	1	0	0	3	1
Baker, c	2	0	0	2	0
Joost, 2b	3	0	0	2	1
Myers, ss	2	0	0	2	0
Thompson, p	1	0	0	0	0
Moore, p	0	0	0	0	0
*Frey	1	0	0	0	0
Vander Meer, p	0	0	0	0	0

The Umpire

By H. G. Salsinger

CINCINNATI, O., Oct. 7—Pitching is Cincinnati's forte. The Reds rode to two National League championships on pitching and they were cocksure that their pitching would win the World Series for them, but with five games played the pitching honors belong to Detroit.

Cincinnati has rarely encoun-

NATIONAL LEAGUE 1940

BOSTON

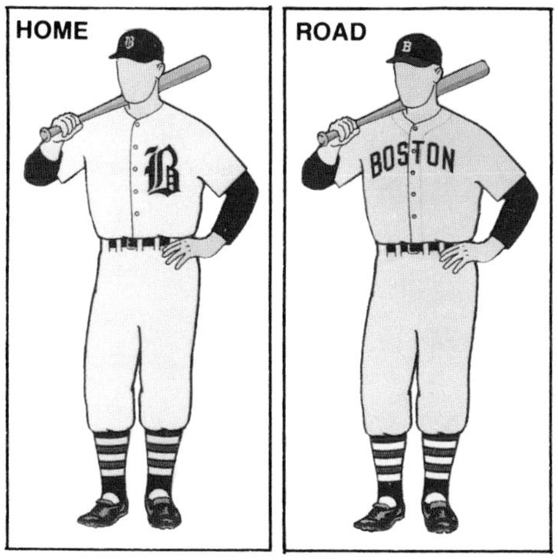

BROOKLYN

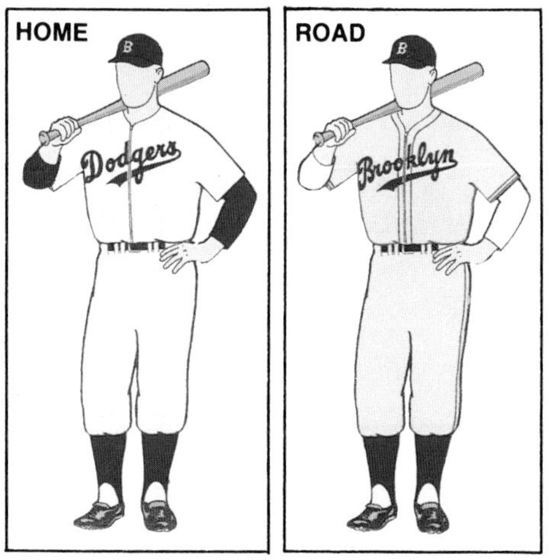

ST. LOUIS

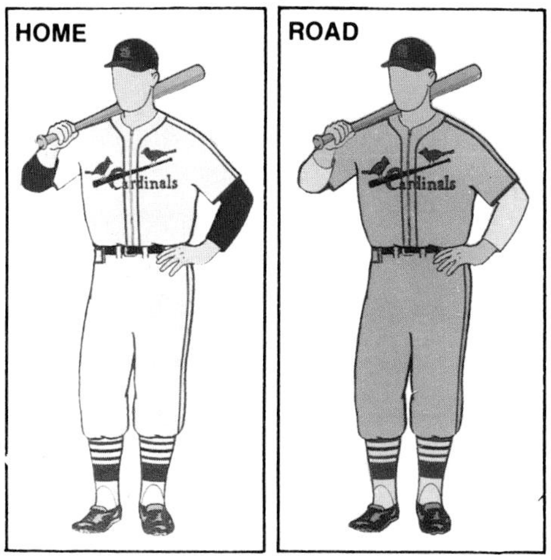

PITTSBURGH

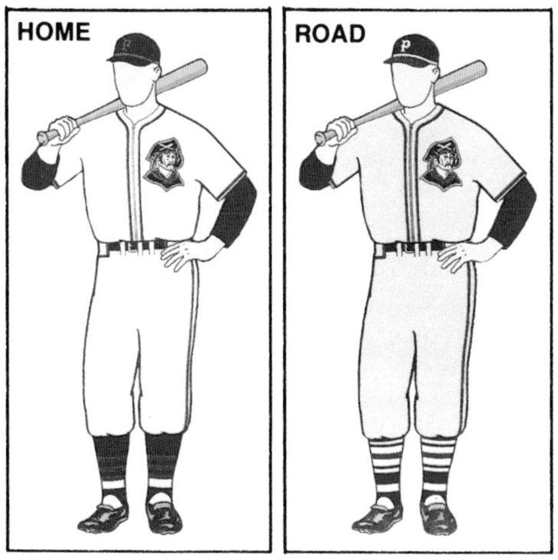

PHILADELPHIA

CHICAGO

CINCINNATI

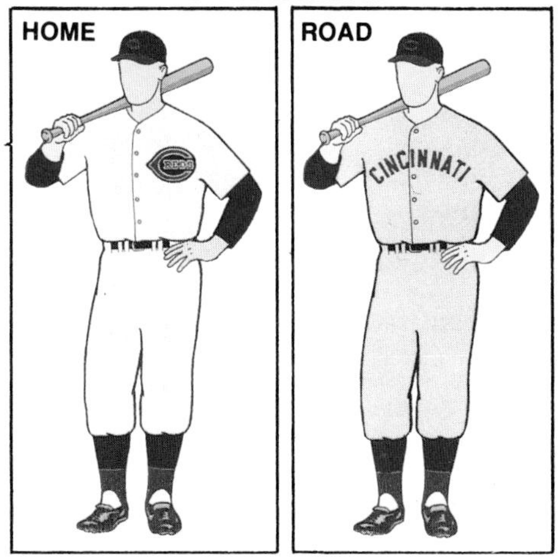

NEW YORK

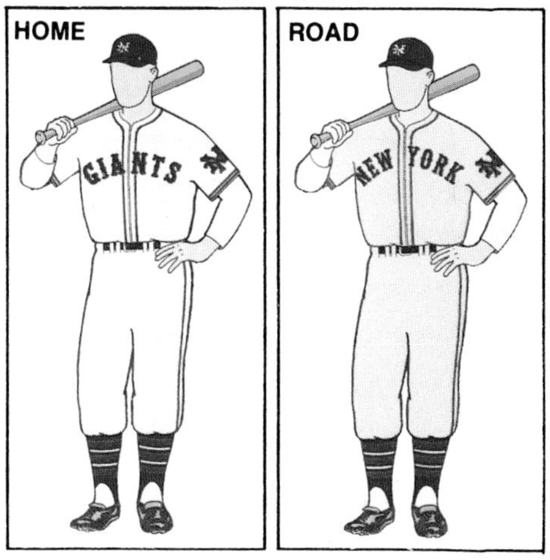

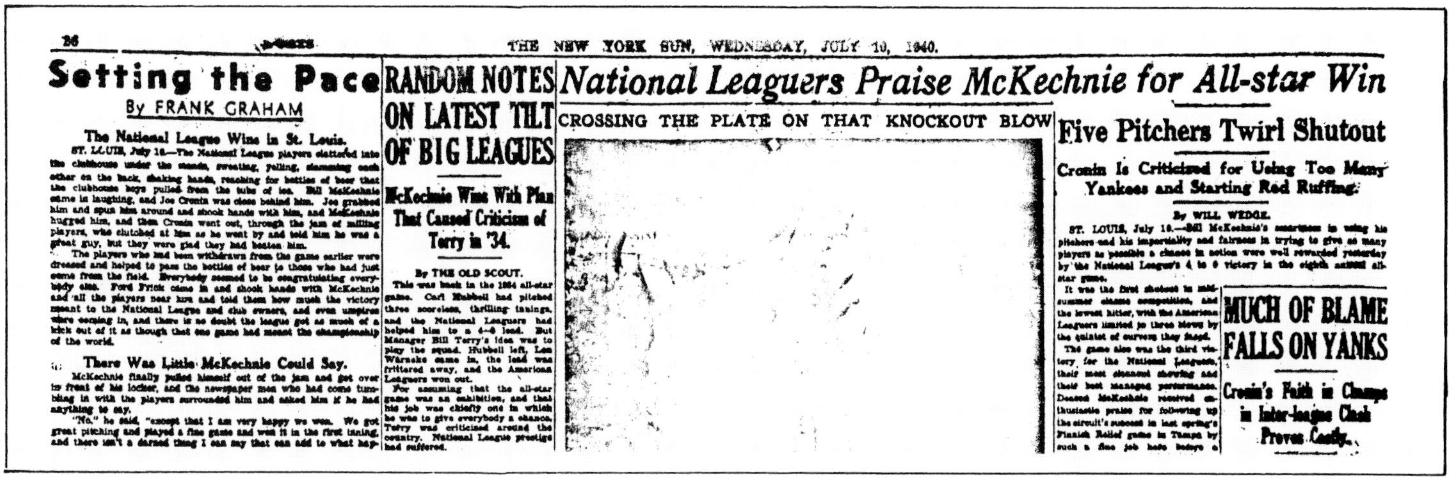

26 THE NEW YORK SUN, WEDNESDAY, JULY 10, 1940.

National Leaguers Praise McKechnie for All-star Win

Setting the Pace

By FRANK GRAHAM

The National League Wins in St. Louis.

ST. LOUIS, July 10.—The National League players clattered into the clubhouse under the stands, sweating, yelling, slamming each other on the back, shaking hands, reaching for bottles of beer that the clubhouse boys pulled from the tubs of ice. Bill McKechnie came in laughing, and Joe Cronin was close behind him. Joe grabbed him and spun him around and shook hands with him, and McKechnie hugged him, and then Cronin went out, through the jam of milling players, who clutched at him as he went by and told him he was a great guy, but they were glad they had beaten him.

The players who had been withdrawn from the game earlier were dressed and helped to pass the bottles of beer to those who had just come from the field. Everybody seemed to be congratulating everybody else. Ford Frick came in and shook hands with McKechnie and all the players near him and told them how much the victory meant to the National League and club owners, and even umpires were coming in, and there is no doubt the league got as much of a kick out of it as though that one game had meant the championship of the world.

There Was Little McKechnie Could Say.

McKechnie finally pulled himself out of the jam and got over in front of his locker, and the newspaper men who had come tumbling in with the players surrounded him and asked him if he had anything to say.

"No," he said, "except that I am very happy we won. We got great pitching and played a fine game and won it in the first inning, and there isn't a darned thing I can say that can add to what hap-

RANDOM NOTES ON LATEST TILT OF BIG LEAGUES

McKechnie Wins With Plan That Caused Criticism of Terry in '34.

By THE OLD SCOUT.

This was back in the 1934 all-star game. Carl Hubbell had pitched three scoreless, thrilling innings, and the National Leaguers had helped him to a 4—0 lead. But Manager Bill Terry's idea was to play the squad. Hubbell left, Lon Warneke came in, the lead was frittered away, and the American Leaguers won out.

For assuming that the all-star game was an exhibition, and that his job was chiefly one in which he was to give everybody a chance, Terry was criticized around the country. National League prestige had suffered.

CROSSING THE PLATE ON THAT KNOCKOUT BLOW

Five Pitchers Twirl Shutout

Cronin Is Criticized for Using Too Many Yankees and Starting Red Ruffing.

By WILL WEDGE.

ST. LOUIS, July 10.—Bill McKechnie's smartness in using his pitchers and his impartiality and fairness in trying to give as many players as possible a chance in action were well rewarded yesterday by the National League's 4 to 0 victory in the eighth annual all-star game.

It was the first shutout in midsummer classic competition, and the lowest hitter, with the American Leaguers limited to three blows by the quintet of curvers they faced.

The game also was the third victory for the National Leaguers, their most pleasant showing and their best managed performance. Deacon McKechnie received enthusiastic praise for following up the circuit's success in last spring's Finnish Relief game in Tampa by such a fine job here before a

MUCH OF BLAME FALLS ON YANKS

Cronin's Faith in Champs in Inter-league Clash Proves Costly.

1941 AMERICAN LEAGUE

BOSTON

CLEVELAND

DETROIT

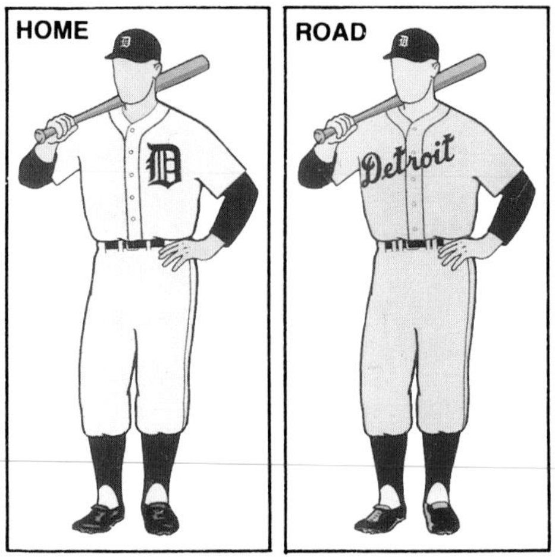

ST. LOUIS

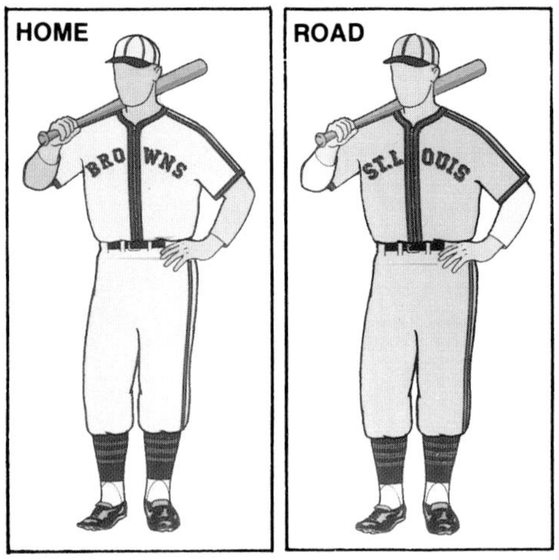

NEW YORK

PHILADELPHIA

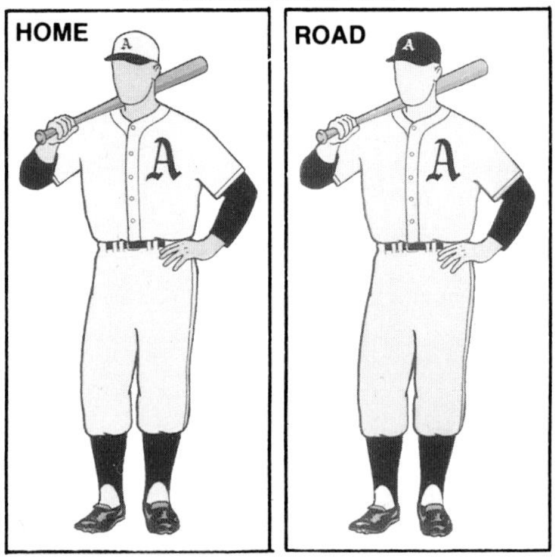

CHICAGO

WASHINGTON

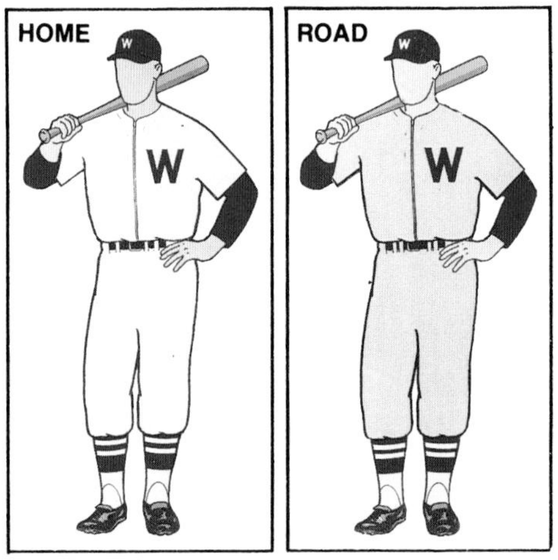

Greenberg Bids Farewell with 2 Homers as Yankees Fall, 7 to 4

Victory Lifts Detroit into Second Place

Campbell Also Gets 2 Circuit Clouts as Johnny Gorsica Hurls 5-Hit Ball

BY CHARLES P. WARD

... Henry Greenberg said farewell ... the Tigers and hail to ... Tuesday by hitting two ... as the Tigers defeated ... 7 to 4, to sweep the ... series. The victory ... Tigers fifth straight and ... them into second place ... American League standings ... games behind the Cleve- ...

... first home run of ... game and the season was ... the offerings of Ernie ... the second inning. The

3,000 Enthusiastic Fans Turn Out to Free Press Golf School

'This Is How It's Done'

Chandler Draws 1,500 Students

Women Outnumber Men at Rackham as Threats of Rain Are Completely Ignored

Close to 3,000 persons braved threatening weather Tuesday evening to attend the opening classes of the Free Press Golf School—and they were well rewarded for their bravery.

Until dark the district pros stuck with their classes adjusting grips and answering questions

Leaders Examine Cards

Nats Snap Tribe String at 11 in Row

Two-Run Homer by Vernon Leads Attack as Griffs Score 5-3 Victory

By the Associated Press

CLEVELAND, May 6—With the assistance of Cleveland's Ken Keltner, the Washington Senators today finally snapped the league-leading Indians' victory streak at 11 games.

Pitcher Emil (Dutch) Leonard ...

Free Press Sports

Wednesday, May 7

Hank Smiles

NATIONAL LEAGUE 1941

BOSTON

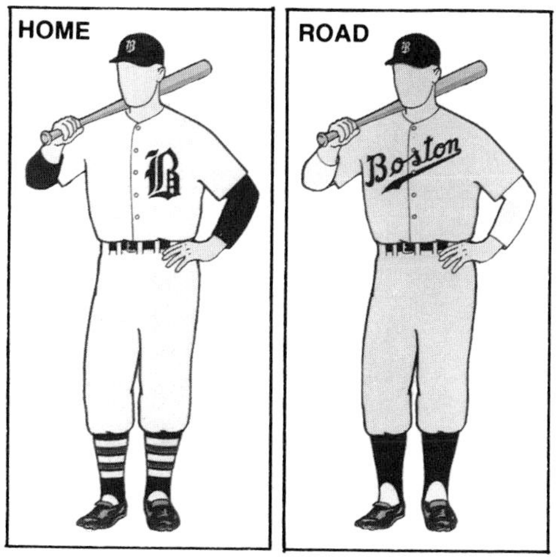

BROOKLYN

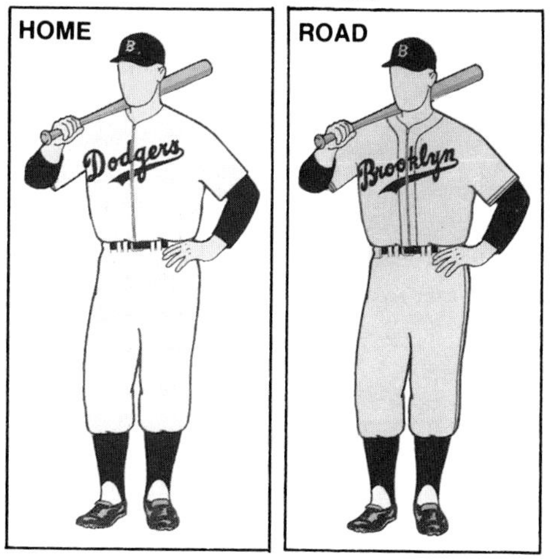

ST. LOUIS

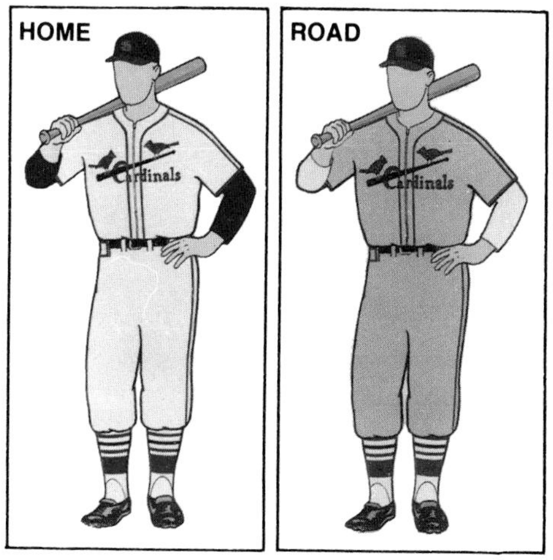

PITTSBURGH

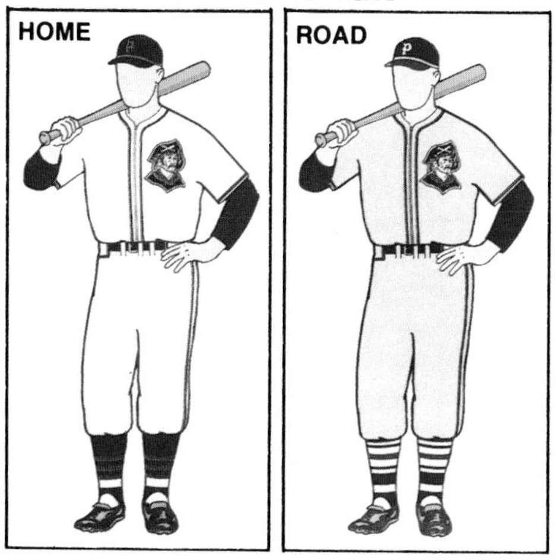

PHILADELPHIA

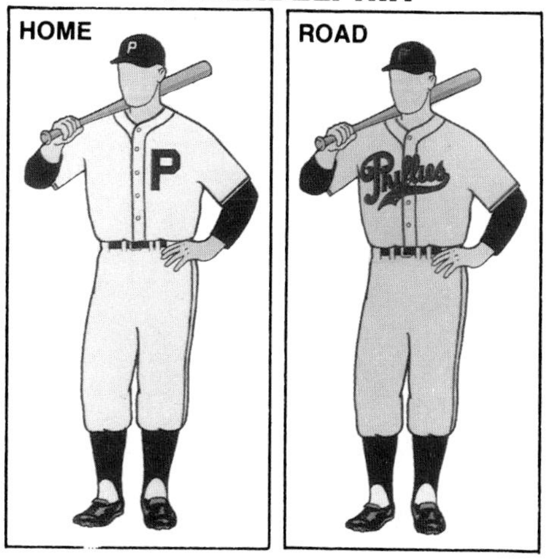

CHICAGO

CINCINNATI

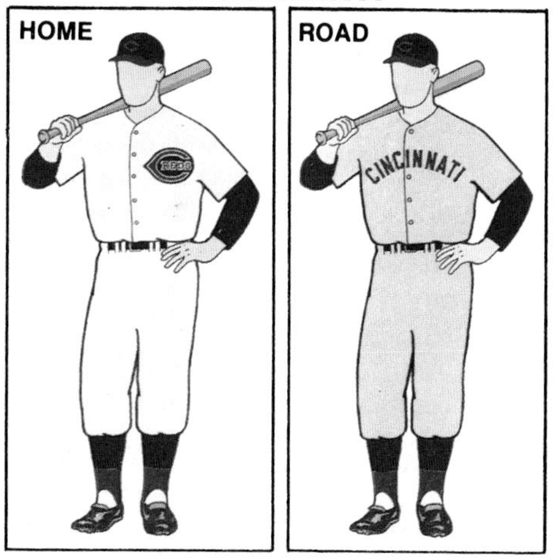

NEW YORK

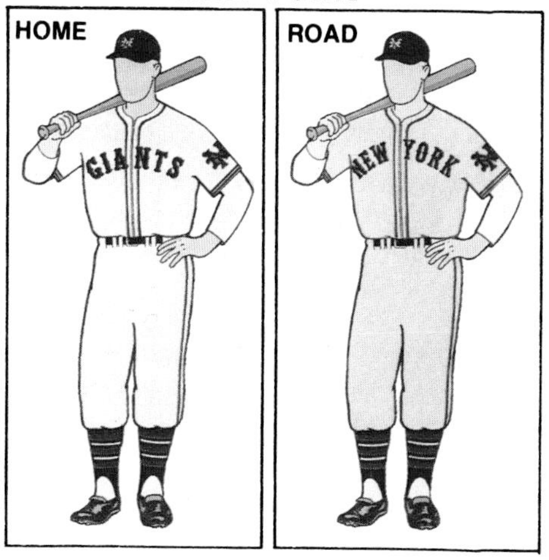

30 SPORTS THE NEW YORK SUN, WEDNESDAY, JUNE 18, 1941. SPORTS

Setting the Pace

By FRANK GRAHAM

There Is Something About Conn.

A slim, nice looking young man who came in here from Pittsburgh a couple of years ago to fight Freddy Apostoli fights Joe Louis for the heavyweight championship at the Polo Grounds tonight. He hasn't changed very much in appearance since the time when he was fighting middleweights. He has put on only ten pounds or so and still is only a light heavyweight. But somehow he has grown in the public mind, so that there are many who believe that tonight he will beat Louis and take the title from him.

Actually, he has done little as a heavyweight. His opponents in that division have been second raters or worse and although he has beaten them he hasn't been too impressive. But there is something about the young man that the public likes. Something besides his engaging smile, because when he goes in there to fight he doesn't smile but is grim and hard. Maybe his manager, Johnny Ray, has the right slant.

"No matter who he is fighting," Johnny said last night, "he lets everybody know he is the boss in the ring, even before the fight starts. Just the way he walks out there to get his instructions from the referee lets you know that he ain't afraid of nobody."

Maybe that's it. Maybe the crowd has learned not only to accept but to admire Conn on his poise.

He Is Contemptuous of Louis.

He has plenty of that. Other men who have fought Louis . . . at least a few of them . . . have not been afraid of him. But Conn is the only one who has been contemptuous of him.

"I wanted to fight him from the time I was a middleweight," he told you at his training camp. "I was fighting good fighters. And I knew all that Louis could do was punch."

Crowd of 40,000 Is Expected to See Louis and Conn Box Tonight

DYKES VALUES FELLER ABOVE JOE DIMAGGIO

Jimmy Compares Two Stars as Assets in Building New Ball Club.

By THE OLD SCOUT.

"Whom would you prefer, Joe DiMaggio or Bob Feller, if you were starting from scratch to build a ball club?"

Jimmy Dykes never batted an eye. He listened to the question, blew a few smoke rings into the ceiling, and said: "Feller."

Dykes's audience did not have to ask the White Sox manager for a reason. It came without

TITLE TILT. By Pap.

Champion Is Logical Choice To Keep Heavyweight Title

Bomber Carries Big Advantage in Punching Power, but the Challenger Is Faster of Foot and a Clever Boxer.

By WILBUR WOOD.
(Sports Editor)

Joe Louis risks the heavyweight boxing championship tonight for the eighteenth time, meeting Billy Conn of Pittsburgh in a scheduled fifteen-round match at the Polo Grounds that has produced more dissension among the experts, and pseudo experts, than any of the Bomber's other battles since his second meeting with Max Schmeling.

Every one was set for the fray except Old Man Weather, who wore a cloudy look, but even he was expected to be smiling by tonight. The prediction was that the skies would be partly cloudy this afternoon and tonight with no rain in sight. The temperature would be moderately warm, it was reported.

In some respects this figures to be one of Louis's softest touches.

FIGHT FACTS.

By Associated Press.

Title at Stake—World heavyweight championship.

Principals—Joe Louis, Detroit, champion, vs. Billy Conn, Pittsburgh, challenger.

Place—Polo Grounds.

Bout—Fifteen rounds to a

1942 AMERICAN LEAGUE

BOSTON

CLEVELAND

DETROIT

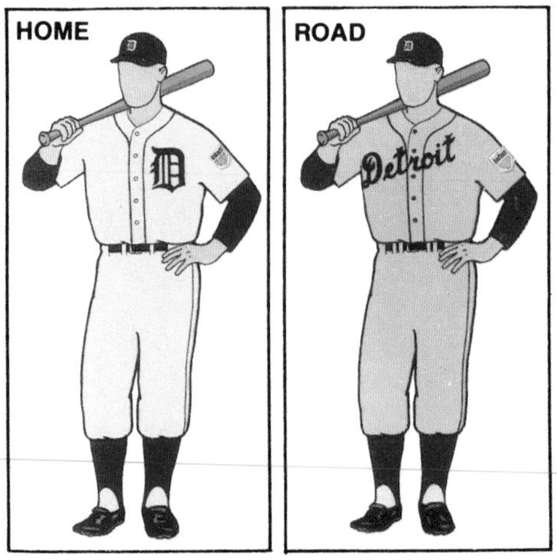

ST. LOUIS

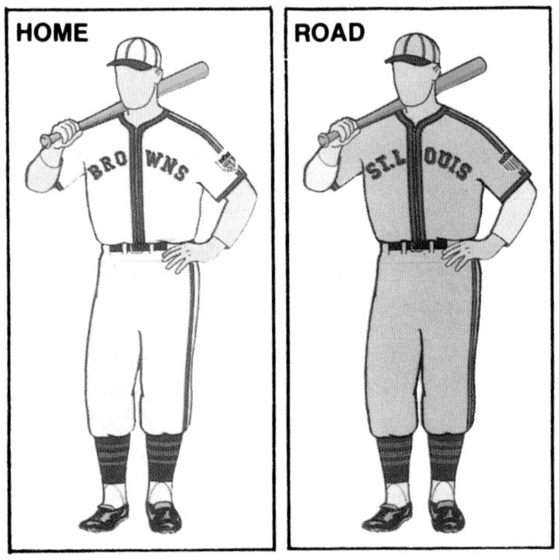

NEW YORK

PHILADELPHIA

CHICAGO

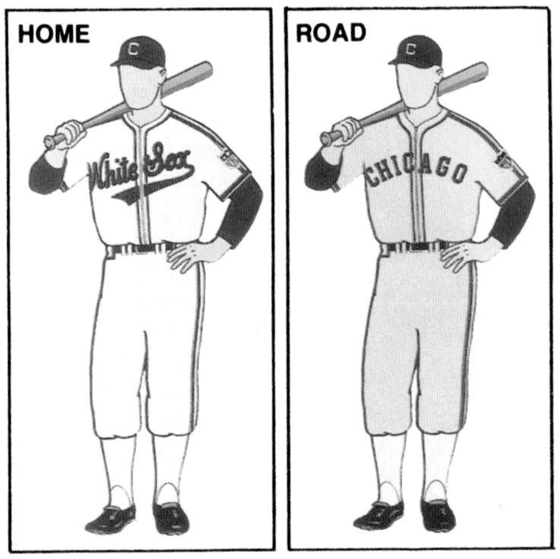

WASHINGTON

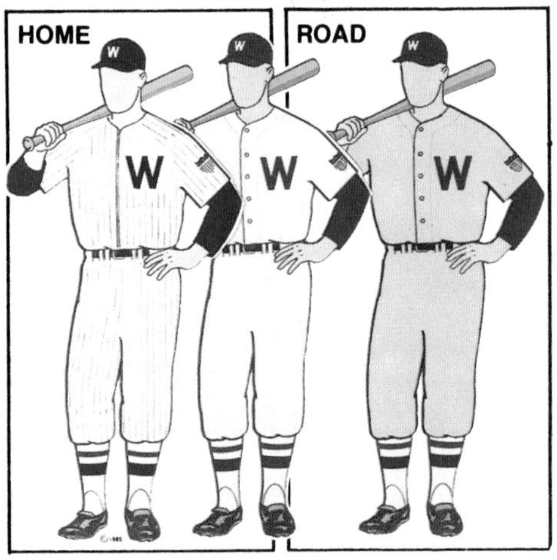

Braves .... 6 | Pirates ... 7 | Dodgers ... 7 | Cardinals .. 5 | Senators ... 4 | Indians .... 6 | Browns ... 3 | Red Sox ... 6
Cubs ..... 3 | Phillies ... 1 | Reds ..... 3 | Giants .... 4 | White Sox .. 3 | Athletics .. 4 | Yankees ... 1 | Tigers 1

THE CHICAGO DAILY NEWS

RED STREAK

TUESDAY, APRIL 28, 1942—TWENTY-TWO PAGES. THREE CENTS

R. A. F. POUNDS FAR-FLUNG FRONT

ONE BAD INNING

CHICAGO GETS ADVANCE VIEW OF CARAVAN

VICTORY IN '42 SOVIET CRY FOR

The War Today

PACIFIC AREA

BRITISH BLAST NEW NAZI BASE

NATIONAL LEAGUE 1942

BOSTON

BROOKLYN

ST. LOUIS

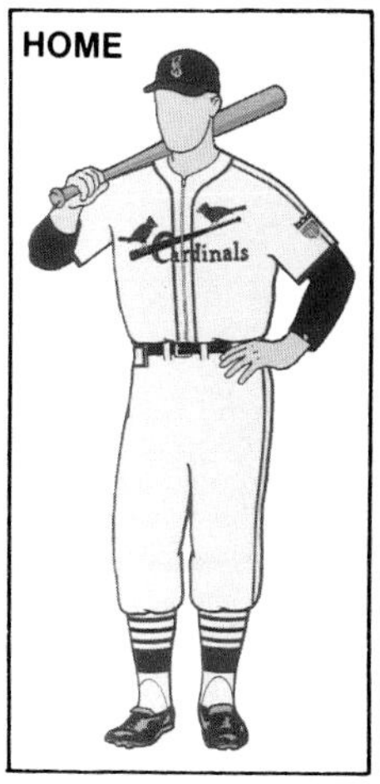

PITTSBURGH

PHILADELPHIA

CHICAGO

CINCINNATI

NEW YORK

The Pittsburgh Press

FINAL STOCKS

PRICE THREE CENTS

VOLUME 58, No. 296 — 30 PAGES — PITTSBURGH, PA., SATURDAY, APRIL 18, 1942

U. S. FLIERS BOMBARD TOKYO

Other Cities Raided, Flames Rage

1943 AMERICAN LEAGUE

BOSTON

CLEVELAND

DETROIT

ST. LOUIS

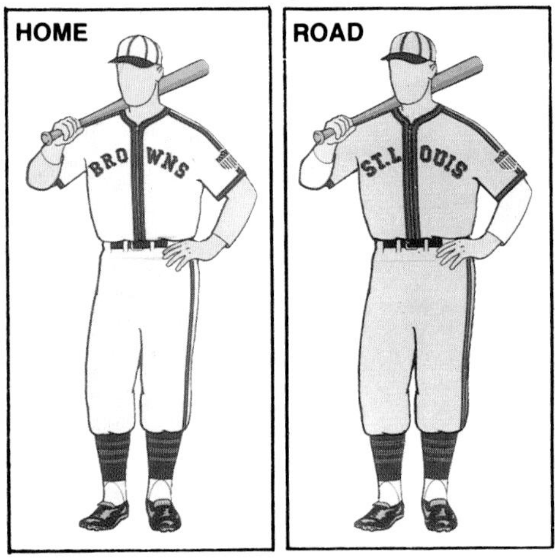

NEW YORK

PHILADELPHIA

CHICAGO

WASHINGTON

THE NEW YORK SUN, FRIDAY, APRIL 22, 1943.

Baseball Men Up in Arms Over Apparent Deadening of 1943 Ball

Setting the Pace

By FRANK GRAHAM

A Small Crowd at the Stadium.

The Yankees and the Senators opened the season before a crowd of about … Well, make it … That wasn't the way it used to be. There was a time when a fellow couldn't get to the Stadium … an opening day and saunter up a ramp to the mezzanine and take any seat he wanted. And, after a few innings, get up and wander around all by himself in the back of the stand and buy a sandwich and a cup of coffee . . . and go back to his seat and light his pipe and stretch his legs and be completely at his ease. Time was when, if he was fortunate enough to get a seat just back of first base ten or fifteen minutes after the game started, he would have been in the middle of a roaring mob, and if he wanted to go back and get a sandwich and a cup of coffee he would have had to fight his way to the counter.

But this . . . why this, save for the coolness in the air, might have been a Monday afternoon in midsummer with the Yankees out in front and the rest of the league nowhere. The field boxes were pretty well filled, but back of them the crowd was scattered. There was a fairish settlement in the right field bleachers, but the gatherings in center and left fields were sparse and there was practically nobody in the mezzanine.

But There Will Be Many a Day—

In all this, however, there is no cause for alarm. The edge had been taken off the opening by the big show last week, when … out in the cold to see the Yankees, Giants and Dodgers in the inter-borough double header. And the weather yesterday was such that the prudent fan, bound for the Stadium, called up first to find out whether or not there would be a ball game. And, of course, if he had been really prudent he would have stayed home, ball game or no.

There will be many a day at the Stadium this year when the …

RICK DESCRIBES 10 MILLION FUND AS GREAT CAUSE

Famous Airman Talks of Post-war Aid for Lost Flyers' Families.

By LAWRENCE PERRY.

As Eddie Rickenbacker stood talking about the $10,000,000 fund for post-war aid of the families of Army aviators which he and other civilians—but principally Eddie himself—are now trying to raise, his eyes had a far away look as though he were seeing our flyers, "more children in arms," winging over combat areas, giving their all for their country.

He was at a luncheon table in …

HE STARTS WITH A BANG!

OTT ONLY GRINS AFTER END OF A PERFECT DAY

Giants' Pilot Hits Four for Four While Dodgers Win Opening Joust.

By FRANK C. TEUR.

It probably would be easier to convince the world that … doesn't slice most of his drives than to make anybody believe a ball player went to the showers dissatisfied after hitting 1,000, or four for four, in an opening day game.

Nevertheless, Manager Mel Ott of the Giants, who had a perfect day at bat in Brooklyn yesterday, had cause to grumble, but he did not do so. Rather, he grinned at what could have …

Demand a Change in Sphere

Rickey and Klem Comment on Lack of Zing as They Watch Dodgers Defeat Giants.

By EDWARD T. MURPHY.

When the weather warms up and the hitters are defrosted, it may be a different story. But thus far the evidence produced by laboratory tests and the reaction of the new baseball against hard-swung bats in actual competition is indisputably to the effect that the 1943 sphere is less lively than the brand used last year.

Baseball men everywhere agree that, whatever the cause, the new ball, supposed to be livelier than the 1942 type, is in reality much slower. When one of the new type was cut open by a representative of the manufacturer at Cleveland yesterday it was discovered that the yarn around the cork and balata center was loosely wound and appeared to be damp.

From Cincinnati came a statement by Warren Giles, general manager of the Reds, that he had proved by bouncing the new ball that it is 25 per cent slower than the one formerly used. Giles, who last winter, led the …

SPEEDIER BALL IN TWO WEEKS

Manufacturer Promises That After Finding First Lot Poor.

The first shipment of the new 1943 baseballs employed in the …

NATIONAL LEAGUE 1943

BOSTON

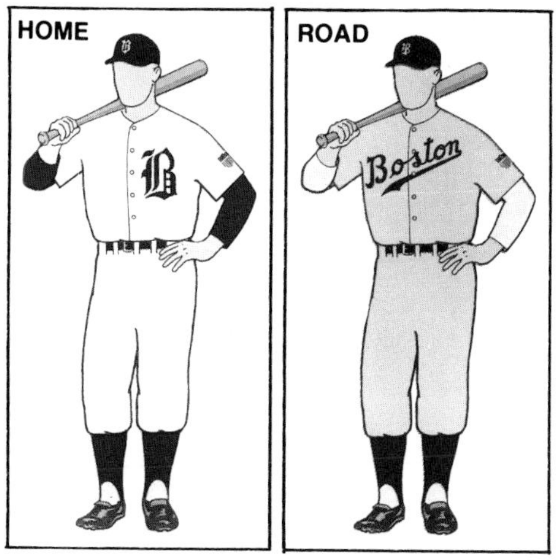

BROOKLYN

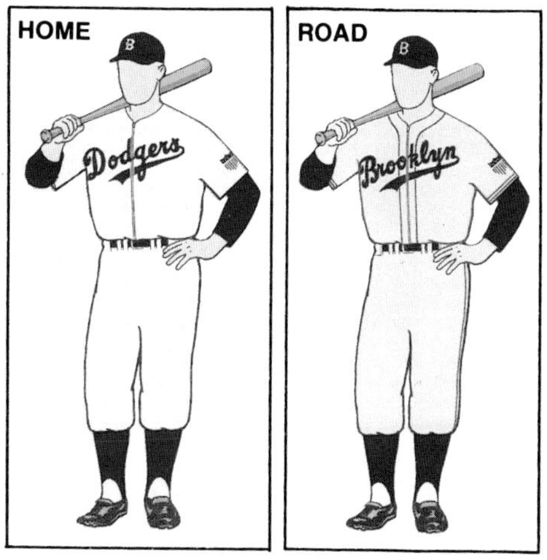

ST. LOUIS

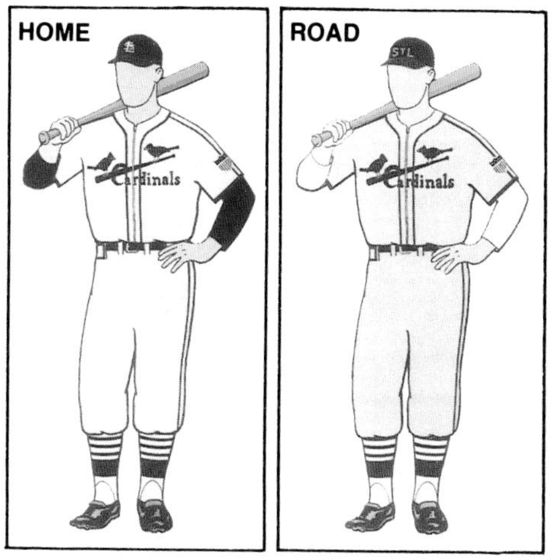

PITTSBURGH

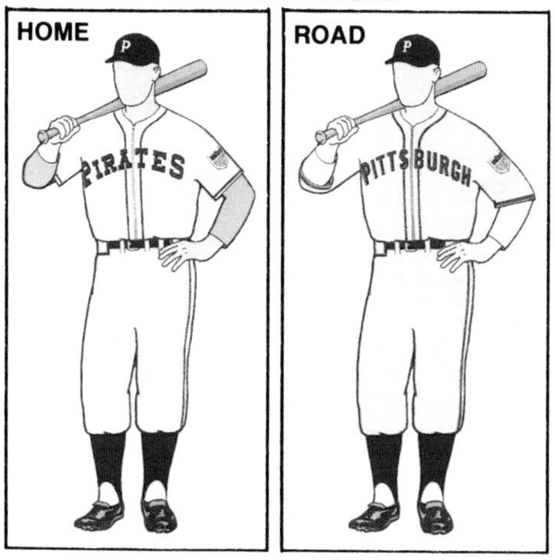

PHILADELPHIA

CHICAGO

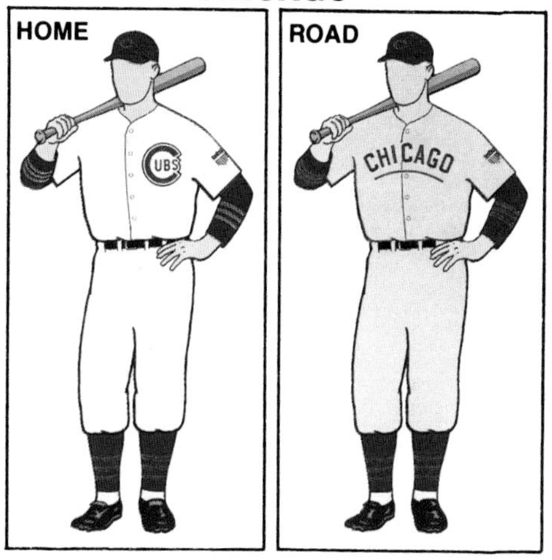

CINCINNATI

NEW YORK

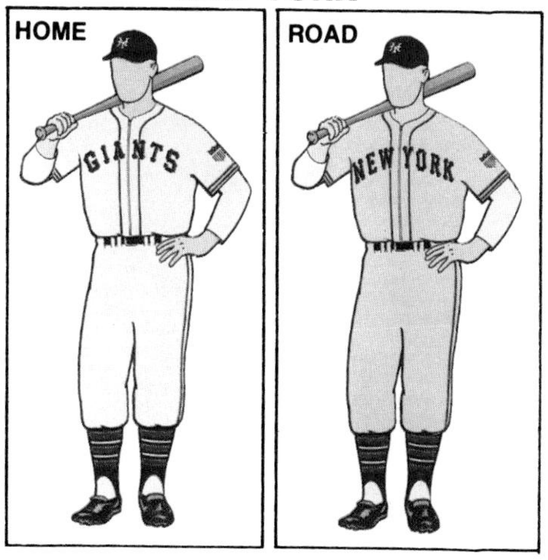

CARDS BAT OUT TWO HOMERS

COMPLETE FINAL ★★★★★★

CLOSING WALL STREET PRICES

The Sun

CLOSING WALL STREET PRICES

VOL. 111—NO. 30. NEW YORK, WEDNESDAY, OCTOBER 6, 1943.

NAZI LINE PIERCED IN ITALY

1944 AMERICAN LEAGUE

BOSTON

CLEVELAND

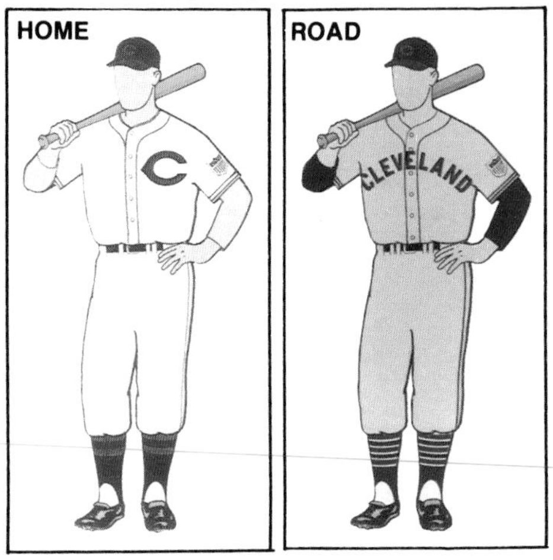

DETROIT

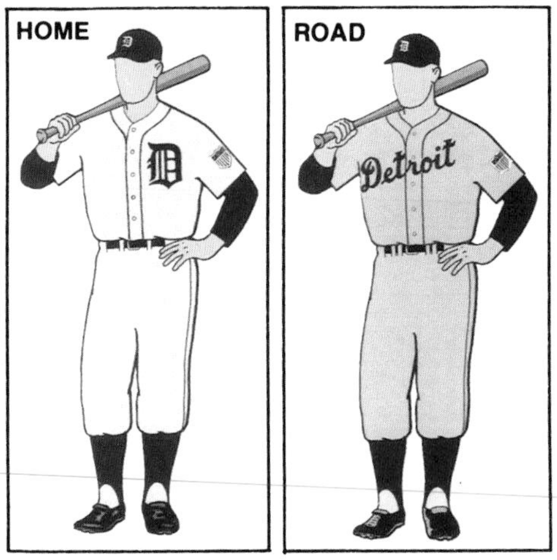

ST. LOUIS

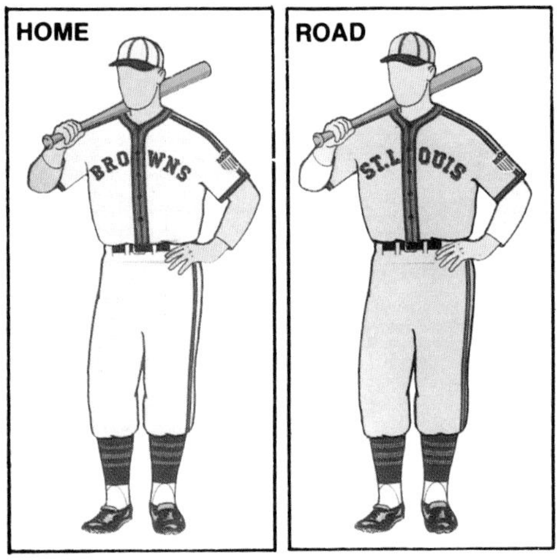

NEW YORK

PHILADELPHIA

CHICAGO

WASHINGTON

PAGE 14A ST. LOUIS POST-DISPATCH SUNDAY MORNING, OCTOBER 1, 1944 ST. LOUIS POST-DISPATCH

BROWNS AND TIGERS WIN AND ARE TIED FOR LEAD WITH FINAL GAMES IN A. L. RACE SCHEDULED TODAY

GALEHOUSE SHUTS OUT YANKS, 2-0, ON FIVE HITS; MOORE GETS A HOME RUN

TO THE WIRE

Hitting It Up and Whooping It Up in the Stretch

NEWHOUSER BAGS NO. 29 AS SENATORS BOW, 7 TO 3

NATIONAL LEAGUE 1944

BOSTON

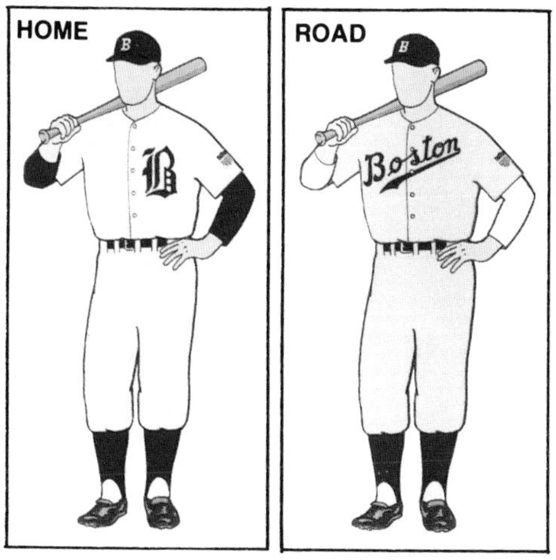

BROOKLYN

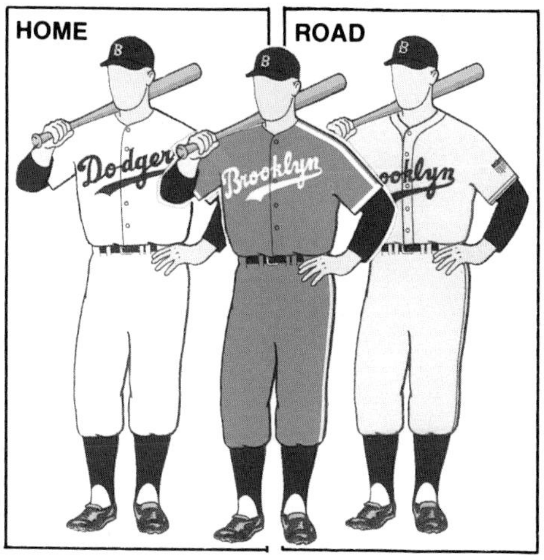

ST. LOUIS

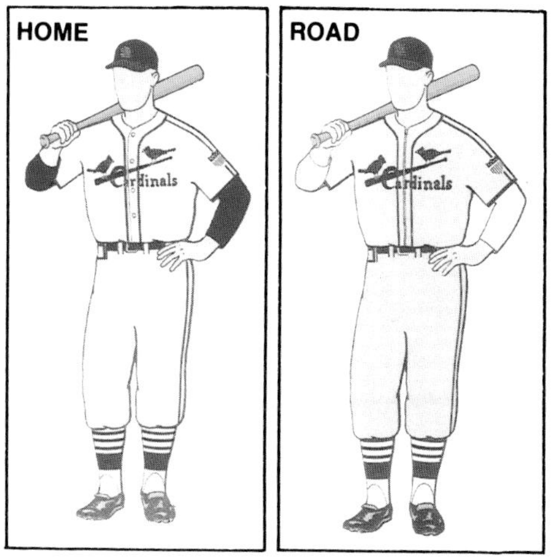

PITTSBURGH

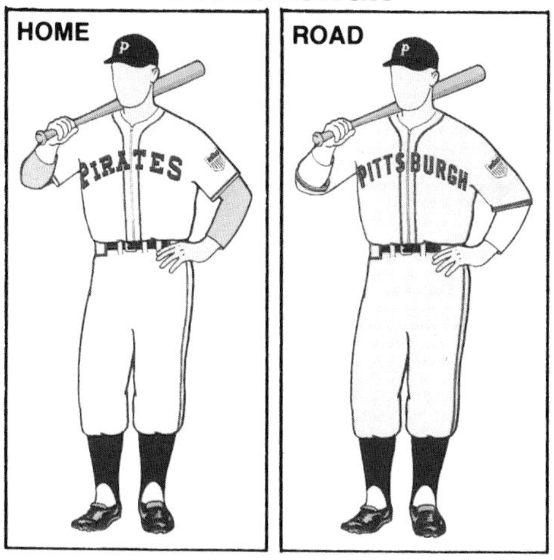

PHILADELPHIA

CHICAGO

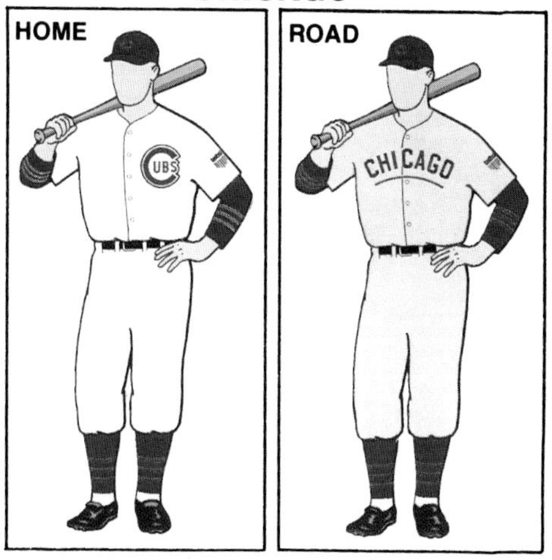

CINCINNATI

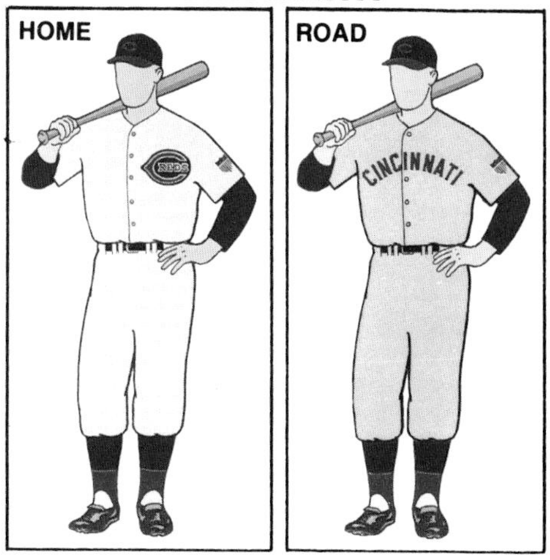

NEW YORK

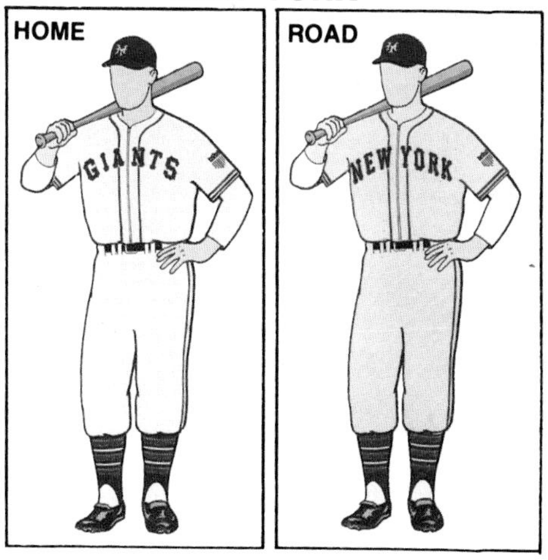

COMPLETE FINAL ★★★★★★ CLOSING WALL STREET PRICES

The Sun

CLOSING WALL STREET PRICES

VOL. 111—NO. 233. NEW YORK, TUESDAY, JUNE 6, 1944.

ALLIED ARMIES SMASH AHEAD

1945 AMERICAN LEAGUE

BOSTON

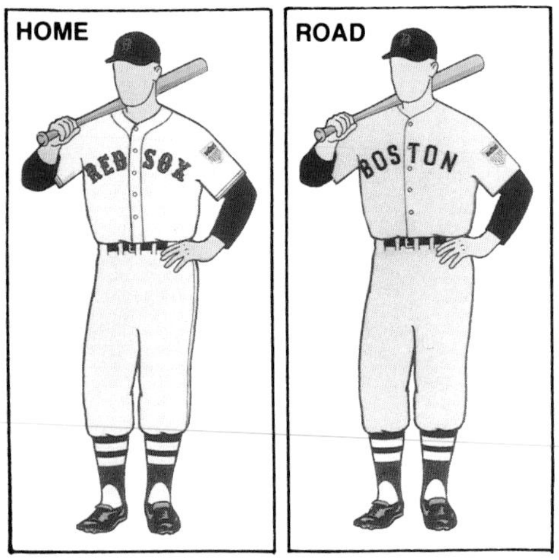

CLEVELAND

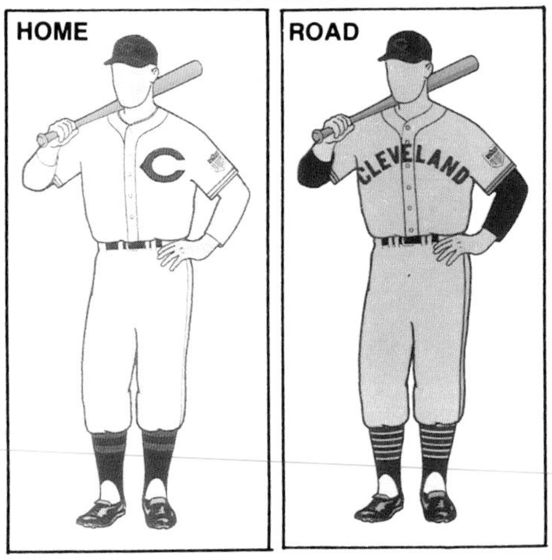

DETROIT

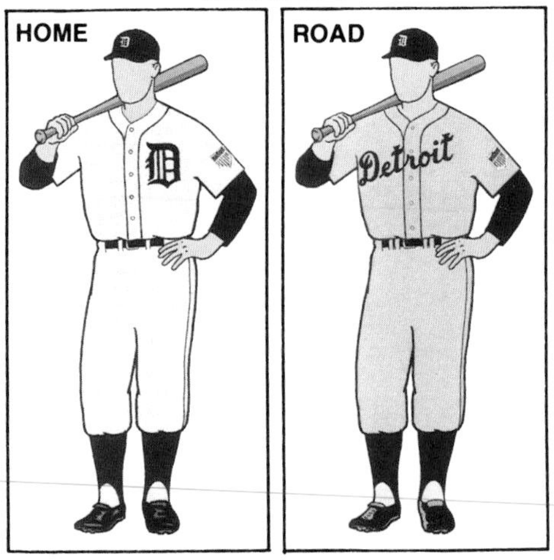

ST. LOUIS

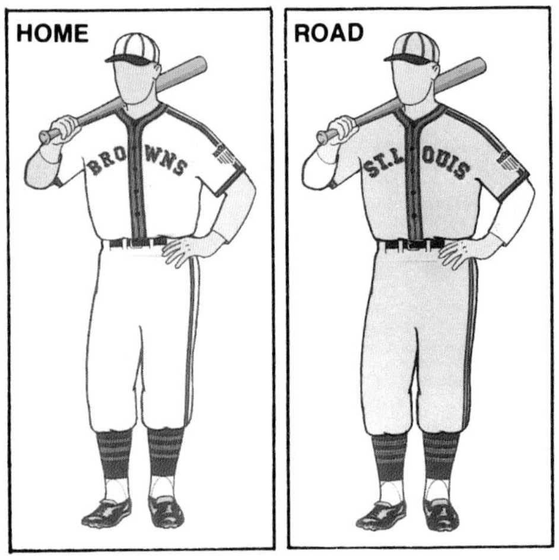

NEW YORK

PHILADELPHIA

CHICAGO

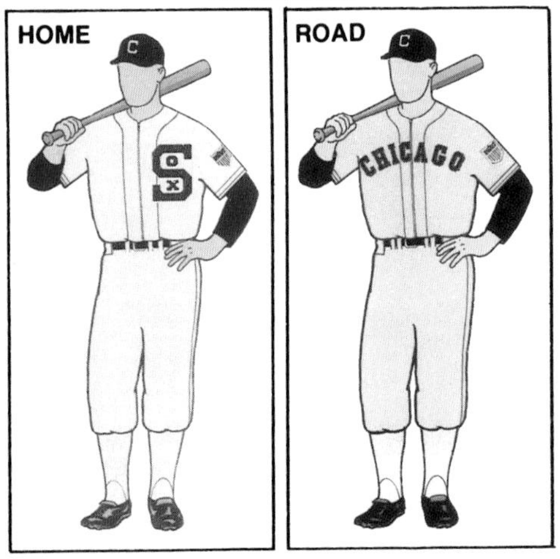

WASHINGTON

OUR 1945 EDITION
OF
WHO'S WHO IN BASEBALL
is now on sale

For further details see advertisement on the back cover of this magazine

14 DETROIT FREE PRESS—Monday, October 1, 1945

Hank's Homer Wins Flag for Tigers

4-Run Smash in 9th Beats Browns, 6-3

Newhouser Gains No. 25 in Relief Job

● Continued from Page One ●

every Tiger on the team. He was hugged and roughed and kissed and pummeled.

It was 1940 all over again. That was the last time the Tigers won the A. L. pennant. They did it that year when Rudy York hit a two-run homer off Bobby Feller to clinch the flag.

But they didn't have to do it under such adverse playing conditions as Sunday. Storms had drenched the field for 10 straight days; the temperature was 57; only 5,582 fans were huddled in the dank park to see baseball history made by a man who hit

Quiet O'Neill Will Match Wits with Colorful Grimm

BY LYALL SMITH
Free Press Sports Editor

They'll be on the third base coaching lines—one or the other—all the time. For the Tigers, stout Stephen O'Neill. For the Cubs, "Jolly Cholly" Grimm.

Two managers so much alike down deep, two managers so far apart on top.

• • •

O'Neill, still relishing the taste of his first league championship in 15 years of handling baseball reins in the minors and big time, is quiet on the base paths, almost demurely so.

Grimm, three times a winner with the Cubs and twice more with Milwaukee, is a rollicking imitation of a roly-poly bear on the diamond. He chugs up and down the base paths waving his huge hands this way and that.

He's filled with more fire than a Mexican tamale. Color drips off him.

O'Neill, firm and intense when angry, keeps his glee in check and

STEVE O'NEILL

buries his disappointment within him. Maybe he'll kick at the bag in disgust at misplaced strategy. That's all.

THIS IS O'Neill's third season as Tiger manager and the joys of hitting a World Series have made him a new man.

One of four baseball playing brothers, Steve broke in with Cleveland as a catcher and crouched behind Indian rivals for 12 seasons through 1923. He dropped into the minors before moving up as manager at Toronto in 1929, '30 and '31.

Toledo was his next managerial step. He directed the Mudhens for three years and then replaced Walter Johnson as manager of the Indians, his old ball club.

Then to Buffalo from 1938 through 1940, when he came to Detroit as a coach before replacing Del Baker as boss man three years ago.

• • •

GRIMM'S career began six years later than O'Neill's. In 1916 he broke in with Philadelphia. After four years in the minors, the big left-handed first baseman joined the Pirates for six full seasons before going to the Cubs as a player in 1925.

CHARLEY GRIMM

He first took over the Cubs in 1932 and promptly led them to a pennant. The next two seasons he finished third and then roared back in 1935 with a string of 21 consecutive September victories to win the National League flag.

After finishing second in '36 and '37, he was replaced by Gabby Hartnett in July of the next season. Then he tried his voice as a baseball narrator and finally wound up at Milwaukee as part owner of the Brewers and a successful manager.

• • •

LAST YEAR, after the Cubs had won only one of their first 12 games, he was called back to the majors and made his second debut as Chicago's manager. He finished fourth that summer and now is back with his third National League pennant.

That's the story up to date [illegible] Managers O'Neill and Grimm. The next chapters will be written [illegible] daily installments, starting Wednesday at Briggs Stadium.

NATIONAL LEAGUE 1945

BOSTON

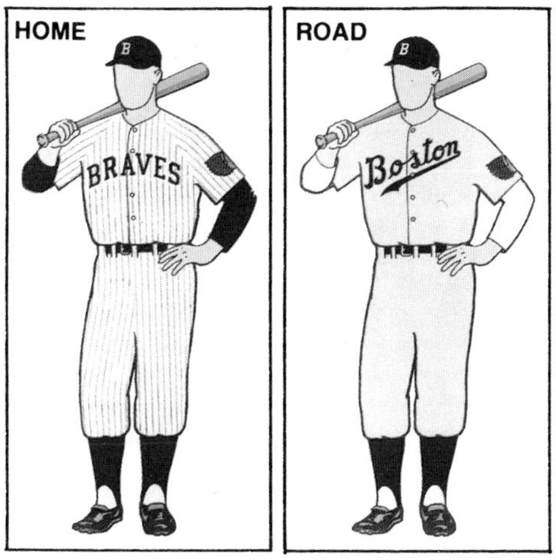

BROOKLYN

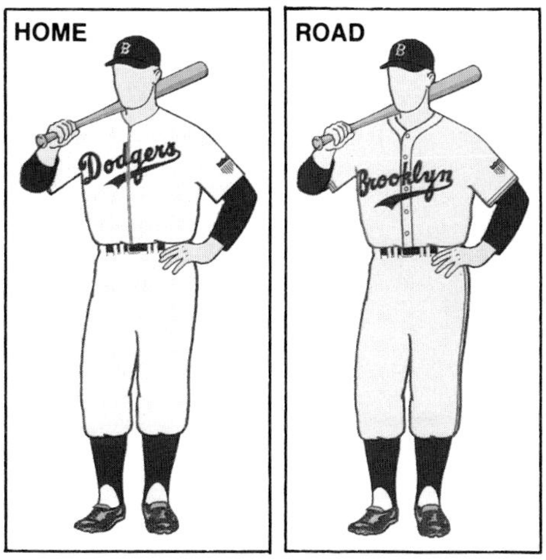

ST. LOUIS

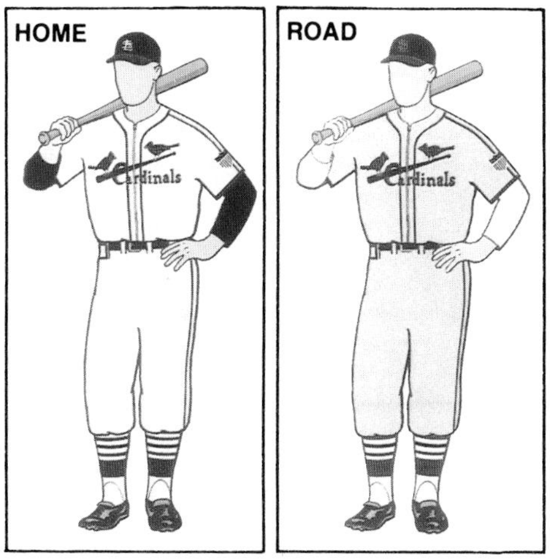

PITTSBURGH

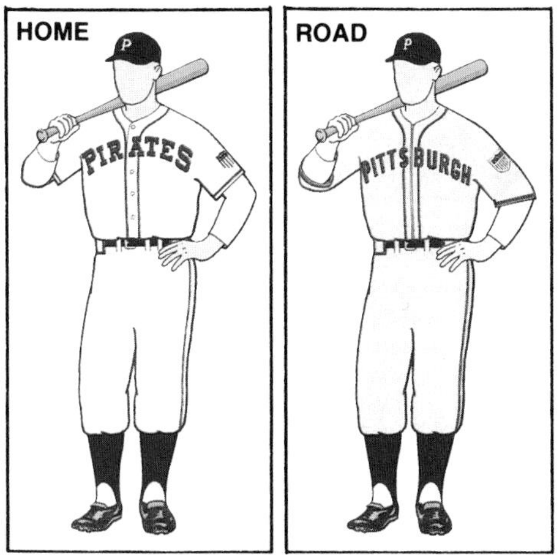

PHILADELPHIA

CHICAGO

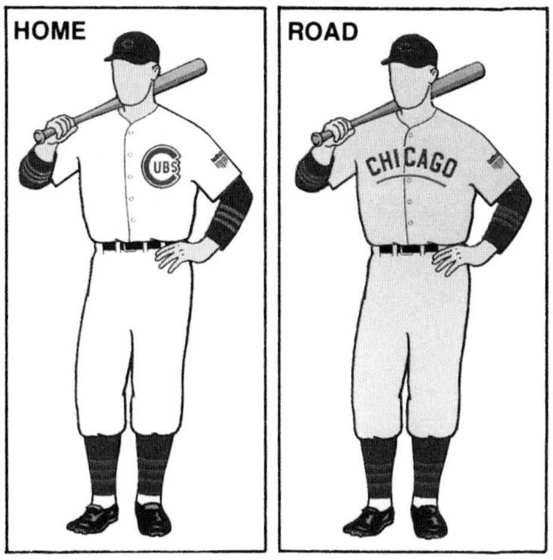

CINCINNATI

NEW YORK

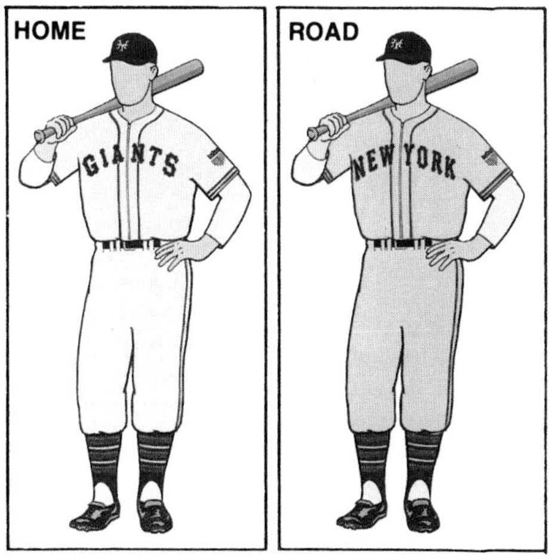

NEW YORK Herald Tribune

V-E DAY EDITION

Vol. V No. 35,968 TUESDAY, MAY 8, 1945

Today Is V-E Day

Truman, Churchill, Stalin to Proclaim War's End; Germans Surrender at Eisenhower's Headquarters

1946 AMERICAN LEAGUE

BOSTON

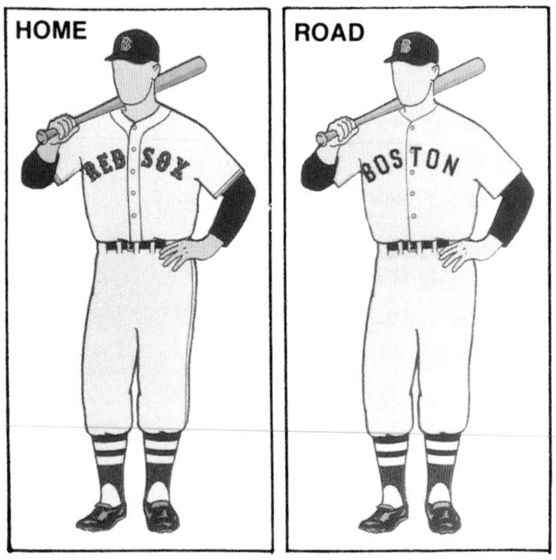

CLEVELAND

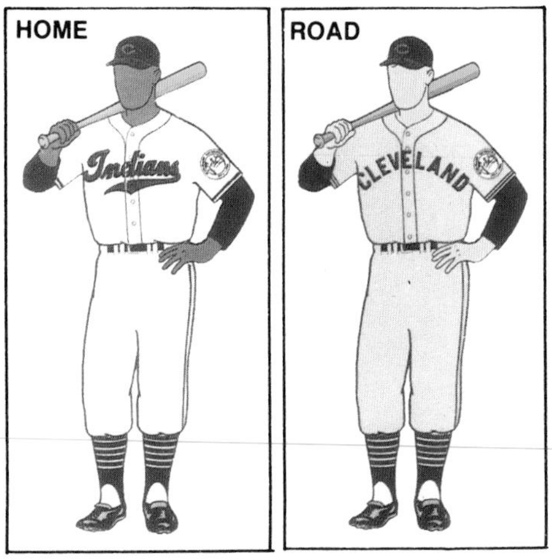

DETROIT

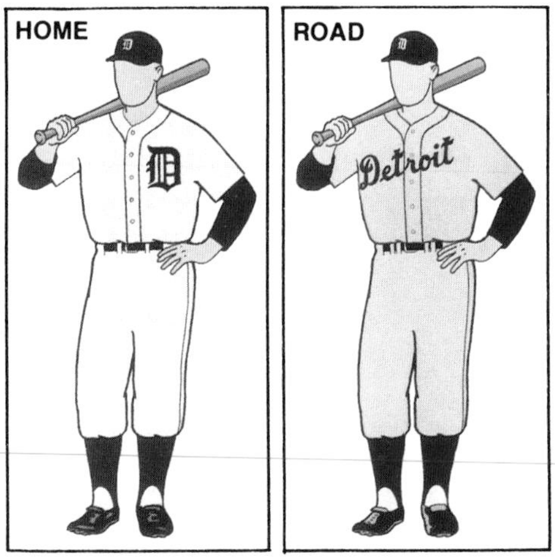

ST. LOUIS

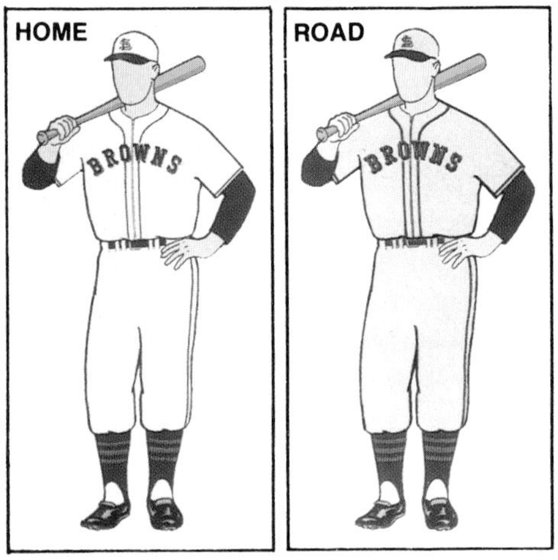

NEW YORK

PHILADELPHIA

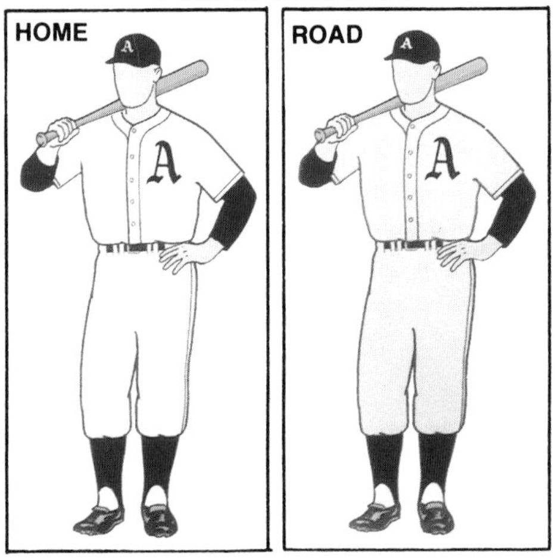

CHICAGO

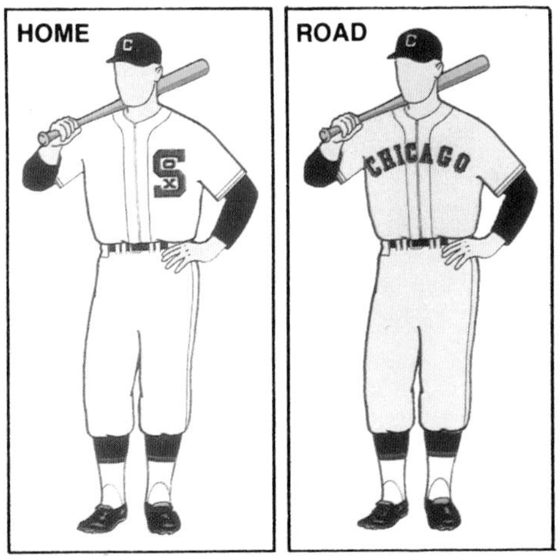

WASHINGTON

PAGE INDEX TO FEATURES

The Boston Post

THE GREAT Breakfast Table Paper OF NEW ENGLAND

FOURTEEN PAGES—TWO CENTS — SATURDAY, SEPTEMBER 14, 1946 ** — FOURTEEN PAGES—TWO CENTS

NEW STRIKE KEEPS SHIPS ALL TIED UP

CIO Seamen Go Out as AFL Walkout Comes to End

PICKET LINES TO KEEP U. S. PORTS PARALYZED

Boston Shipping Men

B. C. COACH'S WIFE PASSES BAR EXAM

Mrs. Denny Myers One of Four Women Winners; Miss Margaret F. McGovern, 21, Youngest to Pass

SOX TAKE PENNANT WITH TED'S HOMER

Red Hose Clinch Top Place in American League Race for Baseball Glory—Beat Cleveland Indians 1 to 0 as Yanks Win Close Battle Over Tigers 5 to 4—

NATIONAL LEAGUE 1946

BOSTON

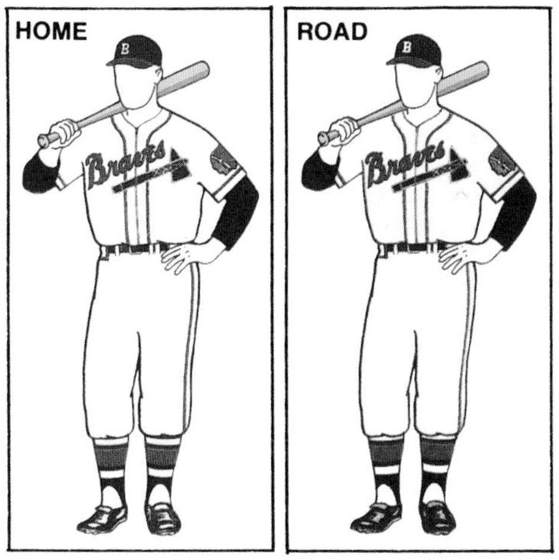

BROOKLYN

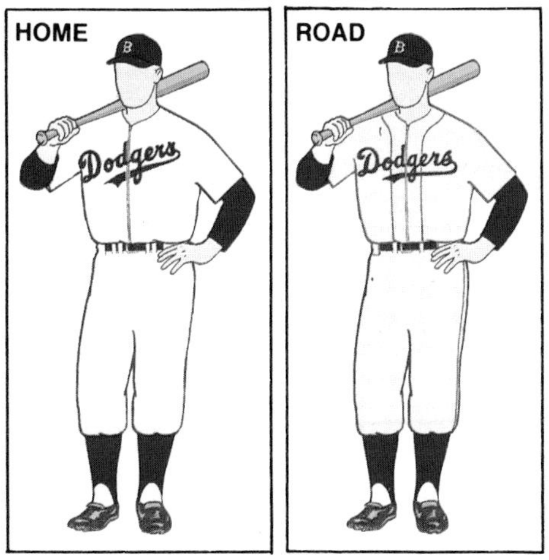

ST. LOUIS

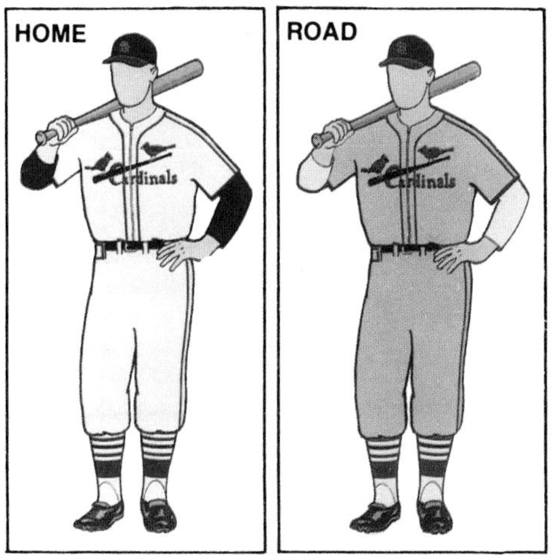

PITTSBURGH

PHILADELPHIA

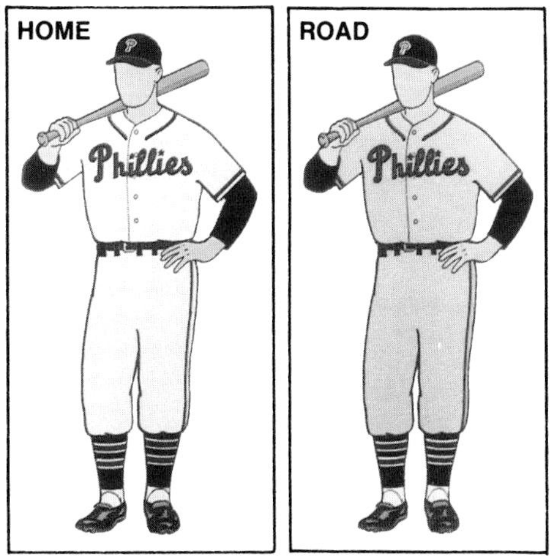

CHICAGO

CINCINNATI

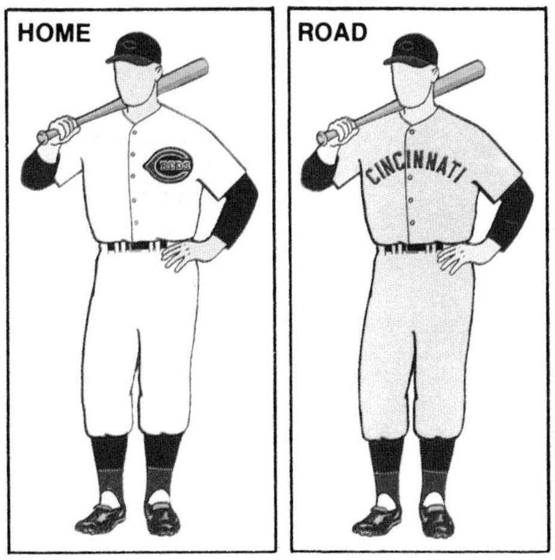

NEW YORK

30 NEW YORK HERALD TRIBUNE, WEDNESDAY, APRIL 17, 1946

Giants Beat Phils, 8-4, in Polo Grounds Debut Before 34,472; Dodgers Lose to Braves,

Ott and Lombardi Pound Judd For Two-Run Homers in First

Circuit Clouts by Murtaugh and Northey Account for Losers' Tallies Against Voiselle; Adams and Trinkle Also Toil; Dewey Tosses Out First Ball

By Al Laney

The New York Giants opened the new baseball season in the old way at the Polo Grounds yesterday, with all the pre-war trappings back on view and a rousing if somewhat jittery victory over the Philadelphia Phillies by a score of 8 to 4. Mel Ott, the popular little manager, and Ernie Lombardi hit home runs in the first inning, each good for two scores, to the huge delight of a crowd of 34,472. Bill Voiselle, the Giants' best pitcher, was the winner, although he had to leave before the end. Governor Thomas E. Dewey, one of the many celebrities present, threw out the first ball.

The weather was far too chilly for comfort and the way the Phils

Giants' Score

Polo Grounds Looking Natural Again Just Before 'Play Ball'

Sain Checks Brooklyn Atta As Gregg Falters in Inaug

Herman Connects for 4 Singles in Losing Hermanski's Fielding Lapses Help Bosto 19,482 Shivering Fans Sit In at Hub's

By Bob Cooke

BOSTON, April 16.—The Boston Braves rode to a 5-to over the Brooklyn Dodgers this afternoon on the wings of fly ball which completed its routine flight to the outfield by Gene Hermanski instead of vice versa.

Few in the opening-day crowd of 19,482 shivering fans anticipated any pleasant effects when Tommy Holmes swatted one of Hal Gregg's pitches in Hermanski's direction in the sixth. The teams were tied at 3-all, two men were out and two runners were in motion. Hermanski's putout would have retired the side. But Hermanski did not make the putout.

236,730 Fans Opening-Day (

The attendance at day's eight major-leag ball openers totaled paid, second only to time high of 249,010 in 1931.

The figures:

1947 AMERICAN LEAGUE

BOSTON

CLEVELAND

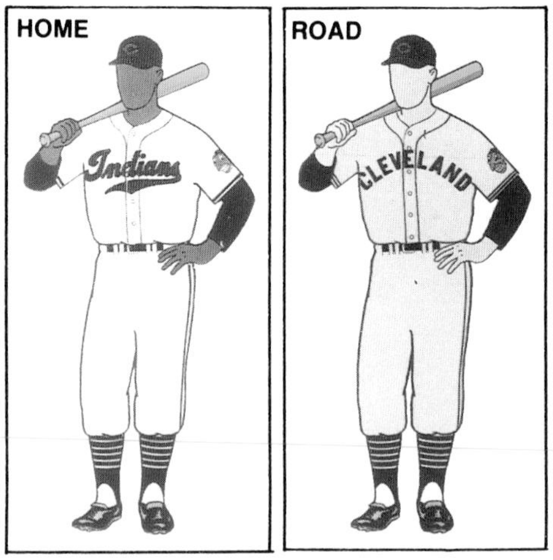

DETROIT

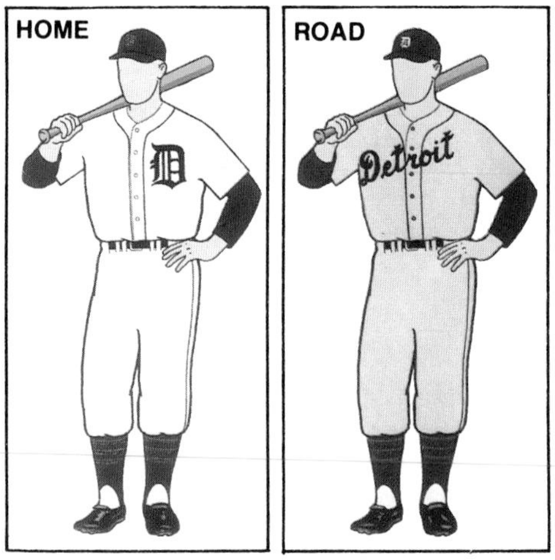

ST. LOUIS

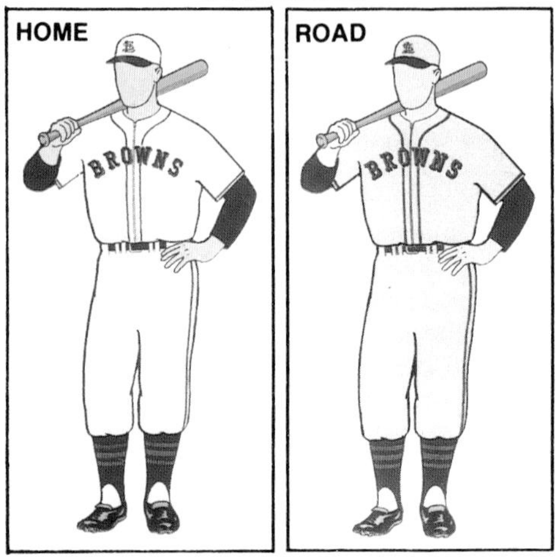

NEW YORK

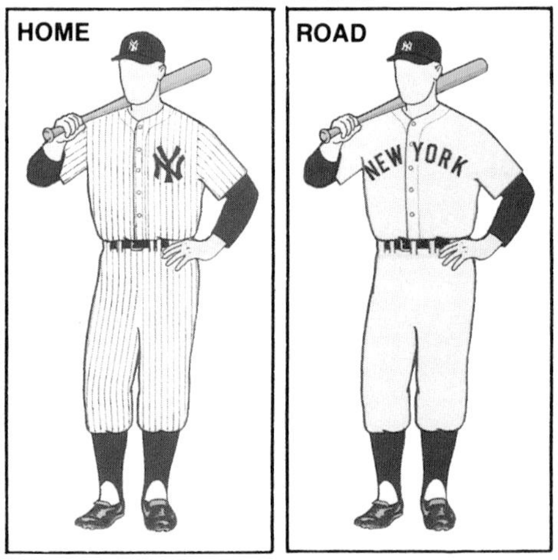

PHILADELPHIA

CHICAGO

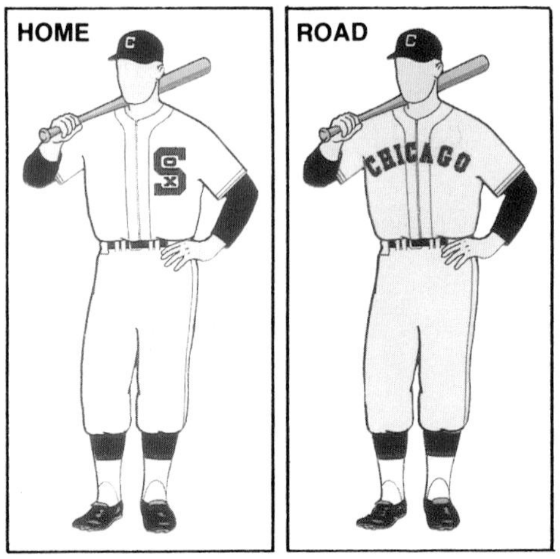

WASHINGTON

NEW YORK HERALD TRIBUNE, TUESDAY, SEPTEMBER 16, 1947 — 23

Idle Yankees Clinch American League Pennant; Giants Overpower Cardinals, 10-5

Bombers Capture Honors As Red Sox Are Defeated

New York Team, Rained Out, Waits in Dressing Room to Hear Result, Celebrates Victory Mildly; MacPhail Pours Champagne, Lauds Harris

By Harold Rosenthal

Pennant Race at Glance

St. Louis Defeat Increases Dodger Lead to 7½ Games

New York Scores Eight Runs in First Two Innings Blasting Brazle and Dickson; Rigney Gets 5 Hits and Cooper Clouts 204th Homer for Club.

By Rud Rennie

ST. LOUIS, Sept. 15 — For the second day in succession the Giants pounded the Cardinals, driving them farther away from their objective — the pace-setting Dodgers and the pennant. Ott's sluggers made eight runs in the first two innings and won, 10 to 5, shoving the defending champions into a discouraging position seven and a half games out of first place.

Giants' Score

NATIONAL LEAGUE 1947

BOSTON

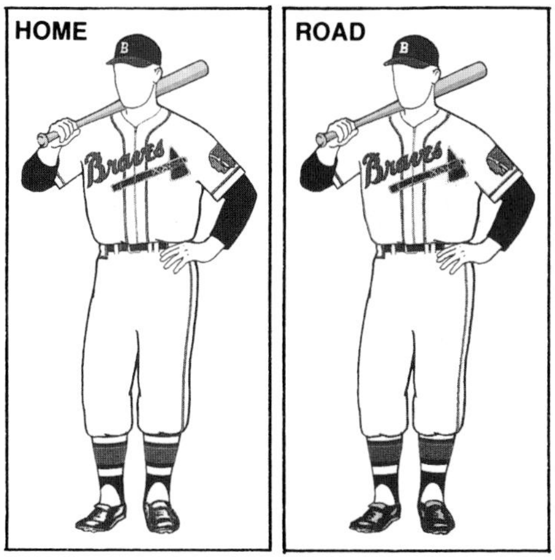

BROOKLYN

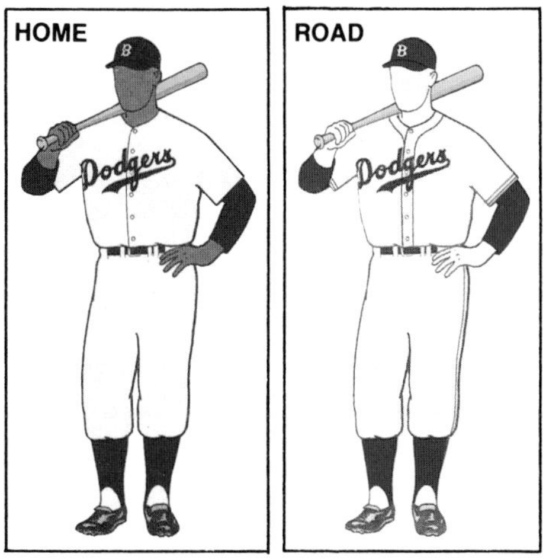

ST. LOUIS

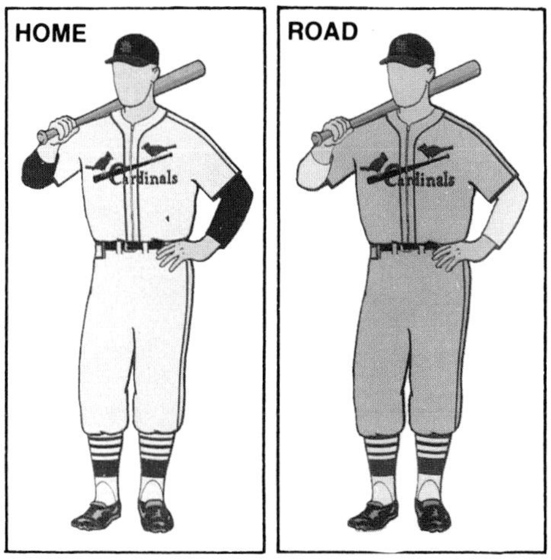

PITTSBURGH

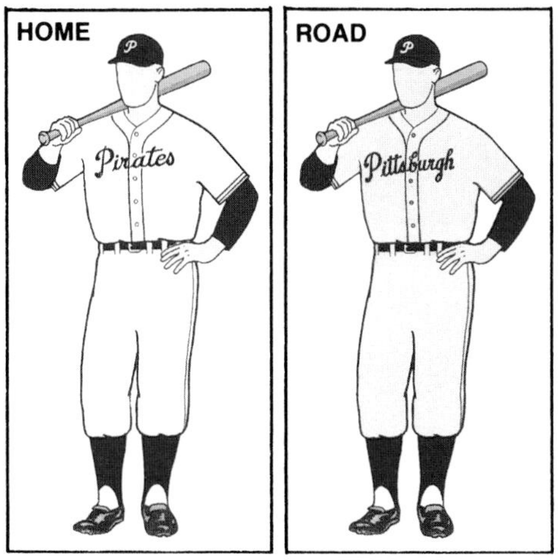

PHILADELPHIA

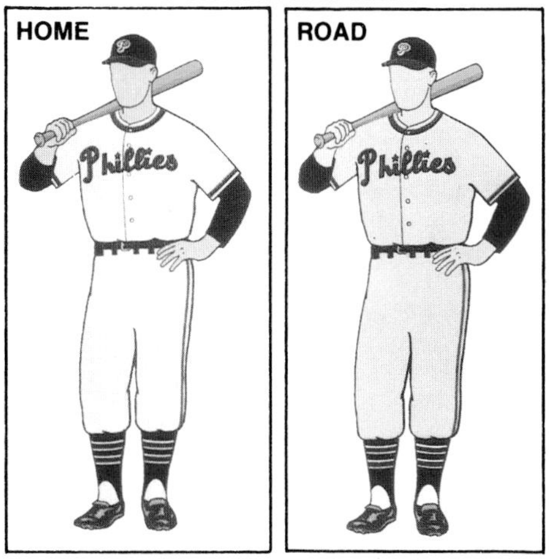

CHICAGO

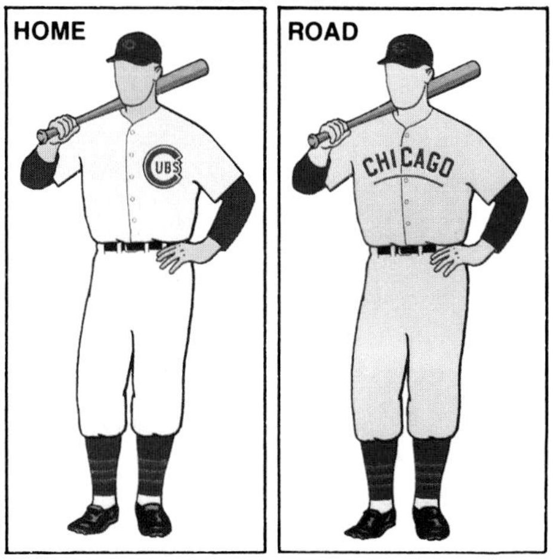

CINCINNATI

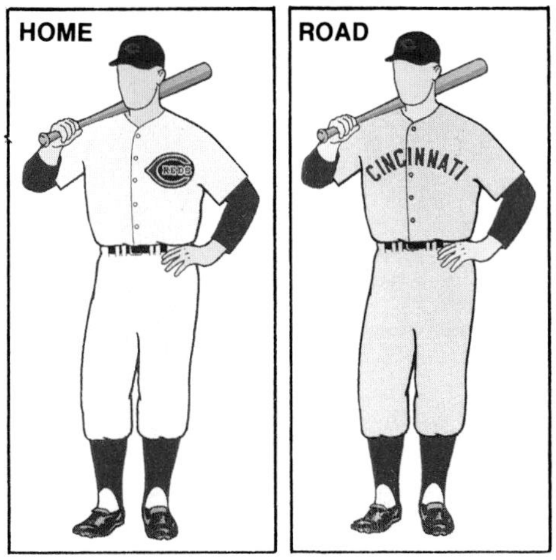

NEW YORK

NOW WE'LL TIE IT UP AGAIN!

Ten Brooklynites Talk About Food for Europe— See Page 21

BROOKLYN EAGLE

5 CENTS EVERYWHERE

WEATHER—Mostly sunny, warm today.

106th YEAR—No. 274—DAILY and SUNDAY   BROOKLYN 1, N. Y., SUNDAY, OCTOBER 5, 1947

YANKEES NIP DODGERS, 2-1, AS SHEA STARS

Ughetta Assigned To Condemnations

Will Sit With Justice Lockwood

REGISTRATION STARTS IN CITY TOMORROW

U. S. Offers U. N. Compromise Plan For Balkan Woes

1948 AMERICAN LEAGUE

BOSTON

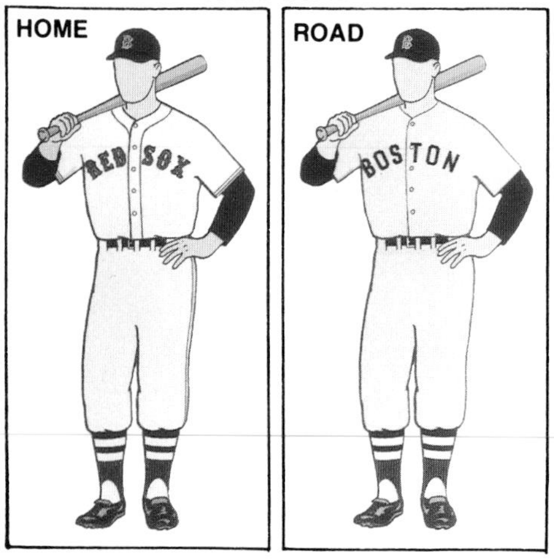

CLEVELAND

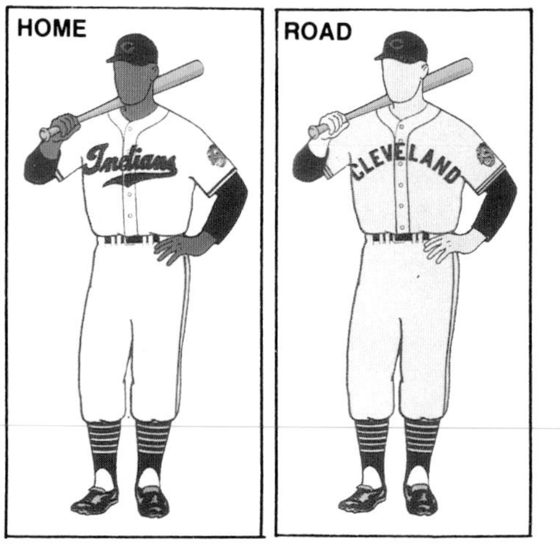

DETROIT

ST. LOUIS

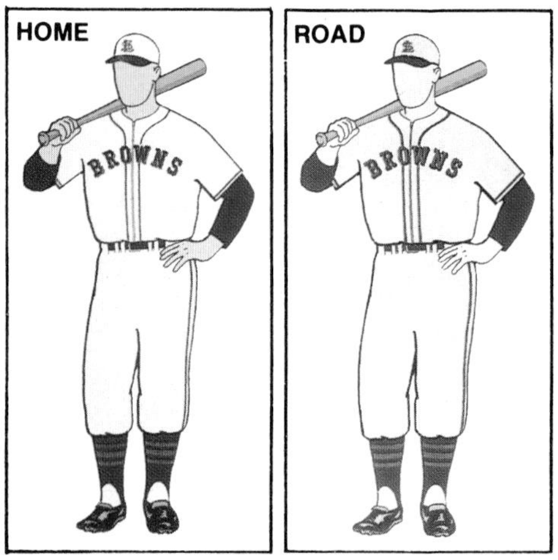

NEW YORK

PHILADELPHIA

CHICAGO

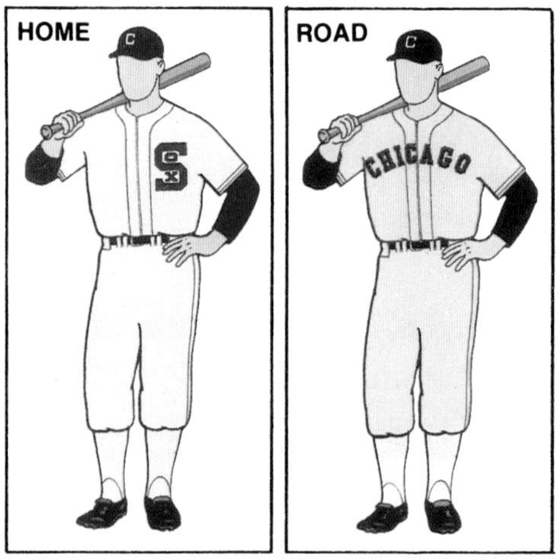

WASHINGTON

Feller Hurls Twice More as Tribe Fights to Clinch Flag

The Press Sports

CLEVELAND, MONDAY, SEPTEMBER 27, 1948

Franklin Lewis

Bits and Bites of Sports Saved for First Place

Mutterings by the Monday Muse and wasn't this once the football season? . . .

You cheered for the Irish or dear old Brown.
You watched new stars gain gridiron renown:
You prayed for Purdue or Cornell or Yale,
You sat in the rain and sometimes in hail.

Braves "In" After 34-Year Wait

BOSTON, Sept. 27—(UP)—For the first time in 34 long and parched years, the Boston Braves today held joyous possession of the National League pennant.

A turnout of 31,172 wild-eyed fans tossed hats, bottles, scorecards and everything else into the air yesterday afternoon as the Braves clinched the senior circuit race with a 8-to-2 victory over the New York Giants.

Bells, sirens, whistles and horns dinned through the city in public celebration a scant minute after a relief hurler retired the last Giant batter in the top of the ninth.

It was Bob Elliott, most valuable National League player in 1947, who knocked in all three runs for the Braves with a two-aboard home run in the first inning, his 22d of the season.

It was freshman Vern Bickford who got credit for the all-important game, his 10th triumph of the year, though he was relieved by Nels Potter in the eighth.

In the first, Tommy Holmes opened the game with a single to center and was followed by Alvin Dark, who singled to right. Earl Torgeson then filed out and Elliott came up.

The broad-shouldered third baseman had a two and one count on him when he picked out a Larry Jansen fast ball and slammed it over the right field fence for three runs, the game and the pennant.

Paintin' Up for War Path . . . . by Darvas

CHICAGO DETROIT

Yanks' Job Is Harder Than Sox

When American League pennant rivals resume action tomorrow, after a day's vacation, the Yankees appear to have a harder

5-Game Drive Opens Tomorrow Night

By FRANK GIBBONS

Back home and blazing with an ever fiercer pennant fire, the Indians rested today preparatory to the Stadium stretch drive of five games, which they hope will bring Cleveland its first pennant in 28 years.

They're one golden game ahead of the Red Sox and Yankees today, the first time they have been out front alone since Aug. 25. They have five games left, beginning tomorrow night against the White Sox, in which to defend their precious lead.

All Alone				
Club	W	L	Pct	GB
INDIANS	93	56	.624	—
New York	92	57	.617	1
Boston	92	57	.617	1

Games Behind Leader

Lou Boudreau speaks for the entire team's spirit when he says.

"We'll win it now and we'll win because of Bob Feller."

Baseball's bouncing boy Master Feller, said that he had more zing on the ball yesterday in

kees out," Boudreau says. "The Red Sox are too tough at home."

Sox Rated No. 1

After what has happened in this most delirious season in the history of the league, it isn't easy to count anybody out, but the

NATIONAL LEAGUE 1948

BOSTON

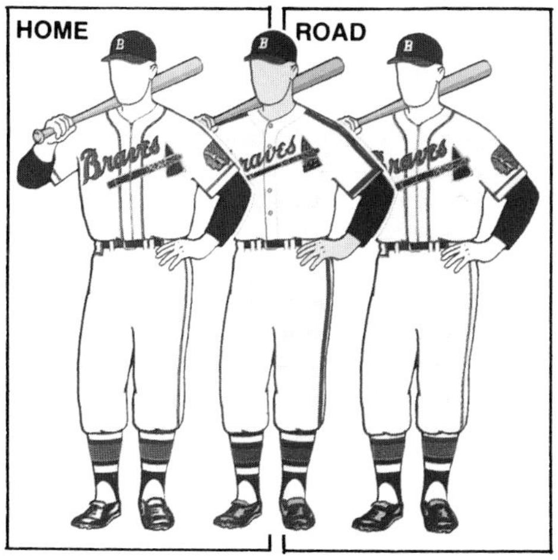

BROOKLYN

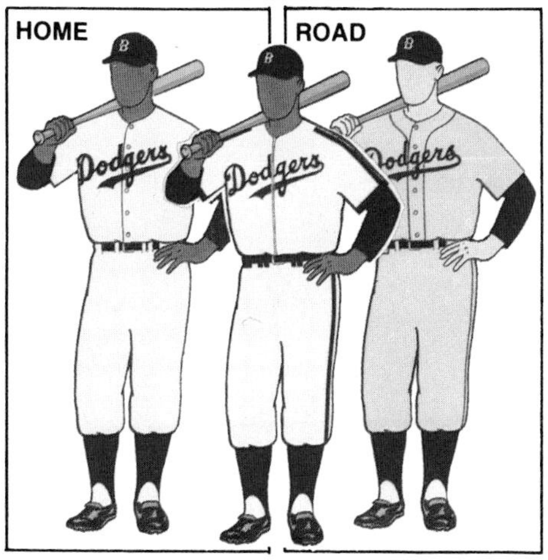

ST. LOUIS

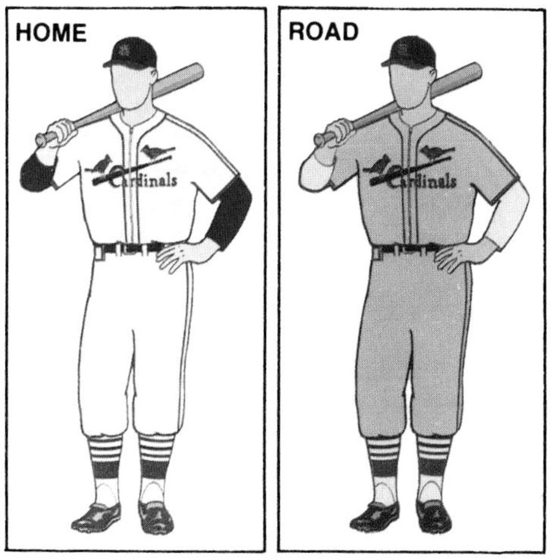

PITTSBURGH

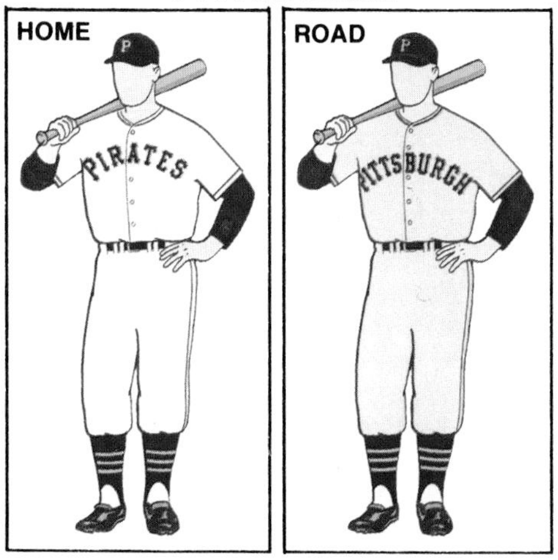

PHILADELPHIA

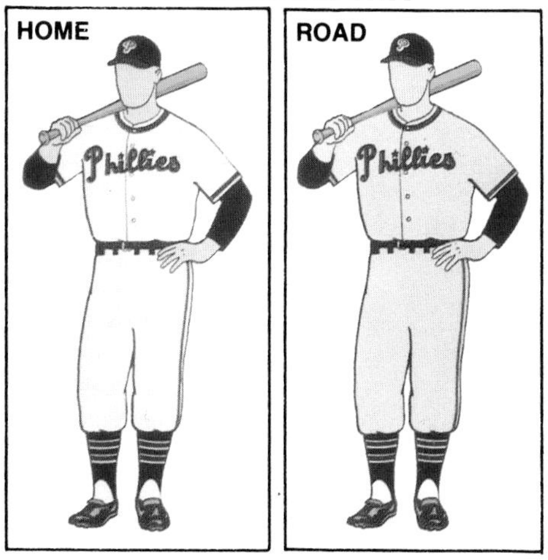

CHICAGO

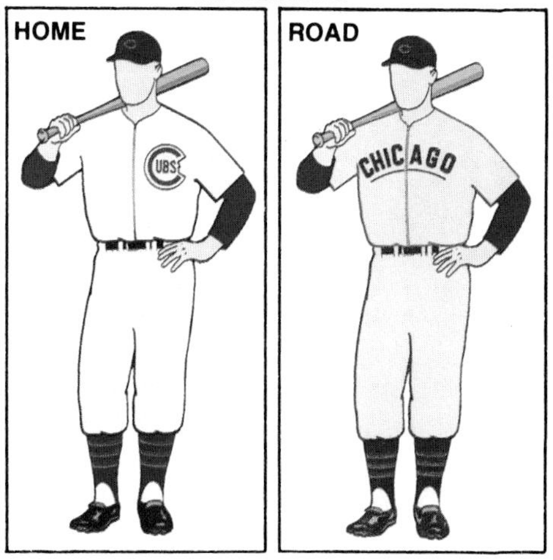

CINCINNATI

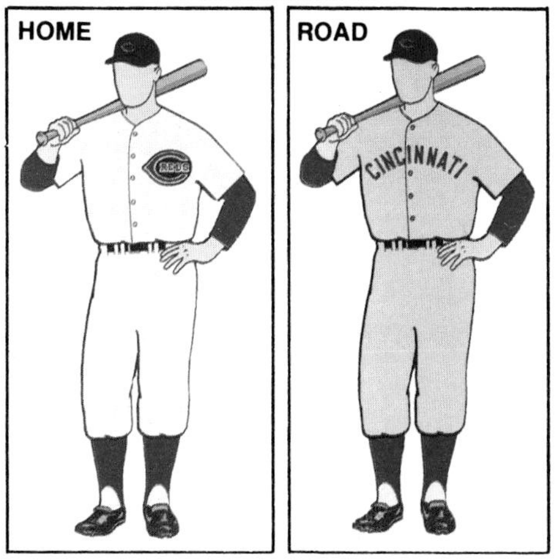

NEW YORK

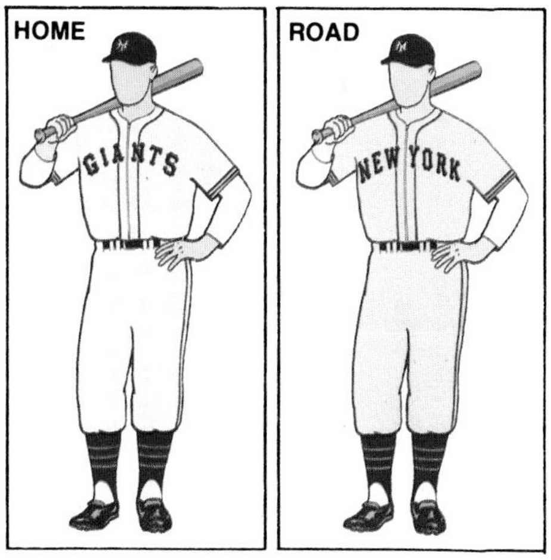

The Boston Post

THE GREAT Breakfast Table Paper OF NEW ENGLAND

TWENTY-FOUR PAGES—THREE CENTS — MONDAY, SEPTEMBER 27 1948 — TWENTY-FOUR PAGES—THREE CENTS

Braves Clinch Pennant, Sox in Second Place

ELLIOTT HOME RUN WINS, 3-2

Feller Tames Tigers, 4-1, as Indians Take American League Lead ---Yanks Beat Hose, 6-2

U. S. BREAKS OFF TALKS WITH SOVIET ON BERLIN

1949 AMERICAN LEAGUE

BOSTON

HOME

ROAD

CLEVELAND

HOME

ROAD

DETROIT

HOME

ROAD

ST. LOUIS

HOME

ROAD

NEW YORK

HOME

ROAD

PHILADELPHIA

HOME

ROAD

CHICAGO

HOME

ROAD

WASHINGTON

HOME

ROAD

30 NEW YORK HERALD TRIBUNE, WEDNESDAY, APRIL 13, 1949

Heel Pains Force DiMaggio to Fly to Johns Hopkins for Second Time in 6 Weeks

$90,000-a-Year Center-Fielder Is Lost to Yankees Indefinitely

Club Officials at Fort Worth Conference Voice Hope Treatments Will Prolong His Career

By Red Rennie

FORT WORTH, Tex., April 12.—Joe DiMaggio, troubled by a painful right heel ever since his first day of spring training, March 1, today had to stop trying to play baseball until something could be done to relieve the pain. The Yankees' star outfielder and slugger left the team and flew to Johns Hopkins Hospital in Baltimore for the second time in six weeks. He will be under treatment for a week or more and will not be in the line-up on the opening day of the season April 19.

Announcement of the decision to send the Yankees' $90,000 outfielder back to the hospital in the hope of prolonging his career as a player was made at a press conference in the Worth Hotel at 11 o'clock this forenoon. DiMaggio was present and Casey Stengel, the manager, and all the newspaper men.

(At Dallas, where his plane stopped for five minutes, DiMaggio told The Associated Press "I certainly am not going to retire from

Cooper Surgeon Finds Knee Very Satisfactory

ST. LOUIS, April 12 (AP).—The surgeon who operated on Walker Cooper's left knee last winter said after an examination today that it appeared "very satisfactory" and should cause the New York Giants' catcher no trouble this season.

Cooper left the Giants at Texarkana, Tex., and came here for the examination by Dr. Robert F. Hyland, club surgeon of the St. Louis Cardinals. Cooper said the knee had been

DiMaggio's Return to Hospital Fails to Alarm Yankee Office

Maggie Regets, Switchboard Chief, Shares Weiss's Optimism That Star Will Soon Rejoin Team

By Bill Lauder Jr.

'Tis said that "as DiMaggio goes, so go the Yankees," but, despite the reports from the Southland concerning the latest affliction of the DiMaggio heel, the local offices of the club were not steeped in gloom yesterday.

Jolting Joe was en route to Johns Hopkins Hospital yesterday afternoon for further treatment on his right heel, from which a bone spur was removed last winter, and will miss the opening game for the eighth time in eleven seasons.

The big ray of sunshine in the Yankee offices was Maggie Regets, custodian of the switchboard and guardian of the gates to the inner-sanctum. "It's not that serious," said smiling Maggie. "Everything will be all right. Joe will be back in there."

Maggie's optimism was echoed in substance by George Weiss, general manager of the Bronx Bombers. Weiss had talked by telephone with Dr. George Bennett, the Johns Hopkins surgeon who performed the operation on

NATIONAL LEAGUE 1949

BOSTON

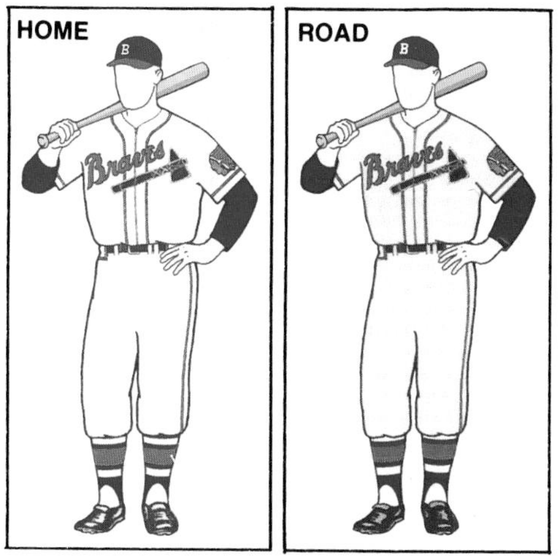

BROOKLYN

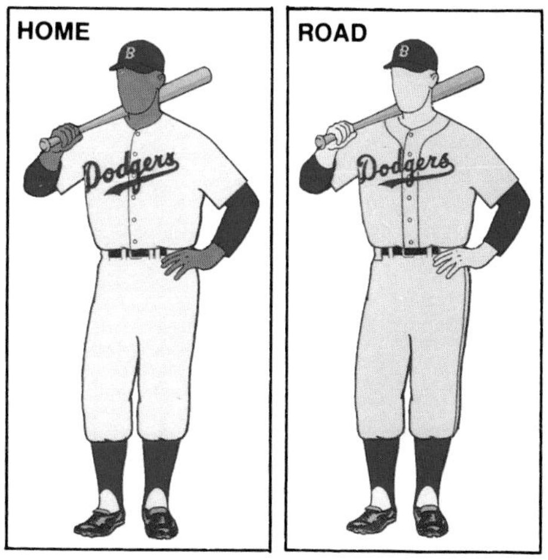

ST. LOUIS

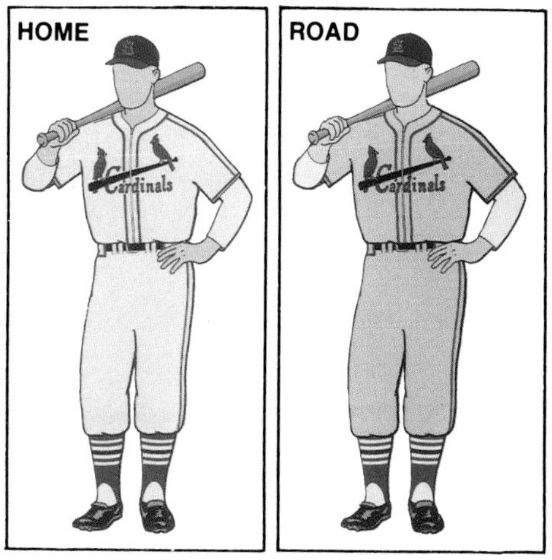

PITTSBURGH

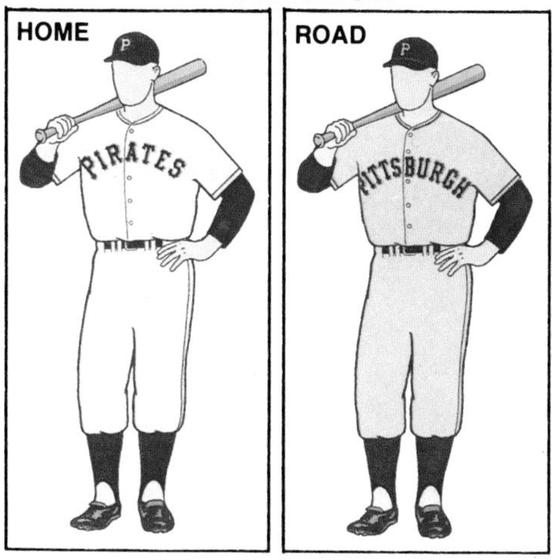

PHILADELPHIA

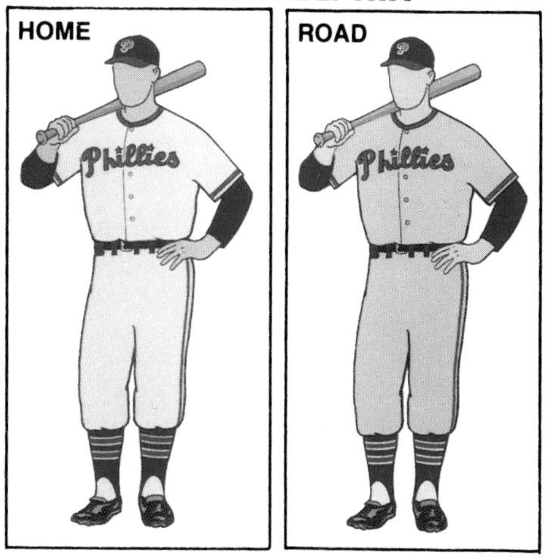

CHICAGO

CINCINNATI

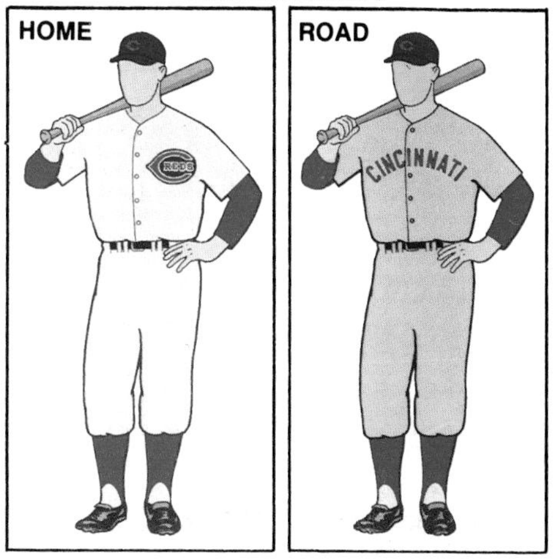

NEW YORK

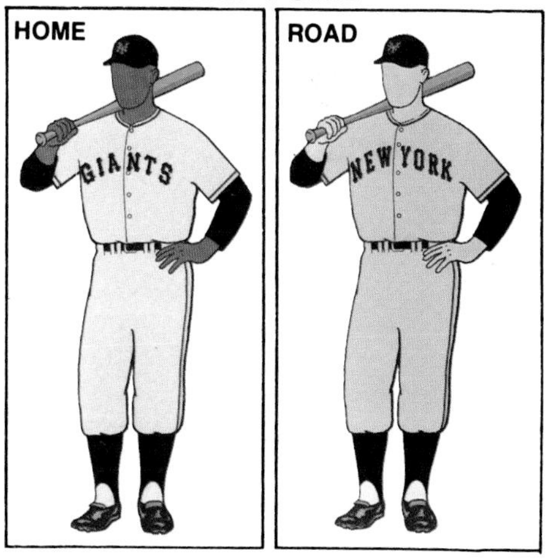

TOMMY HOLMES

Dodgers and Yanks Squeak Into Flags

Yeah, Dodgers! Our Champions Again! And Now Bring On Those Yankees!!

AT THE STADIUM—After all these years you'd think that the proprietor of this corner would have grown up. But I haven't. Here I was, wedged into the jam-packed pressbox at the Yankee Stadium, needing at least two stomachs to accommodate all the butterflies buzzing around inside.

Being a Yankee fan, so far as the American League is concerned, this was a double ordeal. I was trying to root one club home on the ballfield and another one home on the scoreboard.

Finally, it wound up the way I wanted it. But if you think I had fun, you're crazy. So you want to be a sports-writer, huh?

There was that blistering tension from the start . . . Phil Rizzuto's line drive into left field that Ted Williams played into a triple . . . A Yankee run when Tommy Henrich hit a slow bounding ball toward second base . . . Joe DiMaggio dropping another blooper in right and racing for third when Al Zarilla missed a diving catch, but the Yankees failing to cash in further.

Courage Did It—Manager Shotton

Phils Year Away From Being Real Contender—Reese

Manager Burt Shotton does not think that any one Dodger should receive the lion's share of the credit for winning the 1949 National League pennant. They all gave it the old college try.

"The whole team played its heart out," he paid tribute to his players. "They are a great bunch of athletes."

Scared Brooklyn Fans Relax After Near K.O. by Phillies—Snider's Hit in Tenth Clinches

Continued from P[illegible]

[illegible] yesterday when [illegible] Phil[illegible] 9 to 7 in 10 innings after [illegible] Duke Snider delivering the [illegible] The Brook[illegible] to cap[illegible] playoff with the Cardinals [illegible] after four staggering [illegible] St. Louis came alive [illegible] one from the [illegible]

All Brooklyn [illegible] the Dodgers didn't [illegible] pennant. It would have been [illegible]

1950 AMERICAN LEAGUE

BOSTON

CLEVELAND

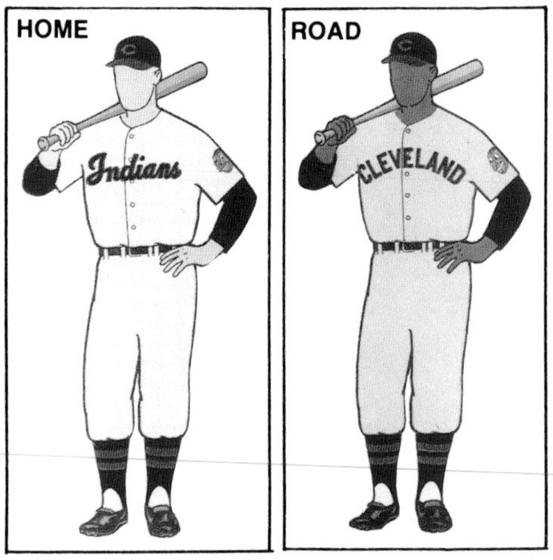

DETROIT

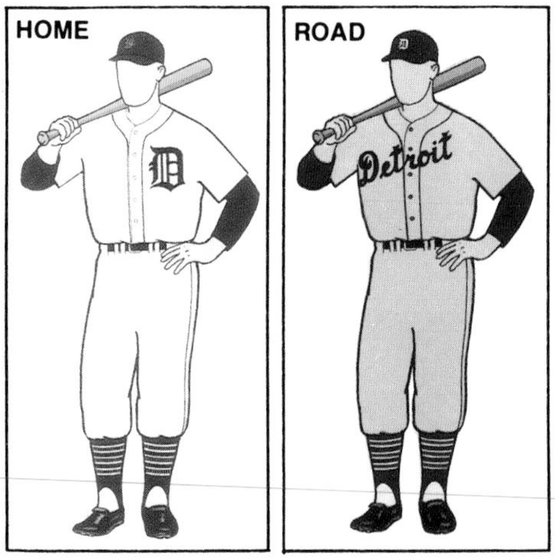

ST. LOUIS

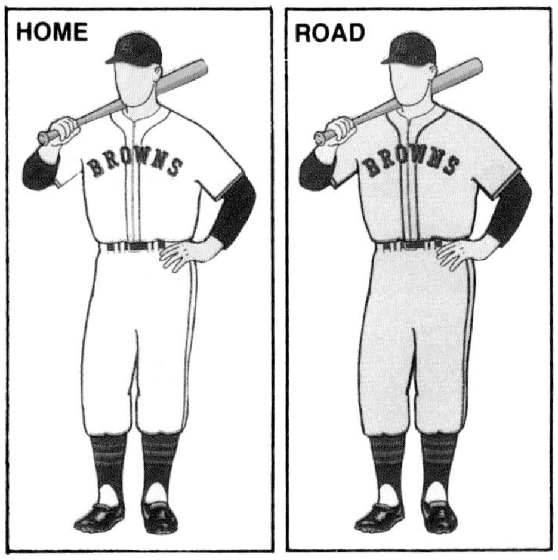

NEW YORK

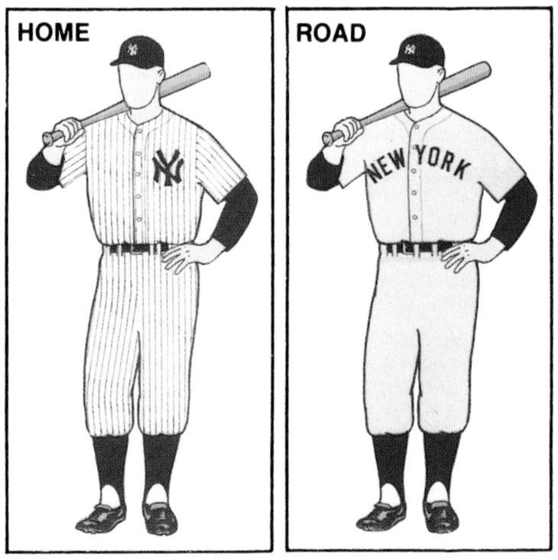

PHILADELPHIA

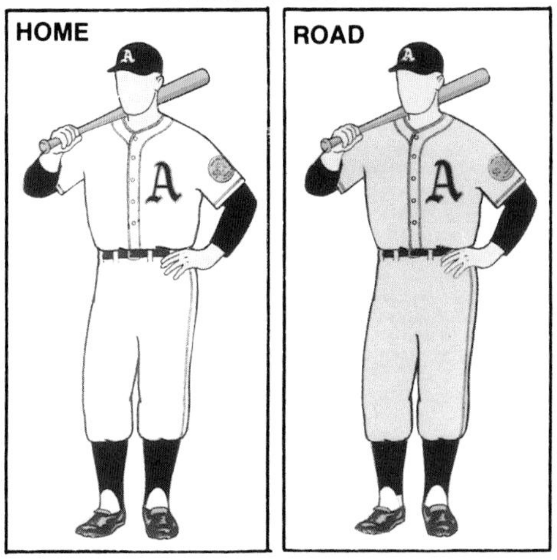

CHICAGO

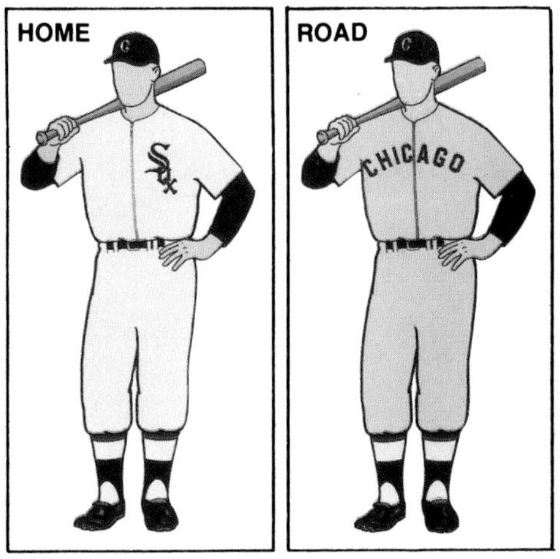

WASHINGTON

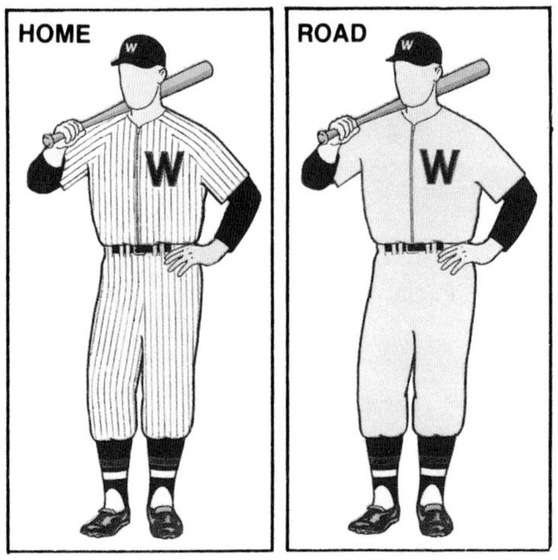

Weather Forecast

Home Delivery

The Sunday Star

WITH DAILY EVENING EDITION

An Associated Press Newspaper

Year. No. 176. ★ WASHINGTON, D. C., JUNE 25, 1950—146 PAGES. TEN CENTS.

REDS INVADE SOUTH KOREA ON WIDE FRONT

Smith Beats Senator Graham By 25,000 Votes in Runoff Primary in North Carolina

Advance Is Reported Stopped After Dawn Assault at 11 Points

NATIONAL LEAGUE 1950

BOSTON

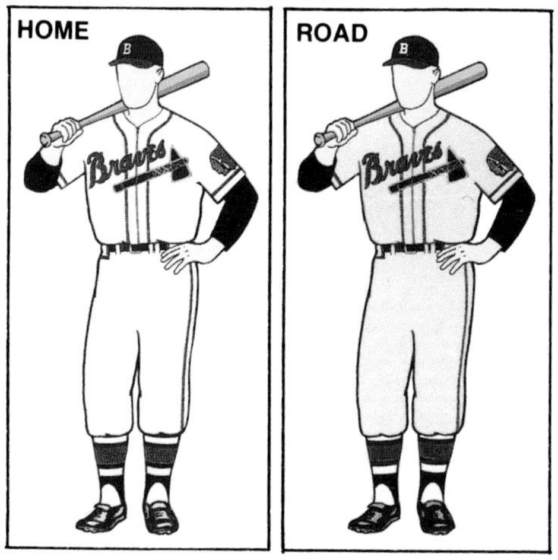

BROOKLYN

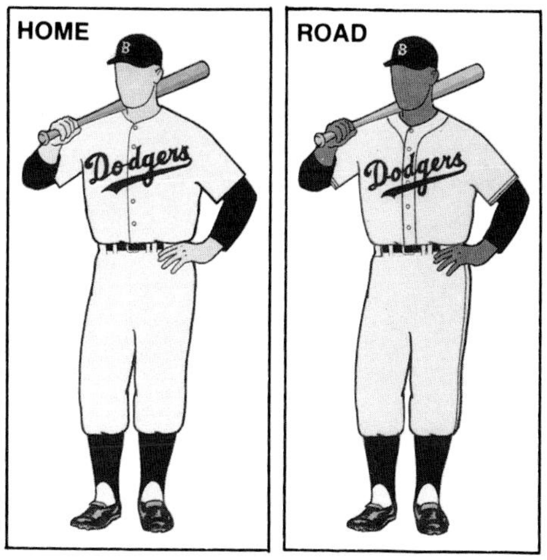

ST. LOUIS

PITTSBURGH

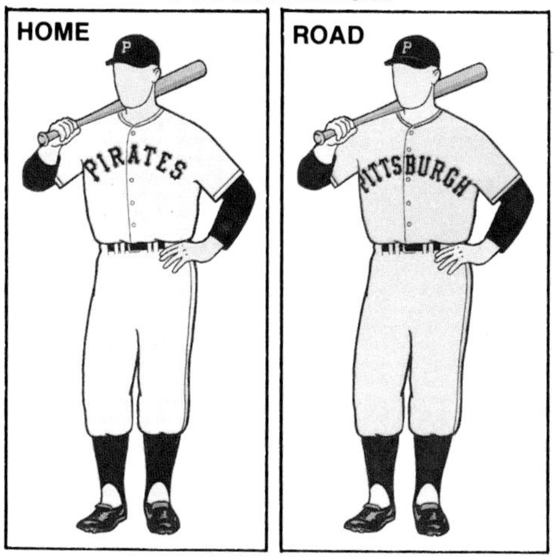

PHILADELPHIA

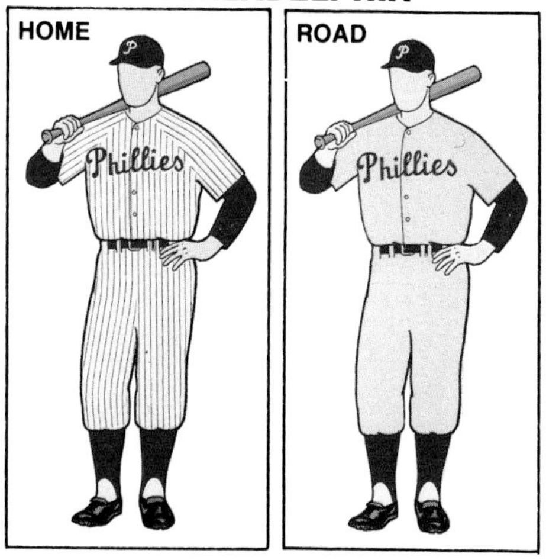

CHICAGO

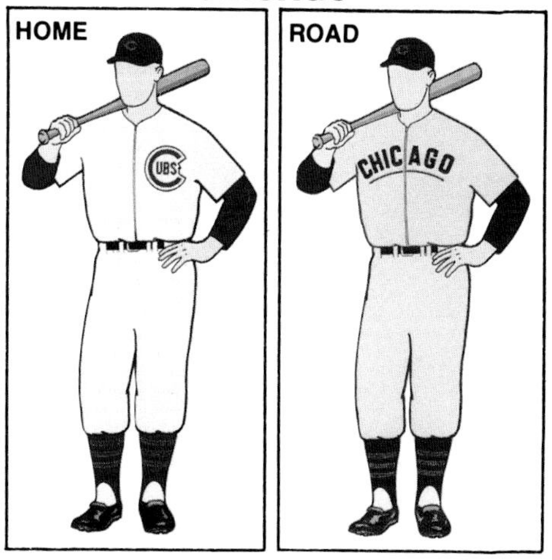

CINCINNATI

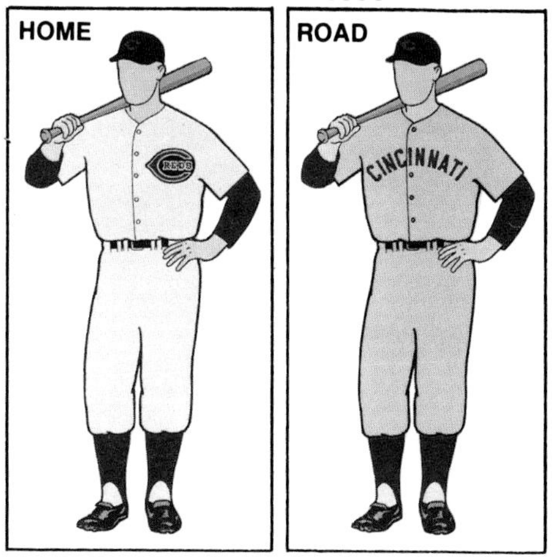

NEW YORK

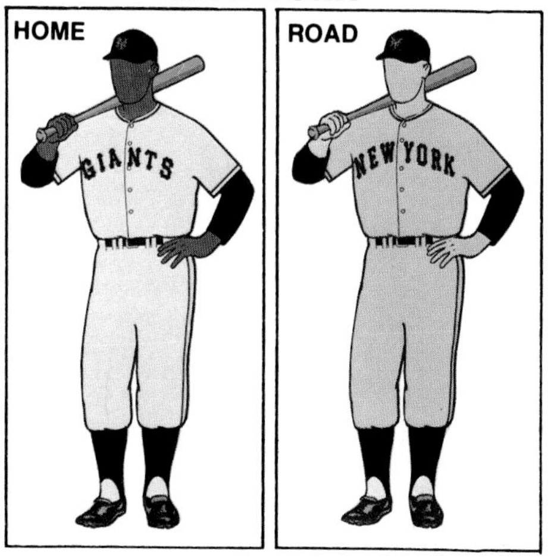

NEW YORK HERALD TRIBUNE, MONDAY, OCTOBER 2, 1950

Phils Win 1st Pennant in 35 Years, Beat Dodgers, 4-1, on Sisler's Homer in 10th

Roberts Escapes Danger in 9th, Hurls 5-Hitter for 20th Victory

Pitcher Strand-3 Runners After Abrams Is Caught at Home; Reese Connects

Dodgers' Score

1951 AMERICAN LEAGUE

BOSTON

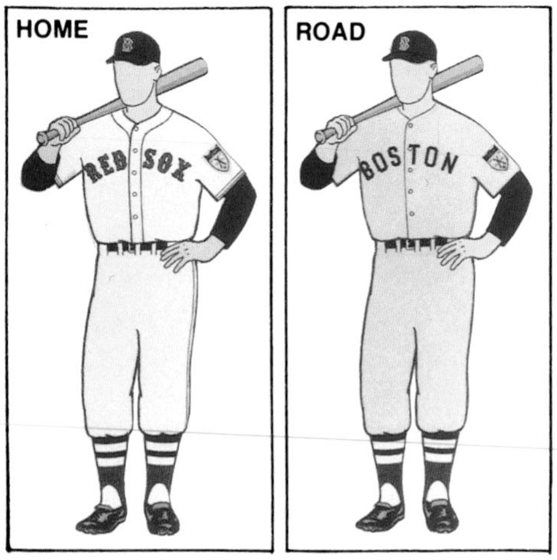

CLEVELAND

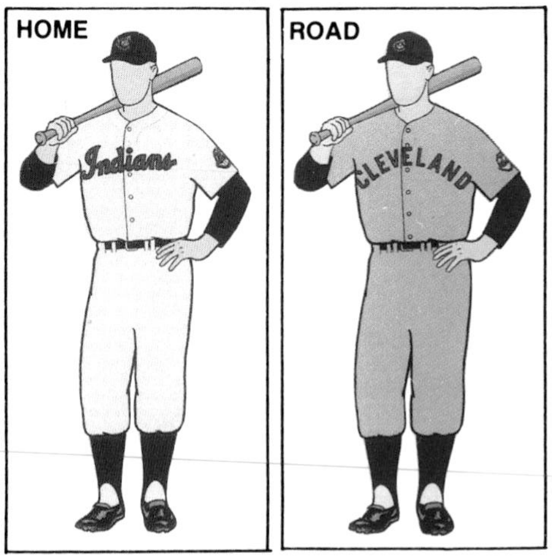

DETROIT

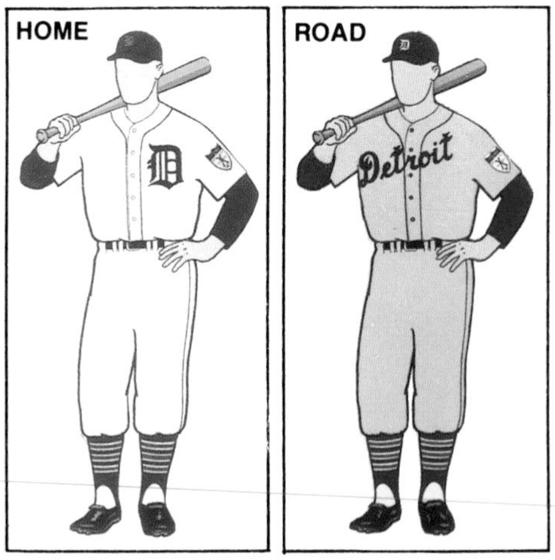

ST. LOUIS

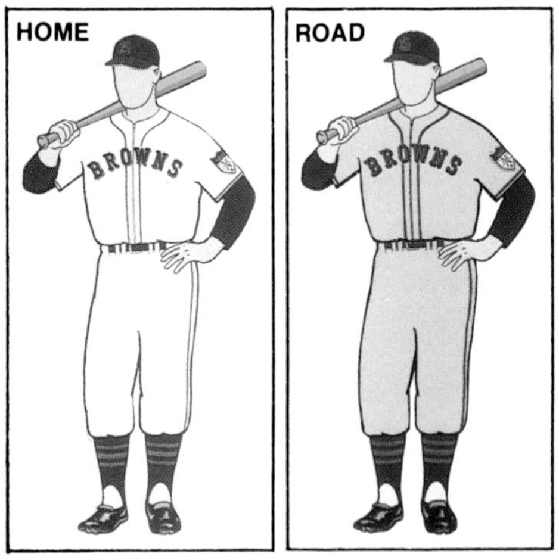

NEW YORK

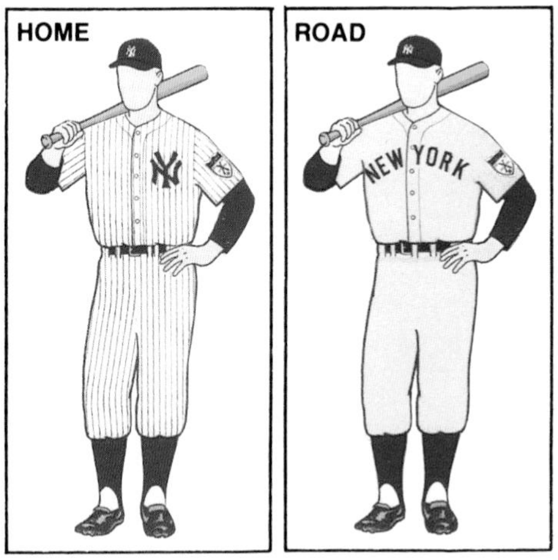

PHILADELPHIA

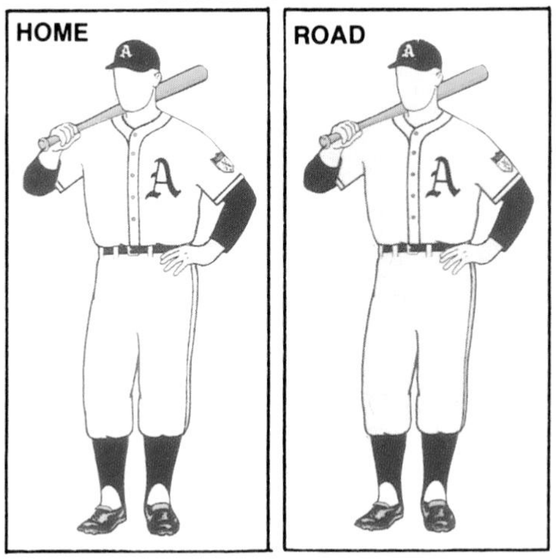

CHICAGO

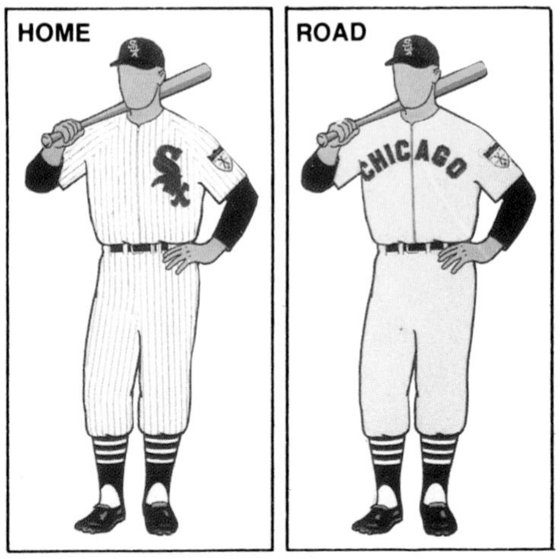

WASHINGTON

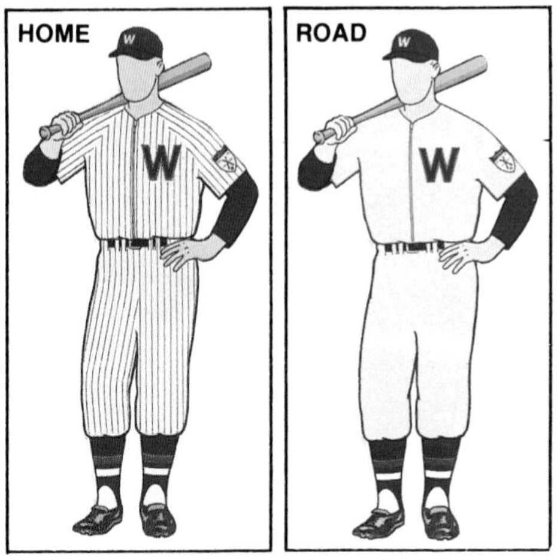

Sports Globe-Democrat

Sat., Sept. 29, 1951 3C

Bears in Grid Debut Today;
Tigers Picked Over Cowpokes
Turn to Page 4C

YANKS CAPTURE PENNANT;
NO-HITTER FOR REYNOLDS

BOSOX SLAUGHTERED
8-0, AND 11-3; ALLIE'S
FEAT SETS A. L. MARK

NATIONAL LEAGUE 1951

BOSTON

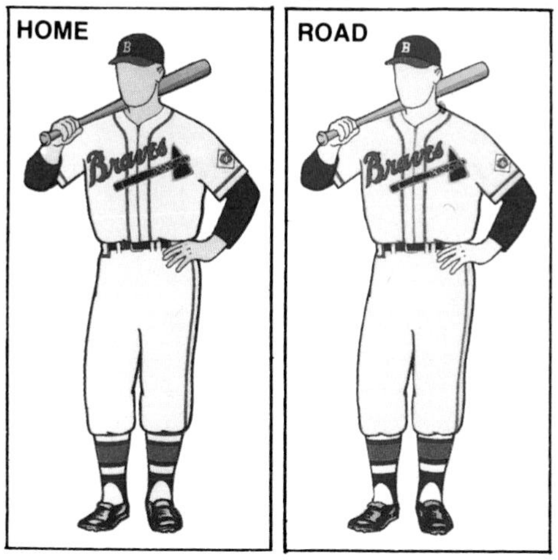

BROOKLYN

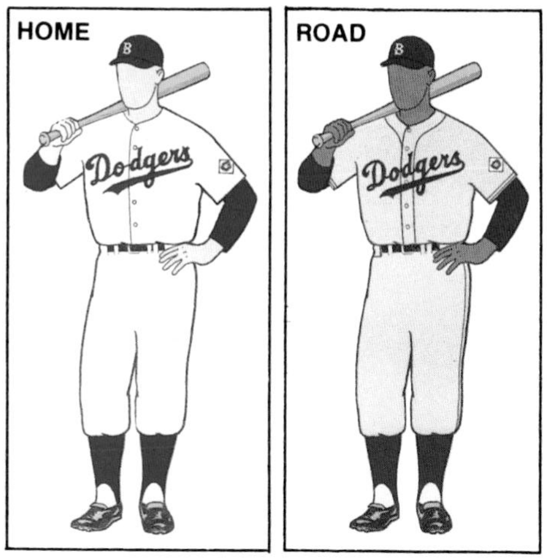

ST. LOUIS

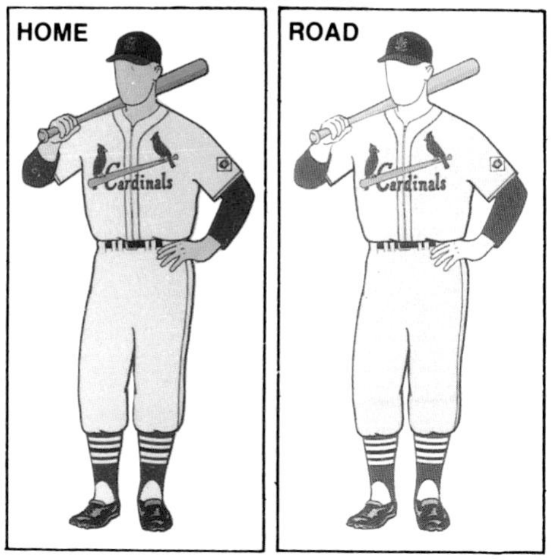

PITTSBURGH

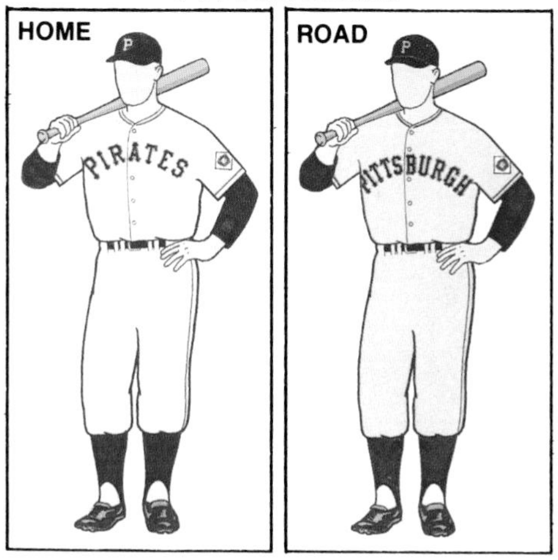

PHILADELPHIA

CHICAGO

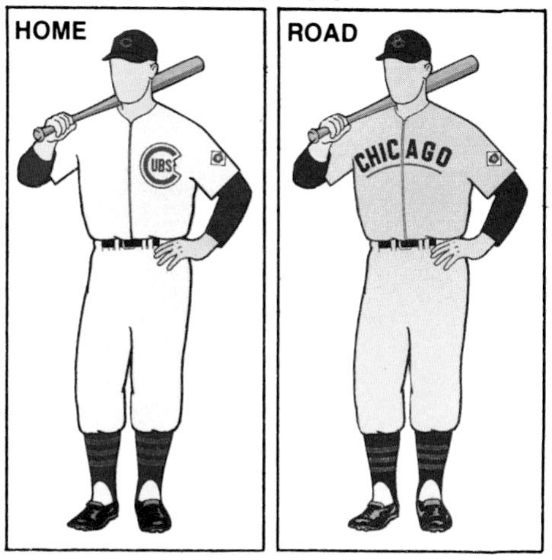

CINCINNATI

NEW YORK

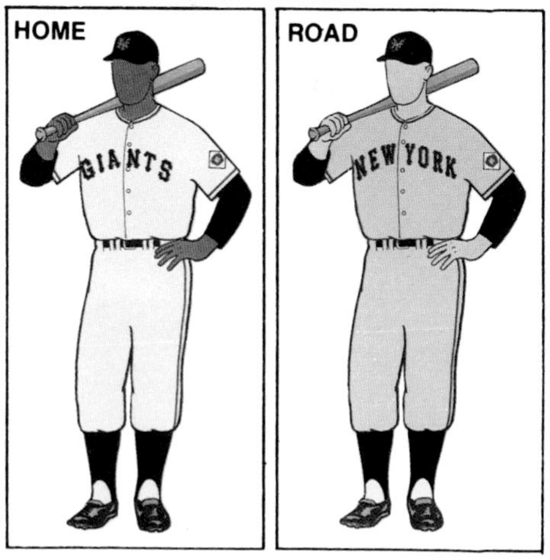

THE WEATHER

Today: Considerable cloudiness and windy; increasing east to northeast winds, becoming 30 to 40 miles an hour and gusty.

Tomorrow: Possible clearing; diminishing northerly winds.

Detailed Report and Map—Page 37

NEW YORK Herald Tribune

European Edition Published Daily in Paris

Late City Edition

111th Year — THURSDAY, OCTOBER 4, 1951 — FIVE-CENTS

Giants Win Pennant in 9th, 5-4, On Thomson's 3-Run Homer

Dodgers Defeated On Hit Off Branca

Newcombe Falters in 9th; Koslo to Face Reynolds

Big U.N. Push Believed On In West Korea

Censors Black Out Most Battle News

Allies Get Reds' Reply on Moving Truce Site; Contents Not Revealed

Reds Set Off Atom Bomb Second Time in 2 Years, White House Announces

Acheson Challenged by Stassen To Deny Effort to Cut China Aid

Explosion Is Placed Inside Soviet Union

1952 AMERICAN LEAGUE

BOSTON

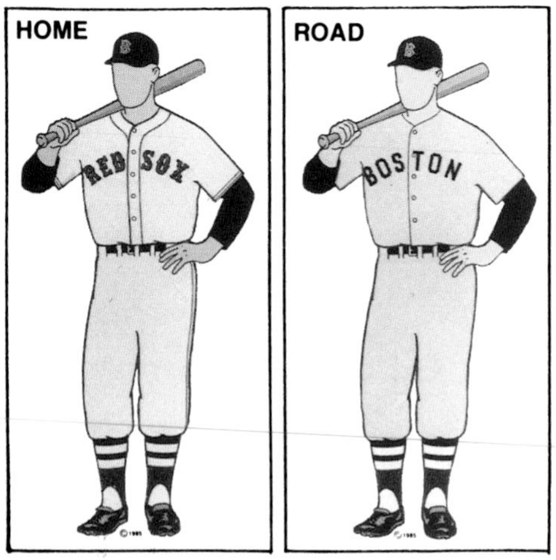

CLEVELAND

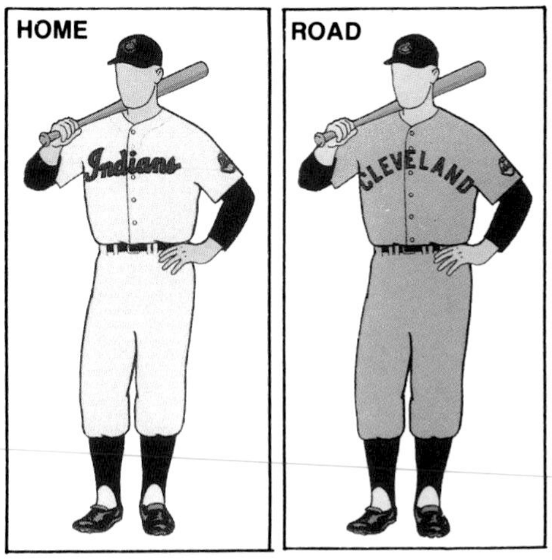

DETROIT

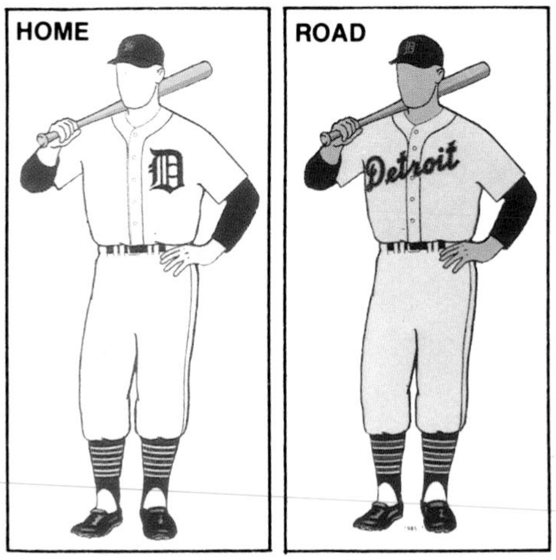

ST. LOUIS

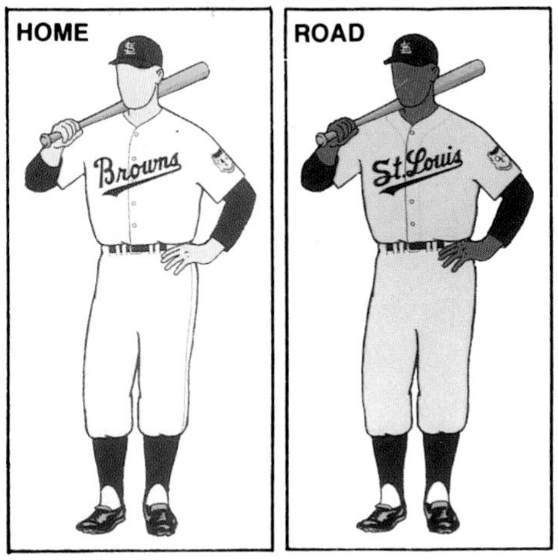

NEW YORK

PHILADELPHIA

CHICAGO

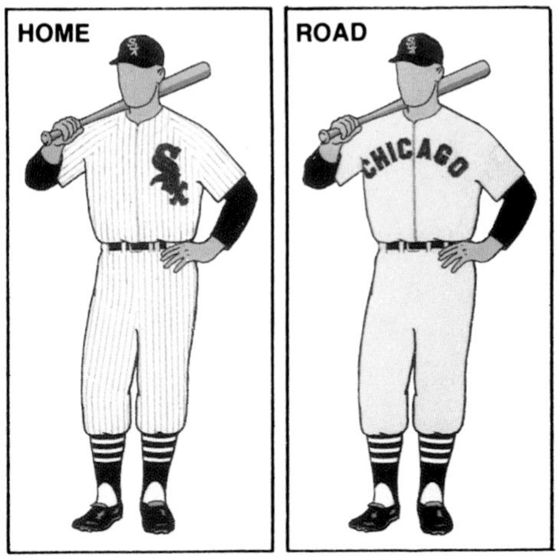

WASHINGTON

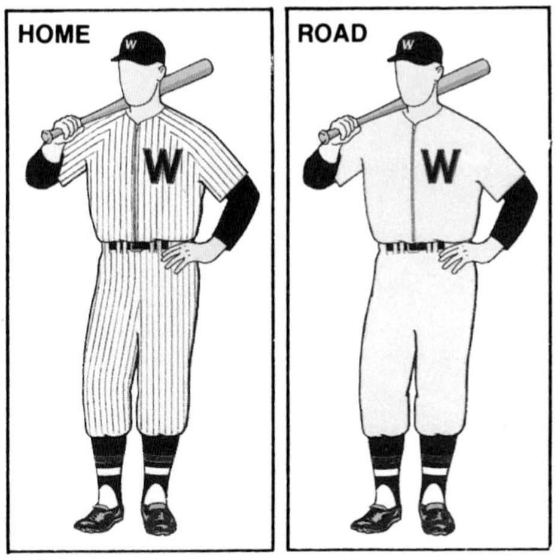

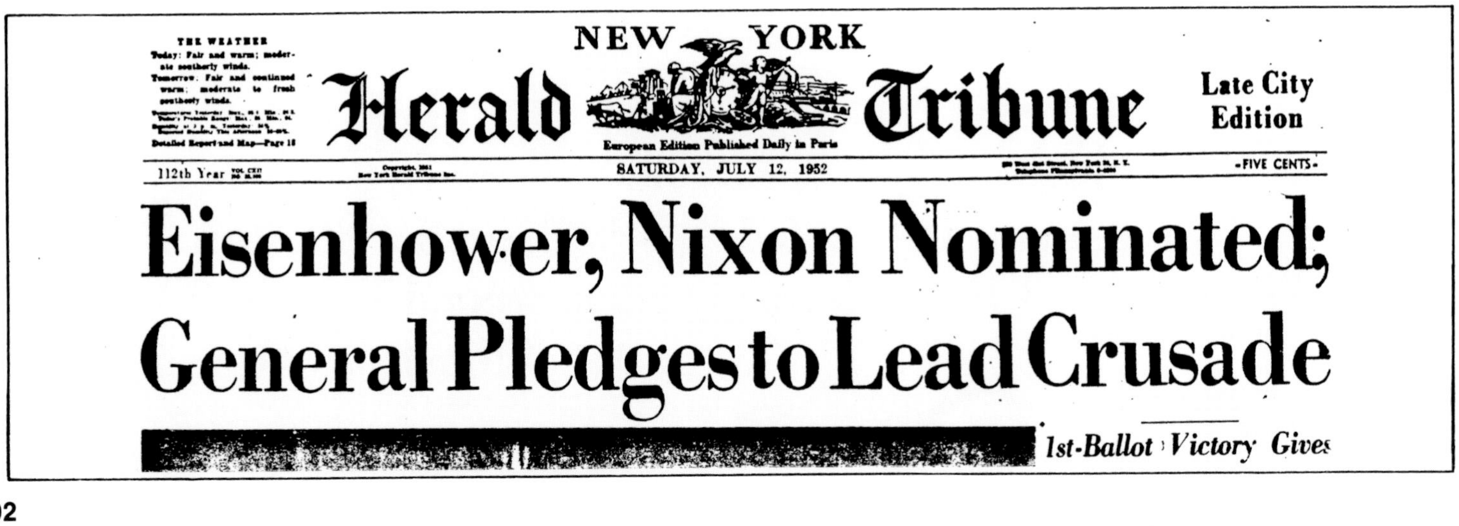
THE WEATHER

Today: Fair and warm; moderate southerly winds.
Tomorrow: Fair and continued warm; moderate to fresh southerly winds.

Detailed Report and Map—Page 10

NEW YORK Herald Tribune

European Edition Published Daily in Paris

Late City Edition

112th Year | SATURDAY, JULY 12, 1952 | FIVE CENTS

Eisenhower, Nixon Nominated; General Pledges to Lead Crusade

1st-Ballot Victory Gives

NATIONAL LEAGUE 1952

BOSTON

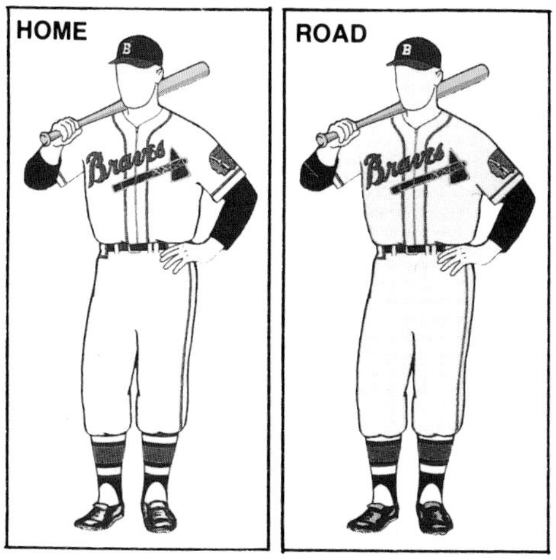

BROOKLYN

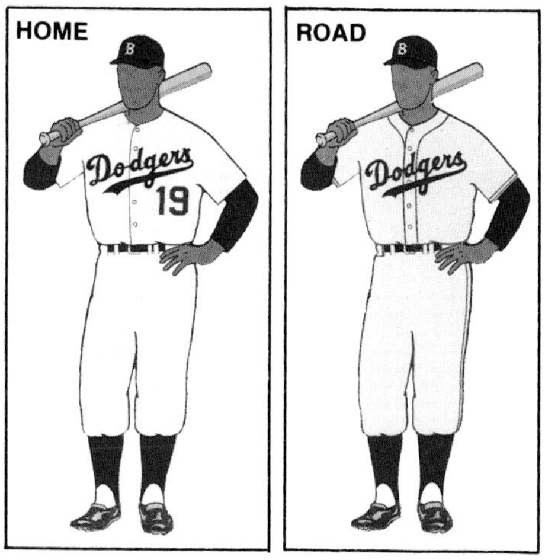

ST. LOUIS

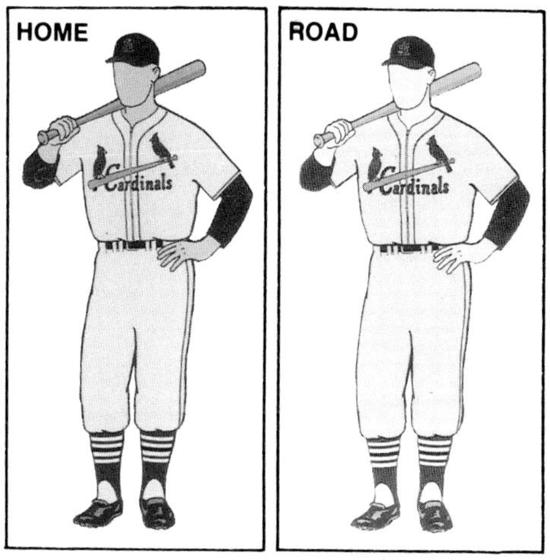

PITTSBURGH

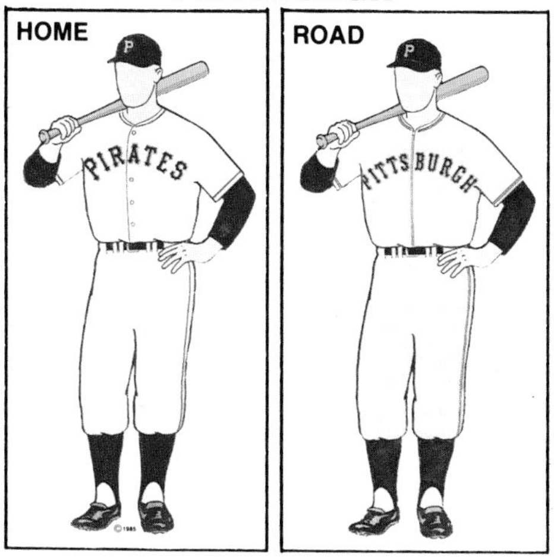

PHILADELPHIA

CHICAGO

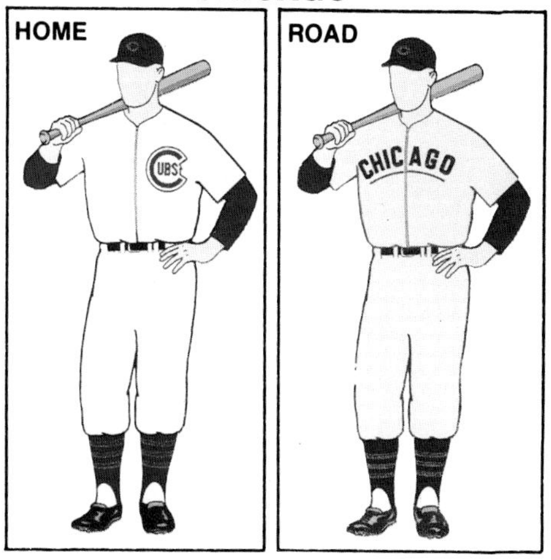

CINCINNATI

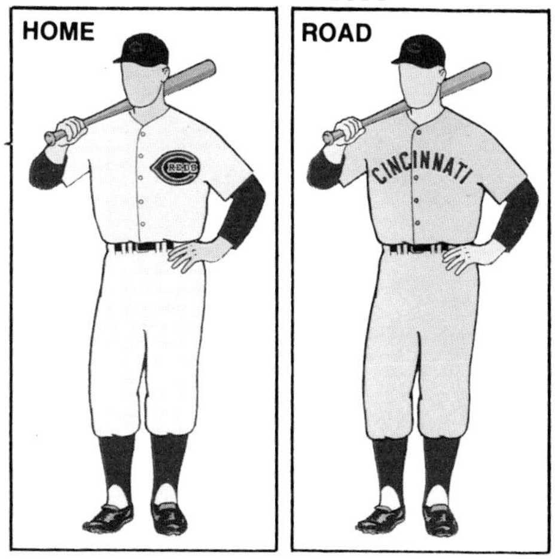

NEW YORK

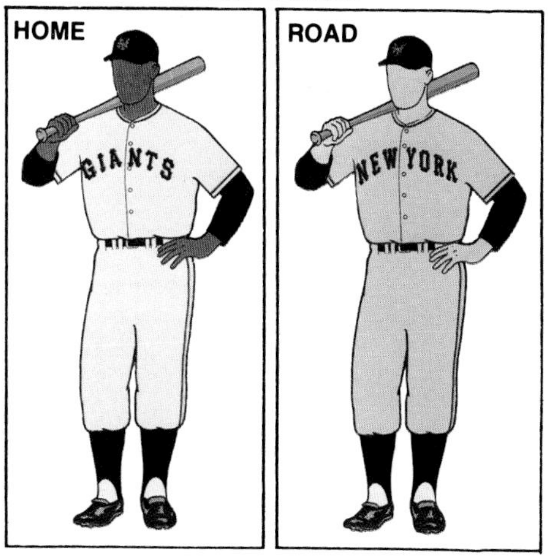

NEW YORK HERALD TRIBUNE, WEDNESDAY, OCTOBER 1, 1952 31

Dodgers and Yankees Open World Series Today With Black Opposing Reynolds

New York Is 8-5 Favorite to Win 4th Straight October Classic

Brooklyn Striving for Its First Series Triumph as Bombers Seek Their 15th World Crown

By Rud Rennie

The forty-ninth World Series, traditional meeting of the major league baseball champions, starts at 1 o'clock this afternoon in Ebbets Field, Brooklyn. For the fourth time in the history of this struggle for the world title and the winners' share of the players' pool, the Brooklyn Dodgers, champions of the National League, will play the Yankees, champions of the American League. The Yankees are favored to win.

Joe Black, a twenty-eight-year-old rookie righthander with a season's record of fifteen victories and four defeats, will be the Dodgers' starting pitcher. It will be his first World Series assignment.

Allie Reynolds, a veteran of four World Series in which he has won four games and lost one, will start for the Yankees. Reynolds, also a righthander, won twenty games this year and lost eight. He is thirty-three years old.

If the Yankees win the series they will be world champions for [illegible]

Frick Clarifies Rules For Series Managers

Managers Casey Stengel, of the New York Yankees, and Chuck Dressen, of the Brooklyn Dodgers, held a meeting with Ford Frick yesterday in the baseball commissioner's office and discussed World Series ground rules.

One of the points agreed upon was that a batter who turns toward the dugout after a dropped third strike would be automatically out.

Heretofore, each league had a different interpretation of the [illegible]

Reese, Robinson Say Yankees Hold No Terrors for Dodgers

Brooklyn Squad, After Its Workout in Stadium, Voices Confidence in Ability to Beat Bombers

By Roger Kahn

The Dodgers went to work at Yankee Stadium at 1 o'clock yesterday, after the proprietors had finished their last World Series drill, and if Brooklyn was impressed by the Yankee intangible, it didn't show.

The intangible, of course, is the ability to win pennants, world championships and big games by the dozen. It's a trademark of the Yankees just like the vertical pinstripe of their uniforms and the star spangled hat on their scoreboard. But it's a trademark the Dodgers say they won't buy.

PeeWee Reese, the Brooklyn captain, spoke for the team. "We're not just satisfied with the pennant. We have to win it all. A lot of teams make the series and figure that the big job is over. No one on our club figures it that way. The Yankees? Our club rises to occasions. I don't think it makes any difference who we're playing."

Jackie Robinson backed his captain. "The younger fellows [illegible]

Call MEridian 7-1212 For World Series Score

Scores by innings of the World Series games between the Yankees and the Dodgers will this year be given every twenty seconds, between each interval of a time announcement at the telephone company's time bureau, Meridian 7-1212. Thus many thousands of fans in the New York metropolitan area will keep posted on the progress of the contests.

A typical announcement will be: "End of — inning, Dodgers —, Yankees —." The final score [illegible]

1953 AMERICAN LEAGUE

BOSTON

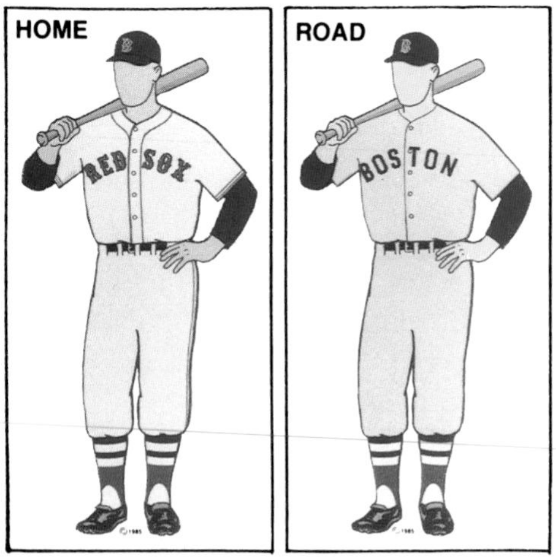

CLEVELAND

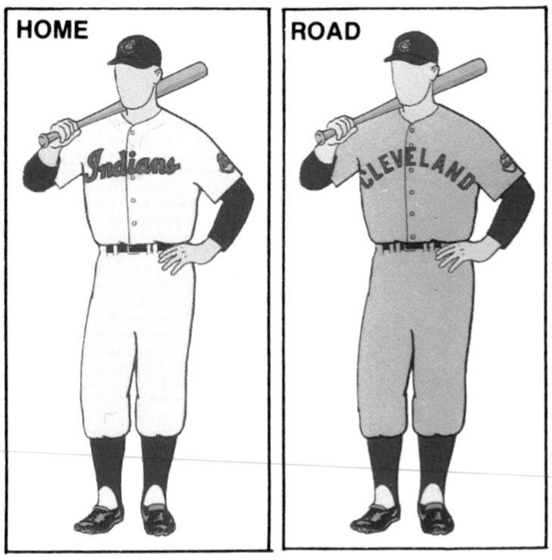

DETROIT

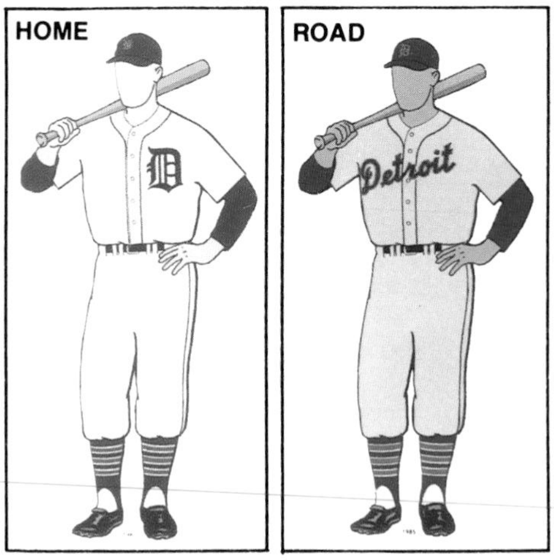

ST. LOUIS

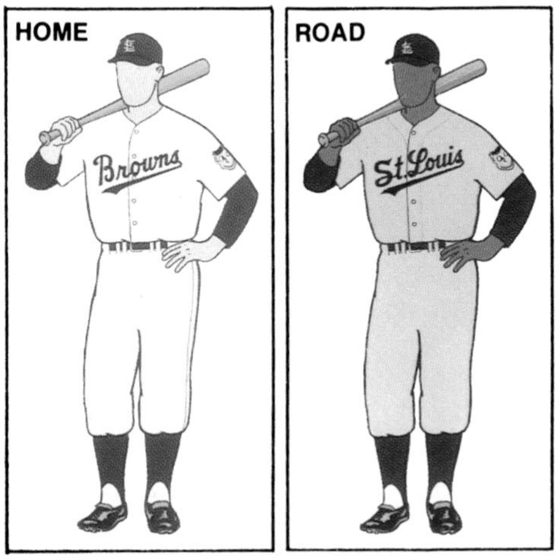

NEW YORK

PHILADELPHIA

CHICAGO

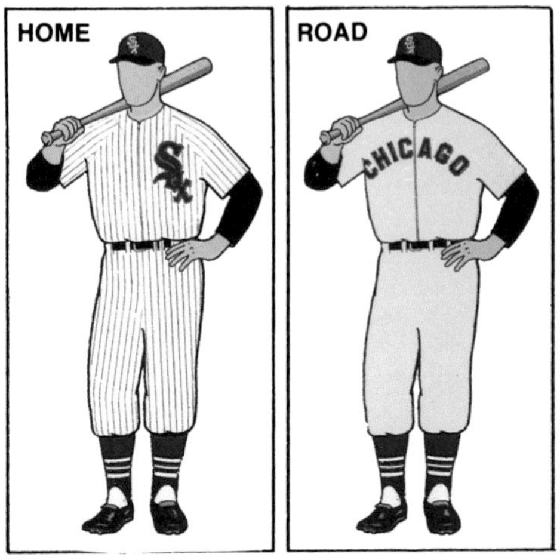

WASHINGTON

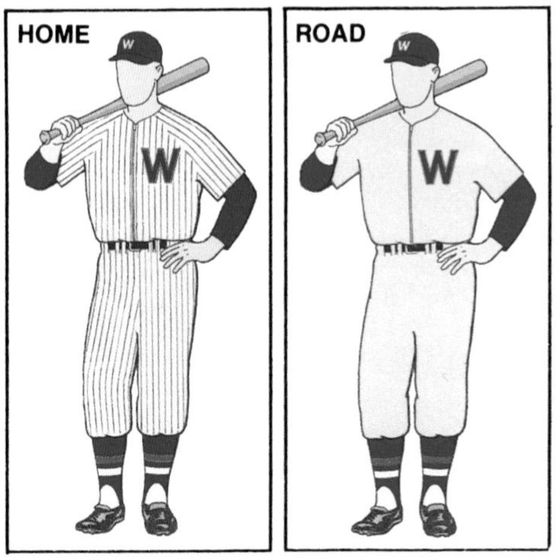

Weather Forecast
Fair and colder tonight, lowest about 40. Tomorrow, fair, cool and windy. (Full report on Page A-2.)
Temperatures Today.
Midnight 53 | 6 a.m. ...49 | 11 a.m. ...50
2 a.m. ...54 | 8 a.m. ...53 | Noon 58
4 a.m. ...49 | 10 a.m. ...57 | 1 p.m. ...60

An Associated Press Newspaper

The Evening Star

WITH SUNDAY MORNING EDITION

The Steeplechasing Set
They'll be off at Middleburg for the annual Hunt Cup Races Saturday. This is naturally the excuse for parties. For more about the entries and their socialite owners, see Page B-3.

New York Markets, Pages C-10-11

101st Year. No. 106. Phone ST. 3-5000 ** WASHINGTON, D. C., THURSDAY, APRIL 16, 1953—EIGHTY PAGES. [illegible] 5 CENTS

Eisenhower Challenges Russia To Match U.S. in Disarmament; Soviet Bloc Makes U.N. Gesture

President Calls For Joint 'War' Against Poverty

The Cost of War . . .

Here, in the words of President Eisenhower, is the human cost of the armaments burden which Russia forces the world to bear:

Polish Peace Plan Withdrawn to Aid Panmunjom Talks

President Opens New Baseball Season Here

Weather Finally Lets Porterfield and Sain Pitch Before 30,000

By Burton Hawkins

With the co-operation of the weatherman and President Eisenhower, baseball got off to its

NATIONAL LEAGUE 1953

MILWAUKEE

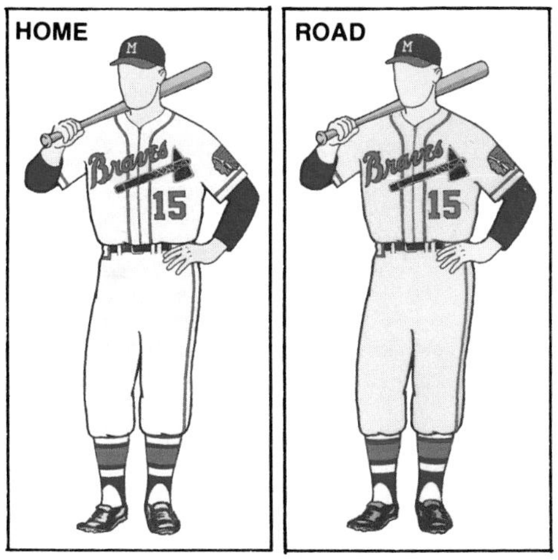

BROOKLYN

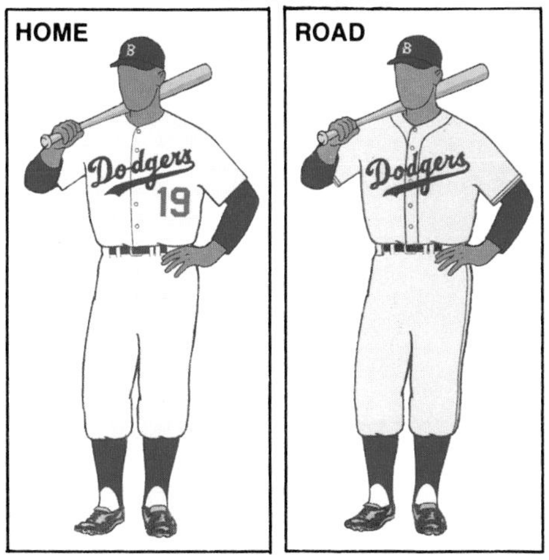

ST. LOUIS

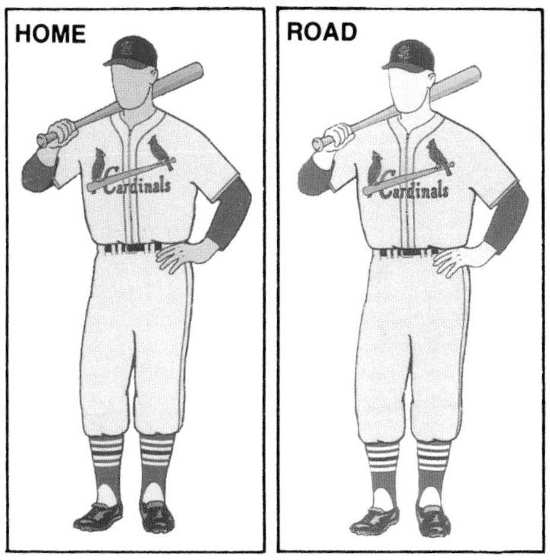

PITTSBURGH

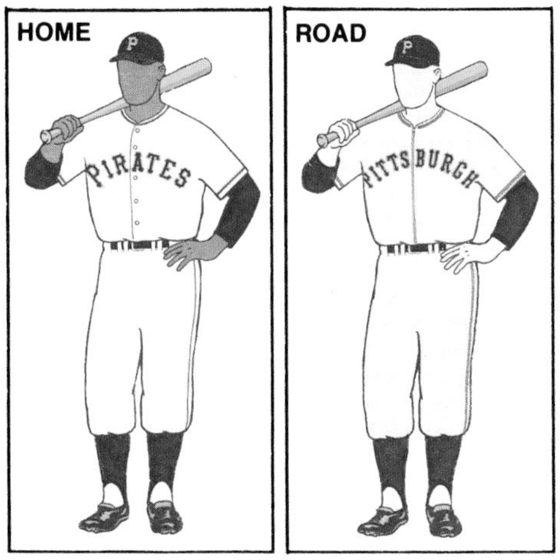

PHILADELPHIA

CHICAGO

CINCINNATI

NEW YORK

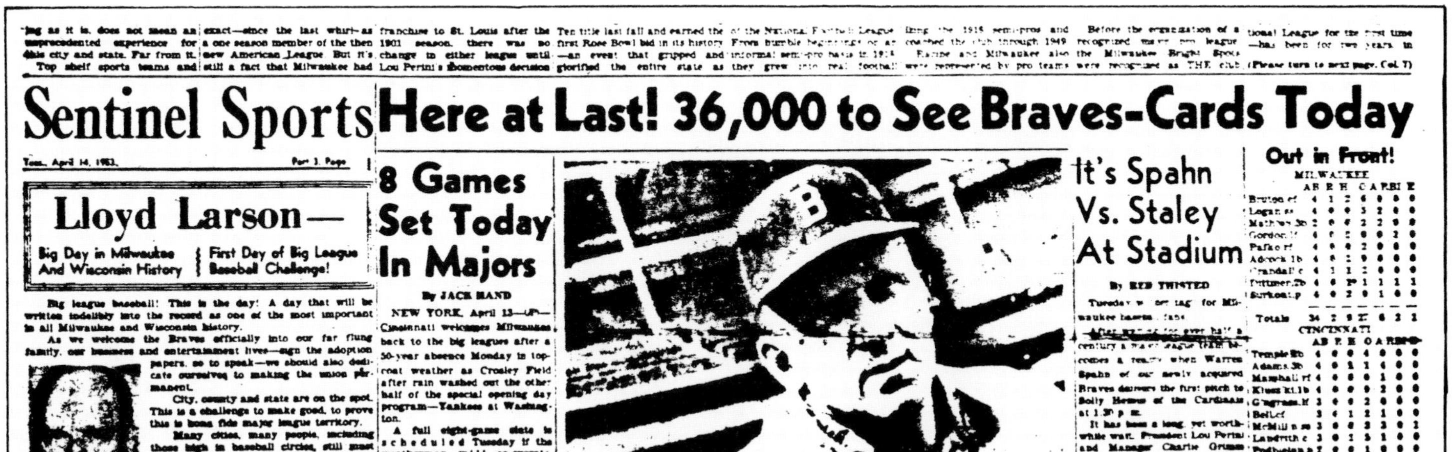

ing as it is, does not mean an unprecedented experience for this city and state. Far from it.

Top shelf sports teams and exact—since the last whirl—as a one season member of the then new American League. But it's still a fact that Milwaukee had franchise to St. Louis after the 1901 season, there was no change in either league until Lou Perini's momentous decision

Ten title last fall and earned the first Rose Bowl bid in its history—an event that gripped and glorified the entire state as of the National Football League. From humble beginnings on an informal semi-pro basis in 1914 they grew into real football during the 1918 semi-pros and coached the club through 1949. Racine and Milwaukee also were represented by pro teams

Before the organization of a recognized major pro league the Milwaukee Bright Spots were recognized as THE club tional League for the first time—has been for two years in

(Please turn to next page, Col. 7)

Sentinel Sports

Tues., April 14, 1953. Part 1, Page 1

Here at Last! 36,000 to See Braves-Cards Today

Lloyd Larson—

Big Day in Milwaukee And Wisconsin History | First Day of Big League Baseball Challenge!

Big league baseball! This is the day! A day that will be written indelibly into the record as one of the most important in all Milwaukee and Wisconsin history.

As we welcome the Braves officially into our far flung family, our business and entertainment lives—sign the adoption papers, so to speak—we should also dedicate ourselves to making the union permanent.

City, county and state are on the spot. This is a challenge to make good, to prove this is bona fide major league territory.

Many cities, many people, including those high in baseball circles, still must be convinced.

8 Games Set Today In Majors

By JACK HAND

NEW YORK, April 13—(UP)—Cincinnati welcomes Milwaukee back to the big leagues after a 50-year absence Monday in topcoat weather as Crosley Field after rain washed out the other half of the special opening day program—Yankees at Washington.

A full eight-game slate is scheduled Tuesday if the weatherman will co-operate.

It's Spahn Vs. Staley At Stadium

By RED THISTED

Tuesday ... for Milwaukee baseball fans.

After ... for over half a century a major league team becomes a reality when Warren Spahn of our newly acquired Braves delivers the first pitch to Solly Hemus of the Cardinals at 1:30 p.m.

It has been a long, yet worthwhile wait. President Lou Perini and Manager Charlie Grimm have put together a good, inter-

Out in Front!

MILWAUKEE

	AB	R	H	O	A	RBI	E
Bruton cf	4	1	2	6	0	0	0
Logan ss	4	0	0	3	2	0	0
Mathews 3b	2	0	0	2	2	0	0
Gordon lf	4	0	2	0	0	2	0
Pafko rf	4	0	0	2	0	0	0
Adcock 1b	4	0	2	9	0	0	0
Crandall c	4	1	1	2	0	0	0
Dittmer 2b	4	0	2*	1	1	1	1
Surkont p	4	0	2	0	1	0	0
Totals	34	2	9	27	6	3	1

CINCINNATI

	AB	R	H	O	A	RBI	E
Temple 2b	4	0	0	4	0	0	0
Adams 3b	4	0	1	1	4	0	0
Marshall rf	4	0	0	0	1	0	0
Kluszewski 1b	4	0	0	9	2	0	0
Greengrass lf	3	0	0	2	0	0	0
Bell cf	3	0	1	2	1	0	0
McMillan ss	3	0	0	2	3	0	1
Landrith c	3	0	1	5	1	0	0
Podbielan p	2	0	0	1	0	0	0
a-Stallcup	1	0	0	0	0	0	0

1954 AMERICAN LEAGUE

BOSTON

CLEVELAND

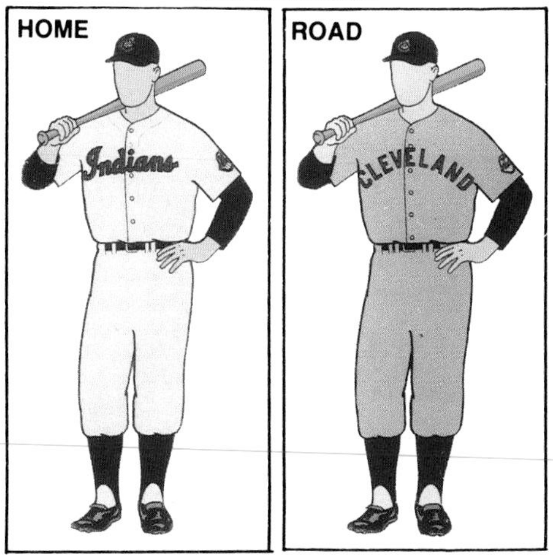

DETROIT

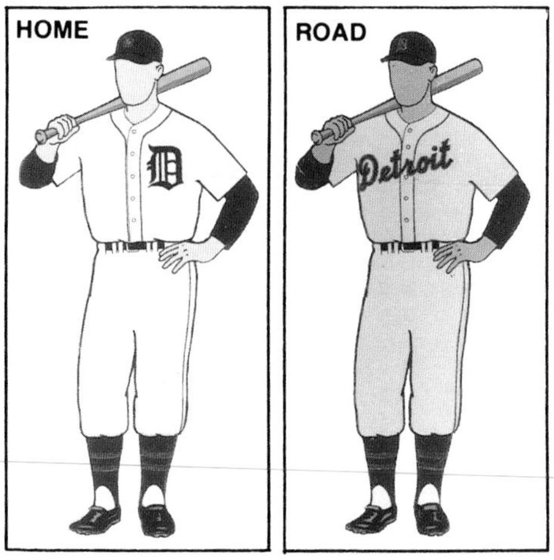

BALTIMORE

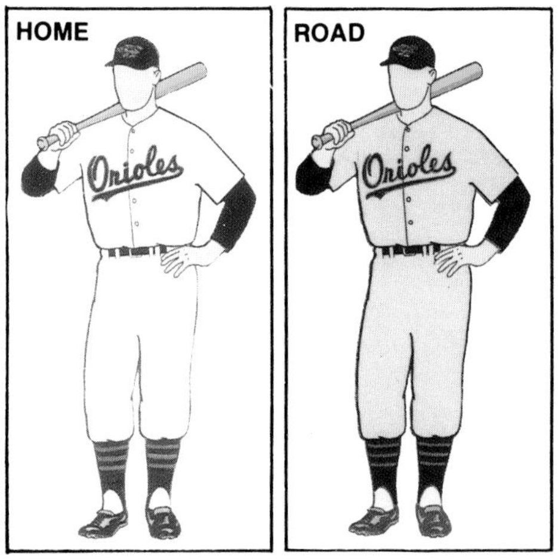

NEW YORK

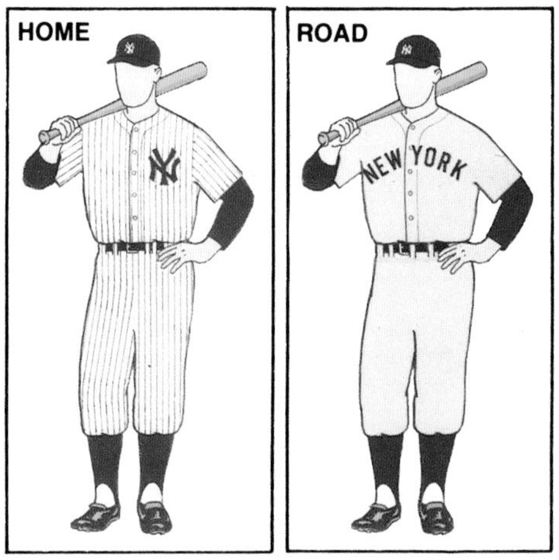

PHILADELPHIA

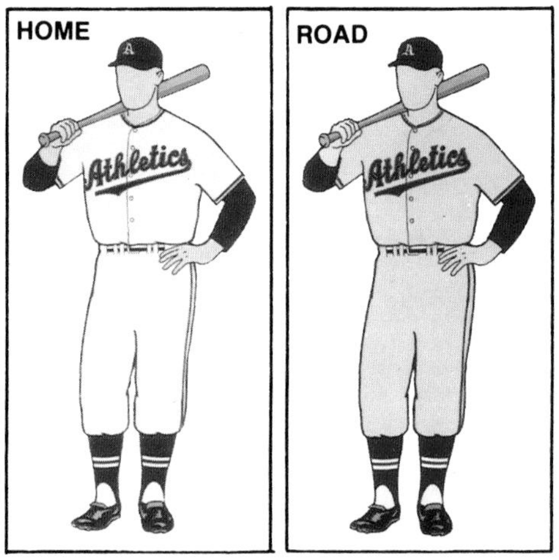

CHICAGO

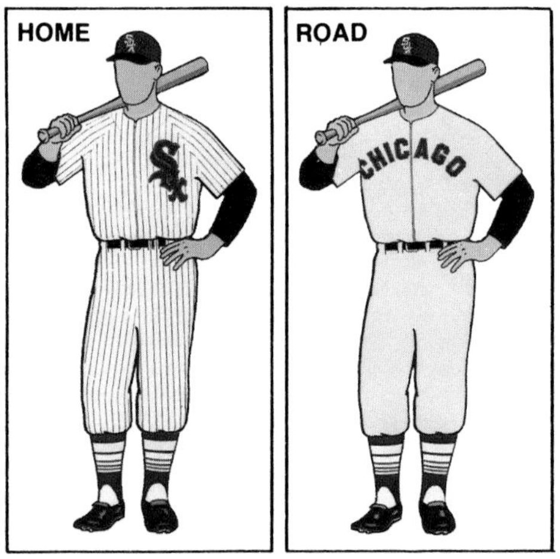

WASHINGTON

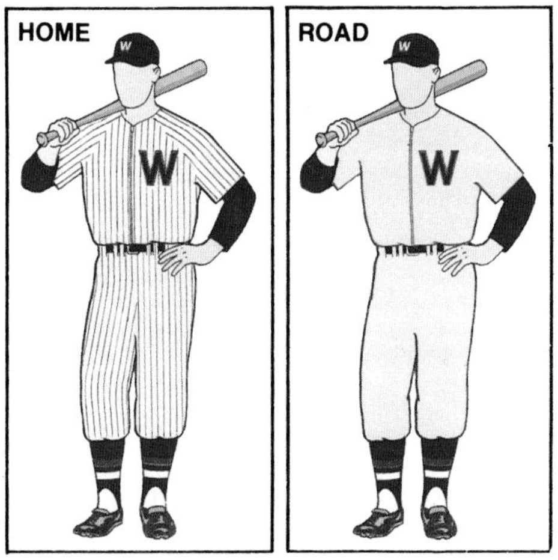

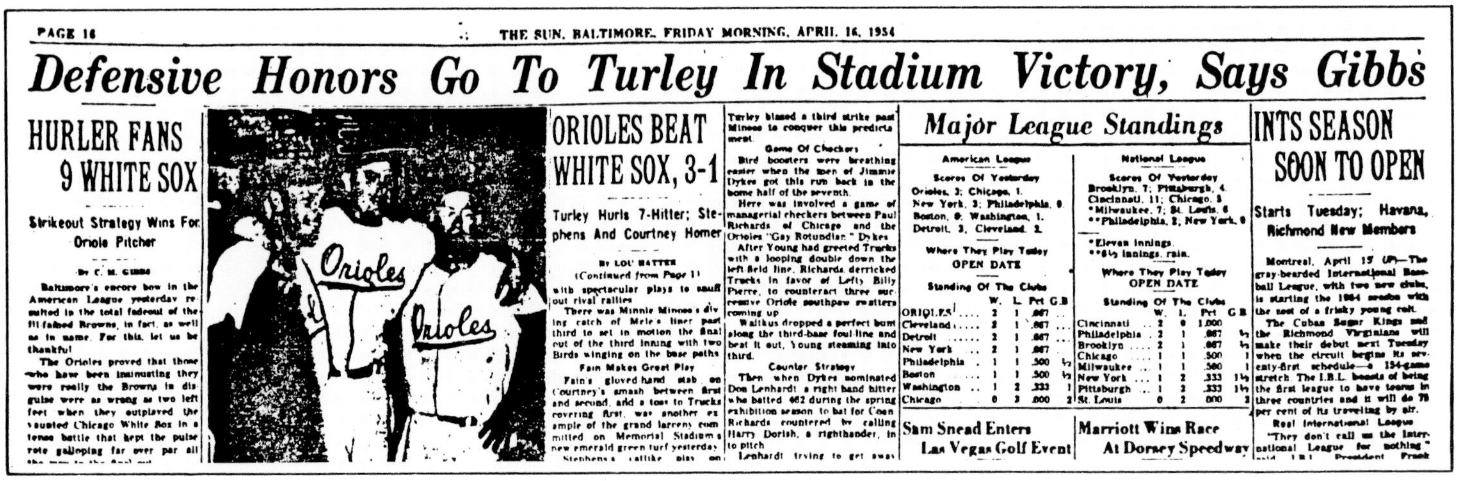

PAGE 16 THE SUN, BALTIMORE, FRIDAY MORNING, APRIL 16, 1954

Defensive Honors Go To Turley In Stadium Victory, Says Gibbs

HURLER FANS 9 WHITE SOX

Strikeout Strategy Wins For Oriole Pitcher

By C. M. GIBBS

Baltimore's encore bow in the American League yesterday resulted in the total fadeout of the ill-famed Browns, in fact, as well as in name. For this, let us be thankful.

The Orioles proved that those who have been insinuating they were really the Browns in disguise were as wrong as two left feet when they outplayed the vaunted Chicago White Sox in a tense battle that kept the pulse rate galloping far over par all the way to the final out.

ORIOLES BEAT WHITE SOX, 3-1

Turley Hurls 7-Hitter; Stephens And Courtney Homer

By LOU HATTER

(Continued from Page 1)

with spectacular plays to snuff out rival rallies.

There was Minnie Minoso's diving catch of Mele's liner past third to set in motion the final out of the third inning with two Birds winging on the base paths.

Fain Makes Great Play

Fain's gloved-hand stab on Courtney's smash between first and second, and a toss to Trucks covering first, was another example of the grand larceny committed on Memorial Stadium's new emerald green turf yesterday.

Stephens's ... play on

Turley blazed a third strike past Minoso to conquer this predicament.

Game Of Checkers

Bird boosters were breathing easier when the men of Jimmie Dykes got this run back in the home half of the seventh.

Here was involved a game of managerial checkers between Paul Richards of Chicago and the Orioles' "Gay Rotundian," Dykes.

After Young had greeted Trucks with a looping double down the left field line, Richards derricked Trucks in favor of Lefty Billy Pierce, to counteract three successive Oriole southpaw swatters coming up.

Waitkus dropped a perfect bunt along the third-base foul line and beat it out, Young steaming into third.

Counter Strategy

Then when Dykes nominated Don Lenhardt, a right hand hitter who batted .462 during the spring exhibition season, to bat for Coan, Richards countered by calling Harry Dorish, a righthander, in to pitch.

Lenhardt, trying to get away

Major League Standings

American League

Scores Of Yesterday

Orioles, 3; Chicago, 1.
New York, 3; Philadelphia, 0.
Boston, 0; Washington, 1.
Detroit, 3, Cleveland, 2.

Where They Play Today

OPEN DATE

Standing Of The Clubs

	W.	L.	Pct	G.B.
ORIOLES	2	1	.667	..
Cleveland	2	1	.667	...
Detroit	2	1	.667	...
New York	2	1	.667	.
Philadelphia	1	1	.500	½
Boston	1	1	.500	½
Washington	1	2	.333	1
Chicago	0	3	.000	2

National League

Scores Of Yesterday

Brooklyn, 7; Pittsburgh, 4.
Cincinnati, 11; Chicago, 3.
*Milwaukee, 7; St. Louis, 6.
**Philadelphia, 2; New York, 0.

*Eleven innings.
**6½ innings, rain.

Where They Play Today

OPEN DATE

Standing Of The Clubs

	W.	L.	Pct	G.B.
Cincinnati	2	0	1.000	
Philadelphia	2	1	.667	½
Brooklyn	2	1	.667	½
Chicago	1	1	.500	1
Milwaukee	1	1	.500	1
New York	1	2	.333	1½
Pittsburgh	1	2	.333	1½
St. Louis	0	2	.000	2

Sam Snead Enters Las Vegas Golf Event

Marriott Wins Race At Dorsey Speedway

INTS SEASON SOON TO OPEN

Starts Tuesday; Havana, Richmond New Members

Montreal, April 15 (AP)—The gray-bearded International Baseball League, with two new clubs, is starting the 1954 season with the zest of a frisky young colt.

The Cuban Sugar Kings and the Richmond Virginians will make their debut next Tuesday when the circuit begins its seventy-first schedule—a 154-game stretch. The I.B.L. boasts of being the first league to have teams in three countries and it will do 75 per cent of its traveling by air.

Real International League

"They don't call us the International League for nothing," said I.B.L. President Frank

NATIONAL LEAGUE 1954

MILWAUKEE

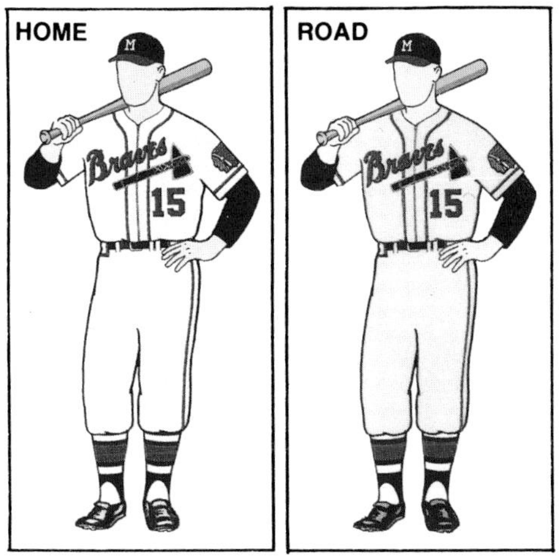

BROOKLYN

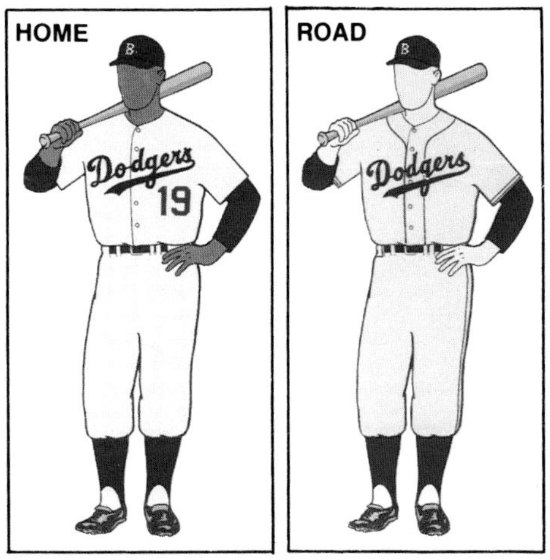

ST. LOUIS

PITTSBURGH

PHILADELPHIA

CHICAGO

CINCINNATI

NEW YORK

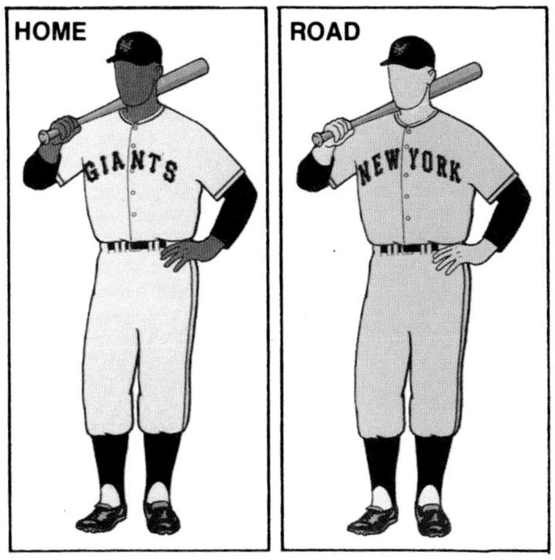

Section 3 SPORTS AUTOMOTIVE STAMPS—BRIDGE

NEW YORK Herald Tribune

SPORTS WEATHER—MARINE MAIL ORDER Section 3

TWELVE PAGES — SUNDAY, OCTOBER [illegible] — TWELVE PAGES

World Champion Giants Sweep Series

Navy, Princeton Win; Irish Upset

Dartmouth Loses, 42-7, To Middies

Antonelli Thwarts Tribe in Relief, 7-4; Dark, Mueller Star

Liddle Gets Credit for Victory; Lemon Routed With 4 in 5th

1955 AMERICAN LEAGUE

BOSTON

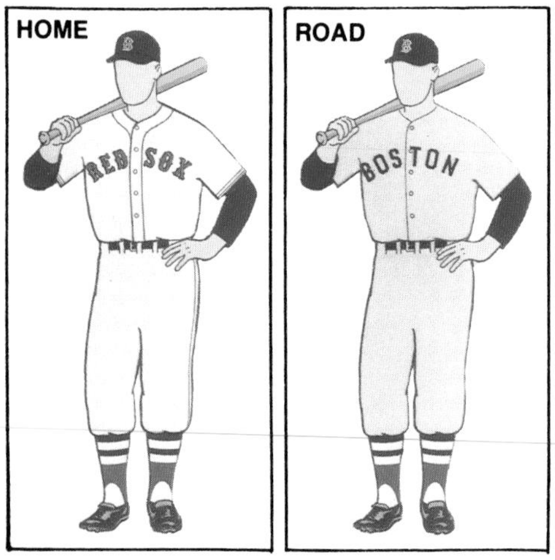

CLEVELAND

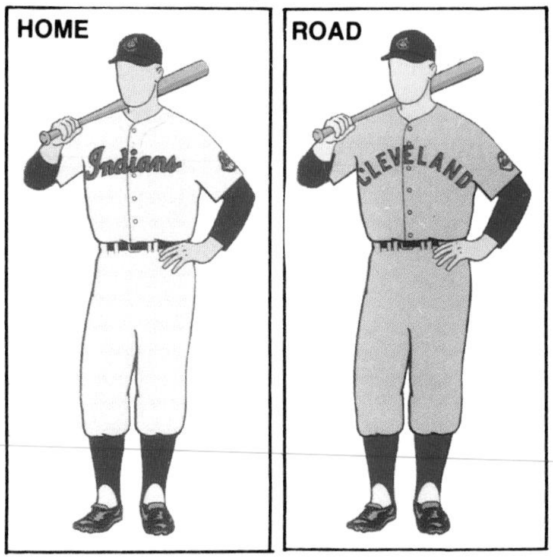

DETROIT

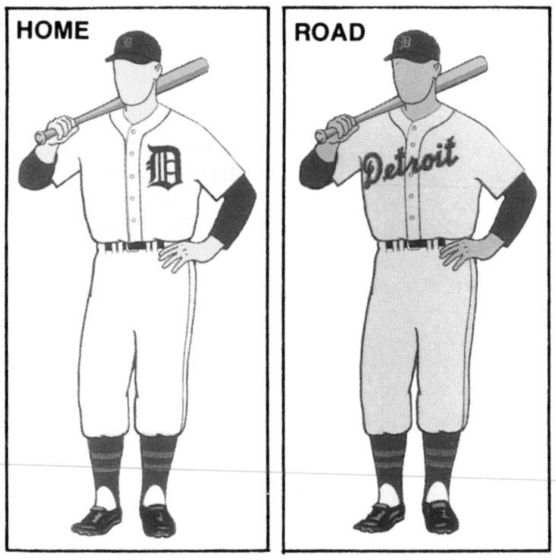

BALTIMORE

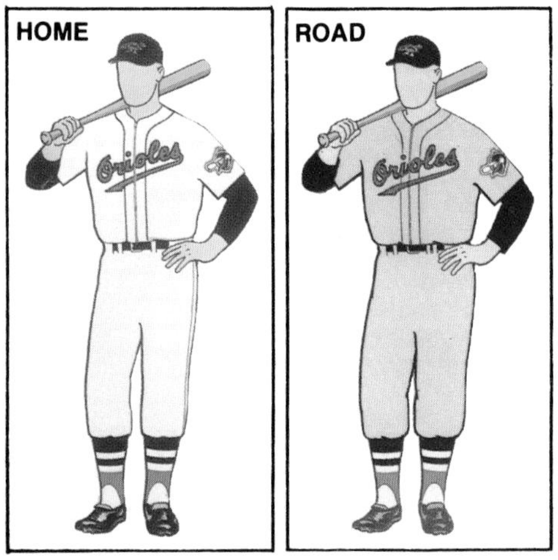

NEW YORK

KANSAS CITY

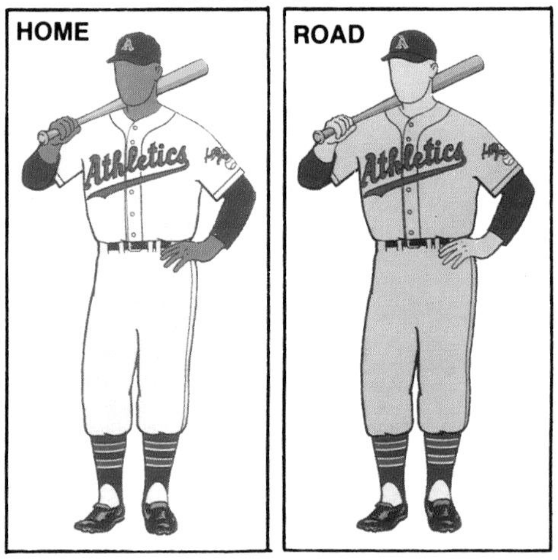

CHICAGO

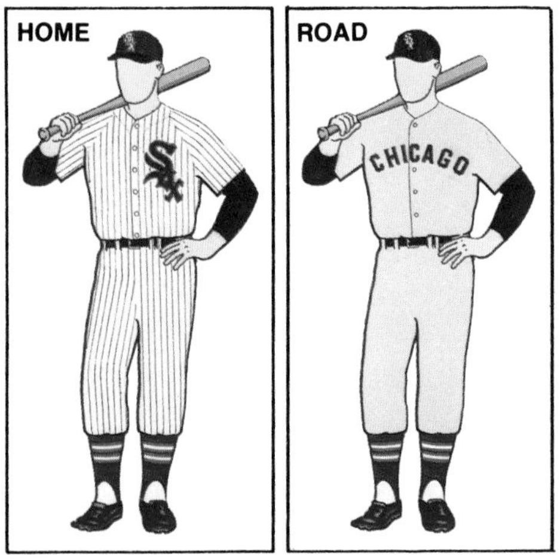

WASHINGTON

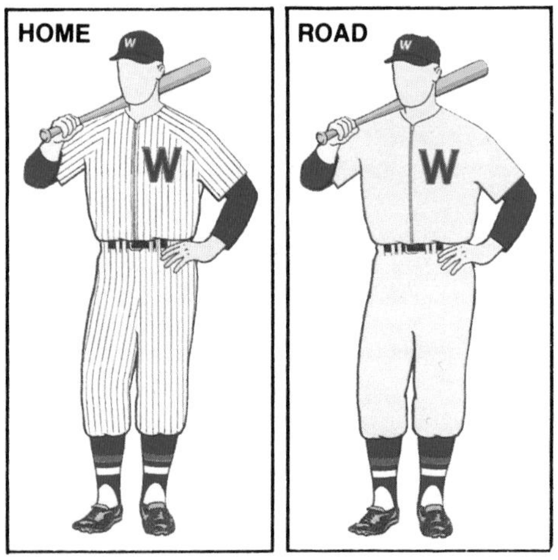

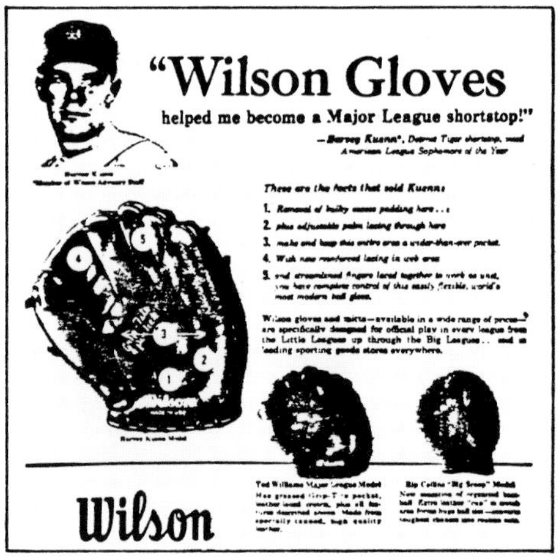

THE KANSAS CITY STAR. MAIN EDITION

VOL. 75. NO. 207. KANSAS CITY, APRIL 12, 1955—TUESDAY—30 PAGES. PRICE 5 CENTS.

SERUM POTENT ON POLIO

Salk Vaccine Also "Safe and Effective," According to Official Verdict After Analyzing Tests Given More Than 1 Million Children.

A PARALYSIS FOE

A Prevention Effectiveness of Between 80 and 90 Per Cent Is Reported.

"SHIELD" TO BULBAR TYPE

Powerful Reaction Is Shown Against Most Terrible Variety of the Disease.

Plan Involving Only Two Shots With a Booster Later Urged by Salk.

Polio Foundation May Now Study Mental Health.

Ann Arbor, Mich., April 12. (UP)—The National Foundation for Infantile Paralysis, which spent 10 million dollars collected from the American people for development and testing the Salk vaccine, will not go out of business.

Basil O'Connor, president of the foundation, said the group's activities would be switched to some other field, the new field may be mental health, he said, but it has not been definitely decided.

Early Surge of Fans for A's Opener.

EARLY ARRIVALS FOR THE FIRST KANSAS CITY ATHLETICS HOME GAME

A's OPENER TO 33,000

Cheering Throng Fills Every Available Space in New Municipal Stadium as Major League Baseball Is Inaugurated in Kansas City.

A SEA OF FACES

Crowd Is the Largest Ever to Attend a Professional Baseball Game Here.

MANY THERE ALL NIGHT

Vigil at Ball Park Ends With Opening of Gates to Stands.

THE WEATHER—OCCASIONAL SHOWERS.

Kansas City and Vicinity: Cloudy with occasional showers tonight with a low in the 40s. Partly cloudy and cooler tomorrow with a high in the 50s.

FIELD IN SHAPE

Grounds Crew Works Entire Morning to Prepare Park After Heavy Rain.

OPEN WITHOUT A CEREMONY

Because of Mud Only the Toss of First Ball by Truman Is Included.

NATIONAL LEAGUE 1955

MILWAUKEE

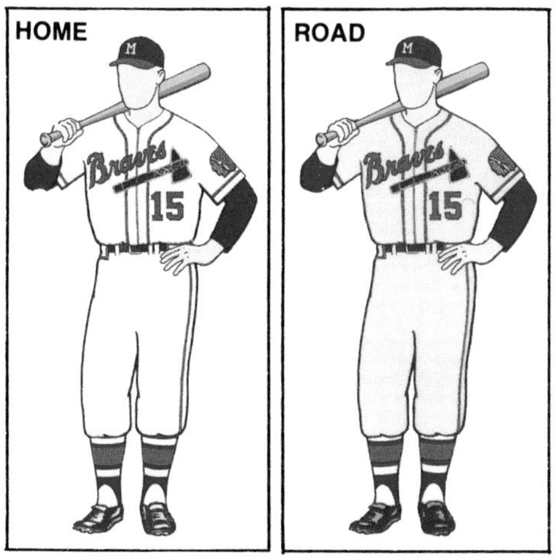

BROOKLYN

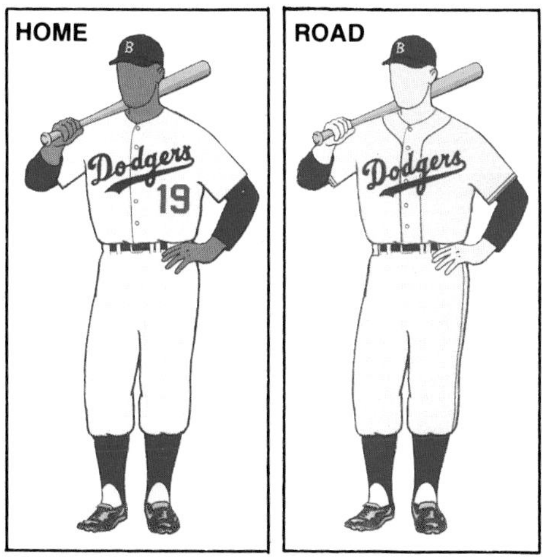

ST. LOUIS

PITTSBURGH

PHILADELPHIA

CHICAGO

CINCINNATI

NEW YORK

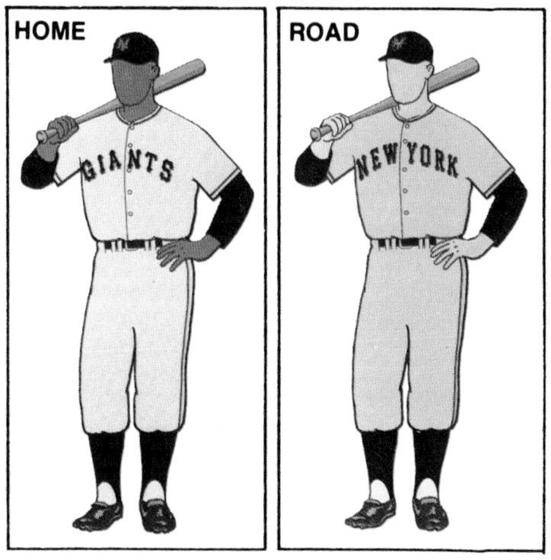

The Village Smithy

★ ★ ★

By CHESTER L. SMITH
Sports Editor

Best of Luck, Fred

This is to wish Mr. Fred Haney, the manager of the Pirates, nothing but the best as he brushes the dust off his desk at Forbes Field and goes into the business of winning baseball games another year.

Let no bloke arise at this point and exclaim, "He's going to need it."

As has been true ever since he came to Pittsburgh, Mr. Haney will be called on to do a sizable chunk of managing. He is at the opposite end of the stick from—say—Leo Durocher who has nothing to do but remember eight names, pick a pitcher to pitch and choose the proper moment to send up Dusty Rhodes to pinch hit.

It isn't that way with Mr. Haney. There are few positions he can go to bed and forget. One of them would be the catching, which

Robinson's Bunt Spoils Buc Opener

Dark Spoils Roberts' No-Hit Bid

Phil Star Misses By Just 'Two Outs'

By THE UNITED PRESS

Robin Roberts of the Phillies, the only pitcher around who is given an outside chance of winning 30 games, was off to his best start in four years today after licking an opening day "jinx" and nearly hurling the first no-hitter of his career in the process.

Usually, Robbie is an opening game dud. He lost the openers

Jackie's Hit Finds Surkont Off Balance, And Pirates Fall, 6-1

By LESTER J. BIEDERMAN

It was only a little bunt and it didn't travel more than 15 or 20 feet but Jackie Robinson executed it perfectly and there lies the story of the Pirates' opening day defeat of the 1955 season at Brooklyn yesterday.

Carl Furillo followed with a three-run line-drive homer into the left-center seats that actually broke up the ball game for the Dodgers but it was Robinson, the 36-year-old star, who caused the Buccos to fall apart in their inaugural 6-1.

Today is another day for the Pirates and they hoped to right themselves as they took on the

1956 AMERICAN LEAGUE

BOSTON

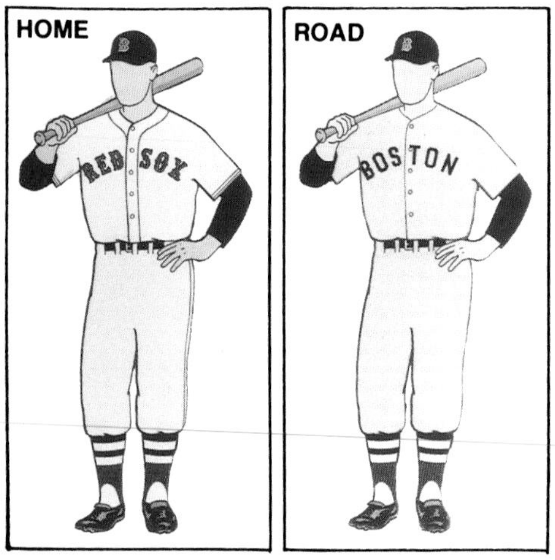

CLEVELAND

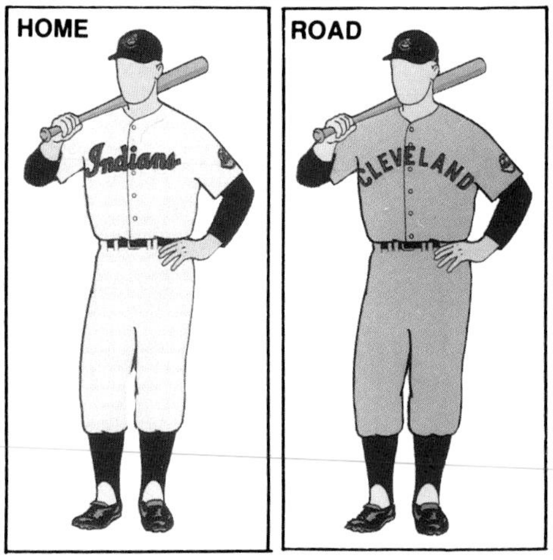

DETROIT

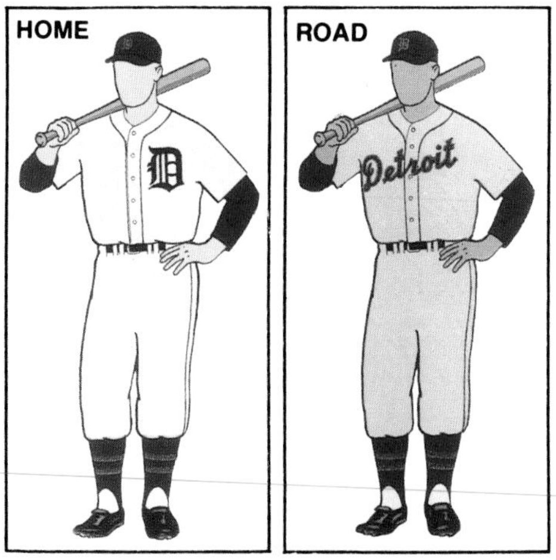

BALTIMORE

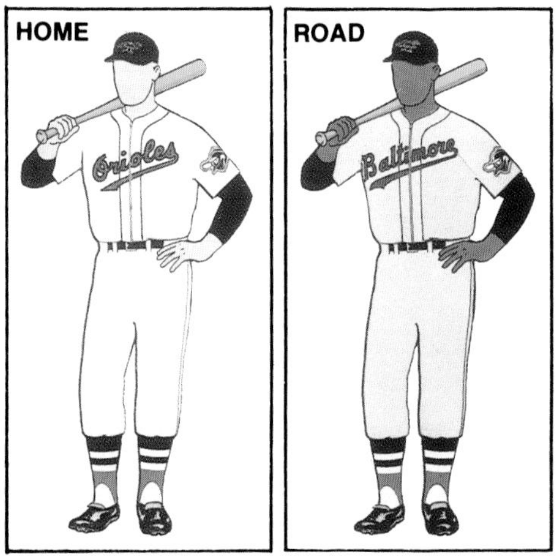

NEW YORK

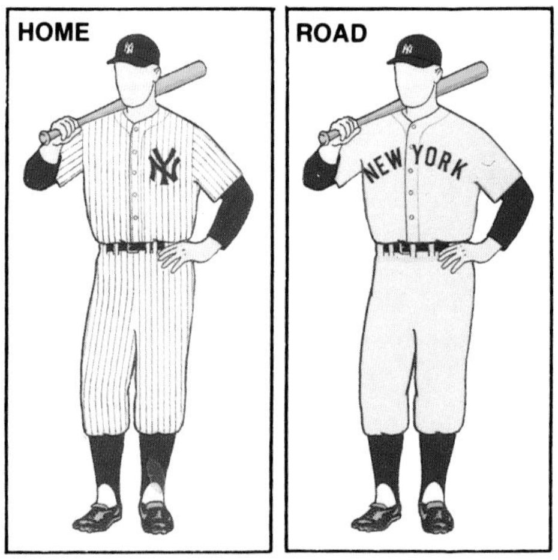

KANSAS CITY

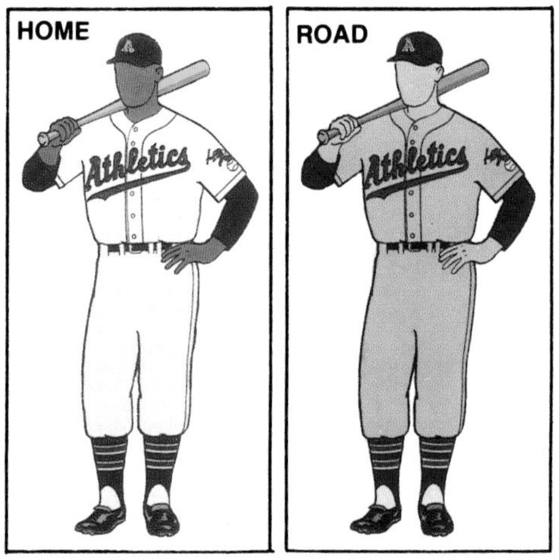

CHICAGO

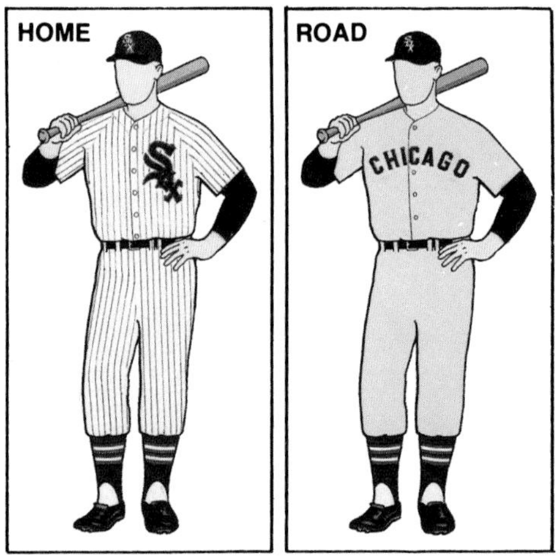

WASHINGTON

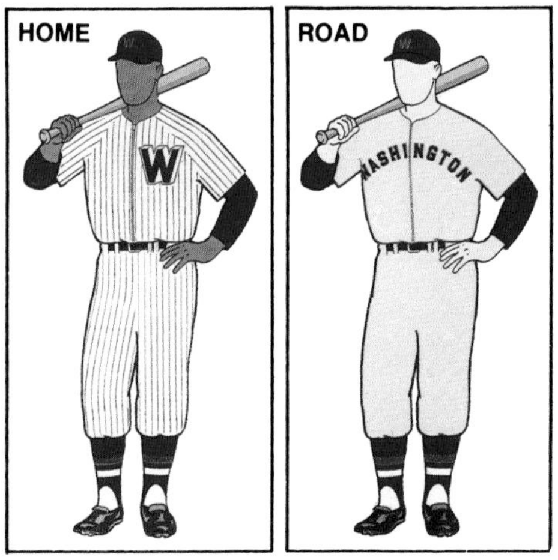

WEATHER FORECAST

Fair tonight, low around 38. Mostly sunny tomorrow, high about 58. (Full report on Page A-2.)

Temperatures Today

Midnight	48	6 a.m.	41	11 a.m.	51
2 a.m.	46	8 a.m.	47	Noon	50
4 a.m.	43	10 a.m.	50	1 p.m.	50

The Evening Star

WITH SUNDAY MORNING EDITION

Metropolitan Edition

New York Markets, Pages A-18-19

104th Year. No. 108. Phone ST. 3-5000 ★★SS WASHINGTON, D. C., TUESDAY, APRIL 17, 1956—FIFTY-TWO PAGES. WMAL—RADIO—TV 5 CENTS

Mantle's Blast In First Matched By Tettelbach

Senators and Yanks Get Off to 1-1 Start In Season Opener

Further Action On Farm Bills Held Unlikely

Congress Seen Cool To 'Advance' Plan For Soil Bank

The outlook was dim on Capitol Hill today for new farm legislation this year.

With Congress taking it easy because of the baseball opener

Text of President's Talk on Farm Bill Veto, Page A-4

Moscow Asks Arabs And Israel for Peace

Offers to Aid Efforts for Settlement

BULLETIN

NATIONAL LEAGUE 1956

MILWAUKEE

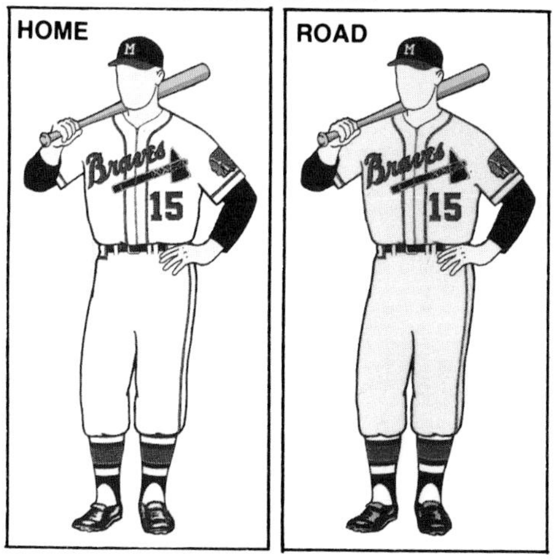

BROOKLYN

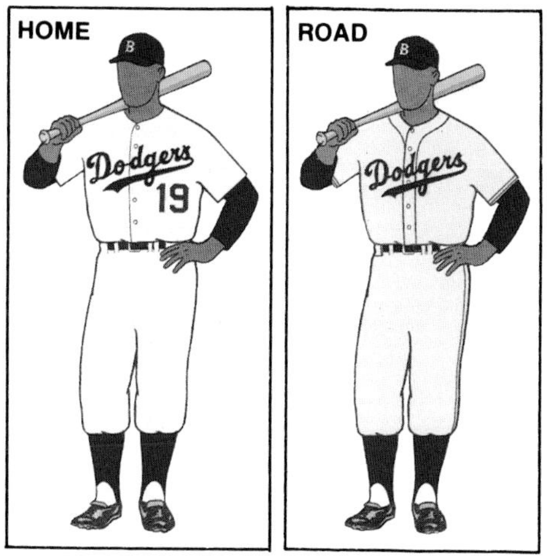

ST. LOUIS

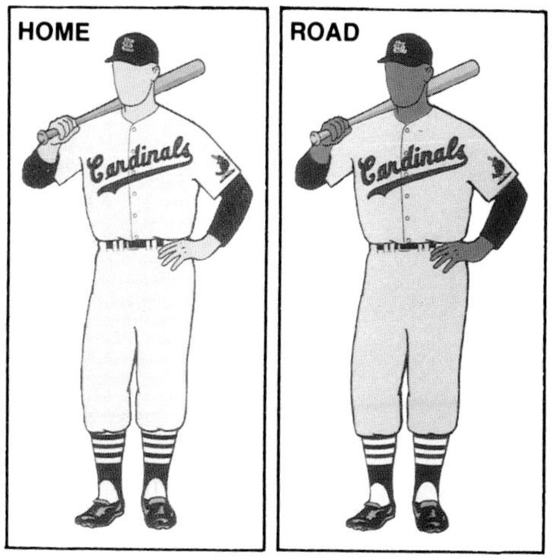

PITTSBURGH

PHILADELPHIA

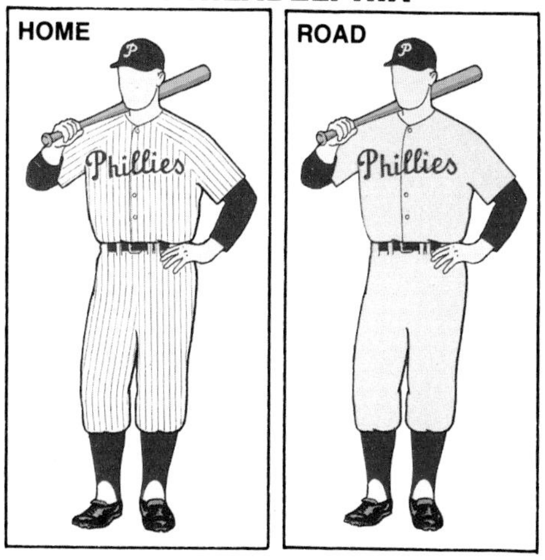

CHICAGO

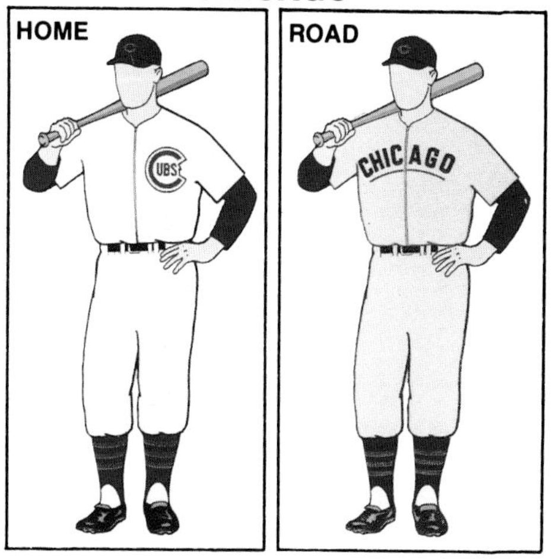

CINCINNATI

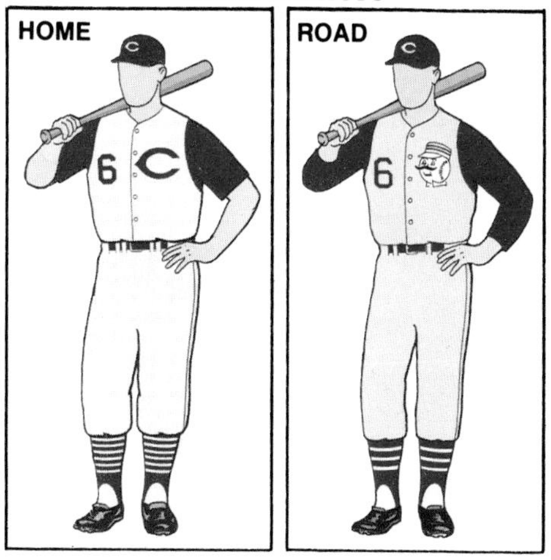

NEW YORK

Sports — NEW YORK Herald Tribune — TV-Radio

Section Three — TUESDAY, OCTOBER 9, 1956 — Section Three

Larsen Hurls 1st Perfect Series Game; Yanks Beat Maglie, 2-0, and Lead 3-2

1957 AMERICAN LEAGUE

BOSTON

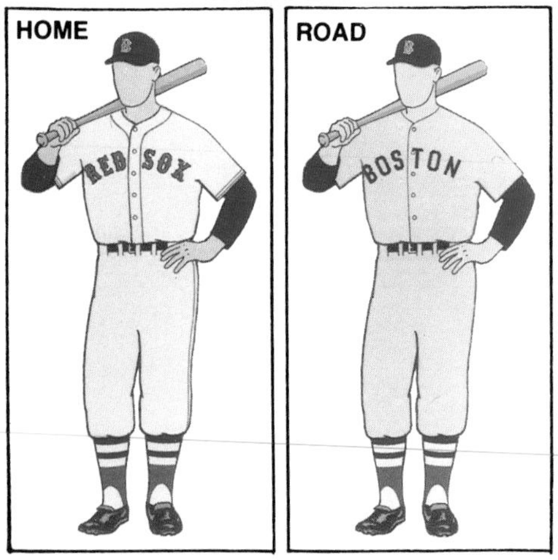

CLEVELAND

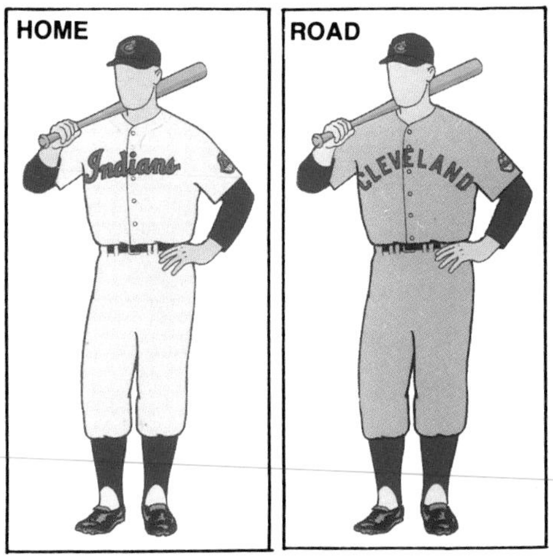

DETROIT

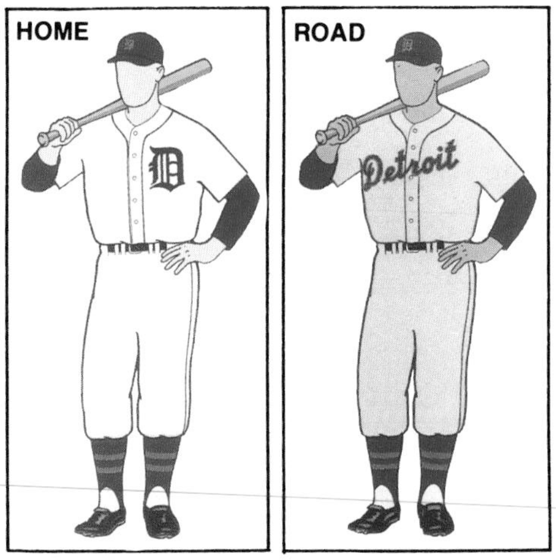

BALTIMORE

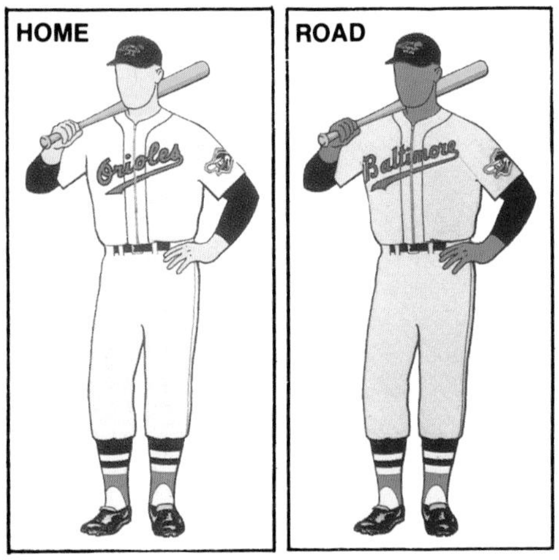

NEW YORK

KANSAS CITY

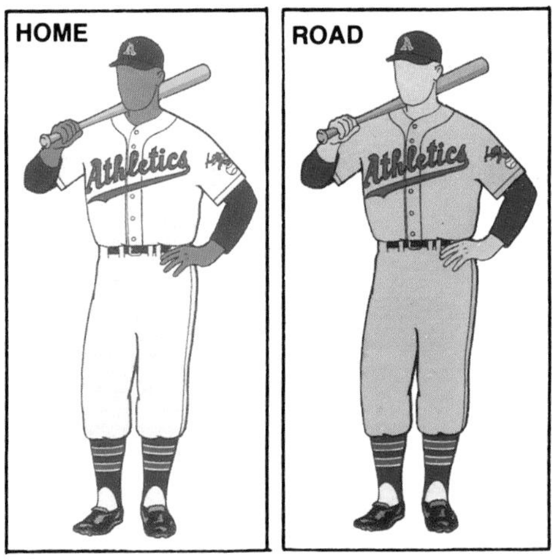

CHICAGO

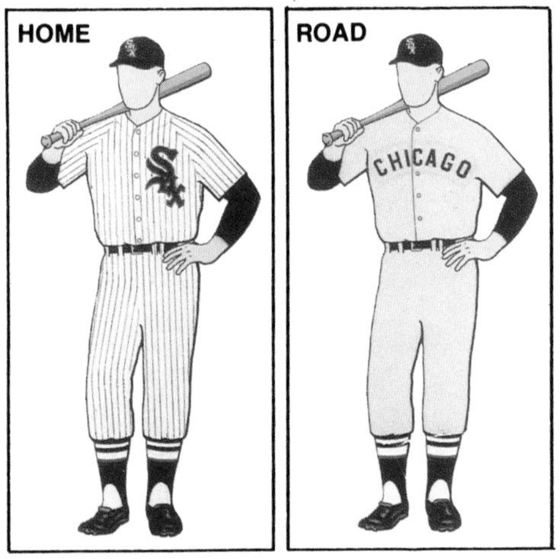

WASHINGTON

THE MILWAUKEE JOURNAL

Copyright, 1957, by The Journal Company

Seventy-fifth Year | 94 Pages | Circulation Yesterday... 378,981 Circulation One Year Ago.. 359,060 | Thursday, October 3, 1957 | Daily ..... 5 Cents Sunday 20 Cents | Pay No More | Latest Edition

Burdette Stops Yanks, Evens Series

Hurless Offers Data to Back Up Check

Shows a Bank Letter Telling of Presence in N. Y. Near Date

state you were there on Jan. 21," commented John F. Cook, an assistant city attorney and the board's special counsel. "Is that a positive statement?"

Three of Quints in France Dead

Toulon, France—AP—Death during the night took three of the quintuplets born prematurely here Wednesday.

A doctor said the chances for survival of the other two babies, Roland and Michele Christofle, was "not too bad."

The mother, Mrs. Camille Christofle, 29, was reported do-

Logan Hits Homer in 4 to 2 Triumph

Three Straight Hits in the Fourth Inning Bat Out Shantz in

Lew's Splitter

MILWAUKEE BRAVES AB R H RBI O A E

NATIONAL LEAGUE 1957

MILWAUKEE

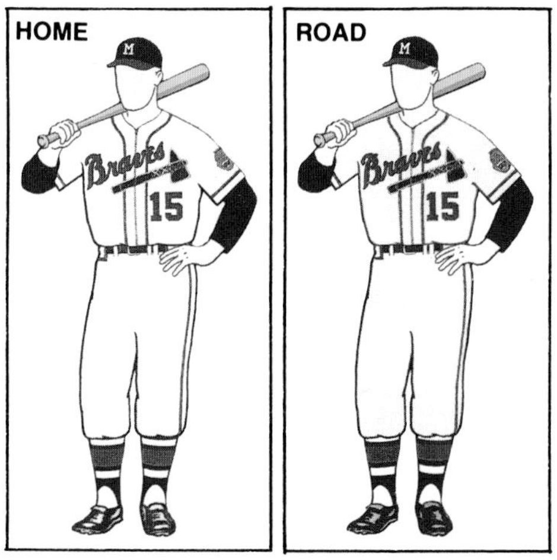

BROOKLYN

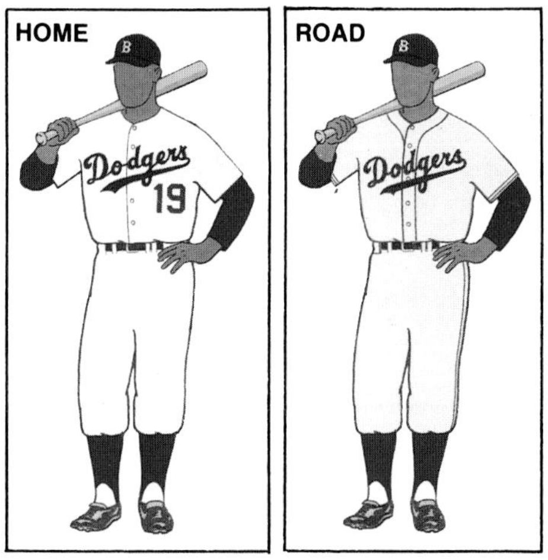

ST. LOUIS

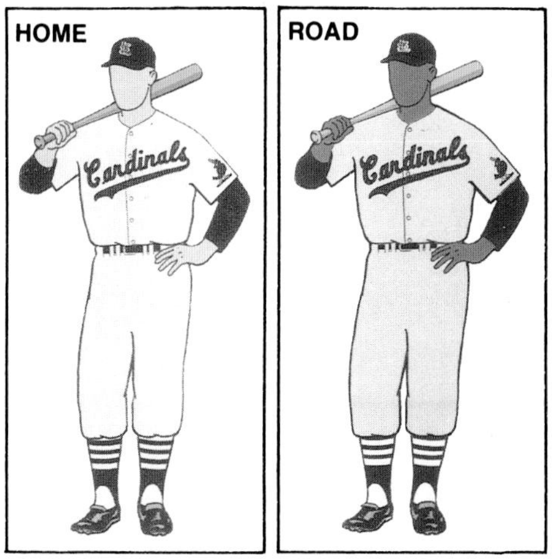

PITTSBURGH

PHILADELPHIA

CHICAGO

CINCINNATI

NEW YORK

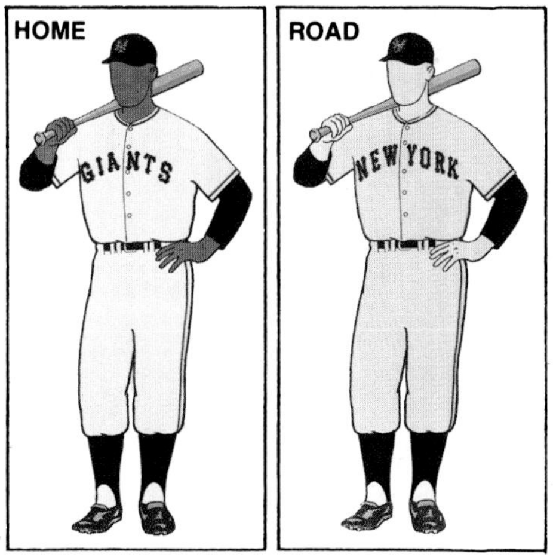

Sports NEW YORK Herald Tribune Sports

Section Three WEDNESDAY, SEPTEMBER 25, 1957 Section Three

Basilio Ready to Fight Robinson Again

Dodgers Top Bucs, 2-0, in Home Finale

But Ray Is Undecided On Future

Ring World Hails New Champion

RED SMITH

Brooklyn's 'Bye Is Won

8th Pennant For Stengel

1958

AMERICAN LEAGUE

BOSTON

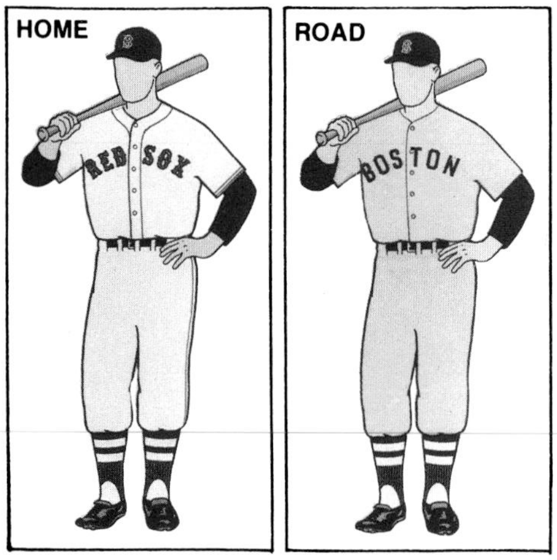

CLEVELAND

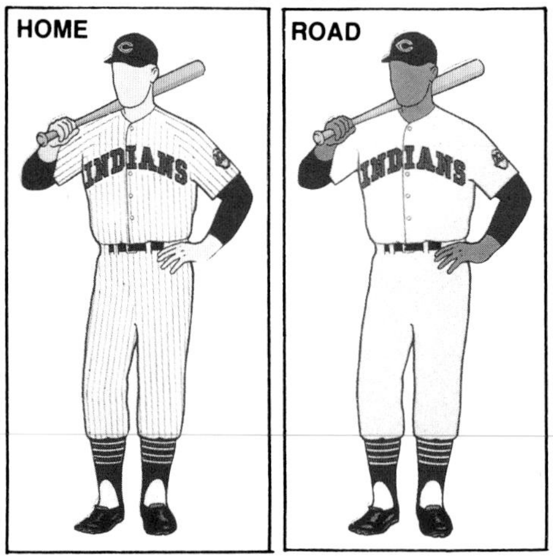

DETROIT

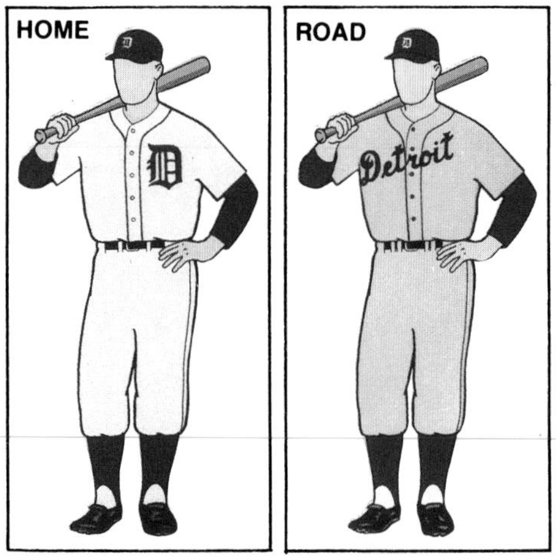

BALTIMORE

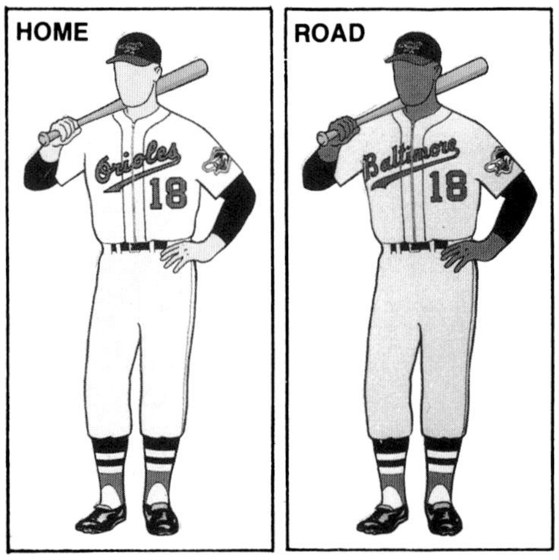

NEW YORK

KANSAS CITY

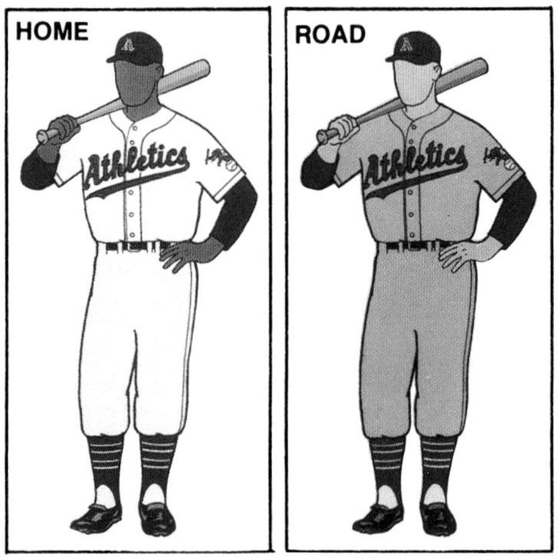

CHICAGO

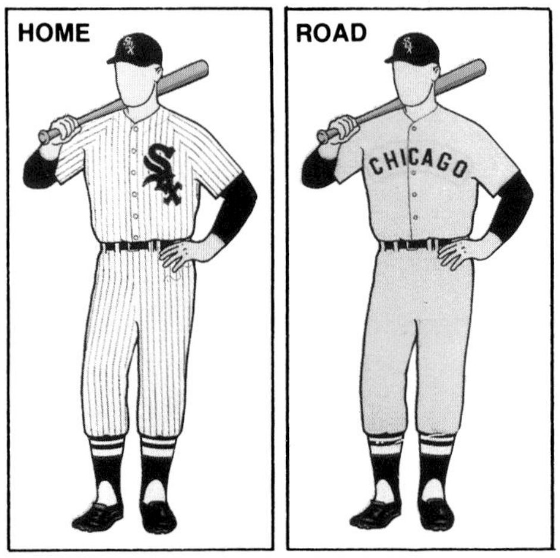

WASHINGTON

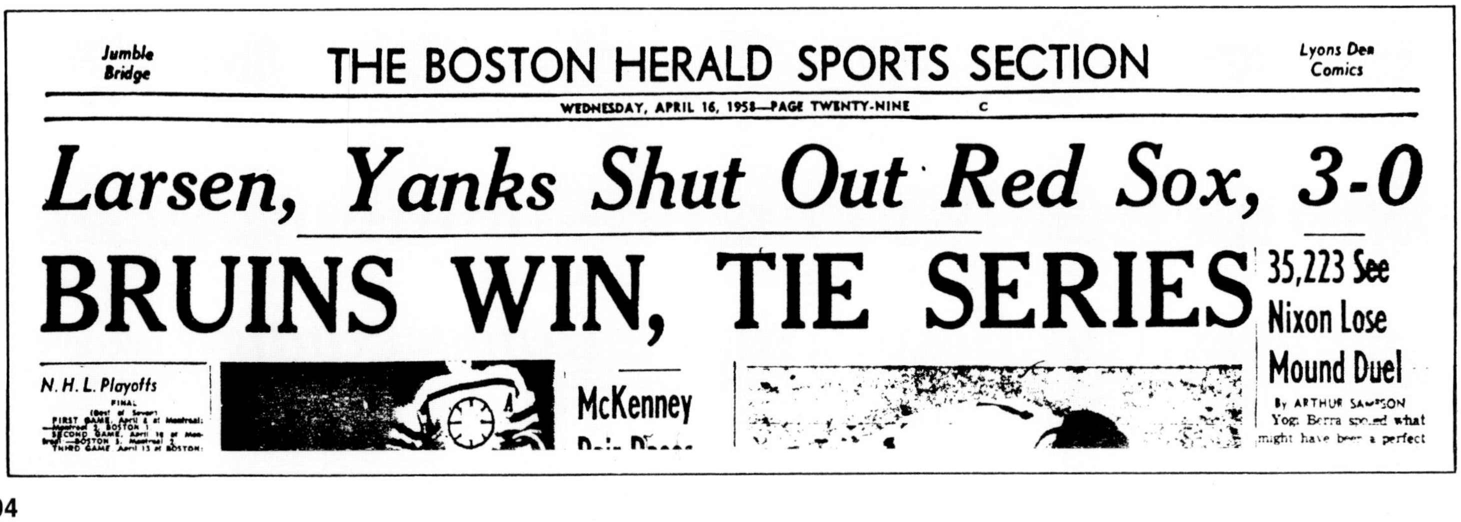

Jumble Bridge

THE BOSTON HERALD SPORTS SECTION

Lyons Den Comics

WEDNESDAY, APRIL 16, 1958—PAGE TWENTY-NINE C

Larsen, Yanks Shut Out Red Sox, 3-0

BRUINS WIN, TIE SERIES

35,223 See Nixon Lose Mound Duel

By ARTHUR SAMPSON

Yogi Berra swung what might have been a perfect

N. H. L. Playoffs

FINAL (Best of Seven)

FIRST GAME, April 8 at Montreal: Montreal 2, BOSTON 1

SECOND GAME, April 10 at Montreal: BOSTON 5, Montreal 2

THIRD GAME April 13 at BOSTON:

McKenney

NATIONAL LEAGUE 1958

MILWAUKEE
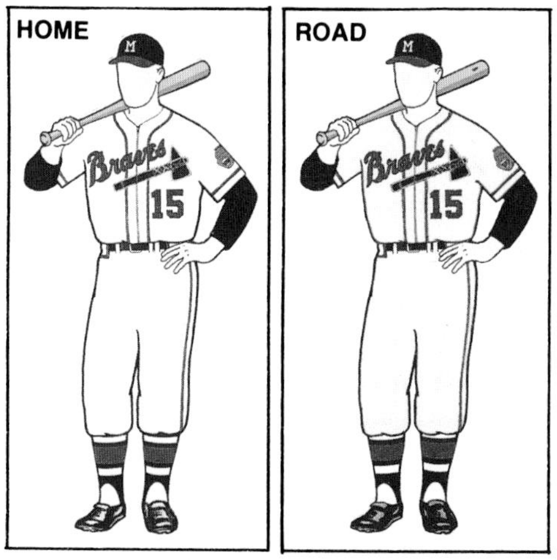

LOS ANGELES
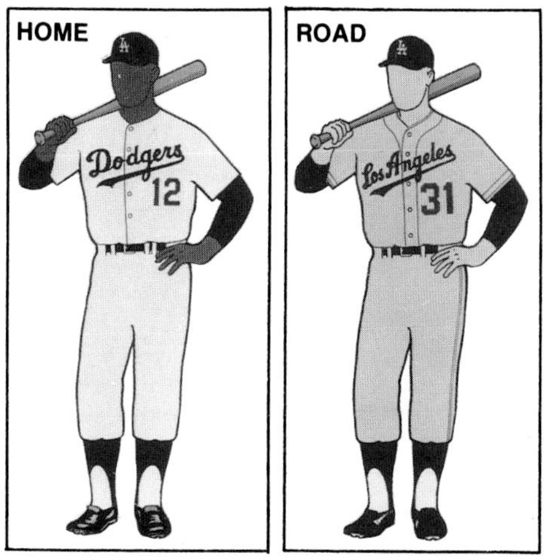

ST. LOUIS
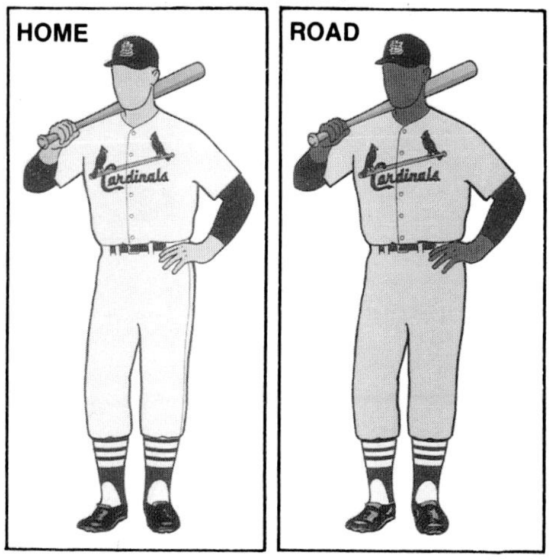

PITTSBURGH

PHILADELPHIA
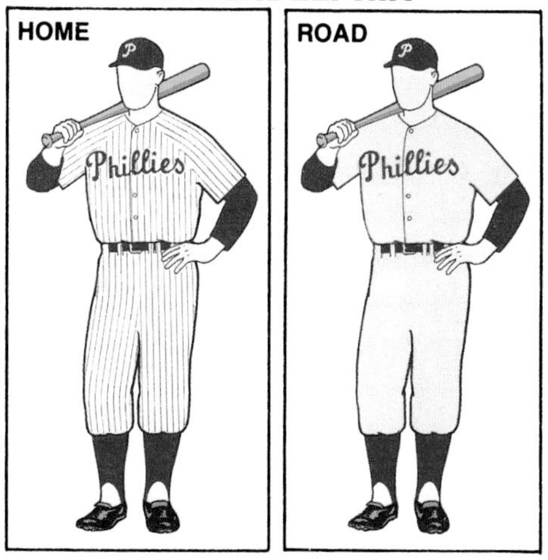

CHICAGO
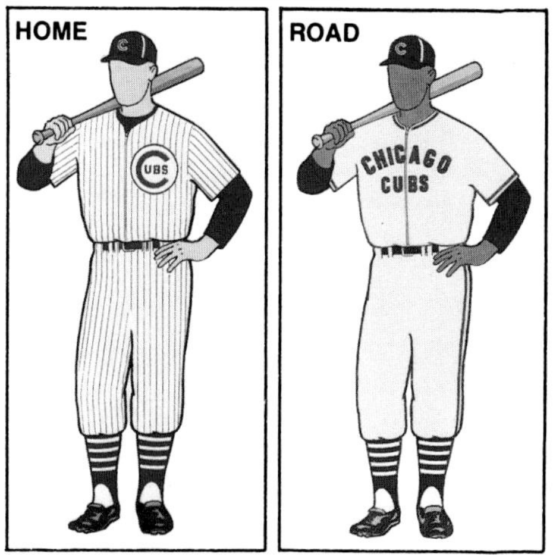

CINCINNATI

SAN FRANCISCO
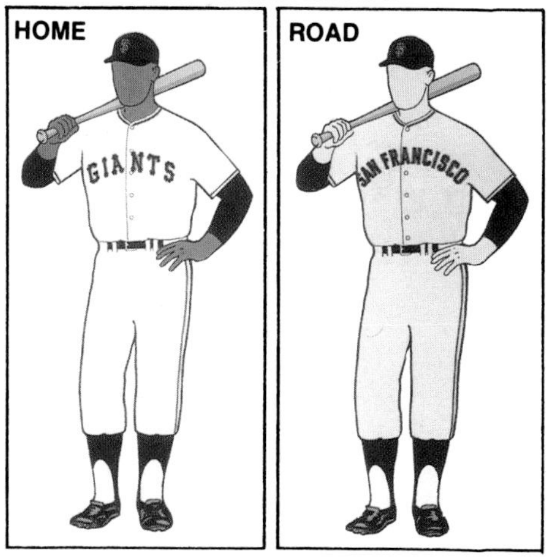

GIANTS BEAT BUMS, 8-0

Mays Dies in Try for Two

San Francisco Chronicle Sporting Green

SAN FRANCISCO, WEDNESDAY, APRIL 16, 1958 PAGE 1H

Gomez Allows Six Hits

Win Them All? Rigney

Spencer, Cepeda Blast Home Runs

1959 AMERICAN LEAGUE

BOSTON

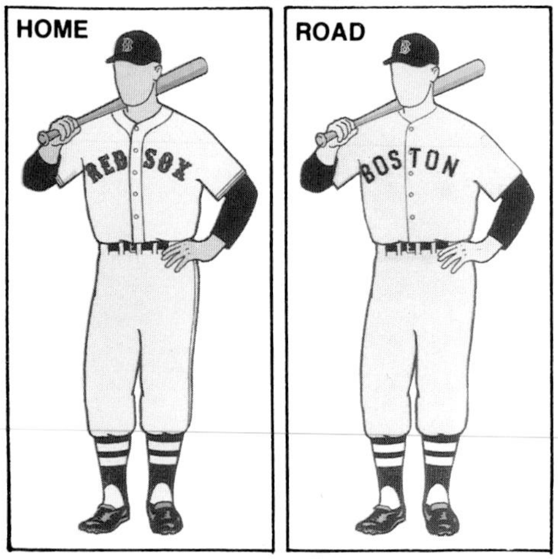

CLEVELAND

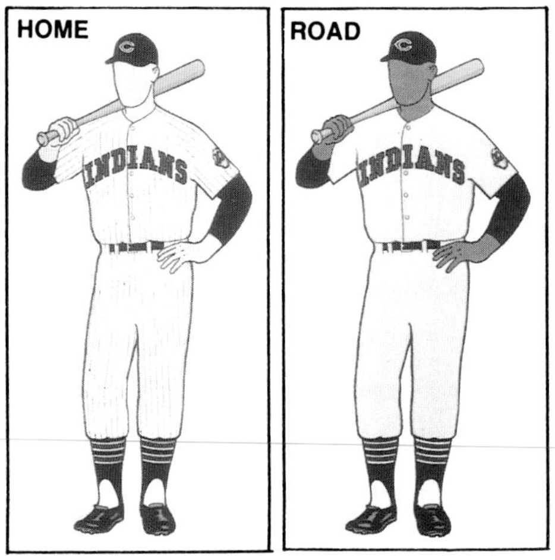

DETROIT

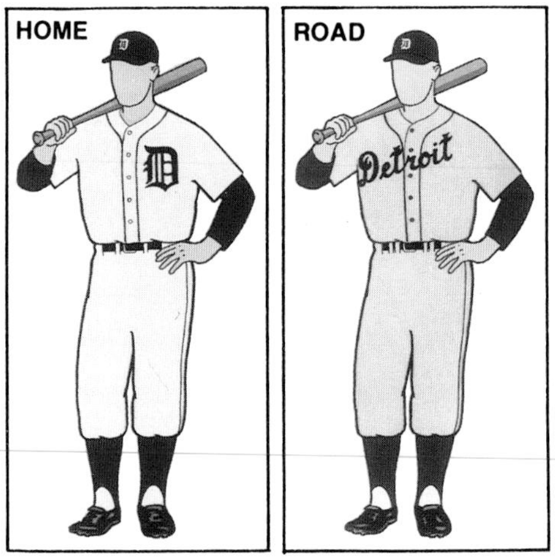

BALTIMORE

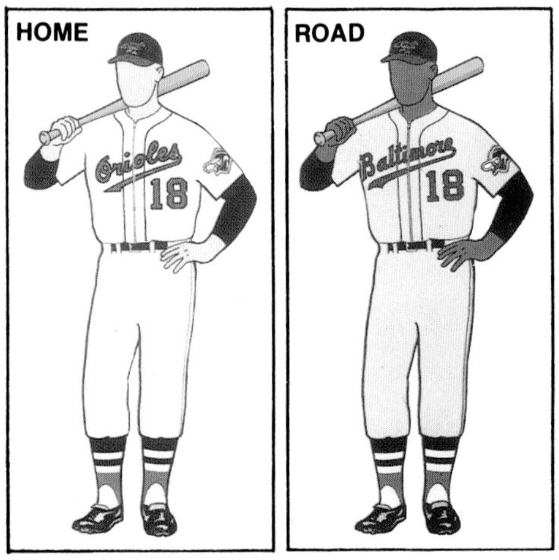

NEW YORK

KANSAS CITY

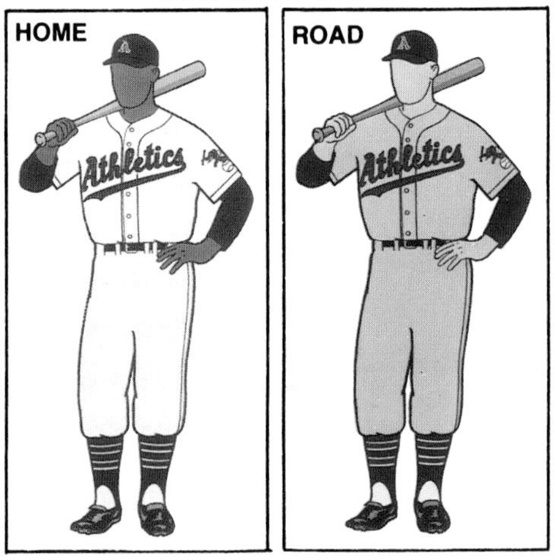

CHICAGO

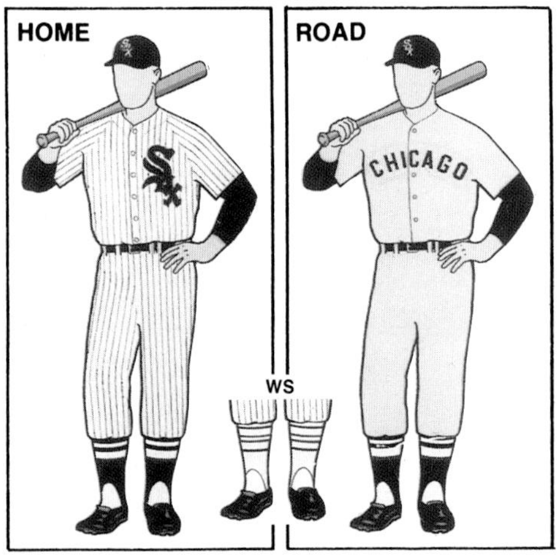

WASHINGTON

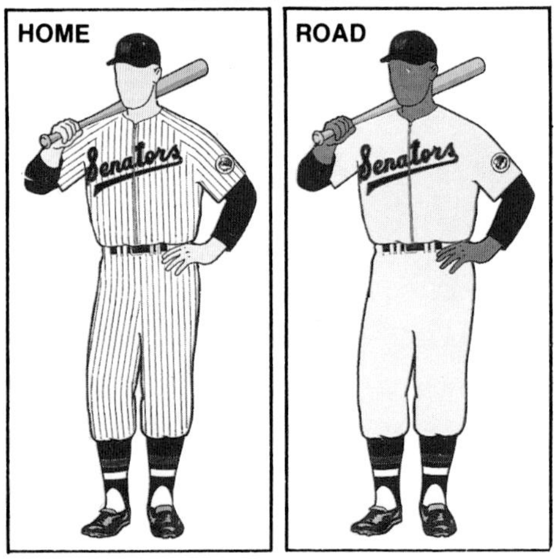

Tonight's The Night!

SOX WANT TO WIN 'AS CHAMPS SHOULD'

Gordon Vows All-Out Bid

He'll Yield Indians' Reins To Harder if Hose Win

Leo Says Indians Bid High

CLEVELAND— (AP) — The Cleveland

Leave It to Old Early, Boys

Wynn, Perry Go for Broke

It's All Over If Hose Can Rack Up This One!

NATIONAL LEAGUE 1959

MILWAUKEE

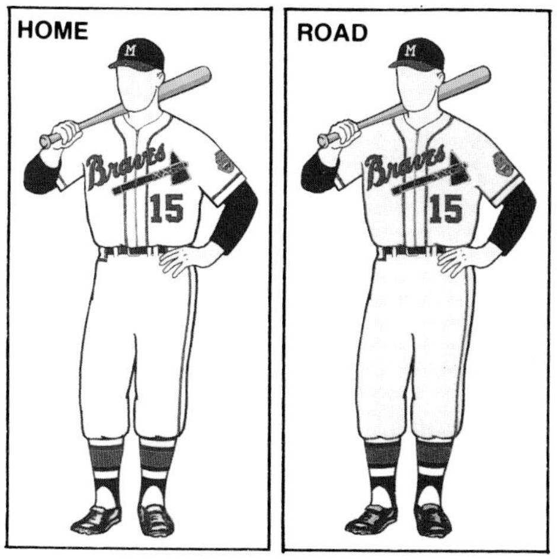

LOS ANGELES

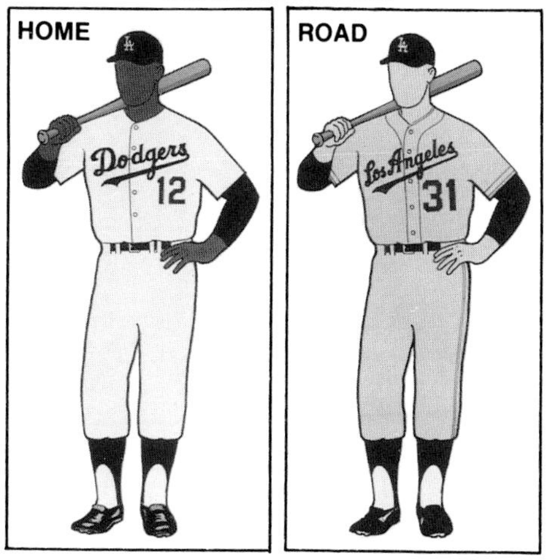

ST. LOUIS

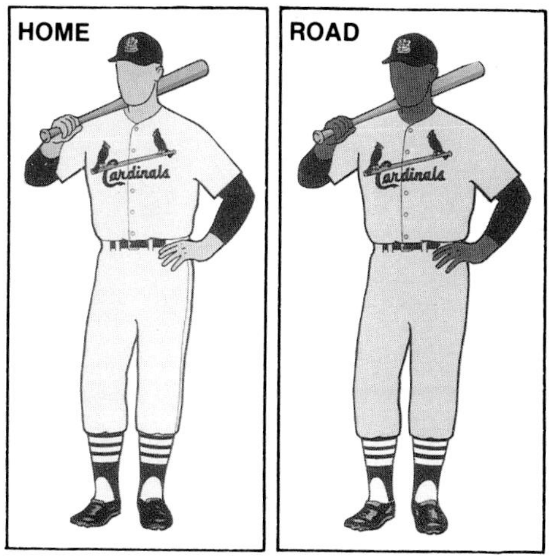

PITTSBURGH

PHILADELPHIA

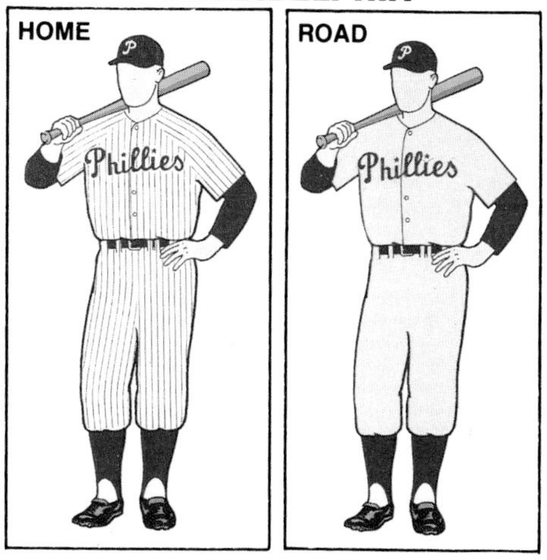

CHICAGO

CINCINNATI

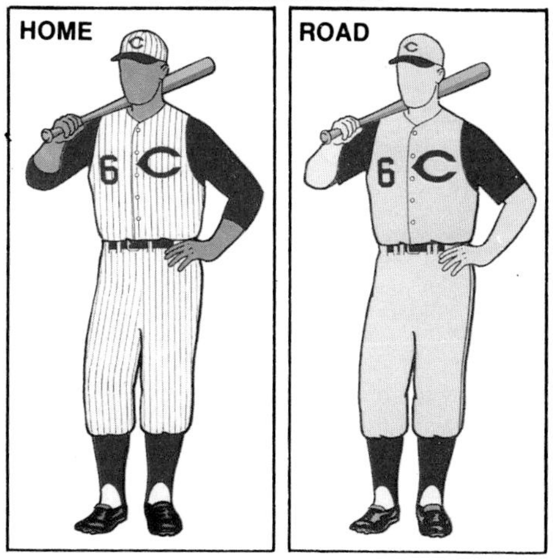

SAN FRANCISCO

WALTER, WOULD YOU THINK YOU'D EVER SEE THE DAY?

Bitter Brooklynites Root for White Sox

By BILL SLOCUM

BROOKLYN, U. S. A., Oct. 3—What hast thou wrought, Walter O'Malley?

Yesterday, in the cool snugness of a bar in the heart of Brooklyn, fine young lads, just come into the joys and responsibilities of manhood, rooted for something called the Chicago White Sox.

There must have been 50 men in the bar. There were two women. Silent women, as behooves a lady in the Jax Bar. The Jax is on Willoughby st., between Jay and Pearl and it's hard by the courthouse. If that ain't the heart of Brooklyn, Walter, what is it?

Do you, dear Walter, know what was the loudest moment of the afternoon as the Los Angeles Dodgers beat the Chicagos? It was that moment in the eighth inning when a man from Chicago, running with the grace and wisdom of Babe Herman at his best, loused up a Chicago rally.

The boys at the bar yelled then. They yelled in the sweet accents of their native borough. They used the words that all America uses but only Brooklynites know how to use.

Naturally, I cannot print these words. But in essence they suggested that Lollar was a poltroon with a fantastic amount of lead centered in a particular portion of his lumbering anatomy.

They were mad at Lollar because, baseball experts as are all Brooklynites, they knew that Lollar was probably losing the game for the White Sox. There were also a few words of deprecation for the wisdom of the coach, a fellow whose parents I could certainly go a long way to look at.

Walter, the young men of Brooklyn were rooting against the Dodgers. They couldn't really get up the heart to root against Gil Hodges. Hell, they once went to mass for him. And, despite their inner hatred, they cheered instinctively when Duke Snider hit one that looked good until it developed into just another high fly.

Neal hit two homers and the boys at the bar weren't happy. Not too long ago a Dodger who hit two homers in a World Series would be posing for statues before nightfall. Another guy hit a home run for the Dodgers and everybody said who is he?

Before your day, Walter, everybody in Brooklyn knew the bat boy. Now they neither know nor know how to pronounce Essegian.

Your name as mentioned only once, Walter, a lady walked in. She sat down in a corner and asked, ever so quietly: "Who is winning? I hope it's the White Sox."

She was told it wasn't. She said "Oh, dear, I want the White Sox to win so much. That O'Malley."

A Brooklyn woman said she wanted the Dodgers to lose. In public, Walter. Not so long ago she would have been thrown in the Gowanus Canal for heresy.

But the worst is yet to come.

I went by Cadman Square. And the kids of Brooklyn, younger even that the lads at Jax', were playing football. Walter. Playing football on a day when the Dodgers were fighting to win a World Series.

For Sake of

Dodgers 6-5 Pick

HERALD EXPRESS

1960 AMERICAN LEAGUE

BOSTON

CLEVELAND

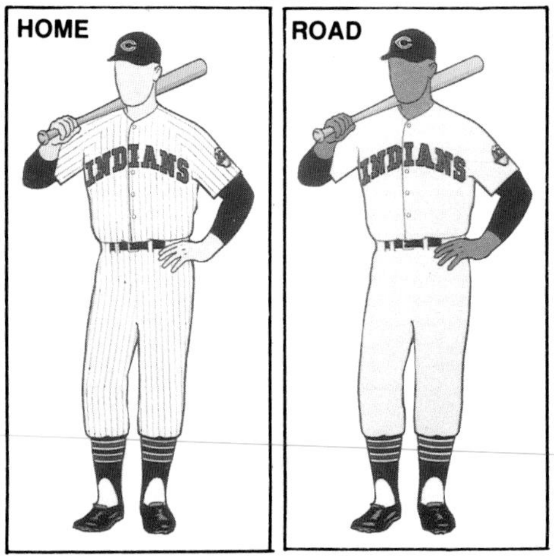

DETROIT

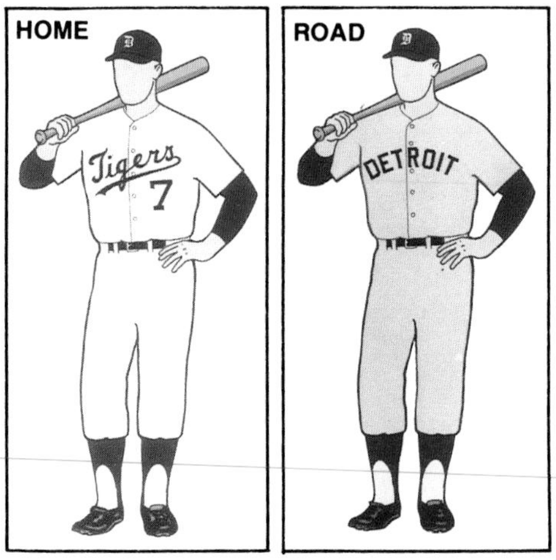

BALTIMORE

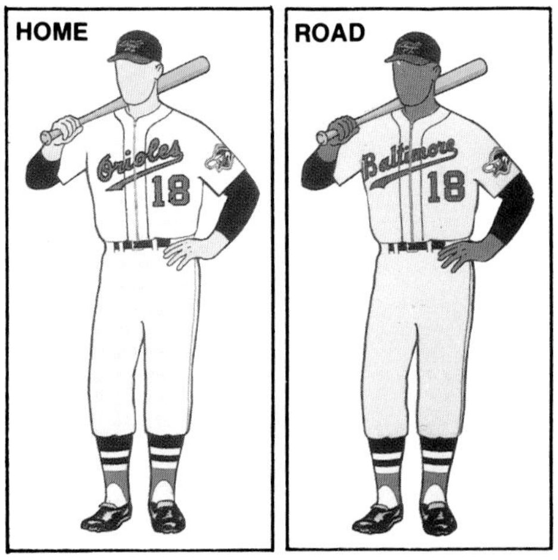

NEW YORK

KANSAS CITY

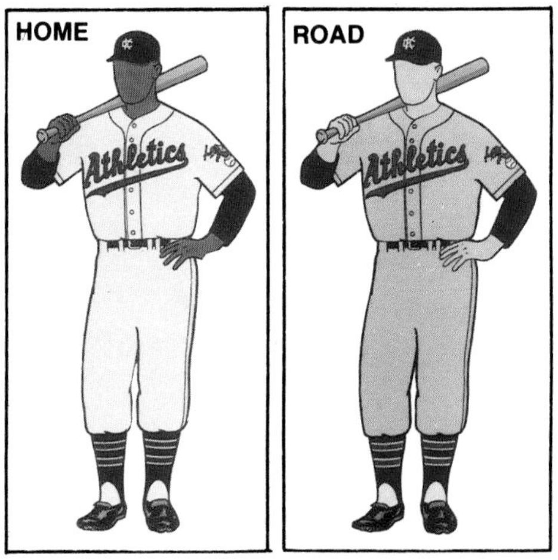

CHICAGO

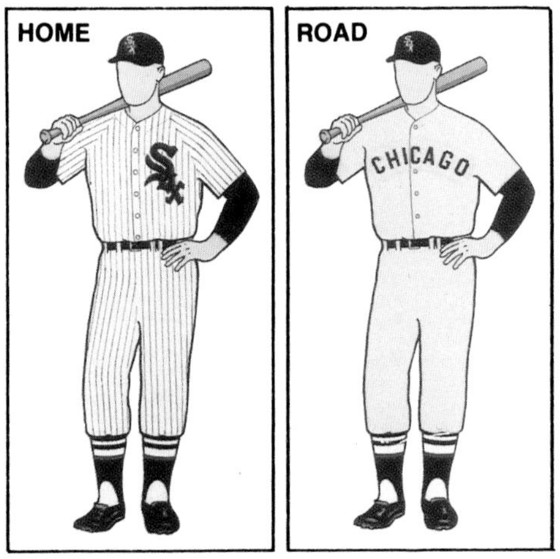

WASHINGTON

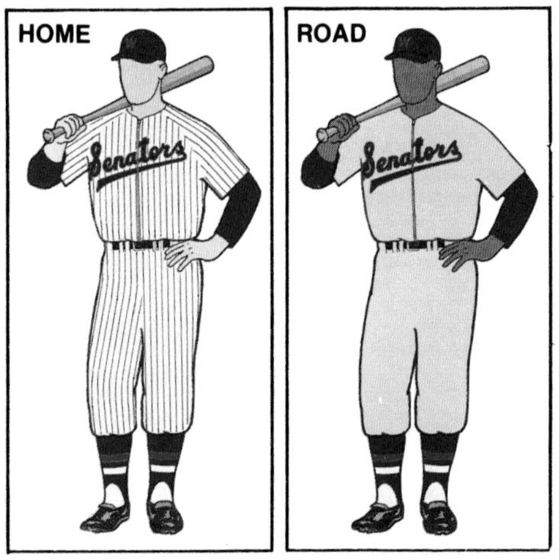

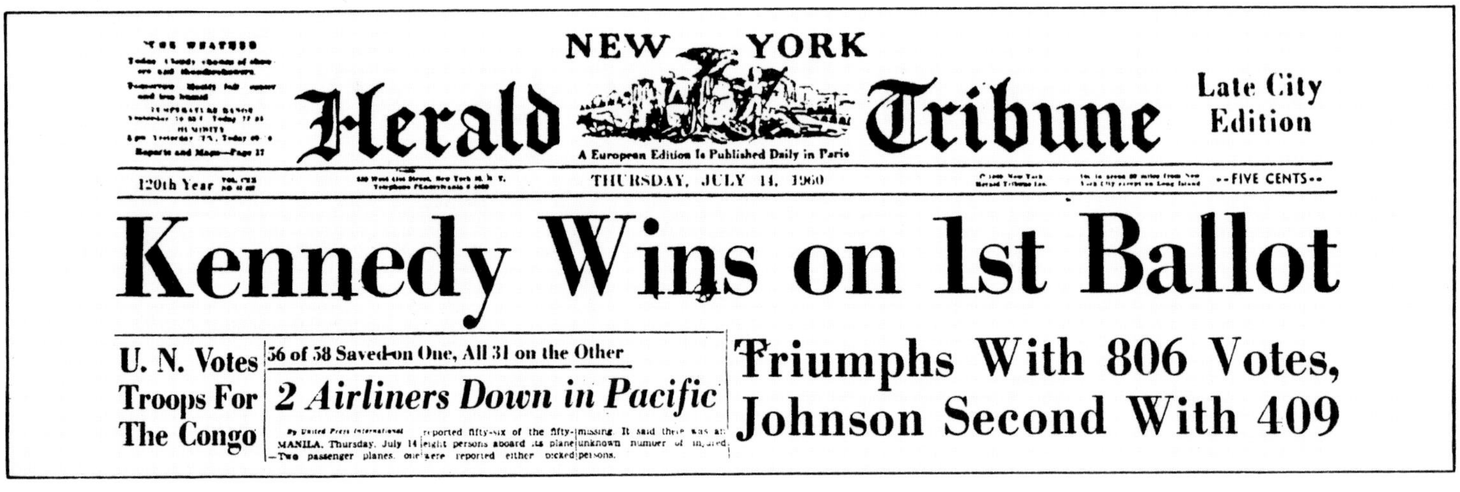

NEW YORK
Herald Tribune
A European Edition Is Published Daily in Paris
Late City Edition
120th Year
THURSDAY, JULY 14, 1960
FIVE CENTS

Kennedy Wins on 1st Ballot

U. N. Votes Troops For The Congo

56 of 58 Saved on One, All 31 on the Other
2 Airliners Down in Pacific

Triumphs With 806 Votes, Johnson Second With 409

NATIONAL LEAGUE 1960

MILWAUKEE

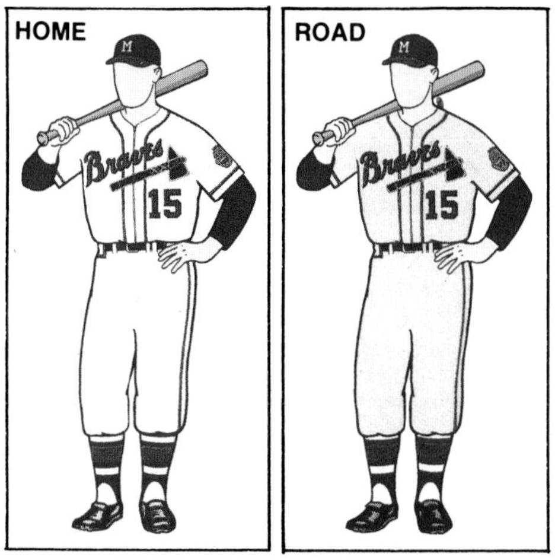

LOS ANGELES

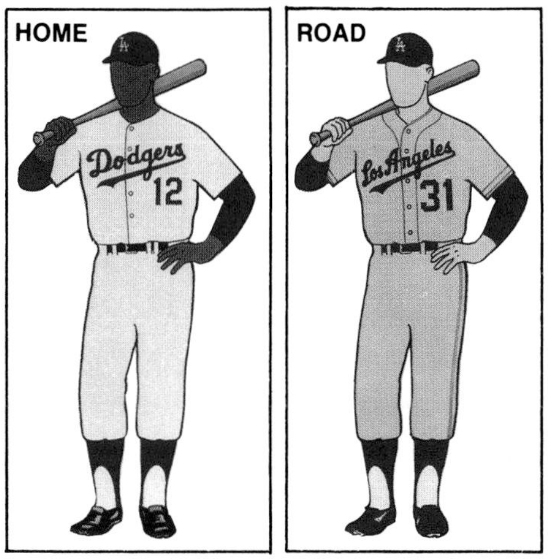

ST. LOUIS

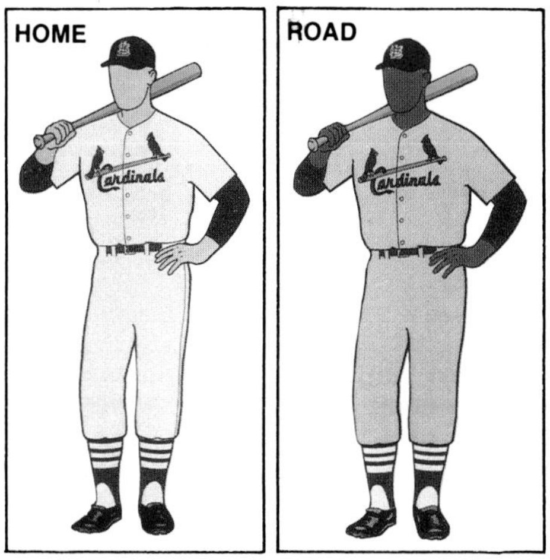

PITTSBURGH

PHILADELPHIA

CHICAGO

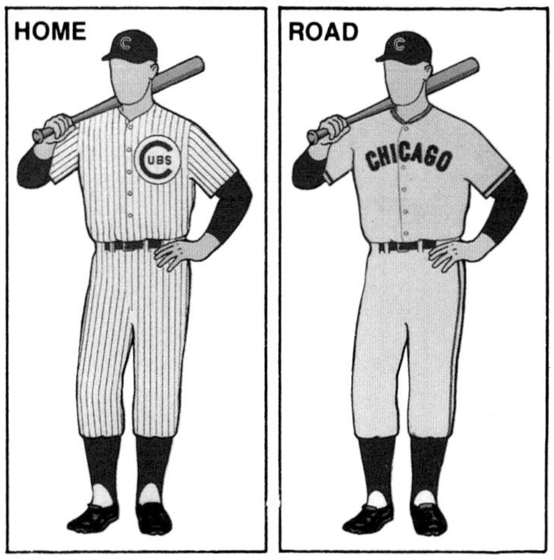

The Masters Tournament
AUGUSTA, GEORGIA
ARNOLD PALMER*
Wins With Wilson
HIT THE LONG BALL!

The 1960 Wilson STAFF Golf Ball

At your Golf Professional Shop NOW
WILSON SPORTING GOODS CO., CHICAGO

CINCINNATI

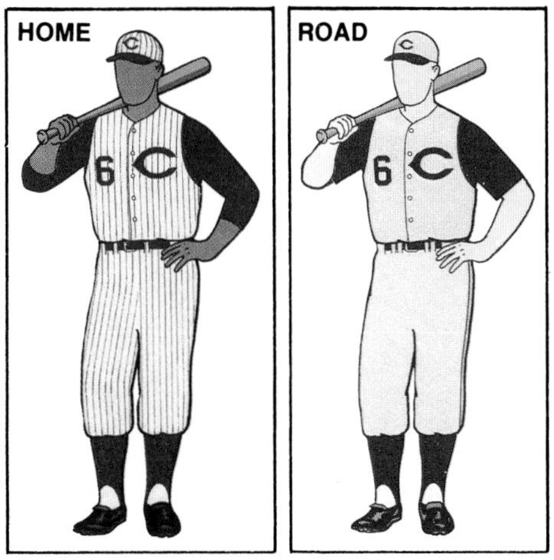

SAN FRANCISCO

The Pittsburgh Press

WORLD SERIES FINAL

VOL. 77, No. 113 | THURSDAY, OCTOBER 13, 1960 | WEATHER—Warm | 76 Pages—5 Cents

PIRATES WORLD CHAMPS

Final Game Box [illegible] Bucs Win 10-9

1961 AMERICAN LEAGUE

BOSTON

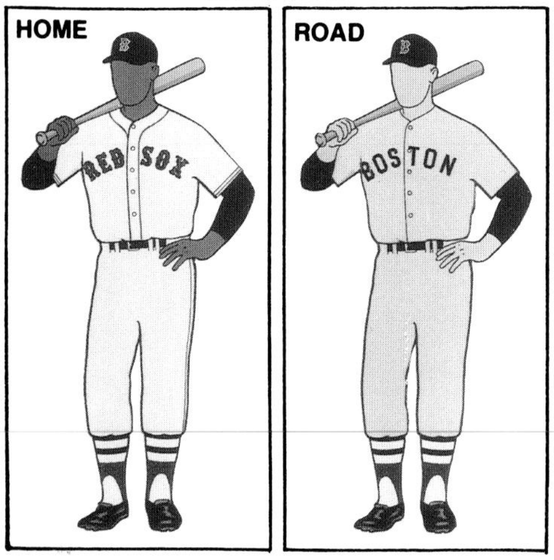

CLEVELAND

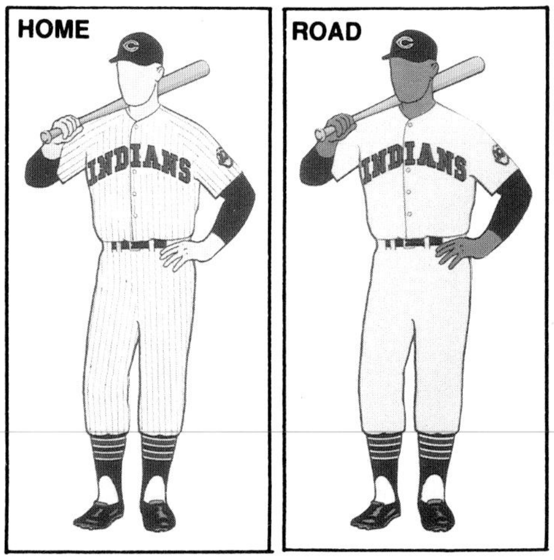

DETROIT

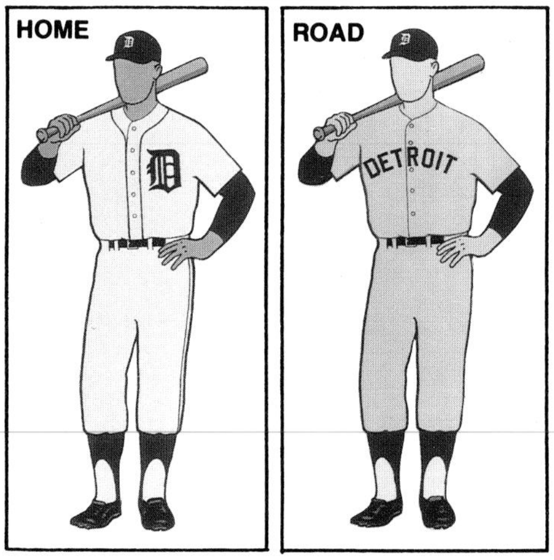

BALTIMORE

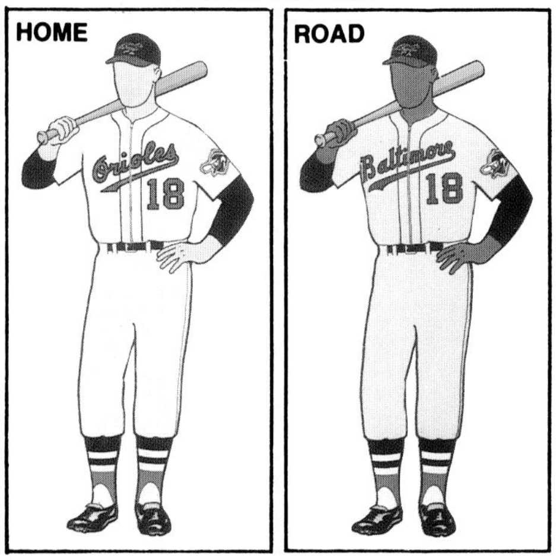

NEW YORK

KANSAS CITY

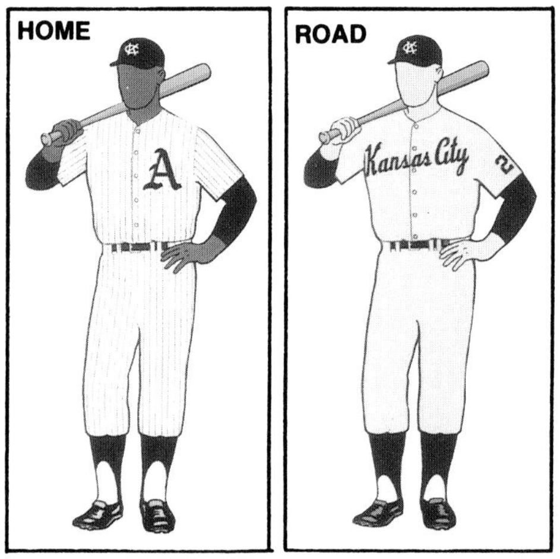

CHICAGO

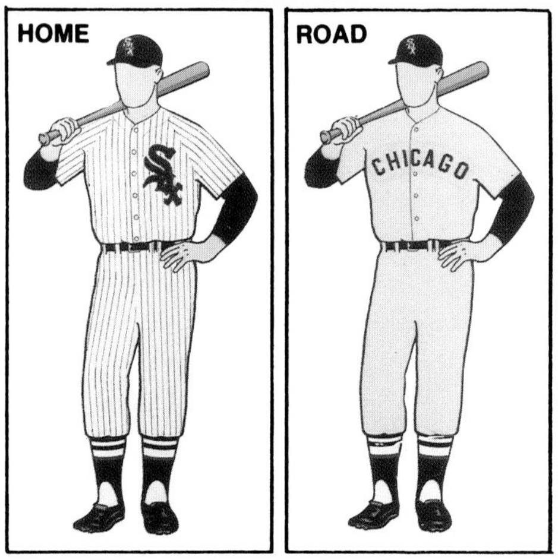

MINNESOTA

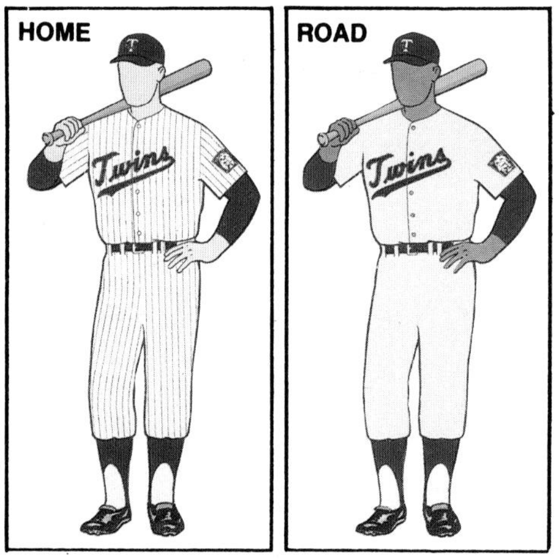

WASHINGTON

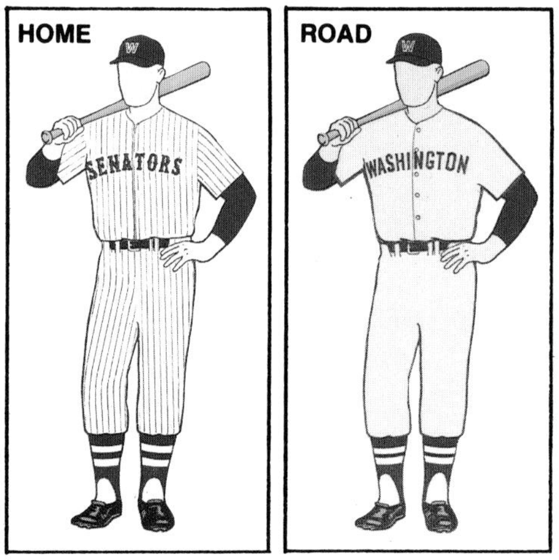

LOS ANGELES

BATTEY'S HOMER RUINS ANGELS' OPENER

1 2 3

SLIDE, ALBIE, SLIDE!—Angel outfielder Albie Pearson hits infield and skids toward second while Minnesota's Billy Gardner prepares to tag in first inning. Gardner dropped ball and Albie was safe. The Twins won 4-2

Los Angeles Times Sports

Ten More Cagers From 6 Schools Named in Scandal

TOO LATE
Wind Shift 'Robs' Hunt

Only 11,931 See Twins Win, 4-2

NATIONAL LEAGUE 1961

MILWAUKEE

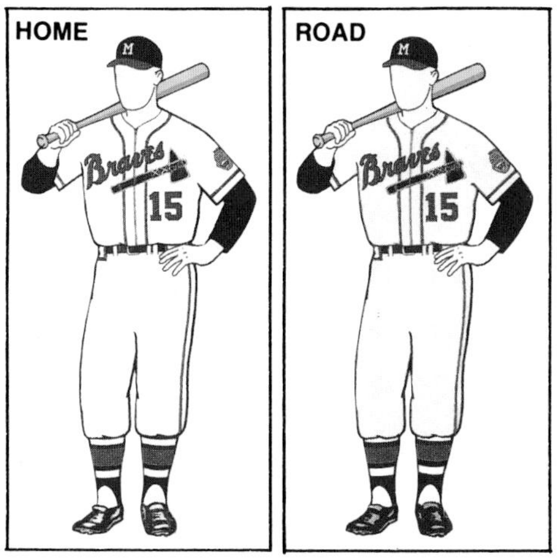

LOS ANGELES

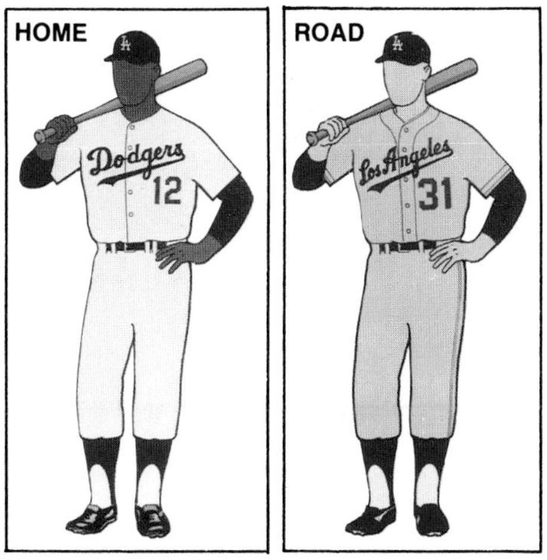

ST. LOUIS

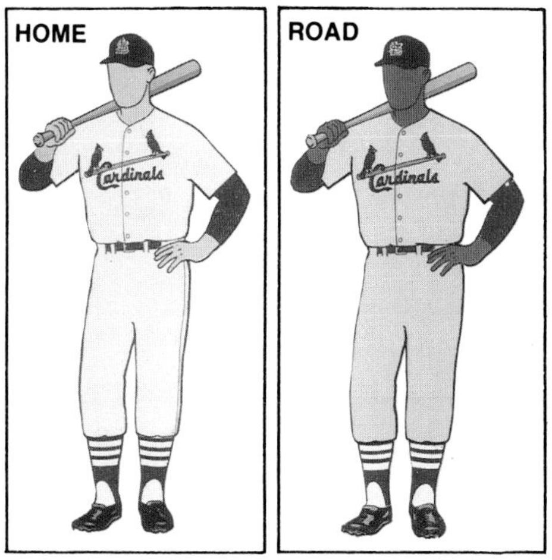

PITTSBURGH

PHILADELPHIA

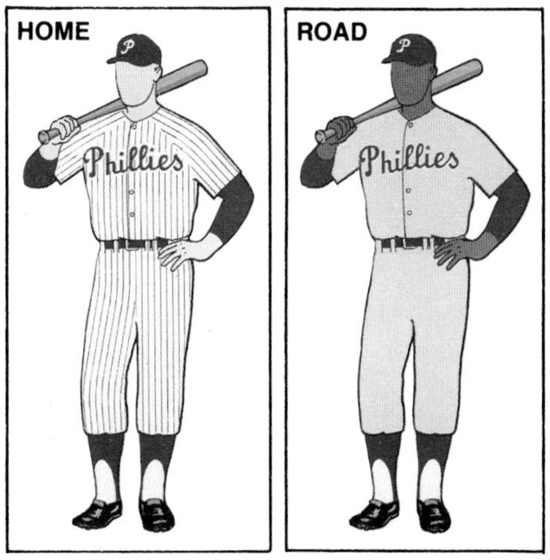

CHICAGO

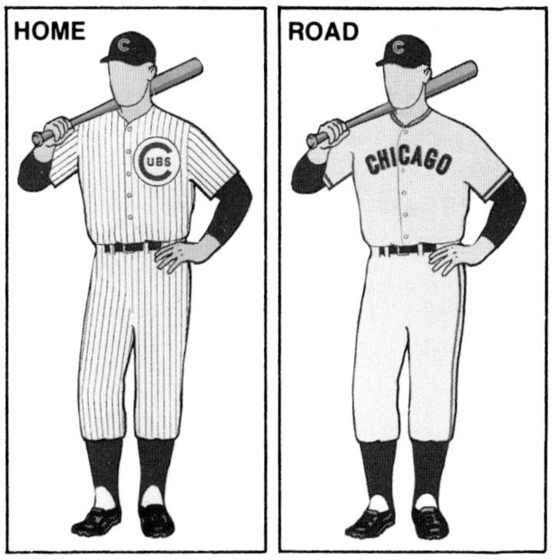

CINCINNATI

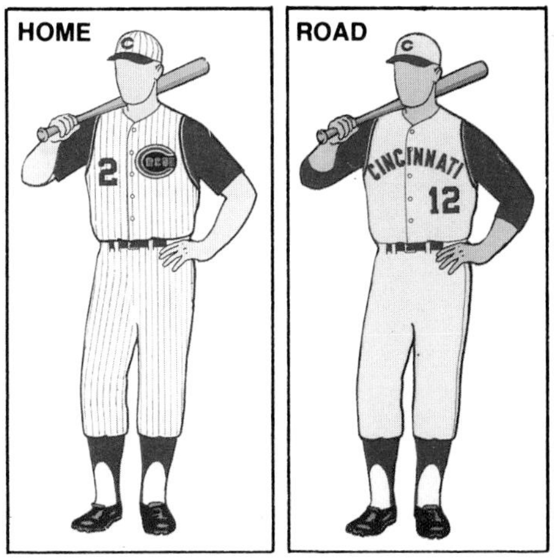

SAN FRANCISCO

New York Herald Tribune — Friday, October 6, 1961

Reds Win, 6-2, to Square Series As Jay's 4-Hitter Halts Yankees

Berra Socks HR; 3 Errors by N.Y.

By Tommy Holmes

Out in the bright Bronx sunshine Cincinnati's Reds bounced

1962 AMERICAN LEAGUE

BOSTON

HOME

ROAD

CLEVELAND

HOME

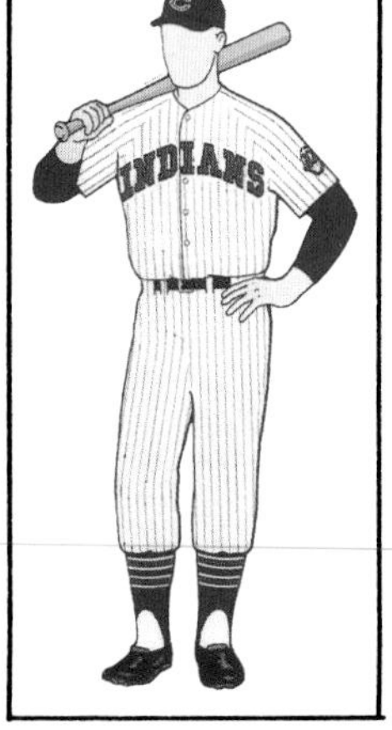

ROAD

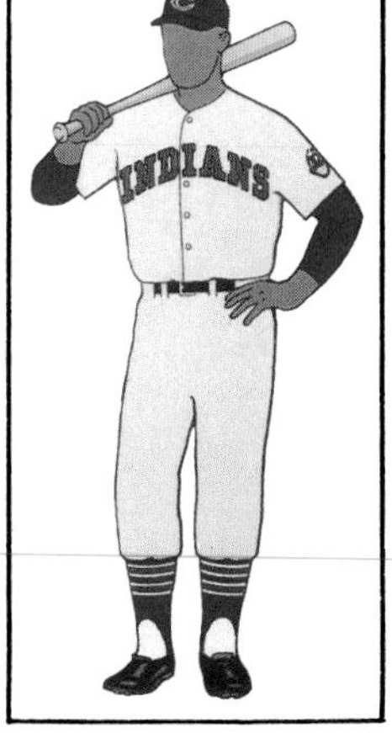

DETROIT

HOME

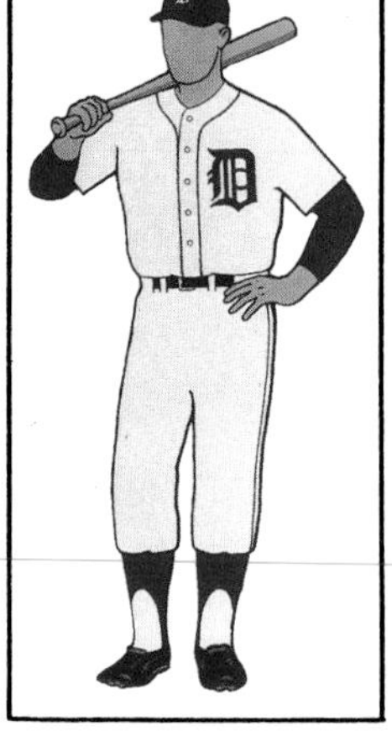

ROAD

BALTIMORE

HOME

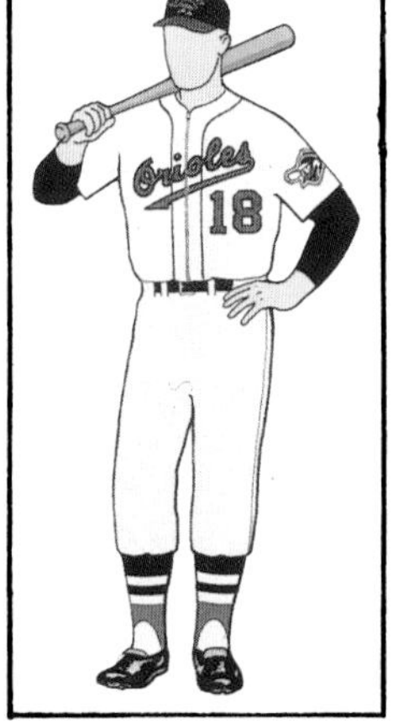

ROAD

NEW YORK

HOME

ROAD

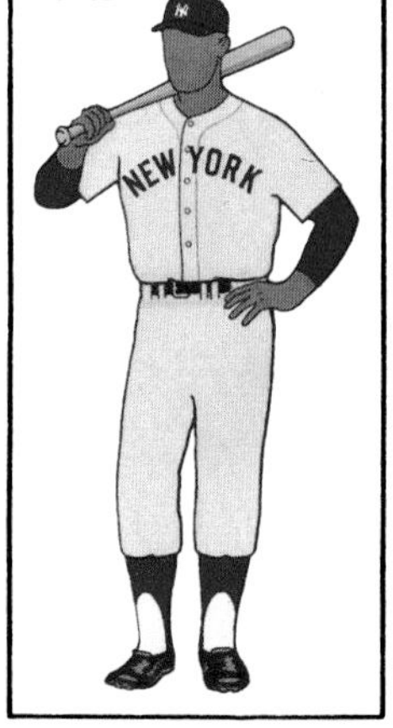

KANSAS CITY

HOME

ROAD

CHICAGO

HOME

ROAD

MINNESOTA

HOME

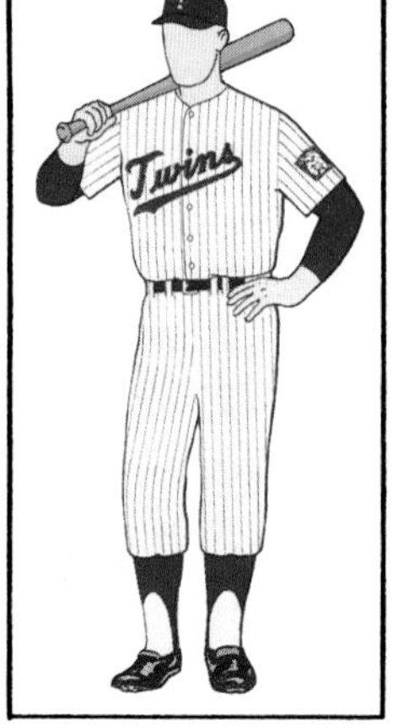

ROAD

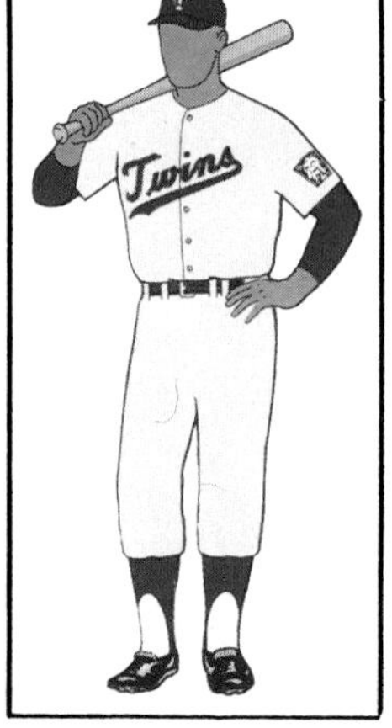

WASHINGTON

HOME

ROAD

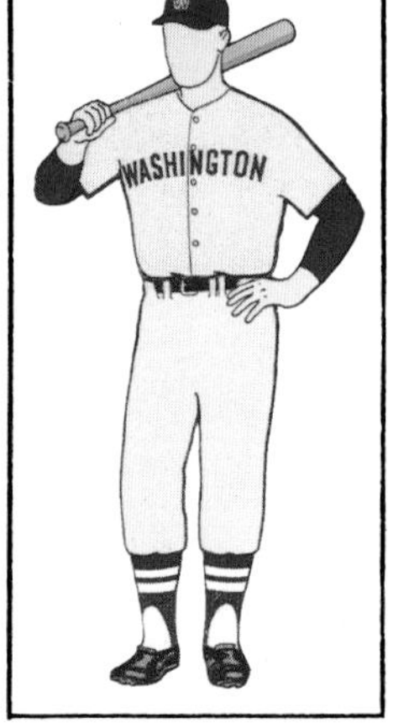

LOS ANGELES

HOME

ROAD

Weather Forecast

The Evening Star

WITH SUNDAY MORNING EDITION

Guide for Readers

110th Year. No. 292. WASHINGTON, D. C., FRIDAY, OCTOBER 19, 1962—64 PAGES 10 Cents

Ranger Loses Power, Fails In Moon Shot

Spacecraft's TV Unable to Take Pictures Planned

Kennedy, in Cleveland, Makes Medicare Plea

Stresses Health Issue as He Starts 3-Day, Cross-Country Campaign Trip

CLEVELAND, Oct. 19 (AP).—President Kennedy brought his off-year election campaign here today with an earnest plea for medical aid to the elderly under social security.

Kennedy Reported Willing To Meet With Khrushchev

Would See Premier on Visit to U. S.

NATIONAL LEAGUE 1962

MILWAUKEE

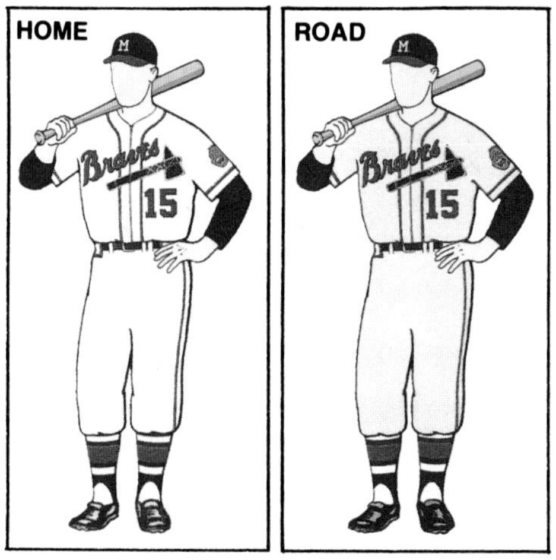

LOS ANGELES

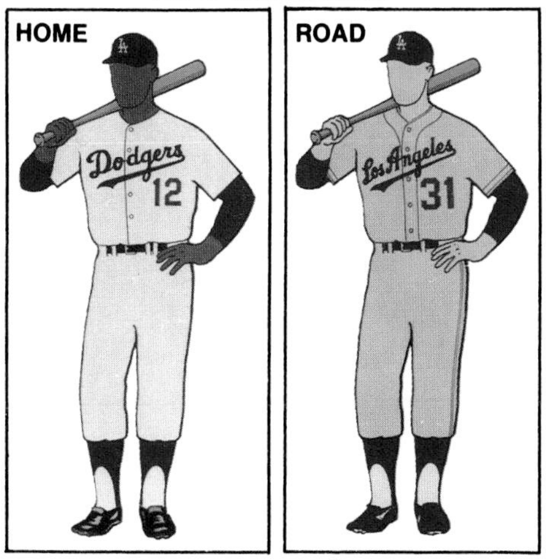

ST. LOUIS

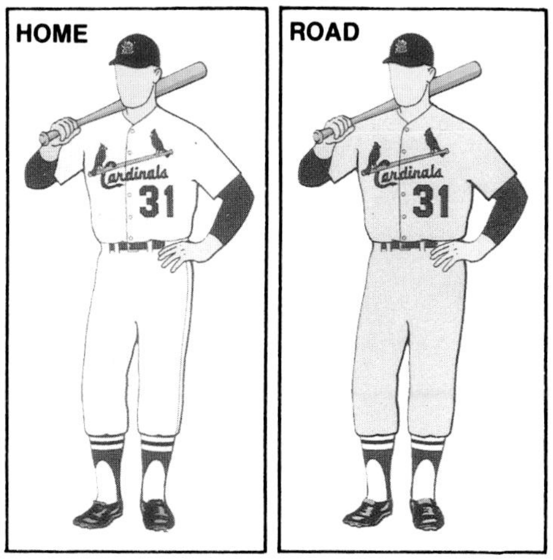

PITTSBURGH

PHILADELPHIA

CHICAGO

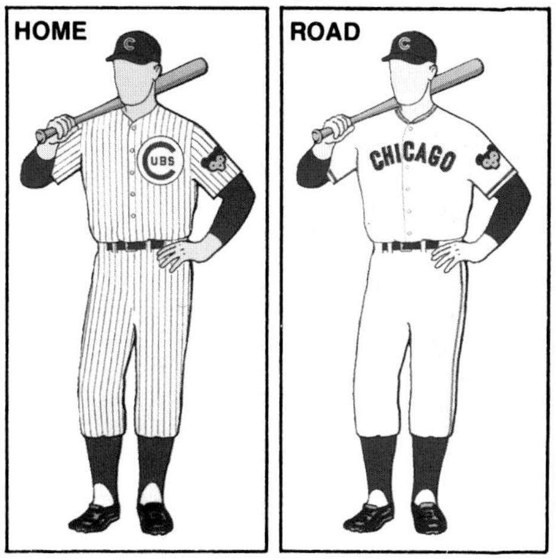

NEW YORK

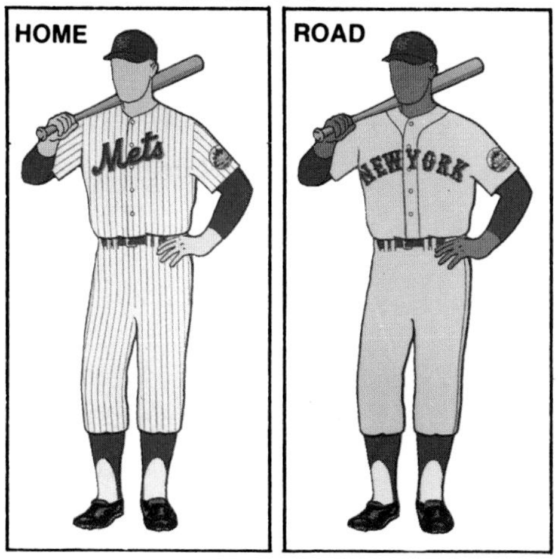

CINCINNATI

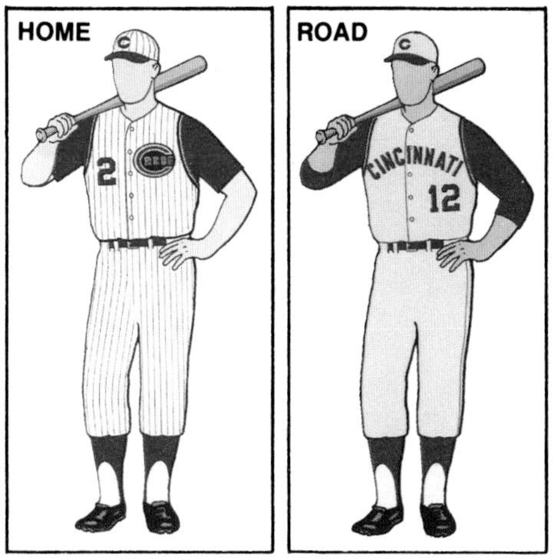

SAN FRANCISCO

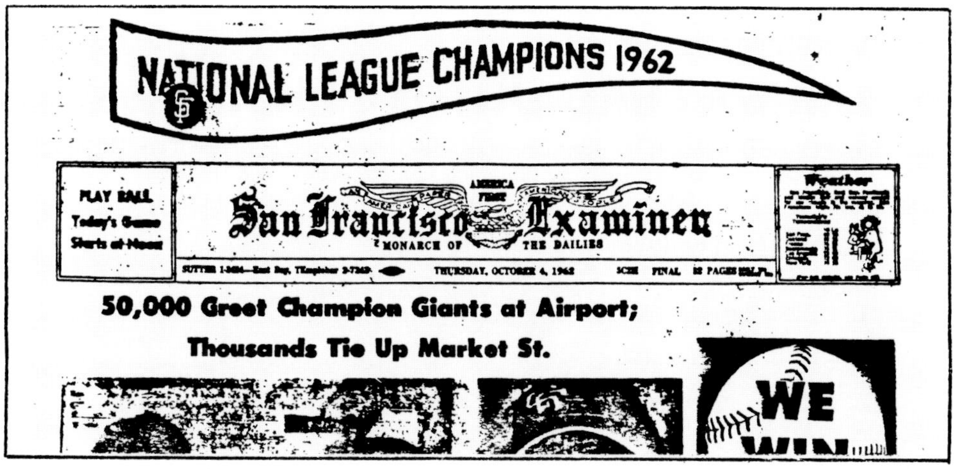

NATIONAL LEAGUE CHAMPIONS 1962

PLAY BALL
Today's Game
Starts at Noon

San Francisco Examiner
MONARCH OF THE DAILIES

THURSDAY, OCTOBER 4, 1962 FINAL

50,000 Greet Champion Giants at Airport;
Thousands Tie Up Market St.

WE

HOUSTON

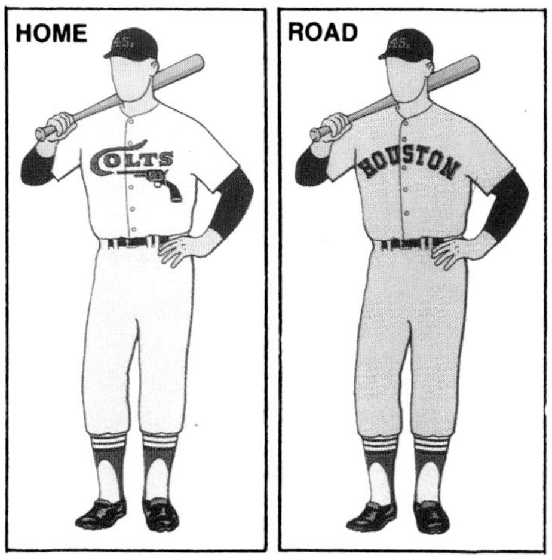

1963 AMERICAN LEAGUE

BOSTON

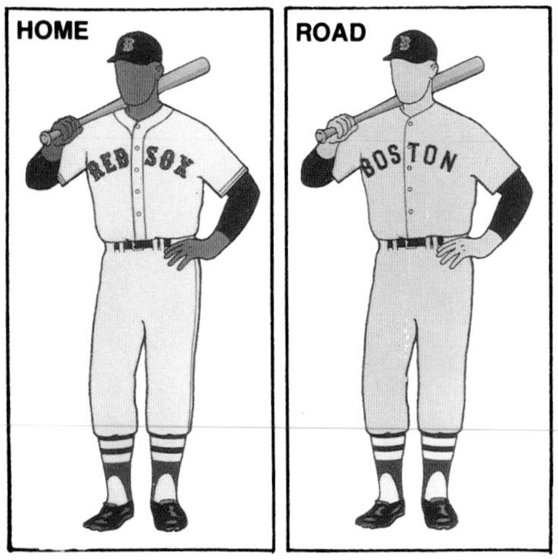

CLEVELAND

DETROIT

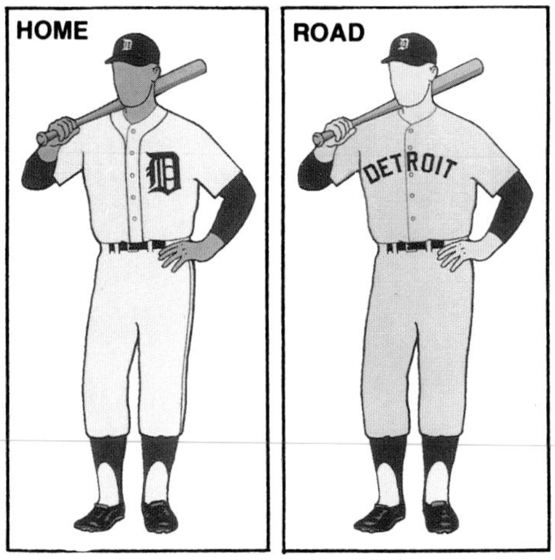

BALTIMORE

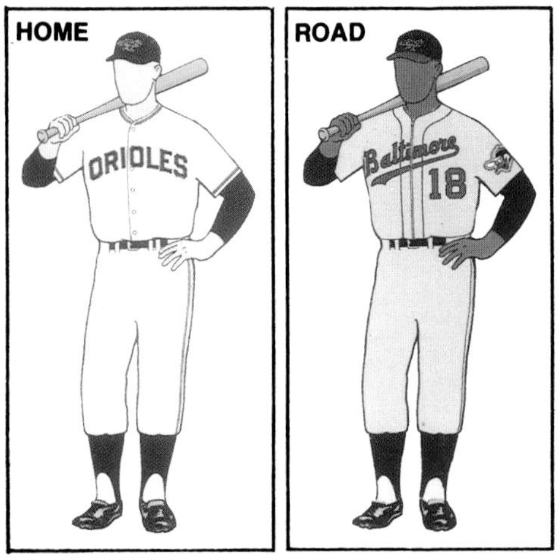

NEW YORK

KANSAS CITY

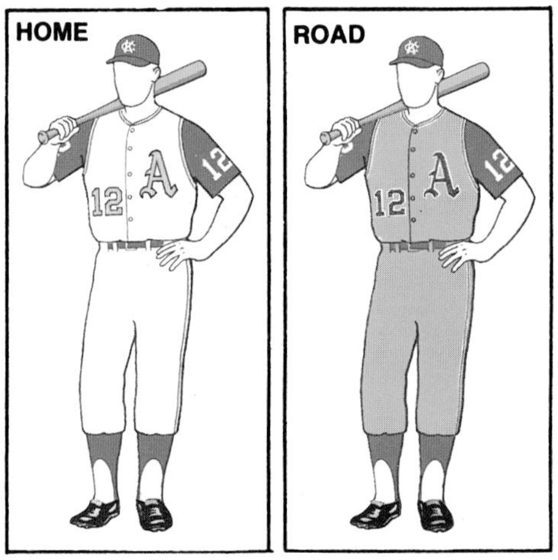

CHICAGO

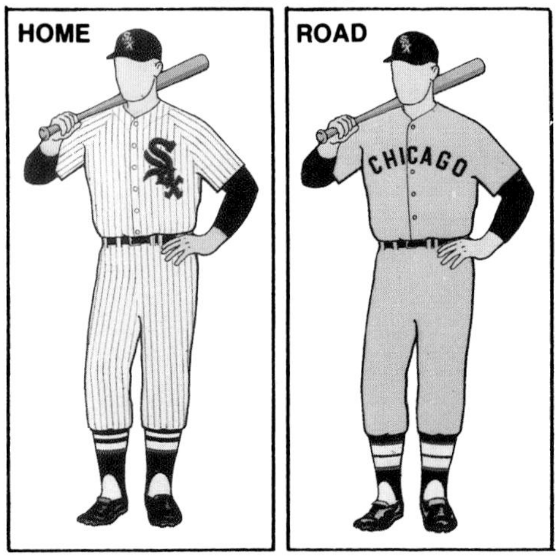

MINNESOTA

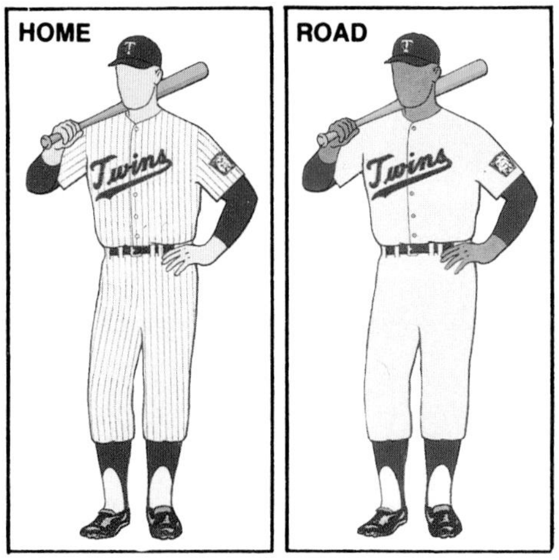

WASHINGTON

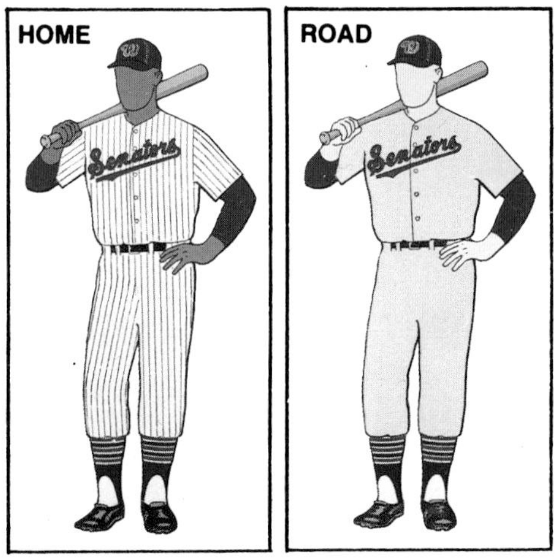

LOS ANGELES

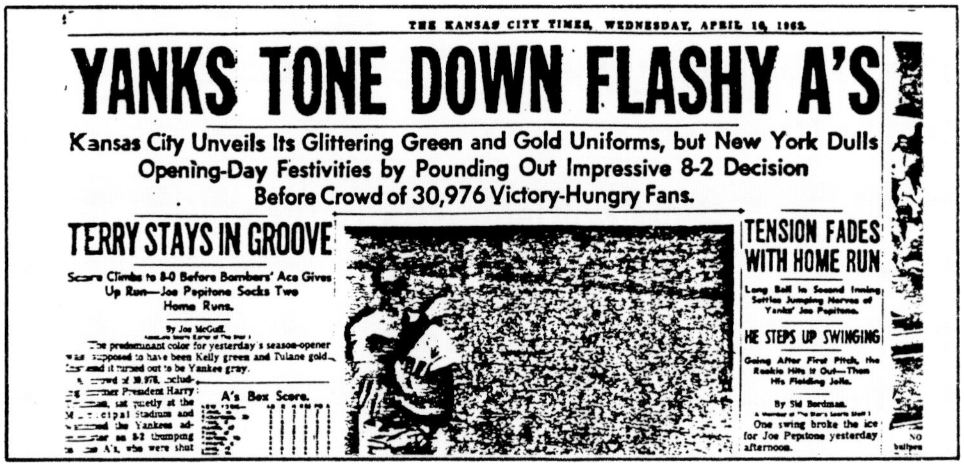

THE KANSAS CITY TIMES, WEDNESDAY, APRIL 10, 1963.

YANKS TONE DOWN FLASHY A'S

Kansas City Unveils Its Glittering Green and Gold Uniforms, but New York Dulls Opening-Day Festivities by Pounding Out Impressive 8-2 Decision Before Crowd of 30,976 Victory-Hungry Fans.

TERRY STAYS IN GROOVE

Score Climbs to 8-0 Before Bombers' Ace Gives Up Run—Joe Pepitone Socks Two Home Runs.

By Joe McGuff.

The predominant color for yesterday's season-opener was supposed to have been Kelly green and Tulane gold, and it turned out to be Yankee gray.

A crowd of 30,976, including former President Harry Truman, sat quietly at the Municipal Stadium and watched the Yankees administer an 8-2 thumping to the A's, who were shut

A's Box Score.

TENSION FADES WITH HOME RUN

Long Ball in Second Inning Settles Jumping Nerves of Yanks' Joe Pepitone.

HE STEPS UP SWINGING

Going After First Pitch, the Rookie Hits It Out—Then His Fielding Jells.

By Sid Bordman.

One swing broke the ice for Joe Pepitone yesterday afternoon.

NATIONAL LEAGUE 1963

MILWAUKEE

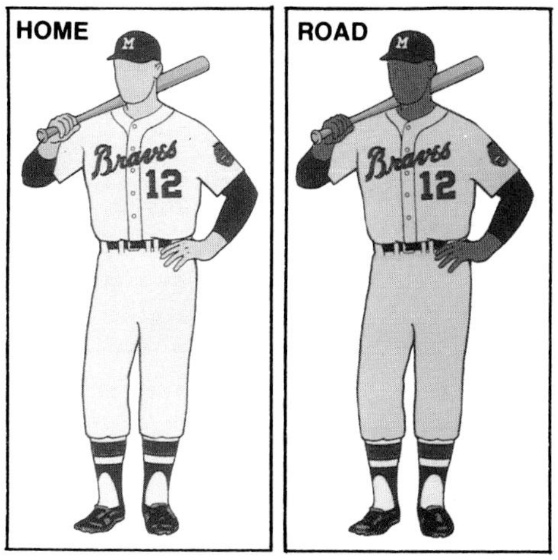

LOS ANGELES

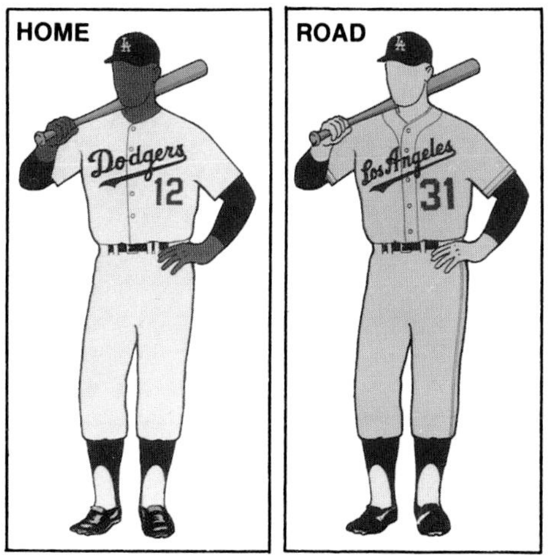

ST. LOUIS

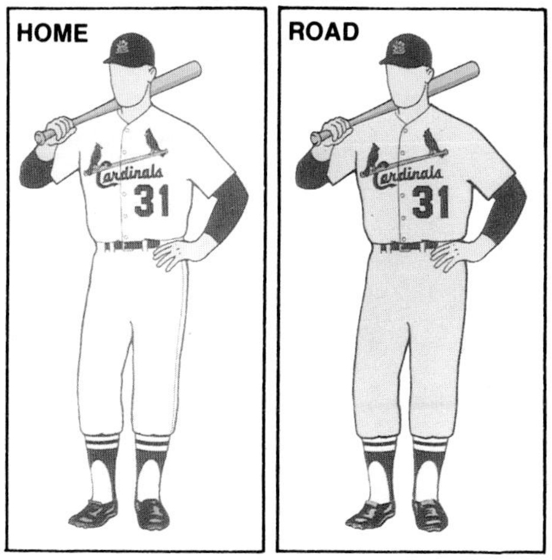

PITTSBURGH

PHILADELPHIA

CHICAGO

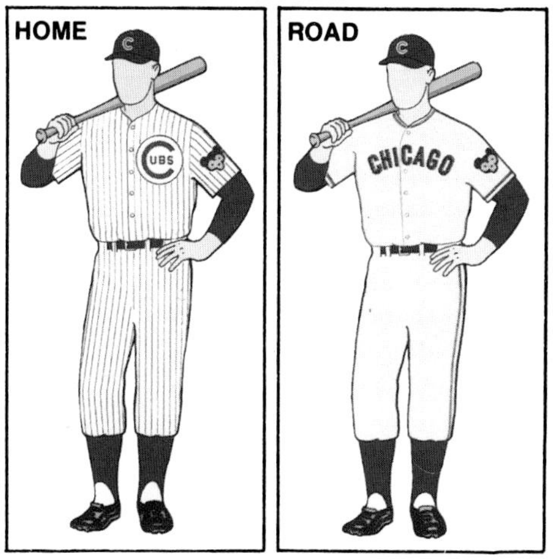

NEW YORK

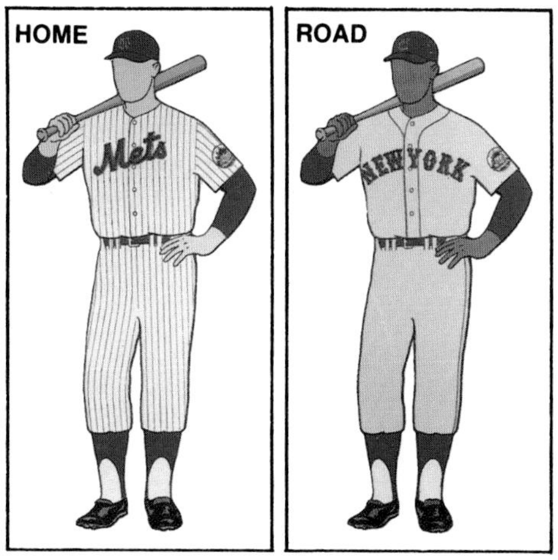

CINCINNATI

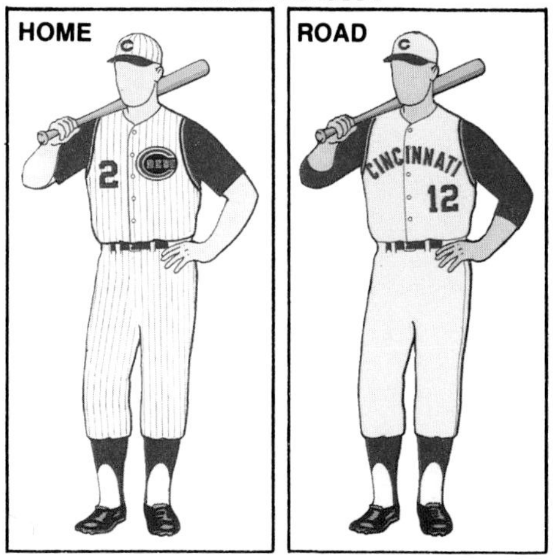

SAN FRANCISCO

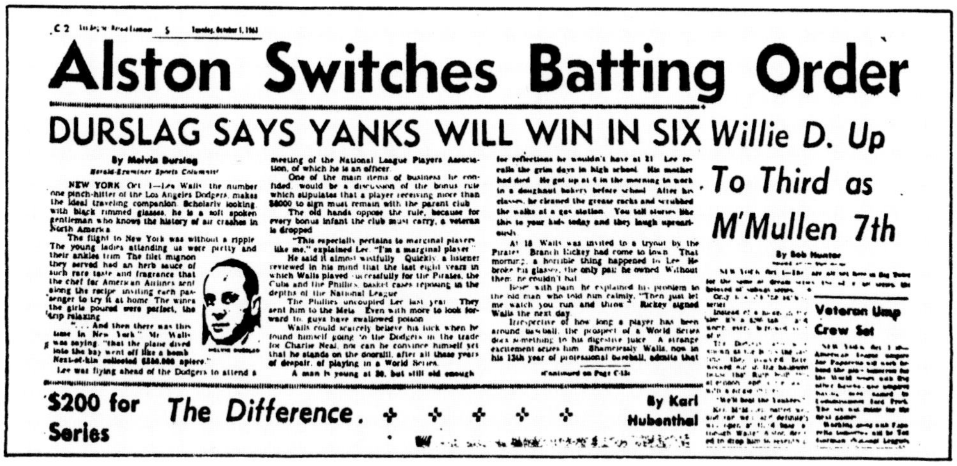

Alston Switches Batting Order

DURSLAG SAYS YANKS WILL WIN IN SIX

By Melvin Durslag
Herald-Examiner Sports Columnist

NEW YORK, Oct. 1—Lee Walls, the number one pinch-hitter of the Los Angeles Dodgers, makes the ideal traveling companion. Scholarly looking, with black rimmed glasses, he is a soft spoken gentleman who knows the history of air crashes in North America.

The flight to New York was without a ripple. The young ladies attending us were pretty and their ankles trim. The filet mignon they served had an herb sauce of such rare taste and fragrance that the chef for American Airlines sent along the recipe, inviting each passenger to try it at home. The wines the girls poured were perfect, the trip relaxing.

". . . And then there was this time in New York," Mr. Walls was saying, "that the plane dived into the bay, went off like a bomb. Next-of-kin collected $250,000 apiece."

Lee was flying ahead of the Dodgers to attend a meeting of the National League Players Association, of which he is an officer.

One of the main items of business, he confided, would be a discussion of the bonus rule which stipulates that a player receiving more than $8000 to sign must remain with the parent club.

The old hands oppose the rule, because for every bonus infant the club must carry, a veteran is dropped.

"This especially pertains to marginal players like me," explained Lee. "I'm a marginal player."

He said it almost wistfully. Quickly, a listener reviewed in his mind that the last eight years in which Walls played successfully for the Pirates, the Cubs and the Phillies, basket cases reposing in the depths of the National League.

The Phillies uncoupled Lee last year. They sent him to the Mets. Even with more to look forward to, guys have swallowed poison.

Walls could scarcely believe his luck when he found himself going to the Dodgers in the trade for Charlie Neal, nor can he convince himself yet that he stands on the doorsill, after all these years of despair, of playing in a World Series.

A man is young at 30, but still old enough for reflections he wouldn't have at 21. Lee recalls the grim days in high school. His mother had died. He got up at 4 in the morning to work in a doughnut bakery before school. After his classes, he cleaned the grease racks and scrubbed the walks at a gas station. You tell stories like this to your kids today and they laugh uproariously.

At 18, Walls was invited to a tryout by the Pirates. Branch Rickey had come to town. That morning, a horrible thing happened to Lee. He broke his glasses, the only pair he owned. Without them, he couldn't hit.

Beset with pain, he explained his problem to the old man, who told him calmly, "Then just let me watch you run and throw." Rickey signed Walls the next day.

Irrespective of how long a player has been around baseball, the prospect of a World Series does something to his digestive juice. A strange excitement seizes him. Shamelessly, Walls, now in his 13th year of professional baseball, admits that

(Continued on Page C-1)

Willie D. Up To Third as M'Mullen 7th

By Bob Hunter

Veteran Ump Crew Set

$200 for Series

The Difference.

By Karl Hubenthal

HOUSTON

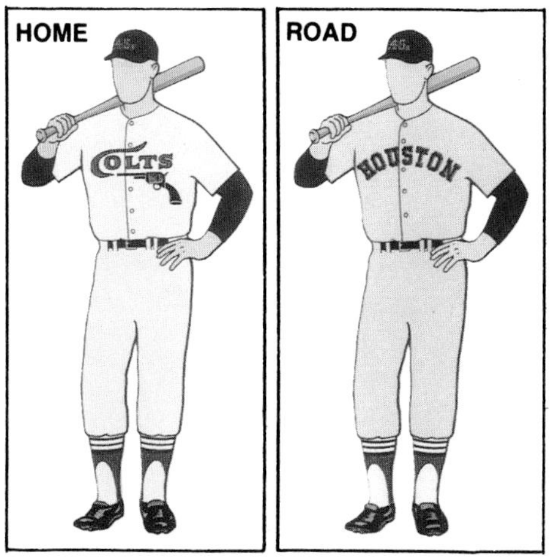

1964 AMERICAN LEAGUE

BOSTON

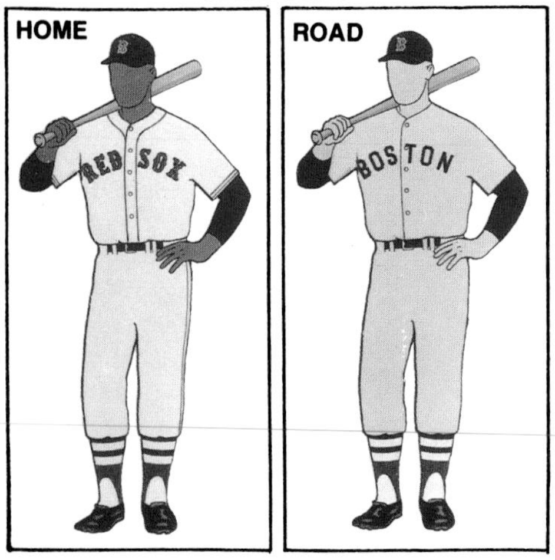

CLEVELAND

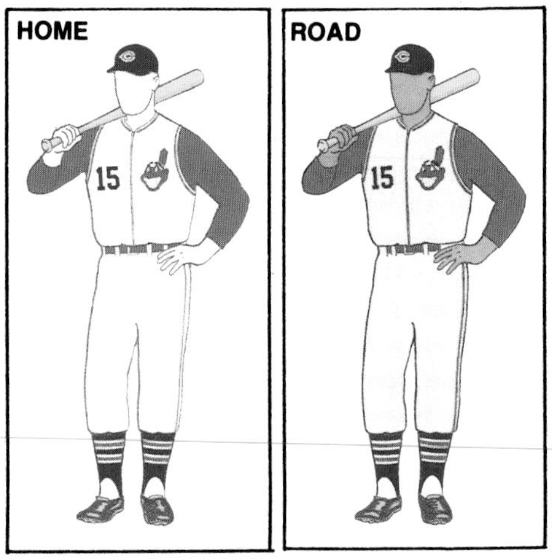

DETROIT

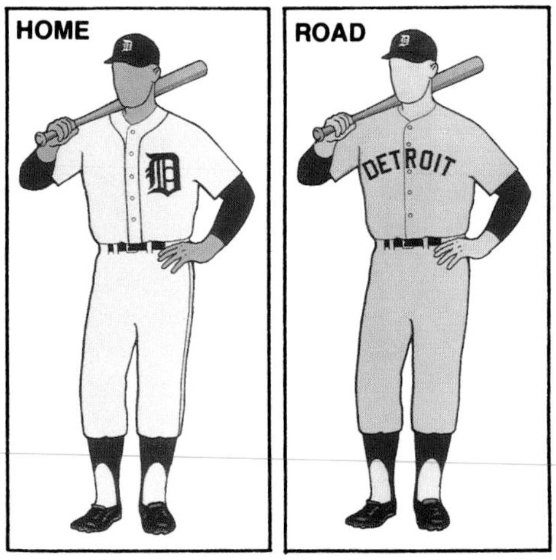

BALTIMORE

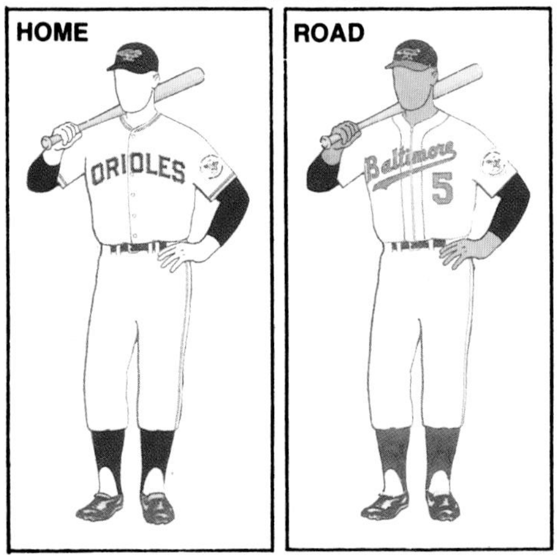

NEW YORK

KANSAS CITY

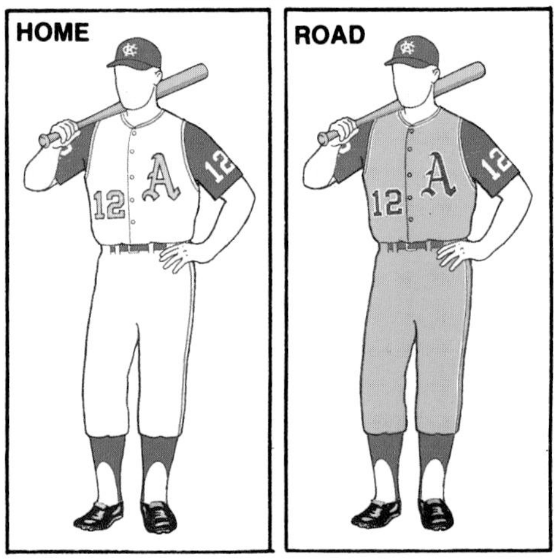

CHICAGO

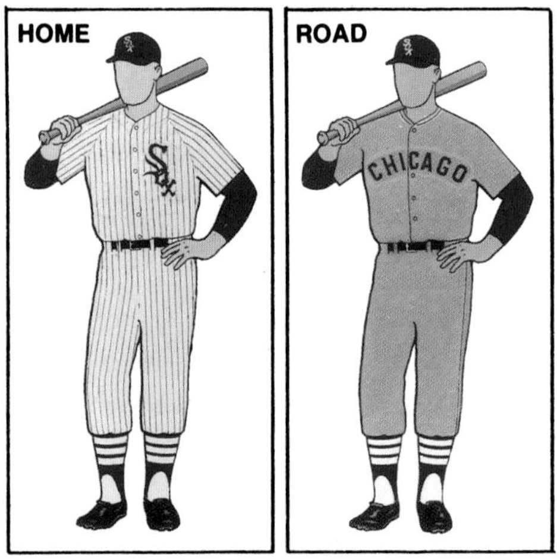

MINNESOTA

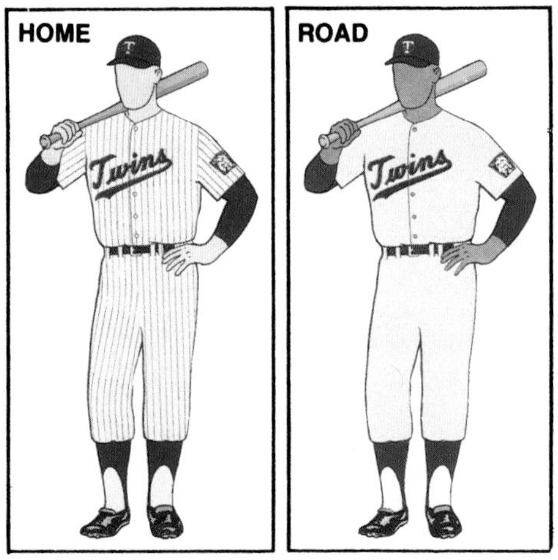

WASHINGTON

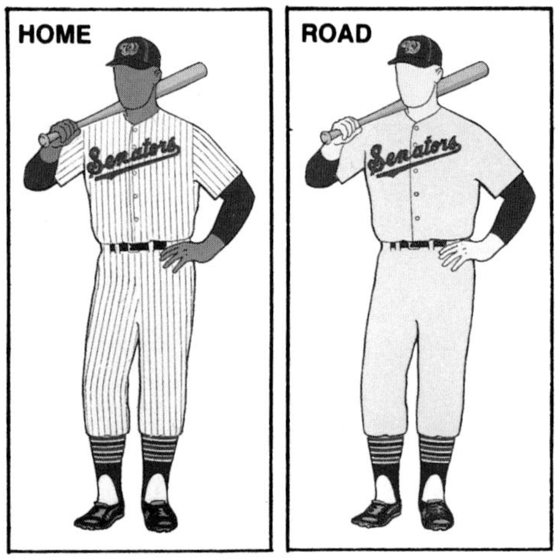

LOS ANGELES

American League Race Shaping Up As 'Old-Fashioned Yankee Cakewalk'

★ ★ ★

Angels Sink Chisox Hopes With Victory

By BOB MYERS

The Knickerbocker News SPORTS Wed., Sept. 23, 1964 4D

By FRED DOWN
UPI Sports Writer

Yogi Berra can tell the world, "I told you so."

"Don't worry, we'll make our move and it'll be a big one," the resident mastermind of the New York Yankee dugout told the experts a month ago when the defending American League champions were floundering.

Only a few believed him. Baltimore and Chicago were running 1-2 and Yogi seemed to be whistling in the dark while the Yankee empire was tumblin' down. Now the race shapes up as an "old-fashioned Yankee cakewalk."

With seven straight victories and nine wins in their last 10 games the Yankees have opened up a 1½-game lead over the Orioles and a 1½-game spread over the White Sox. What's more important is the fact that they hold a four-game advantage over the Orioles and a five-

Berra 'More

NATIONAL LEAGUE 1964

MILWAUKEE

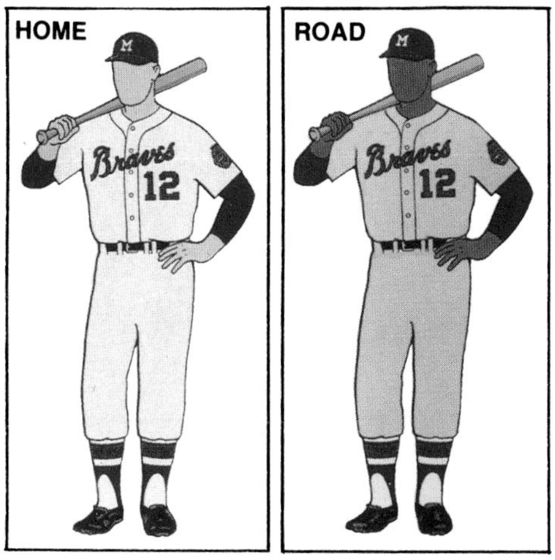

LOS ANGELES

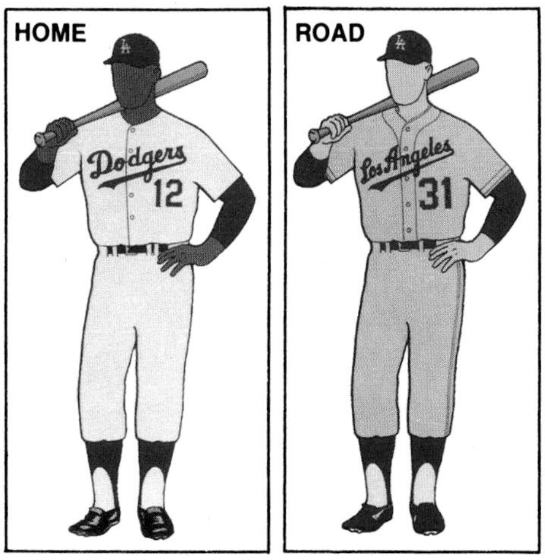

ST. LOUIS

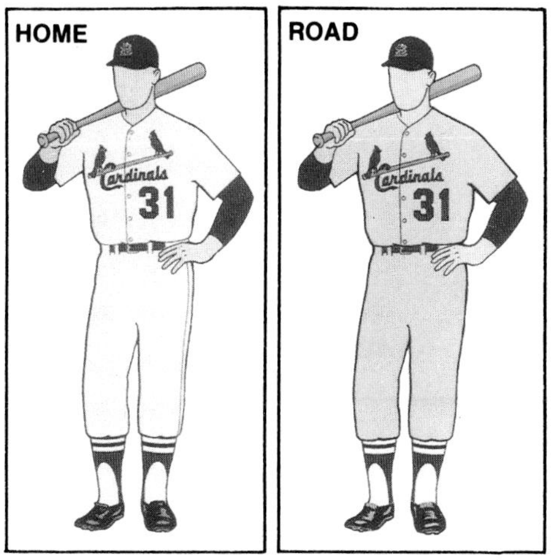

PITTSBURGH

PHILADELPHIA

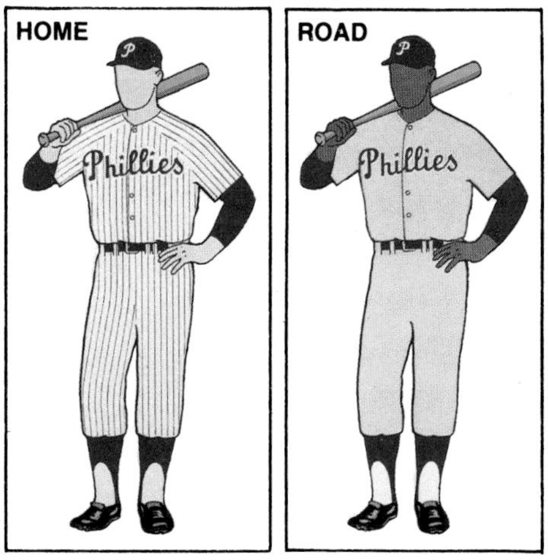

CHICAGO

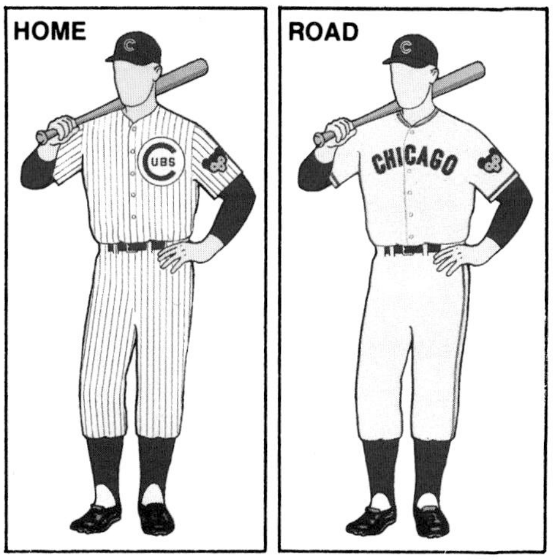

NEW YORK

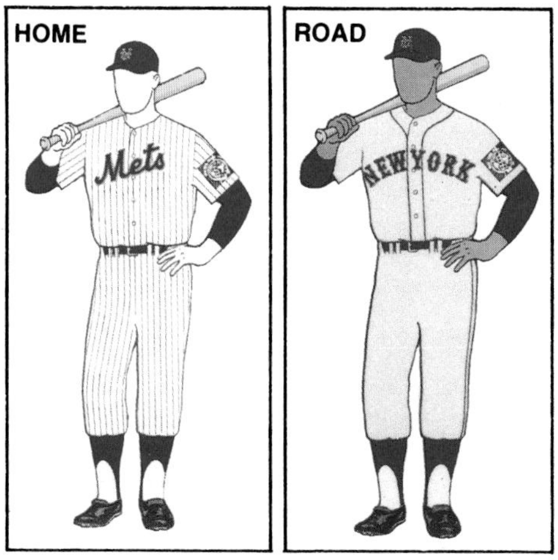

CINCINNATI

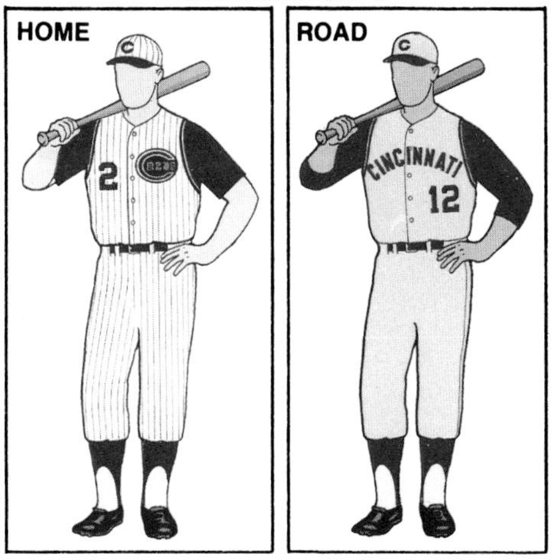

SAN FRANCISCO

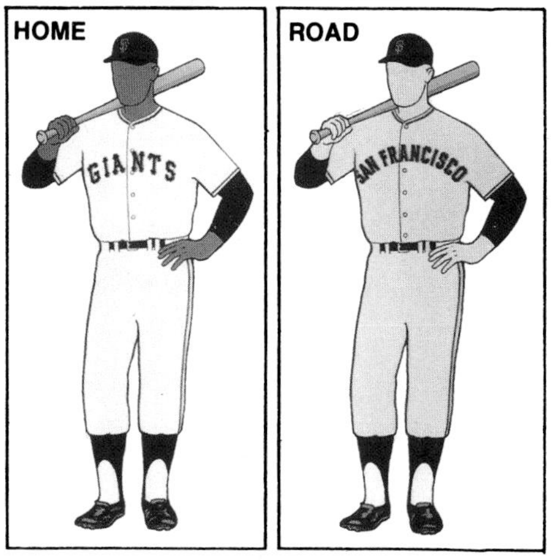

Comics
Classified

St. Louis Globe-Democrat.

Business
Financial

SECTION B — WEDNESDAY, SEPTEMBER 30, 1964 — PAGES 1 TO 14

CARDINALS WIN, 4-2, TIE FOR LEAD

Sadecki, Schultz Kayo Phils; White Raps 19th Homer

By JACK HERMAN

DON'T STOP NOW!

Bucs Topple Reds, 2-0, in Ninth

Mazeroski's 2-Run Single Backs Friend

HOUSTON

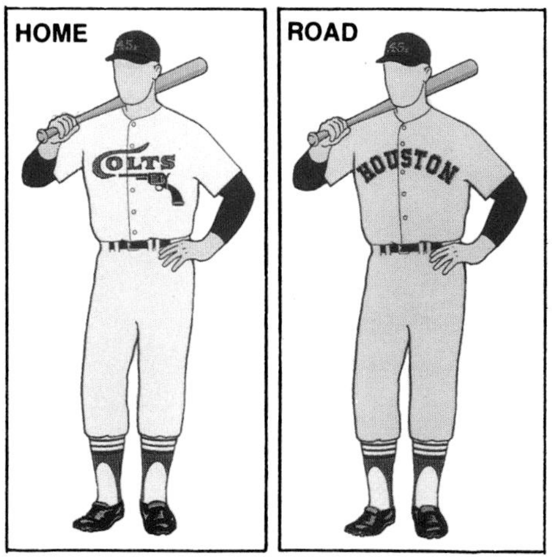

1965 AMERICAN LEAGUE

BOSTON

CLEVELAND

DETROIT

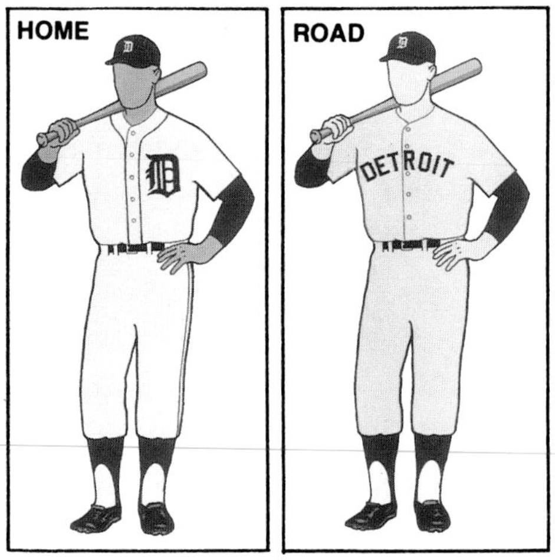

BALTIMORE

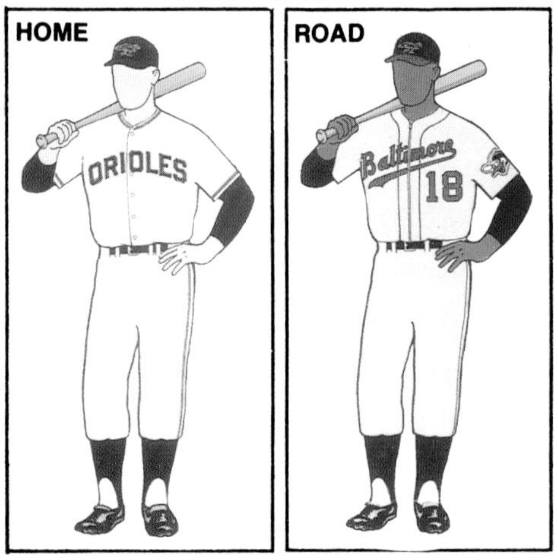

NEW YORK

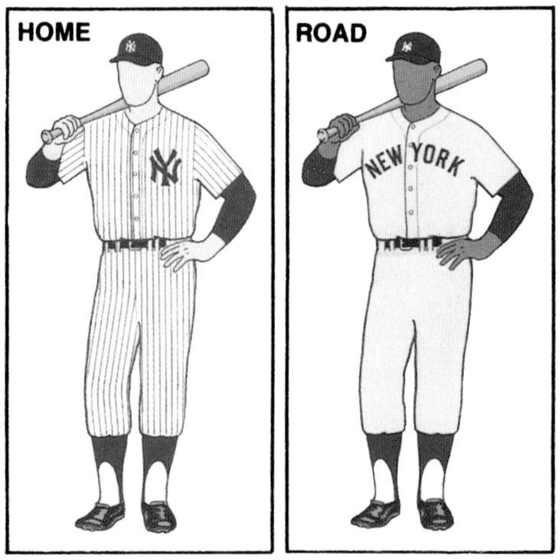

KANSAS CITY

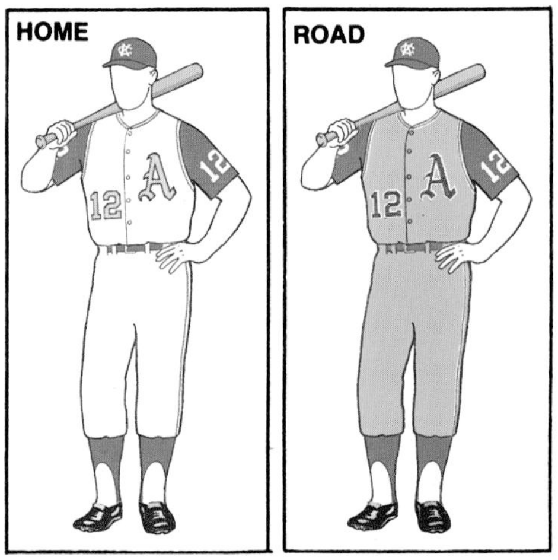

CHICAGO

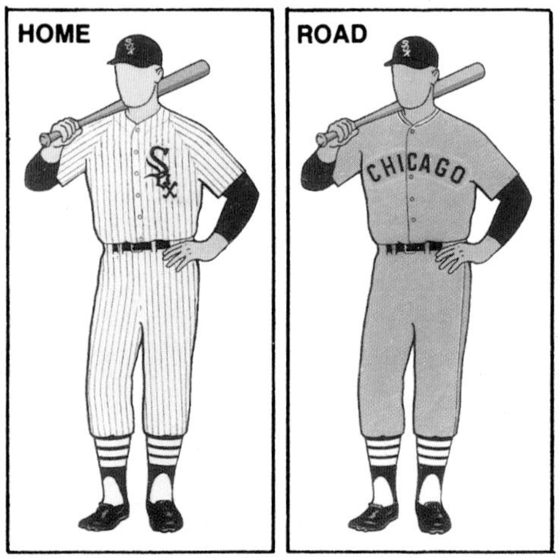

MINNESOTA

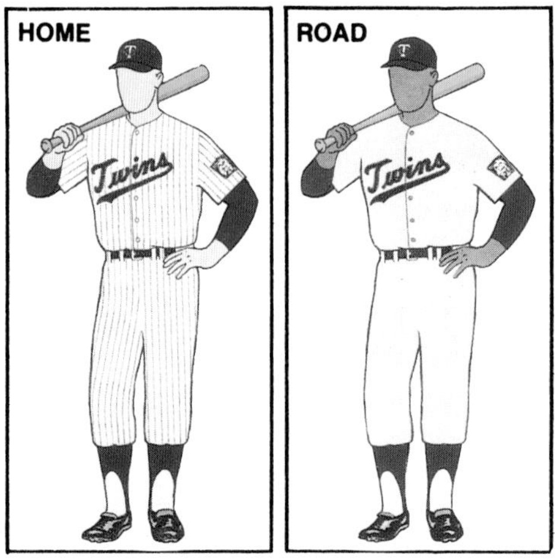

WASHINGTON

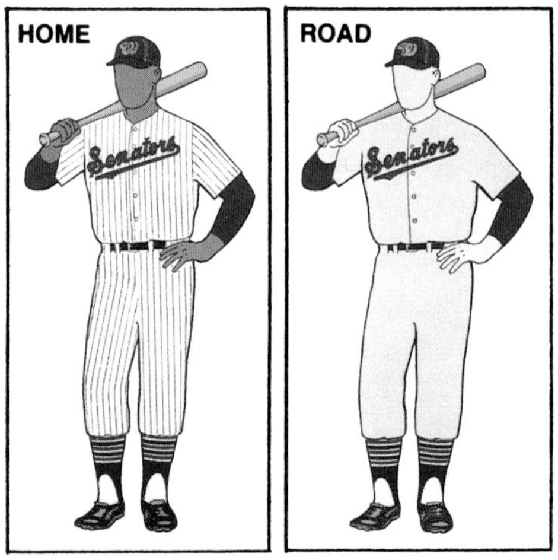

CALIFORNIA

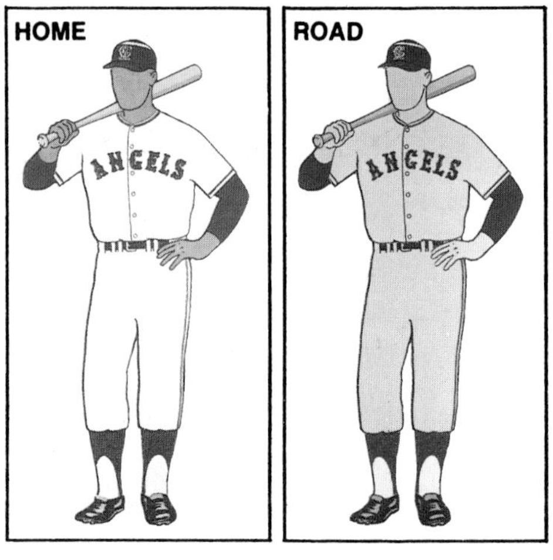

Grant to Start Series; Mele Rests Four Regulars

By MAX NICHOLS
Minneapolis Star Staff Writer

BALTIMORE, Md.—At least four Twins regulars will be rested Tuesday night against the Baltimore Orioles while starting pitchers will continue in regular rotation.

"Zoilo Versalles, Tony Oliva, Earl Battey and Don Mincher will be the first to rest," said Manager Sam Mele. "I'm figuring on Jim Grant, Camilo Pascual and Jim Kaat to start as pitchers in the World Series. But I'm considering Jim Perry, too. He's done a terrific job.

"Grant definitely will pitch the first game."

After clinching the American League pennant Sunday with a 2-1 victory at Washington, Mele must now begin planning for the Series. It is scheduled to open at Metropolitan Stadium Oct. 6.

"Harmon Killebrew will play every day," Mele said. "I want him to have every chance possible to get himself ready."

Killebrew said he definitely feels he will be back in his normal form by the Series. He has only two hits in 10 times at bat, including none in three at bats yesterday, since returning from his elbow dislocation. He has struck out only twice.

"I'm feeling better at the plate, even though I'm not hitting yet," said Harmon. "I am certain I will be ready for the Series."

Any particular feelings about which National League team the Twins will play?

"I don't care," said Killebrew. "We'll take on any team they send."

As far as competing in the Series is concerned, that was the general feelings among the Twins. But the additional seats and therefore money at Los Angeles affected some answers. And Manager Sam Mele was concerned about the difference in the playing fields between Los Angeles and San Francisco.

No one wants to go to Cincinnati, where the ball park is the smallest and the payoff therefore would be below par.

"We never hit too well in Dodger Stadium against the Angels," said Mele. "I think I would rather go to San Francisco. I don't care about the money. There wouldn't be that much difference."

Shortstop Versalles wants no part of Dodger Stadium because of the hard infield there. It makes fielding ground balls and sliding difficult, and these are two of the best parts of his game.

"Anywhere but Los Angeles," said Zoilo.

Mele plans to use numerous rookies and reserves in the Twins' last five games, beginning at 6 p.m. (Minneapolis time) tomorrow.

"I'll rest some of my regulars every other day," he said. "I want them to play enough to keep sharp.

"I will take a look at guys like Cesar Tovar, Andy Kosco, Ted Uhlaender and Dick Reese. John Sevcik definitely will do some catching."

The Twins are off today. Perry is expected to start tomorrow night against the Orioles. Then Grant and Pascual will start in that order to wind up the road trip.

The Twins have two more home games—Saturday at 10 a.m. and Sunday at 1:30 p.m. against Los Angeles.

THE MINNEAPOLIS STAR
Sports
10B ★ Mon., Sept. 27, 1965

A DAY TO REMEMBER IN WINNING TWINS CLUBHOUSE

★ ★ ★ ★ ★ ★ ★ ★

Pennant-hungry Twins Explode in Celebration

Continued from Page One

Manager Sam Mele. "And we went right through the front door. Let the Orioles throwing the water, then ice. Finally they drifted one by one into the showers.

NATIONAL LEAGUE 1965

MILWAUKEE

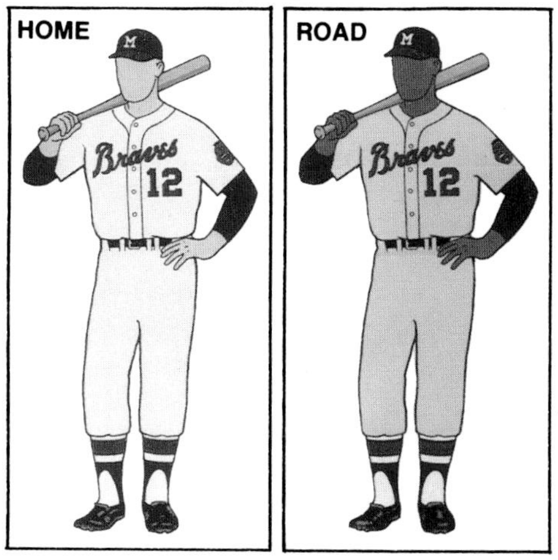

LOS ANGELES

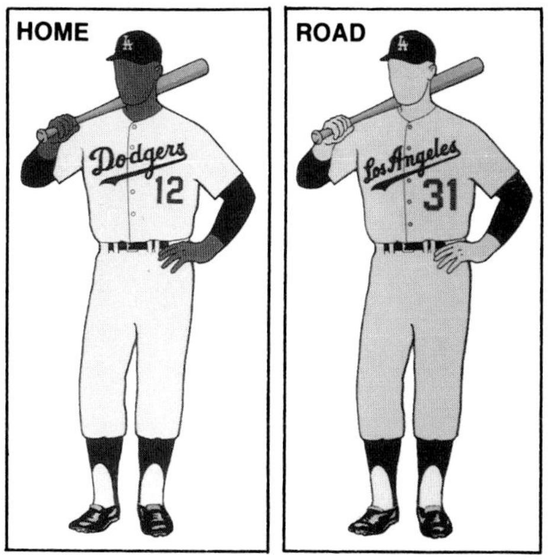

ST. LOUIS

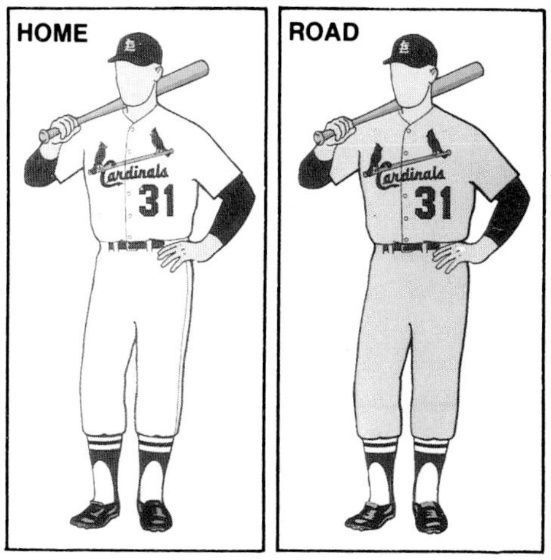

PITTSBURGH

PHILADELPHIA

CHICAGO

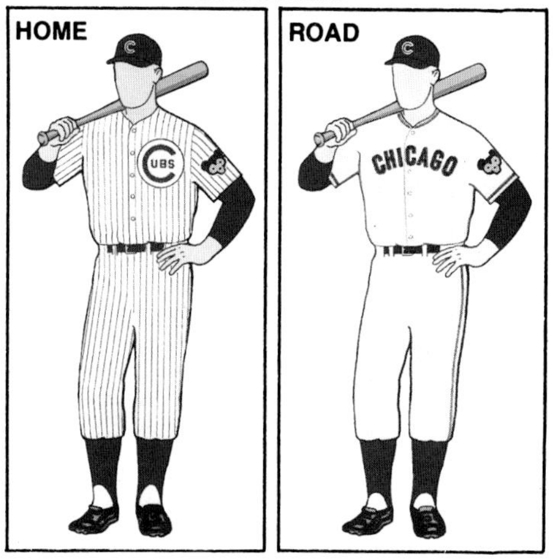

NEW YORK

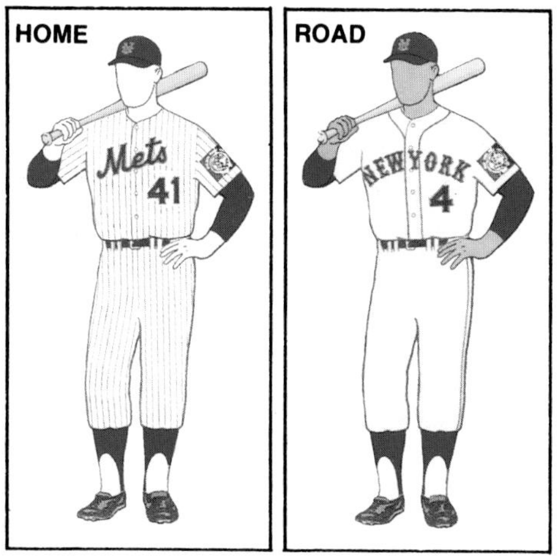

CINCINNATI

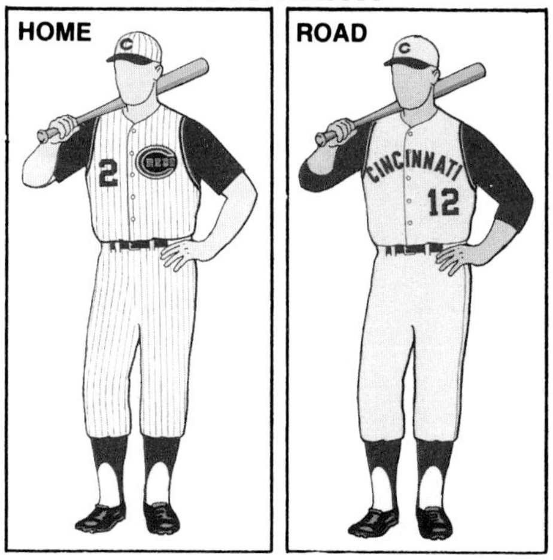

SAN FRANCISCO

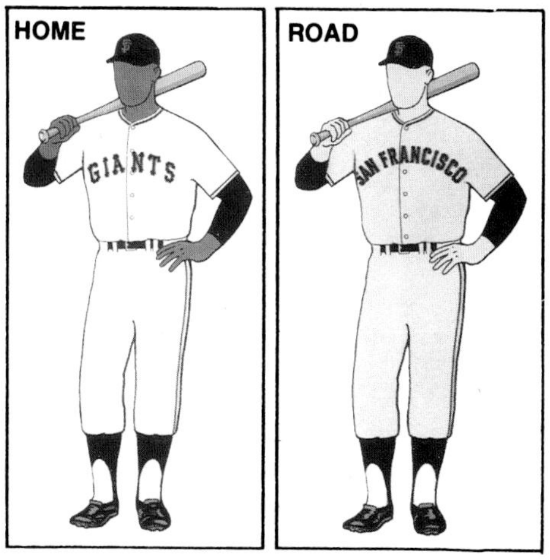

School Aid Bill Approved, Sent To LBJ Sec 1. Page 17

THE HOUSTON POST

Jobs for Teens

Johnson, 47,876 Cheer Astros' Win

In a Mighty Splash, It's Open

1,400 Marines Go To Da Nang

Nellie Fox Singles for 2 to 1 Win

HOUSTON

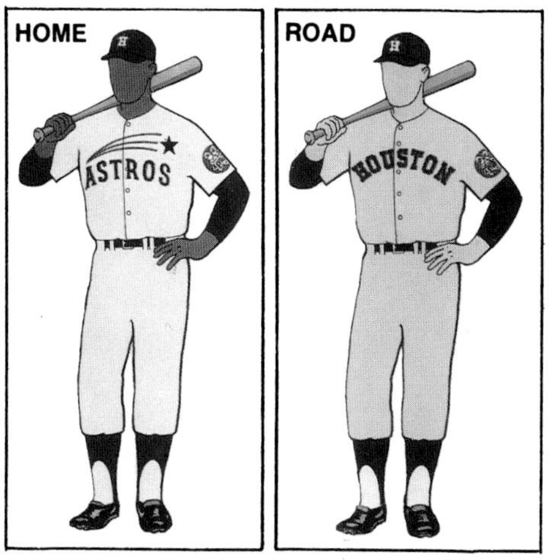

1966 AMERICAN LEAGUE

BOSTON

CLEVELAND

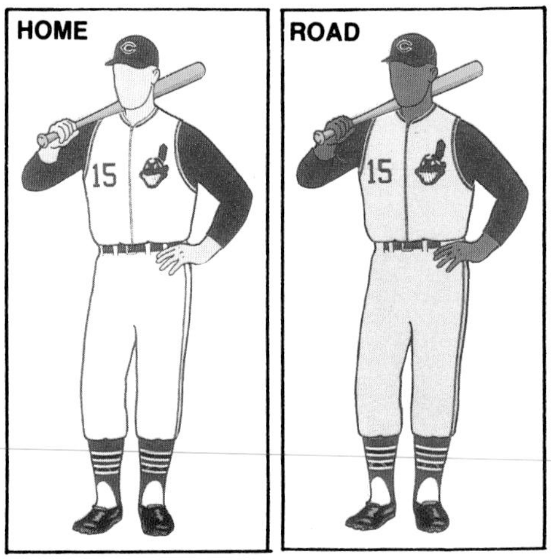

DETROIT

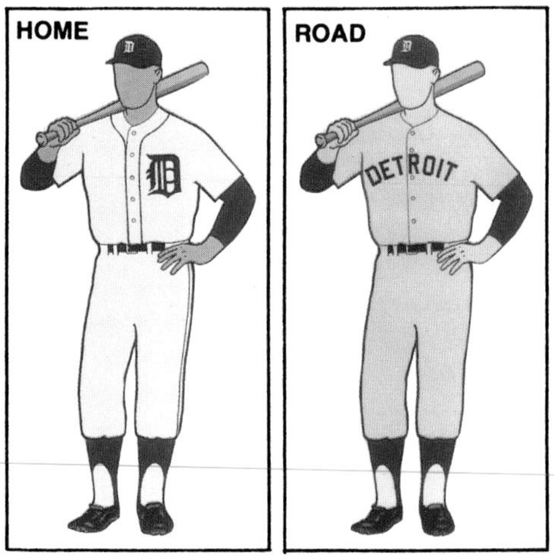

BALTIMORE

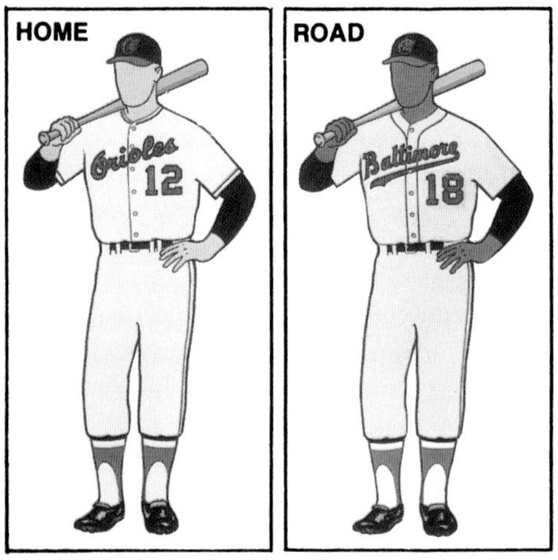

NEW YORK

KANSAS CITY

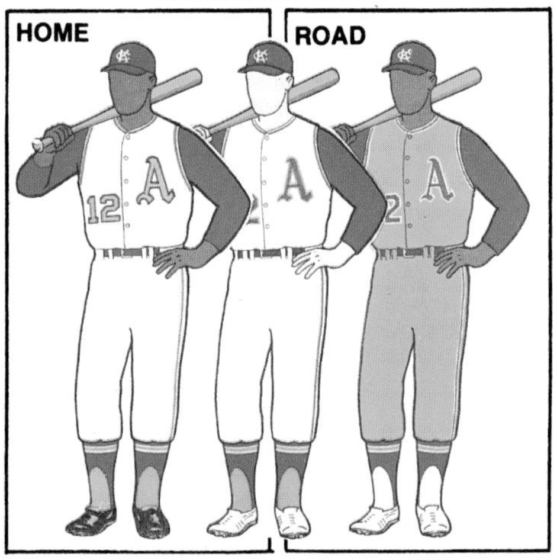

CHICAGO

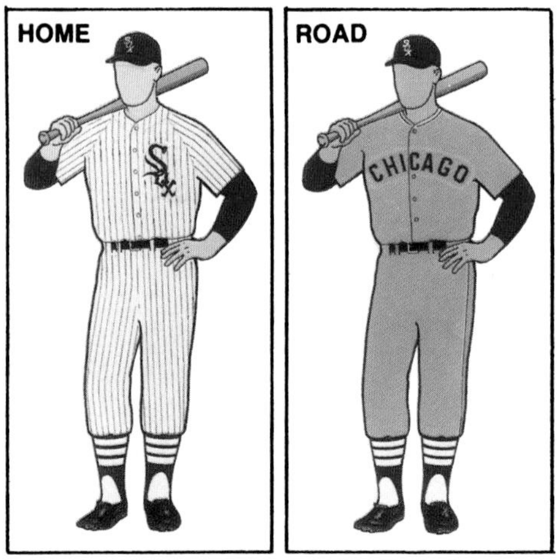

MINNESOTA

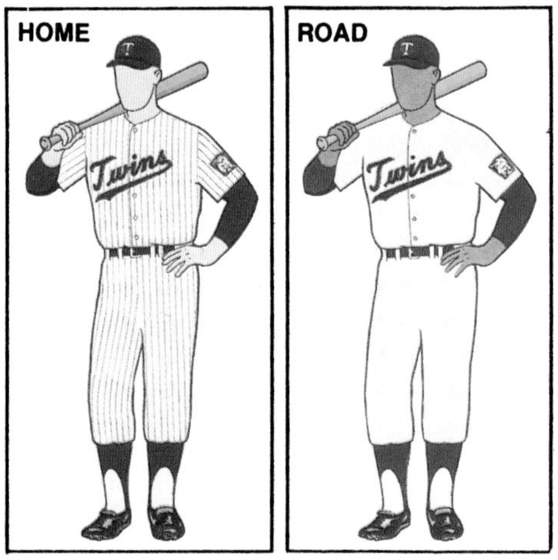

WASHINGTON

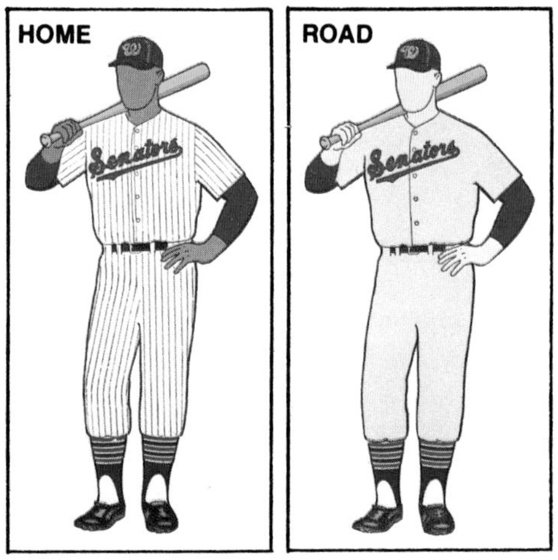

CALIFORNIA

LOVE OUR O-O-ORIOLES!

Home Run The Topper, Says Robinson

World Aghast At Four-Game Sweep

Page of World Series Pictures on Page 8D

The News American

BALTIMORE MARYLAND

Monday Evening, October 10, 1966 — 93rd Year—No. 289 — 10 Cents

RACE SPECIAL

Bauer Calls Club Amazing

Robinson — Orioles

'With Kennedy'—Part 2

NATIONAL LEAGUE 1966

ATLANTA

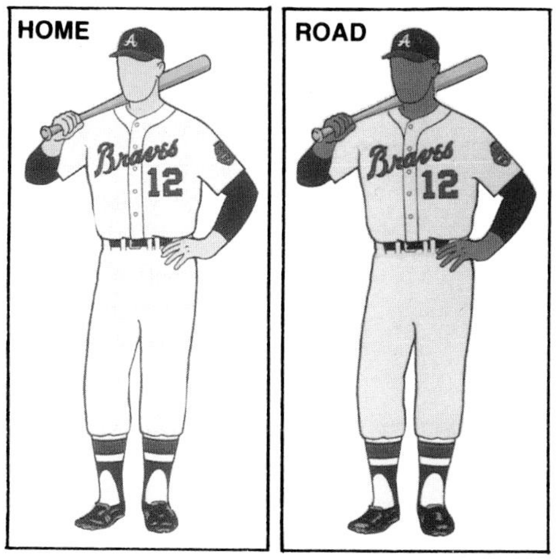

LOS ANGELES

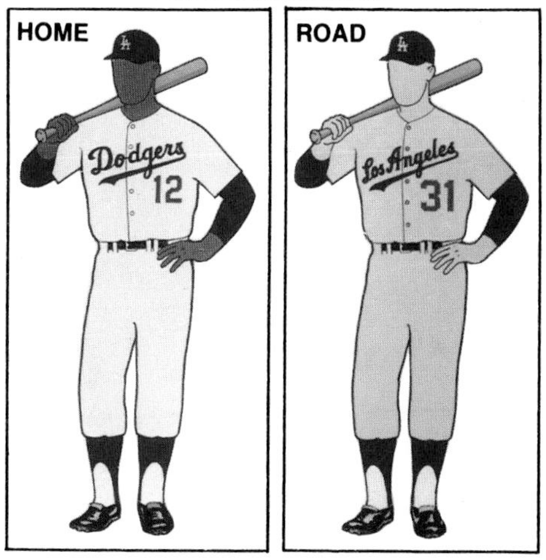

ST. LOUIS

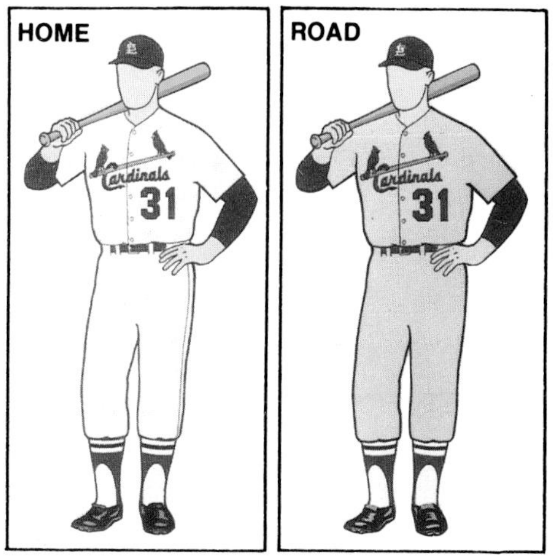

PITTSBURGH

PHILADELPHIA

CHICAGO

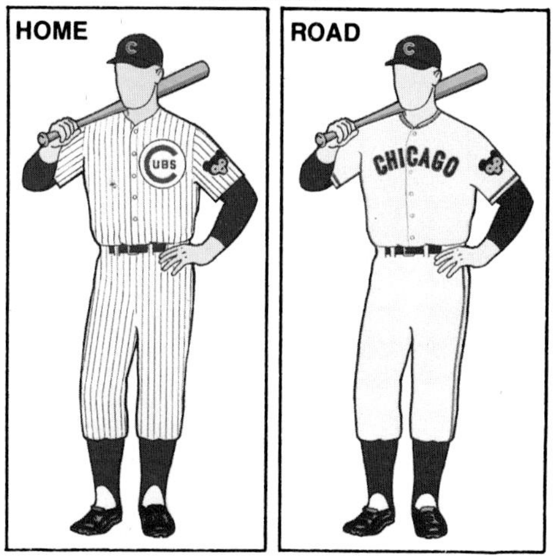

NEW YORK

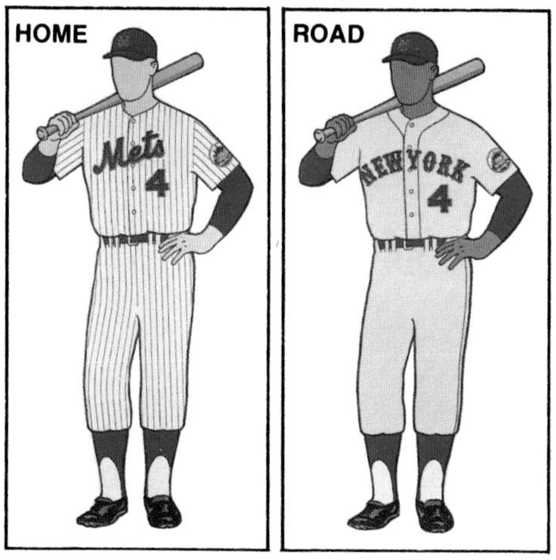

CINCINNATI

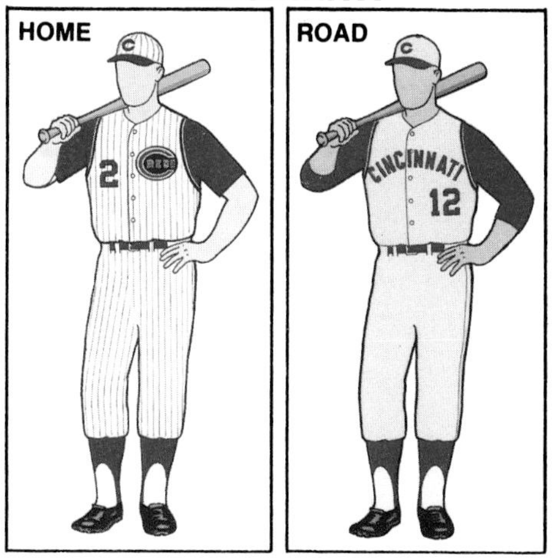

SAN FRANCISCO

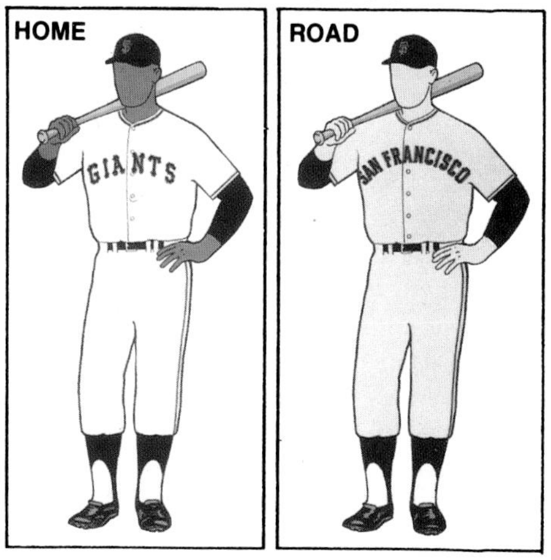

The Atlanta Journal

"COVERS DIXIE LIKE THE DEW"

FINAL HOME EDITION

Atlanta, Ga., 30302, Tuesday Evening, April 12, 1966

Braves Open Here Tonight

50,000 Likely If Rain Threat Goes Away

OLD SMOKEY JUST LIKE A HUMAN

B52s Strike North, Hit Strategic Pass

Big Bombers' 1st Raid One of War's Largest

STREET SCENES

HOUSTON

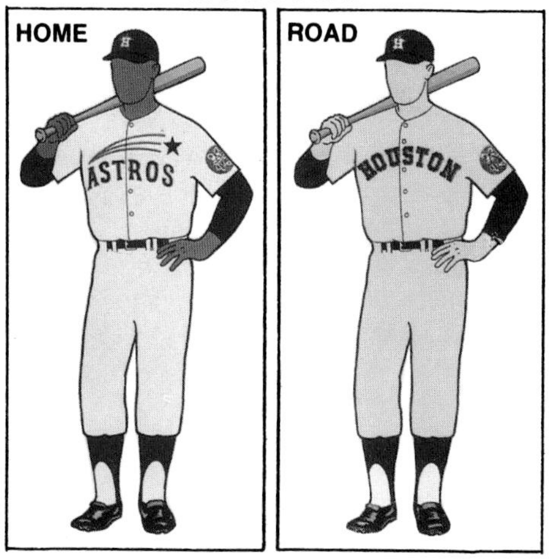

1967 AMERICAN LEAGUE

BOSTON

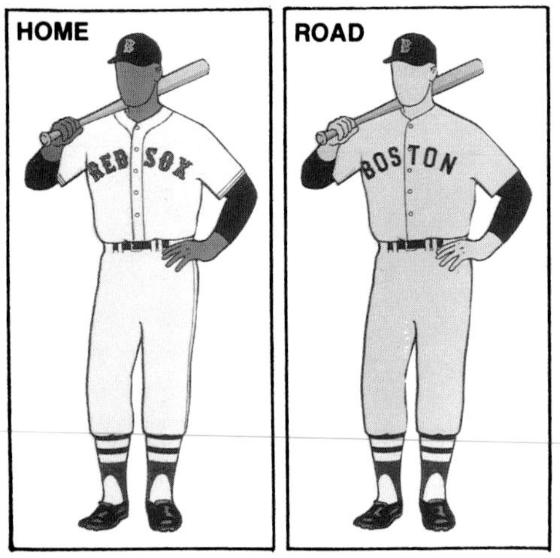

CLEVELAND

DETROIT

BALTIMORE

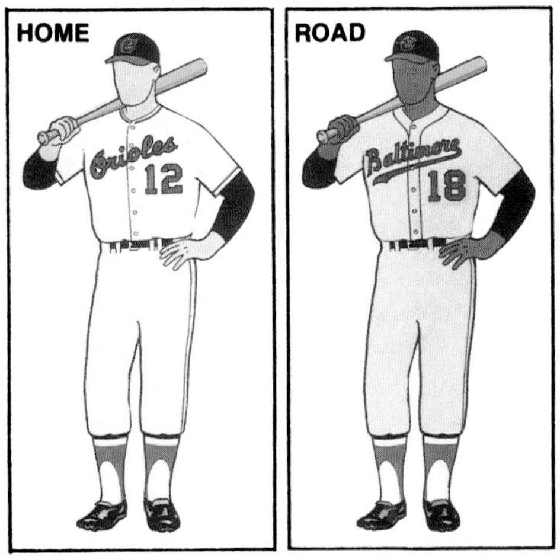

NEW YORK

KANSAS CITY

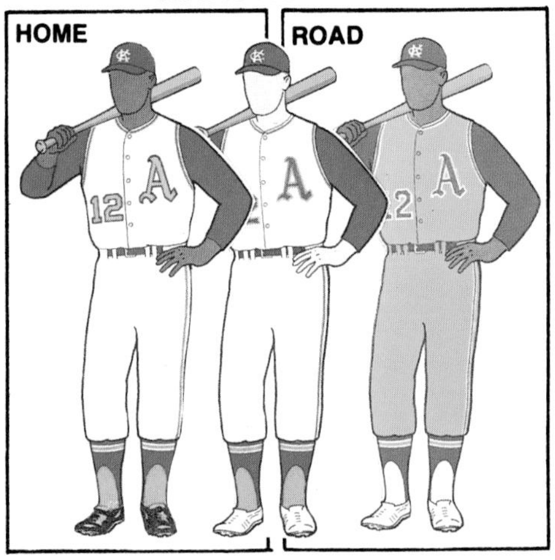

CHICAGO

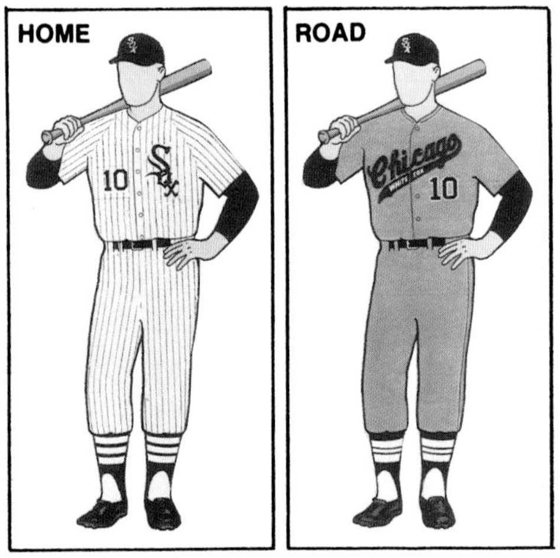

MINNESOTA

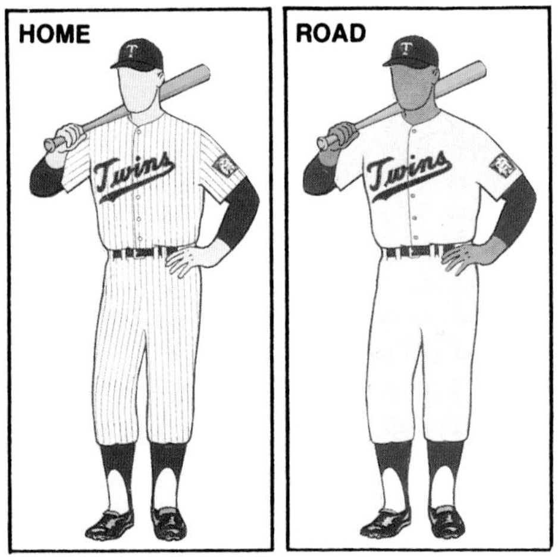

WASHINGTON

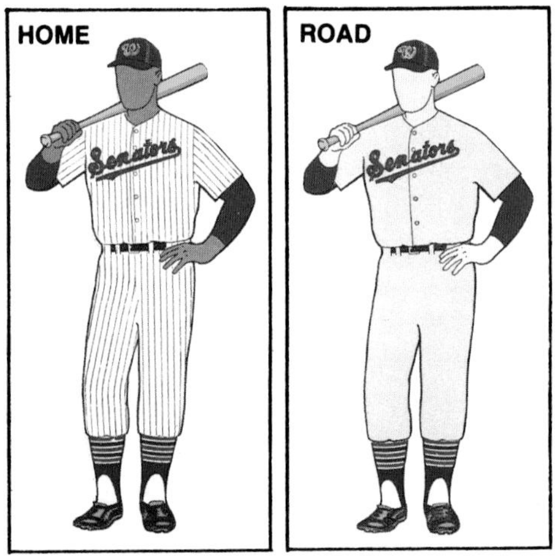

CALIFORNIA

BOSTON HERALD TRAVELER

THE WEATHER—SUNNY, MILD (PAGE 2) —WEDNESDAY, SEPTEMBER 20, 1967— HA 6 3000 TEN CENTS

Sox Do It Again! Tie with Twins at Top

Okay now fellows, you don't have to wait until the ninth inning to win every night. Take Minnesota, for example. The Twins are tied with you for first place in the American League, but they pulled ahead early, 4-2, and then eased by the A's, 8-2. You see, there is another way.

However, you trailed Detroit, 2-1, going into the ninth, tied when George Scott finally fathomed the offerings of Mickey Lolich for a single, and then won it when Earl Wilson loosed a wild pitch in relief. Of course, Wilson was not used to his job. The 21-game winner appeared in relief for the first time.

The setback depressed the Tigers to third place, but the Motor City entry wound up in fourth place after the Chicago White Sox defeated the California Angels, 3-0. The White Sox victory kept them a half game off the pace.

All things considered, though, Minnesota fans don't have as much fun as Red Sox rooters. Some other things they don't have, either. They don't nervously wrench an arm off a chair in front of a TV set, have palpitations, or have the screaming meemies after lights out.

Details Page 53

THE BIG FOUR

	W	L	P.C.	GB	Left
BOSTON	86	66	.566	—	10
Minnesota	86	66	.566	—	10
Chicago	86	67	.562	½	9
Detroit	85	67	.559	1	10

Sox to Accept Series Orders

The Red Sox will accept World Series ticket applications starting Thursday.

Amended Bill Faces Test in House

Senate Approves

NATIONAL LEAGUE 1967

ATLANTA

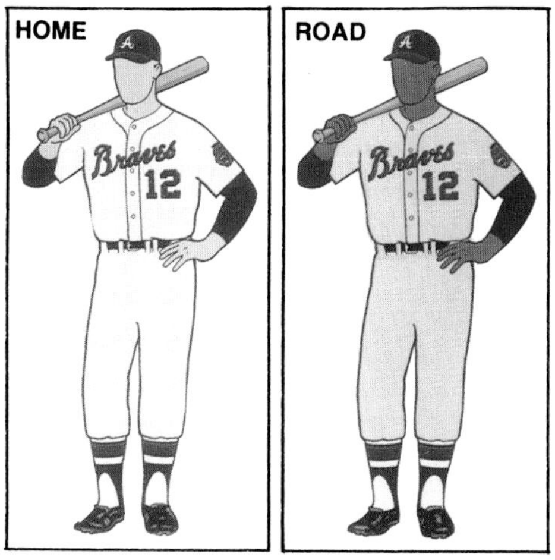

LOS ANGELES

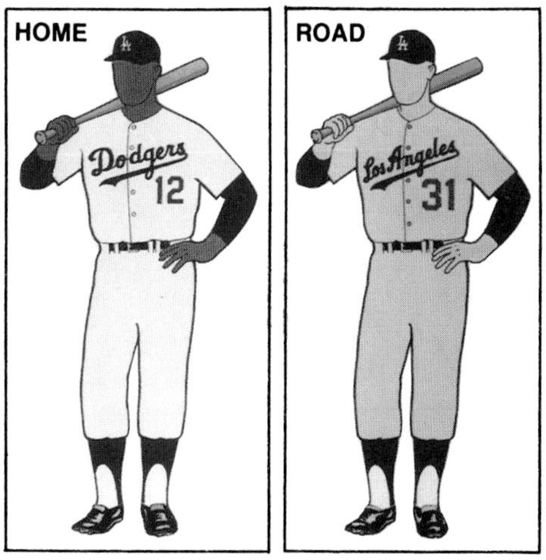

ST. LOUIS

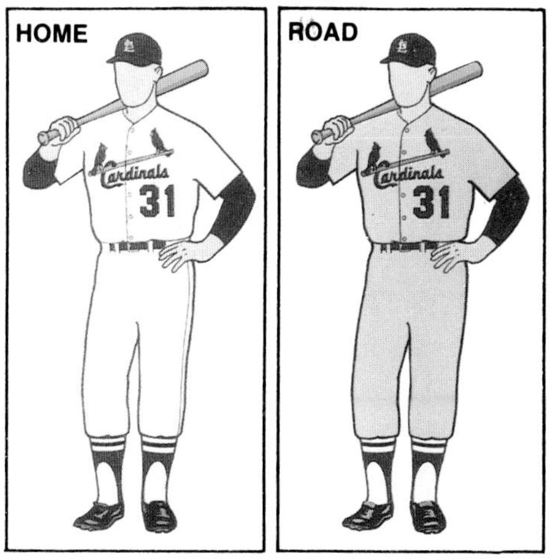

PITTSBURGH

PHILADELPHIA

CHICAGO

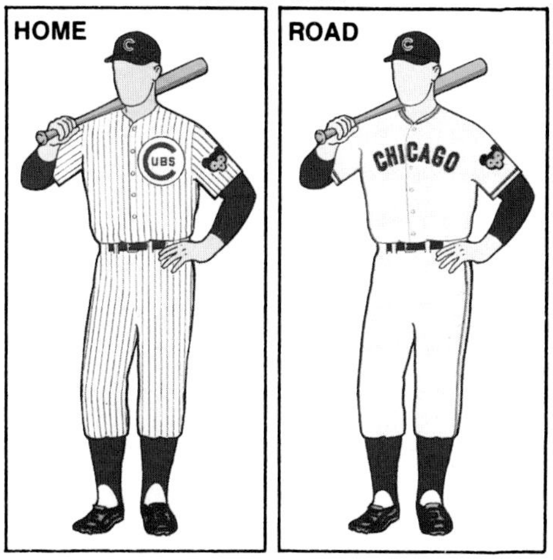

NEW YORK

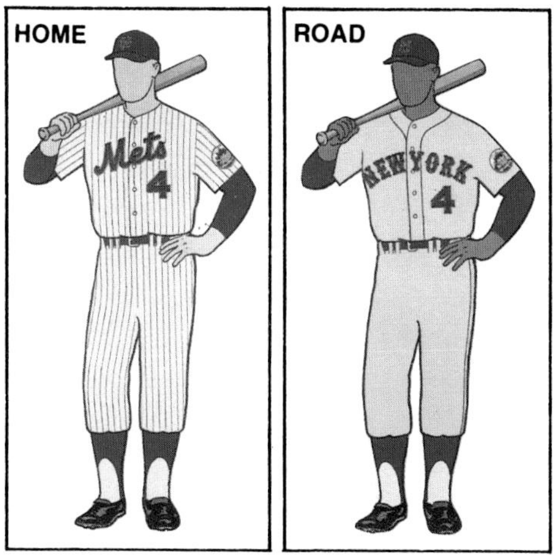

CINCINNATI

SAN FRANCISCO

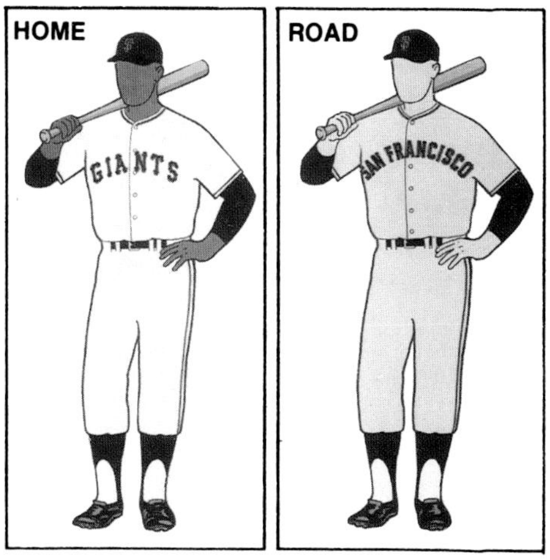

High in 30s

St. Louis Globe-Democrat

One Hundred and Fifteen Years of Public Service

Champions of the World

An Editorial, Page 14A

St. Louis, Friday Morning, October 13, 1967 · 36 Pages · SEVEN CENTS

Cheering, Singing Fans Welcome Red Birds Home

CARDS WORLD CHAMPS!

HOUSTON

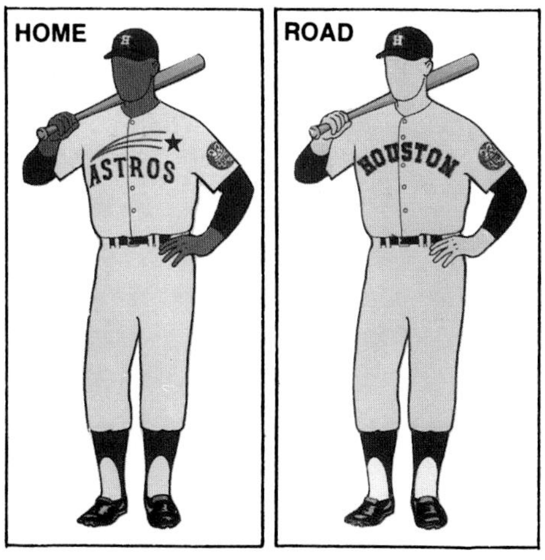

1968 AMERICAN LEAGUE

BOSTON

CLEVELAND

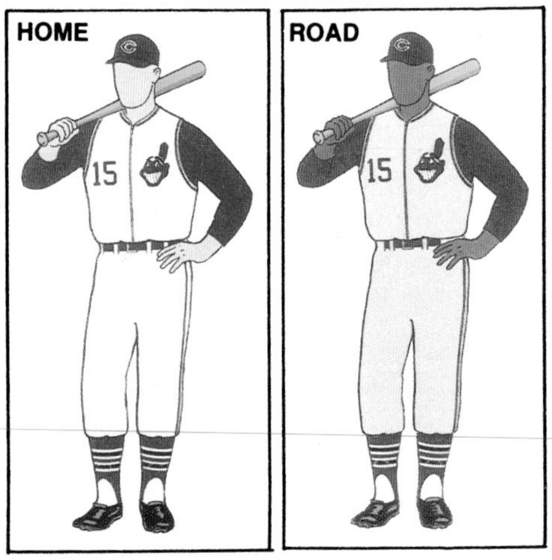

DETROIT

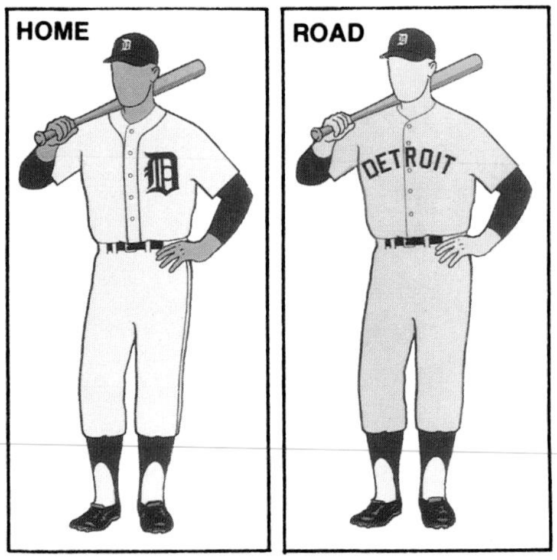

BALTIMORE

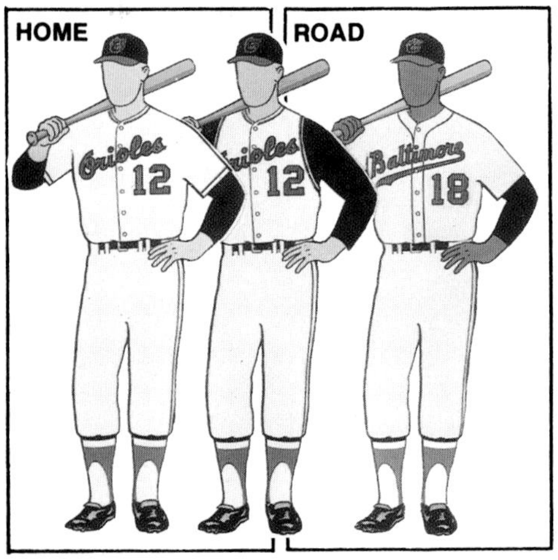

NEW YORK

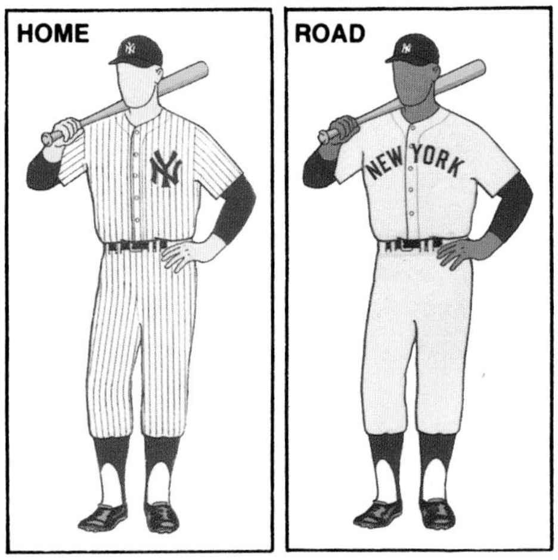

OAKLAND

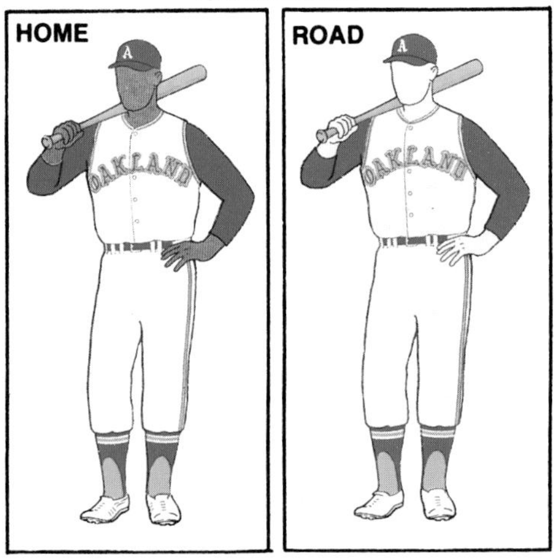

CHICAGO

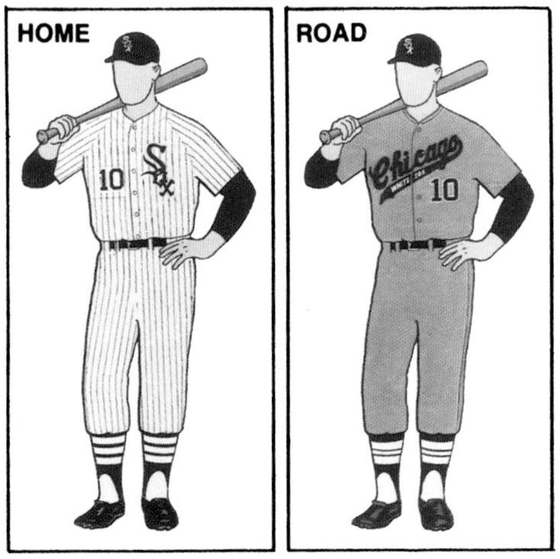

MINNESOTA

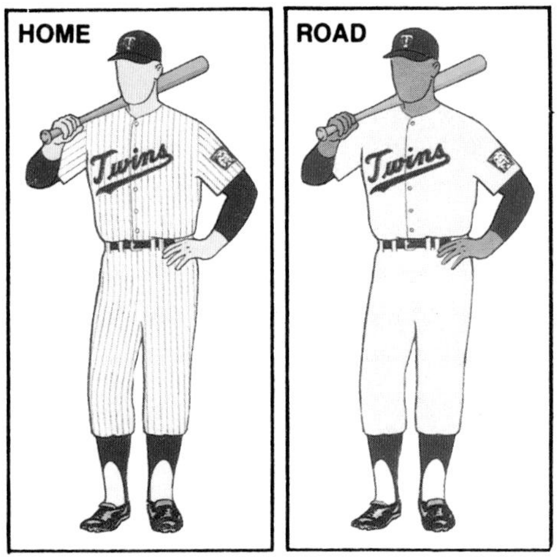

WASHINGTON

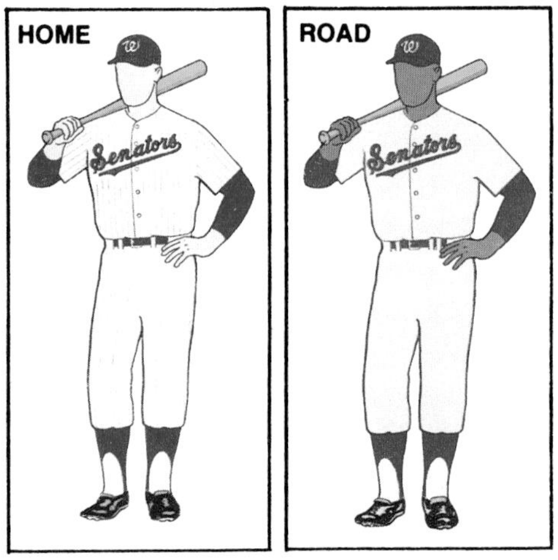

CALIFORNIA

DETROIT FREE PRESS

Cash Belts His Way Past Pretenders

BY GEORGE CANTOR

Tigers Win!

It's All Over—Tigers Win Pennant!

Joe Falls
Sports Editor

Pennant Fever Depends on City

Stop Yanks To Apply Clincher

BY GEORGE CANTOR

Lions' Injured End Out for the Season

NATIONAL LEAGUE 1968

ATLANTA

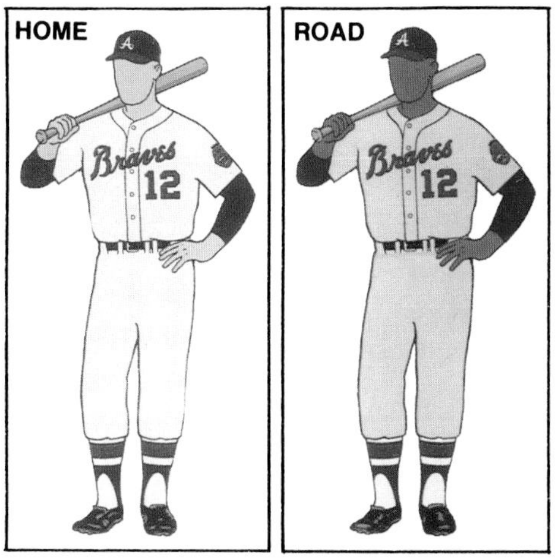

LOS ANGELES

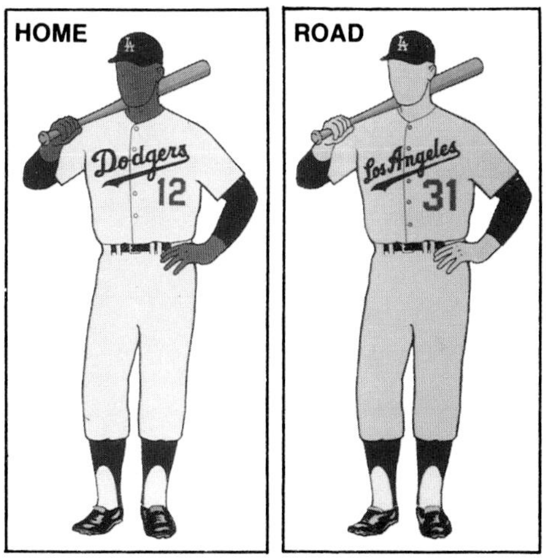

ST. LOUIS

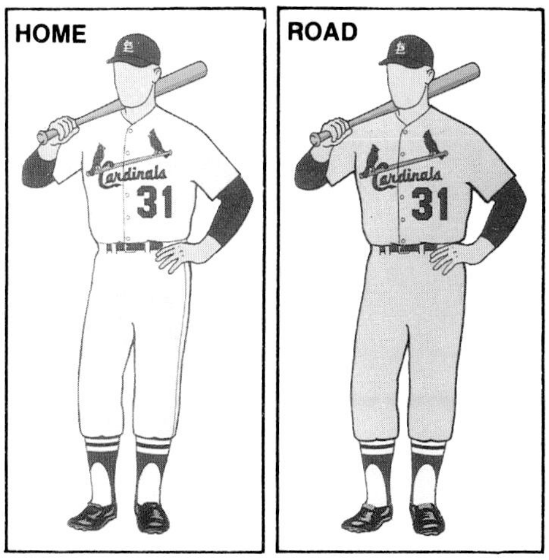

PITTSBURGH

PHILADELPHIA

CHICAGO

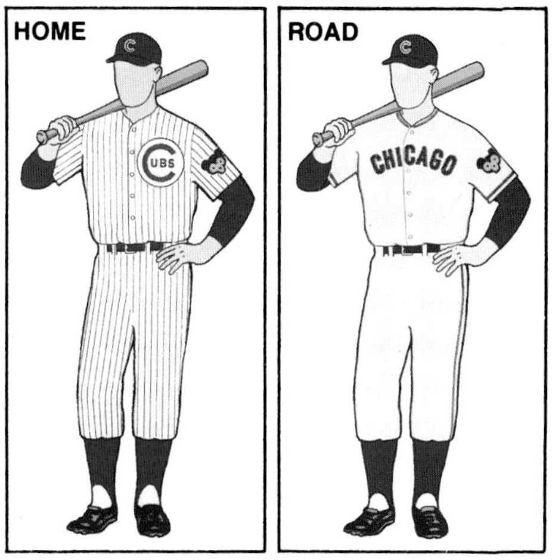

NEW YORK

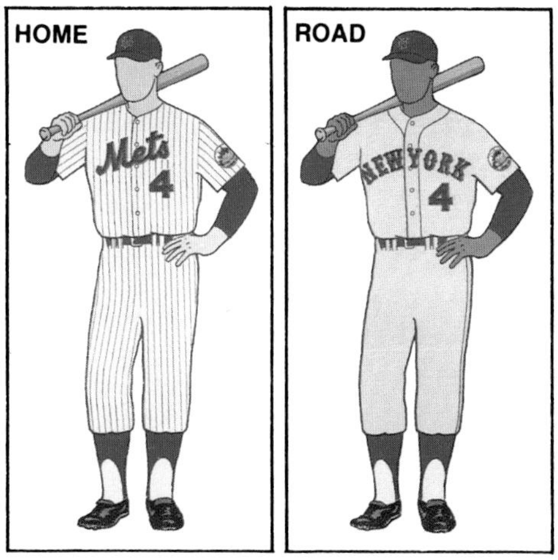

CINCINNATI

SAN FRANCISCO

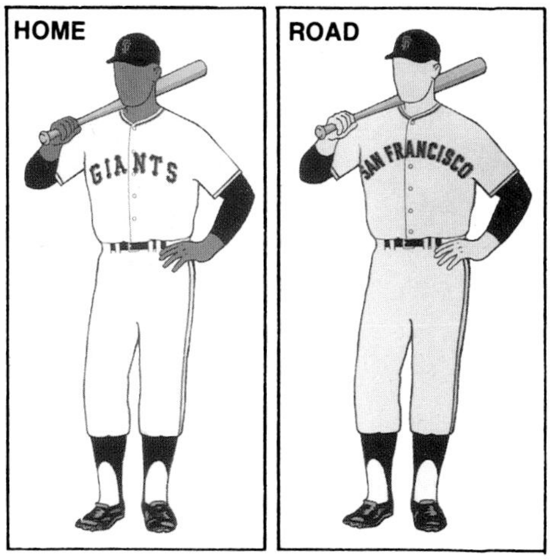

Sports
THE KNICKERBOCKER NEWS
ALBANY, N. Y.
Wed., Apr. 10, 1968 1C

Cardinals Have That Series Look As Dodgers Start Without Alston

By DICK COUCH
Associated Press Sports Writer

The St. Louis Cardinals' World Series line-up should be intact for their belated baseball opener tonight but the Los Angeles Dodgers will be starting a 1968 comeback drive without Manager Walter Alston.

Atlanta takes on the world champion Cardinals at St. Louis, Philadelphia visits the Dodgers and Pittsburgh is at Houston in arclight games, completing a full season opening slate after two days of postponements.

In National League daytime inaugurals—deferred until this afternoon in respect to the memory of Dr. Martin Luther King—the New York Mets were at San Francisco and the Chicago Cubs at Cincinnati.

Washington met Minnesota in

PLAY BALL 1968

CARDINALS

Mick and Mike Yankees' Men For All Seasons

NEW YORK (AP) — Mike Ferraro starts his first season for the New York Yankees today. Mickey Mantle starts his 18th. Everybody else is sort of in between.

After delaying their opening game for a day due to the funeral of Martin Luther King, the

Humphrey Candidate (To Hurl)

By JAMES R. POLK

WASHINGTON (AP) —Vic[e] President Hubret H. Humphre[y] substitute for all seasons, wa[s] nominated as starting pitche[r] today for the belated opening [of] the 1968 baseball campaign.

The Washington Senato[rs] meet the Minnesota Twins [in] the traditional inaugural gam[e] in which everyone starts as [a] loser this year.

HOUSTON

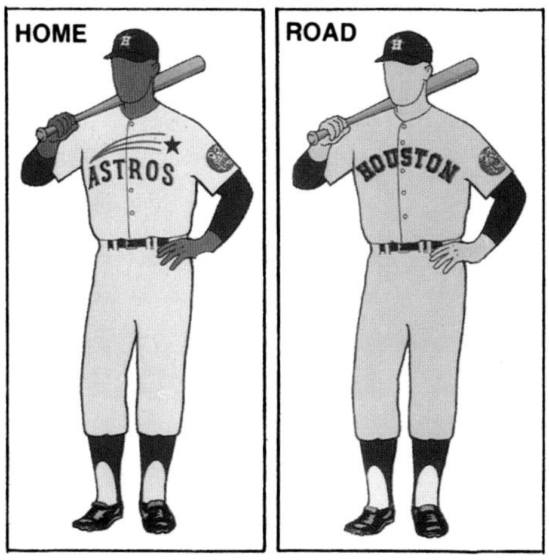

1969 AMERICAN LEAGUE

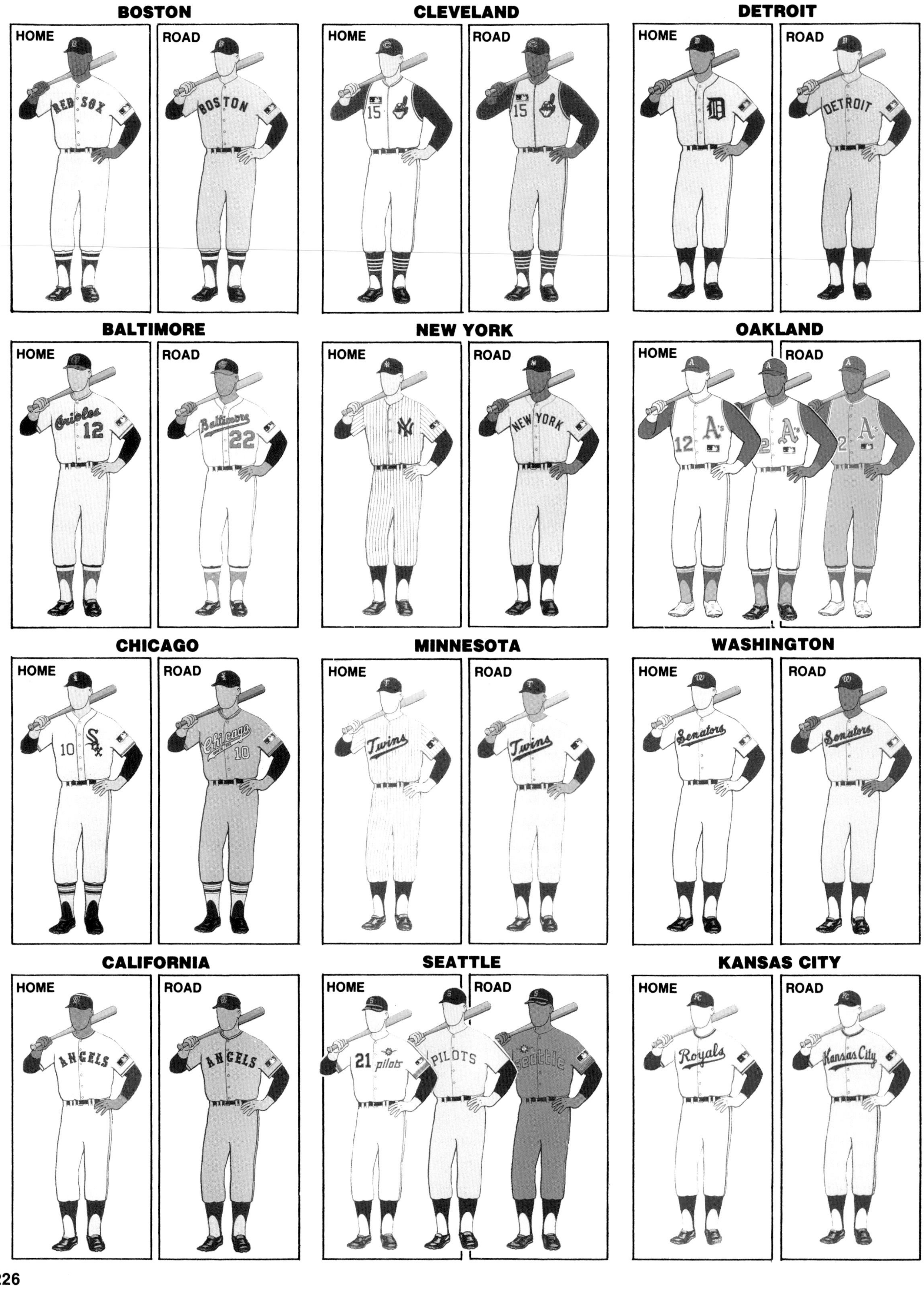

NATIONAL LEAGUE 1969

ATLANTA

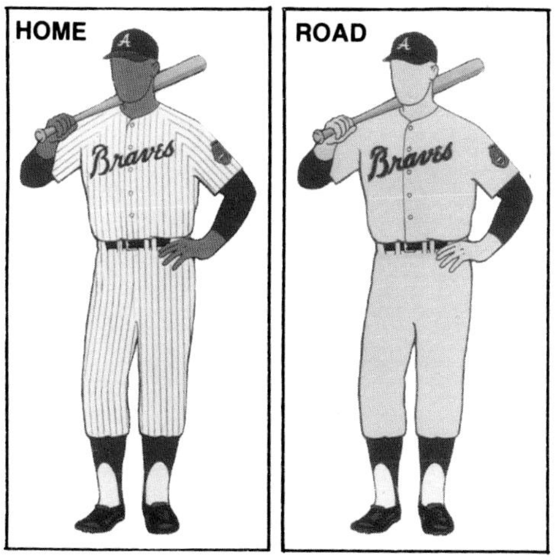

LOS ANGELES

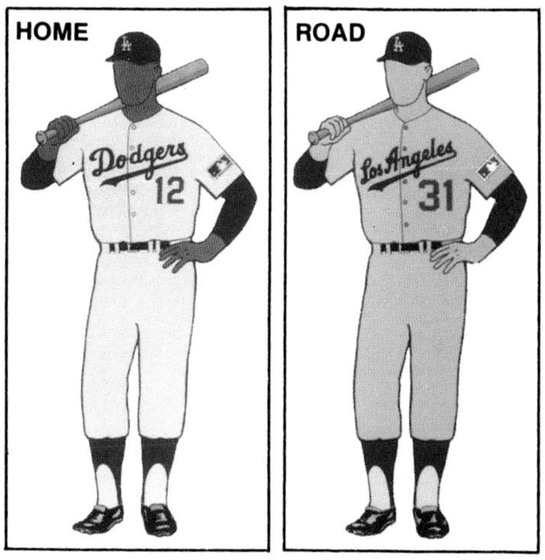

ST. LOUIS

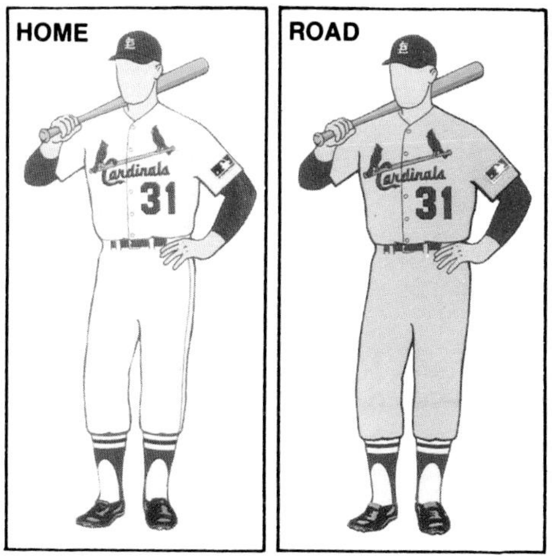

PITTSBURGH

PHILADELPHIA

CHICAGO

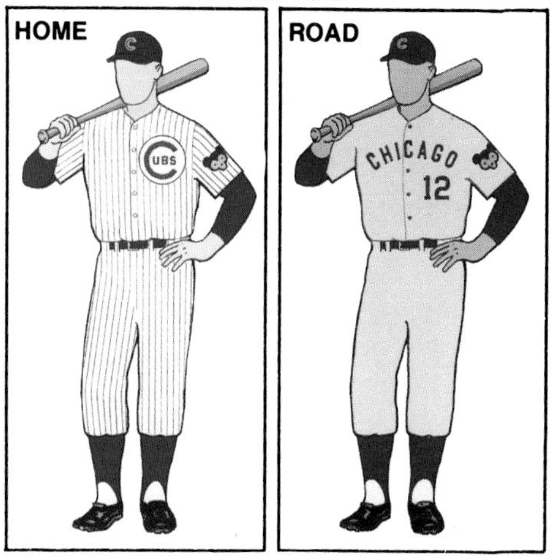

NEW YORK

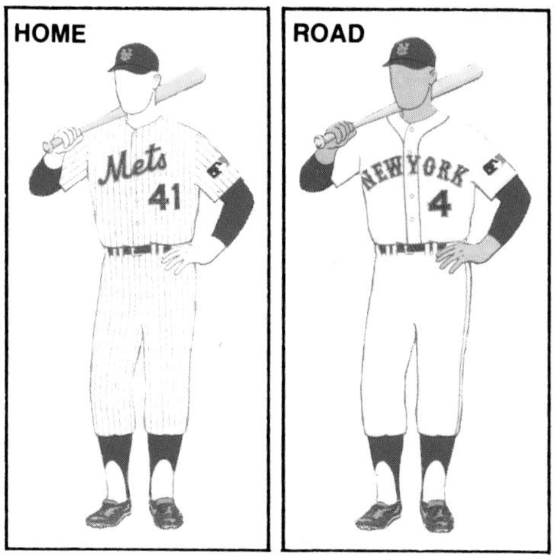

CINCINNATI

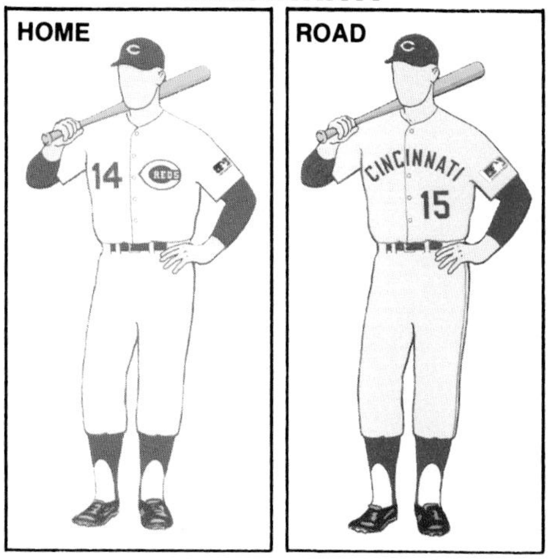

SAN FRANCISCO

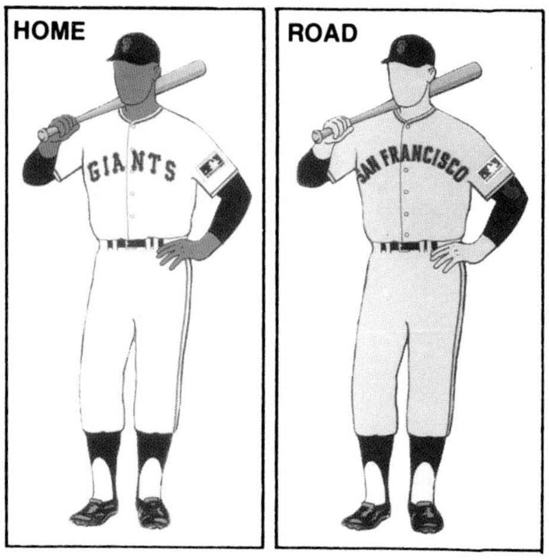

SAN DIEGO

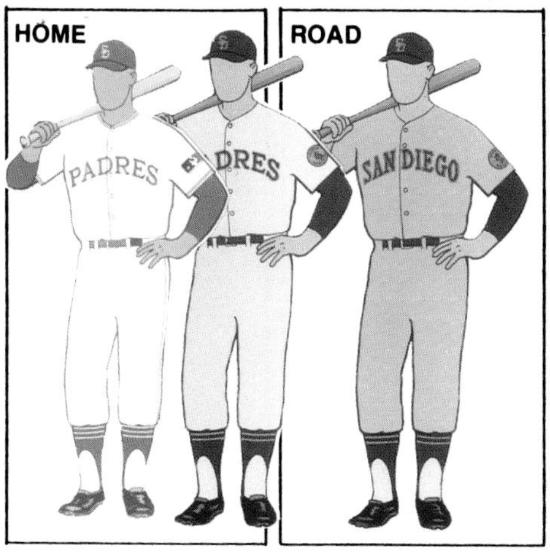

MONTREAL

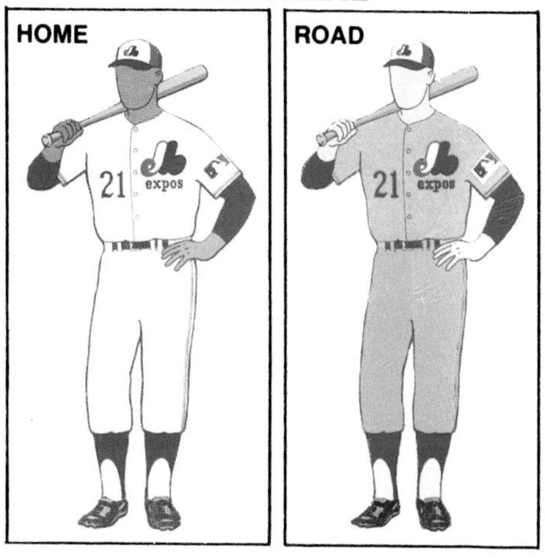

HOUSTON

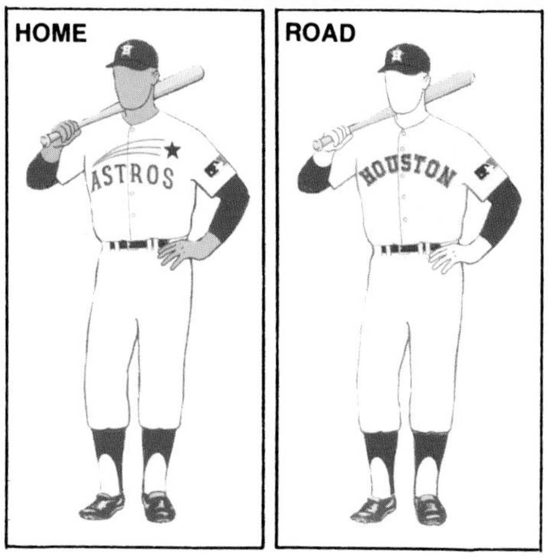

1970 AMERICAN LEAGUE

BOSTON

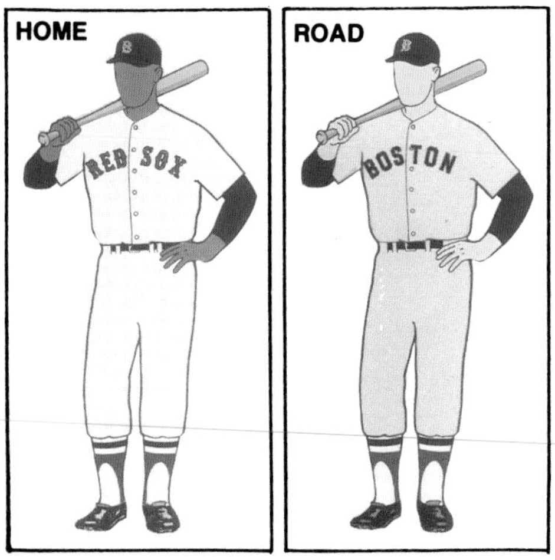

CLEVELAND

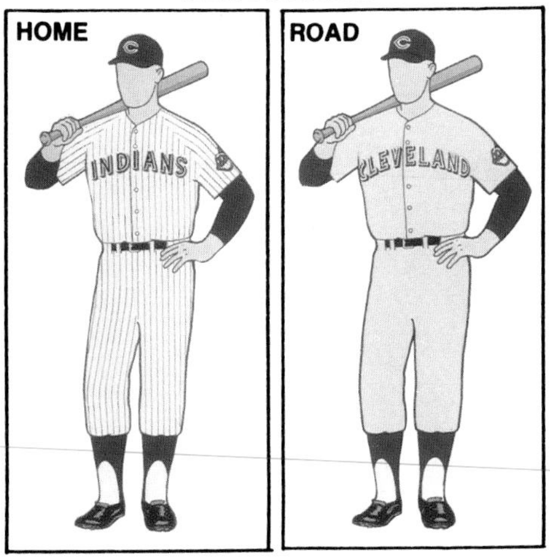

DETROIT

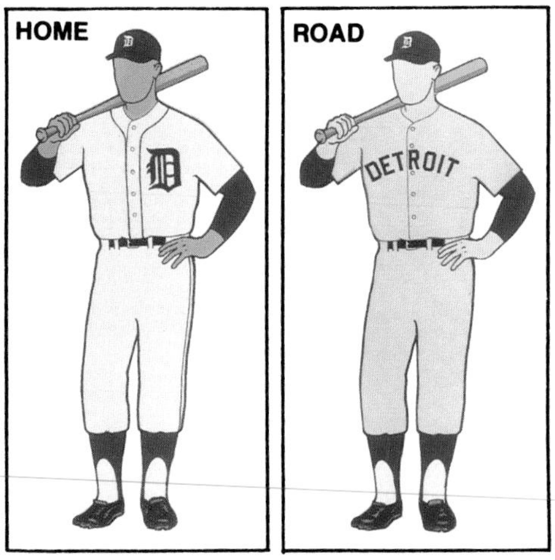

BALTIMORE

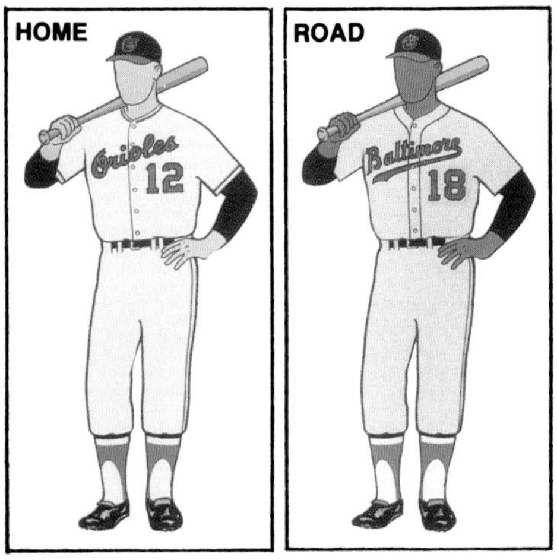

NEW YORK

OAKLAND

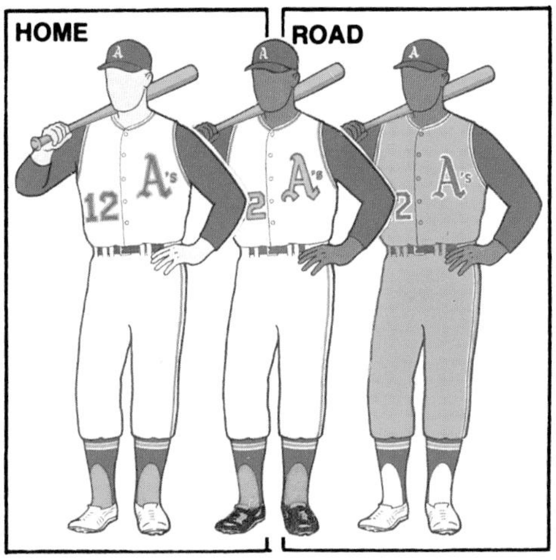

CHICAGO

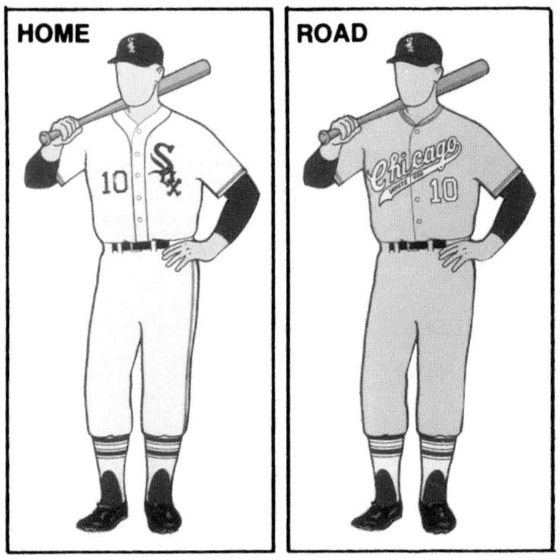

MINNESOTA

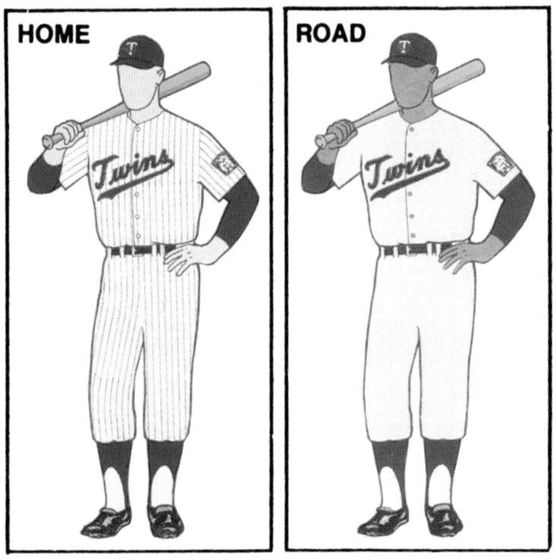

WASHINGTON

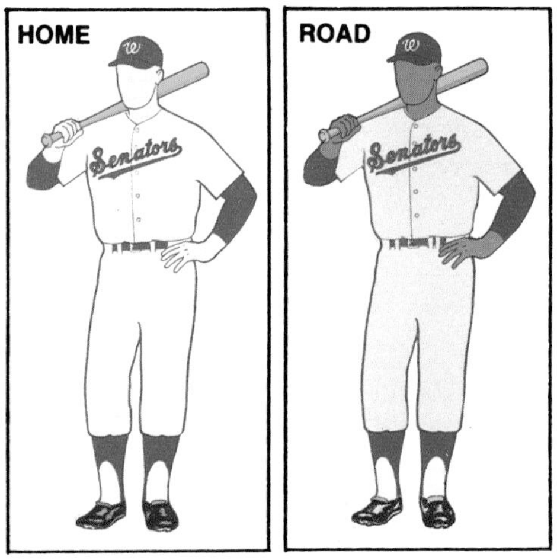

CALIFORNIA

MILWAUKEE

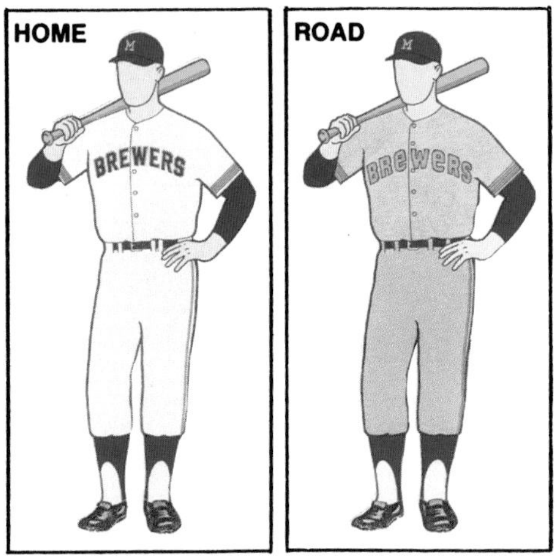

KANSAS CITY

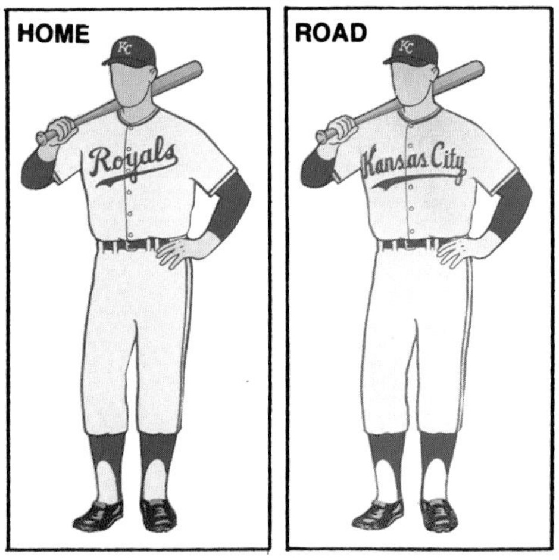

NATIONAL LEAGUE 1970

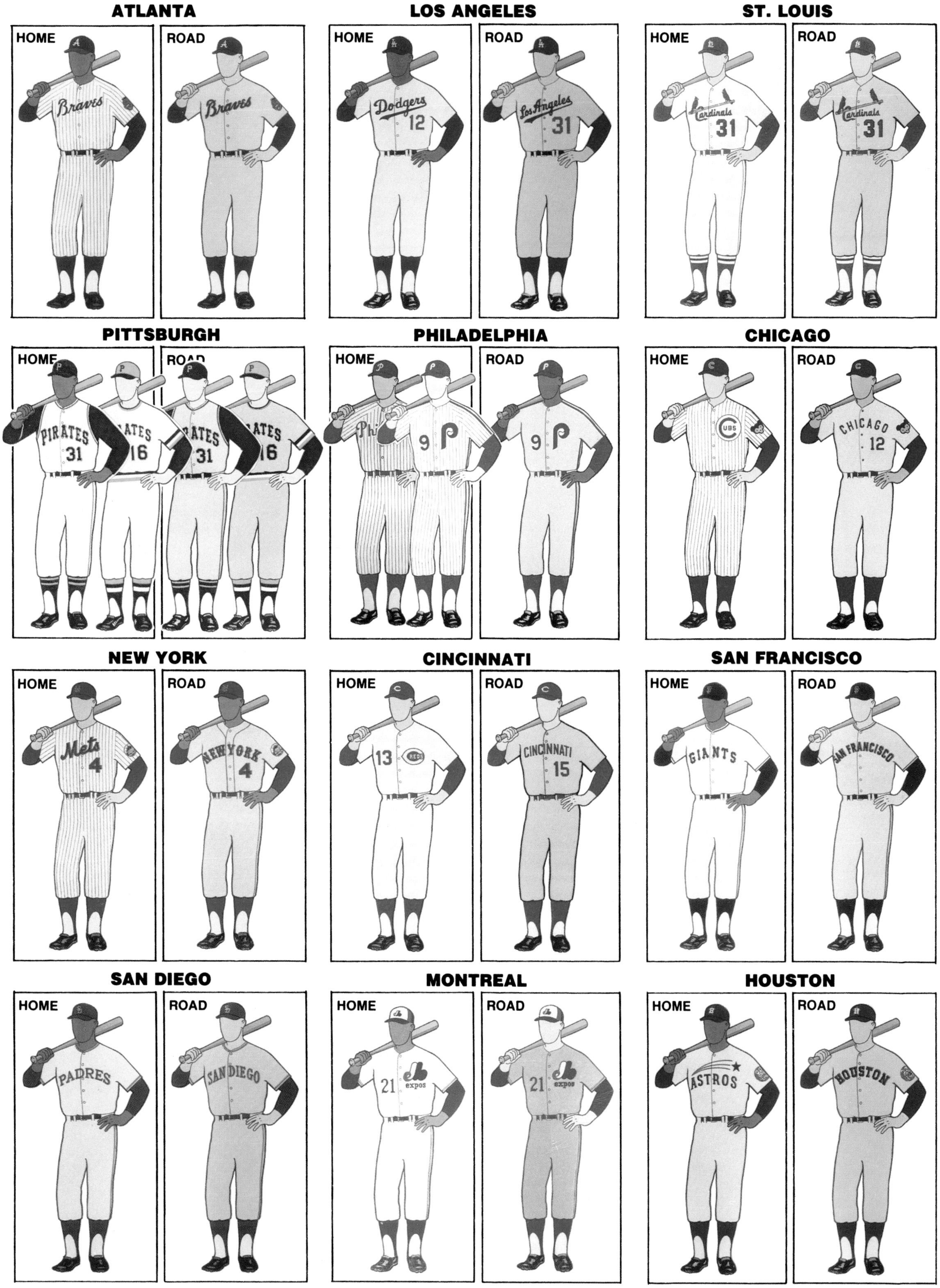

1971
AMERICAN LEAGUE

BOSTON
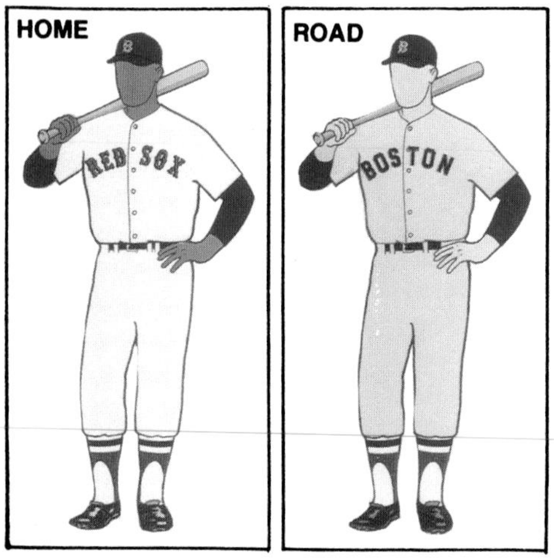

CLEVELAND
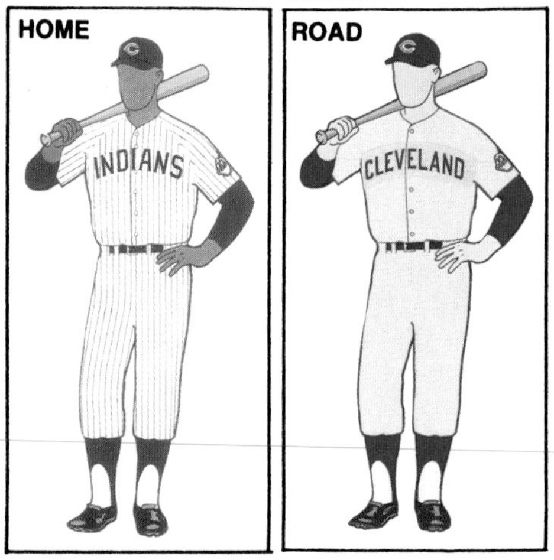

DETROIT
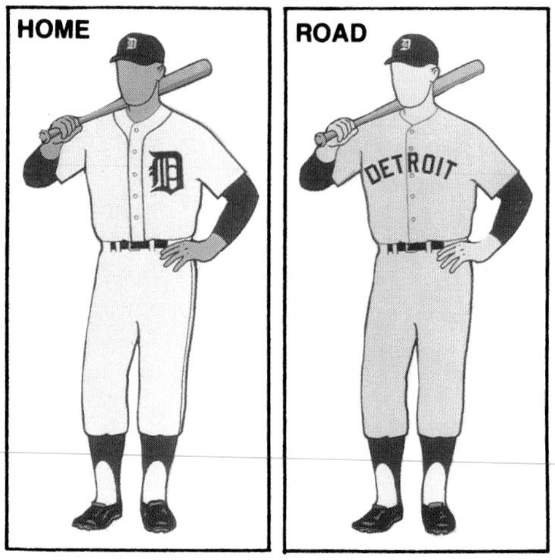

BALTIMORE
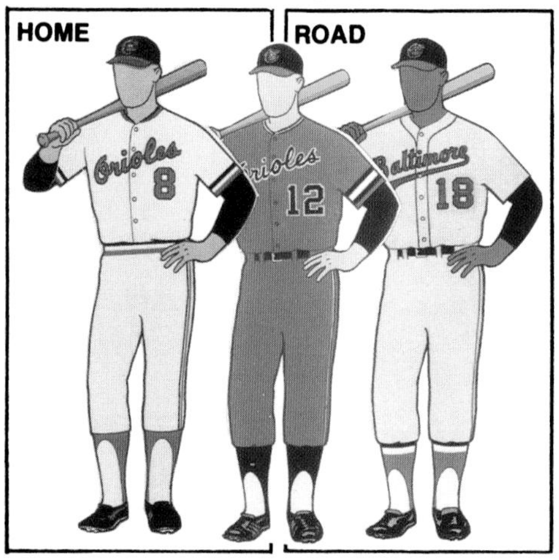

NEW YORK

OAKLAND
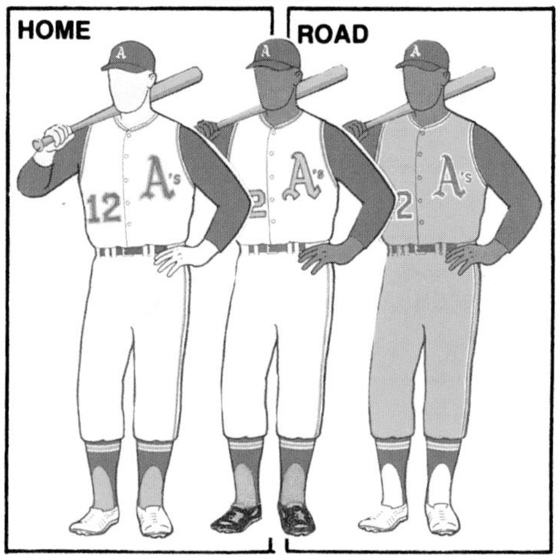

CHICAGO
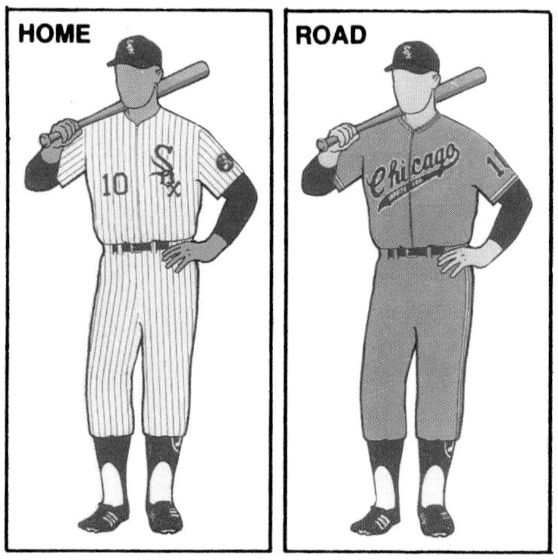

MINNESOTA
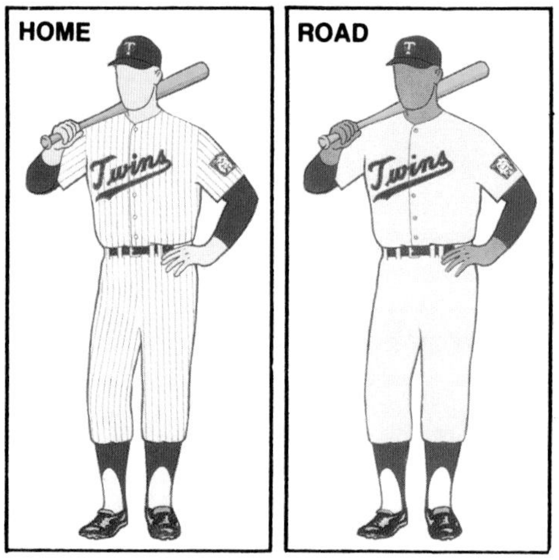

WASHINGTON
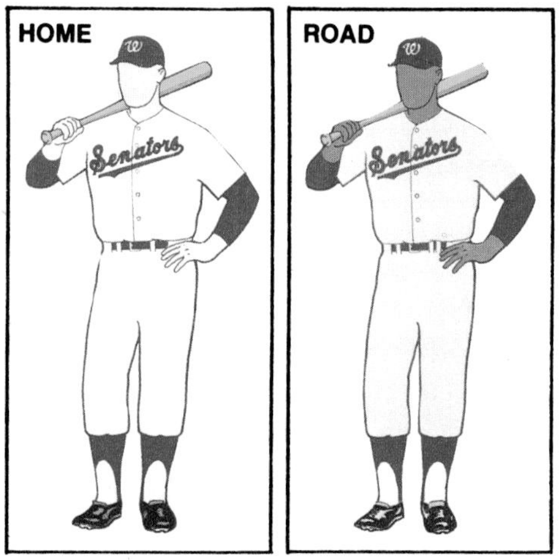

CALIFORNIA
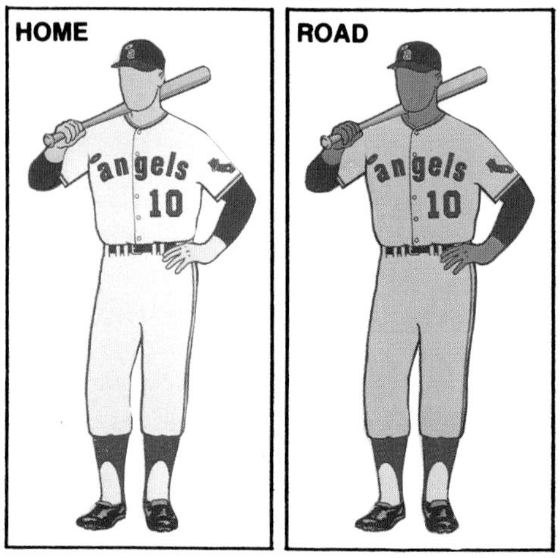

MILWAUKEE
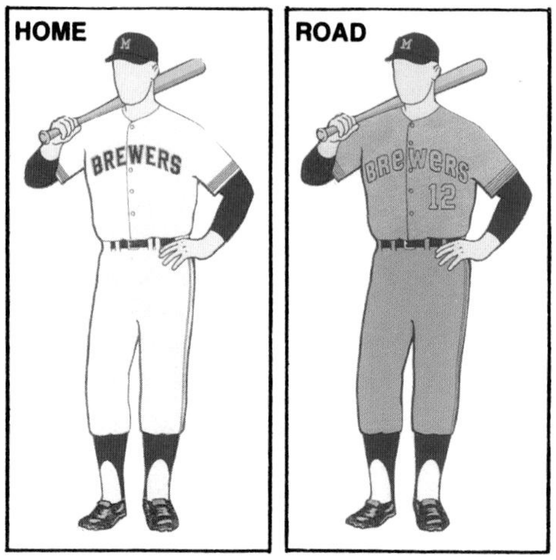

KANSAS CITY
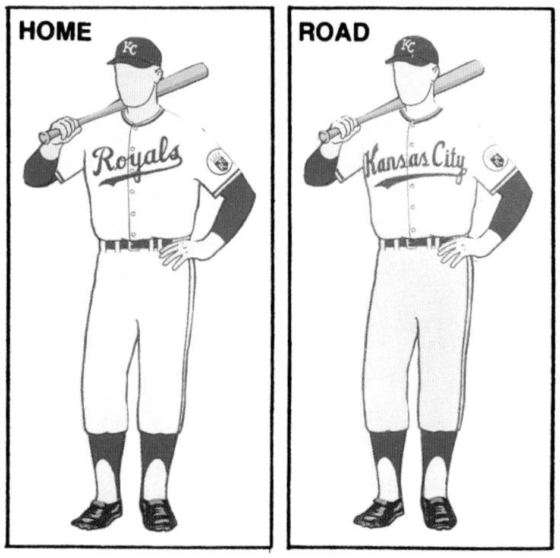

NATIONAL LEAGUE 1971

ATLANTA

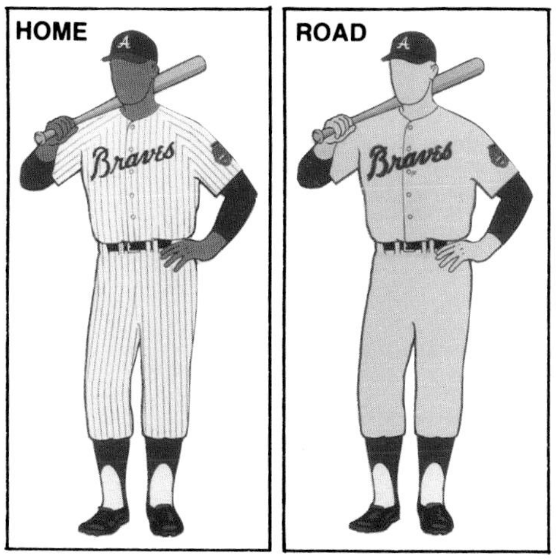

LOS ANGELES

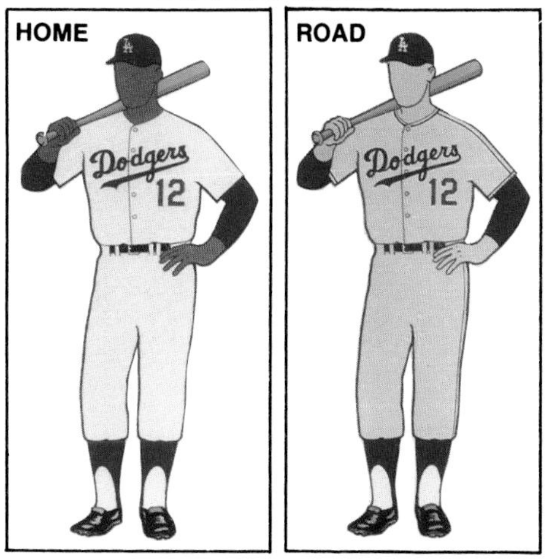

ST. LOUIS

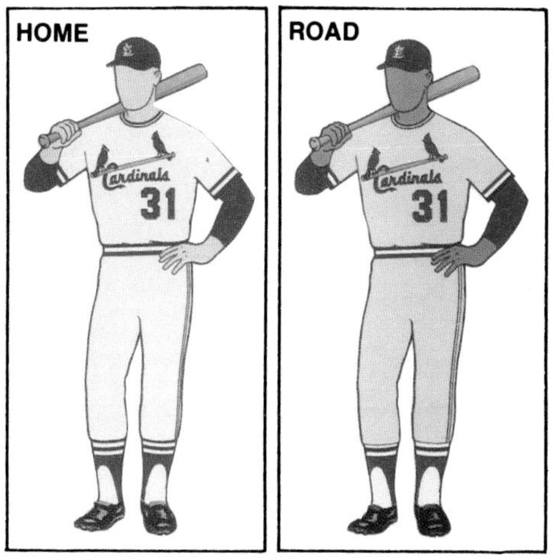

PITTSBURGH

PHILADELPHIA

CHICAGO

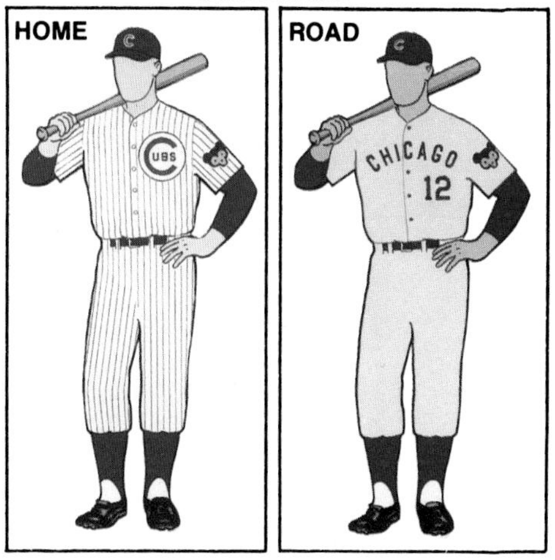

NEW YORK

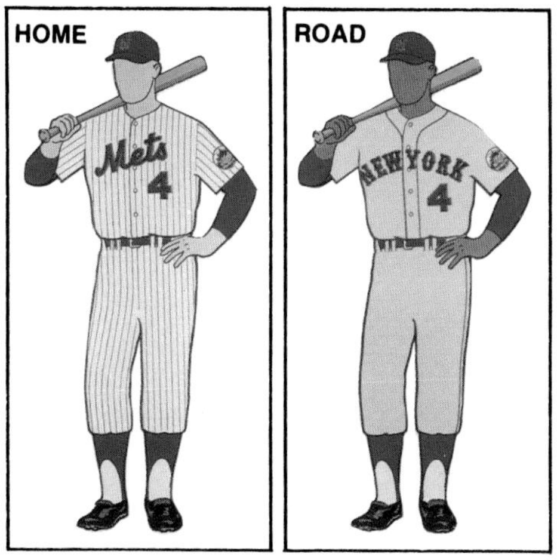

CINCINNATI

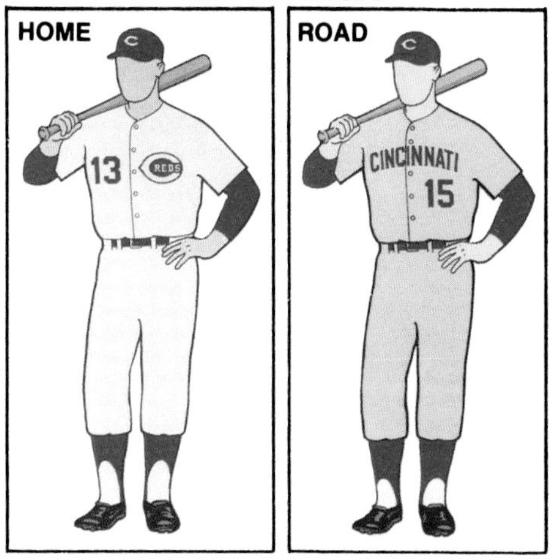

SAN FRANCISCO

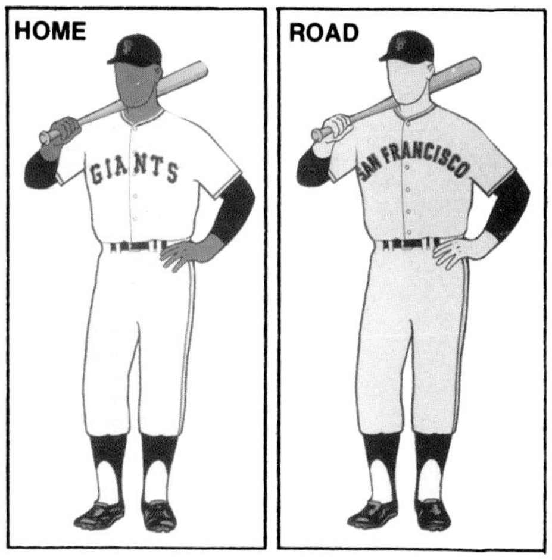

SAN DIEGO

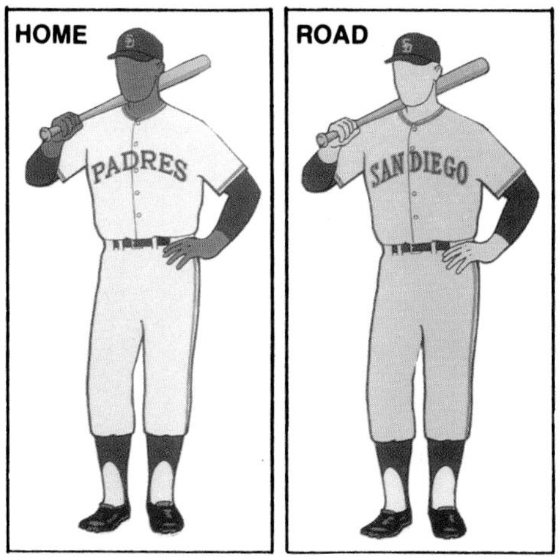

MONTREAL

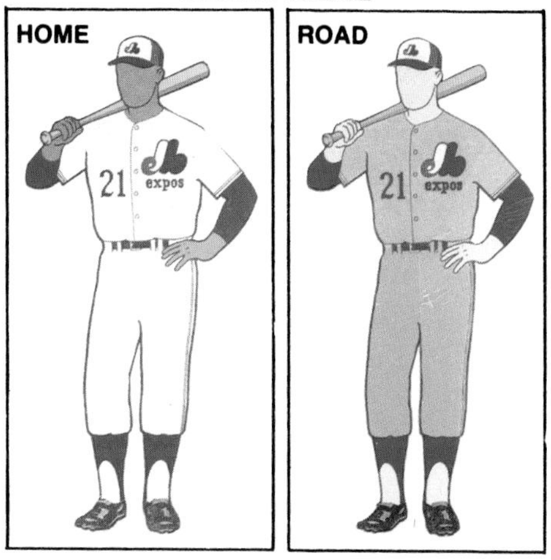

HOUSTON

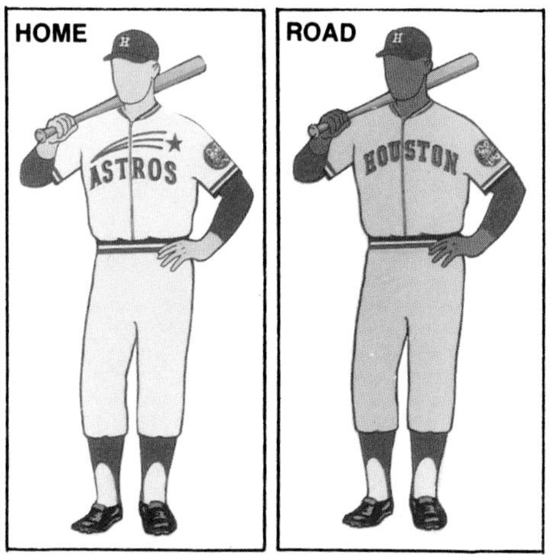

1972 AMERICAN LEAGUE

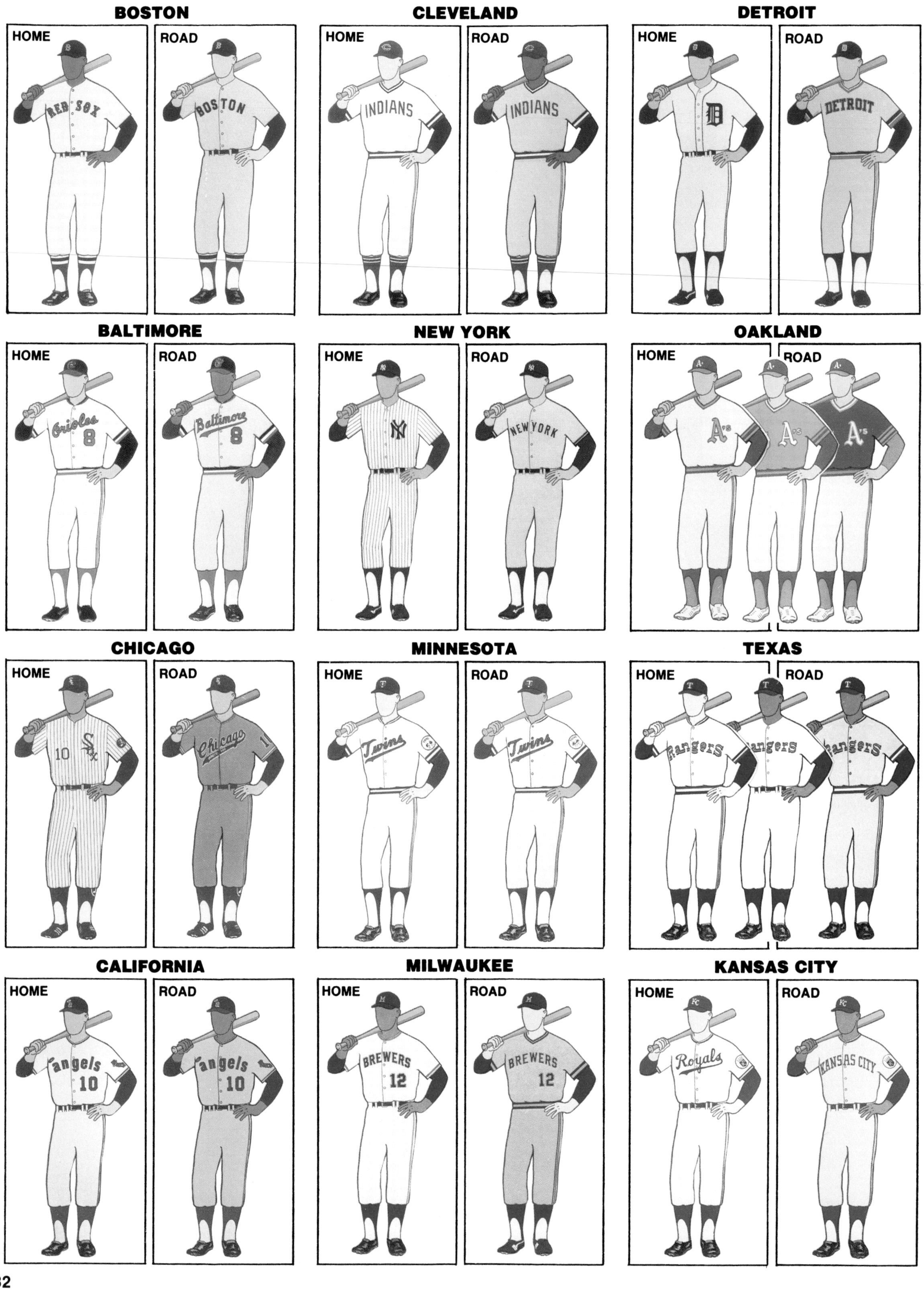

NATIONAL LEAGUE 1972

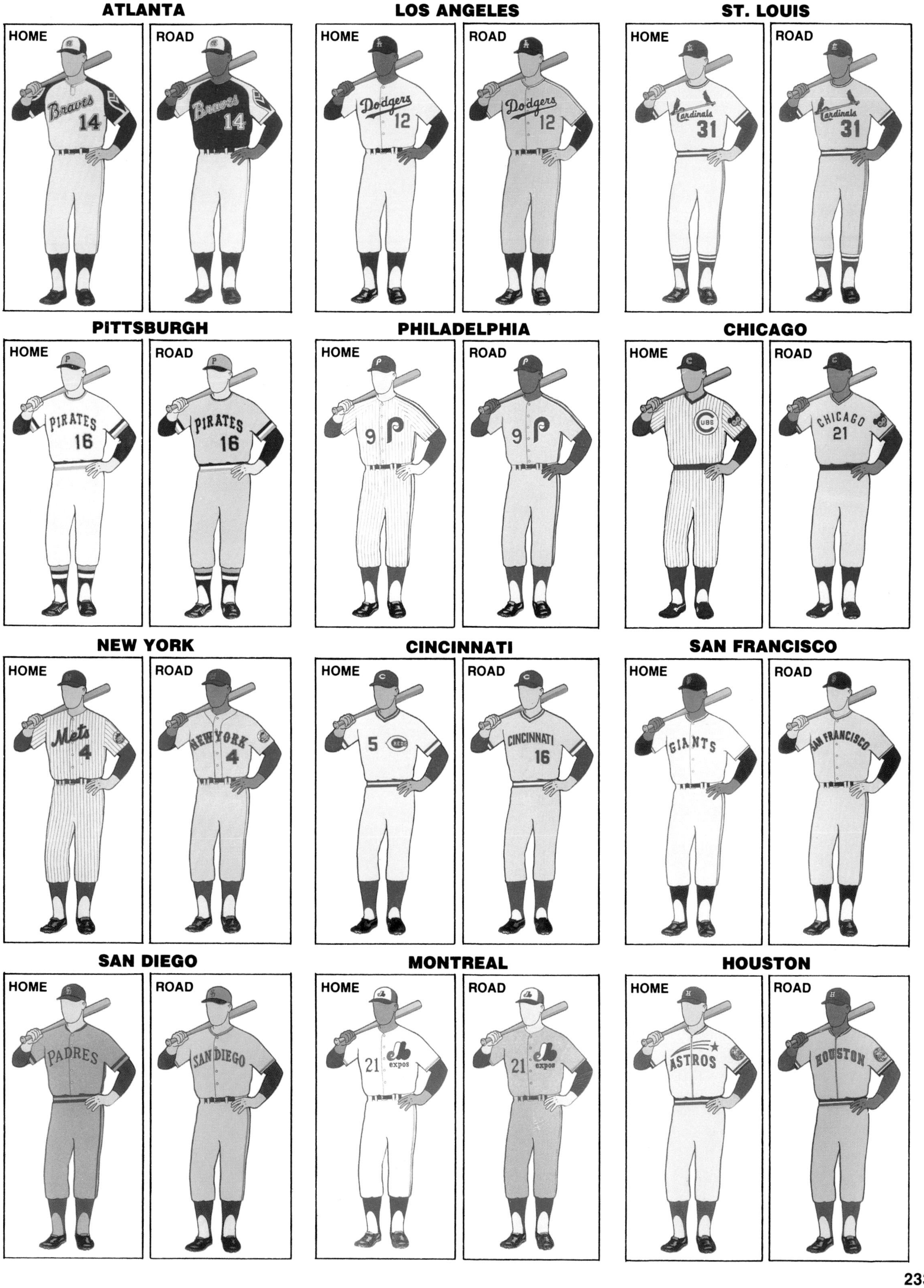

1973 AMERICAN LEAGUE

BOSTON

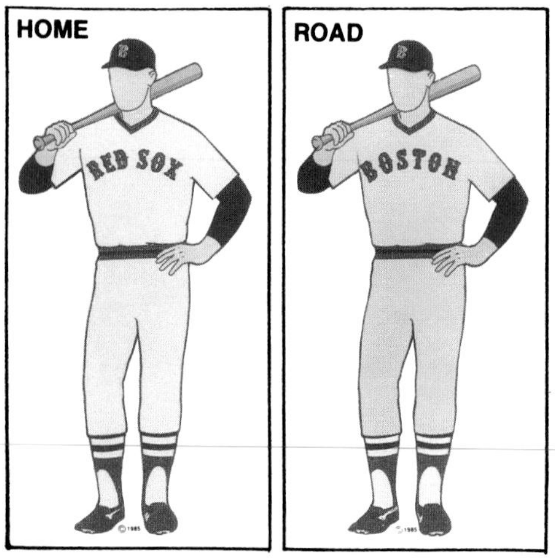

CLEVELAND

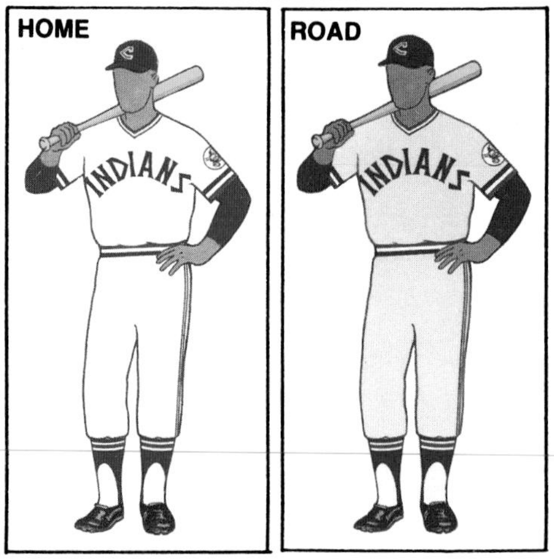

DETROIT

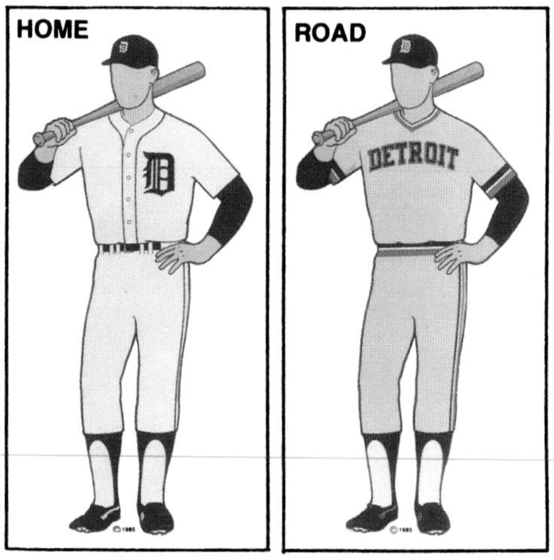

BALTIMORE

NEW YORK

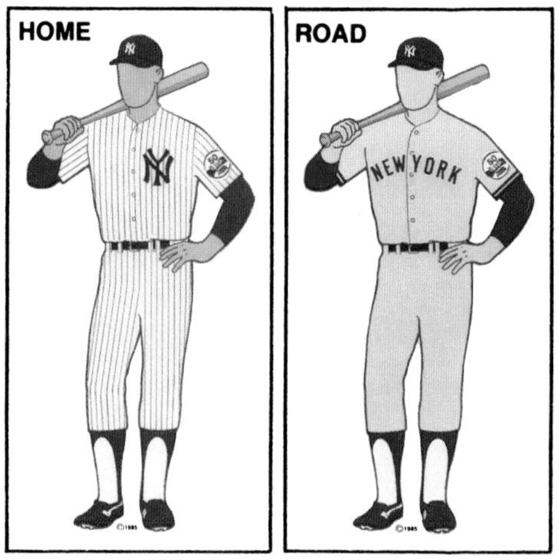

OAKLAND

CHICAGO

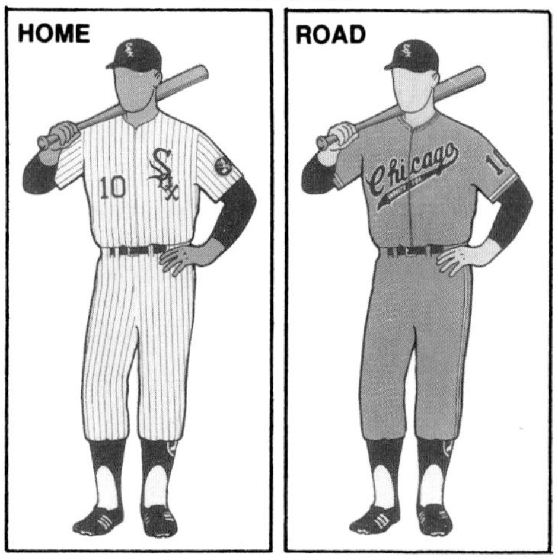

MINNESOTA

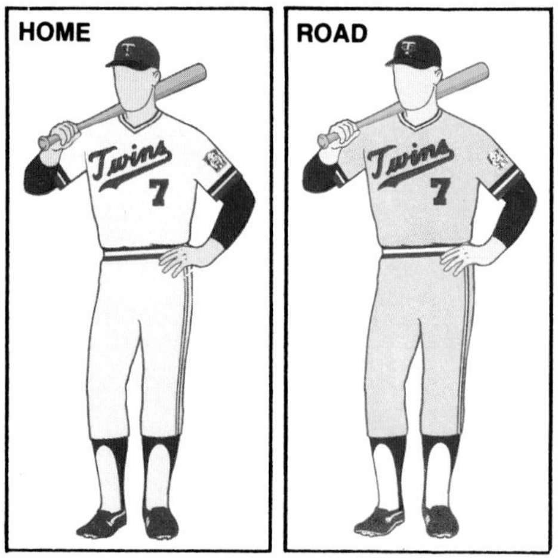

TEXAS

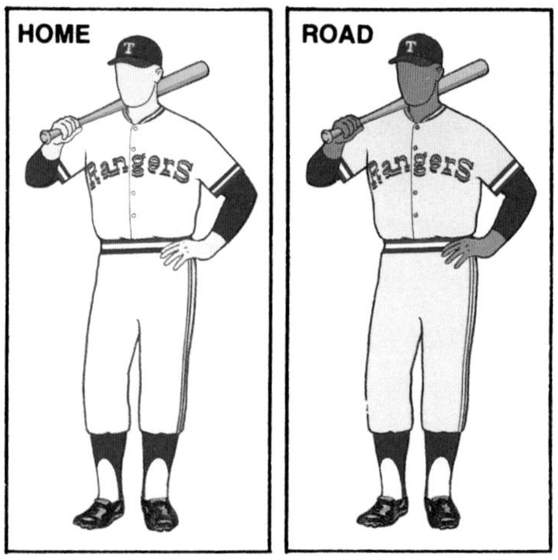

CALIFORNIA

MILWAUKEE

KANSAS CITY

NATIONAL LEAGUE 1973

ATLANTA

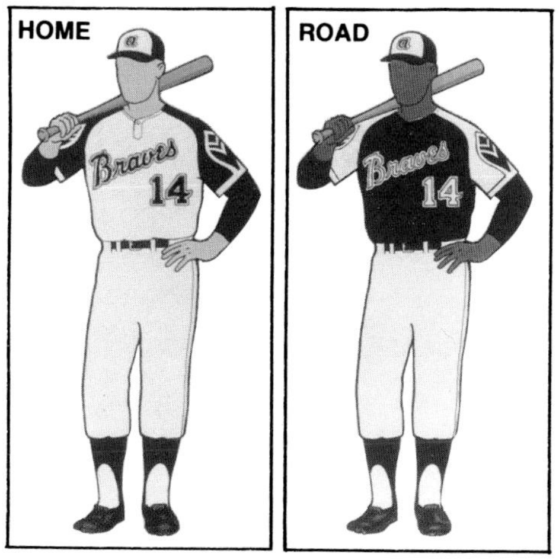

LOS ANGELES

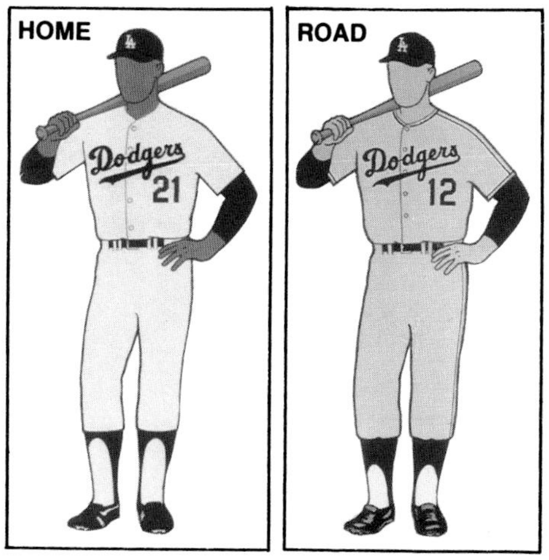

ST. LOUIS

PITTSBURGH

PHILADELPHIA

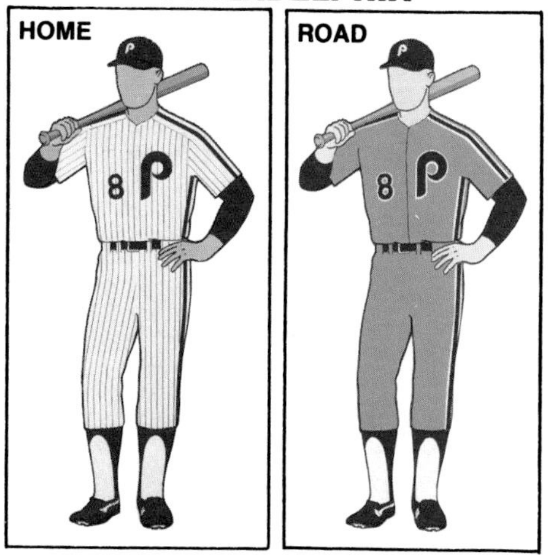

CHICAGO

NEW YORK

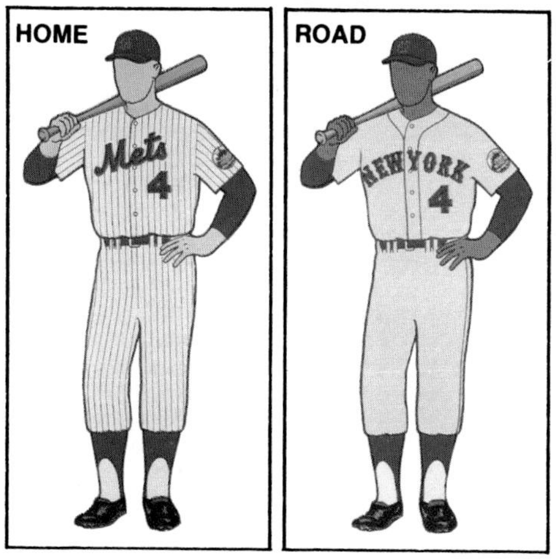

CINCINNATI

SAN FRANCISCO

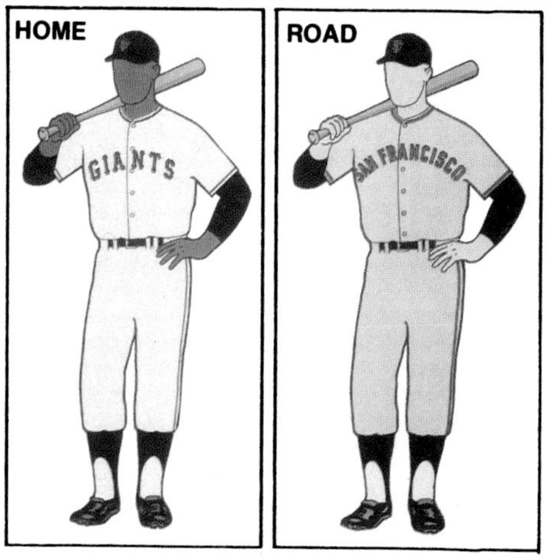

SAN DIEGO

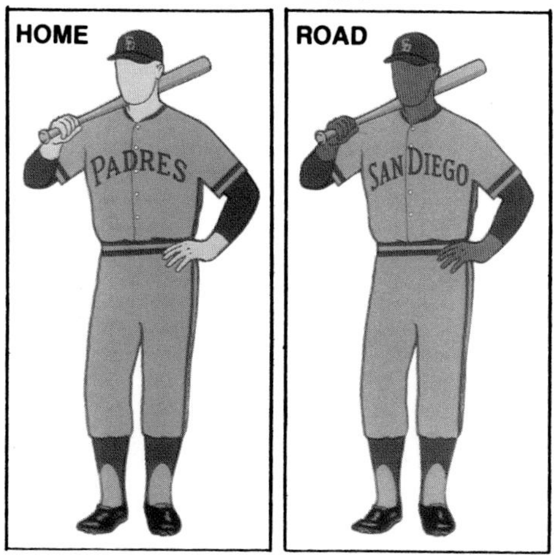

MONTREAL

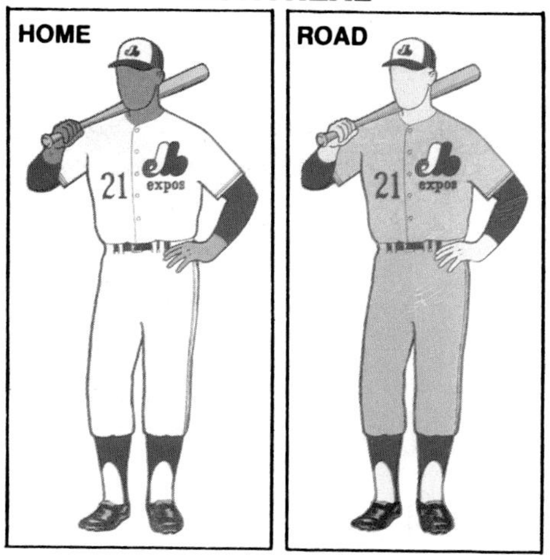

HOUSTON

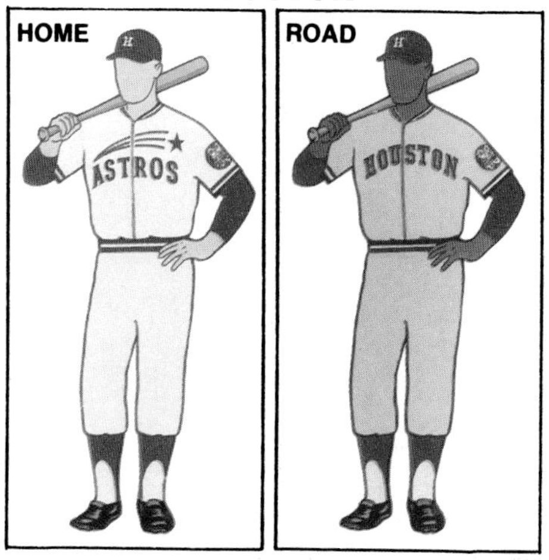

1974 AMERICAN LEAGUE

BOSTON

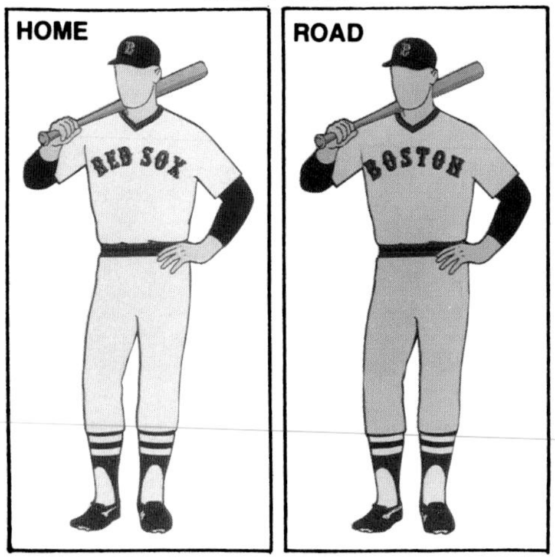

CLEVELAND

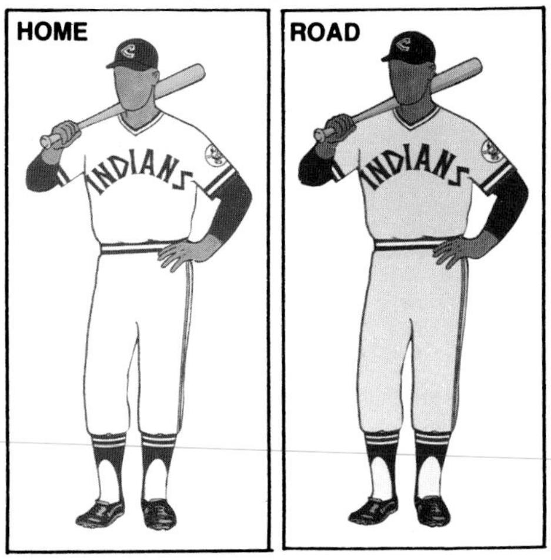

DETROIT

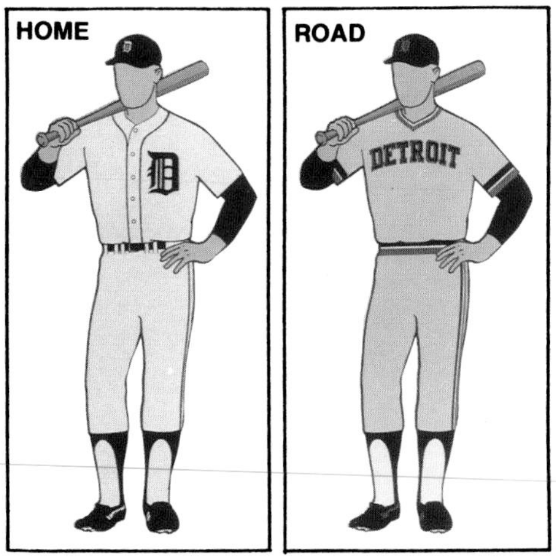

BALTIMORE

NEW YORK

OAKLAND

CHICAGO

MINNESOTA

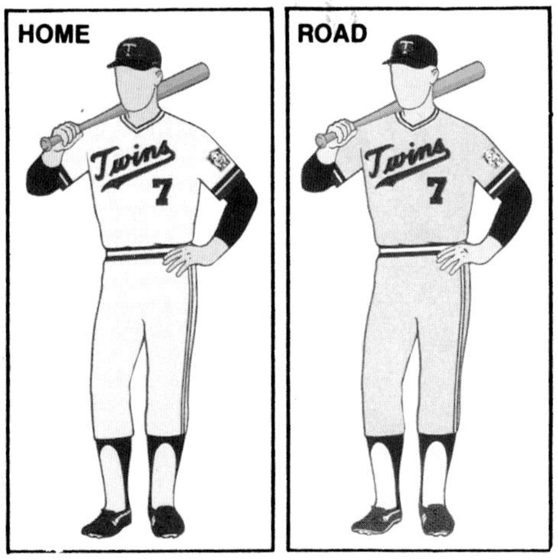

TEXAS

CALIFORNIA

MILWAUKEE

KANSAS CITY

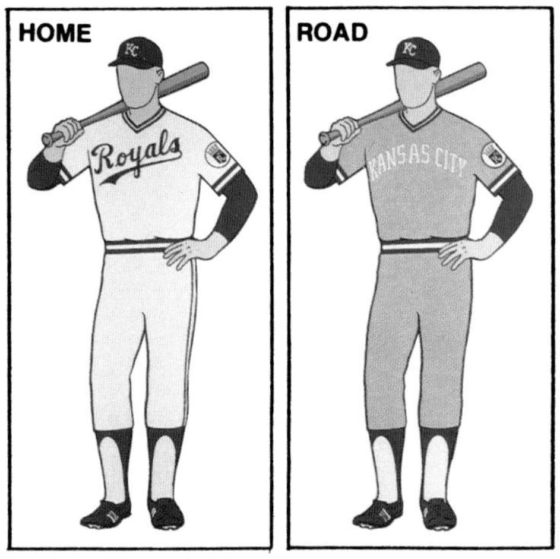

NATIONAL LEAGUE 1974

ATLANTA

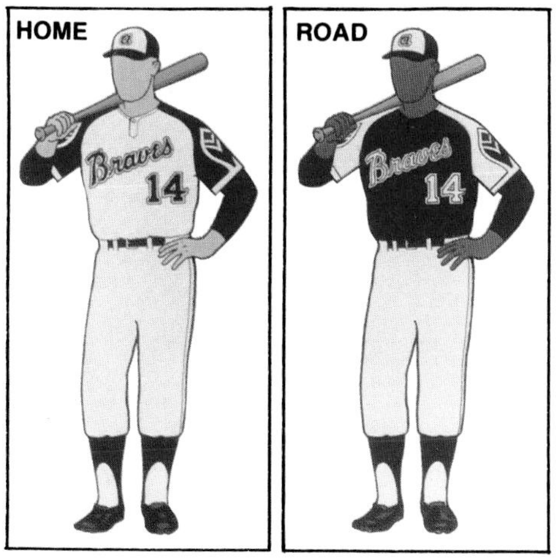

LOS ANGELES

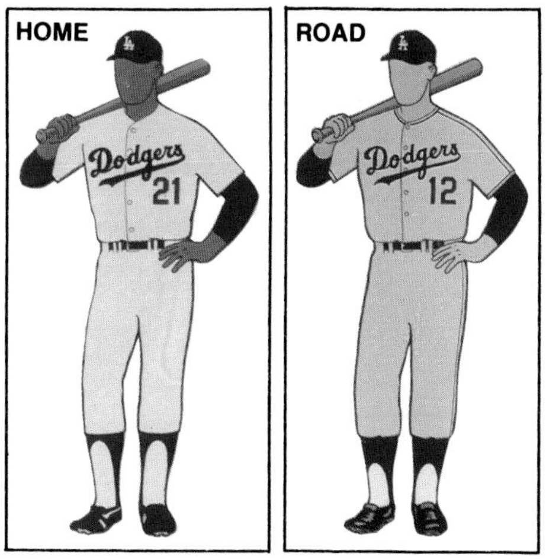

ST. LOUIS

PITTSBURGH

PHILADELPHIA

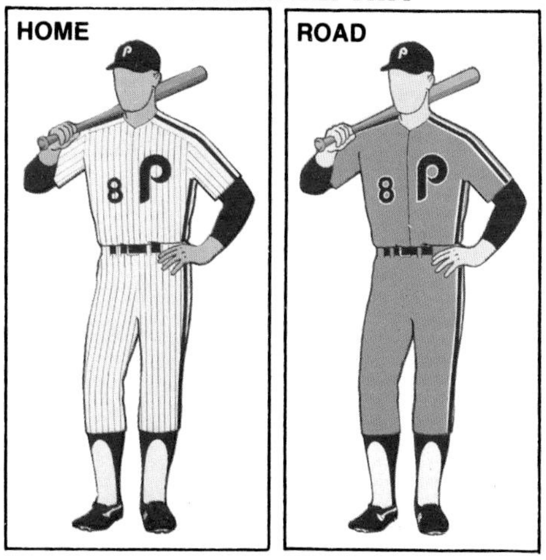

CHICAGO

NEW YORK

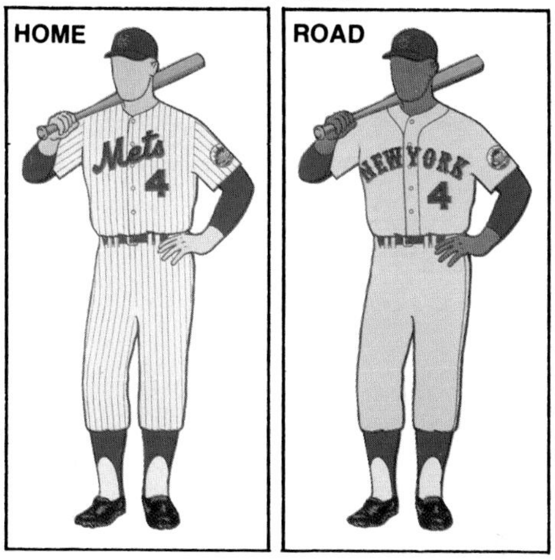

CINCINNATI

SAN FRANCISCO

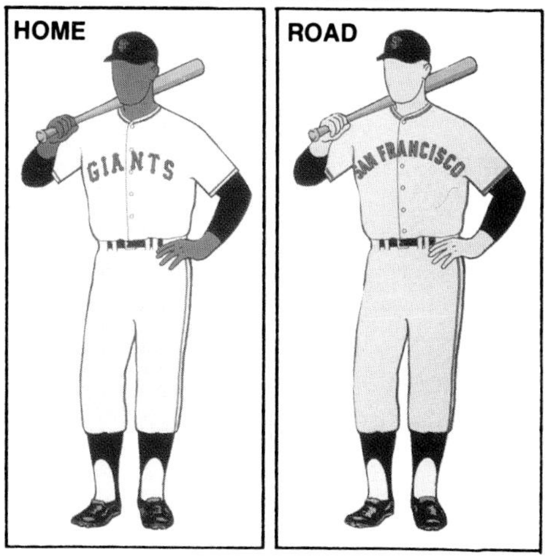

SAN DIEGO

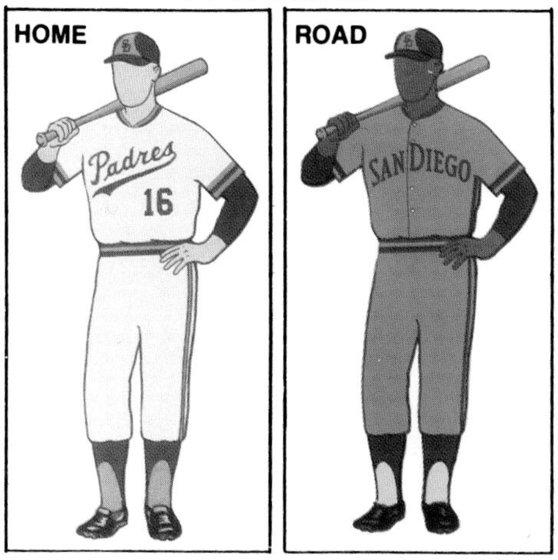

MONTREAL

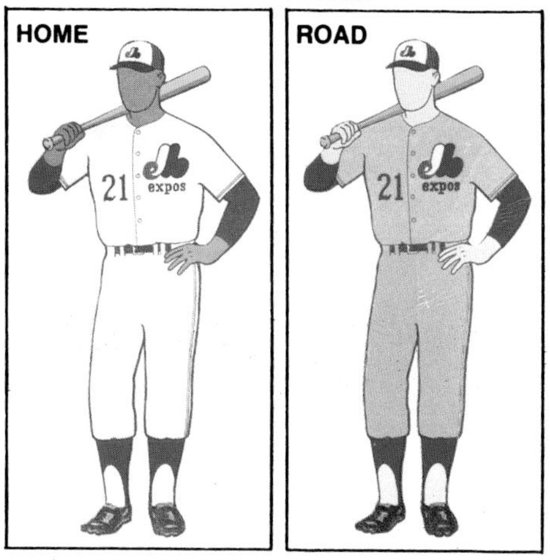

HOUSTON

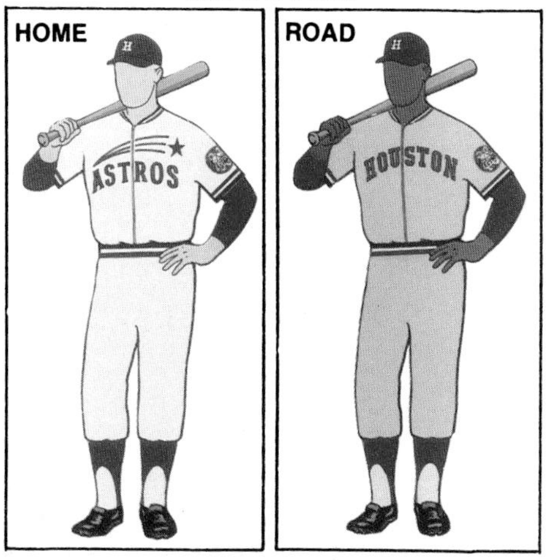

1975 AMERICAN LEAGUE

BOSTON

CLEVELAND

DETROIT

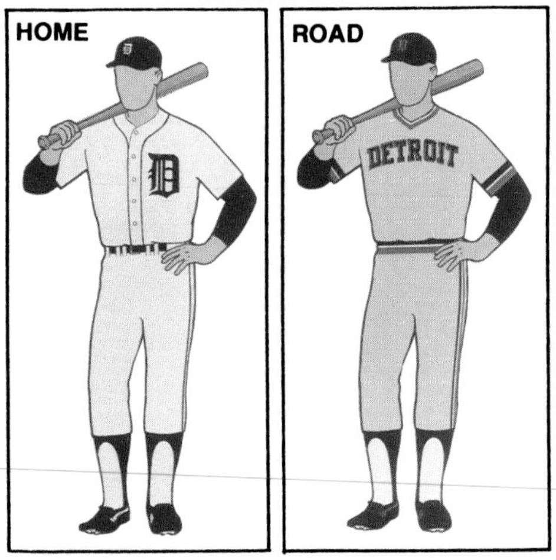

BALTIMORE

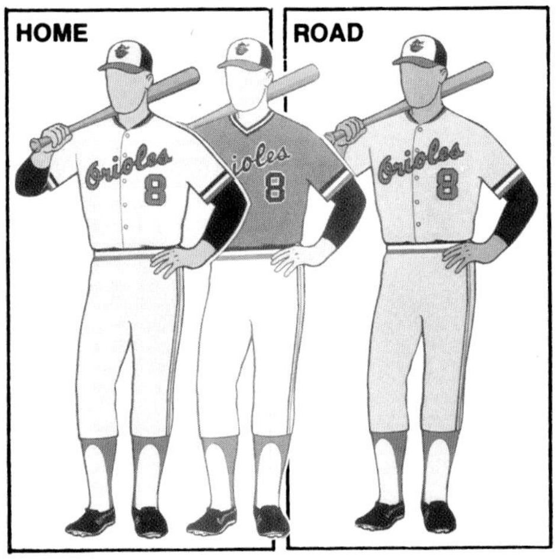

NEW YORK

OAKLAND

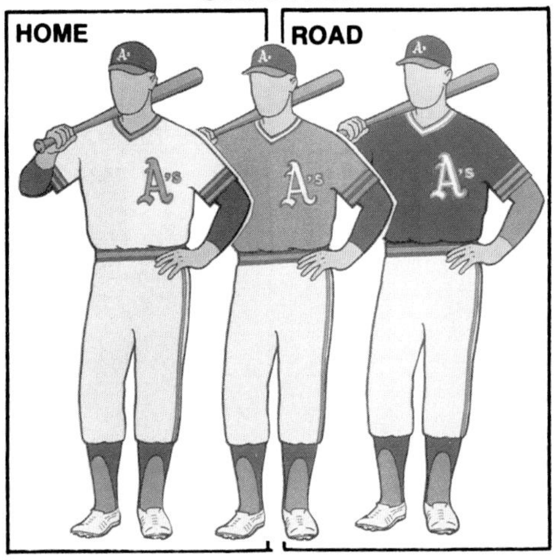

CHICAGO

MINNESOTA

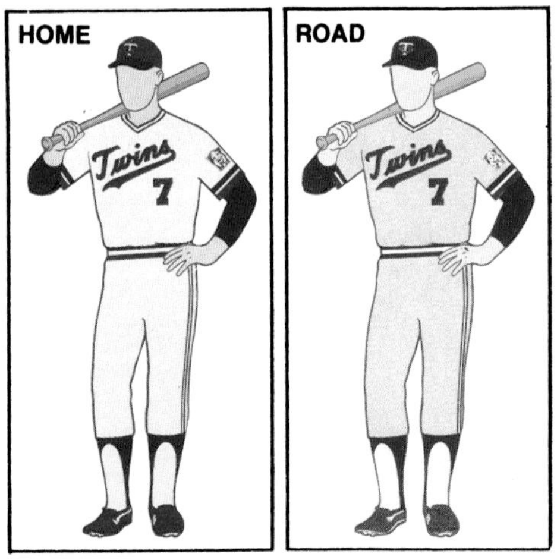

TEXAS

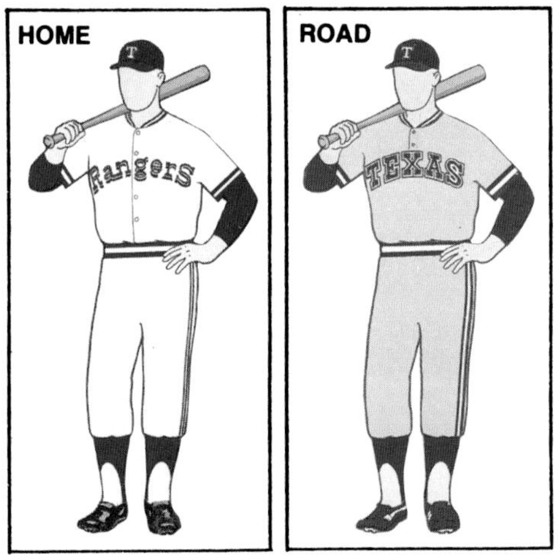

CALIFORNIA

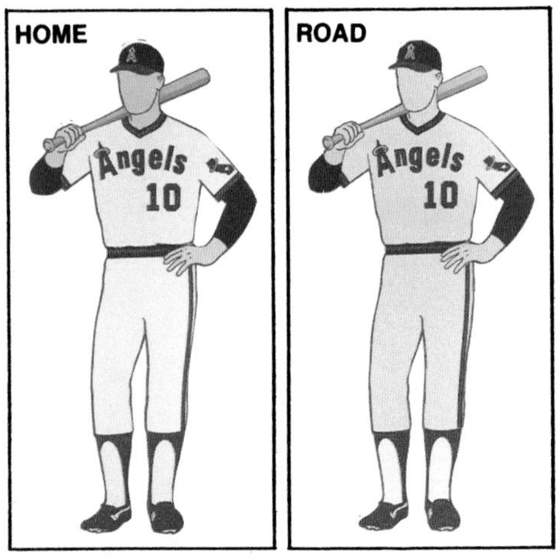

MILWAUKEE

KANSAS CITY

NATIONAL LEAGUE 1975

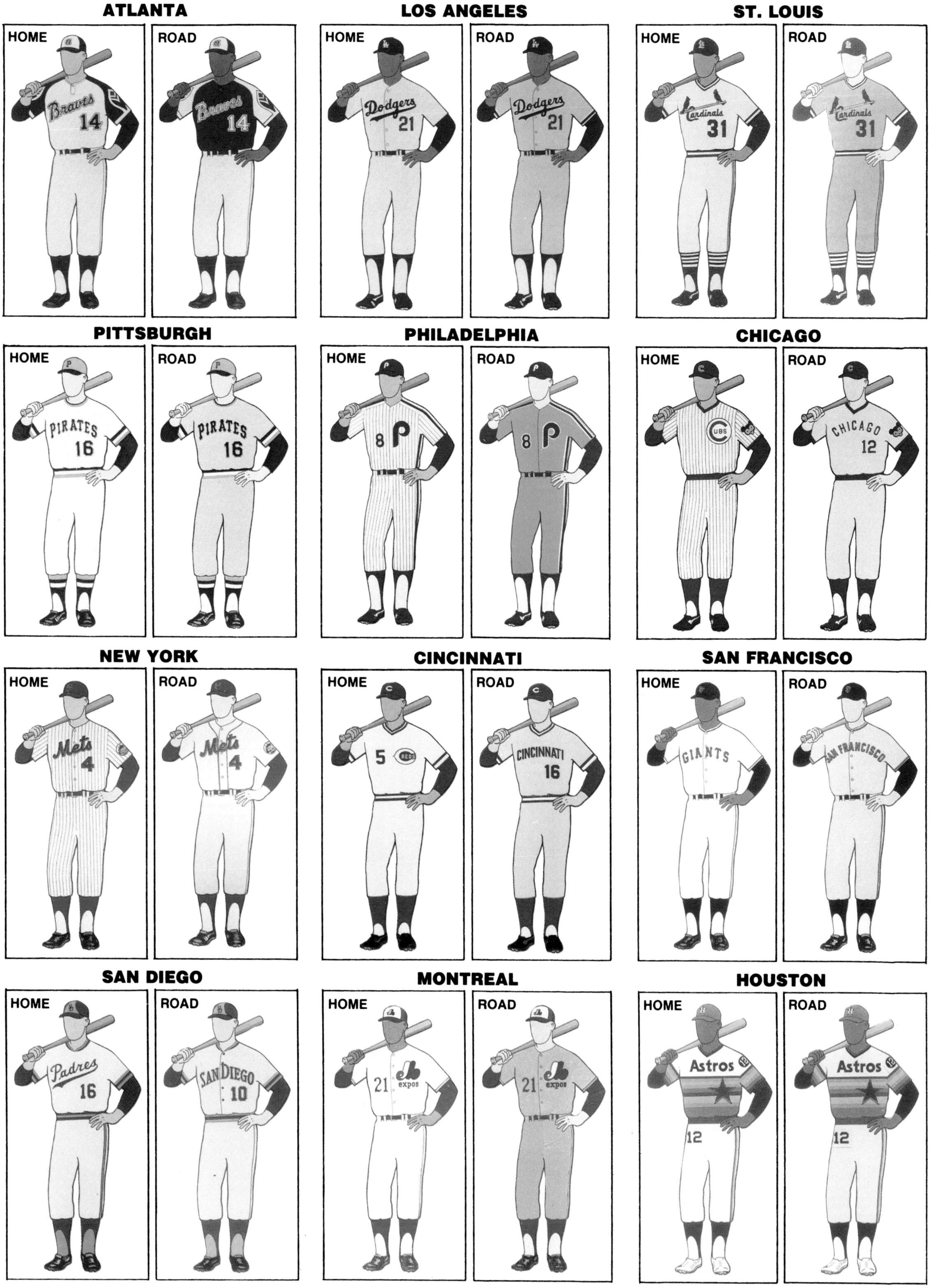

1976 AMERICAN LEAGUE

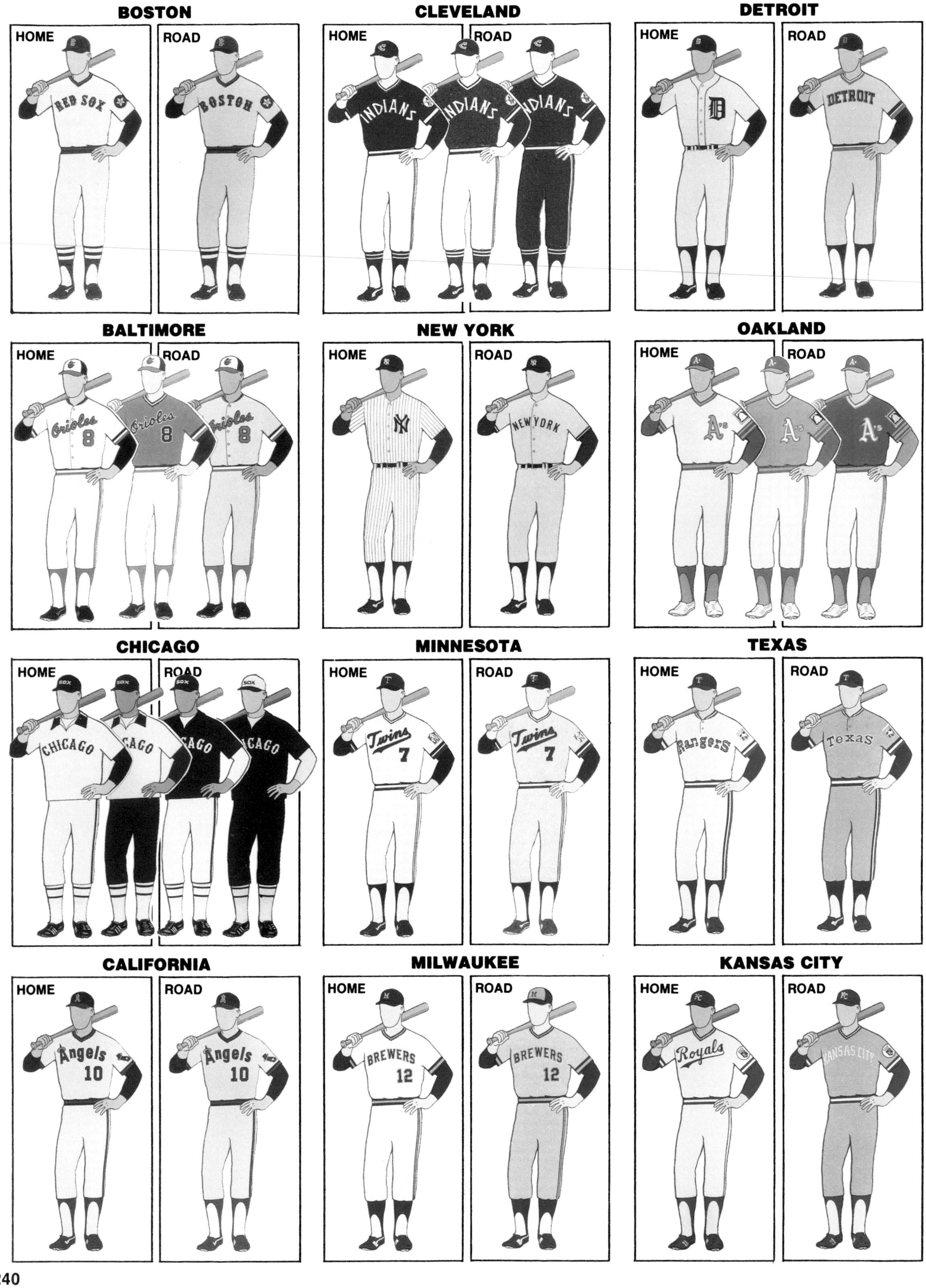

NATIONAL LEAGUE 1976

ATLANTA

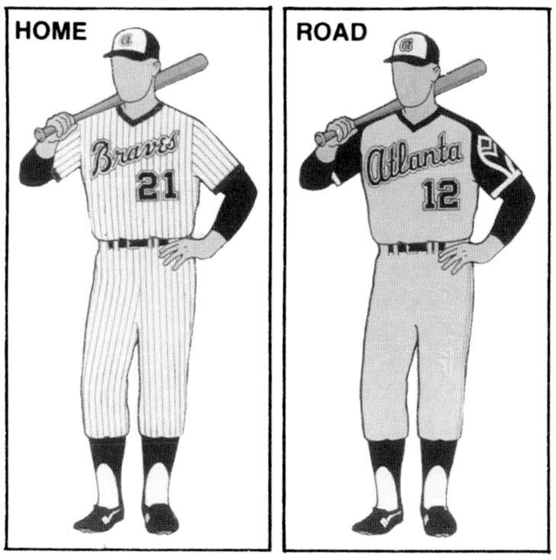

LOS ANGELES

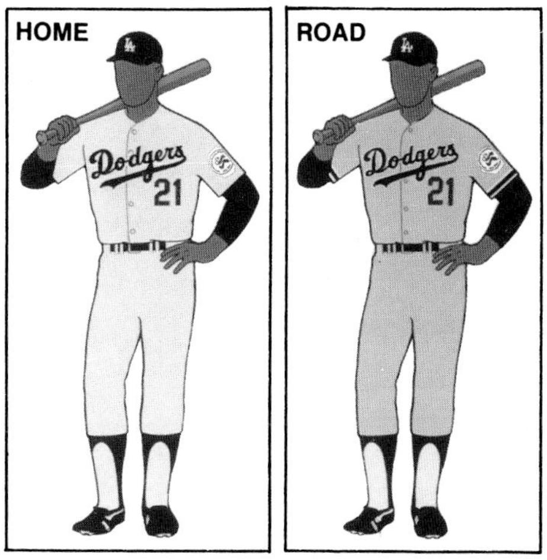

ST. LOUIS

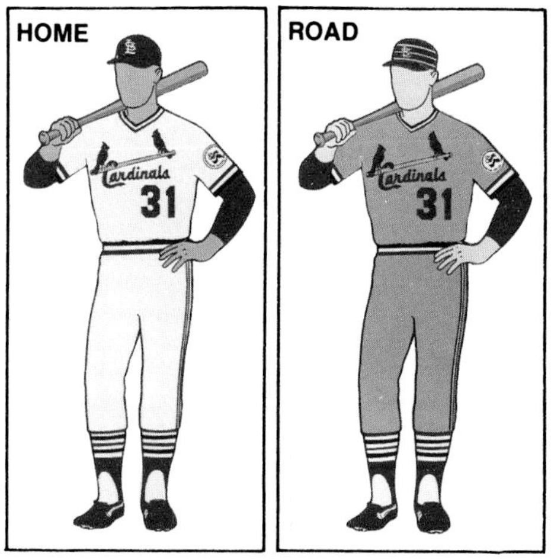

PITTSBURGH

PHILADELPHIA

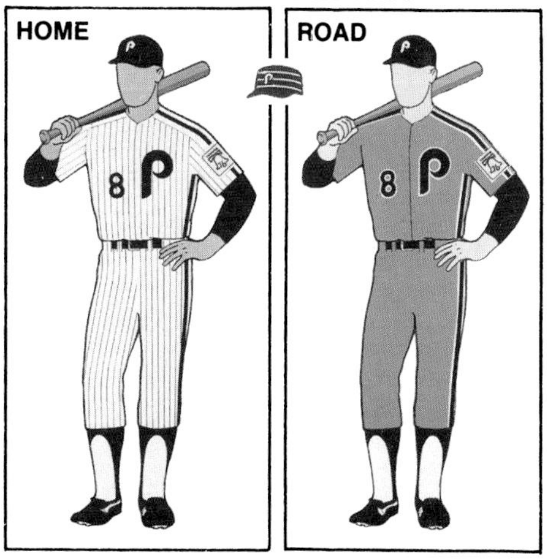

CHICAGO

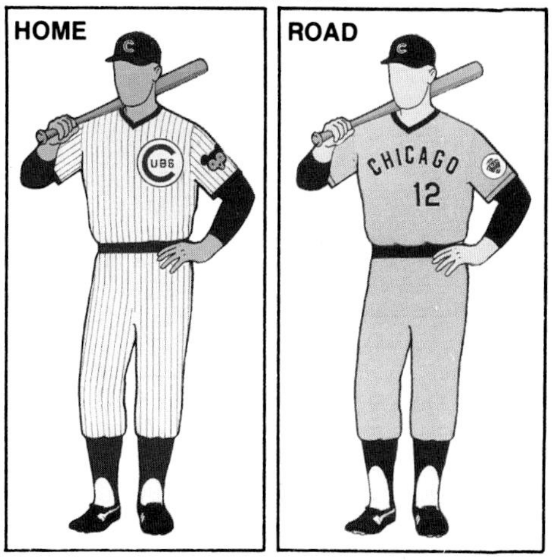

NEW YORK

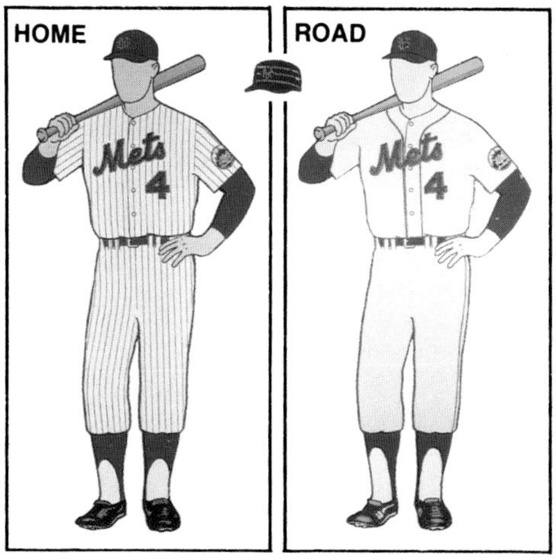

CINCINNATI

SAN FRANCISCO

SAN DIEGO

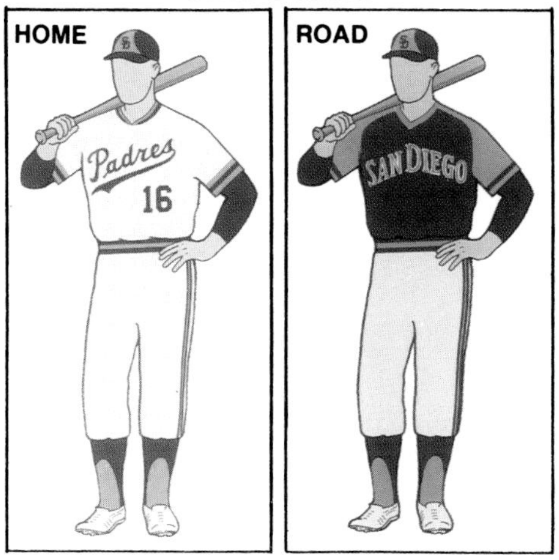

MONTREAL

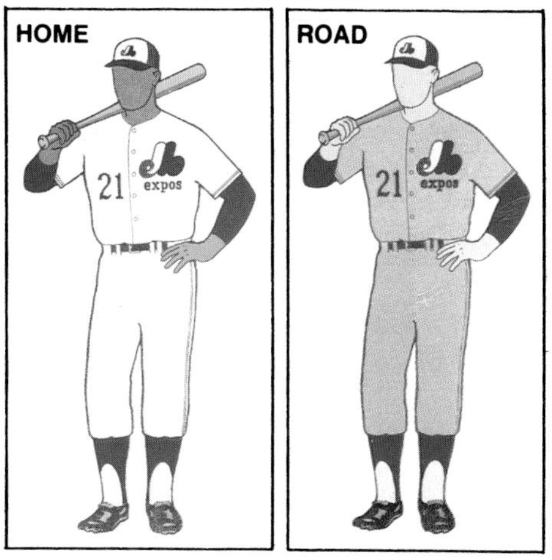

HOUSTON

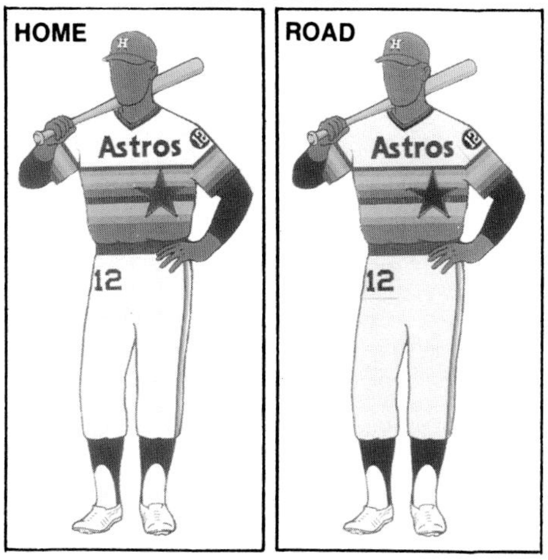

1977 AMERICAN LEAGUE

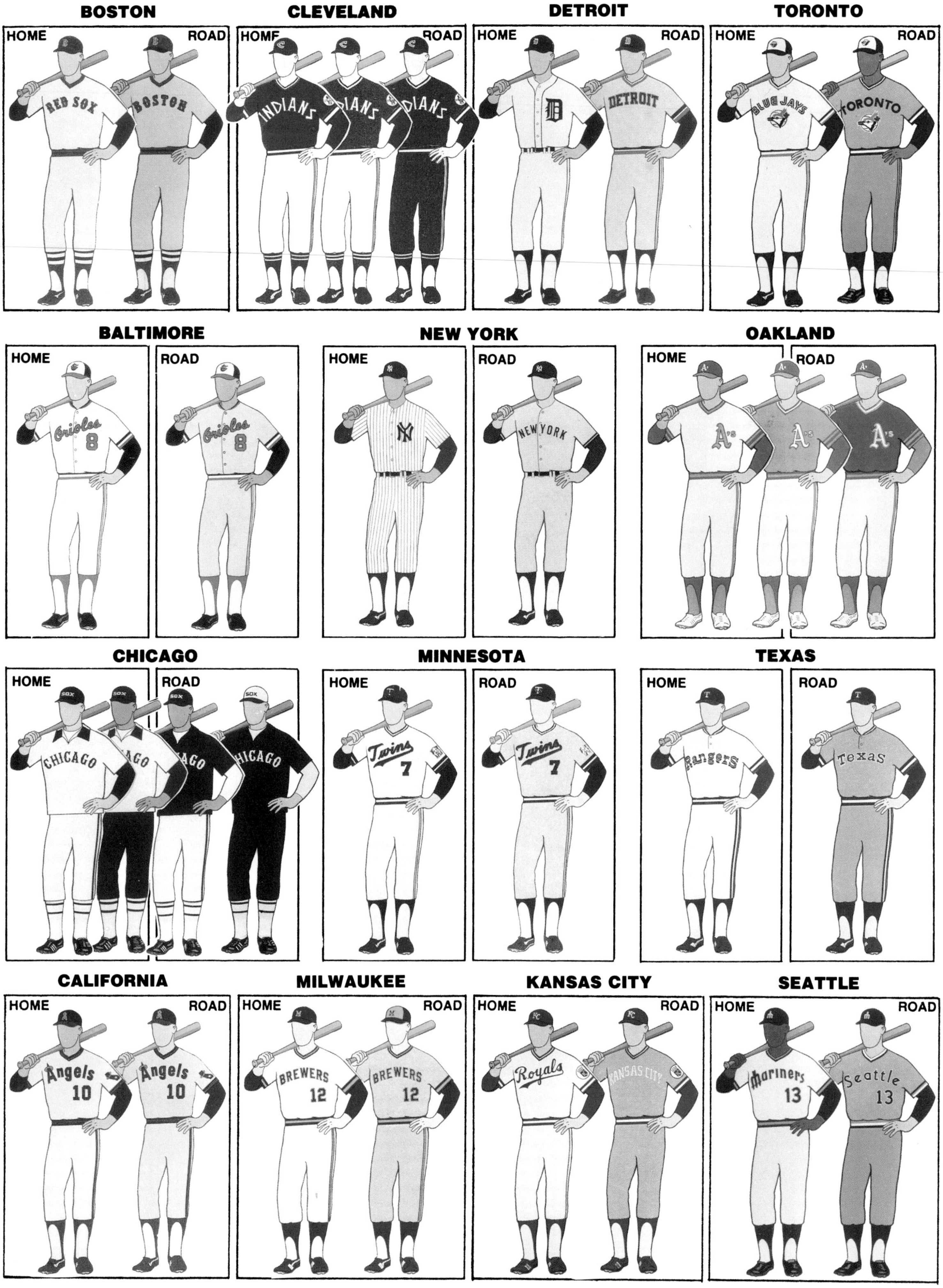

NATIONAL LEAGUE 1977

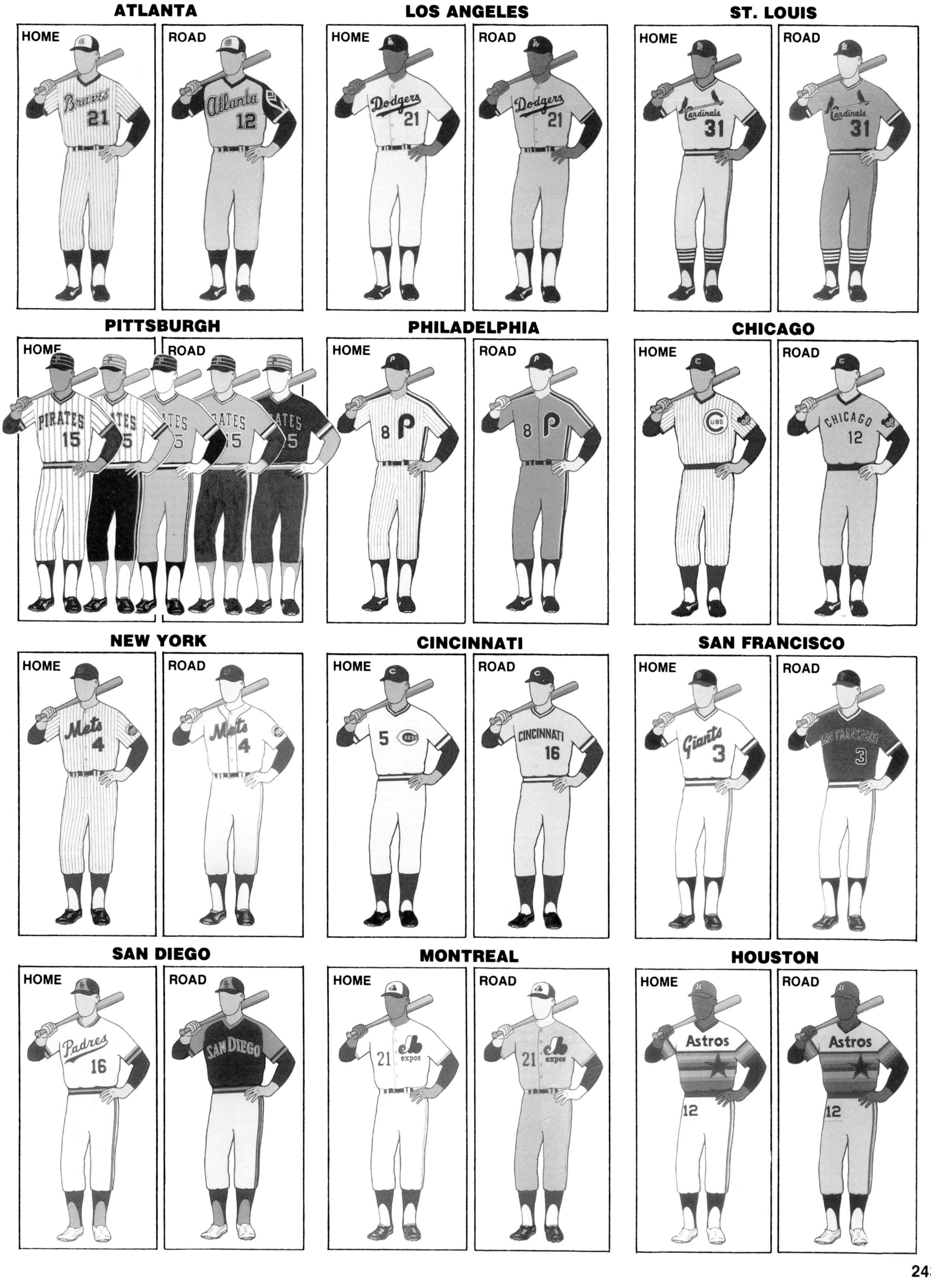

1978 AMERICAN LEAGUE

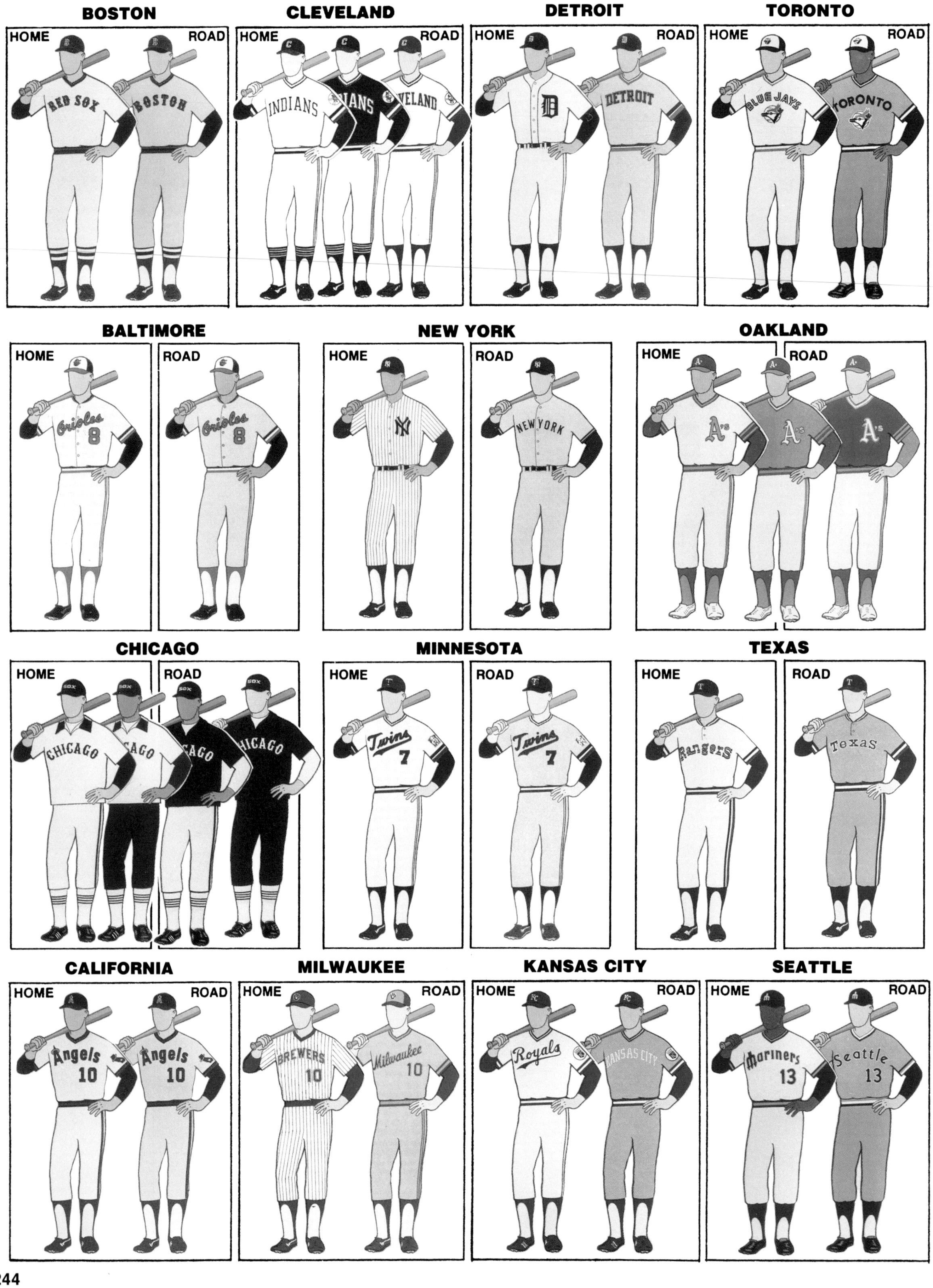

NATIONAL LEAGUE 1978

ATLANTA

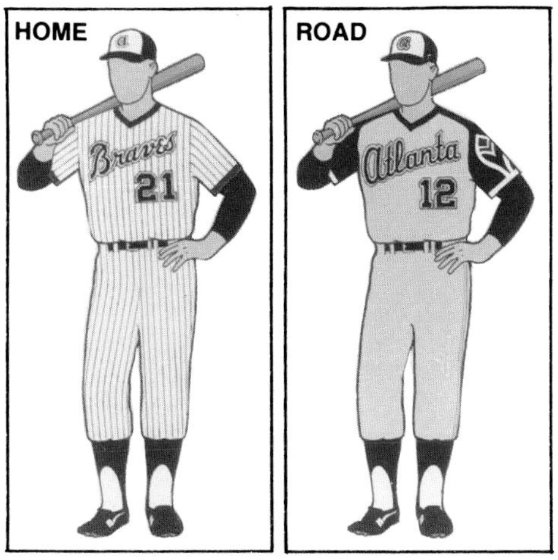

LOS ANGELES

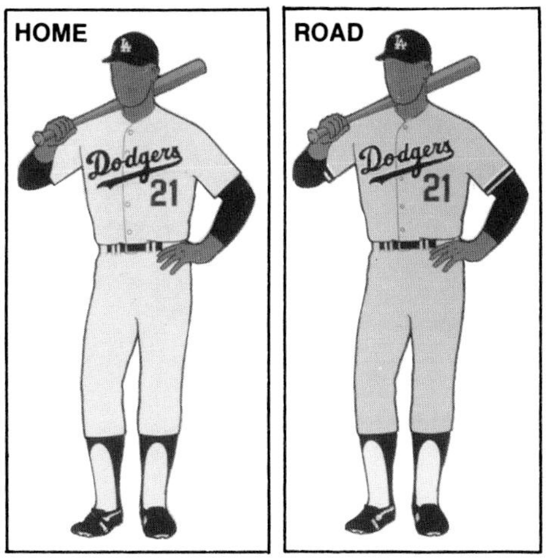

ST. LOUIS

PITTSBURGH

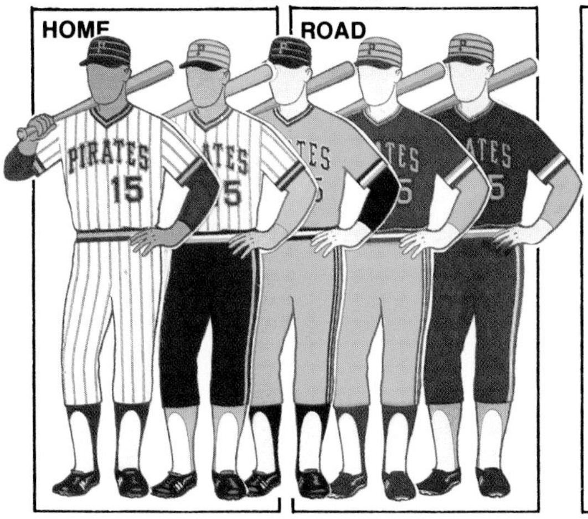

PHILADELPHIA

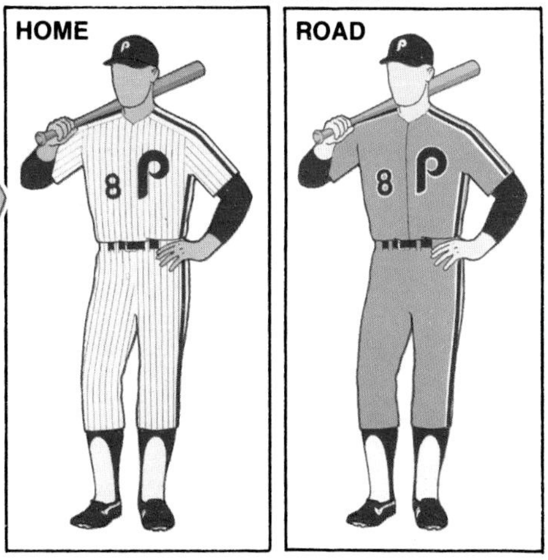

CHICAGO

NEW YORK

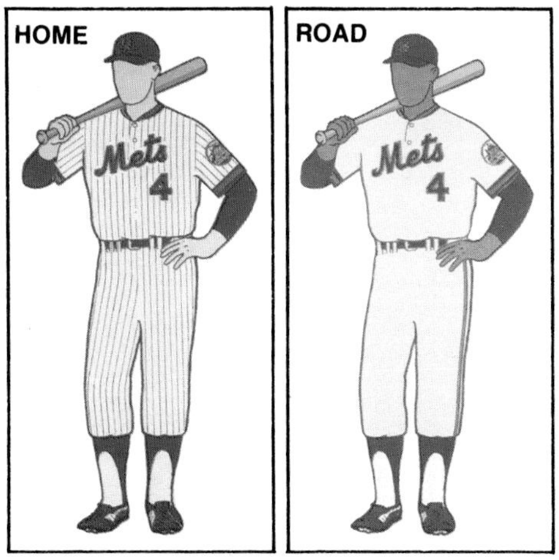

CINCINNATI

SAN FRANCISCO

SAN DIEGO

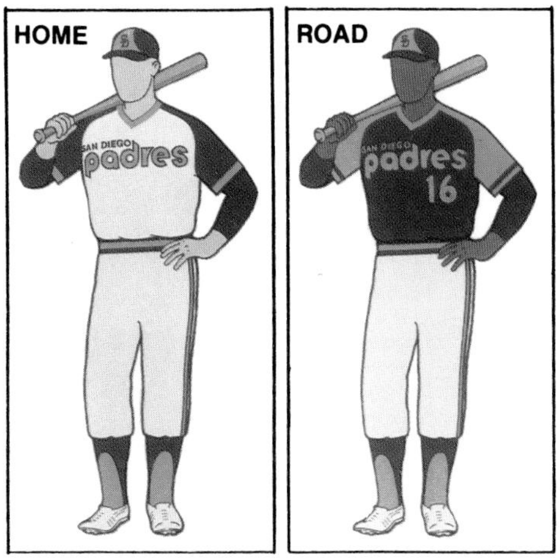

MONTREAL

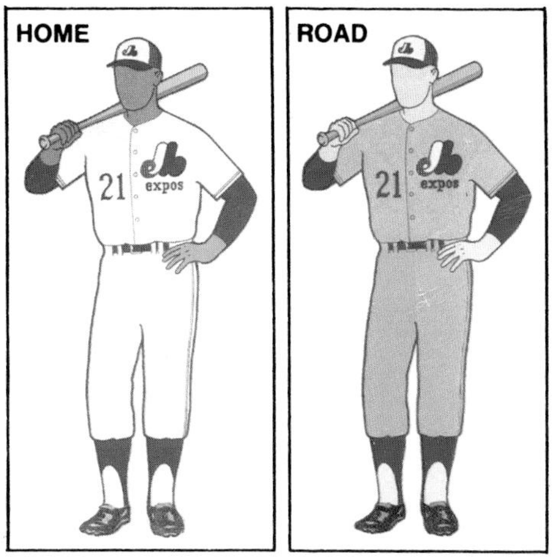

HOUSTON

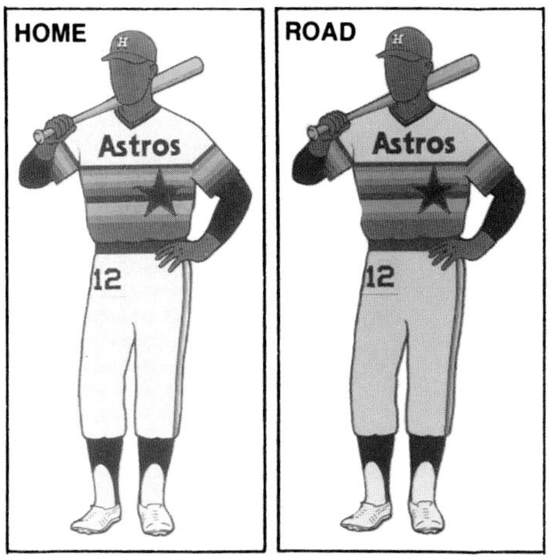

1979 AMERICAN LEAGUE

BOSTON

CLEVELAND

DETROIT

TORONTO

BALTIMORE

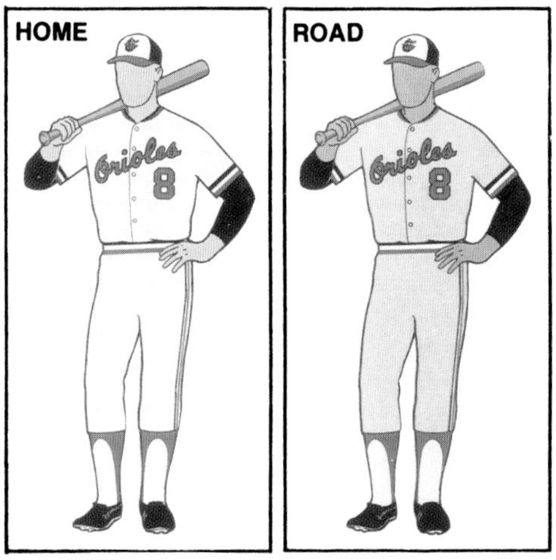

NEW YORK

OAKLAND

CHICAGO

MINNESOTA

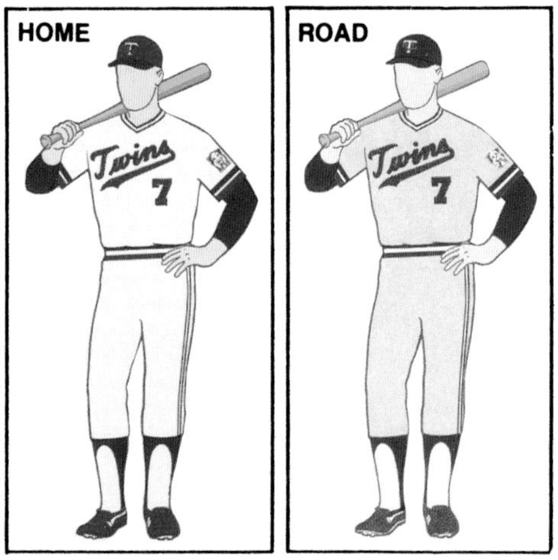

TEXAS

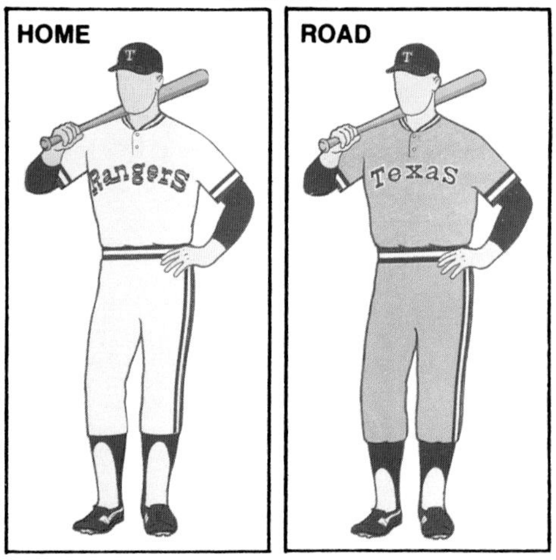

CALIFORNIA

MILWAUKEE

KANSAS CITY

SEATTLE

NATIONAL LEAGUE 1979

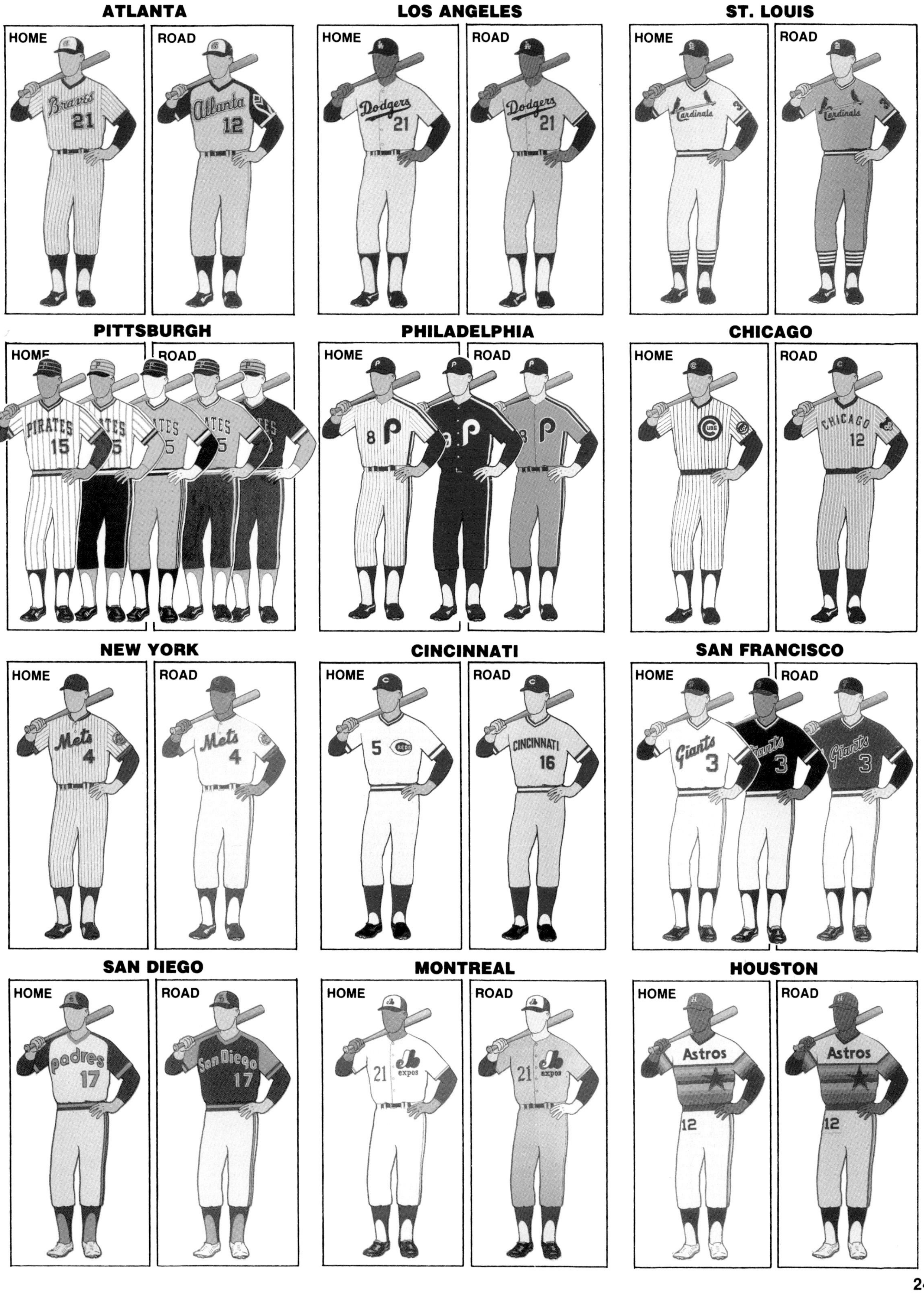

1980 AMERICAN LEAGUE

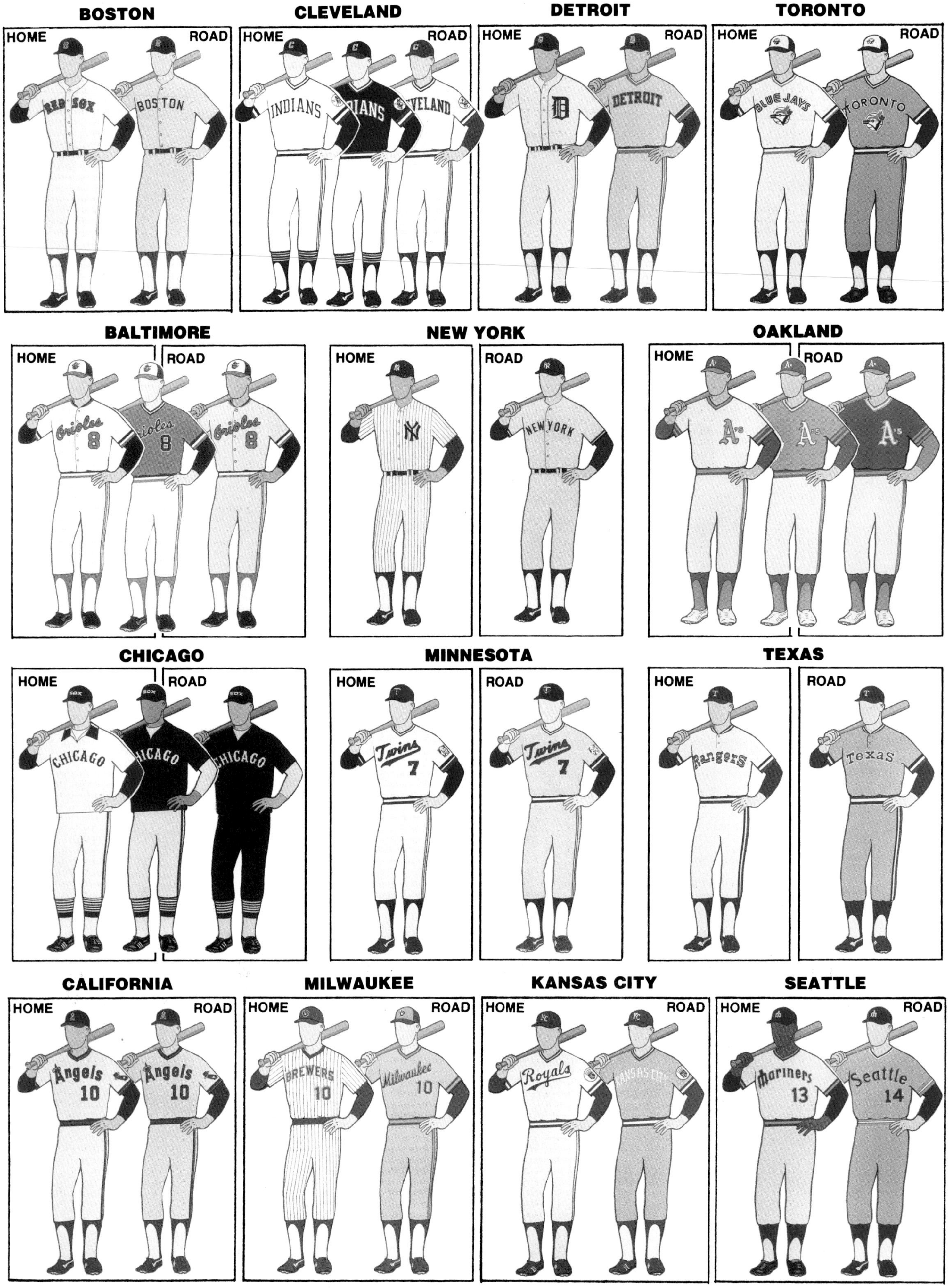

NATIONAL LEAGUE 1980

ATLANTA
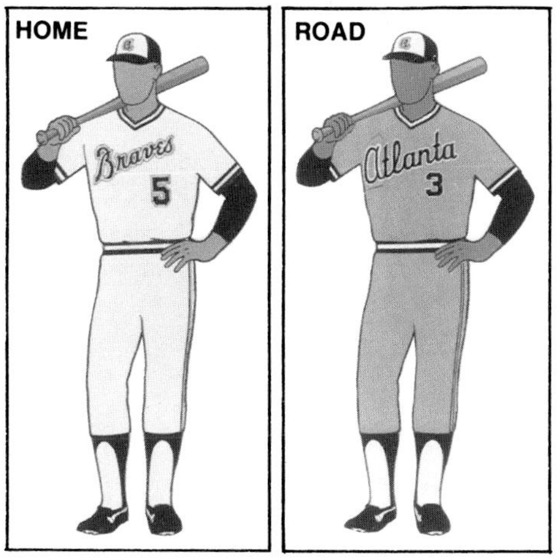

LOS ANGELES
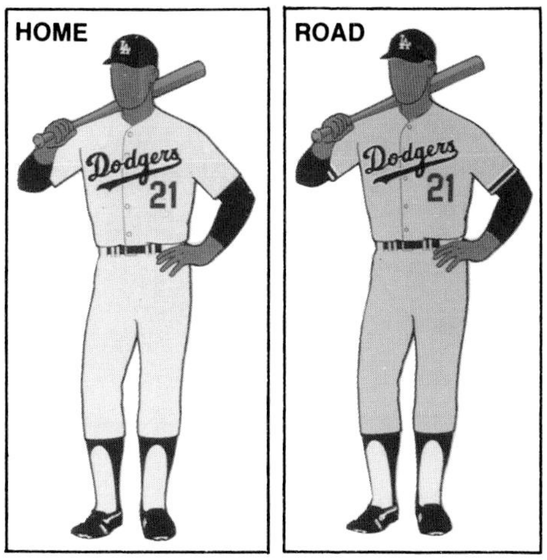

ST. LOUIS
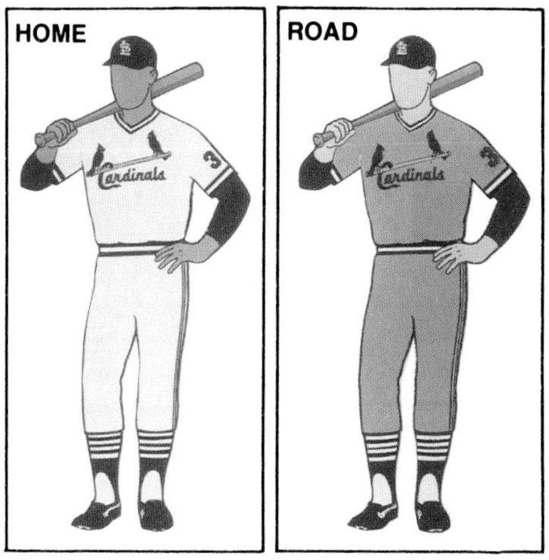

PITTSBURGH

PHILADELPHIA
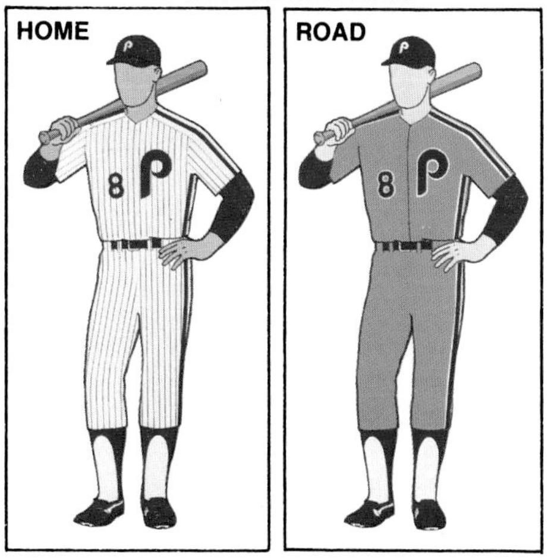

CHICAGO

NEW YORK
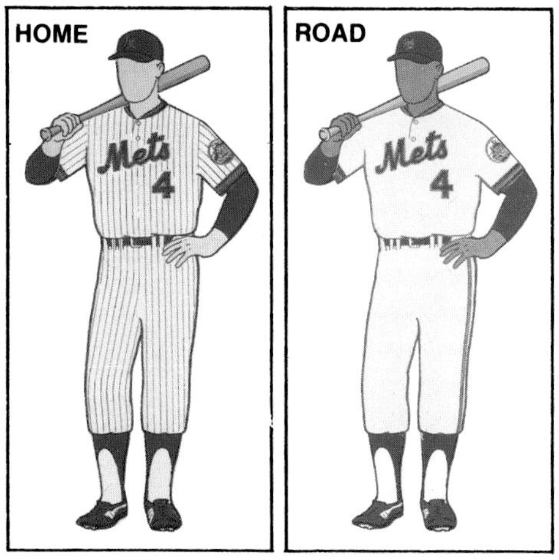

CINCINNATI
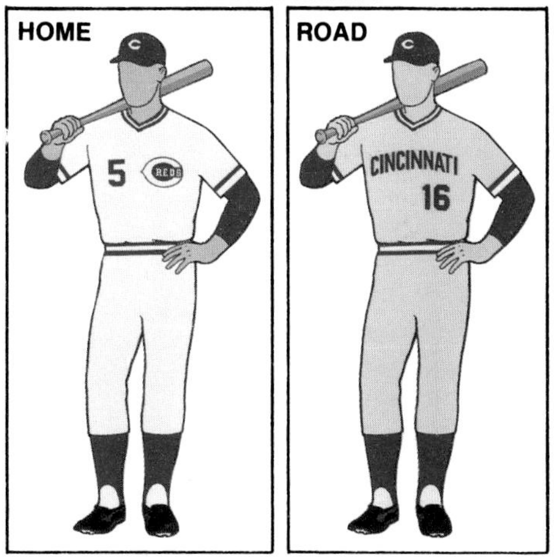

SAN FRANCISCO
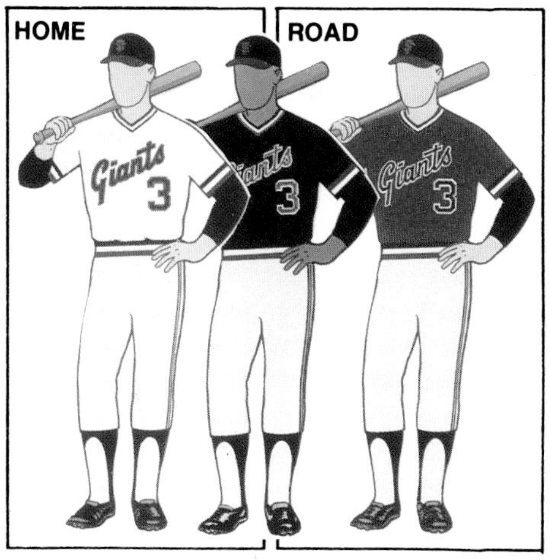

SAN DIEGO
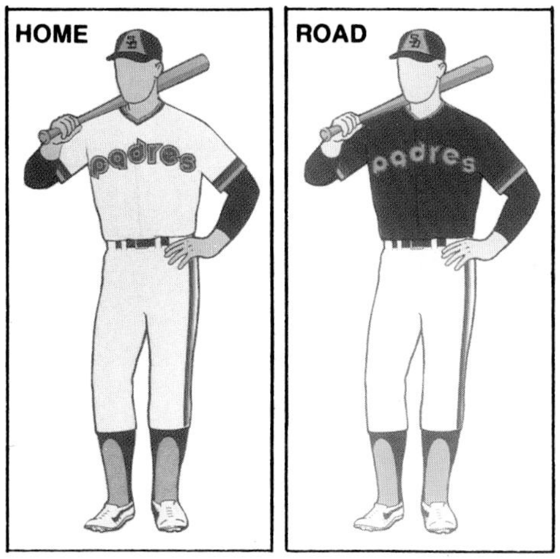

MONTREAL
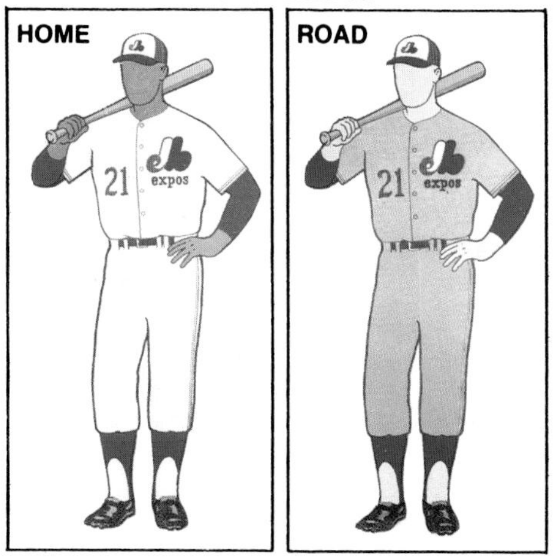

HOUSTON
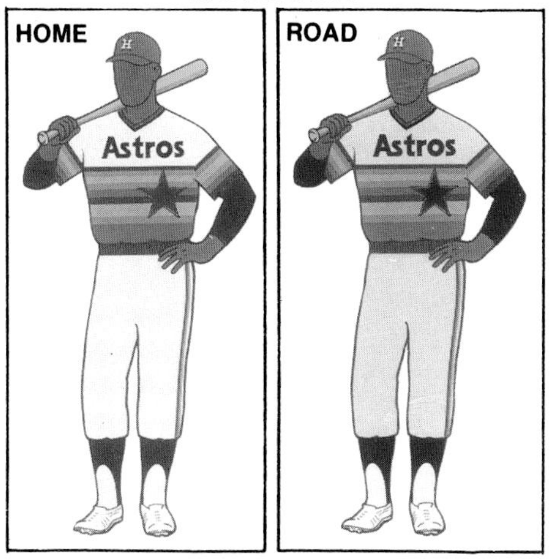

1981 AMERICAN LEAGUE

BOSTON

CLEVELAND

DETROIT

TORONTO

BALTIMORE

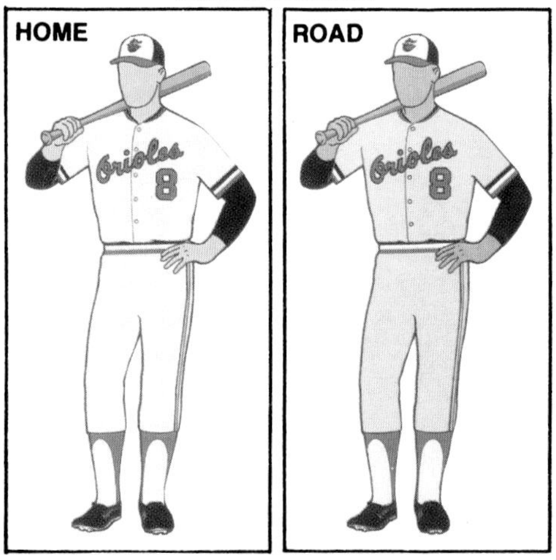

NEW YORK

OAKLAND

CHICAGO

MINNESOTA

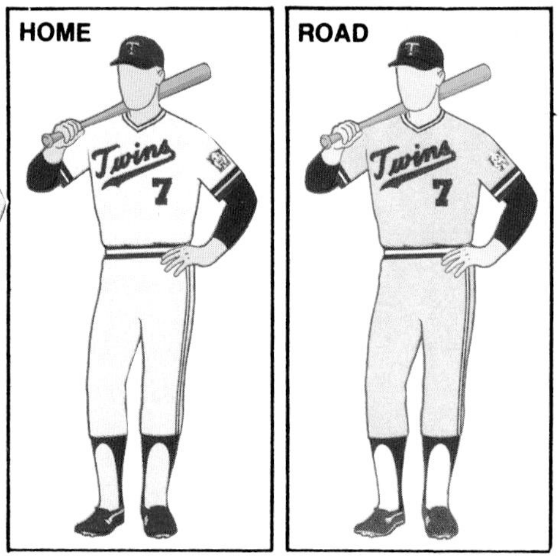

TEXAS

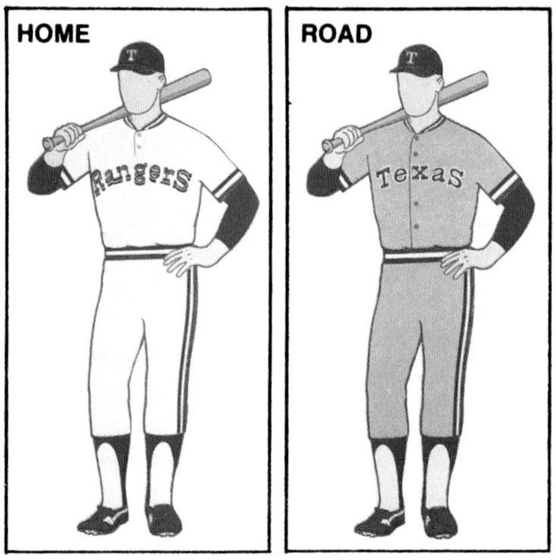

CALIFORNIA

MILWAUKEE

KANSAS CITY

SEATTLE

NATIONAL LEAGUE 1981

ATLANTA

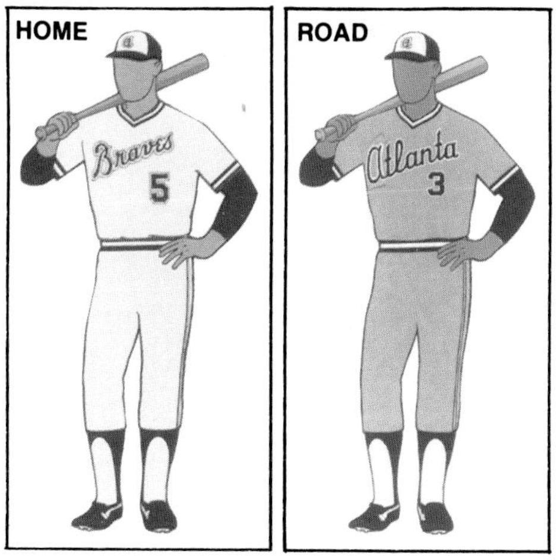

LOS ANGELES

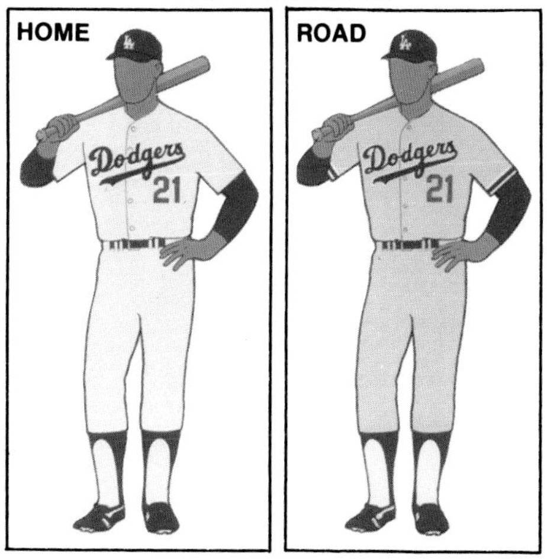

ST. LOUIS

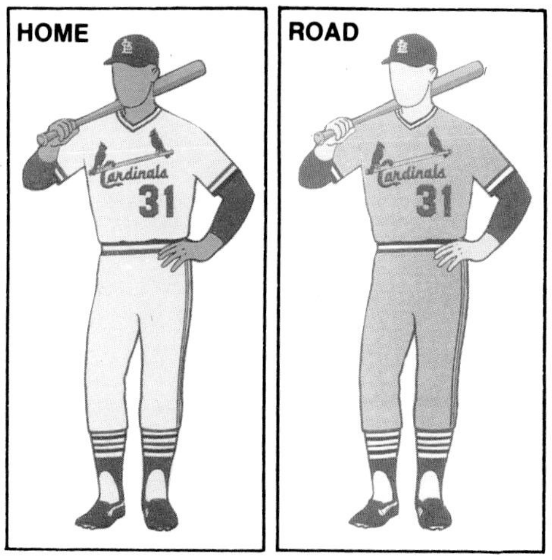

PITTSBURGH

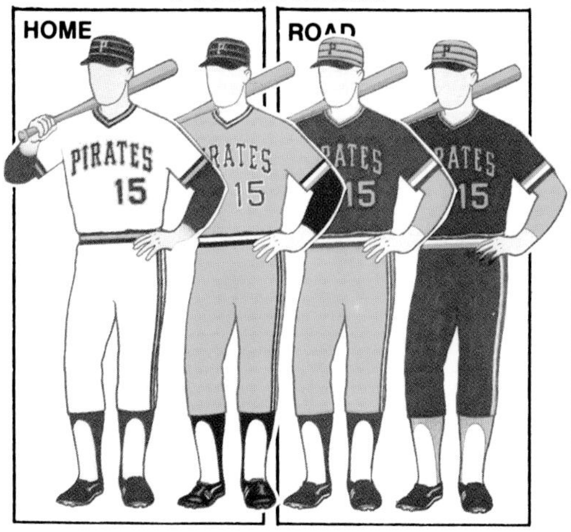

PHILADELPHIA

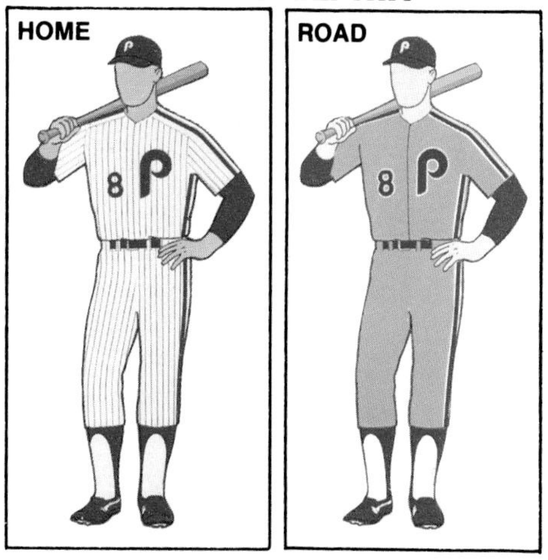

CHICAGO

NEW YORK

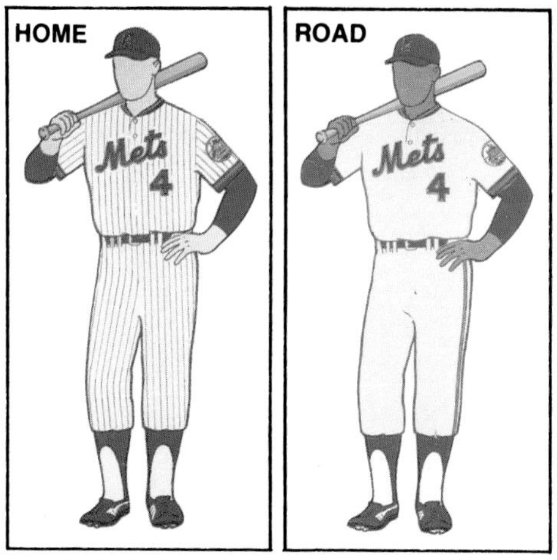

CINCINNATI

SAN FRANCISCO

SAN DIEGO

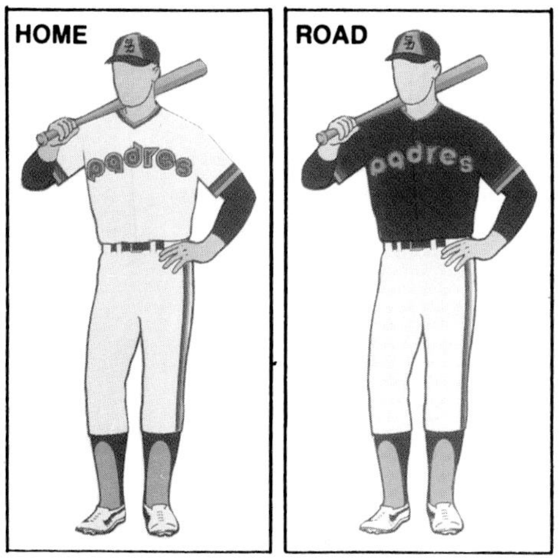

MONTREAL

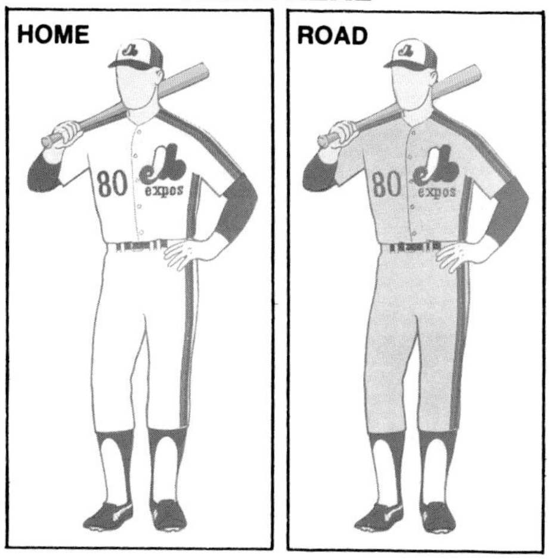

HOUSTON

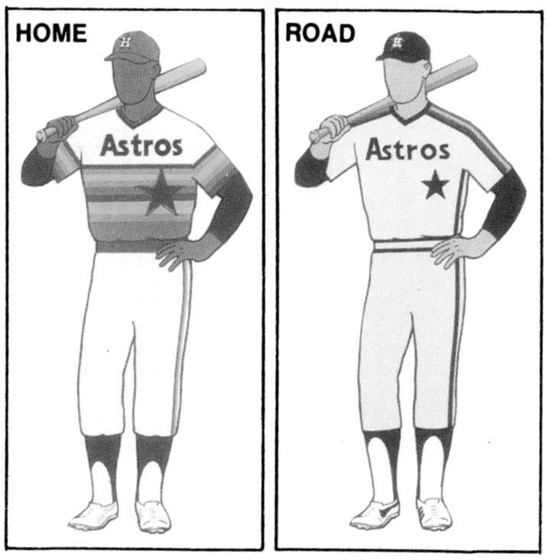

1982 AMERICAN LEAGUE

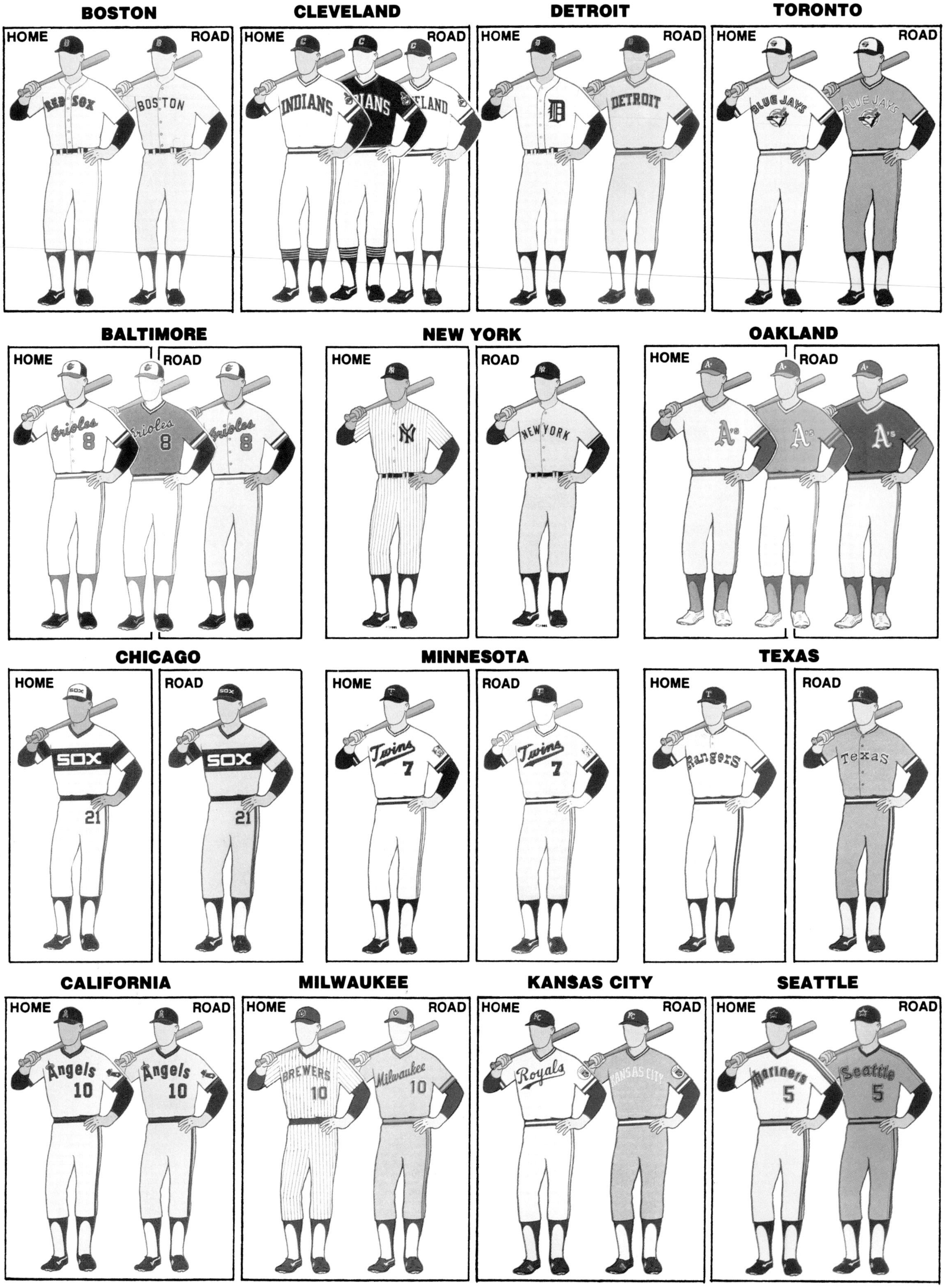

NATIONAL LEAGUE 1982

ATLANTA

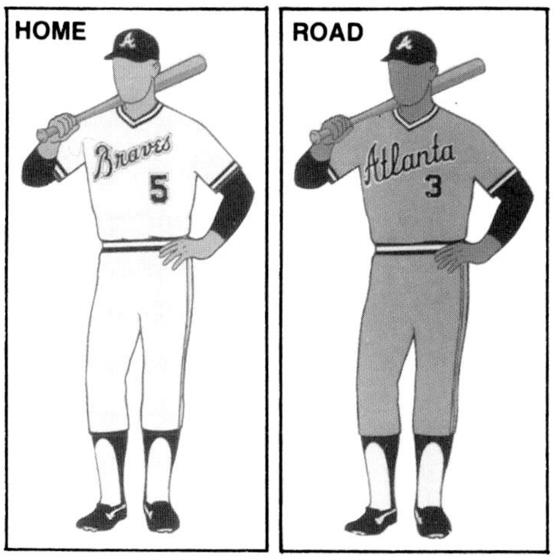

LOS ANGELES

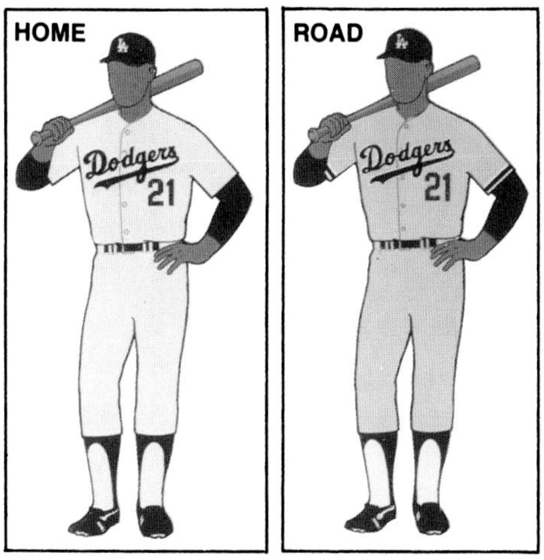

ST. LOUIS

PITTSBURGH

PHILADELPHIA

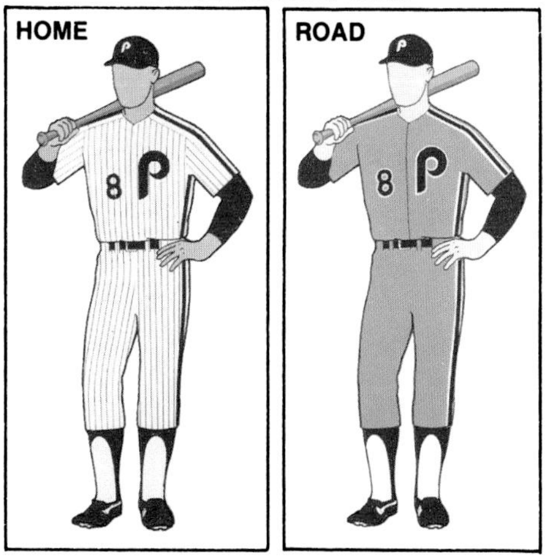

CHICAGO

NEW YORK

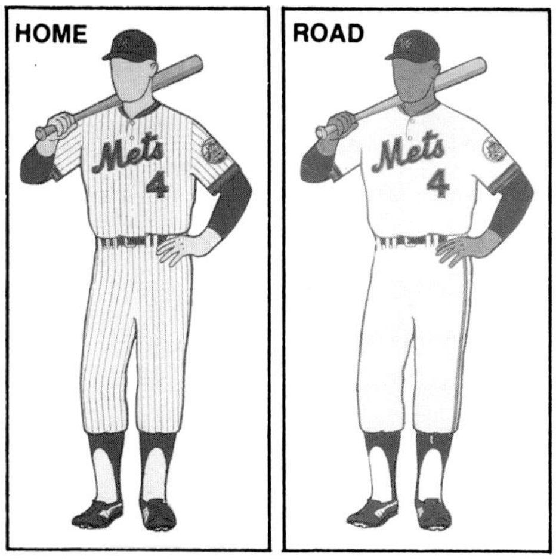

CINCINNATI

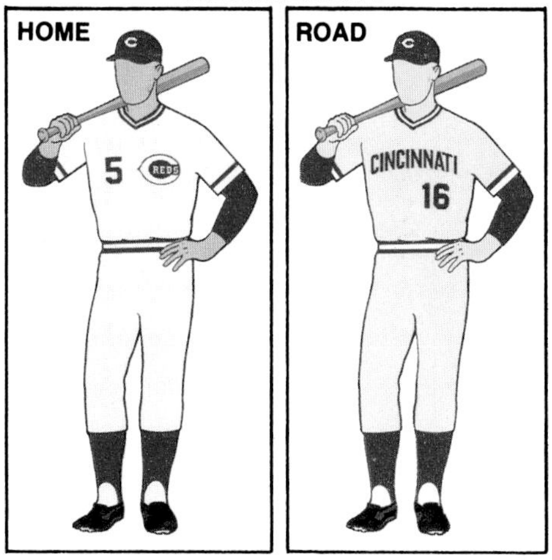

SAN FRANCISCO

SAN DIEGO

MONTREAL

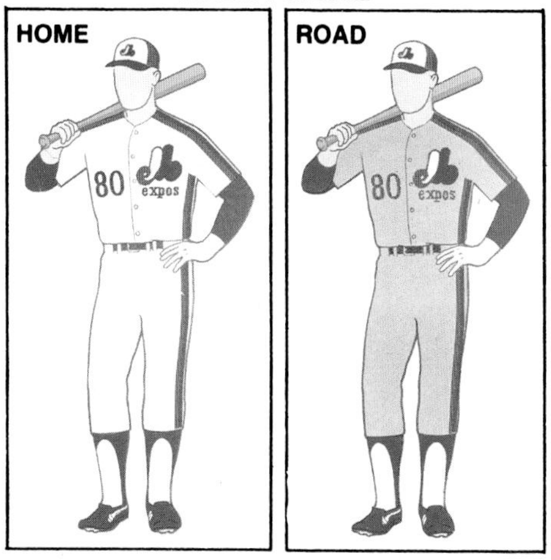

HOUSTON

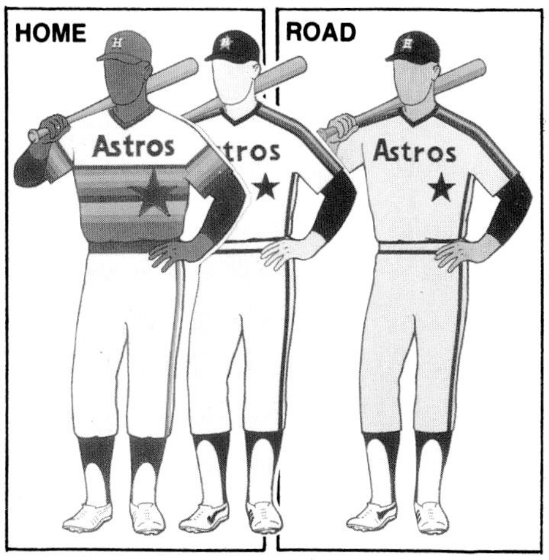

1983 AMERICAN LEAGUE

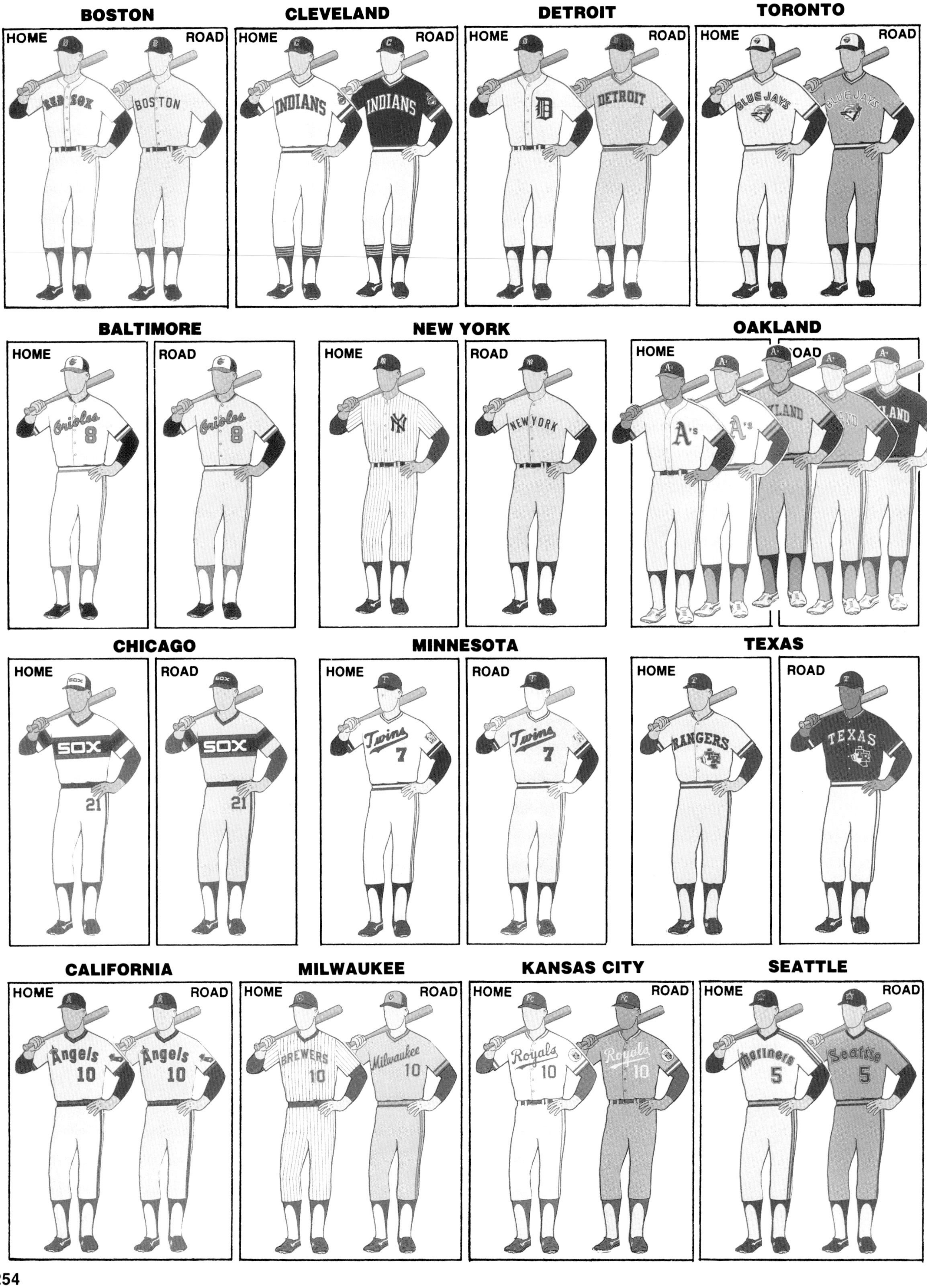

NATIONAL LEAGUE 1983

ATLANTA
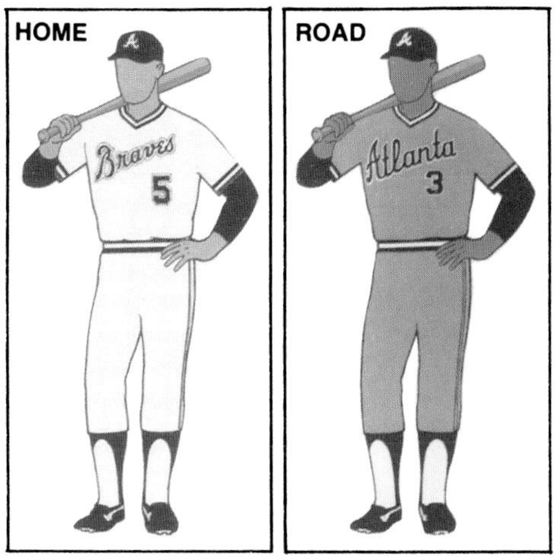

LOS ANGELES
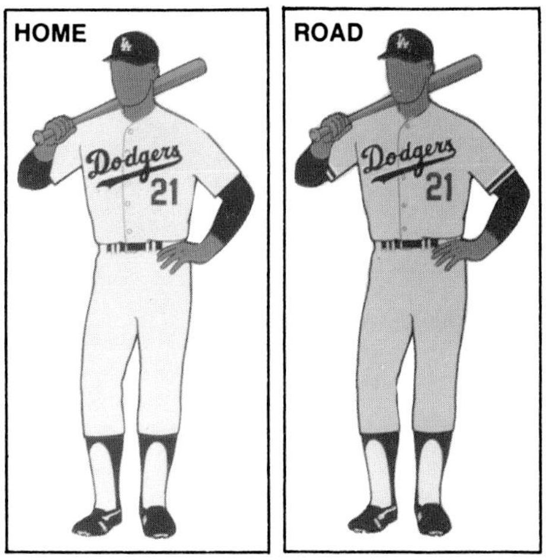

ST. LOUIS

PITTSBURGH
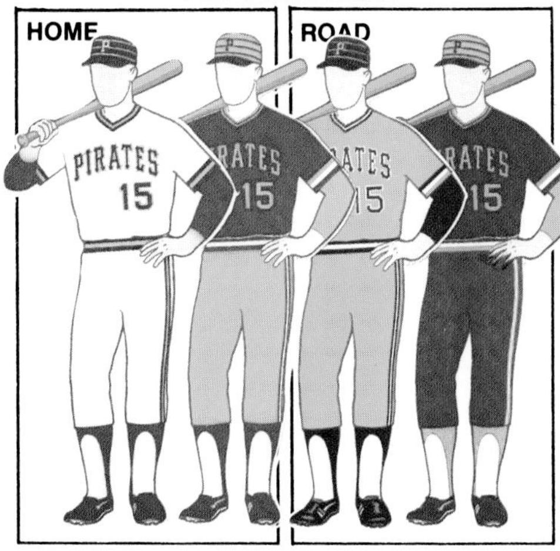

PHILADELPHIA
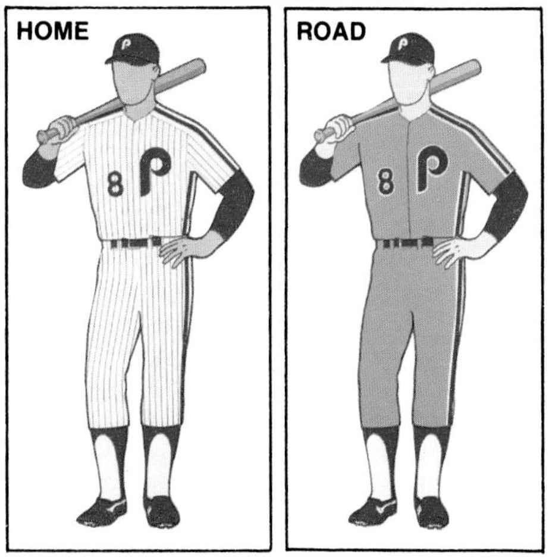

CHICAGO

NEW YORK

CINCINNATI

SAN FRANCISCO

SAN DIEGO
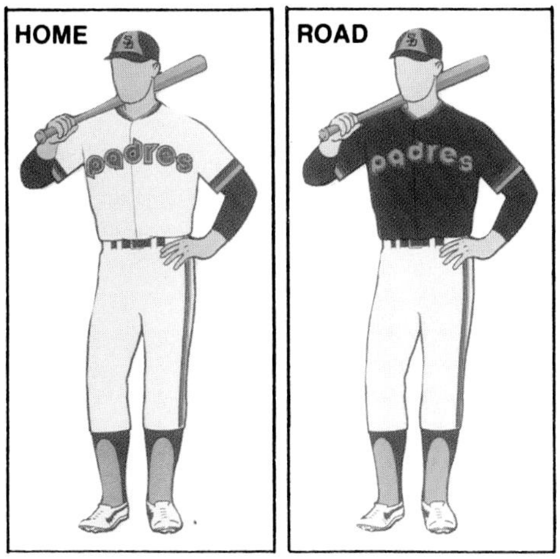

MONTREAL
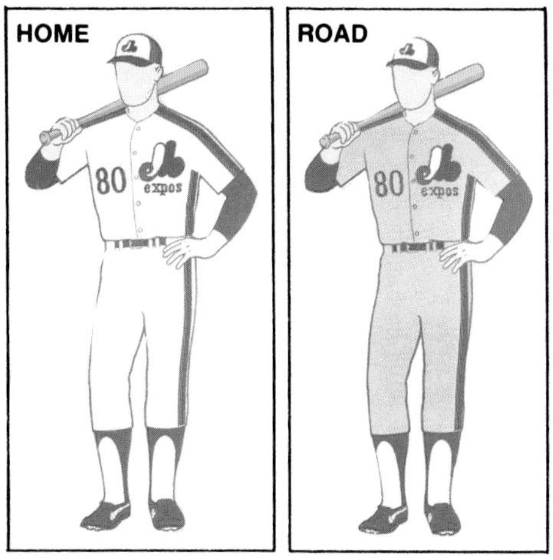

HOUSTON
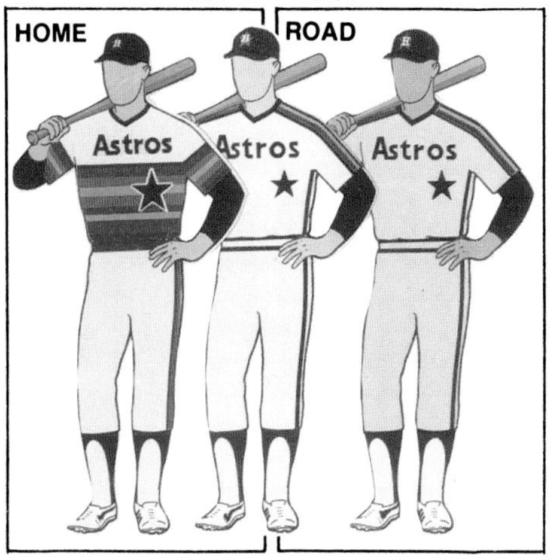

1984 AMERICAN LEAGUE

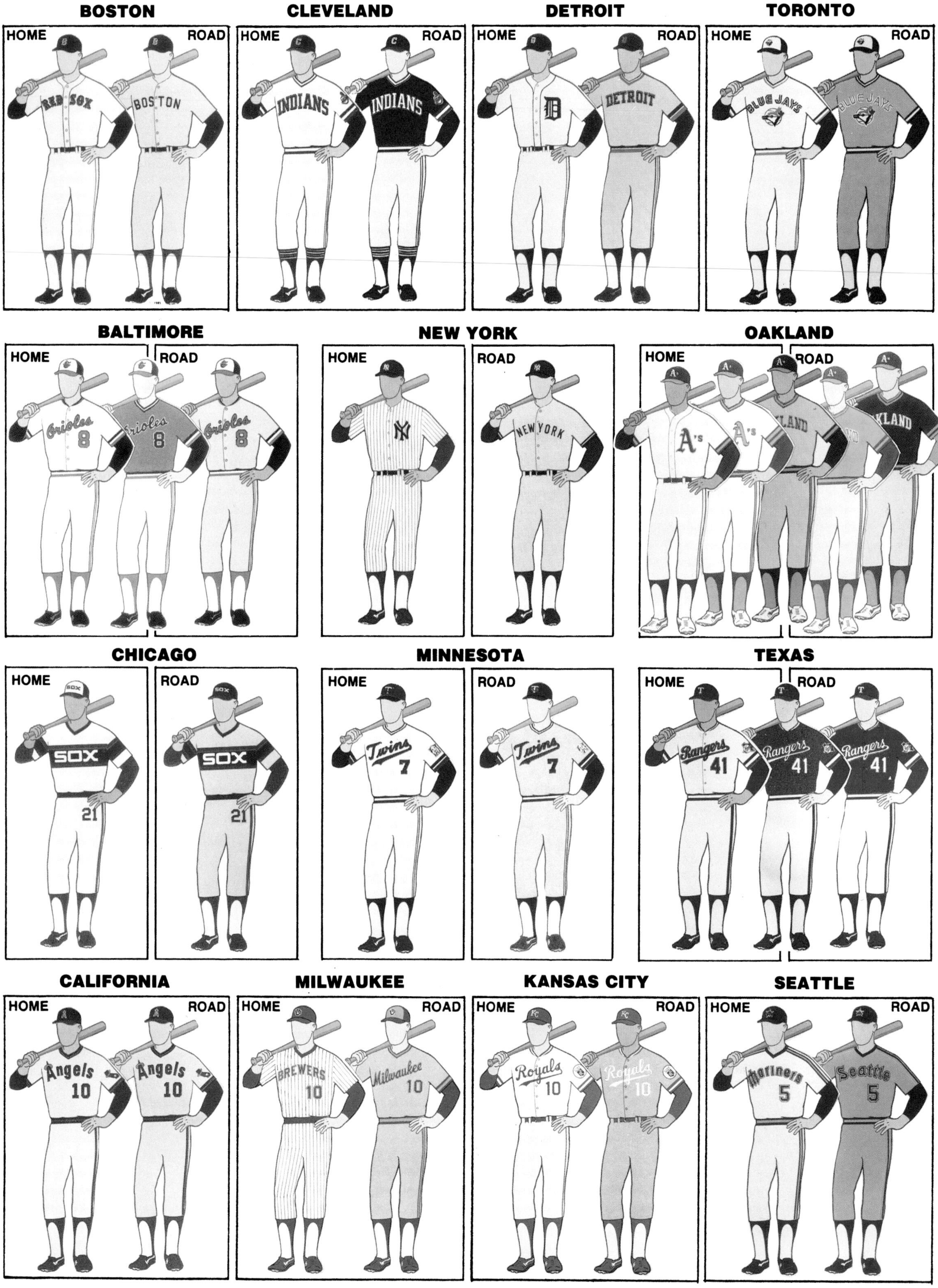

NATIONAL LEAGUE 1984

ATLANTA

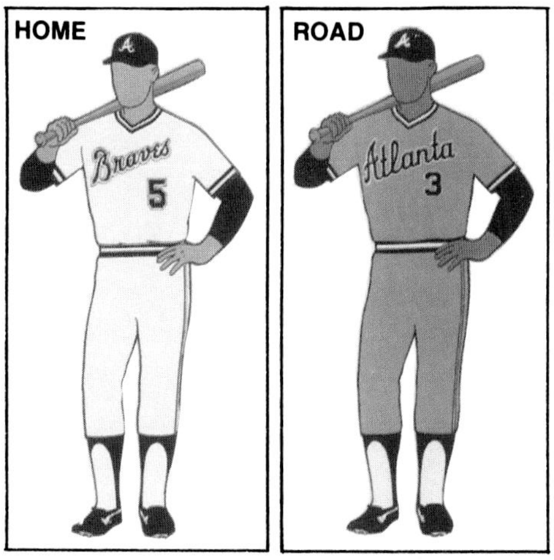

LOS ANGELES

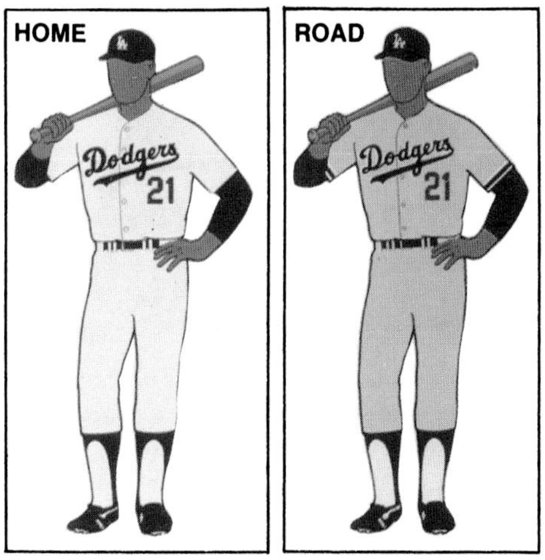

ST. LOUIS

PITTSBURGH

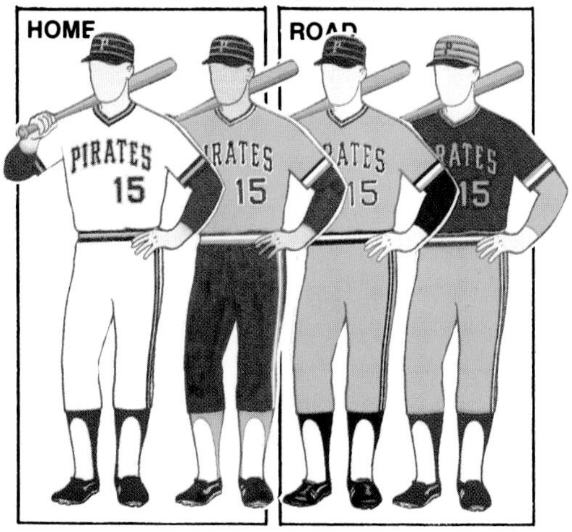

PHILADELPHIA

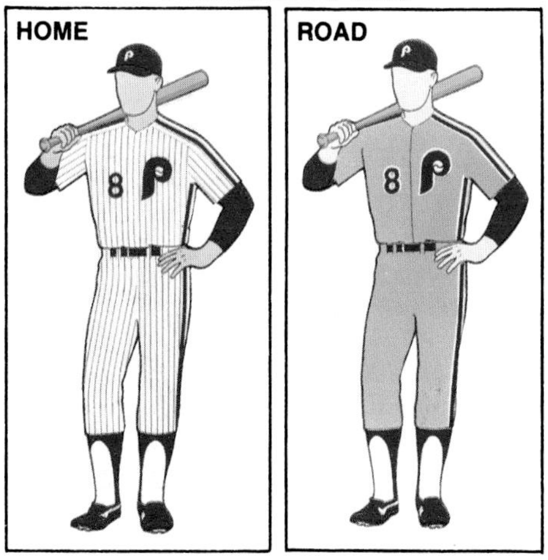

CHICAGO

NEW YORK

CINCINNATI

SAN FRANCISCO

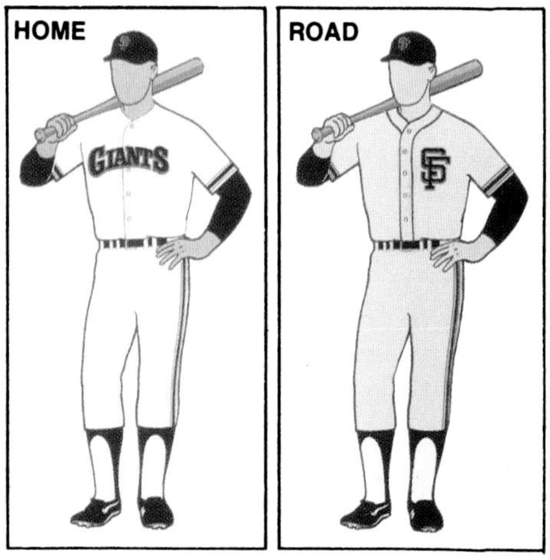

SAN DIEGO

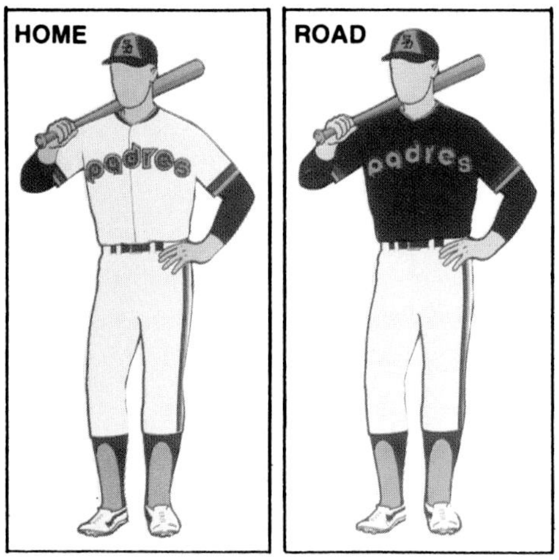

MONTREAL

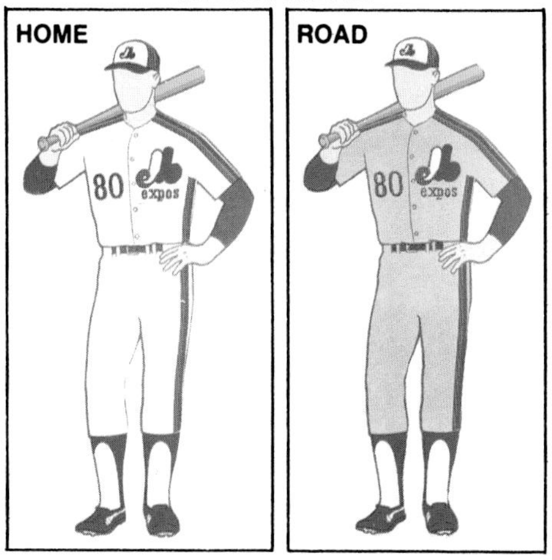

HOUSTON

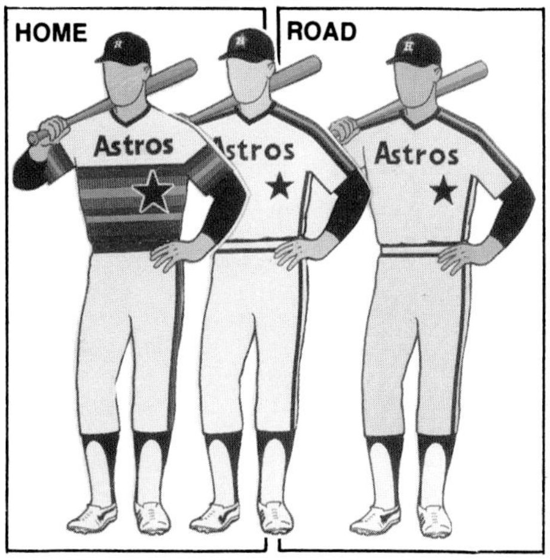

1985 AMERICAN LEAGUE

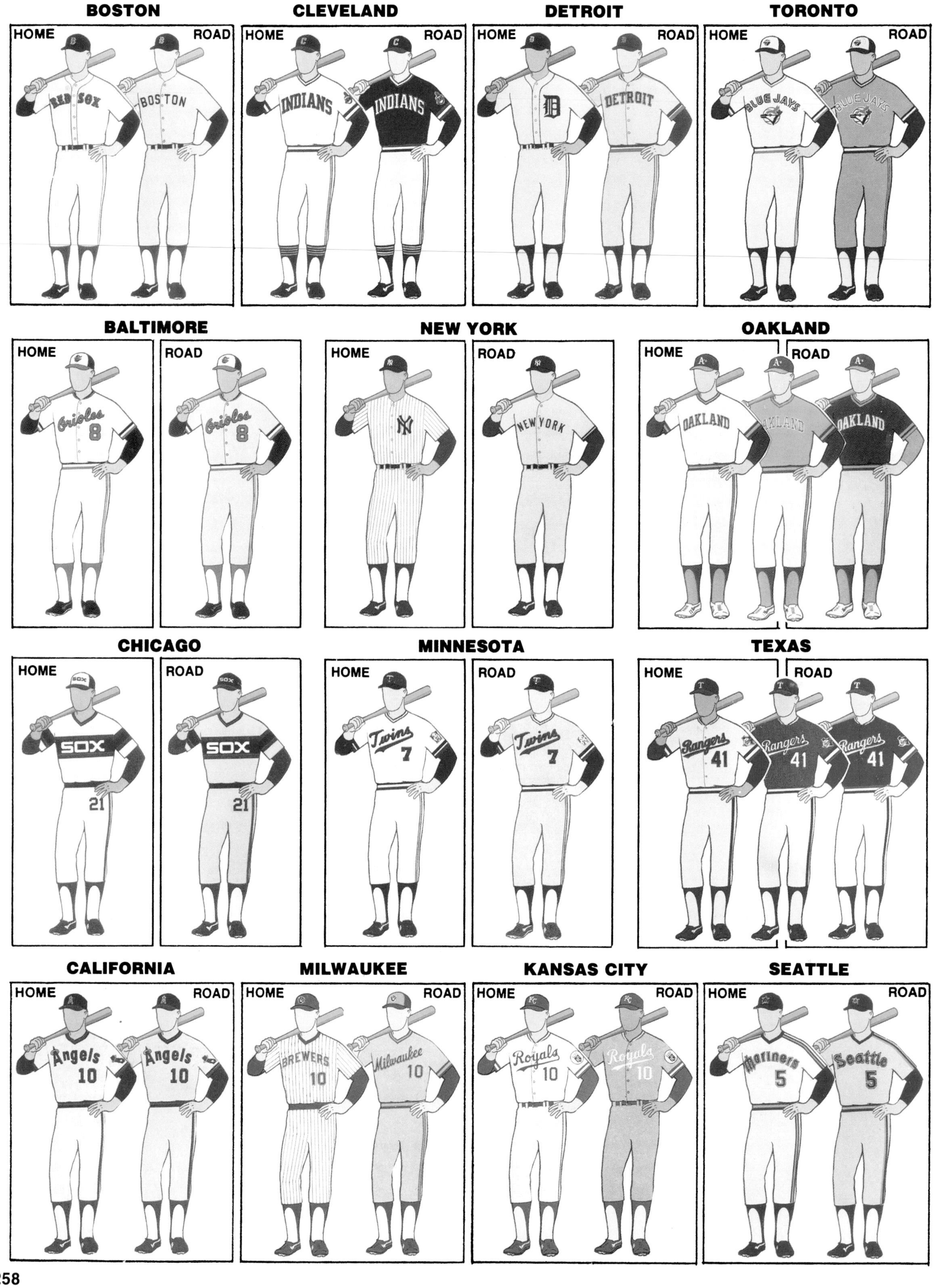

NATIONAL LEAGUE 1985

ATLANTA

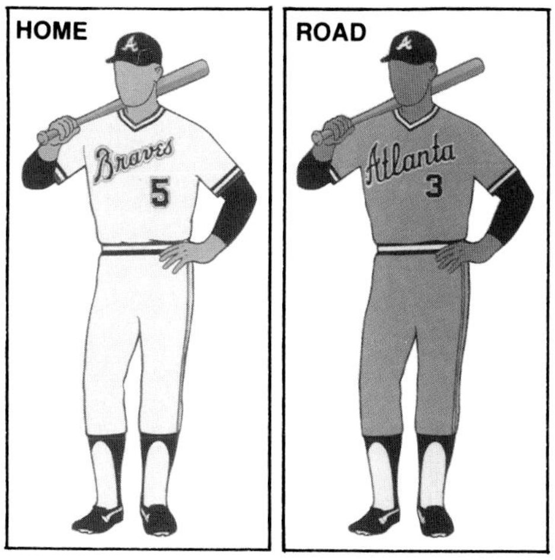

LOS ANGELES

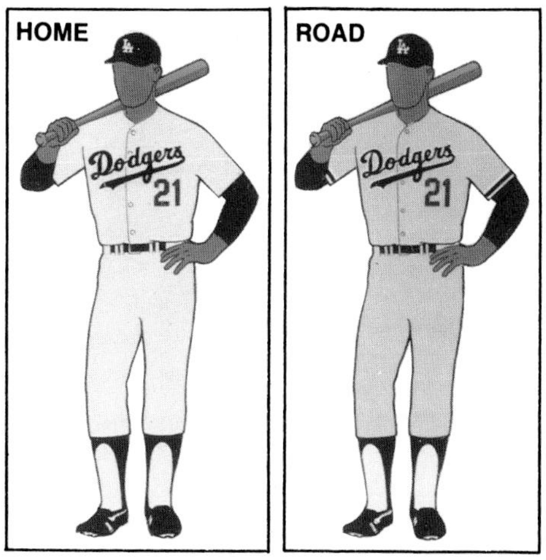

ST. LOUIS

PITTSBURGH

PHILADELPHIA

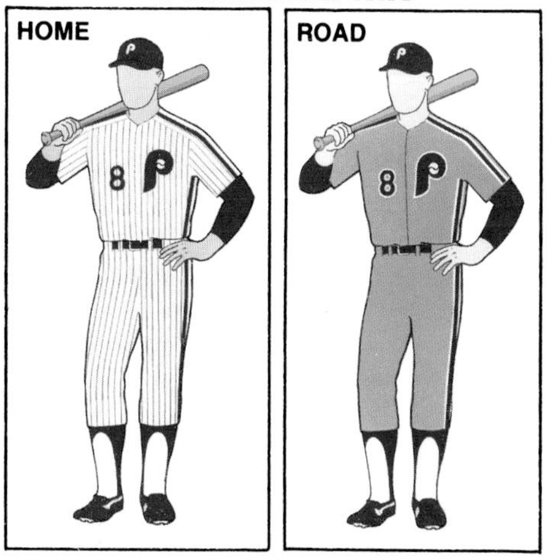

CHICAGO

NEW YORK

CINCINNATI

SAN FRANCISCO

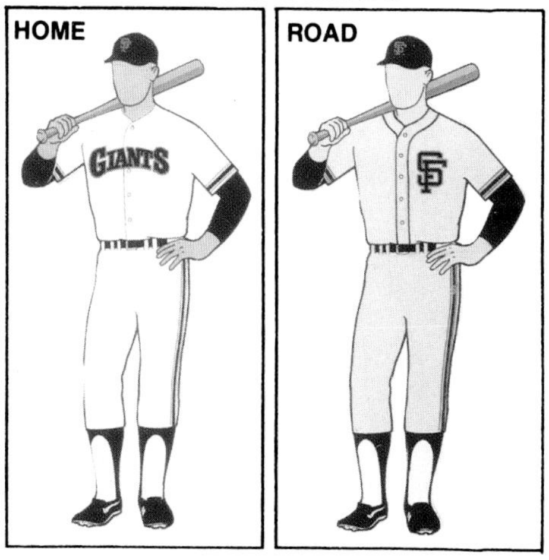

SAN DIEGO

MONTREAL

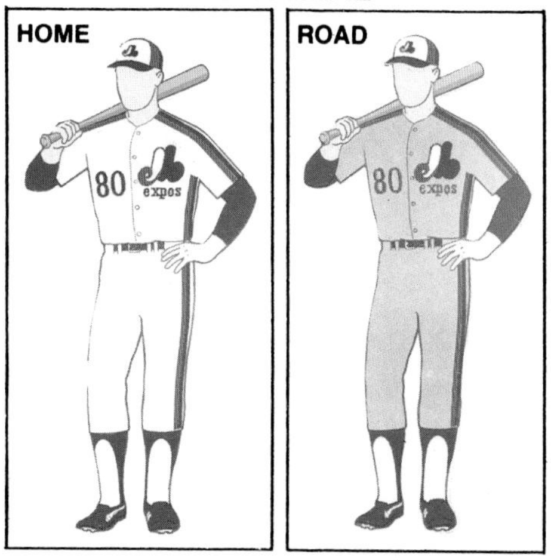

HOUSTON

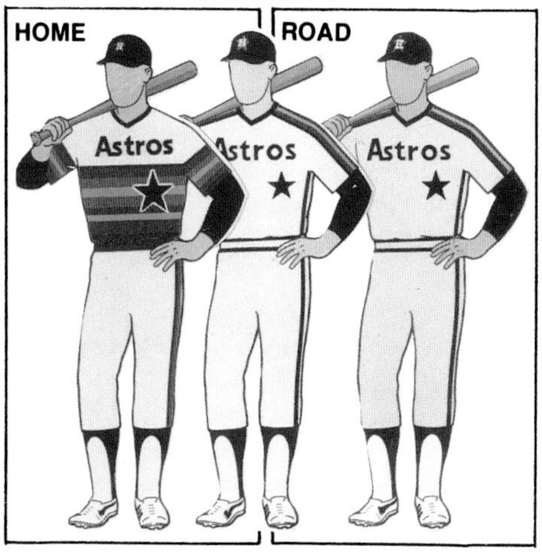

1986 AMERICAN LEAGUE

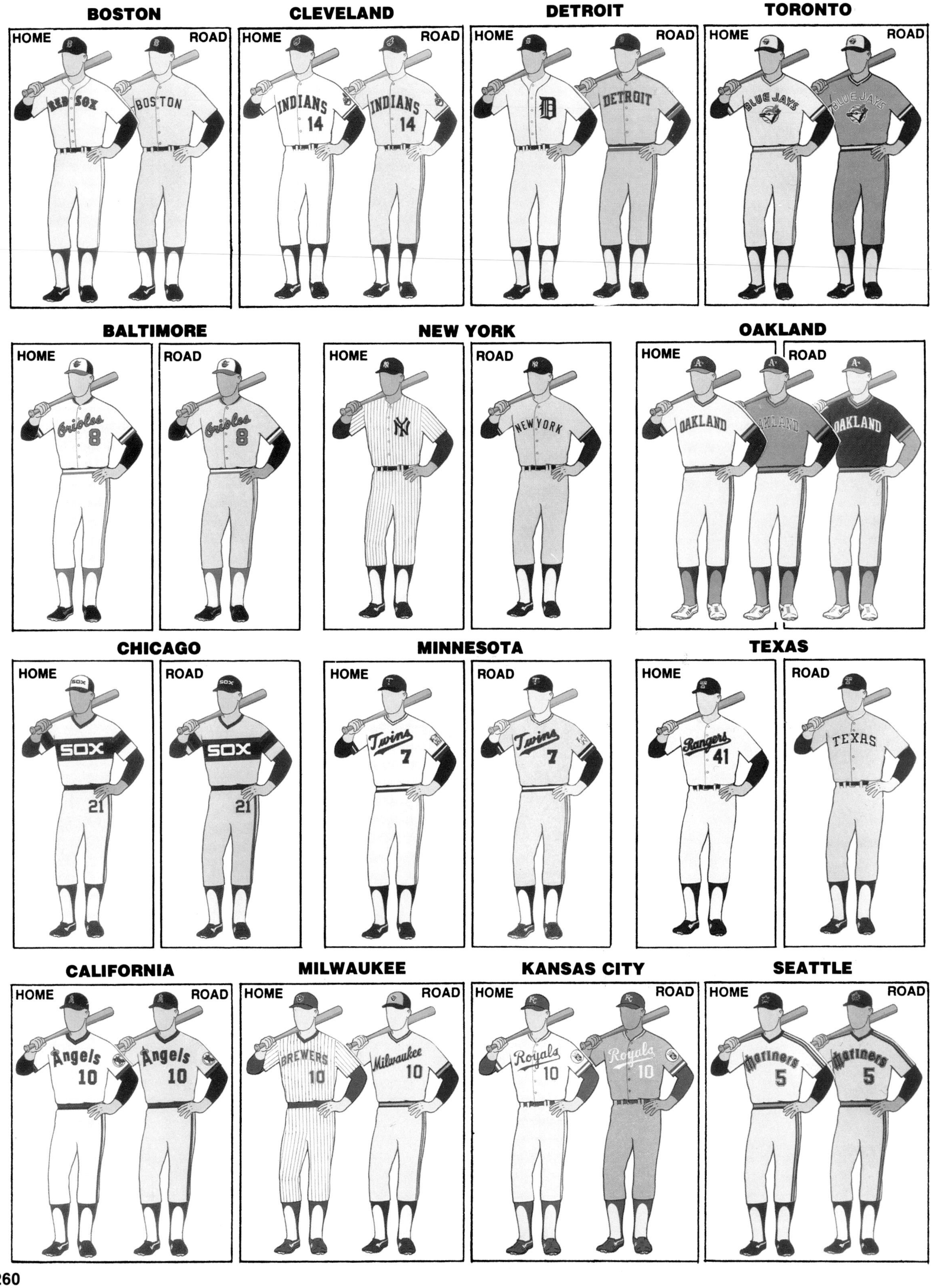

NATIONAL LEAGUE 1986

ATLANTA

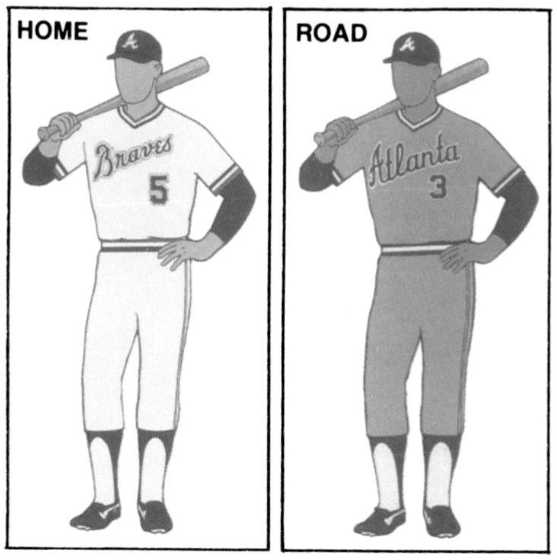

LOS ANGELES

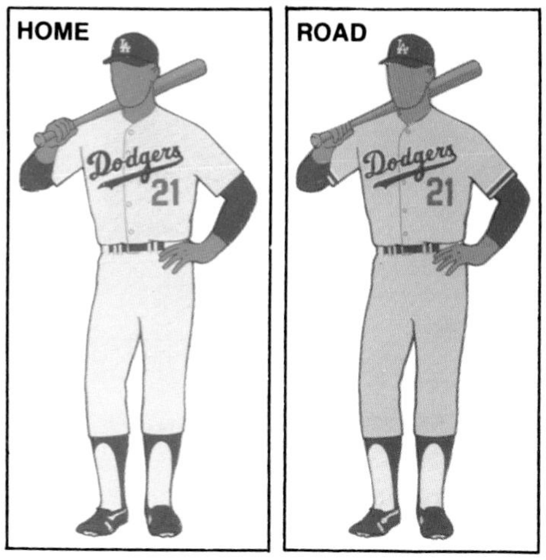

ST. LOUIS

PITTSBURGH

PHILADELPHIA

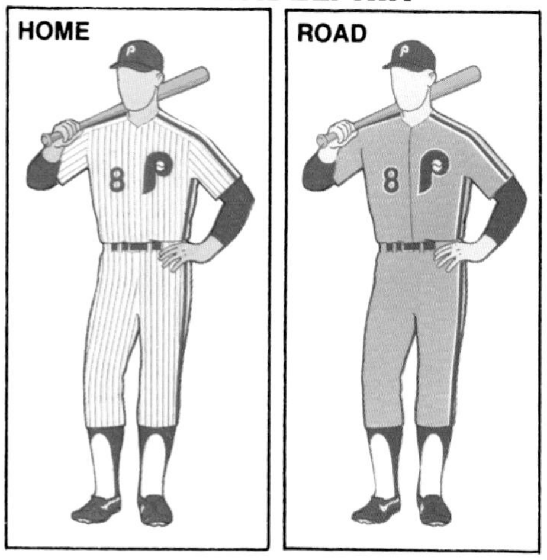

CHICAGO

NEW YORK

CINCINNATI

SAN FRANCISCO

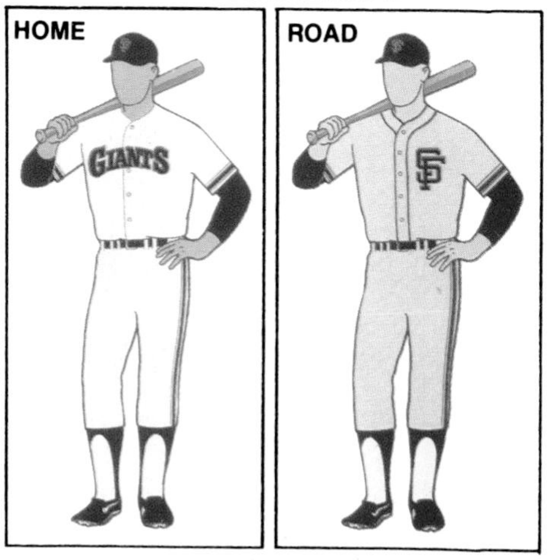

SAN DIEGO

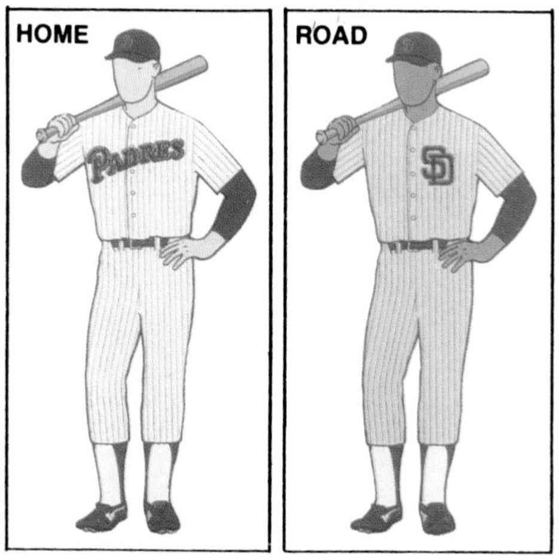

MONTREAL

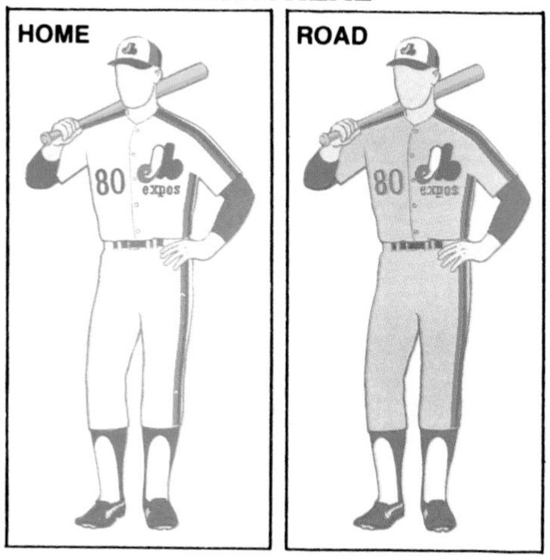

HOUSTON

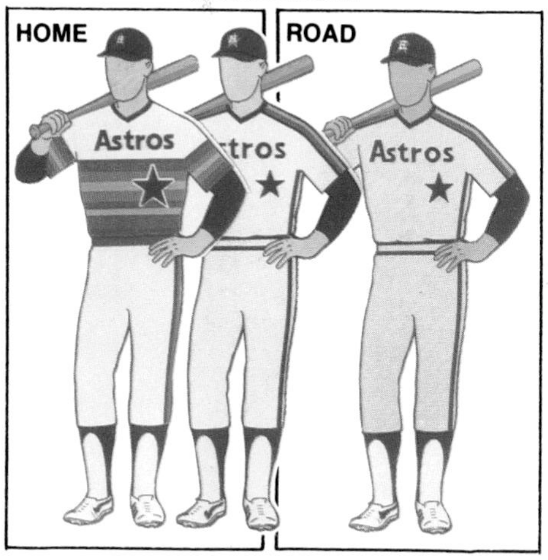

1987 AMERICAN LEAGUE

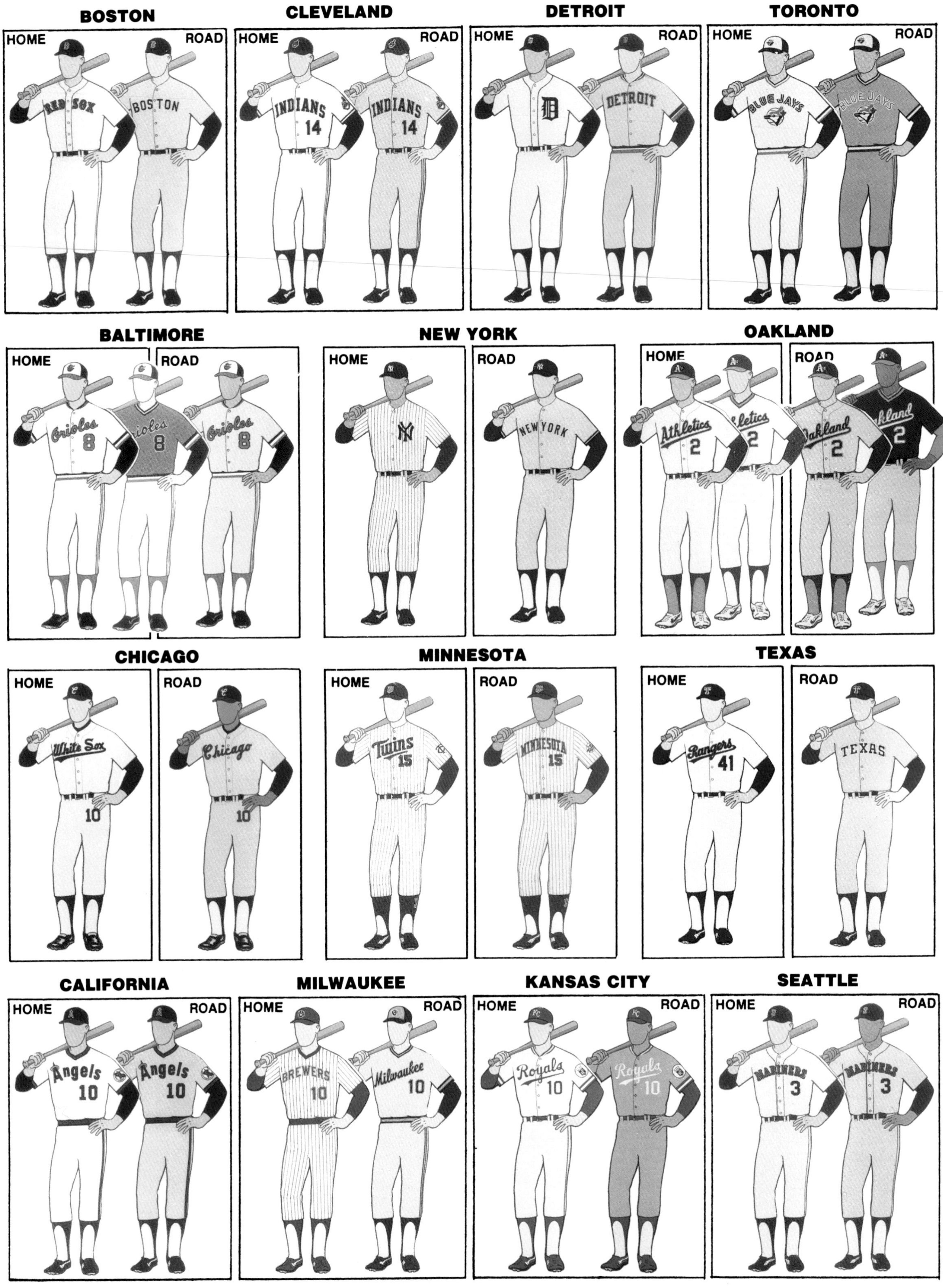

NATIONAL LEAGUE 1987

ATLANTA

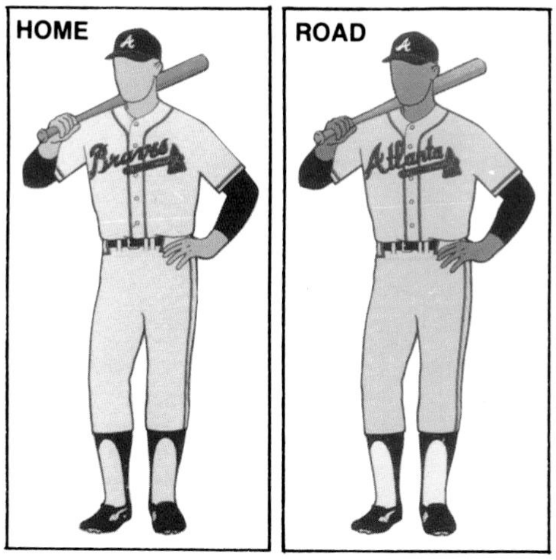

LOS ANGELES

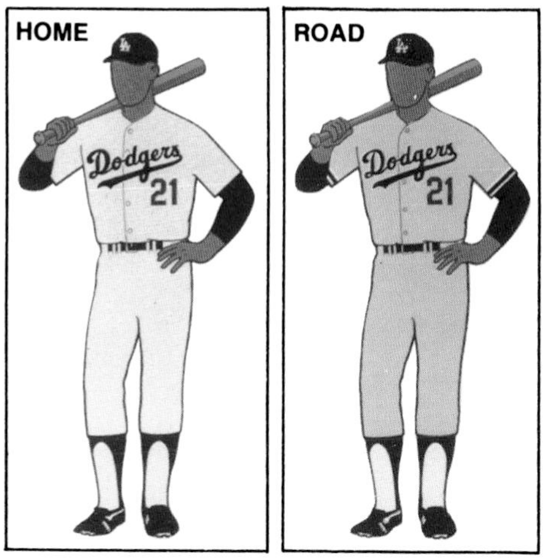

ST. LOUIS

PITTSBURGH

PHILADELPHIA

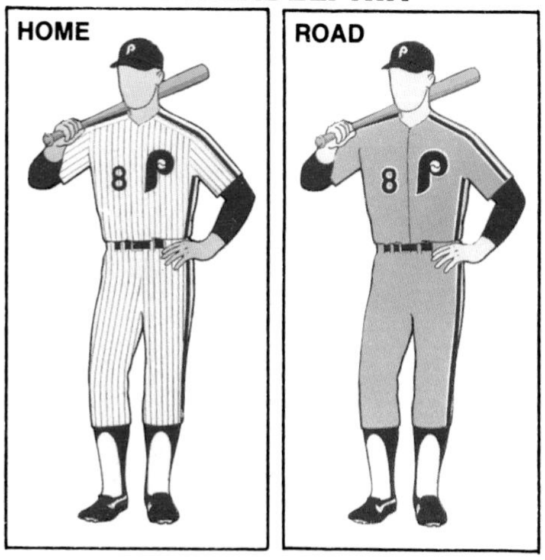

CHICAGO

NEW YORK

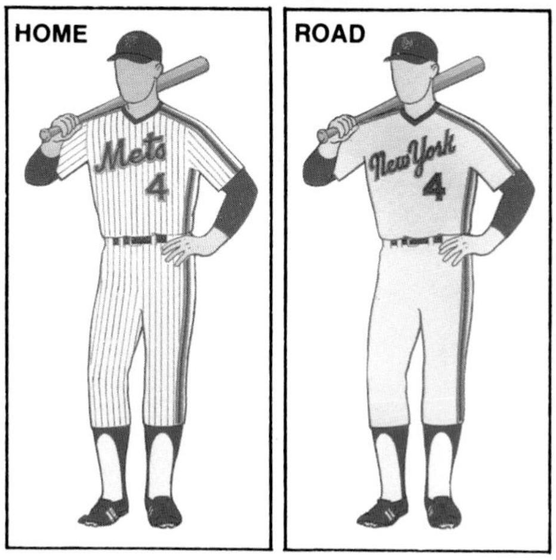

CINCINNATI

SAN FRANCISCO

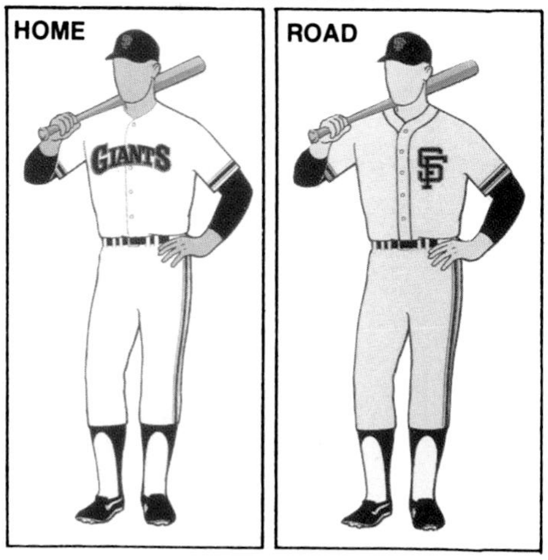

SAN DIEGO

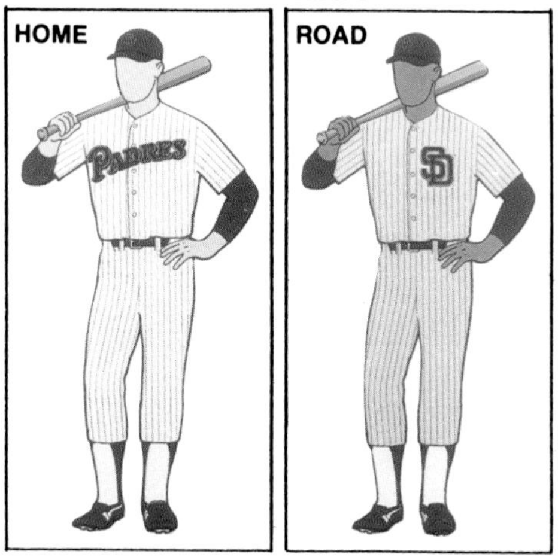

MONTREAL

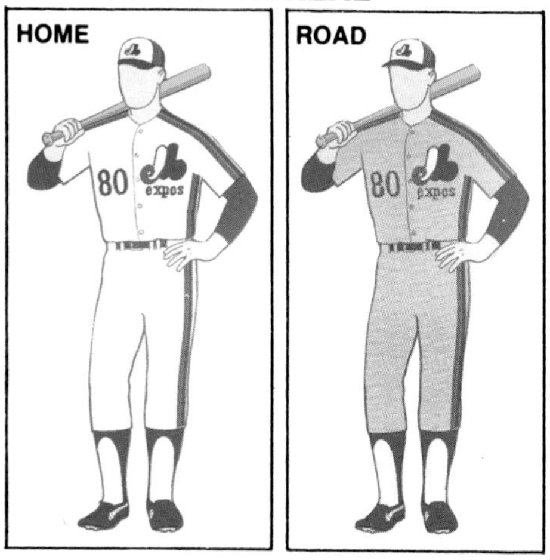

HOUSTON

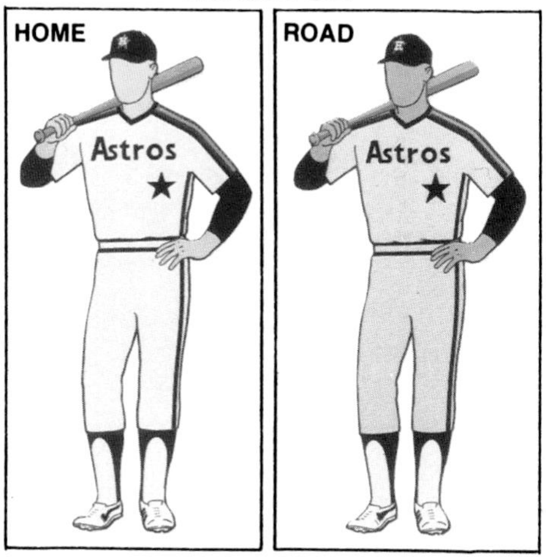

1988

AMERICAN LEAGUE

BOSTON

CLEVELAND

DETROIT

TORONTO

BALTIMORE

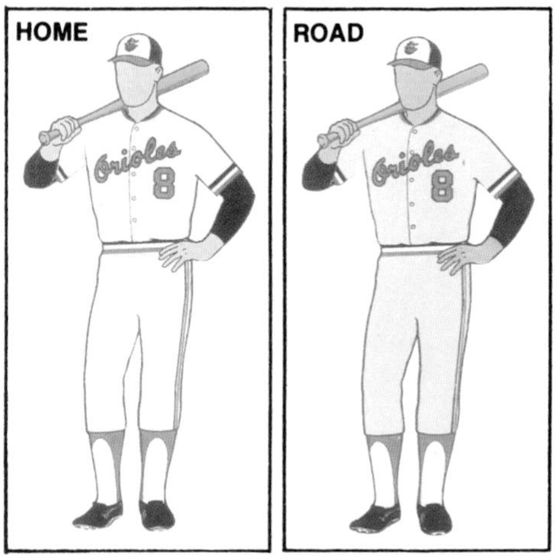

NEW YORK

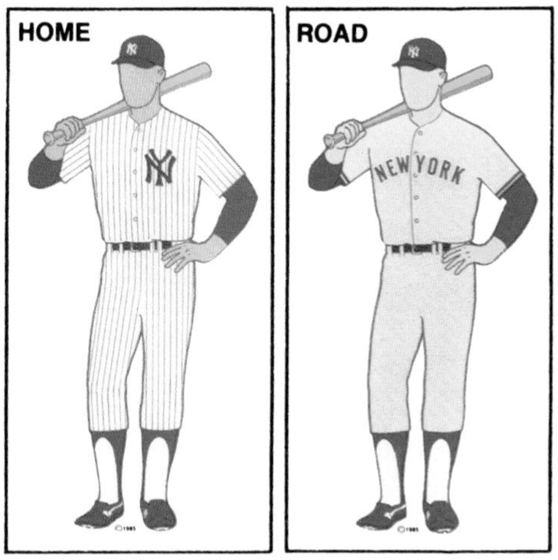

OAKLAND

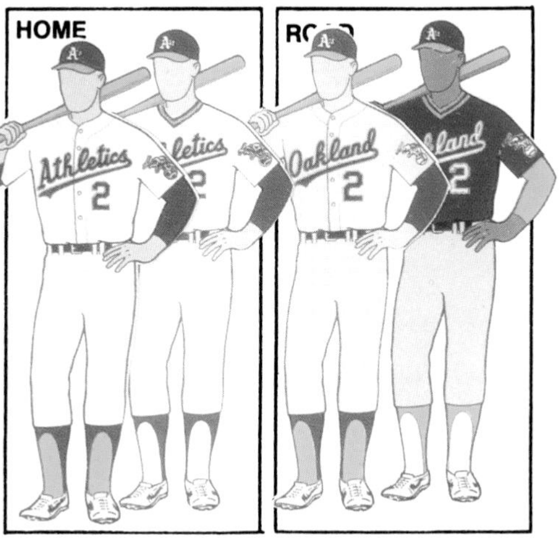

CHICAGO

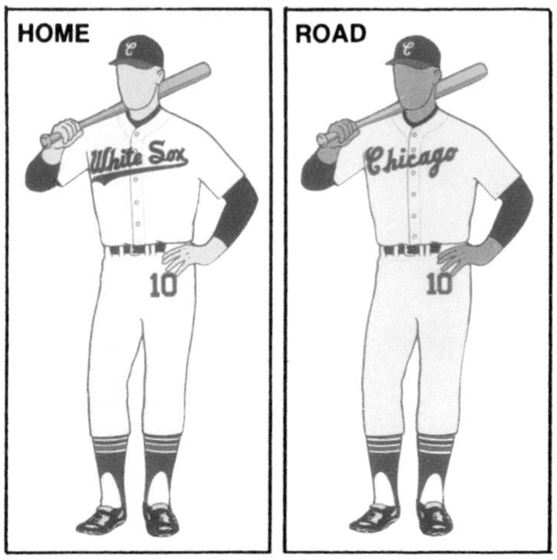

MINNESOTA

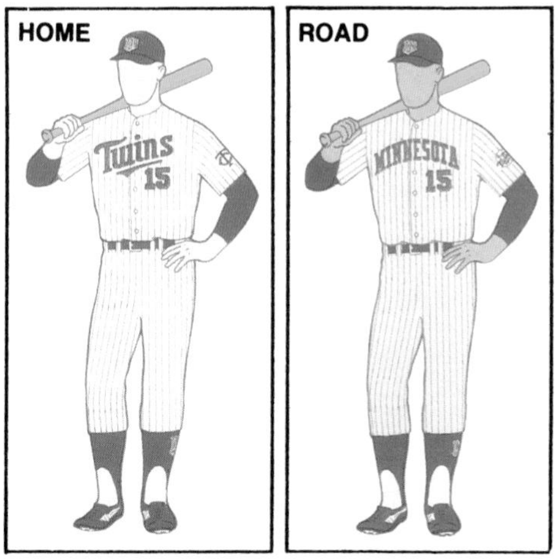

TEXAS

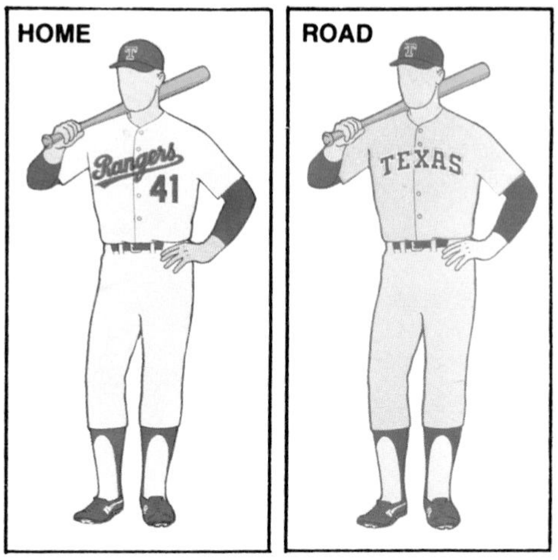

CALIFORNIA

MILWAUKEE

KANSAS CITY

SEATTLE

NATIONAL LEAGUE 1988

ATLANTA

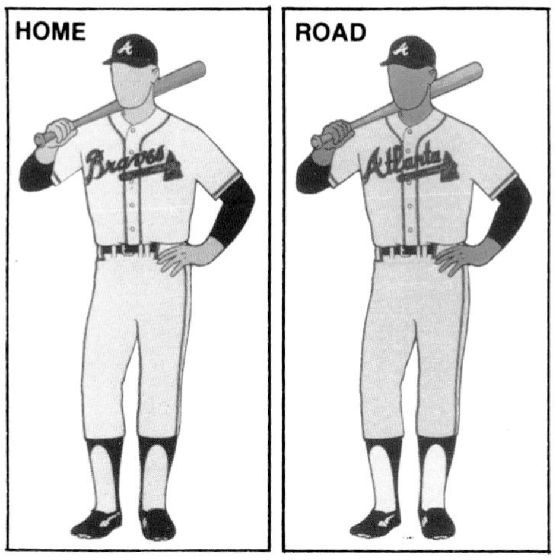

LOS ANGELES

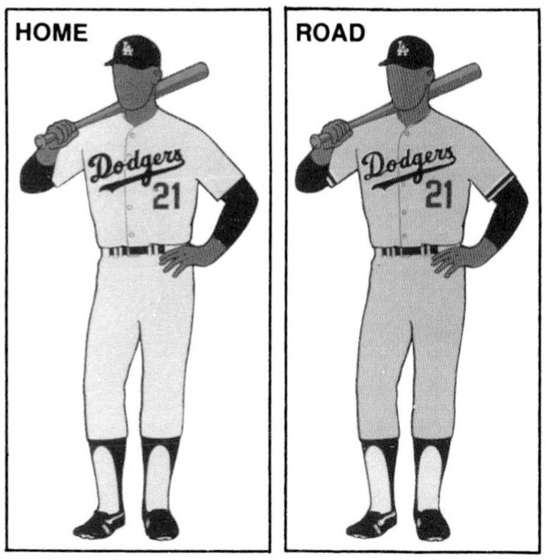

ST. LOUIS

PITTSBURGH

PHILADELPHIA

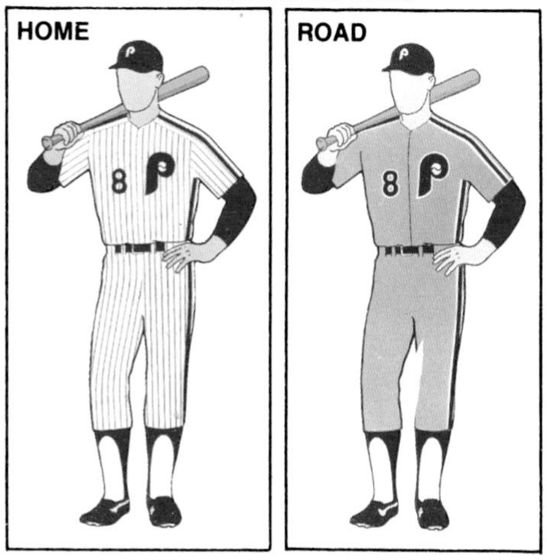

CHICAGO

NEW YORK

CINCINNATI

SAN FRANCISCO

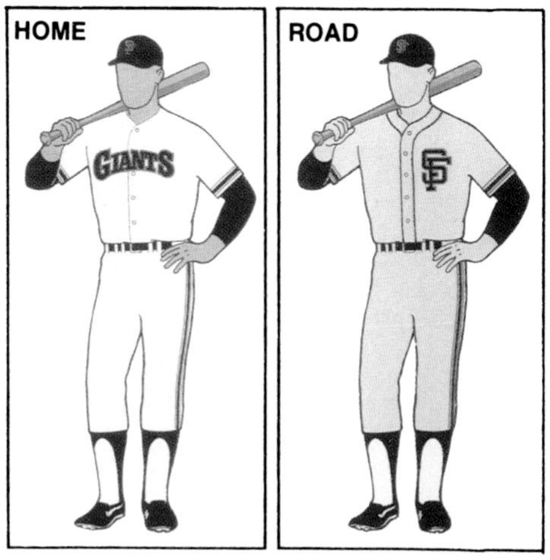

SAN DIEGO

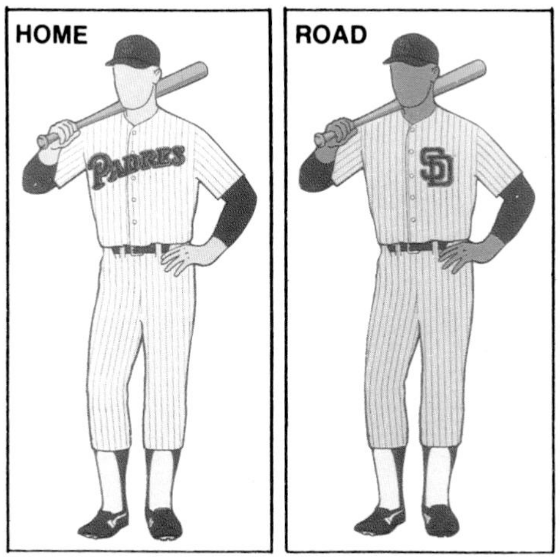

MONTREAL

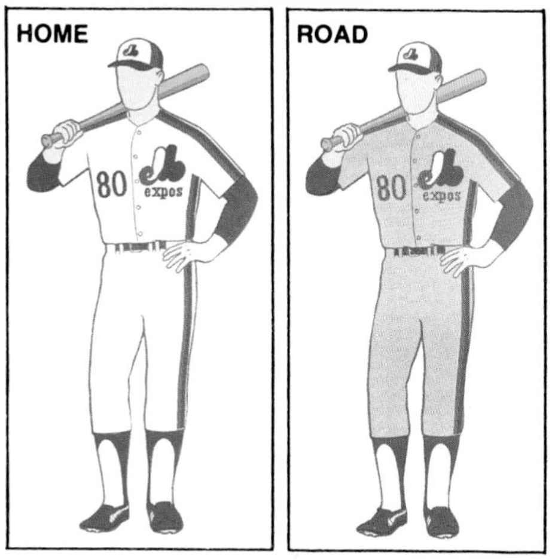

HOUSTON

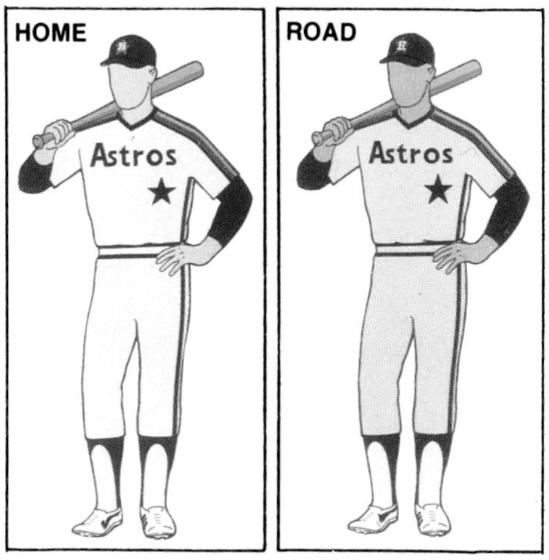

1989 AMERICAN LEAGUE

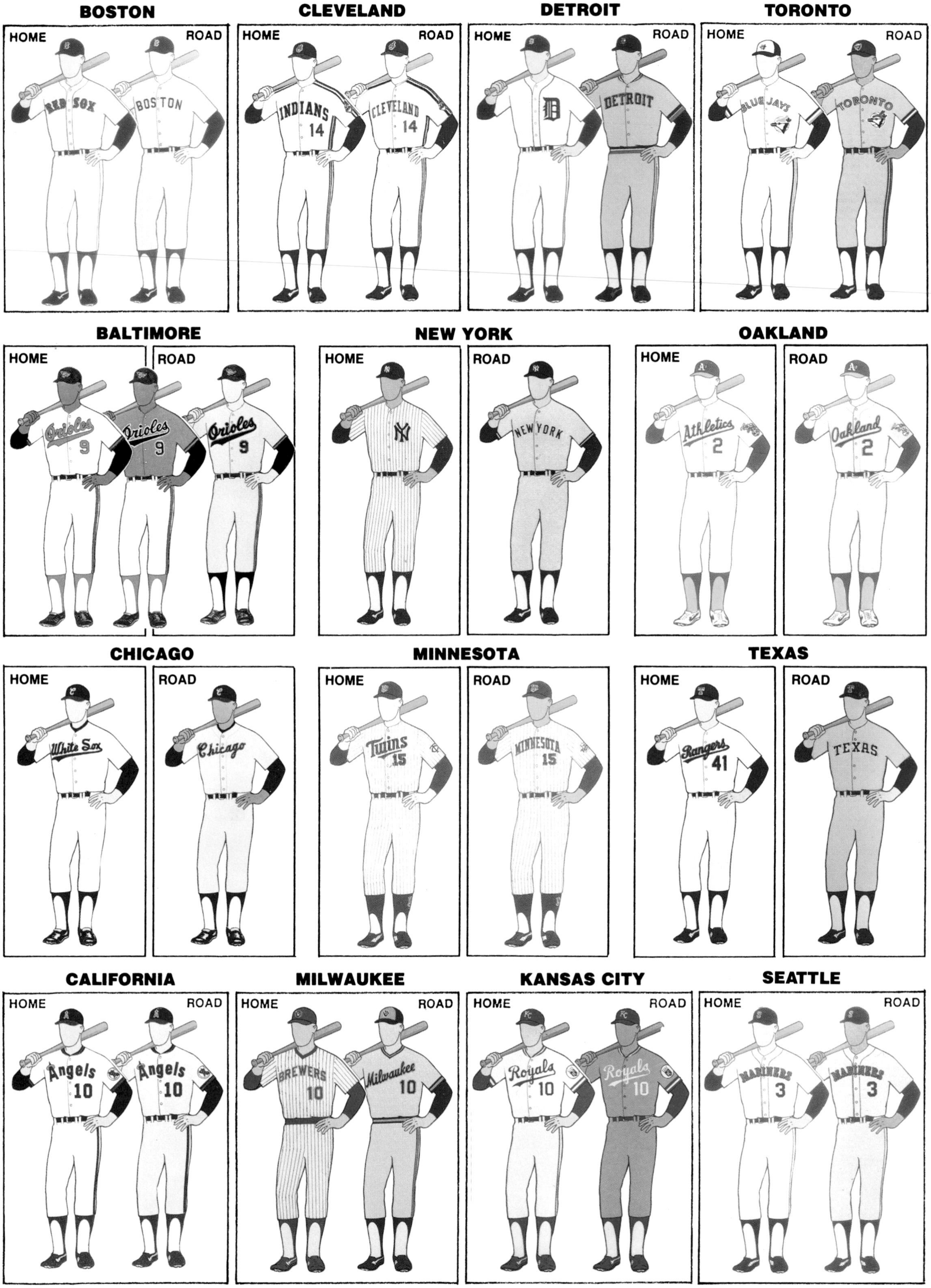

NATIONAL LEAGUE 1989

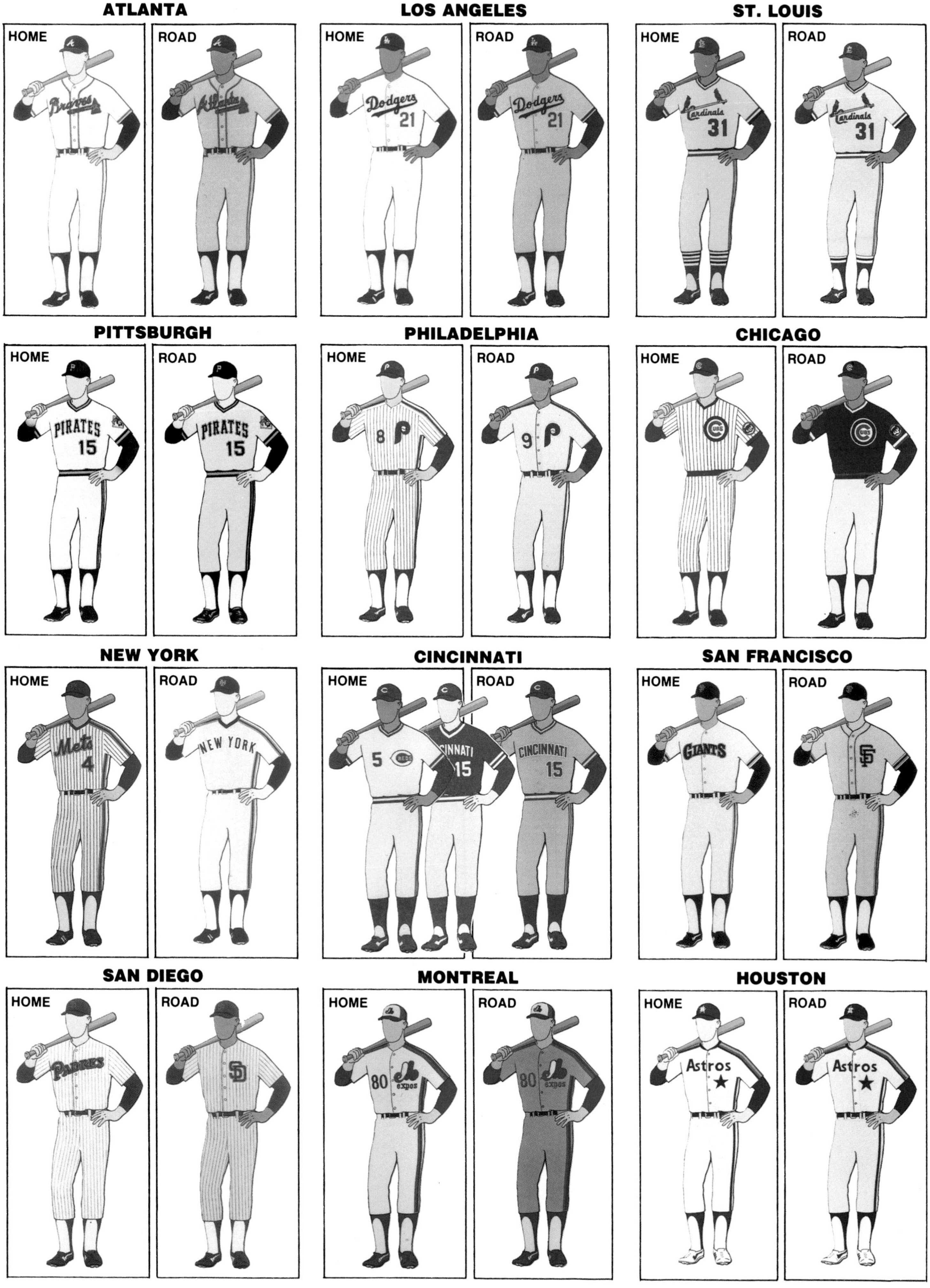

1990 AMERICAN LEAGUE

BOSTON

CLEVELAND

DETROIT

TORONTO

BALTIMORE

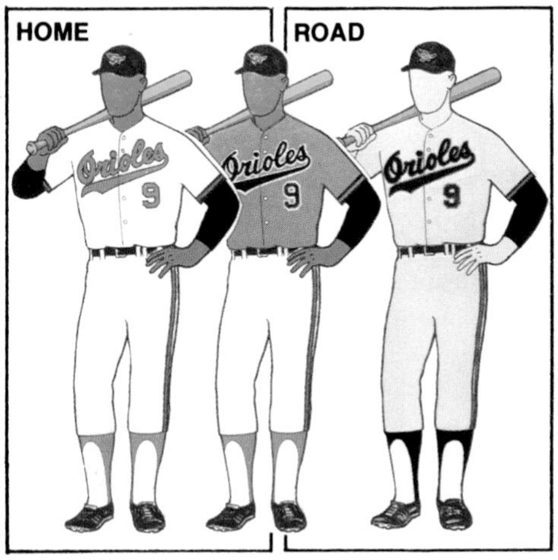

NEW YORK

OAKLAND

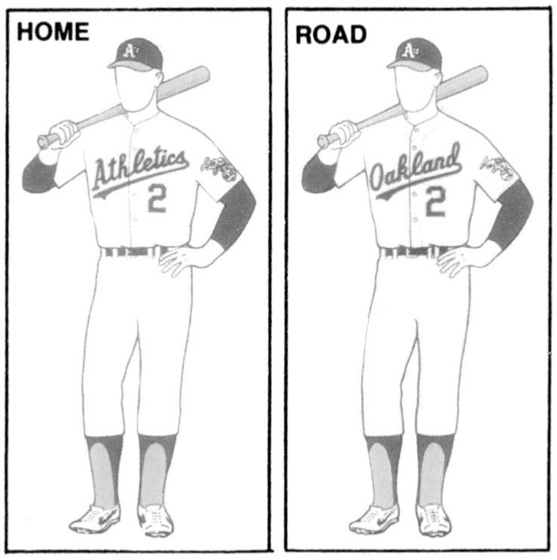

CHICAGO

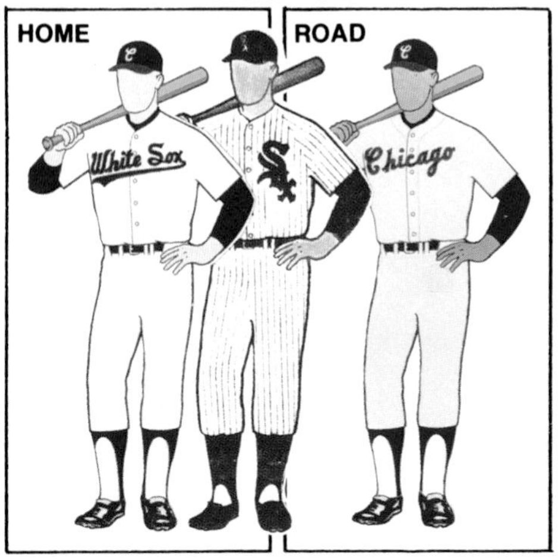

MINNESOTA

TEXAS

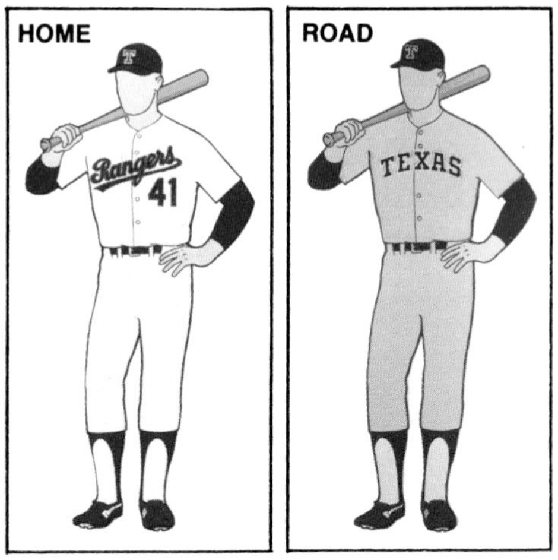

CALIFORNIA

MILWAUKEE

KANSAS CITY

SEATTLE

NATIONAL LEAGUE 1990

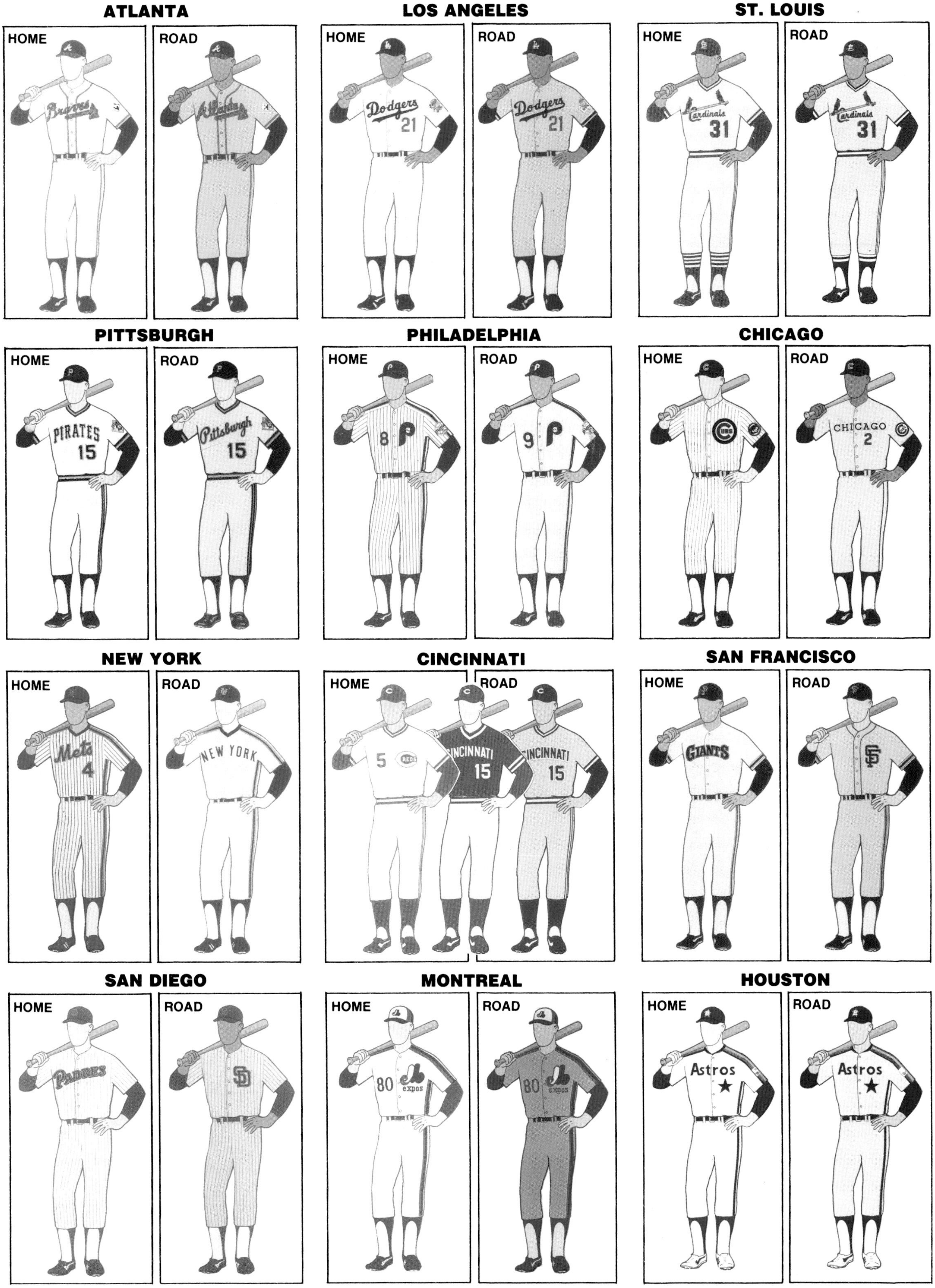

1991 AMERICAN LEAGUE

BOSTON

CLEVELAND

DETROIT

TORONTO

BALTIMORE

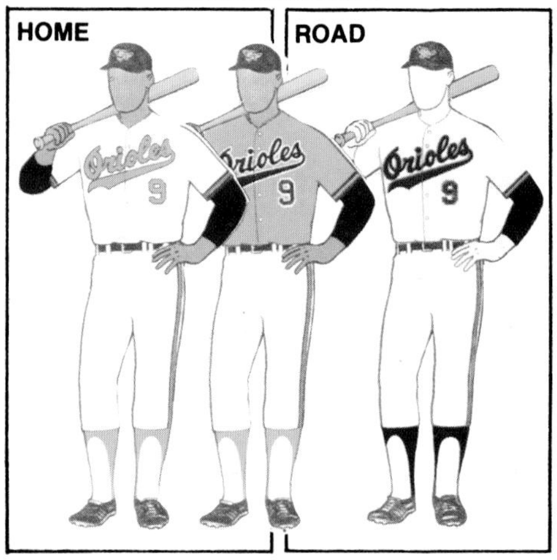

NEW YORK

OAKLAND

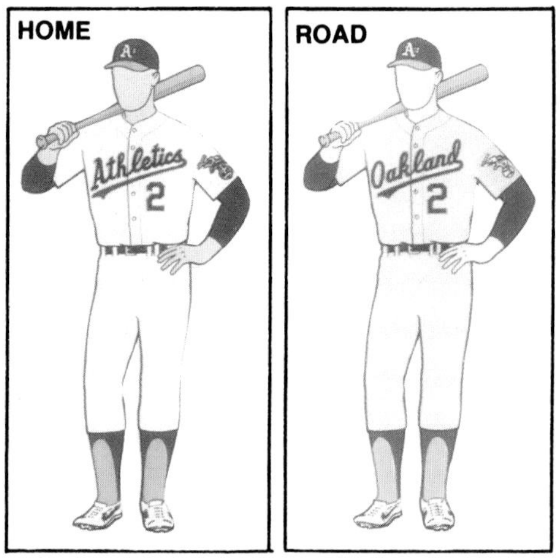

CHICAGO

MINNESOTA

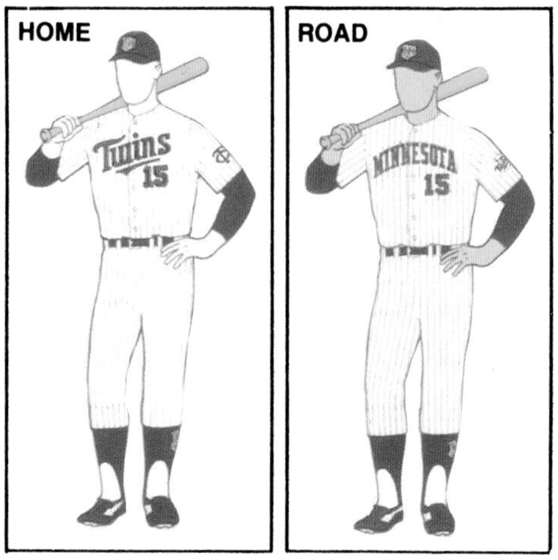

TEXAS

CALIFORNIA

MILWAUKEE

KANSAS CITY

SEATTLE

NATIONAL LEAGUE 1991

ATLANTA
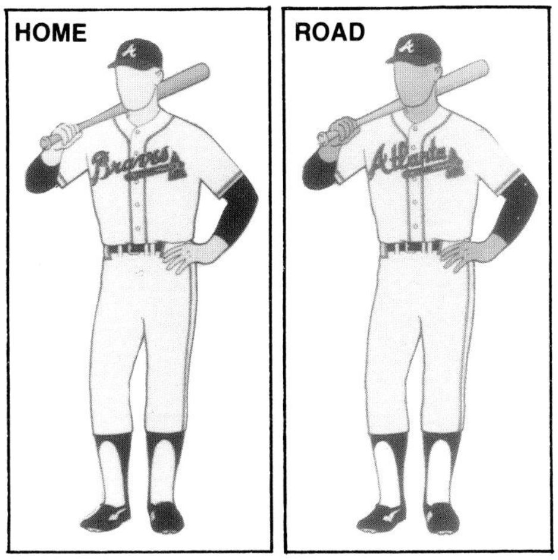

LOS ANGELES
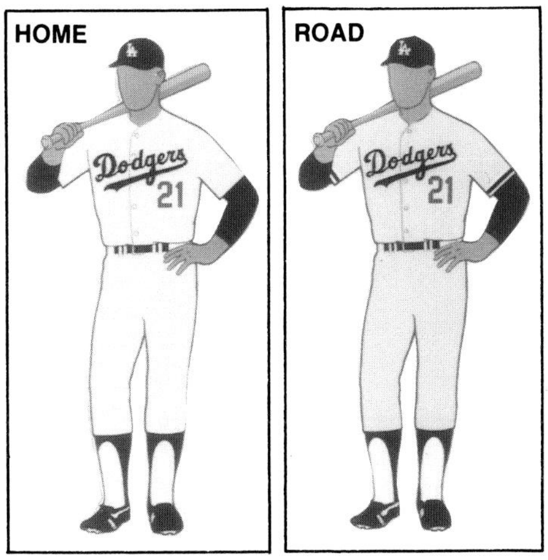

ST. LOUIS

PITTSBURGH
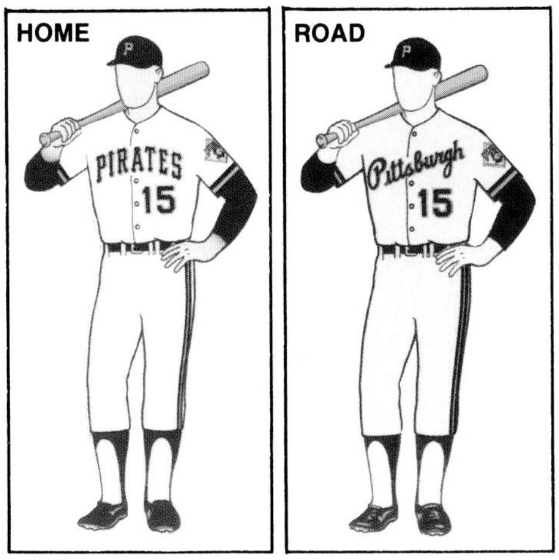

PHILADELPHIA
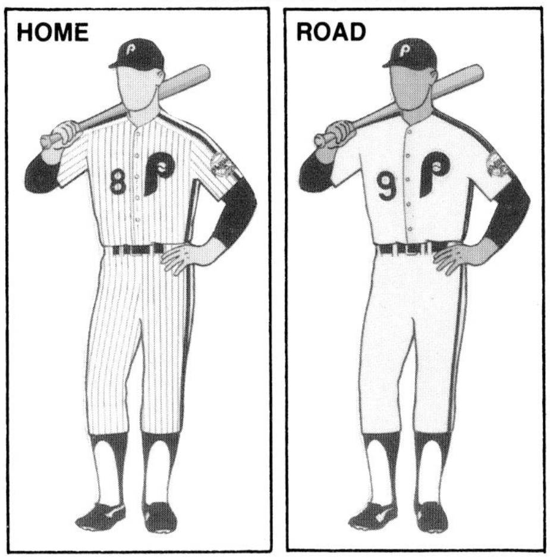

CHICAGO

NEW YORK

CINCINNATI

SAN FRANCISCO
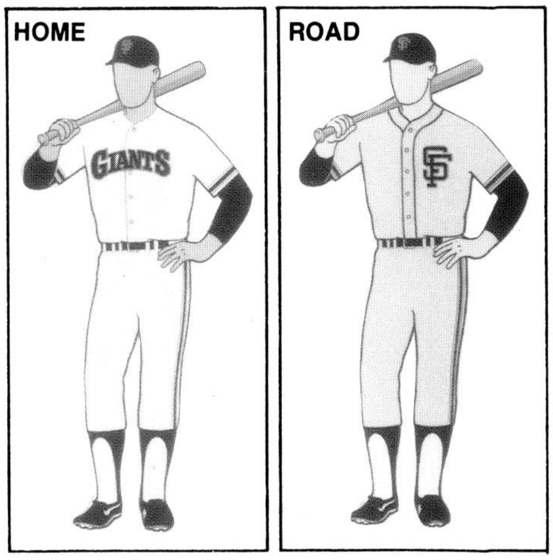

SAN DIEGO
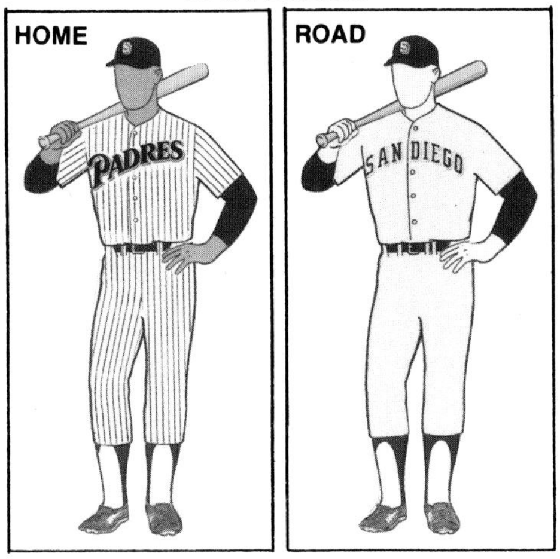

MONTREAL
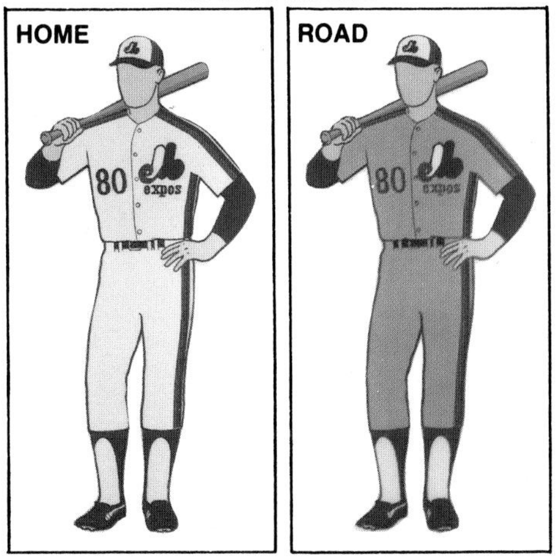

HOUSTON
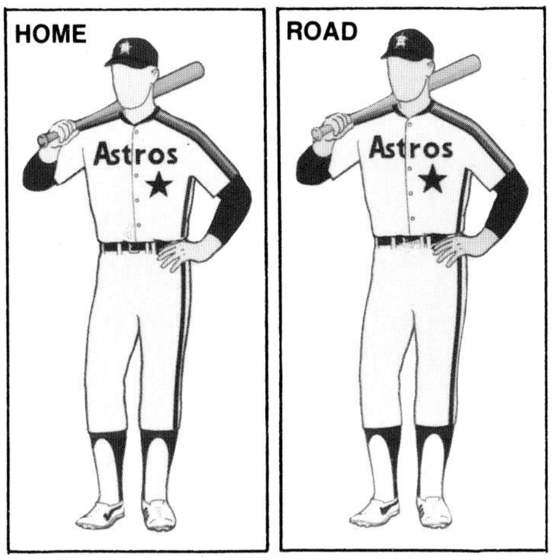

POSTSCRIPT

Since this reference volume attempts to account for a 92-year period of over 3500 major league uniform designs based on a 4-year period of concentrated research, some errors are inevitable. We sincerely hope that subsequent updated editions of this material will eventually be published and that many of the errors will be rectified. In the interest of historical accuracy we invite readers to submit any information regarding incorrect uniform depictions in this volume or legitimate uniform designs which have been inadvertantly omitted (hopefully, your submittal will be supported by some reasonable evidence). Please relay any such information (to my attention) to the NATIONAL BASEBALL LIBRARY, P.O. BOX 590, COOPERSTOWN, NEW YORK 13326, or simply telephone the library at (607) 547-9988.

MARC OKKONEN

INDEX